Aristotle

Politics

Aristotle

Politics

A New Translation

With Introduction and Notes
By

C. D. C. Reeve

Hackett Publishing Company, Inc.
Indianapolis/Cambridge

Printed in the United States of America

20 19 18 17 1 2 3 4 5 6 7

For further information, please address
Hackett Publishing Company, Inc.
P.O. Box 44937
Indianapolis, Indiana 46244-0937

www.hackettpublishing.com

Cover design by Deborah Wilkes
Interior design by Elizabeth L. Wilson
Composition by Aptara, Inc.

Library of Congress Cataloging-in-Publication Data

Names: Aristotle. | Reeve, C. D. C., 1948–
Title: Politics : a new translation / Aristotle ; with introduction and notes by C. D. C. Reeve.
Other titles: Politics. English
Description: Indianapolis, Indiana : Hackett Publishing Company, Inc., [2017] | Series: The new Hackett Aristotle | Includes bibliographical references and index.
Identifiers: LCCN 2016047055| ISBN 9781624665578 (pbk.) | ISBN 9781624665585 (cloth)
Subjects: LCSH: Political science—Early works to 1800.
Classification: LCC JC71.A41 R4413 2017 | DDC 320.01/1—dc23
LC record available at https://lccn.loc.gov/2016047055

The paper used in this publication meets the minimum requirements of American National Standard for Information Sciences—Permanence of Paper for Printed Library Materials, ANSI Z39.48–1984.

♾

For

Deborah Wilkes, Jay Hullett,

&

all at Hackett

Contents

Book IV

Book V

Book VI

Book VII

Preface

This book is a descendant of a translation of the *Politics* published by Hackett in 1988. But it is not the result of making spot revisions to its ancestor. Instead it is an entirely new translation, built from the ground up, and very different in scale and level of annotation from its predecesor. My reason for producing it is in the first instance to have a translation that is in harmony with my *Nicomachean Ethics* (2014), so that readers can more easily read the *Ethics* and then the *Politics* as a relatively seamless whole. The final chapter of the *Ethics* suggests that this is what Aristotle himself intended. A second reason is that readers of the *Politics* find themselves in territory whose apparent familiarity is often deceptive and inimical to proper understanding: *politikê* isn't quite politics, *epistêmê* isn't quite science, *praxis* isn't quite action, *theôria* isn't quite theory, *eudaimonia* isn't quite happiness, *ergon* isn't quite function, *aretê* isn't quite virtue, a *politiea* isn't quite a constitution, and a *polis* isn't quite a city. A translation must try to compensate for this deceptive familiarity, therefore, without producing too much potentially alienating distance and strangeness in its place. Accuracy and consistency are essential to achieving this goal, obviously, and I think that I can now do quite a bit better in these regards than I did before. Indeed, the 1988 version, while sufficiently useful for many purposes to be kept in print, falls short, in my view, of what is required for serious study of this extraordinary work. It is my hope and expectation that this one will eventually replace it entirely.

In addition to accuracy and consistency, extensive annotation and commentary are of the first importance. Some of this can consist, as it does here, of texts selected from other works by Aristotle, so that, while traveling through the region of the Aristotelian world that the *Politics* describes, readers can also travel through other regions of it, acquiring an ever widening and deepening grasp on the whole picture—something that is crucial, in my view, to understanding any part of it adequately or perhaps at all. But much commentary must simply be explanatory, clarificatory, and interpretative.

To make the journey a convenient one, footnotes and glossary entries are replaced by sequentially numbered endnotes, so that the information most needed at each juncture is available in a single location. The non-sequential reader interested in a particular topic will find in the Indexes a guide to places where focused discussion of it occurs. The Introduction describes the book that lies ahead, explaining what it is about, what it is trying to do, what sort of evidence is relevant to its evaluation, and what sort of person has access to such evidence. It is not a comprehensive discussion of all the important topics the *Politics* contains, nor an attempt to situate Aristotle's thought in the history of political thought more generally. Many books are available that attempt these tasks. Nor is it, I should add, an expression of scholarly consensus on the topics it does discuss—insofar as such a thing exists—but rather my own take on them.

I have benefited from the work of previous translators and commentators, especially Carnes Lord and Peter Simpson (into English) and Pierre Pellegrin (into French). The translations in the Clarendon Aristotle Series have also been very helpful, especially those of David Keyt (Books V and VII), Richard Kraut (Books VIII and IX), and Trevor Saunders (Books I and II), as have the translations of parts of the *Politics* by Terence Irwin.

I thank Pavlos Kontos and David Riesbeck for their careful line reading, as well as for their many useful comments, suggestions, and corrections. David's own work on the *Politics* in particular has been a frequent stimulus to new thought on my part.

I renew my thanks to ΔKE, the first fraternity in the United States to endow a professorial chair, and to the University of North Carolina for awarding it to me. The generous research funds, among other things, that the endowment makes available each year have allowed me to travel to conferences and to acquire books, computers, and other research materials and assistance, without which my work would have been much more difficult.

Finally and wholeheartedly, I thank Jay Hullett and Deborah Wilkes for their friendship, encouragement, and faith in me. It is a pleasure to dedicate this new translation to them, and to include all at Hackett in the dedication.

Abbreviations

Aristotle

Citations of Aristotle's works are made to Immanuel Bekker, *Aristotelis Opera* (Berlin: 1831 [1970]), in the canonical form of abbreviated title, book number (when the work is divided into books), chapter number, page number, column letter, and line number. References to the *Politics* typically omit the title. A * indicates a work whose authenticity has been seriously questioned; ** indicates a work attributed to Aristotle but generally agreed not to be by him. The abbreviations used are as follows:

APo.	*Posterior Analytics*
APr.	*Prior Analytics*
Ath.	*Constitution of Athens*
Cael.	*De Caelo (On the Heavens)*
Cat.	*Categories*
DA	*De Anima (On the Soul)*
Div. Somn.	*On Divination in Sleep*
EE	*Eudemian Ethics*
Fr.	*Fragments*
GA	*Generation of Animals*
GC	*On Generation and Corruption* (Joachim)
HA	*History of Animals* (Balme)
Int.	*De Interpretatione*
Juv.	*On Youth and Old Age, Life and Death, and Respiration* (Ross)
Long.	*On Length and Shortness of Life* (Ross)
MA	*Movement of Animals* (Nussbaum)
MM	*Magna Moralia** (Susemihl)

Mem.	*On Memory* (Ross)
Mete.	*Meteorology*
NE	*Nicomachean Ethics*
Oec.	*Economics** (van Groningen and Wartelle)
PA	*Parts of Animals*
Ph.	*Physics*
Po.	*Poetics*
Po. II	*Poetics II* (Janko)
Pol.	*Politics*
Pr.	*Problems**
Protr.	*Protrepticus* (Düring)
Rh.	*Rhetoric*
SE	*Sophistical Refutations*
Sens.	*Sense and Sensibilia*
Somn.	*On Sleep*
Top.	*Topics*
VV	*On Virtues and Vices***

I cite and translate the *Oxford Classical Texts* (OCT) editions of these works, where available, otherwise Bekker or the editions noted:

Balme, D. M. *Aristotle: Historia Animalium* (Cambridge, 2002).

Düring, I. *Aristotle's Protrepticus: An Attempt at Reconstruction* (Göteborg, 1961).

Janko, R. *Aristotle on Comedy: Toward a Reconstruction of Poetics II* (Berkeley, 1984).

Joachim, H. H. *Aristotle on Coming-to-Be and Passing-Away* (Oxford, 1926).

Mayhew, R. *Aristotle: Problems* (Cambridge, Mass., 2011).

Nussbaum, M. *Aristotle's De Motu Animalium: Text with Translation, Commentary, and Interpretative Essays* (Princeton, 1978).

Rose, V. *Aristotelis Fragmenta* 3rd ed. (Leipzig, 1886).

Ross, W. D. *Aristotle Parva Naturalia* (Oxford, 1955).

Susemihl, F. *Aristotelis Magna Moralia* (Leipzig, 1883).

van Groningen, B. A. and A. Wartelle, *Aristote: Économique* (Paris, 1968).

Plato

Ap.	*Apology*
Chrm.	*Charmides*
Ep.	*Letters*
Euthphr.	*Euthyphro*
Grg.	*Gorgias*
Lg.	*Laws*
Men.	*Meno*
Menex.	*Menexenus*
Min.	*Minos**
Phd.	*Phaedo*
Pol.	*Statesman*
Rep.	*Republic*
Tht.	*Theaetetus*
Ti.	*Timaeus*

Translations of Plato in the notes are based on those in J. M. Cooper, (ed.), *Plato: Complete Works* (Indianapolis, 1997) and on my *The Trials of Socrates* (Indianapolis, 2002) and *Plato: Republic* (Indianapolis, 2004).

Xenophon

An.	*Anabasis*
Lac.	*De Republica Lacedaemoniorum*
Cyr.	*Cyropaedia*
Hell.	*Hellenica*
Mem.	*Memorabilia*
Oec.	*Oeconomicus*

Other Abbreviations

Athenaeus = Athenaeus, *Deipnosophistae.*

Barker = A. Barker, *Greek Musical Writings I: The Musician and His Art* (Cambridge, 1984).

Barnes = J. Barnes, *The Complete Works of Aristotle: The Revised Oxford Translation* (Princeton, 1984).

CAG = M. Hayduck, *Commentaria in Aristotelem Graeca* (Berlin, 1882–1909).

Diehl = E. Diehl, *Anthologia Lyrica Graeca* (2 vols., Leipzig, 1925).

Diodorus = Diodorus Siculus, *Library of History.*

DK = H. Diels and W. Kranz (eds.), *Die Fragmente der Vorsokratiker* (6ed., Berlin, 1951).

DL = Diogenes Laertius, *Lives of Eminent Philosophers*, T. Dorandi (ed.) (Cambridge, 2013).

Dreizehnter = A. Dreizehnter, *Aristoteles' Politica* (Munich, 1970).

Gagarin & Woodruff = M. Gagarin and P. Woodruff (eds.), *Early Greek Political Thought from Homer to the Sophists* (Cambridge, 1995).

Herodotus = Herodotus, *Histories.*

Huffman = C. Huffman, *Archytas of Tarentum: Pythagorean, Philosopher and Mathematician King* (Cambridge, 2005).

Justin = *Epitome of the Philippic History of Pompeius Trogus.*

Keyt = D. Keyt, *Aristotle: Politics Books V and VI* (Oxford, 1999).

Kock = T. Kock, *Comicorum Atticorum Fragmenta* (3 vols., Leipzig, 1880).

Kraut = R. Kraut, *Aristotle: Politics Books VII and VIII* (Oxford, 1997).

Lonie = I. Lonie, *The Seed.* In G. Lloyd (ed.), *Hippocratic Writings* (Harmondsworth, 1978).

Nauck = A. Nauck, *Tragicorum Graecorum Fragmenta* 2nd ed. (Leipzig, 1889).

Newman = W. Newman, *The Politics of Aristotle* 4 vols. (Oxford, 1887–1902).

R^3 = Rose, V., *Aristotelis Fragmenta* 3rd ed. (Leipzig, 1886).

Saunders = T. Saunders, *Aristotle: Politics Books I and II* (Oxford, 1995).

Schütrumpf = E. Schütrumpf, and in the case of vol. iii, H-J Gehrke, *Aristotles Politik* 4 vols. (Berlin, 1991–2005).

Strabo = Strabo, *Geographica.*

Susemihl = F. Susemihl and R. Hicks, *The Politics of Aristotle: A Revised Text with Introduction, Analysis, and Commentary* (London, 1894).

TEGP = D. Graham, *The Texts of Early Greek Philosophy: The Complete Fragments and Selected Testimonies of the Major Presocratics* (Cambridge, 2010).

Thucydides = Thucydides, *The Peloponnesian War.*

Introduction

Life and Works

Aristotle was born in 384 BC to a well-off family living in the small town of Stagira in northern Greece. His father, Nicomachus, who died while Aristotle was still quite young, was allegedly doctor to King Amyntas of Macedon. His mother, Phaestis, was wealthy in her own right. When Aristotle was seventeen his guardian, Proxenus, sent him to study at Plato's Academy in Athens. He remained there for twenty years, initially as a student, eventually as a researcher and teacher.

When Plato died in 347, leaving the Academy in the hands of his nephew, Speusippus, Aristotle left Athens for Assos in Asia Minor, where the ruler, Hermias, was a patron of philosophy. He married Hermias' niece, Pythias, and had a daughter by her, also named Pythias. Three years later, in 345, after Hermias had been killed by the Persians, Aristotle moved to Mytilene on the island of Lesbos, where he met Theophrastus, who was to become his best student and closest colleague.

In 343 Aristotle seems to have been invited by Philip of Macedon to be tutor to the latter's thirteen-year-old son, Alexander, later called "the Great." In 335 Aristotle returned to Athens and founded his own institute, the Lyceum. While he was there his wife died and he established a relationship with Herpyllis, also a native of Stagira. Their son Nicomachus was named for Aristotle's father, and the *Nicomachean Ethics* may, in turn, have been named for him or transcribed by him. In 323 Alexander the Great died, with the result that anti-Macedonian feeling in Athens grew stronger. Perhaps threatened with a formal charge of impiety (*NE* X 7 1177^{b}33), Aristotle left for Chalcis in Euboea, where he died twelve months later, in 322, at the age of sixty-two.

Legend has it that Aristotle had slender calves, small eyes, spoke with a lisp, and was "conspicuous by his attire, his rings, and the cut of his hair." His will reveals that he had a sizable estate, a domestic partner, two children, a considerable library, and a large circle of friends. In it Aristotle asks his executors to take special care of Herpyllis. He directs that his slaves be freed "when they come of age" and that the bones of his wife, Pythias, be mixed with his "as she instructed."

Although the surviving writings of Aristotle occupy almost 2,500 tightly printed pages in English, most of them are not works polished for publication but sometimes incomplete lecture notes and working papers. This accounts for some, though not all, of their legendary difficulty. It is unfair to complain, as a Platonist opponent did, that Aristotle "escapes refutation by clothing a perplexing subject in obscure language, using darkness like a squid to make himself hard to catch," but there is darkness and obscurity enough for anyone, even if none of it is intentional. There is also a staggering breadth and depth of intellect. Aristotle made fundamental contributions to a vast range of disciplines, including logic, metaphysics, epistemology, psychology, ethics, politics, rhetoric, aesthetics, zoology, biology, physics, and philosophical and political history. When Dante called him "the master of those who know," he was scarcely exaggerating.

What the Politics *Is*

One thing we might mean by the *Politics* is what we now find inscribed on the pages that make up David Ross's Oxford Classical Text (OCT) edition of the Greek text, first published in 1957, which is the basis of the present translation. This is the descendant of texts derived—via manuscripts copied in the Byzantine period (from the tenth to the fifteenth centuries AD)—from manuscripts that derive from the edition of Aristotle's works produced by Andronicus of Rhodes in the first century BC. Ross's edition, like most other modern editions, records in the textual apparatus at the bottom of the page various manuscript readings alternative to the one he prints in the body of his text. In some cases, I have preferred one of these readings and have indicated so in the notes. Divisions of the text into books and chapters are the work of editors, not of Aristotle himself. Also present in Ross's text are the page numbers of Bekker, *Aristotelis Opera*. These appear here in the margins of the printed version and enclosed in | | in the electronic one. Occasional material in square brackets in the text is my addition.

The second thing we might mean, and are perhaps more likely to mean, by the *Politics* is the work itself—that more abstract thing that is embodied in a good Greek text and (ideally) in any translation of it. Aristotle identifies this as a contribution to "our philosophy of human affairs" (*NE* X 9 1181^{b}15). In the discussion that begins in the opening chapter of the *Ethics* and ends in its successor, he says that the methodical inquiry (*methodos*) pursued in it is "a sort of *politikê*" (*NE* I 2 1094^{b}11)—a sort of politics, a sort of political science. We need to determine, therefore, what this science is, what evidence it is answerable to, and how its success or failure is to be determined.

Aristotelian Sciences

Aristotle usually divides the bodies of knowledge that he refers to as "sciences" (*epistêmai*) into three types: theoretical, practical, and productive (crafts). But when he is being especially careful, he also distinguishes within the theoretical sciences between the *strictly theoretical* ones (astronomy, theology), as we may call them, and the *natural* ones, which are like the strictly theoretical ones in being neither practical nor productive but are unlike them in consisting of propositions that—though necessary and universal in some sense—hold for the most part rather than without exception:

> If all thought is either practical or productive or theoretical, natural science would have to be some sort of theoretical science—but a theoretical science that is concerned with such being as is capable of being moved and with the substance that in accord with its account holds for the most part only, because it is not separable. But we must not neglect to consider the *way* the essence or its account is, because, without this, inquiry produces no result. Of things defined, however, that is, of the "whats" that things are, some are the way the snub is, others the way the concave is. And these differ because the snub is grasped in combination with the matter (for the snub is a concave *nose*), whereas the concavity is without perceptible matter. If, then, all natural things are said the way the snub is (for example, nose, eye, face, flesh, bone, and, in general, animal, and leaf, root, bark, and, in general, plant—for the account of none of these is without [reference to] movement, but always includes matter), the way we must inquire into and define the what-it-is in the case of natural things is clear, as is why it belongs to the natural scientist to get a theoretical grasp even on some of the soul, that is, on as much of it as is not without matter. That natural science is a theoretical science, then, is evident from these considerations. Mathematics too is a theoretical one, but whether its objects are immovable and separable is not now clear; however, it is clear that *some* parts of mathematics get a theoretical grasp on their objects insofar as they are immovable and insofar as they are separable. But if there is something that is eternal and immovable and separable, it is evident that knowledge of it belongs to a theoretical science—not, however, to *natural* science (for natural science is concerned with certain moveable things) nor to mathematics, but to something prior to both. . . .

> If, then, there is no other substance beyond those composed by nature, natural science will be the primary science. But if there is some immovable substance, this will be prior and will be primary philosophy. (*Met.* VI 1 1025^{b}25–1026^{a}30)

When we hear, as we quickly do in the *Ethics* (I 3 1094^{b}14–22), that because the subject matter of politics, which consists of noble, just, and good things and the like, admits of so much difference and variability, its claims hold for the most part, we should bear in mind that all the natural sciences—which for us are the paradigm cases of science—are in a similar boat.

When science receives its focused discussion in the *Ethics*, however, Aristotle is explicit that if we are "to speak in an exact way and not be guided by mere similarities" (VI 3 1139^{b}19), we should not call anything a science unless it deals with eternal, entirely exceptionless facts about universals that are wholly necessary and do not at all admit of being otherwise (1139^{b}22–24). Since he is here explicitly epitomizing his more detailed discussion of science in the *Posterior Analytics* (1139^{b}27), we should take the latter too as primarily a discussion of science in the exact sense, which it calls *epistêmê haplôs*—unconditional scientific knowledge. It follows—and we should acknowledge this—that only the strictly theoretical sciences are sciences in the exact sense. Hence politics is not such a science and neither is physics or biology or any other natural science.

Having made the acknowledgement, though, we must also register the fact—since it is a fact—that Aristotle himself mostly does not speak in the exact way but instead persistently refers to bodies of knowledge other than the strictly theoretical sciences as *epistêmai*. His division of the *epistêmai* into theoretical, practical, and productive is a dramatic case in point. But so too is his use of the term *epistêmê* within the *Politics*, which we first encounter being applied to politics itself, which is a practical and not a theoretical science (I 1 1152^{a}15). Even boxing and wrestling are classed as *epistêmai* (*Cat.* 8 10^{b}3–4).

So the interesting question is not whether politics is a science, since the answer to that is obvious: it is not a science if we are being absolutely exact about the matter, but it is a science if we allow ourselves to be guided by the similarities between it and the strictly theoretical sciences—or by Aristotle's own general use of the term *epistêmê*, on the assumption that he himself was guided by these. The interesting question is, what are these similarities? Just how like a canonical or theoretical science is politics?

An Aristotelian science of any sort, including a theoretical one, is a state of the soul, not a body of propositions in a textbook—although the state does involve having an assertoric grasp on a set of true propositions (*NE* VI 3 1139^{b}14–16). Some of these propositions are indemonstrable starting-points, which are or are expressed in definitions, and others are theorems demonstrable from these starting-points. We can have scientific knowledge only of the theorems, since—exactly speaking—only what is demonstrable can be scientifically known (VI 6). Yet—in what is clearly another lapse from exact speaking—Aristotle characterizes "the most exact of the sciences," which is theoretical wisdom (*sophia*) or primary philosophy, as also involving a grasp by understanding (*nous*) of the truth where the starting-points themselves are concerned (VI 7 1141^{a}16–18). He does the same thing in the *Metaphysics,* where theoretical wisdom is the *epistêmê* that provides "a theoretical grasp on the primary starting-points and causes"—among which are included "the good or the for-sake-of-which" (I 2 982^{b}7–10). Indeed, the grasp we have of such starting-points must result in their being "better known" than the theorems we demonstrate from them if we are to have any scientific knowledge of the exact sort at all (*NE* VI 3 1139^{b}34).

How like that is politics? Are there starting-points here too and theorems demonstrable from them? We might think this is an easy question to answer. After all, the methodical inquiry the *Ethics* employs is a sort of politics, yet it doesn't seem to include any demonstrations whatsoever, and neither does the *Politics.* For a demonstration is, among other things, a deductively valid argument that is syllogistic in form, and deductions of any sort are scarcely to be found in the *Ethics* or *Politics.* This is also a problem with the vast majority of Aristotle's works, even those that are usually classed as "scientific treatises"—for example, *Meteorology* and *Parts of Animals.* For none of them seems to fit the description of a science as developed in the *Posterior Analytics.* Attempts have certainly been made to find elements of demonstration and axiomatic structure in these treatises, but the results are somewhat underwhelming. In large part, this is because the search is somewhat misconceived from the outset.

If we think of a science in the exact sense as consisting exclusively of what is demonstrable, as we have seen that Aristotle himself sometimes does, we will be right to conclude that a treatise without demonstrations in it cannot be scientific. But if, as he also does, we include knowledge of starting-points as parts of science, we will not be right, since a treatise could contribute to a science not by demonstrating anything but by arguing to the starting-points themselves—an enterprise which could not possibly consist of demonstrations from those starting-points, since these would be circular. We might reasonably infer, therefore, that the politics is a sort of science precisely because it contributes to the correct definition and secure grasp on starting-points without which no science can exist. The same idea might be employed in the case of many of Aristotle's other treatises. They too, we might suppose, are scientific in just this sense.

But even if politics has starting-points, it still would not be a science unless it were possible to demonstrate theorems from these. Yet here too we seem to face an obstacle. For Aristotle tells us that we cannot demonstrate things whose starting-points admit of being otherwise (*NE* VI 5 1140^{a}33–35), that politics is the same state of the soul as practical wisdom (VI 8 1141^{b}23–24), and that the starting-points of practical wisdom do admit of being otherwise (VI 5 1140^{a}30–^{b}4). Elsewhere, though, he allows that there *can* be demonstrations of what admits of being otherwise provided it holds for the most part—as the starting-points and theorems of politics are said to do (I 3 1094^{b}19–22):

> What admits of being otherwise is spoken of in two ways: in one, it means what holds for the most part, that is, when the necessity has gaps (*dialeipein*)—for example, a man's turning grey or growing or decaying, or, in general, what belongs to something by nature (for this does not belong by continuous necessity, since a human being does not exist forever, although if a human being does exist, it belongs either necessarily or for the most part); in the other, it means what is indeterminate, which is what is capable of being thus or not thus—for example, an animal's walking or an earthquake's taking place while it is walking, or, in general, what is the result of luck (for it is not more natural for it to be that way rather than the opposite). . . . Science and demonstrative deductions are not concerned with things that are indeterminate, because the middle term is irregular, but there is scientific knowledge of what happens by nature, and argument and investigations are pretty much concerned with things that are possible in this way. (*APr.* I 13 32^{b}4–21)

Apparently, then, the notion of a demonstration is a bit like that of a science. Speaking exactly, there are demonstrations only in the theoretical sciences, since—speaking exactly again—these alone are sciences. Speaking less exactly, though, there are also demonstrations in other bodies of knowledge. Thus we find Aristotle referring to practical demonstrations (*NE* VI 11 1143^{b}2), contrasting the undemonstrated sayings and beliefs of practically-wise people with things they can demonstrate (1143^{b}11–13), telling us about practical deductions (VI 12 1144^{a}31–32), and contrasting what are clearly theoretical deductions with productive ones (VII 3 1147^{a}25–^{b}1). We hear too about starting-points in politics and about reaching conclusions from them (I 3 1094^{b}21–22), and about supposedly having reached some (see I 8 1098^{b}9–10). Finally, if we do not allow there to be demonstrations of what admits of being otherwise in the sense of holding for the most part, it isn't just politics that will lose its putative scientific status; natural science will too.

A penultimate problem: Scientific knowledge seems to be exclusively about universals—about what is common to many particulars (*NE* VI 6 1140^{b}31, X 9 1180^{b}15–16). Yet politics, since it has a deliberative component, must also deal with particulars:

> Of the practical wisdom concerned with the city, the architectonic part is legislative science, while the part concerned with particulars has the name common to both—"politics." This part is practical and deliberative, since a decree is doable in action, as the last thing. (*NE* VI 8 1141^{b}23–28)

It seems an easy inference that politics cannot be a science. The first point to make in response is that even theoretical sciences, though they deal with eternal and unchangeable necessary truths about universals and have no grasp "on any of the things from which a human being will come to be happy" (*NE* VI 12 1143^{b}19–20), can be "coincidentally useful to us where many of the necessities of life are concerned" (*EE* I 6 1216^{b}15–16). Knowledge of astronomy, for instance, helped Thales to make a killing in the olive business (*Pol.* I 11 1259^{a}5–33). The second point to make is that Aristotle allows that sciences dealing with universals can also deal—albeit coincidentally—with (perishable) particulars:

> There is neither demonstration nor unconditional scientific knowledge of what is subject to passing away, but only the coincidental sort, because it does not hold of this universally, but at some time (*pote*) and in some way (*pôs*). (*APo.* I 8 75^{b}24–26)

The scientific theorem that all light meats are healthy (*NE* VI 7 1141^{b}18–19) may enable me to infer that this meat is healthy now, but it does not tell me whether it will still be healthy tomorrow (it may have rotted in the meantime) or whether, though it is healthy for most people, it is healthy for me (I may have a fever that makes meat of any sort a bad choice).

While each of these points does something to take the edge off our problem, even collectively they do not seem to go quite far enough. And the reason is this. It is quite possible to have scientific knowledge of universals without knowing how to apply it in particular cases, but it is not possible, as we have just seen, to have a grasp on politics—which is the same state of the soul as practical wisdom (*NE* VI 8 1141^{b}23–24)—without knowing this. In fact, it is almost the other way around:

> Nor is practical wisdom knowledge of universals only. On the contrary, it must also know particulars. For it is practical, and action is concerned with particulars. That is why, in other areas too, some people who lack knowledge—most of all, those with experience—are more effective *doers* of action than are others who have knowledge. For if someone knows that light meats are digestible and healthy but is ignorant about which sorts of meat are light, he will not produce health; but someone who knows that bird meats are healthy will produce health more. But practical wisdom is practical, so one must possess both sorts of knowledge—or this one more. (*NE* VI 7 1141^{b}14–21)

At the same time, knowledge of universals is a crucial part of politics. This emerges most clearly in the final discussion in the *Ethics,* where we learn not only about the importance of experience of particulars to politics but also about the need to "take steps toward the universal" (X 9 1180^{b}21), on the grounds that "the best supervision in each particular case" will be provided by the person who has "knowledge of the universal and knows what applies in all cases or in these sorts (since the sciences are said to be—and actually are—of what is common)" (1180^{b}13–16).

Once we register the fact that politics must include both a scientific knowledge of universals and an experience of particulars that enables us to apply those universals correctly to them, we can see that it is something like an applied science as opposed to a pure one. And this seems to be what Aristotle has in mind by classifying it as *practical*—that is to say, as bearing on *praxis,* or action, and so on the particulars with which action is irremediably concerned. When we look for the similarities that may justify him in classifying it as a practical *science*, then, we must look not at its particularist component but at its universalist one, since a science, as we saw, is always of what is universal. A practical science, in other words, might to some extent be usefully thought of as a combination of something like a theoretical science (in any case, in the sense in which natural science is theoretical) and the experience-based knowledge of how to apply it.

What the universalist component of politics consists in is uncontroversial, since Aristotle tells us plainly that it is *nomothetikê,* or legislative science:

> Maybe, then, someone who wishes to make people—whether many or few—better because of his supervision should also try to acquire legislative science, if it is through laws that we can become good. For producing a noble disposition in anyone whatever—in anyone put before him—is not a matter for some

> random person, but if indeed anyone can do it, it is a person who knows, just as in medicine and in all other matters that involve a sort of supervision and practical wisdom. (*NE* X 9 1180^{b}23–28)

What legislative science does, as its name suggests, is to produce a set of universal laws—for "all law is universal" (V 10 1137^{b}13)—that will "make citizens good by habituating them" (II 1 1103^{b}3–4). Thus one very important subset of these laws bears on education, since "what produces virtue as a whole are the actions that are ordained by the laws concerned with education that looks to the common good" (V 2 1130^{b}25–26). Another subset, however, governs the actions of already-educated adults:

> It is not enough, presumably, that when people are young they get the correct nurture and supervision. On the contrary, even when they have grown into manhood they must continue to practice the same things and be habituated to them. And so there will need to be laws concerning these matters as well and, in general, then, concerning all of life. (*NE* X 9 1180^{a}1–4)

The phrase "concerning all of life" nicely captures the ideal extent of the laws: "It is above all appropriate that correctly laid down laws themselves define all the things they possibly can and leave the fewest possible to the judges" (*Rh.* I 1 1354^{a}31–33), since "the wish of human beings . . . is not a safe standard" (*Pol.* II 10 1272^{b}6–7).

We are now able to solve a final problem. Theorems in canonical theoretical sciences are not just universal, they are also necessary: they are about relations between universals that do not "*at all* admit of being otherwise" (*NE* VI 3 1139^{b}20–21). The theorems of natural science too, although not as strictly necessary as this, also describe relations between universals that are far from simply being matters of luck or contingency. Were it otherwise, there would, as we noticed, simply be no such thing as natural *science*. Obviously the theorems of politics, which are universal laws, are not like either of these, since they govern voluntary action, which, as something whose starting-point is in us, is up to us to do or not to do (*NE* III 5 1113^{b}7–8). This difference, however, is due to a difference in direction of fit. Theorems of a theoretical science *describe* how things must be; practical laws *prescribe* how they must be. Thus, when Aristotle gives an example of an ethical proposition, it is this: "whether we *should* obey our parents or the laws, if they disagree" (*Top.* I 14 105^{b}22–23). What practical laws prescribe will be correct, if it is what the virtues require of us (*NE* V 2 1130^{b}22–24), and it will be what the virtues require of us if it is what the practical wisdom they presuppose would prescribe, and it will be what practical wisdom would prescribe if it is what best furthers happiness or the human good (VI 9 1142^{b}31–33, 10 1143^{a}8). For the law owes its compulsive force to the fact that it is "reason that derives from a sort of practical wisdom and understanding" (X 9 1180^{a}21–22).

Although it is through laws that we can "become good" (*NE* X 9 1180^{b}25), it is not just through any old laws. Rather, we need *correct* laws—laws that really do further genuine happiness by inculcating genuine virtues. The question arises, therefore, of how such laws are to be found. A good place to start, Aristotle thinks, is by collecting the laws and constitutions that are in use in different places, as well as those ideal ones suggested by wise people, such as Plato, who have thought a lot about the topic. But this by itself will not be enough, since selecting the best ones from these requires "correct discernment" (X 9 1181^{a}17), based on knowledge of what virtue and vice really are. In Aristotle's view, there is only one such constitution:

> [The constitution] consisting of those who are unconditionally best in accord with virtue, and not those who are good men relative to a hypothesis, is the only constitution that it is just to call an aristocracy. For only in it is the same person unconditionally a good man and a good citizen, whereas those who are good in the others are so relative to their constitutions. (*Pol.* IV 7 1293^{b}3–6; compare *NE* V 7 1135^{a}5)

Thus when the topic of the best constitution is taken up in the *Politics*, Aristotle begins by noting that "anyone who is going to make an inquiry into the best constitution in the appropriate way must first determine what the most choiceworthy life is" (VII 1 1323^{a}14–17), referring us for a fuller discussion to "external accounts," whose topics significantly overlap those of the *Ethics*. Other constitutions, however—and this is a point that we shall return to in a moment—can come close enough to the best one that something approximating full virtue can be acquired in them; these are the non-deviant constitutions (kingship, aristocracy, and polity) described in the relevant parts of the *Politics*.

It is scarcely a step at this point to see what the *Ethics* contributes to legislative science. After all, the *Ethics* is devoted to defining the virtues of character, which are starting-points of politics (*Met.* XIII 4 1078^{b}17–30, quoted below), as well as to correctly and clearly defining the yet more fundamental starting-point, happiness, which is the end or target that politics aims at (*NE* I 2 1094^{a}26–^{b}7, *Pol.* VII 1 1323^{a}15–21). It is a contribution to the philosophy of human affairs, as we saw, and "the political philosopher is the architectonic craftsman of the end to which we look in calling each thing unconditionally bad or good" (*NE* VII 11 1152^{b}1–3)—namely, happiness.

This helps us to understand something that is much more mysterious than is usually recognized, namely, how it is that Aristotle can do the following three things: First, characterize the *Ethics* as "not undertaken for the sake of theoretical knowledge . . . but in order to become good people, since otherwise there would be nothing of benefit in it" (II 2 1103^{b}26–29; also I 3 1095^{a}5–6). Second, insist that we become good in large part through habituation, not through reading books (II 2 1103^{b}23–25). And, third, that we must already have been "nobly brought up if, where noble things, just things, and the topics of politics as a whole are concerned, we are to be an adequate audience" (I 4 1095^{b}4–6). For "argument and teaching . . . do not have strength in everyone," but only in those whose souls have been "prepared beforehand through habits to enjoy and hate in a noble way, like earth that is to nourish seed" and may not even be comprehensible to anyone else (X 9 1179^{b}23–31). The heavy lifting of the *Ethics*' practicality is done, then, not so much by the book itself, which presupposes an already existing noble condition in a comprehending reader, but by the contribution it makes to legislative science, ensuring that the laws it selects will habituate people in genuine virtues and that it will have as its end happiness correctly conceived and clearly defined. The *Politics* comes into play at this point to actually find those laws and the constitution to which they belong (II 5 1263^{a}39n).

Because the heavy lifting is done by legislation and habituation, it matters enormously that the legislation and habituation in question is not required to be of the ideal or very best sort available only in a true aristocracy of virtue. For such a constitution does not exist, and never has existed. But even if it had, Aristotle was not brought up in it—Stagira and Athens were certainly not such true aristocracies—and his audience and fellow Lyceum members were not brought up in it either. What *is* required, though, is that we not be "disabled in relation to virtue" (*NE* I 9 1099^{b}19), that we have the natural resources needed to develop it—which may include possession of the so-called natural virtues (VI 13 1144^{b}5–6), that we have been sufficiently well brought up that we do not, like children, pursue each thing in accord with our feelings, but rather form our desires and perform our actions to some extent at least "in accord with reason" (I 3 1095^{a}4–11), and that we have "sufficient experience of the actions of life," since "the arguments are in accord with these and concerned with these" (1095^{a}3–4). Aristotle does not go into detail in the *Ethics* about just how much experience of just what sorts of actions we need, but there is clear evidence in the *Politics* that we may not have it until we have reached the age of around fifty (VII 9 1328^{b}34–1329^{a}17). Because our nature, upbringing, and experience are unlikely to have been ideal, moreover, we must not expect too much, but rather "be content if, when we have all the things through which it seems we become decent people, we achieve some share of virtue" (*NE* X 9 1179^{b}18–20).

We turn now to the particularist part of politics, which is concerned with deliberation:

> The part concerned with particulars has the name common to both—"politics." This part is practical and deliberative, since a decree is doable in action, as the last thing. (*NE* VI 8 1141^{b}25–28)

Precisely because this part is particularist, it cannot itself be a science, since—to repeat—sciences are always (anyway non-coincidentally) about universals. Nonetheless, it is some sort of knowledge or ability that makes its possessor a competent deliberator—someone who is reliably able to deliberate correctly by working out the best means to the best end (*NE* VI 9 1142^{b}28–33), this being happiness or the human good. Since only a practically-wise person is in this position and since practical wisdom is as much if not more concerned with particulars than with universals, the function of such a person is "most of all . . . to deliberate well" (VI 7 1141^{b}9–10).

Now the sphere of deliberation is the part of what admits of being otherwise that deliberators can change through their own actions (*NE* III 3 1112^{a}30–34). Hence it is also the sphere of the practical and productive sciences which help deliberators to make good choices within that sphere. But once these sciences are factored into the equation, the scope of deliberation within the sphere is affected, so that as their scope expands, that of deliberation contracts:

> There is no deliberation, however, where sciences that are both exact and self-sufficient are concerned—where writing the letters of the alphabet is concerned, for example, since we have no hesitation about what way to write them. We do deliberate, however, about those things that come about through ourselves, but not always in the same way (for example, about the things that medicine or moneymaking deals with). And we deliberate more about navigation than about athletic training, insofar as navigation is less exactly developed. Further, deliberation is involved in a similar way where the rest are concerned, but more where crafts are concerned than sciences, since we are more hesitant about them. (*NE* III 3 1112^{a}34–^{b}9)

As Aristotle succinctly puts it at one point: "Craft does not deliberate" (*Ph.* II 8 199^{b}28). He means, as we see, that a craft, insofar as it is exact, fully developed, and self-contained, does not do so.

Even when the productive sciences are less exact or developed, however, as is true, for example, of medicine and wealth acquisition, their universal laws should generally be followed:

> Those who think it advantageous to be ruled by a king hold that laws speak only of the universal, and do not prescribe with a view to particular circumstances, so that it is foolish to rule in any craft accord with what is written down. And so it is a good thing that in Egypt the doctors are allowed to change the treatment [prescribed by the manuals] until after the fourth day—although, if they do so earlier, it is at their own risk. It is evident, therefore, that the best constitution is not one that is in accord with what is written down and laws, due to the same cause. But then, the rulers should possess the universal account as well. And something to which the passionate element is wholly unattached is better than something in which it is innate. This element does not belong to the law, whereas every human soul necessarily possesses it. But presumably it should be said, to balance this, that a human being will deliberate better about particular cases. That he must, therefore, be a legislator is clear, and that laws must be laid down, but they must not be in control insofar as they deviate from what is best, although they should certainly be in control everywhere else. (*Pol.* III 15 1286^{a}9–25; also 16 1287^{a}33–1287^{b}5)

It is when the universal laws fail us—as the Egyptian doctors imagine them doing by the fourth day of a patient's unresponsiveness to the prescribed treatment—that deliberation comes into play. It is then that the practical wisdom possessed by the better practitioners of the science becomes important. We "speak of people as practically-wise *in some area*, when they rationally calculate well about what furthers some excellent end, concerning which no craft [prescription] exists" (*NE* VI 5 1140^{a}28–30).

The element in practical wisdom that is particularly involved in the kinds of cases where the end is "living well as a whole" (*NE* VI 5 1140^{a}27–28) is decency (*epieikeia*):

> All law is universal, but about some sorts of things it is not possible to pronounce correctly in universal terms. . . . So whenever the law makes a universal pronouncement and a particular case arises that is contrary to the universal pronouncement, at that time it is correct (insofar as the legislator has omitted something, and he has made an error in pronouncing unconditionally) to rectify the deficiency—to pronounce what the legislator

> himself would have pronounced had he been present and would have put into his law had he known about the case. . . . And this is the very nature of what is decent—a rectification of law insofar as it is deficient because of its universality. For this is also the cause of not everything's being regulated by law—namely, that there are some cases where it is impossible to set up a law, so that decrees (*psêphismata*) are needed. For the standard of what is indeterminate is itself indeterminate, just like the lead standard used in Lesbian building. For the standard is not fixed but adapts itself to the shape of the stone and a decree adapts itself to the things themselves. (*NE* V 10 1137^{b}13–32)

Though this comment applies primarily to the context of political deliberation by members of a city's ruling deliberative body, it is the model for Aristotle's account of an individual agent's deliberation as well. This is particularly clear when an individual's action-controlling beliefs—the guiding premises of his deliberative reasoning—are analogized to decrees (*NE* VII 9 1151^{b}15, 10 1152^{a}20–21). But it is similarly in operation when the last thing reached in deliberation is identified as a decree (VI 8 1141^{b}26–28). Practical wisdom is prescriptive (VI 10 1143^{a}8) indeed because it issues in decrees which, like laws, have prescriptive force.

The picture that finally emerges of politics, therefore, is of a science that has three elements. The first is legislative science, which, since it issues universal laws that have the right sort of modal status (allowing for differences of direction of fit), makes politics similar enough to a canonical theoretical science to justify its classification as a science. The second is deliberative ability (*bouleutikê*), which is particularistic enough to justify its classification as practical. The third is the judicial science (*dikastikê*), which is primarily exercised in the administration of legal justice (*dikê*) (VI 8 1141^{b}33, *Pol.* I 2 1253^{a}36–38). But this is a picture of politics that has, as it were, a concealed element, which is the one providing an argument for the starting-points—happiness, the virtues—that are crucial to it. These, we learned, it was the job of the methodical inquiry of the *Ethics* to provide. We must now see what it consists in.

The Foundations of Politics

We know that scientific starting-points cannot be demonstrated. They are what we construct demonstrations from, not to. Of scientific starting-points, therefore, we have understanding, not scientific knowledge (*Pol.* I 5 1254^{b}5n, *NE* VI 6 1141^{a}7–8)—even if, when we do have understanding of them combined with demonstrations from them, what we have is a more exact form of such knowledge (*NE* VI 7 1141^{a}16–18). It is in this less exact way, remember, that we saw we should speak when considering the scientific status of politics. How, then, do we get this understanding? Where do we start the process? "We must," Aristotle says, "start from things that are knowable. But things are knowable in two ways, since some are knowable to us, some unconditionally. So presumably we should start from things knowable to us" (I 4 1095^{b}2–4). For the sake of clarity, let us call these *raw starting-points*. These are what we start from when we are arguing to *explanatory scientific starting-points*. It is important not to confuse the two.

In the case of the methodical inquiry of the *Ethics*, we are told that a raw starting-point is "the fact that something is so" (I 4 1095^{b}6; also I 7 1098^{b}2–3) and that this fact concerns "noble things, just things, and the topics of politics as a whole" (I 4 1095^{b}5–6). But since no explicit examples are given of these starting-points, we need to do some detective work to get a better understanding of what exactly they are.

An important clue to their nature derives from the way that we gain access to them: "it is virtue, whether natural or habituated, that teaches correct belief about the starting-point" (*NE* VII 8 1151^{a}18–19). Hence Aristotle's insistence on the importance of being well or nobly brought up: "it makes no small difference whether people are habituated in one way or in another way straight from childhood; on the contrary, it makes a huge one—or rather, *all* the difference" (II 1 1103^{b}23–25). Equally important is the account of the way that failure to be brought up well affects or blocks our access to raw starting-points:

> Ordinary people naturally obey not shame but fear, and abstain from base things not because of their shamefulness but because of the sanctions involved. For living by feeling as they do, they pursue the pleasures that are properly their own as well as the things through which these come about, and avoid the opposing pains. Of what is noble and what is truly pleasant, however, they have no understanding at all, not having tasted it. What sort of argument, then, could reform such people? For it is not possible—or not easy—to alter by argument what has long since been locked up in traits of character. (X 9 1179^{b}11–16)

By being habituated badly where pleasures and pains are concerned, people are prevented from experiencing what is noble and truly pleasant. When such people read in the *Ethics* that we should sacrifice wealth, power, honor, the satisfaction of their appetites, and other such so-called external goods (*Pol.* VII 1 1323^{a}25n) in order to gain what is noble for ourselves, they should suppose it mere words (*NE* X 8 1179ᵃ22). After all, their own life experience, which is what casts "the controlling vote" (1179ᵃ20) in practical matters, tells them in no uncertain terms that words is all it is. For ordinary people "judge by external goods, since these are the only ones they can perceive" (1179ᵃ16), and so when they see someone who lacks these, they cannot see how he could be happy, and when they see him sacrifice these for the sake of what is noble, they cannot do otherwise than take him to be sacrificing his self-interest for an empty dream (IX 8, *Pol.* VII 1).

One kind of raw political starting-point, then, is a belief about the sort of value that noble things (as well as just things) have. People who have been correctly habituated to enjoy and hate in a noble way see correctly that these things are intrinsically valuable or choiceworthy for their own sake and that they are more valuable than external goods. People who have been inadequately habituated cannot see this, and so reject one of the raw starting-points of politics right off the bat. When they read the *Ethics* and *Politics*, therefore, they simply cannot see the truth in them, and so these works are of no practical value to them. They do what virtue requires of them to the extent that they do from fear of penalties rather than for the sake of what is noble (*NE* X 9 1180ᵃ4–5).

Happiness is also a raw starting-point of politics (*Pol.* VII 1 1323ᵃ15–21, *NE* I 12 1102ᵃ2–4), about which people quite reasonably get "their suppositions . . . from their lives" (*NE* I 5 1095ᵇ15–16). Hence happiness too can seem as variable as good things generally (I 3 1094ᵃ16–17). As a result, ordinary people—anyway "the most vulgar ones"—suppose that happiness is pleasure, since their bad habituation, especially where bodily pleasures and pains are concerned, leads them exclusively to pursue "money, honors, and bodily pleasures . . . on the supposition that they are the best goods" (IX 8 1168ᵇ16–18). Yet, as Aristotle points out, they "have an argument for their choice," since people in positions of power, like Sardanapalus, who are able to do what they want, pursue these goods too. It is this argument that makes their views worth examining (I 4 1095ᵃ28–30). The same goes for people whose upbringings have led them to pursue honor as if it were the best good.

Raw political starting-points, we now see, are socially mediated and language-mediated facts (or putative facts) that are accessible only to properly socialized subjects and so only to subjects who are members of societies—that is, of groups that socialize or habituate their members into some common form of life. Here is Aristotle himself on the topic:

> The voice is a signifier of what is pleasant or painful, which is why it is also possessed by the other animals (for their nature does extend this far, namely, to having the perception of pleasure and pain and signifying them to each other). But speech is for making

> clear what is advantageous or harmful, and so too what is just or unjust. For this is special to humans, in comparison to the other animals, that they alone have perception of the good and the bad, the just and the unjust, and the rest. And it is community in these that makes a household and a city. (*Pol.* I 2 $1253^{a}10$–18)

It follows, then, that the beliefs of properly socialized subjects—or the way things noble, just, and so on appear to them as a result of such socialization—are the rawest data available. It is to these that politics is ultimately answerable.

It is useful to juxtapose this picture of politics to a picture Aristotle gives of the canonical sciences and of the importance in them of experience and ultimately of perception:

> What causes our inability to take a comprehensive view of the agreed-upon facts is lack of experience. That is why those who dwell in more intimate association with the facts of nature are better able to lay down [explanatory] starting-points which can bring together a good many of these, whereas those whom many arguments have made unobservant of the facts come too readily to their conclusions after looking at only a few facts. (*GC* I 2 $316^{a}5$–10)

We might advisedly see "those who dwell in more intimate association with the facts of nature," in other words, as the equivalent in a canonical science of the well brought up or properly socialized and habituated subjects of the *Ethics* and *Politics*, who, "because they have an eye formed from experience, . . . see correctly" (*NE* VI 11 $1143^{b}13$–14). And one reason we might do so is that canonical scientists too are socialized subjects, albeit of a somewhat specialized sort. For it is only within scientific communities or communities of knowledge that, through complex processes of habituation and teaching, canonical scientists are produced: we learn science from other scientists (X 9 $1180^{b}28$–34). But communities of knowledge, both in Aristotle's view and in reality, are parts of the political community and are regulated and sustained by it. When we first meet politics, in fact, it is as an architectonic science that oversees the others, ensuring that all sciences work together to further human happiness (*NE* I 2 $1094^{a}26$–$^{b}7$, *Pol.* I 13 $1260^{a}18$–19n).

Because the things that appear to be so to appropriately socialized subjects are the raw starting-points in canonical sciences just as much as in politics, the only difference between them lying in the sort of socialization involved, we must be careful not to think of an appeal to "the things we say (*ta legomena*)" (*NE* I 8 $1098^{b}10$, VII 1 $1145^{b}20$) as an appeal to evidence of a sort quite different from the sort appealed to in a canonical science.

We are not in the one case appealing to conceptual considerations or intuitions and in the other to empirical facts or findings. We are not looking at analytic matters as opposed to synthetic ones. Instead, what we have in both cases are socially mediated facts, some closer to the conceptual or the analytic, some closer to the empirical or synthetic. Political subjects who disagree about the intrinsic choiceworthiness of what is noble, for example, are not disagreeing about a concept or about the meaning of a word but about a substantive issue concerning how to live. Aristotle's account of happiness and his definition of virtue of character as a sort of medial state are to be evaluated not by appeal to our intuitions but by appeal to the facts of our lives (X 8 1179^{a}17–22).

The significance of these conclusions about raw political starting-points and the kinds of subjects who can detect them is most easily seen when we run across—as readers of the secondary literature on the *Ethics* and *Politics* inevitably will—topics related to the "foundations" of Aristotle's politics. Often a central exhibit in these discussions is the famous function (*ergon*) argument (*NE* I 7 1097^{b}22–1098^{a}20), where it is thought that the notion of a function is introduced into politics as something already so grounded in the facts (or putative facts) of Aristotle's biological or metaphysical investigations that politics then inherits these grounds and becomes hostage to these facts—facts that are not themselves political facts or putative facts. Another frequent exhibit is the use Aristotle makes, at various junctures, of his own account of the soul—an account supported not by political facts or putative facts, apparently, but by biological or psychological ones (*NE* I 13 1102^{a}14–26, *Pol.* I 5 1254^{a}34–^{b}4, 13 1260^{a}4–14).

What these discussions fail to give proper weight to is the difference between *empirical* foundations, or the facts to which politics or any other body of knowledge is ultimately answerable, and *explanatory* foundations, or the explanatory notions that politics makes use of in explaining those facts. To be sure, these notions may also often play explanatory roles in various other Aristotelian bodies of knowledge, including various theoretical sciences, and may for that reason recommend themselves to Aristotle for use elsewhere. It would be strange if it were otherwise. These notions may well, then, be epistemically sanctioned within these other bodies of knowledge too, providing correct explanations of the relevant sorts of facts. But this does not mean that politics must be committed to them as fixed points of its own explanatory enterprise. Rather, it takes them on board wholly and entirely as answerable to raw political starting-points and must reject them if they prove inadequate for those purposes. In the only really important sense, then, politics has political facts as its sole foundations. Biology, metaphysics, and other bodies of knowledge have no foundational role in politics whatsoever.

Explanatory Starting-points and Dialectic

In the case of canonical sciences, the most important explanatory starting-points consist of definitions that specify the genus and differentia of the real (as opposed to nominal) universal essences of the beings with which the science deals (*APo.* II 10 93^{b}29–94^{a}19). Since scientific definitions must be apt starting-points of demonstrations, this implies, Aristotle thinks, that the "extremes and the middle terms must come from the same genus" (I 7 75^{b}10–11). As a result, a single canonical science must deal with a single genus (I 28 87^{a}38–39). The conclusion we reached earlier—that politics deals with and is empirically based only on political facts—thus marks another potential similarity between politics and a canonical science, since it suggests that politics does deal with a single genus and so meets a crucial condition definitive of a canonical science.

It should come as no surprise, then, that in defining the virtues of character, which are the explanatory starting-points of politics and are those states of the soul with which noble and just actions must be in accord, Aristotle first specifies their genus (*NE* II 5 1106^{a}12–13). They are, he says, states (*hexeis*)—where a state is a condition "by dint of which we are well or badly off in relation to feelings" (1105^{b}25–26). Then, making use of the so-called doctrine of the mean, he goes on to tell us what the differentiae are of the states that are virtues:

> Virtue . . . is a deliberately choosing state, which is in a medial condition in relation to us, one defined by a reason and the one by which a practically-wise person would define it. (*NE* II 6 1106^{b}36–1107^{a}1)

At that point he implies he has discovered virtue's "substance and the account that states its essence" (*NE* II 6 1107^{a}6–7). It is just what a definition or account in a canonical science is supposed to do (*APo.* II 3 90^{b}16, 10 93^{b}29).

There is an important difference, though, which Aristotle takes pains to register but whose significance is nonetheless easy to miss. If politics is a science at all, it is a practical one, which aims to make us good. This means that the definitions it produces must be of a sort that can guide the actions of politicians, legislators, and individual agents. They must, in a word, be definitions that can be put into practice. Thus Aristotle's major criticism of Plato's form of the good is that it is impractical:

> Even if there is some single good predicated in common of all intrinsic goods, a separable one that is itself an intrinsic good, it

> is clear that it will not be something doable in action or acquirable by a human being. But that is the sort we are now looking for. (*NE* I 6 1096^{b}32–35)

Moreover, it is even impractical in a more attenuated sense, namely, as a sort of regulative ideal, unachievable in action yet guiding it from beyond. For to treat it as such results in a clash with the productive sciences as these are actually practiced, since the practitioners of the productive sciences, though seeking some good, ignore the form of the good altogether, "yet for all craftsmen not to know—and not even to look for—so important an aid would hardly be reasonable" (1097^{a}6–8).

It is true that Aristotle's own definition of happiness as activity of the soul in accord with the best and most complete virtue seems to end up entailing that a certain leisured theoretical activity—the contemplation of the god—is the best kind of happiness (*NE* X 7–8). But it is not a theoretical definition for all that, if by "theoretical" we mean, as we should, that truth alone is the measure of its correctness. What matters most is that what it defines, unlike Plato's good itself, is something we can put into practice—something we can *do*. That is why the measure of its success is an entirely practical one:

> When we examine what has been previously said, . . . it must be by bringing it to bear on the facts of our life, and if it is in harmony with the facts, we should accept it, but if it clashes, we should suppose it mere words. (*NE* X 8 1179^{a}20–22)

With similar concerns in mind, Aristotle prefaces his definition of virtue of character with an account of how we think such virtue is acquired (II 1) and with a reminder that the goal of the *Ethics* and *Politics* is practical, not theoretical (II 2). When the definition is finally developed (II 5–6), we see that it is in keeping with these prefatory comments, since it is one that can guide us in both inculcating and maintaining the virtues of character in others and in ourselves (II 9).

Nowadays philosophy is for the most part a theoretical subject with few pretensions to having much bearing on practical affairs. So it is easy to forget that Aristotle thinks of some branches of philosophy, anyway, in quite a different way. His discussion of voluntariness and involuntariness, for example, is intended to be "also useful to legislators regarding honors and punishments" (*NE* III 1 1109^{b}34–35). When we evaluate that discussion, therefore, we shouldn't just do so in standard philosophical fashion—by looking for clever counterexamples, however far-fetched they might be. We should think rather of how well it would work in practical life, where the far-fetched seldom occurs and requires special provision when it does. Here the discussion of decency (V 10) should serve as our guide.

Understanding, then, that definitions of starting-points in politics must be practical, let us return to the question of how we arrive at these definitions by beginning from raw starting-points. Well, first we have to have the raw starting-points ready to hand. Aristotle is clear about this, as he is indeed about what is supposed to happen next:

> The way [of inquiry] (*hodos*) is the same in all cases, in philosophy as well as in the crafts or any sort of learning whatsoever. For one must observe for both terms what belongs to them and what they belong to, and be supplied with as many of these terms as possible. . . . When it is in accord with truth, it must be from the terms that are catalogued (*diagegrammennôn*) as truly belonging, but in dialectical deductions it must be from premises that are in accord with [reputable] belief. . . . Most of the starting-points, however, are special to each science. That is why experience must provide us with the starting-points where each is concerned—I mean, for example, that experience in astronomy must do so in the case of astronomical science. For when the appearances had been adequately grasped, the demonstrations in astronomy were found in the way we described. And it is the same way where any other craft or science whatsoever is concerned. Hence if what belongs to each thing has been grasped, at that point we can readily exhibit the demonstrations. For if nothing that truly belongs to the relevant things has been omitted from the collection, then concerning everything, if a demonstration of it exists, we will be able to find it and give the demonstration, and if it is by nature indemonstrable, we will be able to make that evident. (*APr.* I 30 46ᵃ3–27)

So once we have a catalogue of the raw starting-points, the demonstrative explanation of them from explanatory scientific starting-points is supposedly fairly routine. We should not, however, demand "the cause [or explanation] in all cases alike. Rather, in some it will be adequate if the fact that they are so has been correctly shown (*deiknunai*)—as it is indeed where starting-points are concerned" (*NE* I 8 1098ᵃ33–ᵇ2). But what exactly is it to show a starting-point correctly or adequately? It can't be to demonstrate it, we know that.

Aristotle describes what he is undertaking in the *Ethics* specifically as a "methodical inquiry (*methodos*)," as we saw, that like the *Politics* is a contribution to the "philosophy of human affairs" (*NE* X 9 1181ᵇ12–15). And to the explanatory scientific starting-points of these, he claims, there is a unique route:

> Dialectic is useful in the philosophical sciences because the capacity to go though the puzzles on both sides of a question will make it easier to discern what is true and what is false in each. Furthermore, dialectic is useful as regards the primary [starting-points] (*ta prôta*) in each science. For it is impossible to say anything about these based on the starting points properly belonging to the science in question, since these starting-points are, of all of them, the primary ones, and it is through reputable beliefs (*endoxa*) about each that it is necessary to discuss them. This, though, is a task special to, or most characteristic of, dialectic. For because of its ability to examine (*exetastikê*) it has a route toward the starting-points of all methodical inquiries. (*Top.* I 2 101^{a}34–^{b}4)

Prima facie, then, the *Ethics*—and also the *Politics* to the extent that it involves new starting-points beyond those found there, such as the definitions of a citizen and a city—should correctly show the explanatory starting-points of politics by going through puzzles and solving them by appeal to reputable beliefs. But before we rush to the *Ethics* or *Politics* to see whether that is what we do find, we need to be clearer about what exactly we should be looking for. Writers on Aristotle's politics often go astray by failing to do this.

Dialectic is recognizably a descendant of the Socratic elenchus, which famously begins with a question like this: *Ti esti to kalon?* What is the noble? The respondent, sometimes after a bit of nudging, comes up with a universal definition, what is noble is what all the gods love, or whatever it might be (I adapt a well-known answer from Plato's *Euthyphro*). Socrates then puts this definition to the test by drawing attention to some things that seem true to the respondent himself but that conflict with his definition. The puzzle, or *aporia,* that results from this conflict then remains for the respondent to try to solve, usually by reformulating or rejecting his definition. Aristotle understood this process in terms that reveal its relationship to his own:

> Socrates . . . busied himself about the virtues of character, and in connection with these was the first to inquire into universal definition. . . . It was reasonable, though, that Socrates was inquiring into the what-it-is. For he was inquiring in order to deduce, and the what-it-is is a starting-point of deductions. . . . For there are two things that may be fairly ascribed to Socrates—inductive

> arguments and universal definition, both of which are concerned with a starting-point of scientific knowledge. (*Met.* XIII 4 1078^{b}17–30; also I 6 987^{b}1–4)

In Plato too dialectic is primarily concerned with scientific starting-points, such as those of mathematics, and seems to consist in some sort of elenchus-like process of reformulating definitions in the face of conflicting evidence so as to render them puzzle free (*Rep.* VII 532a1–533d1). Aristotle can reasonably be seen, then, as continuing a line of thought about dialectic which, in the *Topics* and the *Sophistical Refutations,* he explores, systematizes, and elaborates.

Think now about the respondent's first answer, his first definition: what is noble is what the gods love. Although it is soon shown to be incorrect, there is something quite remarkable about its very existence. Through experience shaped by acculturation and habituation involving the learning of a natural language, the respondent is confident that he can say what nobility is. He has learned to apply the word "noble" to particular people, actions, and so on correctly enough to pass muster as knowing its meaning, knowing how to use it. From these particular cases he has reached a putative universal, something the particular cases have in common, but when he tries to define that universal in words, he gets it wrong, as Socrates shows. Here is Aristotle registering the significance of this:

> What is knowable to each person at first is often knowable to a very small extent and possesses little or nothing of what is real [or true]. All the same, we must start from what is but badly knowable to us and try . . . to proceed through this to a knowledge of what is entirely knowable. (*Met.* VII 3 1029^{b}8–12)

The route by which the respondent reaches the universal that he is unable to define correctly is what Aristotle calls "induction" (*epagôgê*), or that variant of induction, which also involves the shaping of feelings and the development of character, namely, habituation (*ethismos*).

Induction begins with (1) perception of particulars, which leads to (2) retention of perceptual contents in memory, and, when many such contents have been retained, to (3) an experience, so that for the first time "there is a universal in the soul" (*APo.* II 19 100^{a}3–16). The universal reached at stage (3), which is the one the respondent reaches, is described as "indeterminate" and "better known by perception" (*Ph.* I 1 184^{a}22–25). It is the sort of universal, often quite complex, that constitutes a nominal essence corresponding to the nominal definition or meaning of a general term. Finally, (4) from experience come craft knowledge and scientific knowledge, when "from many intelligible objects arising from experience one universal supposition about similar objects is produced" (*Met.* I 1 981^{a}5–7).

The *nominal* (or analytic, meaning-based) definition of the general term "thunder," for example, might pick out the universal *loud noise in the clouds*. When science investigates the things that have this nominal essence, it may find that they also have a real essence or nature in terms of which their other features can be scientifically explained:

> Since a definition is said to be an account of what something is, it is evident that one sort will be an account of what its name, or of what some other name-like account, signifies—for example, what "triangle" signifies. . . . Another sort of definition is an account that makes clear the explanation of why it exists. So the former sort signifies something but does not show it, whereas the latter will evidently be like a demonstration of what it is, differing in arrangement from a demonstration. For there is a difference between giving the explanation of why it thunders and saying what thunder is. In the first case you will say: because fire is being extinguished in the clouds. And what is thunder? The loud noise of fire being extinguished in the clouds. Hence the same account is given in different ways. In one way it is a continuous demonstration, in the other a definition. Further, a definition of thunder is "a noise in the clouds," and this is a conclusion of the demonstration of what it is. The definition of an immediate item, though, is an indemonstrable positing (*thesis*) of what it is. (*APo.* II 10 93^{b}29–94^{a}10)

A real (or synthetic, fact-based) definition analyzes this real essence into its "constituents (*stoicheia*) and starting-points" (*Ph.* I 1 184^{a}23), which will be definable but indemonstrable. It makes intrinsically clear what the nominal definition made clear only to us by enabling us to recognize instances of thunder in a fairly—but imperfectly—reliable way. As a result, thunder itself, now clearly a natural and not just a conventional kind, becomes better known not just to us but entirely or unconditionally (*NE* I 4 1095^{b}2–8). These analyzed universals, which are the sort reached at stage (4), are the ones suited to serve as starting-points of the sciences and crafts: "People with experience know the fact that but not the explanation why, whereas those with craft knowledge know the explanation why, that is, the cause" (*Met.* I 1 981^{a}28–30).

Socrates too, we see, wanted definitions that were not just empirically adequate but also explanatory. Thus in telling Euthyphro what he wants in the case of piety, he says that he is seeking "the form itself *by dint of* which all the pieties are pieties" (*Euthphr*. 6d10–11). That is why he rejects the definition of piety as being what all the gods love. This definition is in one way correct, presumably, in that if something is pious, it is necessarily loved by all the gods, and vice versa, but it is not explanatory, since it does not tell us what it is about pious things that makes all the gods love them, and so it does not identify the form by dint of which they are pious (9e–11b).

Let's go back. We wanted to know what was involved in showing a scientific starting-point. We were told how we could *not* do this, namely, by demonstrating it from scientific starting-points. Next we learned that dialectic had a route to it from reputable beliefs. At the same time, we were told that induction had a route to it as well—something the *Ethics* also tells us: "we get a theoretical grasp on some starting-points through induction, some through perception, some through some sort of habituation, and others through other means" (I 7 1098^{b}3–4). This suggests that induction and dialectic are in some way or other the same process. It is a suggestion to keep in mind.

What shows a Socratic respondent to be wrong is an example that the respondent's definition does not fit. The presentation of the example might be quite indirect, however. It might take quite a bit of stage setting, elicited by the asking of many questions, to bring out a puzzle. But if the example is one the definition does not fit, it shows that the universal grasped by the respondent and the definition he produces are not entirely or unconditionally knowable and that his state is not one of clear-eyed understanding:

> A puzzle in thought reveals a knot in its subject matter. For thought caught in a puzzle is like people who are tied up, since in either case it is impossible to make progress. That is why one must get a theoretical grasp on all the difficulties ahead of time, both for these reasons and because those who inquire without first going through the puzzles are like people who don't know where they have to go, and, in addition, don't even know whether they have found what they were inquiring about, since the end is not clear to them. But to someone who has first gone through the puzzles it is clear. (*Met*. II 1 995^{a}30–^{b}2)

But lack of such clear-eyed understanding of a scientific starting-point has serious downstream consequences:

> If we are to have scientific knowledge through demonstration, . . . we must know the starting-points better and be better persuaded of them than of what is being shown, but we must also not find anything more persuasive or better known among

> things opposed to the starting-points from which a contrary mistaken conclusion may be deduced, since someone who has unconditional scientific knowledge must be incapable of being persuaded out of it. (*APo.* I 2 72ᵃ37–ᵇ4; also see *NE* VI 3 1139ᵇ33–35)

If dialectical examination reveals a puzzle in a respondent's thought about a scientific starting-point, then he cannot have any unconditional scientific knowledge even of what he may well be able to demonstrate correctly from it. Contrariwise, if dialectical examination reveals no such puzzle, then he apparently does have clear-eyed understanding, and his route to what he can demonstrate is free of obstacles.

At the heart of dialectic, as Aristotle understands it, is the dialectical deduction (*dialektikos sullogismos*). This is the argument lying behind the questioner's questions, partly dictating their order and content and partly determining the strategy of his examination. In the following passage it is defined and contrasted with two relevant others:

> Dialectical arguments are those that deduce from reputable beliefs in a way that reaches a contradiction; peirastic arguments are those that deduce from those beliefs of the respondent that anyone must know (*eidenai*) who pretends to possess scientific knowledge. . . . Contentious (*eristikos*) arguments are those that deduce or appear to deduce from what appear to be reputable beliefs but are not really such. (*SE* 2 165ᵇ3–8)

If we think of dialectical deductions in this way, a dialectician, in contrast to a contender, is an honest questioner, appealing to genuinely reputable beliefs and employing valid deductions. "Contenders and sophists use the same arguments," Aristotle says, "but not to achieve the same goal. . . . If the goal is apparent victory, the argument is contentious; if it is apparent wisdom, sophistic" (*SE* 11 171ᵇ27–33). Nonetheless, Aristotle does also use the term *dialektikê* as the name for the craft that honest dialecticians and sophists both use:

> In dialectic a sophist is so called in accord with his deliberate choice, and a dialectician is so called not in accord with his deliberate choice but in accord with the capacity he has. (*Rh.* I 1 1355ᵇ20–21)

If dialectic is understood in this way, a dialectician who deliberately chooses to employ contentious arguments is a sophist (*Rh.* I 1 1355ᵃ24–ᵇ7).

We need to be careful, therefore, to distinguish *honest dialectic* from what we may call *plain dialectic*, which—like all crafts—can be used for good and ill (*NE* V 1 1129ª13–17).

The canonical occasion for the practice of the Socratic elenchus, obviously, is the examination of someone else. But there is nothing to prevent a person from practicing it on himself: "How could you think," Socrates asks Critias, "that I would refute you for any reason other than the one for which I would refute myself, fearing lest I might inadvertently think I know something when I don't know it?" (*Chrm.* 166c7–d2). Dialectic is no different in this regard:

> The premises of the philosopher's deductions, or those of a person who is investigating by himself, though true and knowable, may be refused by the respondent because they lie too near to the original proposition, and so he sees what will happen if he grants them. But the philosopher is unconcerned about this. Indeed, he will presumably be eager that his axioms should be as familiar and as near to the question at hand as possible, since it is from premises of this sort that scientific deductions proceed. (*Top.* VIII 1 155b10–16)

What we are to imagine, then, is that the political philosopher, to focus on him, surveys the raw political starting-points (the empirical foundations of politics), constructing detailed catalogues of these. He then tries to formulate definitions of the various universals involved in them that seem to be candidate scientific starting-points (virtue, happiness, and so on), testing these against the raw political starting-points by trying to construct demonstrations from them. But these definitions will often be no more than partial; our political philosopher is on his way to complete definitional starting-points, just as the demonstrations will often be no more than proto or nascent demonstrations. The often rudimentary demonstrations that we find in Aristotle's scientific treatises are parts of this process of arguing *to*, not *from* starting-points: we argue to them in part by seeing whether or to what extent we could demonstrate from them.

So, first, we have the important distinction between dialectic proper, which includes the use of what appear to be deductions from what appear to be reputable beliefs, and honest dialectic, which uses only genuine deductions from genuine reputable beliefs. Second, we have the equally important distinction between the use of dialectic in examining a potentially hostile respondent and its use by the philosopher in a perhaps private pursuit of the truth. Third, we have an important contrast between honest dialectical premises and philosophical ones or scientific ones. Honest dialectical premises are reputable beliefs; philosophical and scientific premises must be true and knowable. Fourth, we have two apparently equivalent routes to scientific starting-points, one inductive, which starts from raw political starting-points, and the other dialectic, which starts from reputable beliefs.

According to the official definition, genuine reputable beliefs are "things that are believed by everyone, by the majority, or by the wise—either by all of them, or by most, or by the most well known and most reputable" (*Top.* I 1 100^{b}21–23). Just as the scientist should have a catalogue of scientific truths ready to hand from which to select the premises of his demonstrations, so a dialectician ought also to select premises "from arguments that have been written down and produce catalogues (*diagraphas*) of them concerning each kind of subject, putting them under separate headings—for example, 'Concerned with good,' 'Concerned with life'" (*Top.* I 14 105^{b}12–15). We should be reminded of the collections of laws and constitutions that enjoy "a good reputation (*eudokimountas*)," from which the legislative scientist selects the best ones (*NE* X 9 1181^{a}12–^{b}12, *Pol.* II 5 1263^{a}39n).

Clearly, then, there will be considerable overlap between the scientist's catalogue of raw starting-points and the honest dialectician's catalogue of genuine reputable beliefs. For, first, things that are believed by reputably wise people are themselves reputable beliefs, and, second, any respondent would accept "the beliefs of those who have investigated the subjects in question—for example, on a question of medicine he will agree with a doctor, and on a question of geometry with a geometer" (*Top.* I 10 104^{a}8–37). The catalogues also differ, however, in that not all reputable beliefs need to be true. If a proposition is a reputable belief, if it would be accepted by all or most people, it is everything an honest dialectician could ask for in a premise, since his goal is simply this: to reveal by honest deductions that a definition offered by any respondent whatsoever conflicts—if it does—with other beliefs that the respondent has. That is why having a complete or fairly complete catalogue of reputable beliefs is such an important resource for a dialectician. It is because dialectic deals with things only "in relation to belief," then, and not as philosophy and science do, "in relation to truth" (I 14 105^{b}30–31) that it needs nothing more than reputable *beliefs*.

Nonetheless, the fact that all or most people believe something leads us "to trust it as something in accord with experience" (*Div. Somn.* 1 426^{b}14–16), and—since human beings "are naturally adequate as regards the truth and for the most part happen upon it" (*Rh.* I 1 1355^{a}15–17)—as containing some truth. That is why, having catalogued some of the things that people believe happiness to be, Aristotle writes:

> Some of these views are held by many and are of long standing, while others are held by a few reputable men. And it is not

> reasonable to suppose that either group is entirely wrong, but rather that they are correct on one point at least or even on most of them. (*NE* I 8 1098ᵇ27–29).

Later he generalizes the claim: "things that seem to be so to everyone, these, we say, are" (X 2 1172ᵇ36–1173ᵃ1). Raw starting-points are just that—raw. But when refined, some shred of truth is likely to be found in them. So likely, indeed, that if none is found, this will itself be a surprising fact needing to be explained: "when a reasonable explanation is given of why an untrue view appears true, this makes us more convinced of the true view" (VII 14 1154ᵃ24–25). It is in the perhaps mere grain of truth enclosed in a reputable belief that a philosopher or scientist is interested, then, not in the general acceptability of the surrounding husk, much of which he may discard.

The process of refinement in the case of a candidate explanatory starting-point is that of testing a definition of it against reputable beliefs. This may result in the definition being accepted as it stands or in its being altered or modified. The same process applies to the reputable beliefs themselves, since they may conflict not only with the definition but also with each other. Again, this may also result in their being modified, often by uncovering ambiguities within them or in the argument supporting them or by drawing distinctions that uncover complexities in these. Thus Aristotle's view that it is "from oneself that all the features fitted to friendship also extend to others" is in accord with the reputable beliefs embodied in "all the proverbs" (*NE* IX 8 1168ᵇ5–10). But both conflict with the view that there is something shameful about being a self-lover, since a base person "does all his actions for the sake of himself," whereas a decent one "seems to act because of what is noble . . . and for the sake of a friend, disregarding his own interests" (1168ᵃ31–35). As a result, "it is reasonable to be puzzled . . . as to which side we should follow, since both carry conviction." Hence, to ease our puzzlement not just in this case but in all others like it, "we need to draw distinctions in connection with the arguments and determine to what extent and in what ways they grasp the truth. If, then, we were to find out what those on each side mean by 'self-love,' perhaps this would be clear" (1168ᵇ10–15). By the end of the chapter, this is precisely what has been accomplished. If, as ordinary people do, we think of self-lovers as those who gratify the non-rational part of their soul (as if it were their true self) with money, honors, and bodily pleasures (as if these were the greatest goods), we can see why they are right to think that "self-love" is a term of reproach. But if we recognize that noble things are better than these other goods, and that the true self is the understanding, we will also see what is wrong in their view and what is right in the opposing one, and agree that we should be "self-lovers" in that sense of the term. Just what it means to say that our true self is the understanding, however, is something we will return to at the appropriate juncture.

A more extreme possibility, as we saw, is that a reputable belief is not modified at all but is rejected entirely and has its appearance of truth explained away. This is what happens in the case of bodily pleasures. These are not more choiceworthy, Aristotle argues, yet they appear to be. So we must explain away their false appearance of choiceworthiness, one source of which is that they "knock out pain," and "get their intensity (which is why they are pursued) from the fact that they appear alongside their contrary" (*NE* VII 14 1154ᵃ26–31). Sometimes all the reputable beliefs on a certain topic stemming from a certain group can be excluded *en masse*:

> To investigate all the beliefs about happiness held by different people is superfluous, since little children, sick people, and lunatics apparently have many views, but no one with any understanding would go through these. For these people need not arguments but, in some cases, time in which to mature, in others, medical or political correction [or punishment]—for a drug is no less correctional than a flogging. Similarly there is no need to investigate the beliefs of the majority, since they speak baselessly on pretty much every topic but most of all this one. On it, only the beliefs of wise people need be investigated. (*EE* I 3 1214ᵇ28–1215ᵃ2)

We might see Aristotle's account of the distorting effects on beliefs about happiness of inadequate habituation where pleasures and pains are concerned as the justification of this bold claim. Readers who think that Aristotle gives the life of indulgence shrift that is much too short (*NE* I 5 1095ᵇ19–22, X 6 1176ᵇ9–1177ᵃ1) should not overlook its bearing on their concern. False consciousness, at least in one of its forms, was as familiar to Aristotle as it subsequently became to Hegel and Marx.

The canonical occasion for the use of honest dialectic, as of the Socratic elenchus and plain dialectic, is the examination of a respondent. The relevant premises for the questioner to use, therefore, are the reputable beliefs in his catalogue that his respondent will accept. Just how wide this set of beliefs is in a given case depends naturally on how accessible to the untrained subject the subject matter is on which he is being examined. In this regard our target candidate science, politics, is in a somewhat special position, since all adequately socialized subjects have access to the relevant subject matter and are even likely to have received some—however vestigial—training in politics itself. That is no doubt why Socrates' respondents are so confident, prior to examination, that they do know how to define the virtues. We might usefully compare the case of religious beliefs about the nature of human beings and the origins of life and cosmos in a society where all the citizens practice the same religion and all the schools teach it. In other more esoteric areas the class of reputable beliefs may be substantially narrower. We may all have some beliefs about thunder and other phenomena readily perceptible to everyone, that are—for that very reason—reputable. But about Mandelbrot sets, Bell's theorem, or messenger RNA we may have none at all.

When a scientist is investigating by himself, the class of premises he will select from is the catalogue of *all* the raw starting-points of his science, despite a natural human inclination to do otherwise:

> Yet . . . people seem to inquire up to a certain point but not as far as it is possible to take the puzzle. It is what we are all inclined to do, to make our inquiry not with an eye to the thing itself but with an eye to the person who says things that contradict him. For even a person inquiring on his own continues up to the point at which he is no longer able to contradict himself. That is why a person who is going to inquire correctly should be able to raise objections to a position by using objections that are proper to the relevant genus, and this will be when he has acquired a theoretical grasp on all the differentiae. (*Cael.* II 13 294^{b}6–13)

Hence our scientist will want to err on the side of excess, adding any reputable belief that appears to have any relevance whatsoever to his catalogue. When he formulates definitions of candidate scientific starting-points from which he thinks he can demonstrate the raw ones, he must then examine himself to see whether he really does in this case have the scientific knowledge he thinks he has. If he is investigating together with fellow scientists, others may examine him: we all do better with the aid of co-workers (*NE* X 7 1177^{a}34), among whom time figures as one (I 7 1095^{a}23–24). What he is doing is using honest dialectic on himself or having it used on him. But this, we see, is little different from the final stage—stage (4)—of the induction we looked at earlier. Induction, as we might put it, is, in its final stage, (possibly self-directed) honest dialectic.

In a famous and much debated passage of the *Ethics*, Aristotle writes:

> We must, as in the other cases, set out the things that appear to be so and first go through the puzzles, and, in that way show preferably all the reputable beliefs about these ways of being affected, or, if not all of them then most of them, and the ones with the most control. For if the objections are resolved and the

> reputable beliefs are left standing, that would be an adequate showing. (VII 1 1145^{b}1–7)

The specific topic of the comment is "these ways of being affected," which are self-control and its lack as well as resilience and softness. Some people think that the comment applies only to this topic and should not be generalized, even though "as in the other cases" surely suggests a wider scope. And as we can now see, that scope *is* in fact entirely general, since it describes the honest dialectical or inductive route to the starting-points of *all* the sciences and methodical inquiries, with *tithenai ta phainomena* ("setting out the things that appear to be so") describing the initial phase in which the raw starting-points are collected and catalogued.

Earlier we asked whether the *Ethics* took a route like this to the starting-points of politics. Now that we know what exactly it is we are asking, we must follow in Aristotle's footsteps both there and in the *Politics* to see what the answer is. But that is a task that a reader can be safely left to undertake for her- or himself. The fact that the *Ethics* explicitly refers to puzzles over thirty times, while the *Politics* does so around fifty,* might be taken as one measure, however, of the importance of honest dialectic in these works. But if we take this as the only measure, we are likely not to recognize the honest dialectic that is present in the many discussions in which no puzzles arise because none are encountered. This would be a mistake, as we saw, that our understanding of the *Ethics* and *Politics* would inherit from a mistake we had already made about the nature of honest dialectic and its role in all canonical sciences. When appearances, or what appears so, or what is evident to properly socialized subjects is appealed to—as happens repeatedly in the *Ethics* and *Politics*—honest dialectic is silently there, even if no puzzles are present.

Is politics, then, sufficiently similar to count as a science—provided that we are guided by similarities and are not speaking in an exact way? If we look, as we should, to politics' universalist component, the answer is that politics is as much like a canonical theoretical science as a natural science is. If we look to politics' particularist component, the answer is that it is not a science. All of which is to say that politics is a *practical* science, one with both a universalist and a particularist component. The contribution the *Ethics* makes to this science, so conceived, is to give it its capstone or "head"—a clear-eyed understanding of its primary starting-points (VI 7 1141^{a}19) that is at once true and (unlike Plato's form of the good) practical.

---

*As a glance at the Index of Terms s.v. "puzzle" will attest.

Happiness and the Human Function

Aristotle attributes functions to parts of bodies and souls, to instruments or tools of various sorts, and to human beings, insofar as they play certain sorts of roles (*Pol.* I 2 1252^b4n). Thus "a flute player, a carpenter, and every craftsman" have a function, since each has a characteristic activity or type of action that he does, namely, playing the flute or doing woodwork (*NE* I 7 1097^b25–26). But instead of arguing directly that human beings have a function, he treats the uncontroversial fact that craftsmen have "certain functions and actions," and that bodily parts, such as eyes, hands, and feet do (1097^b28–33), as making it absurd to think that they do not have one. The first thought seems to be that if in his roles as craftsmen of various sorts a human being has a function, he must also have a function of a more general type that suits him to play those roles, and to adapt himself to the rational principles and norms of the associated crafts and sciences. The second thought seems to reach the same conclusion by something like the reverse route: if each part of the human body has a function, the whole of which they are the parts must also have one, to which each of theirs contributes, so that its function explains theirs.

Whatever the human function turns out to be, then, it must be something we can intelligibly think of as explaining the functions of the parts of the human body, and how it is that human beings can be craftsmen, subject to the rational principles or norms of their craft. These are the requirements that shape Aristotle's search (F-prefaced numerals will help us keep track of its various steps and stages):

> [F1] What, then, could this [human function] be? For living (*zên*) is evidently shared with plants as well, but we are looking for what is special. Hence we must set aside the living that consists in nutrition and growth. Next in order is some sort of perceptual living. But this too is evidently shared with horse and ox and every animal. [F2] There remains, then, some sort of practical (*praktikê*) living of the part that has reason. And of what has reason, [F3] one part has it by dint of obeying reason, the other by dint of actually having it and exercising thought. [F4] But "living" is said of things in two ways, and we must take the one in accord with activity, since it seems to be called "living" in a fuller sense. (*NE* I 7 1097^b33–1098^a7)

Zôê refers to the sorts of life processes studied by biologists, zoologists, and other scientists (including psychologists and theologians): growth and reproduction are such processes, as are perceiving and understanding. As a result it is, as [F4] tells us, ambiguous, referring either to the potential to grow, reproduce, or perceive, or to the process or activity of growing, reproducing, perceiving, or understanding (*Protr.* B79–83). A second word, *bios*, refers to the sort of life a natural historian or (auto)biographer might investigate—the life of the otter, the life of Pericles—and so to a span of time throughout which someone possesses *zôê* as a potentiality: "The good and the bad person are least distinct while asleep, which is why happy people are said to be no worse off than wretched ones for half their life (*bios*)" (*NE* I 13 1102^{b}5–7). Hence, in the conclusion of the function argument, we are reminded that a *zôê* will not be happiness for a human being unless it occurs "in a complete *bios*" (I 7 1098^{a}18–20).

What is characterized as *praktikê* in [F2] is the *zôê* of what possesses reason, which might lead us to think that what is being referred to is a peculiarly practical as opposed to theoretical or contemplative rational activity. What is *praktikê*, however, often includes what is theoretical or contemplative, rather than excluding it:

> Yet it is not necessary, as some suppose, for an action-involving life to be lived in relation to other people, nor are those thoughts alone action-involving that arise for the sake of the consequences of doing an action, rather, much more so are the acts of contemplation and thought that are their own ends and are engaged in for their own sake. For doing well in action is the end, and so action of a sort is the end too. (*Pol.* VII 3 1325^{b}16–21)

[F3] seems intended to remind us of just this fact. Rational activity, it tells us, is twofold—that of the part that obeys reason, which is the desiring part, and that of the part that possesses reason autonomously, which comprises the scientific part, the deliberative part, and the understanding (I 5 1254^{b}5–9n, VII 14 1333^{a}16–18n, 15 1334^{b}20). But when we consider the desiring part in the way that [F4] requires, as actively obeying reason, it also involves the activity of the deliberative calculative subpart of the part that possesses reason autonomously. The twofold activity of what possesses reason is not (a) non-rational active desiring and (b) practical thinking, therefore, but rather (c) active desiring in accord with practical thinking or deliberation and (d) theoretical thinking or contemplation. It is the distinction between (c) and (d) indeed that paves the way for the disjunctive conclusion of the argument as a whole: "the human good turns out to be activity of soul in accord with virtue, and, if there are more virtues than one, in accord with the best and most complete" (*NE* I 7 1098^{a}16–18). For the most complete virtue is theoretical wisdom, which is the virtue of the scientific part, and is responsible for theoretical thinking or contemplation, while the less complete one is the amalgam of practical wisdom and the virtues of character, which is the virtue of the calculative and desiring parts, and is responsible for practical thinking or deliberation (*NE* X 7–8).

The implicit argument by elimination that Aristotle uses in [F1–2] to identify the human function with rational activity of a sort presupposes his own account of the soul (*NE* I 13). But whichever account we appeal to, rational activity of some sort is likely to emerge as best fitted for the double explanatory duty the human function must perform. For the crafts and choice-relevant sciences are rational enterprises, and the parts of the body, since they can be moved in accord with their norms, are arguably adapted by nature to subserve and further their ends and goals:

> Just as every instrument is for the sake of something, the parts of the body are also for the sake of something, that is, for the sake of some action, so that the whole body must evidently be for the sake of some complex action. Just as the saw is there for the sake of sawing, not sawing for the sake of the saw, since sawing is a certain use [of a saw], so the body, too, is somehow for the sake of the soul, and the parts of the body for the sake of those functions for which each is naturally adapted. (*PA* I 5 645^b14–20)

That is why [F2] the human function, as a rational activity of the soul, is something beyond all the functions of the bodily parts (*NE* I 7 1097^b32–33).

Once the human function is identified with a type of rational activity, the conceptual or analytic connection between a thing's functions and its virtues is used to legitimate the introduction of these virtues:

> [F5] If, then, the function of a human being is activity of the soul in accord with reason or not without reason, and the function of a sort of thing, we say, is the same in kind as the function of an excellent thing of that sort (as in the case of a lyre player and an excellent lyre player), and this is unconditionally so in all cases when we add to the function the superiority that is in accord with the virtue (for it is characteristic of a lyre player to play the lyre and of an excellent one to do it well)—if all this is so, and a human being's function is supposed to be a sort of living, and this living is supposed to be activity of the soul and actions that involve reason, and it is characteristic of an excellent man to do these well and nobly, and each is completed well when it is in accord with the virtue that properly belongs to it—if all this is so, [F6] the human good turns out to be activity of the soul in accord with virtue and, if there are more virtues than

> one, then in accord with the best and most complete (*teleiotatên*). [F7] Furthermore, in a complete life, for one swallow does not make a spring, nor does one day. Nor, similarly, does one day or a short time make someone blessed and happy. (*NE* I 7 1098^{a}7–20)

The investigation of happiness then focuses on the various candidate virtues governing rational activity, with the aim, finally, of discovering which of them is most complete. Once we know that, we will have the clearer account of what happiness is—or what its essence is—that readies it to be a scientific starting-point.

Before we can take that step, however, we need to understand [F6] more fully. The adjective *teleion*, which there occurs in the superlative, derives from *telos* ("end," "goal"), is discussed in the following entry in Aristotle's philosophical lexicon:

> What is said to be complete is, [C_1] in one way, that outside which not even one part is to be found—for example, the complete time of each thing is the one outside which there is no time to be found that is part of that time. [C_2] That which, as regards virtue or the good, cannot be surpassed relative to its kind (*genos*)—for example, a doctor is complete and a flute player is complete when they lack nothing as regards the form of their own proper virtue. (It is in this way, transferring the term to bad things, we speak of a complete scandalmonger and a complete thief—indeed we even say that they are good, for example, a good thief and a good scandalmonger.) Also, virtue is a sort of completion. For each thing is complete and every substance is complete when, as regards the form of its proper virtue, it lacks no part of its natural magnitude. [C_3] Further, things that have attained their end, this being something excellent, are said to be complete. For things are complete in virtue of having attained their end. So, since the end is a last thing, we transfer the term to base things and say that a thing has been completely ruined and completely destroyed, when there is no deficiency in its destruction and badness but it has reached its last. This is why death, too, is by metaphorical transference said to be an end, because both are last things. And the end—that is, the for-the-sake-of-which—is a last thing. (*Met.* V 16 1021^{b}12–30)

When Aristotle speaks of virtue as being complete, then, he often means that it is [C_1] *part-whole* complete. In the *Eudemian Ethics*, for example, he identifies complete virtue with virtue as a whole, incomplete virtue with its parts: "life (*zôê*) is either complete or incomplete, and similarly virtue, since in the one case it is whole (*holê*), in the other a part (*morion*)" (II 1 1219^{a}36–37). There and in the *Magna Moralia* he also identifies complete virtue with the amalgam of practical wisdom and the virtues of character that he calls *kalokagathia* or noble-goodness (II 8 1207^{b}20–27, *EE* VIII 3 1249^{a}16–17)—a notion he also employs in the *Politics* (I 13 1259^{b}34–35). In both these ethical treatises, he identifies happiness with activity in accord with complete virtue in a complete life (*MM* I 4 1184^{a}35–^{b}9, *EE* II 1 1219^{a}38–39). At the same time, he acknowledges the existence of practical wisdom as a virtue of thought, not of character, characterizes it as inferior to theoretical wisdom, and recognizes the contemplative activity that theoretical wisdom perfects or completes as of the greatest possible import to happiness (*MM* I 34 1197^{b}3–11, *EE* VII 15 1249^{a}24–^{b}25). What he does not do is explain how all these claims can be consistent with each other.

The *Nicomachean Ethics* might seem to inherit this problem. For there, too, general justice is "the complete use of complete virtue" (V 1 1129^{b}31), not "a part (*meros*) of virtue, but virtue as a whole (*holê*)" (V 1 1130^{a}9). Yet theoretical wisdom, which is also "a part (*meros*) of virtue as a whole (*holês*)" (VI 12 1144^{a}5–6), is not a part of general justice or its use. For "the virtue of understanding is separate" from the virtues of character and practical wisdom, which are virtues of the matter-form compound of soul and body (X 8 1178^{a}9–23), just as understanding is separate from the compound itself. Thus the problem implicit in the *Magna Moralia* and the *Eudemian Ethics* now seems to be right out in the open.

In all three ethical treatises, virtues are divided into those of character and those of thought, but once the (full) virtues of character are shown to be inseparable from practical wisdom, this distinction fades in prominence, and the distinction between the complete virtue of the merely human matter-form compound of body and soul and the virtue of the fully human or divine constituent in us in accord with which we contemplate on the other gains prominence—implicitly in the *Magna Moralia* (II 3 1199^{b}38–1200^{a}5) and *Eudemian Ethics* (VIII 1 1246^{b}32–33), explicitly in the *Nicomachean Ethics* (X 8 1178^{a}16–22). Thus in the latter happiness is no longer activity in accord with complete virtue but is activity in accord with the *best* and most complete virtue. Moreover, theoretical wisdom is the virtue of the best thing and the one with most control, so that its activity is complete happiness (*NE* I 7 1098^{a}16–18, X 7 1177^{a}12–17). Thus it is now recognized as a more complete virtue than full virtue of character. Yet the sense in which it is more or most complete cannot be a matter of [C_1] part-whole completeness, since, again, full virtue of character is not part of theoretical wisdom. Instead, it seems that the completeness it possesses to the greatest extent is something more akin to [C_2] *value* completeness, so that theoretical wisdom is more value complete than full virtue of character, because relative to the kind *virtue*, it cannot be surpassed in value.

While theoretical wisdom may be more value complete than full or complete virtue of character, it is apparently less part-whole complete than human virtue as a whole, which includes both of them (*NE* VI 12 1144^{a}5–6). In the case of virtues, in other words, it might seem that the two sorts of completeness can come apart. It is signal, therefore, that while the *Eudemian Ethics* seems not to distinguish complete virtues from whole virtues, the *Nicomachean Ethics*, while it recognizes human virtue to be a whole, of which theoretical wisdom and full or complete virtue of character are both parts, never characterizes it as complete. Full virtue of character is *a* virtue, as are its constituents, practical wisdom and the individual virtues of character. It is something with which activity can be in accord. The same is true of theoretical wisdom. Human virtue as a whole, by contrast, is not *a* virtue, *a* state, or something with which activity can be in accord: for activity in accord with theoretical wisdom is leisured, while activity in accord with full virtue is unleisured (X 7 1177^{b}4–26). Hence it is not something that is even a candidate for being a complete virtue, let alone the most complete one. The *Nicomachean Ethics* avoids a problem in the conception of a complete virtue present in the *Magna Moralia* and *Eudemian Ethics*, then, in a way that might reasonably be taken to suggest an awareness of its existence.

A problem similar to the one we have been exploring in the case of the virtues arises, too, in the case of ends or goods. The *Magna Moralia* is explicit that that thing "is better for the sake of which the rest are." Nonetheless, it uses this fact not to define the completeness of ends, as the *Nicomachean Ethics* does (I 7 1097^{a}30–34), but to establish the superior value of goods that are ends over that of goods that are not ends but means to them (*MM* I 2 1184^{a}3–7). The relative value of ends, on the other hand, is established by a kind of completeness that is part-whole:

> Among ends themselves, the complete is always better than the incomplete. A complete end is one whose attainment leaves us not still needing anything in addition, whereas an incomplete one is one whose attainment does leave us needing something in addition. For instance, if we attain justice alone, there are many things we need in addition, but when we attain happiness, there is nothing additional we still need. This, therefore, is the best end we are searching for, the complete end. The complete end, then, is the good and the end of the [other] goods. . . . But the complete end, unconditionally speaking, is nothing other

> than happiness, it seems, and happiness is composed of many goods. . . . For happiness is not something separate from these, but is these. (*MM* I 2 1184ᵃ7–29)

The conclusion reached is that happiness "cannot exist apart from external goods, and they come about as a result of good luck" (II 8 1207ᵇ16–18). Nonetheless, happiness does not consist in these goods but "in actively living in accord with the virtues" of character (I 4 1184ᵇ35–36), in a complete life (I 4 1185ᵃ1–9). Implicitly, then, the distinction is recognized between goods that are parts of happiness and those that are necessary or enabling conditions of it, as in the *Eudemian Ethics* (I 2 1214ᵇ26–27). Since the many goods of which happiness is composed are the activities of the various virtues of character, this again leaves the relationship of *theoretical wisdom* to happiness in an unstable situation—now because of how happiness is being conceived. In the *Nicomachean Ethics* (X 7–8) this instability is removed by recognizing two different types or grades of happiness, one incomplete, constituted by activity in accord with full virtue of character, another complete, constituted by activity in accord with theoretical wisdom.

The *Nicomachean Ethics* recognizes in [F7] that if activity in accord with theoretical wisdom is to constitute complete happiness, it must receive "a complete span of life (*bios*)" (X 7 1177ᵇ25) or must occur in or throughout "a complete life (*bios*)" (I 7 1098ᵃ18). What it does not do is explain what a complete life is or what makes it complete. The *Eudemian Ethics* refers to the "life (*bios*) with most control" (I 3 1215ᵃ4–5), emphasizes the importance of ordering "one's life (*bios*) in relation to some end" (I 2 1214ᵇ10), and replaces *bios* with *zôê* in requiring happiness to be "activity of a complete life (*zôê*)" (II 1 1219ᵃ38–39) but is equally silent about what makes a *bios* or *zôê* complete. In spelling out what a complete life is, the *Magna Moralia* stands alone:

> Since, then, happiness is a complete good and end, we should not overlook the fact that it will also exist in what is complete. For it will not exist in a child (since a child is not happy) but in a man, since he is complete. Nor will it exist in an incomplete time, but in a complete one, such as that of a human life (*bios*). For it is correctly said among the masses that a life's happiness should be discerned in its longest time, since what is complete should exist in a complete time and a complete human being. (I 4 1185ᵃ1–9)

As in the case of virtues and ends, then, the completeness attributed to lives is [C_1] part-whole completeness.

The completeness assigned to a life in the *Nicomachean Ethics*, by contrast, cannot be of this part-whole variety, since what is said there to virtue seems plainly inconsistent with it:

> It is true of an excellent person too that he does many actions for the sake of his friends and his fatherland, even dying for them if need be. For he will give up wealth, honors, and fought-about goods generally, in keeping for himself what is noble. For he will choose intense pleasure for a short time over weak pleasure for a long one; living life nobly for a year over many years lived in random fashion; and a single noble and great action over many small ones. This is presumably what happens with those who die for others. (IX 8 1169^a18–25)

It may be true, of course, that a happy life is presumptively of normal length, and so is part-whole complete—just as long as it is recognized that a shorter life can also be happy, provided its shortness is compensated for in some way.

In characterizing one sort of compensation, Aristotle again appeals to the notion of completeness. A virtuous person, he says, who has suffered many great strokes of bad luck will not return "to being happy again in a short time but—if indeed he does do so—in a long and complete one in which he achieves great and noble things" (I 10 1101^a12–13). Again, this sort of completeness, while clearly some sort of measure of life extent, cannot be that of normal life expectancy or part-whole completeness. The sort of life (*bios*) to which a natural life expectancy belongs, indeed, is primarily a biological life: elephants and plants also have life expectancies in this sense. But an individual human being's life, as we saw, is also an *(auto)-biographical* life, which can be a success—can be worthwhile and in need of nothing—even if it is not of normal length. One way it might be so is by containing, like the life of a great hero, "a single action that is noble and grand"—that is to say, an action of the sort the *Iliad* or *Odyssey* is built around, "an action that is unified, and a whole as well, whose parts, consisting of the events that happen, so constructed that the displacement or removal of any one of them will disturb and disjoint the whole" (*Po.* 8 1451^a32–35). Such a life may in a way be part-whole complete, but what is really important is that by achieving a good end it is [C_3] *end* complete.

Whether we consider virtues, ends, or lives, then, Aristotle seems to move away from thinking of their completeness in part-whole terms and toward thinking of it in terms of the completeness appropriate to ends. The reason he does so, in the case of virtues, seems to be the tension that otherwise results in how to include theoretical wisdom among the virtues.

Where life itself is concerned, the reason seems to have more to do with the virtues themselves and the demands they make—demands that cannot be made subservient to a formula, of the sort provided in the *Magna Moralia,* for how long a virtuous or happy life must be.

In one way it is easy to say what the human function is: it is [F5] activity of the soul in accord with reason. It is when we try to be more specific that we run into difficulties. For there seem to be three possibilities for what such activity could be: contemplative activity in accord with reason of the sort that theoretical wisdom completes or perfects; practical activity involving reason of the sort that practical wisdom and the virtues of character perfect; or some sort of activity involving reason that all of these virtues together somehow complete or perfect.

In the *Protrepticus*, we find Aristotle apparently confronting this problem in an interesting way, unparalleled in his other works:

> [F8] When each thing completes in the best way that which—not coincidentally but intrinsically—is its function, the thing in question must be said to be good too, and the virtue by which each thing can by nature accomplish this should be deemed to have the most control. [F9] What is composite and divisible into parts has several different activities, but what is by nature simple and does not have its substance in relation to something else must have one controlling virtue intrinsically. [F10] If then a human being is a simple animal and his substance is ordered in accord both with reason and with understanding, he has no other function than this alone, namely, the attainment of the most rigorous truth about the beings. [F11] But if he is naturally co-composed of several potentialities, and it is clear that he has by nature several functions to be completed, the best of them is always *his* function, as health is the function of the doctor, and safety of a ship's captain. We can, however, name no function of thought or of the understanding part of our soul that is better than truth. Truth, therefore, is the function of this part of the soul that has most control. [F12] But this it attains in accord with unconditional scientific knowledge, or rather in accord with what is scientific knowledge to a higher degree [than anything else], and of this the end that has most control is contemplation. For when of two things one is choiceworthy for the sake of the other, the latter is better and more choiceworthy, precisely because the other is choiceworthy for it, as, for example, pleasure is more choiceworthy than pleasant things, and health than healthy ones, since the latter, we say, produce the former.

> Than wisdom, however, which we say is the potentiality in us that has most control, nothing is more choiceworthy, when one state is discerned in relation to another, for the part that has knowledge, whether taken separately or jointly, is better than all the rest of the soul, and its virtue is [a sort of unconditional] scientific knowledge [namely, theoretical wisdom]. (B63–67)

[F8] reprises doctrine familiar from the function argument, making plain what is implicit there, that a thing's function is what the virtue with most control completes or perfects. [F9] contrasts two kinds of beings: a simple being—the primary god (*Pol.* III 6 1287^{a}29n)—who has only one function (implied in [F10]), and so only one virtue with most control; and a complex being, which has many parts. If a human being were a simple animal, his function would be "the attainment of the most rigorous truth," and so [F12] his one virtue would be the wisdom ensuring such attainment, namely, theoretical wisdom. But [F11] he is not a simple animal. Instead, he has many potentialities and functions to be completed, and so (by implication), many virtues too. Nonetheless, it is the best of these functions that is *his* function, so that the virtue of his that has most control, like the virtue of the simple being, is theoretical wisdom.

To take the next step we need first to acknowledge complexity in Aristotle's use of the term *anthrôpos*—or, if you like, in his conception of what a human being is. An *anthrôpos* in the most general sense is a human being of either sex, whereas an *anêr*, by contrast, is specifically a male human being—a man. The associated adjective *anthrôpinos*, while it can certainly mean "human," often seems to mean something more like "*merely* human":

> We should not, however, in accord with the makers of proverbs, "think human things (*anthrôpina*), since you are human" or "think mortal things, since you are mortal" but, rather, we should as far as possible immortalize, and do everything to live in accord with the element in us that is most excellent. (*NE* X 7 1177^{b}31–33)

Anthrôpikos (also "human") sometimes has similar connotations:

> Happiest, but in a secondary way, is the life in accord with the other virtue, since the activities in accord with it are human (*anthrôpikai*). . . . Indeed, some of them even seem to arise from the body. . . . But the virtues of the compound [of soul and body] are human (*anthrôpikai*). So too, then, are both the life and the happiness that is in accord with them. The virtue

> of understanding [= theoretical wisdom], though, is separated. (*NE* X 8 1178ᵃ9–22)

Indeed, even *anthrôpos* itself is sometimes used to refer to the whole human animal, sometimes to the human element in human beings by contrast with the divine one:

> But such a [contemplative] life would be more excellent than one in accord with the human element (*anthrôpon*), since it is not insofar as he is a human being (*anthrôpos*) that someone will live a life like that but insofar as he has some divine element (*theion ti*) in him, and to the degree that this element is superior to the compound, to that degree will its activity also be superior to that in accord with the other sort of virtue. (*NE* X 7 1177ᵇ26–29)

But *anthrôpos* is equally well used to refer to that divine element itself, since it is what makes human beings distinctively human:

> Of those pleasures that seem to be decent, however, which sort or which particular one should we say is characteristic of a human being? Or isn't this clear from the corresponding activities, since the pleasures are entailed by these? So whether the activities of a complete and blessed man are one or more than one, the pleasures that complete these will be said to be characteristically human (*anthrôpou*) pleasures in the full sense, and the rest will be so in a secondary or many-times-removed way, as are the activities. (*NE* X 5 1176ᵃ24–29)

Here the pleasures that are characteristically human are those not of the body, since many of these we share with wild beasts, but of the soul, especially the understanding:

> We think that pleasure must be mixed in with happiness, and the most pleasant of the activities in accord with virtue is agreed to be the one in accord with theoretical wisdom. (*NE* X 7 1177ᵃ22–25)

Thus when we ask what the special human function is, we need to be clear about what we think a human being in the relevant sense is.

It is at this point that we come face to face with an initially quite puzzling doctrine:

> [F13a] But just as a city too or any other complex system, seems to be most of all (*malist'*) its most controlling part, so also does a human being. (*NE* IX 8 1168^{b}31–33)

> [F13b] It would seem too that each person actually *is* this, if indeed it is the controlling and better element. So it would be strange if he were to choose not his own life but that of something else. Moreover, what we said before will fit now as well. For what properly belongs to each thing by nature is best and most pleasant for each of them. For each human being, then, the life in accord with understanding is so too, if indeed this most of all is a human being. Hence, this life will also be happiest. (*NE* X 7 1178^{a}2–8; also *Protr.* B58–70)

[F13a] tells us that a human being is *malista* ("most of all") its most controlling element, which [F13b] identifies with the divine element in him—understanding. [F13b] goes further in one dimension, since it drops the adverb *malista*, and speaks of a human being simply as being—as being one and the same as—his understanding. At the same time, it is more tentative about this identity—"if indeed it is the controlling and better element"—and in the end even restores the adverb: "if indeed this most of all is a human being."

Now it is certainly true that we cannot make much sense of one thing being most of all one and the same as another if this means that it has a very high degree, or the highest degree, of numerical identity to it. For numerical identity, like existence, does not come in degrees: things either exist or they don't and are either one and the same as each other or they aren't. However, the fact that [F13a] mentions a city as an example of the sort of complex system that is most of all its most controlling element gives us a way to understand it in more familiar, and less apparently paradoxical terms.

In *Politics* III 6, Aristotle squarely states that "the governing body controls the city everywhere, and the constitution is governing body" (1278^{b}10–11). What is revealing about this statement is that, like [F13a–b], it mentions the notion of control, which is itself characterized in terms of degree: "most controlling" in [F13a] and "controls the city everywhere (*pantachou*)." And the reason it is revealing is this:

> [F14a] A person is called "self-controlled" or "lacking in self-control" depending on whether or not his understanding is in control, on the supposition that this is what each person *is*, and it is actions involving reason that people seem most of all to do themselves and to do voluntarily. So it is clear enough that this

> part is what each person is or is most of all and that a decent person likes this part most. (*NE* X 8 1168^{b}34–1169^{a}2)
>
> [F14b] Just as in the whole it is the [primary] god, so it is too in us. For the divine constituent in us [= understanding or reason] in a way does all the moving. Of reason, however, the starting-point is not reason, but something superior. But what besides the [primary] god is superior to both scientific knowledge and understanding, since virtue [of character] is an instrument of understanding? (*EE* VIII 2 1248^{a}25–29)

Without going into all the details involved in interpreting [F14b], we can see that together with [F14a] it licenses us to understand [F13a–b] as a doctrine that is as much about control as it is about identity.

When contemporary philosophers try to understand human agency, they often find themselves wanting to distinguish actions that originate in—or have their causal source in—the agent from actions that stem from the agent's "real self" or "will" or what the agent "identifies" with. A reforming smoker, for example, may succumb to temptation and exhibit lack of self-control by smoking a cigarette, without thereby returning to being a smoker. Why? Because that action stems from a desire that is no longer a part of his true self, no longer part of his will or what he identifies with. However precisely we are best to understand the psychology of agency that makes these distinctions fully intelligible, it is attractive to see Aristotle as making an early contribution to it, since this allows us to make good sense of [F13a–b]. For on this way of looking at them degrees of identity have no place in them. We are most of all our understanding because our understanding is our "true self"—the source of those actions that are most our own, that we most identify with. And our function—even though unlike the primary god we are complex beings—is our function for the same reason. It is, so to speak, the function that is most of all ours—the function of what we most of all identify with.

The Happiest Human Life 1: Education

Since practical wisdom includes politics, it shares its status as the most architectonic sort of knowledge. Yet there are limits even to its control. Practical wisdom "does not control either theoretical wisdom or the better part [of the soul], any more than medicine controls health, since it does not use it, but sees to its coming into being. So it prescribes for its sake, but not to it" (*NE* VI 13 1145^{a}6–9). To think otherwise would be like thinking that politics "rules the gods, because it prescribes with regard to everything in the city" (1145ᵃ10–11). For while politics does indeed enact laws concerning the distribution of priesthoods, the location of temples, and other things pertaining to the public worship of the gods, these are for the sake of the gods, ensuring their proper honor and worship, not laws to which the gods themselves are subject (*Pol.* VII 9 1329ᵃ27–34, 10 1330ᵃ11–13). Similarly, the divine constituent of the soul and its virtue (theoretical wisdom) do not operate in accord with politics' prescriptions, but rather these prescriptions are for their sake. True, politics "uses the other practical sciences" (*NE* I 2 1094ᵇ4–5), but that means that it uses them to further happiness, which, as we saw, just is the activity of theoretical wisdom. It does not use theoretical wisdom itself, since it does not use *it* to further anything. In this regard, politics is like medicine, which does not issue prescriptions to the already healthy, or use health to further some additional end, but rather prescribes to the sick to see to it that health comes to be in them.

Theoretical wisdom is a state of the soul's scientific part. Hence, to see to its coming into being, politics must arrange for its acquisition by some group in the city it supervises, and then arrange for those in the group to have the leisure necessary to actualize their acquired state in active contemplation, throughout a life that is sufficiently long to count as complete. In the case of the best kind of city and constitution described in *Politics* VII–VIII, the implication seems to be that *all unconditional citizens* should have access to happiness, so that all should acquire and, to the extent possible, exercise theoretical wisdom. There seems to be no question of restricting theoretical wisdom to some intellectual elite, or to those who are actual or future political leaders, or heads of households. Aristotle does, of course, restrict membership of the class of unconditional citizens of the best city, but the way he does it shows him to be entirely unconcerned about issues of this sort.

Because a city must be a self-sufficient community, it needs "a multitude of farmers to provide the food; and craftsmen; and a fighting element; and a rich element; and priests; and judges of necessary matters and advantageous ones" (*Pol.* VII 8 1328ᵇ20–23). It is from these groups that the unconditional citizens must be selected. One way constitutions differ, indeed, is by making the selection in different ways: "in democracies everyone shares in everything, whereas in oligarchies it is the contrary" (VII 9 1328ᵇ32–33). So the task is to determine how in the best circumstances the selection should be made:

> Since we are investigating the best constitution, however, the one in accord with which a city would be most happy, and happiness cannot exist separate from virtue, as was said earlier, it evidently follows that in a city governed in the best way, possessing men who are unconditionally—not relative to a hypothesis—just, the citizens should not live a vulgar or a trading life. For lives of these

> sorts are ignoble and entirely contrary to virtue. Nor should those who are going to be citizens be farmers, since leisure is needed both for the development of virtue and for political actions. But since the best city contains both a military part and one that deliberates about what is advantageous and renders judgment about what is just, and since it is evident that these are most of all parts of the city, should these functions also be assigned to distinct people, or are both to be assigned to the same people? [The answer to] this is evident too, because in one way the functions should be assigned to the same people and in another they should be assigned to distinct ones. For insofar as the prime time for each of the two functions is different, in that one requires practical wisdom and the other strength, they should be assigned to different people. On the other hand, insofar as it is impossible for those capable of using and resisting force to tolerate being always ruled, to that extent they should be assigned to the same people. For those who control the weapons also control whether a constitution will endure or not. The only course remaining, therefore, is for the constitution to assign both functions to the same people, but not at the same time. Instead, just as it is natural for strength to be found among younger men and practical wisdom among older ones, so it is advantageous and just to assign the functions to each group in this way, since this division is in accord with worth. Moreover, the property too should be assigned to them. For it is necessary for the citizens to be well supplied with resources, and these people are the citizens. For the vulgar element does not share in the city, and nor does any other kind (*genos*) of person who is not a craftsman of virtue. This is clear from our hypothesis. For happiness necessarily involves virtue, and a city must not be called happy by looking at just a part of it, but by looking at all the citizens. It is also evident that the property should be theirs, if indeed the farmers must either be slaves, either barbarians or subject peoples. (*Pol.* VII 9 1328^{b}33–1329^{a}26)

The phrase "a craftsman of virtue" is borrowed from Plato, who uses it to characterize the work of the philosopher rulers in drafting the constitution of his own best city or *kallipolis*:

> The philosopher, by associating with what is orderly and divine [that is, the Platonic Forms] becomes as divine and orderly as a human being can. . . . And if he should come to be compelled to make a practice—in private and in public—of stamping what he

> sees there into the people's characters, instead of shaping only his own . . . he will [not] be a poor craftsman of temperance, justice, and the whole of popular virtue (*dêmiourgon . . . tês dêmotikês aretês*). (*Rep.* 500d)

It is hard to believe that Aristotle would use this phrase were he not also planning to educate *his* ideal citizens in philosophy. But that is a small point on which we have no need to lean.

The prime time for a man's military service is that of his body, which is somewhere between the ages of thirty and thirty-five, while the prime time for that of his soul or his potentiality for thought is forty-nine or fifty (*Pol.* VII 16 1335b32–35, *Rh.* II 14 1390b9–11). Until the age of forty or so, then, male citizens lack the experience necessary for practical wisdom and deliberative ruling office, and thereafter possess it. Yet, though full virtue of character is something they can develop only in middle age, all are presumed capable of developing it. No elaborate tests are countenanced, as they are in Plato's best city, to segregate the future philosopher rulers from other citizens equally mature but less gifted in, for example, mathematics. A politician aims at "happiness for himself and for his fellow citizens" (*NE* X 7 1177b14), not for the happiness of some narrower few. As an end additional to the unleisured activities of the virtues of character themselves, such happiness must be contemplative in nature.

The mature citizens of the best city are all unconditionally just, which involves their possessing full virtue of character. Moreover, all of them are as happy as possible, which involves their also possessing theoretical wisdom. But theoretical wisdom cannot be acquired except through lengthy education and experience (*NE* II 1 1103a14–17). Hence the natural place to begin an investigation of how politics arranges more specifically for theoretical wisdom's acquisition is with the discussion in *Politics* VII–VIII of the education that the best city and constitution provides.

A community could not really be a city, Aristotle thinks, if it did not educate its citizens in virtue, since it is by means of education that people are unified and made into a city (*Pol.* II 5 1263b36–37, III 9 1280b1–8). Consequently, education should be suited to the constitution and provided to the citizens by it, so that it is communal or public rather than private (I 13 1260b15, VIII 1 1337a14–26). Although most of the discussion of education in the best city concerns that of (future) male citizens, communal education is also provided to girls and women (I 3 1260b13–20, VII 16 1335b11–12). Since women's virtues of character are different from men's, part of their education must also be different. Just how different it will be when these virtues are no longer the issue is hard to say. Women cannot have unconditional practical wisdom and virtue of character, since the deliberative part of their soul lacks authority

(I 13 1260ª12–13n). The scientific part, on the other hand, seems unaffected by this difference. So perhaps women are capable of acquiring theoretical wisdom, or some close approximation to it. Aristotle does not explicitly rule it out, but he does not explicitly discuss it either. (Among the students in Plato's Academy, where Aristotle spent twenty years, Diogenes Laertius (III [46], IV [2]) lists two women, Lasthenia of Mantinea and Axiothea of Plus, citing Dicaerarchus, one of Aristotle's pupils, as a source of his information. So Aristotle cannot have been ignorant of the existence of women philosophers.)

Education from infancy to early adulthood seems to have four stages:

1. The first concerns the treatment of infants, and their informal training up to the age of five (*Pol.* VII 17 1336ª3–ᵇ35). The emphasis here is on diet, on the shaping and conditioning of the body, and especially on the use of leisure appropriate to free citizens.
2. From age five to seven, children observe the lessons they will later learn for themselves (1336ᵇ35–37).
3. From seven to fourteen, their education includes lighter gymnastic exercises (VIII 4 1338ᵇ40–42).
4. From fourteen to twenty-one, the first three years are devoted in part to "other sorts of learning," and the next four to arduous athletic training combined with a strict diet (VIII 4 1339ª5–7).

Much of what is included here falls under the rubric of the "education through habituation" provided by physical trainers and coaches, which precedes "education through reason" (VIII 3 1338ᵇ4–7) and helps lead to habituated virtue. The "other sorts of learning" mentioned at stage 4 are not explicitly identified. They could be restricted to reading, writing, music, and drawing (1337ᵇ24–25), but then the only thing that children would be taught at stage 3—a period of seven whole years—would be light gymnastics. This is sufficiently implausible in its own terms, and a sufficiently large departure from common Greek practice that we would expect Aristotle to acknowledge it as an innovation and defend it carefully. The fact that he does neither suggests that he is intending to follow tradition and include reading, writing, drawing, and music at stage 3.

A promised discussion of a sort of education that sons must be given "not as something useful or necessary but as something noble and free" (*Pol.* VIII 3 1338ª30–34) is not a part of Aristotle's works as we have them. Nonetheless, what we do have contains some clues as to the nature of such studies. We know, for example, that music and drawing are both to be taught in part because they are free subjects and contribute to leisure (VIII 3 1338ª21–22, 1338ᵇ1–2). We also know that a free person must have theoretical knowledge of various aspects of wealth-acquisition

(I 11 1258^{b}9–11). Stage 4 seems a plausible location for some level of training in these subjects.

Aristotle also sometimes refers to what he calls "a well-educated person" (*pepaideumenos*)—someone who studies a subject not to acquire scientific knowledge of it but to become a discerning judge:

> Regarding every sort of theoretical knowledge and every methodical inquiry, the more humble and more estimable alike, there appear to be two ways for the state to be, one that may be well described as scientific knowledge of the subject matter, the other a certain sort of educatedness. For it is characteristic of a person well educated (*pepaideumenos*) in that way to be able accurately to discern what is well said and what is not. We think of someone who is well educated about the whole of things as a person of that sort, and we think that being well educated consists in having the capacity to do that sort of discerning. But in one case, we consider a single individual to have the capacity to discern in, so to speak, all subjects, in the other case, we consider him to have the capacity to discern in a subject of a delimited nature—for there might be a person with the same capacity as the person we have been discussing but about a part of the whole. So it is clear in the case of inquiry into nature too that there should be certain defining marks by reference to which we can appraise the way of its demonstrations, separately from the question of what the truth is, whether thus or otherwise. (*PA* I 1 639^{a}1–15)

> Not being well educated is just the inability to discern in each subject which arguments belong to it and which are foreign to it. (*EE* I 6 1217^{a}7–10)

Thus a person well educated in medicine, for example, is capable of discerning whether someone has treated a disease correctly (*Pol.* III 11 1282^{a}3–7), and the "unconditionally well-educated person," who is well educated in every subject or area, "seeks exactness in each area to the extent that the nature of its subject matter allows" (*NE* I 3 1094^{b}23–1095^{a}2).

Since a well-educated person is discerning, he knows who is and is not worth listening to on any topic, and so is free from intellectual enslavement to self-proclaimed experts. He is also free from the sort of intellectual enslavement that is often the lot of the narrow specialist, whose imagination is often straitjacketed by the one thing he knows too well. A well-educated person has studied all the "free sciences," but he has done so only "up to a point" and not so assiduously as "to make thought unleisured and low"

(*Pol.* VIII 3 1337[b]14–17). Presumably, then, the citizens of the best city, who are all free and well-educated people, must be trained in these subjects at some stage, if not at stage 4, then later in their lives: "a young person," notoriously, is not "a suitable audience for politics" (*NE* I 3 1095[a]2–3).

That there must be public education in philosophy generally, and not just in ethics or political science, is certain, since philosophy is required for leisure and education in it is needed to make a city good (*Pol.* II 5 1263[b]37–40, 7 1267[a]10–12). Besides, since theoretical wisdom (*sophia*) is at least part of the *sophia* of which *philosophia* is the love, it must be education in *philosophia* that leads to *sophia*'s acquisition, and so to the happiness it constitutes.

Aristotle sometimes applies the term *philosophia* to any science aiming at truth rather than action: "It is also correct that philosophy should be called scientific knowledge of the truth. For the end of theoretical science is truth, while that of practical science is the result (*ergon*) [of action]" (*Met.* II 1 993[b]19–21). In this sense of the term, all the broadly theoretical sciences count as branches of philosophy, and *philosophia* is more or less equivalent in meaning to *epistêmê*. *Philosophia* also has a narrower sense, however, in which it applies exclusively to sciences providing knowledge of starting-points. Thus "natural—that is, secondary, philosophy" has the task of providing theoretical knowledge of the starting-points of perceptible substances (VII 11 1037[a]14–16), whereas "the determination of the unmoving starting-point is a task for a distinct and prior philosophy" (*GC* I 3 318[a]5–6). Since there are just "three theoretical philosophies, mathematical, natural, and theological" (*Met.* VI 1 1026[a]18–19), theological philosophy must be primary, mathematical philosophy tertiary (although it is not, I think, ever referred to as such).

Besides these theoretical philosophies, Aristotle occasionally mentions practical ones, such as "the philosophy of human affairs" (*NE* X 9 1181[b]15). It is among these that his own ethical writings belong:

> It seems to everyone that justice is some sort of equality, and up to a point, at least, they agree with what has been determined in those philosophical accounts in which ethical matters were discussed. For justice is something to someone, and they say it should be something equal to those who are equal. But we should not neglect to consider what sort of equality and what sort of inequality. For this also involves a puzzle for political philosophy. (*Pol.* III 12 1282[b]18–23)

Since puzzles—especially those about starting-points—are the provenance of dialectic and philosophy, as we saw, it seems that political philosophy, like its theoretical fellows, should be primarily concerned with the starting-points of political science, and with the puzzles to which these give rise. And in fact, as we also saw, puzzles are explicitly mentioned around fifty times in the *Politics*.

In its early stages, at least, the education that politics provides to citizens in the best city overlaps with the habituation designed to cultivate in the young the habits of being pleased and pained that will lead them to form true beliefs about the noble and just things that the subject matter of ethics comprises. Once such habits are acquired, the task remains of explaining why the beliefs these habits support are true by demonstrating them from the appropriate starting-points (*NE* I 4 1095ᵃ30–ᵇ8). This is a task for ethics and politics. By showing that the various conventionally distinguished virtues of character are mean states that help us complete or fulfill our function well, for example, politics shows that they are genuine virtues, and provides a demonstration (or the raw materials for a demonstration) of them, by revealing their relationship to its own starting-point—happiness:

> In every methodical inquiry, there is a difference between what is said philosophically and what is said un-philosophically. That is precisely why even politicians (*tôn politikôn*) should not regard as irrelevant to their work the sort of theoretical knowledge (*theôrian*) that makes evident not only the fact, but also the reason why. For in every line of inquiry this is how the philosopher proceeds. (*EE* I 6 1216ᵇ35–39)

In the process, it explains why the virtues are worth having, and why the beliefs they help sustain are true. Likewise, it explains why a certain constitution is in fact the best one because it is the one in which those virtues are best cultivated, and genuine happiness best achieved. Once political science has accomplished this task, it falls to political *philosophy* to give us clear understanding of the starting-point by solving the relevant puzzles. Political science and the related philosophy, then, are what transform habituated virtue into full virtue and practical wisdom, by providing them with understanding of the target or end they further: "to those who form their desires and do their actions in accord with reason," knowledge of politics will be "of great benefit" (*NE* I 3 1095ᵃ10–11), since it is through "habits, *philosophy*, and laws" that cities are made virtuous or good (*Pol.* II 5 1263ᵇ39–40).

The focus of the various philosophies on starting-points is indicative of their reflective or higher-order status—their being not so much science as *meta*-science. Hence it is by reflecting on first-order sciences generally that primary philosophy begins, seeking insight not so much into the subject matter of each one as into the structure of the whole of the reality—the beings as such or qua being—these sciences collectively characterize and explain:

> The starting-points and causes of beings are what we are inquiring into, and clearly qua beings. For there is some cause of health and of good physical condition, and there are starting-points and elements and causes of the objects of mathematics, and in general every science that proceeds by thinking or that has some share in thinking is concerned with causes and starting-points, whether more exactly or more simply considered. All these sciences, however, mark off a certain being, a certain genus, and busy themselves with it, but not with being unconditionally or qua being, nor do they produce any account of the what-it-is. Instead, starting from the what-it-is—some making it clear by means of the perceptual capacities, some getting hold of it as a hypothesis—they in this way proceed to demonstrate the things that belong intrinsically to the genus with which they are concerned, either in a more necessary or in a weaker way. Which is why it is evident from such an induction that there is no demonstration of substance nor of the what-it-is, but some other way of making it clear. Similarly too they say nothing as to whether the genus they busy themselves with does or does not exist, because it belongs to the same sort of thinking to make clear both what-it-is and whether it exists. (*Met.* VI 1 1025^{b}3–18)

What induction reveals is that the familiar special sciences, each of which deals with a single genus, are all to some degree demonstrative in structure, have essences as their starting-points, and give no arguments for these or demonstrations of them. Hence they "say nothing" about the existence of the genus of beings with which they deal. Induction also reveals that the special sciences fall into three distinct types: natural, mathematical, and theoretical, these being distinguished by the kinds of essences that serve as their starting-points, and whether or not they involve matter. These types are not genera, however, since natural and mathematical beings, for example, belong to multiple genera.

Although theorems of mathematics are usually special to some branch of it, such as arithmetic or geometry, there are also "certain mathematical theorems of a universal character" (*Met.* XIII 2 1077^{a}9–10):

> That proportionals alternate might be thought to apply to numbers qua numbers, lines qua lines, solids qua solids, and times qua times, as used to be demonstrated of these separately,

> although it is possible to prove it of all cases by a single demonstration. But because all these things—numbers, lengths, times, solids—do not constitute a single named [type] and differ in form from each other, they were treated separately. But now it is demonstrated universally: for what is supposed to hold of them universally doesn't hold of them qua lines or qua numbers, but qua this [unnamed] type. (*APo.* I 5 74ᵃ17–25)

That proportionals alternate is a theorem of universal mathematics, but its universality is open to challenge, since lines, numbers, and so on belong to different genera. For the tight unity of the definitions that are scientific starting-points makes it "necessary for the extreme and middle terms in a demonstration to come from the same genus" (I 7 75ᵇ10–11). Consequently, transgeneric demonstrations seem to be ruled out: "it is impossible that what is proved should cross from one genus to another" (I 23 84ᵇ17–18). Yet even though the explanation of why the theorem about proportionals holds "in the case of lines and of numbers is different, qua such-and-such an increase in quantity, it is the same" (II 17 99ᵃ8–10). What the theorem does hold of, in other words, are *quantities* (*Met.* XI 4 1061ᵇ19–21). *Quantity*, however, is not a genus, since it is unified analogically:

> Of the items used in the demonstrative sciences some are special to each science and others common, but common by analogy, since they are only useful in so far as they bear on the genus falling under the science. Proper, for example, that a line is such-and-such, and straight so-and-so. Common, for example, that if equals are taken from equals, the remainders are equal. (*APo.* I 10 76ᵃ37–41)

It is an analogically unified *category*, therefore, that serves as the ontological correlate or truth-maker for theorems of universal mathematics (I 32 88ᵇ1–3).

The status of universal natural science is similar:

> Natural science too has the same way of inquiring as mathematics. For natural science gets a theoretical grasp on the [intrinsic] coincidents and starting-points of beings insofar as they are moving and not qua beings (whereas the primary science, we have said, is concerned with these, only insofar as the underlying subjects are beings, and not insofar as they are anything else). That is why both this science and mathematical science must be posited as *parts* of theoretical wisdom. (*Met.* XI 4 1061ᵇ27–33)

There must be theorems of universal natural science, then, that, like those of universal mathematics, require distinctive analogically unified ontological correlates. These are what are needed to explain change generally:

> The causes and starting-points of distinct things are distinct in a way, but in a way—if we are to speak universally and analogically—they are the same for all. For we might raise a puzzle as to whether the starting-points and elements of substances and of relations are distinct or the same, and similarly, then, in the case of each of the categories. . . . Or as we say, there is a way in which they are and there is a way in which they are not. For example, the elements of perceptible bodies are presumably: as *form*, the hot and, in another way, the cold, which is the *lack*; and, as *matter*, what is potentially these directly and intrinsically. And both these and the things composed of them are substances, of which these are the starting-points. . . . But since not only the things present in something are causes, but also certain external things, for example, the moving cause, it is clear that starting-point and element are distinct. Both, though, are causes, while what is so in the sense of moving or causing rest is a sort of starting-point, and the starting-point is divided into these two [sorts]. So analogically there are three elements, and four causes and starting-points. But distinct things have distinct ones, as was said, and the direct cause in the sense of a moving cause is distinct for distinct things. . . . And, furthermore, beyond these there is what as the first of all [movers] moves all things. (*Met.* XII 4 1070^{a}31–^{b}35)

The upshot for universal natural science is that the ontological correlates or truth-makers for its theorems are not species or genera, but beings that, as a type, are characterized in terms of analogical unities: the three fundamental constituents (matter, form, privation) and the four analogically characterized causes (material, formal, final, and efficient) (5 1071^{a}29–1071^{b}2).

Once the fundamental constituents and starting-points of the various universal sciences have been identified, it falls to the associated philosophy to give an account and—where appropriate—a demonstration of them. Matter, form, the various causes are among philosophy's topics, therefore, but so too are the other transgeneric attributes: being and nonbeing, unity and plurality, likeness and unlikeness, sameness and difference, equality and inequality, priority and posteriority, whole and part (*Met.* IV 2 1003^{b}22–1004^{a}25). It is because all beings share in these that the various transgeneric principles or axioms hold of them. Since substantial beings are the kind on which all the other kinds (qualitative, relational, quantitative, and so on) depend, the same branch of philosophy deals with both:

> We do, however, have to say whether it belongs to one science or to distinct ones to get a theoretical grasp both on what in mathematics are called "axioms" and on substance. It is evident, then, that the investigation of these does also belong to one science and, besides, that the one in question is the philosopher's. For these axioms hold of all beings, and not of some special genus separate from the others. Also, because they are true of being qua being and each genus is a genus of being, all people do use them. However, they use them only so far as is adequate for their purposes, that is, so far as the genus extends about which they are carrying out their demonstrations. So, since it is clear that these axioms hold of all things qua beings (for this is what is common to them), it belongs to the person who knows being qua being to get a theoretical grasp on them as well. That is why none of those who investigate a part [of being]—neither geometer nor arithmetician—attempts to say anything about them, as to whether or not they are true. But some natural scientists, as makes perfect sense, did do this, since they were the only ones who thought that they were both investigating nature as a whole and investigating being. But since there is someone further, higher than the natural scientist (for nature is one particular kind (*genos*) of being), it will belong to him whose theoretical grasp is universal and concerned with primary substance also to investigate these axioms. Natural science, however, is a sort of wisdom too, but it is not the primary sort. (*Met.* IV 3 1005ᵃ19–1005ᵇ2)

The implication that primary or theological philosophy investigates these matters is one we should for now simply register.

The transgeneric axioms, which serve as starting-points of the universal sciences, also have a starting-point, since the principle of noncontradiction is "by nature the starting-point of all the other axioms too" (*Met.* IV 4 1005ᵇ33–34). For though the other logical axioms, such as the law of excluded middle, which are "the starting-points of a syllogism" (1005ᵇ5–8), also apply to beings as such, noncontradiction is the most stable of them:

> And it is fitting for the one who knows best about each kind (*genos*) to be able to state the most stable starting-points of his subject matter, and so when this is beings qua beings, the

> most stable starting-points of all things. And this person is the philosopher. The most stable starting-point of all, however, is the one it is impossible to be deceived about. For such a starting-point must be both the best known—since it is things that people do not know that they can all be fooled about—and unhypothetical. For a starting-point that must be possessed by anyone who is going to apprehend *any* beings is no hypothesis. And what someone must know who knows anything at all, he must already possess. It is clear, then, that such a starting-point is the most stable of all. What it is, however, we must next state. It is, that the same thing cannot at the same time belong and also not belong to the same thing and in the same respect. (*Met.* IV 3 1005^{b}10–20)

The reason noncontradiction has this especially stable status is that we cannot think falsely about it but must "always . . . be grasping the truth" (*Met.* XI 5 1061^{b}35–36). This does not mean that we cannot sincerely deny it or say that we do not believe it, since "it is not necessary for what someone says to be what he takes to be so" (IV 3 1005^{b}25–26). What it does mean is that a demonstration of the principle of noncontradiction to someone who denies it cannot, except perhaps in cases of confusion, constitute his primary reason for believing it, since there is no reason more basic than it. For a demonstration "is not related to external argument, but to the one in the soul, since a syllogism is not either, for one can always object to external argument, but not always to internal argument" (*APo.* I 10 76^{b}24–25).

As a starting-point of all sciences, the principle of noncontradiction cannot be unconditionally demonstrated, since no science can demonstrate its own starting-points:

> While there is no unconditional demonstration of such things, against a given person there is one. For it is not possible to produce a deduction of this from a more convincing starting-point, and yet we at any rate must do so, if indeed we are to demonstrate it unconditionally. (*Met.* XI 5 1062^{a}2–5)

Nonetheless, it can be demonstrated "by refutation" (*Met.* IV 4 1006^{a}11–12) or "against someone" (1062^{a}3):

> And by "demonstrating by refutation" I mean something different from demonstrating, because in demonstrating we might seem to be assuming the starting-point at issue, but if the other person is responsible for an assumption of this sort, it would

> be refutation not demonstration. The starting-point for all such arguments is to ask the disputant not to *state* something to be or not to be (since someone might take this to be assuming the starting-point at issue), but rather to *signify* something both to himself and to another person, since that is necessary if indeed he is to say something. For if he does not grant this, no argument is possible for such a person, either with himself or with another person. But if he does grant it, demonstration will be possible, since there will already be something definite. The one responsible for it, however, is not the one who gives the demonstration but the one who submits to it, since in doing away with argument, he submits to argument. Further, anyone who agrees to this has agreed that something is true without a demonstration, so that not everything will be so-and-so and not so-and-so. (*Met.* IV 4 1006^{a}15–28)

The *say-or-signify-something requirement* is the starting-point common to all demonstrations by refutation of the principle of noncontradiction. If the denier satisfies this requirement, *he* takes on the responsibility that allows the philosopher to escape the charge of assuming what is at issue. Hence the denier, in complying with the say-or-signify-something requirement, must unwittingly reveal his commitment to noncontradiction:

> To show to the person who makes opposite affirmations that he speaks falsely, one must get the sort of thing from him that *is* the same as that it is not possible for the same thing to be and not to be at the same time, but that does not *seem* to be the same. (*Met.* XI 5 1062^{a}5–9)

Whatever the say-or-signify-something requirement amounts to, and in whatever way Aristotle's use of it to defend the principle of noncontradiction is supposed to work, one salient point is uncontroversial: the principle itself is not an outré one, uncovered through specialized scientific research, but one we all already accept, even if confusion leads us to deny that we do.

A second principle with a status comparable to that of noncontradiction is the principle that natural beings are subject to change (*Ph.* I 2 185^{a}12–13). Because this principle is a transgeneric starting-point of universal natural science, a defense of it "is not a contribution to natural science" (184^{b}25–185^{a}5) but belongs instead (since the principle does not apply to all beings as such) to secondary or natural philosophy. Hence natural philosophy should provide a demonstration—or demonstration by refutation—of it. The following, whether intended as such or not, seems a plausible candidate:

> Even if it is truly the case that being is infinite and unchanging, it certainly does not appear to be so according to perception; rather, many beings appear to undergo change. Now if indeed there is such a thing as false belief or belief at all, there is also change; similarly if there is imagination, or if anything is thought to be one way at one time and another at another. For imagination and belief are thought to be changes of a sort. (*Ph.* VIII 3 254ᵃ24–30)

As someone can deny the principle of noncontradiction in words, so he can deny that natural beings are subject to change. To do so internally, however, seems impossible, since the denial of it itself involves self-conscious change.

As a product of confusion, the demand to have it demonstrated that natural bodies are subject to change shows not intellectual probity but lack of discernment:

> To investigate this at all, to seek an argument in a case where we are too well off to require argument, implies poor discernment of what is better and what is worse, what commends itself to belief and what does not, what is a starting-point and what is not. It is likewise impossible that all things should be changing or that some things should always be changing and the remainder always at rest. For against all these, this one thing provides sufficient assurance: we *see* some things sometimes changing and sometimes at rest. (*Ph.* VIII 3 254ᵃ30–ᵇ1)

In the case of the principle of noncontradiction too, the demand for a demonstration is a bad sign:

> Now some people do demand that we demonstrate even this, but this is due to lack of educatedness. For it is lack of educatedness not to know what things we should look for a demonstration of and what things we should not. For it is in general impossible to demonstrate everything (for it would go on without limit, so that even then there would be no demonstration). But if there are things we should not look for a demonstration of, these people would not be able to say what starting-point they think has more of a claim to be such. (*Met.* IV 4 1006ᵃ5–11)

To grasp such fundamental starting-points, then, we do not need specialized training in a science, just the discernment that comes with being well educated. To defend them against skeptics, of course, one needs to be dialectically or philosophically proficient, but such proficiency is what leads the well educated to a clear understanding of them in the first place, free of the intellectual knots that unsolved puzzles constitute.

The Happiest Human Life 2: Leisure and Contemplation

Theology, which is the science dealing with the primary god, is this god's own science in a very strong sense:

> A science would be most divine in only two ways: if the [primary] god most of all would have it, or if it were a science of divine things. And this science alone is divine in both these ways. For the [primary] god seems to be among the causes of all things and to be a sort of starting-point, and this is the sort of science that the [primary] god alone, or that he most of all, would have. (*Met.* I 2 983^{a}5–10)

And what this god does in theologizing is to actively contemplate or understand himself:

> It is itself, therefore, that it [the primary god] understands, if indeed it is the most excellent thing, and the active understanding is active understanding of active understanding. (*Met.* XII 9 1074^{b}33–35)

As "a judge is meant to be, as it were, justice ensouled" (*NE* V 4 1132^{a}21–22), so the primary god is, as it were, theology ensouled—theology actively understood.

A second of Aristotle's thoughts about theology, as we saw in passing, is that it is identical to primary philosophy:

> The most estimable [philosophy] must be concerned with the most estimable genus. Thus, the theoretical are the more choiceworthy of the various sciences, and this [theology] of the theoretical. . . . But if there is some immovable substance, this [theology] will be prior and will be primary philosophy, and it will be universal in this way, namely, because it is primary. And it will belong to it to get a theoretical grasp on being qua

> being, both what it is and the things that belong to it qua being. (*Met.* VI 1 1026^{a}21–30)

The primary god is his own starting-point, his own cause, and always and eternally has clear understanding of himself, and so of theology—the science of himself. Hence he does not need dialectic to clarify his understanding by solving the puzzles that muddy it and knot it up. In our case, of course, things are different. Our understanding of theology is darkened by puzzles, so that we do need dialectic. In the limit, however, that need evaporates even for us. For the most exact scientific knowledge of theology comes only at the end of the dialectical process that renders our understanding clear and puzzle free. In the end, then, when we become truly well educated, primary philosophy is replaced by theology in our case too.

We might analogize this conclusion to a more familiar one. In some versions of Christianity, complete happiness consists in the eternal, untrammeled vision of the Christian god, which is achievable by anyone, once they have accepted Christ as their savior and been cleansed of their sins, since all have in their immortal souls a spark of the divine. There is no one, as a result, who is too intellectually humble to see this god. Aristotle does not go that far, but he is recognizably traveling a parallel road. Each human being has understanding, which is something divine. It is darkened by incarnation and by puzzles, which prevent it from seeing clearly. And being well educated in the Aristotelian sense can often resolve these puzzles. In the case of theology, the distinction between being well educated in it and having scientific knowledge of it, like the distinction between theology itself and theological philosophy, breaks down or is overcome. To be sure, the "free" education, in which dialectic and philosophy figures so prominently, may still seem much too demanding to expect of all free citizens. This may be true, but we can at last see why Aristotle thought it was not true, and why his well-educated free citizens do not compromise their status as such when they acquire, in becoming theoretically wise, the most exact form of scientific knowledge:

> Clearly we do not inquire into it [theology] because of its having another use, but just as a human being is free, we say, when he is for his own sake and not for someone else, in the same way we pursue this as the only free science, since it alone is for its own sake. (*Met.* I 2 982^{b}24–28)

No doubt, too, it is important to remember that Aristotle is talking about the kinds of human beings that a legislator would pray to have as the citizens of the best of all possible cities (*Pol.* VII 4 1325^{a}38–40).

Life for a human being is twofold, as we saw, consisting in *bios*, or (auto)-biographical life, and *zôê*, the life activities that take place within it. In the case of the primary god, on the other hand, *bios* just is the life activity of contemplation to which he is identical:

> And life (*zôê*) too certainly belongs to him [the primary god]. For the activity of understanding is life, and he is that activity; and his intrinsic activity is life that is best and eternal. We say, indeed, that the god is a living being who is eternal and best, so that living and a continuous and everlasting eternity belong to the god, since this is the god. (*Met.* XII 7 1072^{b}26–30)

The more of the life activity of contemplation our *bios* contains, therefore, the more like the god's it is in its happiness:

> So the activity of a god, superior as it is in blessedness, will be contemplative. And so the activity of humans, then, that is most akin to this will most bear the stamp of happiness. (*NE* X 8 1178^{b}21–32)

In its best form, such activity consists in theologizing, since that is the most exact and most excellent kind of scientific knowing. When we are urged to "immortalize," it is this that we are being urged to do (*NE* X 7 1178^{b}33). That is why the *Nicomachean Ethics*, whose focus is on virtues or excellences, and on the best kind of happiness, mentions no form of theoretical activity besides the very best sort in connection with the contemplative life. Elsewhere, however, the picture is somewhat different:

> Among the substances formed by nature, some [such as the heavenly bodies] never for all eternity either come to be or pass away, while others share in coming to be and passing away. Yet, as it happens, our theoretical knowledge (*theôria*) of the former, though they are estimable and divine, is slighter, since as regards both those things on the basis of which one would investigate them and those things about them that we long to know, the perceptual appearances are altogether few. Where the plants and animals that pass away are concerned, however, we are much better off as regards knowledge, because we live among them. For anyone willing to take sufficient trouble can grasp a lot about each genus of them. Each type of theoretical knowledge has its attractions. For even if our contact with eternal things is but slight, all the same, because of its esteem, this

> knowledge is a greater pleasure than our knowledge of everything around us, just as even a chance, brief glimpse of those we love is a greater pleasure than the most exact view of other things, however many or great they are. On the other hand, because we know more of them and know them more fully, our scientific knowledge of things that pass away exceeds that of the others. Further, because they are nearer to us and because their nature is more akin to ours, they provide their own compensations in comparison with the philosophy concerned with divine things. . . . For even in the theoretical knowledge of animals that are disagreeable to perception, the nature that crafted them likewise provides extraordinary pleasures to those who can know their causes and are by nature philosophers. . . . That is why we should not be childishly disgusted at the investigation of the less estimable animals, since in all natural things there is something wondrous. (*PA* I 5 644^{b}22–645^{a}17)

As in the *Ethics*, a glimpse of the divine remains the best kind of theoretical knowing. The difference is that now the extraordinary pleasures offered by the vaster scientific knowledge of the sublunary realm are also part of the picture.

It is in discussing pleasures, indeed, that Aristotle acknowledges an obvious fact about our nature:

> That it is in connection with each of the perceptual capacities that pleasure arises is clear, since we say that sights and sounds are pleasant. It is clear too that it does so most when the perceptual capacity is at its best and is active in relation to an object that is in the same condition. And when the perceptual capacity and the object being perceived are in conditions like that, there will always be pleasure, so long, at any rate, as what will produce the effect and what will be affected are both present. . . . So long, then, as the intelligible object or the perceptible one and what discerns or contemplates are as they should be, there will be pleasure in the activity. For when what is affected and the thing producing the effect are similar and keep in the same relation to each other, the same thing naturally arises. How is it, then, that no one is pleased continuously? Or is it that we get tired (*kamnei*)? For continuous activity is impossible for all things human. So no continuous pleasure arises either, since it is entailed by the activity. Some things delight us when they are novelties, but later delight us less, because of the same thing. For

> at first thought is called forth and is intensely active regarding them, as happens in the case of our sight when we look hard at something, but later the activity is no longer like that but has grown relaxed, so that the pleasure is dimmed as well. (*NE* X 4 1174b26–1175a10)

The tiredness that explains why we cannot be continuously pleased might be the sort a good night's sleep relieves, which is what the verb *kamnein* usually signifies. The immediate mention of novelties, however, suggests that boredom rather than fatigue may be the issue—especially since the reason no activity pleases us for long isn't simply that our batteries wear down:

> In no case, though, is the same thing always pleasant, because our nature is not simple but also has another element in it, in that we are mortals. As a result, if one of the two is doing something, it is contrary to the nature of our other nature, and when the two are equally balanced, what we are doing seems neither painful nor pleasant. For if the nature of some being were simple, the same action would always be most pleasant. That is why the god always enjoys a single simple pleasure. For there is not only an activity of moving but also an activity of unmoving, and pleasure is found more in rest than in movement. "Change in all things is sweet," as the poet says, because of a sort of wickedness. For just as a wicked human being is an easily changeable one, a nature that needs change is also wicked, since it is neither simple nor decent. (*NE* VII 14 1154b20–31)

Usually, the fault line in human nature seems to coincide with the divide between action and contemplation, between the merely human practical life of politics and the truly human or divine contemplative life. Now, however, it has opened up within the contemplative life itself. Not even theologizing, it seems, will continuously charm us. At some point boredom or tedium will set in, and we will crave the delights of contemplating something else, something closer to home. *Historia Animalium* offers plenty of examples to choose from. But again we should register that if we were the truly virtuous citizens of the best city, this sort of issue might be less of a problem.

The focus on theoretical wisdom, as the very best kind of contemplation of the very best intelligible object, makes the task that politics faces seem somewhat simpler than it is, suggesting that maximizing the time we spend theologizing will make us happiest. It would be truer to say, it seems, that it will do so by giving us as much theologizing as we can tolerate, and as many contemplative alternatives to it as we may need. This doesn't quite turn the dazzling brightness of theory into nature's green, but it makes the contemplative life look much less monochrome.

The education that politics provides to citizens of the best city must already include sufficient exposure to the special sciences to enable the induction that leads to the universal sciences and their associated philosophies, since only in that way can theoretical wisdom be reached. It might seem that with this enrichment of the contemplative life comes a need for something closer to firsthand expert scientific knowledge of the special sciences themselves, rather than reflective, meta-level, secondhand knowledge of their starting-points. Consequently, it is of some importance that even in the case of the special sciences, it is those who "can know their causes and are by nature philosophers" who get the extraordinary pleasures they have to offer. It may be less the narrow specialist who is being described, therefore, than the well-educated person, who sees the beauty even in naked mole rats or other unattractive living things because he has had a clear-headed glimpse of the divine, and so can see that:

> The order is not such that one thing has no relation to another but rather there is a relation. For all things are jointly ordered in relation to one thing. (*Met.* XII 10 1075ᵃ17–19)

The one thing referred to is, of course, the primary god. What distinguishes "those doctors who pursue their craft more philosophically" is that their search for the "primary starting-points of health and disease" leads them to begin by considering nature in general (*Sens.* 1 436ᵃ17–ᵇ1). It can hardly be an accident, in any case, that Aristotle's longest paean to well educatedness forms a preface to *Parts of Animals* (quoted in the previous section), suggesting that this biological treatise itself is a contribution to the very thing praised within it.

One sort of simplification the *Nicomachean Ethics* engages in when portraying the contemplative life is a result of its focus on the *virtues* whether of character or thought, since this has the effect of making the star of the contemplative show—the most virtuous or excellent kind of contemplation—look like the entire cast. A second sort of simplification is caused by its focus on the question of what activity in accord with what virtue *happiness* is, which tends to make the contemplative components of the leisured life look like the leisured life as a whole. This has the further effect of overheightening the contrast between the leisured contemplative life and the unleisured political life that supports it.

As Aristotle conceives of it, political activity is already a step up from productive work, since, as activity in accord with practical wisdom and full virtue of character, it is choiceworthy at least in part because of itself.

Unleisured, productive work, by contrast, is choiceworthy only because of the additional ends that are its products. Engaging in it, therefore, or in certain sorts of it anyway, such as farming or the vulgar crafts, unfits one to be a free citizen of many constitutions, including the best one. Leisure for a productive worker may well just be time off from work. This, no doubt, is how we sometimes conceive of it ourselves. We are at leisure when our time is our own to do with as we please. Aristotle's view is different: we are at leisure not when we are, as we say, doing nothing, or doing as we please, but when what we are doing is choiceworthy because of itself. Much practical activity is, in that sense, already somewhat leisured, even if, because it also has an additional end, it is also somewhat unleisured.

The reason leisure should not consist exclusively of playing games or amusing oneself is that amusement is choiceworthy for the sake of relaxation, and relaxation is not something choiceworthy for its own sake but only because the pains and exertions of unleisure require it:

> Happiness does not lie in amusement, since it would indeed be strange if the end were amusement and we did all the work we do and suffered evils all our lives for the sake of amusing ourselves. For, in a word, we choose everything—except happiness, since end *it* is—for the sake of something else. But to engage in serious matters and to labor for the sake of amusement would evidently be silly and utterly childish. On the contrary, "amusing ourselves so as to engage in serious matters," as Anacharsis puts it, seems to be correct. For amusement is like relaxation, and it is because people cannot labor continuously that they need relaxation. End, then, relaxation is not, since it occurs for the sake of activity. (*NE* X 6 1176^{b}27–1177^{a}1)

Nonetheless, because, as political animals, we do have to engage in unleisured practical activities, the best city will "introduce amusement, but watch for the appropriate time to use it, as if dispensing it as a medicine [for the ills of unleisure]" (*Pol.* VIII 3 1337^{b}40–42). Amusement is a bridge, in other words, between the unleisured life of politics and the leisured one—included in the latter only because of its connection to the former.

Free people should be educated in drawing, in part because it helps them better discern the quality of a craftsman's work, so that they do not "make errors in their private purchases and avoid being cheated when buying or selling products," but also as a leisured pursuit that "makes them good at contemplating the beauty of bodies" (*Pol.* VIII 3 1338^{a}41–^{b}2). Likewise, they should be educated in reading and writing, because they are "useful for making money, managing a household, acquiring learning, and for many political actions" (VIII 3 1338a15–19), but also, no doubt, because they too can be leisured pursuits: Aristotle's own love of books was legendary and he refers to his own philosophical works as "leisured discussions" (VII 1 1323b39–40). Finally, he should be educated in *mousikê*, a combination of poetry, dance, and music proper, which was a staple of traditional Greek education, solely because it is "a pastime characteristic of free people" (VIII 3 1338a22–23). We are already a long way, then, from thinking of the leisured life as consisting of contemplation alone. The peak is not the whole range.

Within that life, moreover, a variety of different virtues have roles to play:

> Since the end is evidently the same for human beings both communally and individually, and since it is necessary for there to be the same defining mark for the best man and for the best constitution, it is evident that the virtues for leisure must be present. For, as has often been said, the end of war is peace, and that of unleisure is leisure. But the virtues useful with a view to leisure and passing the time include both those whose function lies in leisure and those whose function lies in unleisure. For many necessities must be present in order for being at leisure to be possible. That is why temperance is appropriate for our city as are courage and resilience. For as the proverb says, there is no leisure for slaves, and those who are incapable of facing danger courageously are the slaves of their attackers. Now, courage and resilience are for unleisure, philosophy for leisure, and temperance and justice are useful during both, and particular when people remain at peace and are at leisure. For war compels people to be just and temperate, but the enjoyment of good luck and the leisure that accompanies peace make them wantonly aggressive instead. Much justice and temperance are needed, therefore, by those who seem to do best and who enjoy all the things regarded as blessings—people like those, if there are any, as the poets say there are, who live in the Isles of the Blessed. For these above all will need philosophy, temperance, and justice, to the extent that they are at leisure amidst an abundance of such goods. (*Pol.* VII 15 1334a11–40)

Philosophy, which must be theoretical wisdom here, since it is exclusively useful in leisure, is also theoretical wisdom in the following passage: "if certain people wish to find enjoyment through themselves, they should not look for a remedy beyond philosophy, since all other pleasures require [other] human beings" (II 7 1267ᵃ10–12). For it is the theoretically wise person, who is able—"and more able the wiser he is"—to engage in contemplation "even by himself" (*NE* X 7 1177ᵃ32–34).

The mention of good luck and arrogance in connection with the virtues needed in leisure strongly suggest that the use temperance and justice (and so practical wisdom) have there concerns external goods, since it is these that luck controls, these whose possession in abundance arrogance commonly accompanies:

> The sorts of character that wealth entails are on the surface for all to see. For the wealthy are wantonly aggressive and arrogant, since they are affected somehow by the possession of wealth (for their general disposition is that of those who possess every good thing, since wealth is a sort of standard of value for the other ones, which is why all of them appear to be purchasable by it). (*Rh.* II 16 1390ᵇ32–1391ᵃ2)

Add to this the fact that very abundant external goods are positive hindrances to contemplation (*NE* X 8 1178ᵇ3–5) and something like the following picture is suggested. As human beings whose lives are not self-sufficient for contemplation, we must live together with others in a city, where—if we are lucky and our city is the best possible—abundant external goods will be available (*Pol.* VII 13 1332ᵃ28–31). For unless we possess an abundance of such goods, we cannot exercise all the virtues of character—generosity and great-souledness being obvious examples. When we are at leisure, some of these virtues, such as courage and endurance, are inactive, while others, temperance and justice, are active. Since these are inseparable parts of full virtue of character, however, all must be possessed together with practical wisdom, if any are. We must be fully virtuous and practically-wise, it follows, not just when being unleisured activities but also when being at leisure.

The best human life, then, has an unleisured part, consisting of practical political activities, and a leisured one, consisting of contemplative activities of various sorts, as well as other activities of a non-contemplative sort, such as relaxing amusements. The ordering of all these into a single life-structure that best furthers the contemplation of the primary god is a politician's primary task:

> This is always what is most choiceworthy for each individual, to attain what is the topmost. . . . The politician must legislate, therefore, looking to all these things in a way that is in accord with the parts of the soul and their actions, but more to those that are better and those that are ends. . . . But reason and

> understanding are our nature's end, and so it is to further the coming to be and the training of our habits should be established. . . . Supervision of desire must be for the sake of the understanding, and that of the body for the sake of the soul. (*Pol.* VII 14–15 1333ᵃ29–1334ᵇ28; also *Protr.* B17–30)

Since every organized system, as we saw, is identified most of all with the constituent in it that has most control (*NE* IX 8 1168ᵇ31–32), and a life with the structure described is clearly such a system, there is good reason to call it the contemplative life, since contemplation is the end or target that controls it.

If abundant external goods are not to hinder contemplation, however, we must not overindulge in them, or become involved in the sort of competition for them to which greed gives rise. We need temperance, therefore, which pertains to the private use of such goods, and justice, which pertains to their fair and equal distribution. Leisure time itself is also a sort of good, of course, which needs to be used temperately and justly for the same reason. Theoretical wisdom—philosophy—is needed in this regard, too, because it is only if we have experienced contemplation for ourselves that we can grasp as a practical truth that *it* is what complete happiness consists in. That is why, having provided a theoretical argument in support of contemplation's claim to be complete happiness, Aristotle insists that the proof of the pudding, where a practical treatise like the *Ethics* is concerned, lies ultimately in the eating:

> The truth in practical matters must be discerned from the facts of our life, since these are what have the controlling vote. When we examine what has been previously said, then, it must be discerned by bringing it to bear on the facts of our life, and if it is in harmony with the facts, we should accept it, but if it clashes, we should suppose it mere words. (*NE* X 8 1179ᵃ17–22)

This is what gives the virtues of character a more intimate role to play even within those leisured activities that are strictly contemplative. In the case of the gods, contemplation always appears as the happiness it really is. This is not so for us: to experience contemplation *as happiness*, we must have the virtues of character, since it is they—and they alone—that make our target, and our suppositions about it, correct: "it is virtue, whether natural or habituated, that teaches correct belief about the starting-point [namely, happiness]" (*NE* VII 8 1151ᵃ18–19). Without the virtues of character, therefore, even if we did engage in contemplation of the god, we could not possibly see it as what all by itself made a life choiceworthy and in need of nothing. Other activities in which we found much greater pleasure and satisfaction might seem far stronger contenders. We would then be entirely justified from the practical point of view in dismissing Aristotle's arguments to the contrary as mere words. For human beings, then, if not for gods, it is impossible to have theoretical wisdom without also having practical wisdom and the virtues of character.

In the best city, practical wisdom (politics) is something that all the male citizens achieve when, at around the age of forty, they have acquired an experienced eye to complement their theoretical knowledge. But one does not need to have been brought up in the best city to be practically-wise. Even an oligarchy or a democracy, provided it is not too extreme, can provide someone with good enough habits to make him an adequate student of noble and just things, once he is old enough. At the beginning of his ethical studies, he will already have a grasp on the pertinent facts, a grasp on what the noble and just things are, since this good habits can provide unaided. What he does not have is an explanation of these things. That is what, by the end of his studies, he will have acquired. He will have seen how and why noble and just things further happiness.

In the best city, practical wisdom (politics) is ideally placed and rules everything, but it can get by with much less:

> Nonetheless, we should not think that a person who is going to be happy needs many things and grand ones, even if it is not possible for him to be blessed without external goods. For self-sufficiency does not lie in an extreme amount of these and neither does action. But it is possible to do many noble actions even without ruling land and sea, since even from moderate resources a person can do actions in accord with virtue. (This is plain enough to see, since private individuals seem to do decent actions no less, or even more, than people in positions of power.) It is enough, then, to have that amount, since the life of a person who is active in accord with virtue will be happy. (*NE* X 8 1179^{a}1–9)

Aristotle's own will reveals that he had a sizable estate, including houses in Chalcis and Stagira, significant capital, a domestic partner, two children, a number of slaves, a large library, and a wide circle of friends (DL V [11–16]). Adequate resources, one would suppose. When he was seventeen, there was the Academy, where he spent twenty years studying under the greatest philosopher there has ever been, himself perhaps excepted. No doubt, the best city would do much better, but adequate training in philosophy the Academy surely provided. Later in life, there was the Lyceum, and the company of distinguished colleagues and co-workers, his friend Theophrastus prominent among them.

That Aristotle had something approaching practical wisdom—something approaching what he took to be a scientific knowledge of politics—by the time he composed the *Ethics* and *Politics* seems a safe assumption, then, given his own account of what it takes to acquire it (II 5 1263^{a}39n). We might infer that he nonetheless somewhat lamented his exclusion from active participation in politics, since as a resident alien in Athens, not a citizen, he was debarred from holding office, participating in the assembly, serving on a jury, owning land, or building a house, since the best life, as he describes it, involves ruling a city as one of its free and unconditional citizens. But it is also possible that he thought that luck had landed him in a better situation, one in which he was free to pursue what he thought of as the leisured life in a way untrammeled by a citizen's responsibilities.

The World of the *Politics*

Politics

Book I

I 1

1252a1 Since we see every city to be a sort of community, and every community to be formed for the sake of some good (for everyone does every action for the sake of what seems to be good), clearly, then, while every community aims at some good, the community that has the most control of all, and encompasses all the others, aims both at the good that has the most control of all and does so to the highest degree.[1] And this community is the one called a city, the community that is political.[2]

Now those who think that the positions of politician, king, household manager, and master [of slaves] are the same, are not correct.[3] For they think that each of these differs with regard to large or small number, but not in kind (*eidos*)—for example, if someone rules few people, he is a master, if more, a household manager, if still more, he has the position of politician or king—the assumption being that there is no difference between a large household and a small city.[4] And as for the positions of politician and king, they say that someone who is himself in charge has the position of king, whereas someone who, in accord with the reasons belonging to this sort of science, takes his turn at ruling and being ruled, has the position of politician.[5] But these claims are not true.

What I am saying will be clear, if we investigate the matter in accord with the method of inquiry that has guided us elsewhere.[6] For as in other cases, a composite must be analyzed until we reach things that are incomposite, since these are the smallest parts of the whole, so too it is by investigating the parts of which a city is composed that we shall see better both how these differ from each other, and whether or not it is possible to gain some craft-like expertise concerning each of the things we have mentioned.[7]

I 2

If we were to see how these things grow naturally from the start, we would in this way, as in other cases, get the best theoretical grasp on them.[8] First, then, those who are incapable of existing without each other necessarily form a couple, as female and male do for the sake of procreation (they do not do so from deliberate choice, but, like other animals and plants, because the urge to leave behind something of the same sort as themselves is natural), and as what rules by nature and what is by nature ruled do for the sake of preservation.[9] For if something is capable of looking ahead by using its thought, it is by nature a ruler and by nature a master, whereas whatever can labor by using its body is ruled and is by nature a slave.[10] That is why the same thing is advantageous for both master and slave.[11]

Now by nature female is distinguished from slave. For, unlike the blacksmiths who make the Delphian knife, nature produces nothing in a stingy way, but instead makes one thing for one [function].[12] For each one of the instruments will be completed best if it serves one function rather than many.[13] Among barbarians, however, a woman and a slave occupy the same position. The cause of this is that they have no element that is by nature a ruler, but rather their community is that of male and female slave. That is why the poets say "it is reasonable for Greeks to rule barbarians," on the supposition that a barbarian and a slave are by nature the same.[14] 1252b1

From these two communities, then, the household was first to arise, and Hesiod was correct when he said in his poem, "First and foremost a house, a woman, and an ox for the plow."[15] For to poor people an ox takes the place of a servant.[16] The community that is formed to satisfy everyday needs, then, is the household in accord with nature, whose members are called "meal-sharers" by Charondas and "manger-sharers" by Epimenides the Cretan.[17]

The first community, consisting of several households, for the sake of satisfying needs other than everyday ones, is the village. And above all the village in accord with nature seems to be a colony of the household, consisting as it does of what some have called "sharers of the same milk," sons and the sons of sons.[18] That is why cities were at first ruled by kings, as [barbarian] nations still are.[19] For those who came together were living under kingly rule, since every household is ruled by the eldest as a king. And so the same holds in the colonies, because of the kinship [of the villagers].[20] This is what Homer is describing when he says: "Each one lays down the law for his own wives and children."[21] For they were scattered about, which is how people used to dwell in ancient times. And it is because of this that all people say that the gods too are ruled by a king, namely, that they themselves were ruled by kings in ancient times, and some still are. And human beings model not only the forms of the gods on their own, but their way of life as well.

The community, coming from several villages, when it is complete, is the city, once it has already reached (one might almost say) the limit of total self-sufficiency.[22] It comes to be for the sake of living, but it exists for the sake of living well. That is why every city exists by nature, since the first communities also do.[23] For this one is their end, and nature is an end. For what each thing is when its coming to be has been completed, this we say is the nature of each—for example, of a human, of a horse, or of a household. Further, its for-the-sake-of-which—namely, its end—is best, and self-sufficiency is both end and best.

1253a1 From these considerations, then, it is evident that a city is among the things that exist by nature, that a human is by nature a political animal, and that anyone who is without a city, not by luck but by nature, is either a wretch or else better than human, and, like the one Homer condemns, he is "clanless, lawless, and homeless."[24] For someone with such a nature has at the same time an appetite for war, like an isolated piece in a game of checkers.[25]

It is also clear why a human is more of a political animal than any bee or any other gregarious animal. For nature does nothing pointlessly, as we say, and a human being alone among the animals has speech.[26] Now, the voice is a signifier of what is pleasant or painful, which is why it is also possessed by the other animals (for their nature does extend this far, namely, to having the perception of pleasure and pain and signifying them to each other). But speech is for making clear what is advantageous or harmful, and so too what is just or unjust. For this is special to humans, in comparison to the other animals, that they alone have perception of the good and the bad, the just and the unjust, and the rest.[27] And it is community in these that makes a household and a city.[28]

Also the city is prior in nature to the household and to each of us individually.[29] For it is necessary for the whole to be prior to the part. For if the whole body is put to death, there will no longer be a foot or a hand, except homonymously, as one might speak of a stone "hand" (for, once dead, the hand will be like that).[30] For everything is defined by its function and by its capacity, so that when they are no longer in that condition they should not be said to be the same things but homonymous ones.[31] It is clear, then, that the city both exists by nature and is prior in nature to the individual. For if an individual is not self-sufficient when separated, he will be in a similar state to that of the other parts in relation to the whole.[32] And anyone who cannot live in a community with others, or who does not need to because of his self-sufficiency, is no part of a city, so that he is either a wild beast or a god.[33]

Now, although the impulse toward this sort of community exists by nature in everyone, the person who first put one together was also the cause of very great goods. For just as when completed a human is the best of the animals, so when separated from law and judicial proceeding he is worst of all.[34] For injustice is harshest when it possesses weapons, and a human grows up possessed of weapons for practical wisdom and virtue to use, which may be used for absolutely contrary purposes.[35] That is why he is the most unrestrained and most savage of animals when he lacks virtue, as well as the worst as regards sex and food. But justice is something political.[36] For justice is a political community's order, and justice is judgment of what is just.[37]

I 3

Since it is evident from what parts the city is composed we must first 1253b1 discuss household management, for every city is composed of households. And the parts of household management correspond in turn to the parts of which the household is composed, and a complete household is composed of slaves and free people.[38] But since we must first inquire into each thing in terms of its smallest parts, and the primary and smallest parts of a household are master and slave, husband and wife, and father and children, we shall have to investigate these three things to see what each of them is and what sort of thing each must be.[39] The three in question are: mastership, "marital" science (for we have no word to describe the union of woman and man), and, third, "procreative" science (this too has not been given a name that is special to it).[40] Let these three that we mentioned stand. But there is also a part, which some believe to be identical to household management, and others believe to be its largest part. We shall have to get a theoretical grasp on how things stand with it too. I am speaking of what is called the craft of wealth acquisition.[41]

But let us first discuss master and slave in order to see the things that are related to necessary use, and also to see whether we can acquire something in the way of knowledge about these things that is better than what it is supposed at present.[42] For some people believe that mastership is a sort of science, and that household management, mastership, politics, and kingship are all the same, as we said at the start.[43] But others believe that it is contrary to nature to be a master.[44] For it is by law that one person is a slave and another free, whereas by nature there is no difference between them.[45] That is why to be a master is not just either, since it is based on force.

I 4

Since property is part of the household, the craft of property acquisition is also a part of household management.[46] For we can neither live nor live well without the necessities. So, just as the specialized crafts must have their proper instruments if they are going to perform their functions, the same applies to a household manager. Of instruments, however, some are inanimate and some are animate—for example, for the ship's captain a rudder is an inanimate instrument, whereas his lookout is an animate one. For in the crafts an assistant belongs in the kind (*eidos*) that consists of instruments. So too a piece of property is an instrument for living, and property [in general] a number of such instruments, a slave is a sort of animate piece of property, and all assistants are like instruments for [using] instruments.[47] For if each instrument could perform its own function on command or by anticipating instructions, and if—like the statues of Daedalus or the tripods of Hephaestus (which the poet describes as having "entered the assembly of the gods of their own accord")—shuttles wove cloth by themselves, and plectra played the lyre, an architectonic craftsman would not need assistants and masters would not need slaves.[48]

1254a1 Now, what are commonly said to be instruments are instruments for production, whereas a piece of property is action-involving.[49] For something comes from a shuttle beyond the use of it, but from a piece of clothing or a bed we get only the use. Further, since production and action differ in kind (*eidos*), and both need instruments, their instruments must differ in the same way as they do.[50] Life (*bios*), though, is action, not production.[51] That is why a slave is an assistant in the things related to action.[52] And something is said to be a piece of property in the same way as it is said to be a part. For a part is not just a part of another thing, but is *wholly* that thing's, and the same also holds of a piece of property. That is why a master is just his slave's *master*, not simply his, while a slave is not just his master's *slave*, but wholly his.

From these considerations it is clear what the nature and capacity of a slave are. For anyone who, though human, is by nature not his own but someone else's is by nature a slave. And a human being is someone else's when, though human, he is a piece of property, and a piece of property is an instrument that is for action and separate [from its owner].[53]

I 5

But whether anyone is like that by nature or not, and whether it is better and just for anyone to be a slave or not (all slavery being, on the contrary, against nature)—these are the things we must investigate next. And it is neither difficult to get a theoretical grasp on the answer by argument nor to learn it from what actually happens. For ruling and being ruled are not only necessary, they are also advantageous, and some things are set apart straight from birth, some to rule, others to be ruled. And there are many kinds (*eidos*) of rulers and ruled, and the rule is always better when the ruled are better—for example, rule over humans is better than rule over wild beasts.[54] For a function that is accomplished by something better is a better function, and where one thing rules and another is ruled, there is a certain function belonging to these. For in whatever is composed of a number of things, whether continuous with each other or discontinuous, and becomes one communal thing, a ruler and a ruled are always seen, and this is present in animate beings on the basis of their entire nature. For even in things that do not share in living some rule exists—for example, in a harmony.[55] But these topics presumably lie far outside our investigation.

In the first place, a living being is composed of soul and body, and of these the first is by nature the ruler, the latter by nature the ruled. And one must investigate what is natural in things whose condition is in accord with nature, not in corrupted ones. That is why we must also get a theoretical grasp on the human being who is in the best possible condition, both of soul and of body, since in him this is clear. For in depraved people, and those in a depraved condition, the body will often seem to rule the soul, because their condition is base and in disaccord with nature.

But it is, as we were saying, in a living being, that we can first get a theoretical grasp on both the rule of a master and political rule. For the soul rules the body with the rule of a master, whereas the understanding rules desire with political rule or kingly rule.[56] In these cases, it is evident that it is in accord with nature and advantageous for the body to be ruled by the soul, and for the affective part to be ruled by the understanding and the part that has reason, whereas if the relation were equal or reversed it would be harmful to all concerned. And again in the case of a human being and the other animals the same holds. For domestic animals are by nature better than wild ones, and it is better for all of them to be ruled by human beings, since in this way they secure their preservation.[57] Further, the relation of male to female is that of what is better by nature to what is worse, and that of ruler to ruled. And it must be the same way in the case of all human beings.

Those people, then, who are as different [from others] as body is from soul or beast from human (and they are in this condition if their function is to use their bodies, and this the best thing to come from them)—those people are by nature slaves. And it is better for them to be subject to this rule, if indeed it is also better for the other things we mentioned. For he is by nature a slave who is capable of belonging to someone else, belongs to someone else because of this, and shares in reason to the extent of perceiving it but not to the extent of having it himself. For the other animals assist not because they perceive the reason but because of feelings.[58] Also, the difference in the use made of them is small. For in relation to the necessities bodily help comes from both, both from slaves and from domestic animals.

Now, nature tends indeed to make the bodies of free people and slaves different, the latter strong enough to be used for necessities, the former upright in posture and useless for that sort of work, but useful for political life—which is itself divided into what is useful for war and what is useful for peace. But the contrary also often happens, namely, some have the bodies of freemen, whereas others have the souls.[59] For this at any rate is evident: if people were to become in body alone as distinguished as the statues of the gods, everyone would say that those who fell short deserved to be their slaves.[60] And if this is true in the case of the body, it is even more just to make this distinction in the case of the soul. But it is not as easy to see the beauty of the soul as it is to see that of the body.

It is evident, therefore, that by nature some people are free and others are slaves, for whom slavery is both advantageous and just.

I 6

But that those who make the contrary claim are also correct in a way is not difficult to see.[61] For someone is said to be being ruled as a slave, or to be a slave, in two ways, since *by law* too a person can be a slave or be ruled as a slave. For the law [in question] is a sort of agreement by which what is conquered in war is said to belong to the conquerors. Against the justice of this, then, many of those versed in the law bring a writ of illegality, analogous to that brought against a [legislative] speaker, on the grounds that it is a terrible thing if what is overcome by force is going to be the slave of, and ruled by, what is able to use force and is superior in power.[62] And some hold the latter view, others the former, even among the wise.

The cause of this dispute, and what produces a going back-and-forth in the arguments, is that in a way virtue, when it is equipped with resources, is most able to use force, and what conquers is always superior in something good, so that it seems that there is no force without virtue, the dispute being only about justice.[63] For because of this view one side believes that justice is goodwill, whereas the other believes that justice is precisely this—the rule of the stronger.[64] At any rate, if these arguments are left aside, the other arguments have neither strength nor anything to persuade us that the one who is better in virtue should not rule, that is, be master.

Some people, though, cleave exclusively to what they think is a sort of justice (since the law is something just), and maintain that enslavement in war is just. But at the same time they say that it is not just. For it is possible for wars to be started unjustly, and there is no way in which someone would say that the person who does not deserve to be in a condition of slavery is a slave—otherwise, it could turn out that those believed to be the most well bred are slaves or the children of slaves, if any of them happen to be taken captive and sold. That is why indeed the people who hold this view are not willing to say that *these* are slaves, but only that barbarians are. And yet, in saying this, what they are seeking is nothing other than what is by nature a slave—which is just what we talked about at the start. For they have to say that some people are slaves everywhere, others nowhere.

It is the same way with good-breeding.[65] For people think of themselves as well bred not just when they are in their own country, but wherever they are, whereas they think of barbarians as well bred only at home, on the supposition that it is one thing to be *unconditionally* well bred and free, and another to be so but not unconditionally—as the Helen of Theodectes does when she says: "Sprung from divine roots on both sides, who would think that I deserve to be called a hired servant?"[66] But when people say this, it is by nothing but virtue and vice that they are defining slave and free, well bred and ill bred. For they think that in just the way that human comes from human, and wild beast from wild beast, so too good people come from good ones. But, though nature tends to do this, it is nonetheless often unable to do so.[67]

It is clear, then, that there is some reason for the dispute and that the one lot are not always slaves by nature nor the other free. But it is also clear that in some cases there is such a distinction—cases where it is advantageous and just for the one to be ruled as a slave and the other to rule as a master, and where the one should be ruled and the other should exercise the rule that is natural for him (so that he is in fact ruling as a master), and where misrule is disadvantageous to both.[68] For the same thing is advantageous for both part and whole, body and soul, and a slave is a sort of part of his master—a sort of living but separate part of his body. That is why there is in fact a sort of mutual advantage and mutual friendship for such masters and slaves as deserve to be by nature so related.[69] When their relationship is not that way, however, but is in accord with law, and they have been subjected to force, the contrary holds.

I 7

It is also evident from these considerations that the rule of a master and the rule of a politician are not the same, and that the sorts of rule are not all the same as each other either, as some people claim. For one is rule over people who are by nature free, the other over slaves. Rule by a household manager is a monarchy, since every household has one ruler; rule of a politician is rule over people who are free and equal.[70]

Now, someone is said to be a master not in virtue of his scientific knowledge but in virtue of being such-and-such a sort of person.[71] The same is true of both slave and free. Nevertheless, there *could* be such a thing as mastership or slavecraft—for example, of the sort that was taught by the man in Syracuse, who, for a fee, used to teach slave boys their day-to-day services.[72] Lessons in such things as these might well be extended to include cooking and other services of that kind (*genos*). For distinct slaves have distinct functions, some of which are more estimable, others more concerned with providing the necessities—"slave before slave, master before master," as the proverb says.[73]

All such sciences, then, are the business of slaves, whereas mastership is the science of using slaves. For being a master does not consist in the acquiring of slaves but in the using of them. But there is nothing grand or dignified about this science. For what the slave needs to scientifically know how to do is what the master needs to scientifically know how to prescribe. That is why for those who have the resources not to bother with such things a steward takes on this office, while they themselves engage in politics or do philosophy.[74] As for the science of acquiring slaves (that is, the just variety of it), it is distinct from both of these, and is a kind of warfare or hunting.[75]

Where master and slave are concerned, then, let the distinctions be made in this way.

I 8

Let us now get a general theoretical grasp on all property and the craft
1256a1 of wealth acquisition, in accord with our guiding way [of inquiry], since in fact a slave has turned out to be a part of property.[76] The first puzzle we might raise is whether the craft of wealth acquisition is the same as household management, or a part of it, or an assistant to it.[77] And if it is an assistant, whether it is in the way that shuttle-making is to weaving, or in the way that bronze-smelting is to statue-making. For these do not assist in the same way, but rather the first provides instruments, the second the matter. (By the matter I mean the underlying subject from which the product is made—for example, wool for the weaver and bronze for the statue-maker.)

Now, it is clear that household management is not the same as the craft of wealth acquisition, since the former uses resources, while the latter provides them. For [if they are identical] what science will there be that uses what is in the household, except that of household management? But whether the craft of wealth acquisition is a part of household management or a science of a distinct kind (*eidos*) is a matter of dispute. For if it belongs to someone who possesses the craft of wealth acquisition to get a theoretical grasp on the various sources of wealth and property, and property and wealth include many parts, we shall first [have to investigate] whether farming—and, in universal terms, the supervision and acquisition of food—is a part of wealth-acquisition or some distinct kind (*genos*) of thing.[78]

But then there are indeed many kinds (*eidos*) of food, because the ways of life of both animals and humans are also many. For it is impossible to live without food, so that differences in food have produced distinct ways of life among the animals. For some beasts live in herds and others live scattered about, whichever is advantageous for getting their food, because some of them are carnivorous, some herbivorous, and some omnivorous. And so with a view to their convenience and their preference in these matters, nature has made their ways of life different. And since the same things are not naturally pleasant to each, but rather distinct things to distinct ones, among the carnivores and herbivores themselves the ways of life are different.

The same is also true of human beings. For their ways of life differ greatly. The most idle are herders. For they—without effort and while at leisure—get their food from their domestic animals. Although, when it is necessary for their herds to change pasture, they too have to move around with them, as if they were farming a living farm. Others live from hunting, and distinct sorts from distinct sorts of it: some from raiding; some—those who live near lakes, marshes, rivers, or a suitable sort of sea—live from fishing; and some off birds or wild beasts. But the kind (*genos*) of human being that is most numerous lives off the land and off cultivated crops.

The ways of life, then, at any rate those that naturally develop of themselves and do not provide food through exchange or commerce, are pretty much these: nomadic, raiding, fishing, hunting, farming. But some people live pleasantly by mixing together several of these, supplementing their way of life where it happens to be deficient with regard to self-sufficiency—for example, some live both a nomadic and a raiding life, others, both a farming and a hunting one, and similarly in the case of the others, each passing their time in the way need, together with other things, necessitates.

Property of this sort, then, is evidently given by nature itself to all living things straight from when they are first conceived, and similarly too when they have reached completion. And in fact some animals produce at the start, together with their offspring, enough food to last the latter until such time as it is able to get it for itself—for example, those that produce grubs or eggs. Animals that give birth to live offspring, on the other hand, carry food for their offspring in their own bodies for a certain period—namely, the natural substance called milk. It is clear, then, in the case of developed things too, that we must suppose both that plants are for the sake of animals, and that the other animals are for the sake of humans, domestic ones both for using and eating, and if not all, nonetheless most, wild ones for food and other sorts of support, so that clothes and other instruments may be got from them. If then nature makes nothing incomplete and nothing pointlessly, it must be that nature made all of them for the sake of humans.[79] That is why even warfare, since hunting is a part of it, will in a way be by nature a craft of property acquisition—one that should be used not only against wild beasts but also against those humans who are naturally suited to be ruled but unwilling to be, on the supposition that this sort of warfare is by nature just.

One kind (*eidos*) of craft of property acquisition, then, is by nature a part of household management, in that either there must be available, or it itself must arrange to make available, a store of what is both necessary for living and useful to the community of city or household. At any rate, true wealth seems to consist of such things. For self-sufficiency in this sort of property, with a view to living the good life, is not unlimited, as Solon in his poetry says it is: "No boundary to wealth has been laid down for human beings."[80] For one has been laid down just as in the other crafts. For there is no instrument of any craft that is unlimited in quantity or size, and wealth is a collection of instruments for politicians and household managers.[81]

It is clear, then, that there is a natural sort of craft of property acquisition for household managers and politicians, and what the cause of this is.

I 9

But there is another kind (*genos*) of craft of property acquisition, which they most of all call—and justly so—*the craft of wealth acquisition*. It is
1257b1 because of it that wealth and property seem to have no limit. For many people think that the craft of wealth acquisition is one and the same thing as what we talked about, because the two are close neighbors. But it is neither the same as what we were talking about nor all that far from it. One of them, though, exists by nature, whereas the other does

not exist by nature, but comes more from a sort of experience and craft knowledge.[82]

Concerning the latter, let us take the following as our starting-point.[83] Each piece of property has two uses, both of which are uses of it intrinsically, but not uses of it intrinsically in the same way.[84] Instead, one properly belongs to the thing, while the other does not properly belong to it—for example, as regards a shoe, its use in wearing it and its use in exchange.[85] For both are uses to which a shoe can be put. For someone who exchanges a shoe in return for money or food with someone who needs a shoe is using the shoe insofar as it is a shoe. But this is not the use that properly belongs to it. For it does not come to exist for the sake of exchange. And it is the same way with other pieces of property as well. For the craft of exchange applies to all of them, and first started from the natural circumstance of some human beings having more than enough and others less. (It is also clear from this that the craft of commerce does not by nature belong to the craft of wealth acquisition, since it was up to the point at which they had enough that it was necessary for them to engage in exchange.[86]) It is evident, then, that in the first community, that is, the household, there is no function for exchange, but only when the community already consists of more members. For the members of the household used to share all their own things, whereas those in separate households in turn shared many other things, and it was necessary to make a trade of these in accord with the need, as many barbarian peoples still do, through exchange. For they exchange useful things for other useful things, but nothing more than that—for example, they take and give wine in return for corn, and so on with everything else of this sort.

This sort of craft of exchange, then, is neither contrary to nature nor is it any kind (*eidos*) of craft of wealth acquisition. For it existed as a replenishment of a self-sufficiency that is in accord with nature.[87] Nevertheless, the craft of wealth acquisition arose from it, and did so in accord with reason. For when supplies came from increasingly foreign sources, because of importing what was needed and exporting the surplus, the use of money had of necessity to be devised. For not all the natural necessities are easily transportable. And that is why with a view to exchange people agreed with each other to give and take something that was itself one of the useful things and that was easily adaptable to the needs of living—for example, iron, silver, and anything else of that sort. At first, its value was determined simply by size and weight, but finally people also put a stamp on it, in order to save themselves the trouble of measuring it. For the stamp was put on to signify the amount.

1257b1 Once money was devised, necessary exchange gave rise to the second of the two kinds (*eidos*) of crafts of wealth acquisition, namely, the craft of commerce. At first, it was presumably a simple affair, but then through experience it became more of a craft of how and from what sources the greatest profit could be made through exchange. That is why it seems that the craft of wealth acquisition is most of all concerned with money, and that its function is to be able to get a theoretical grasp on the sources from which a quantity of wealth will come. For it is productive of wealth and money. For wealth is often assumed to be a quantity of money, because this is what the craft of wealth acquisition and the craft of commerce are concerned with.

But sometimes, contrariwise, money seems to be empty trash and to exist entirely by convention and not by nature at all, because, when changed by its users, it has no value and is useless for acquiring the necessities, and often someone who is rich in money will be unprovided with the food that is necessary. Yet it is absurd for something to be wealth if someone well provided with it will die of hunger, like Midas in the fable, when everything set before him turned to gold in answer to his own greedy prayer. That is why people seek another notion of what wealth and the craft of wealth acquisition are, and correctly so. For the craft of natural wealth acquisition and natural wealth are of another sort, and it is [a part of] household management, whereas the craft of commerce is productive of goods, not in every way, but through their exchange. And it seems to be concerned with money, since money is the element and limit of exchange.[88]

And the wealth that derives from this sort of craft of wealth acquisition *is* unlimited. For just as the craft of medicine aims at unlimited health, and each of the crafts aims to achieve its end in an unlimited way (since each tries to achieve it as fully as possible), whereas the things that further the end are not unlimited (for the end is the limit of all of them), so too of this sort of craft of wealth acquisition there is no limit where its end is concerned, since its end is wealth of this sort, namely, the possession of money. The sort of craft of wealth acquisition that is a part of household management, on the other hand, does have a limit. For this [providing unlimited wealth] is not the function of household management. That is why, in one way it appears to be necessary for all wealth to have a limit, and yet, if we look at what actually happens, the contrary seems true, since all acquirers of wealth go on increasing their money without limit.[89] The cause of this is the close relation between the two. For the use, being of the same thing, goes back and forth between the two sorts of crafts of wealth acquisition.[90] For the use is of the same property in both cases, but not with respect to the same thing. Instead, in one case the end is increase, in the other, something else. So it seems to some people that this is the function of household management, and so they end up thinking that they should either preserve the substantial amount of money they have or increase it without limit.

The cause, though, of their being so disposed is that what they take seriously is living, not living well.[91] And since their appetite for living is unlimited, they also have an appetite for an unlimited amount of what is productive of it. But even those who do aim at living well seek what furthers bodily gratification, so that since this too appears to depend on having property, they spend all their time acquiring wealth. And the other kind (*eidos*) of craft of wealth acquisition arose because of this. For since their gratification lies in excess, they seek the craft that is productive of the excess needed for gratification. And if they cannot provide it through the craft of wealth acquisition, they try to do so by means of some other cause of it, using each of their capacities not in accord with nature. For it does not belong to courage to produce wealth but to produce confidence in the face of danger, nor does it belong to generalship or medicine to do so, but rather to produce victory and health, respectively. These people, however, make all of these into the craft of wealth acquisition, on the supposition that acquiring wealth is the end, and that everything must further the end.

About the craft of unnecessary wealth acquisition, what it is, and what the cause is of our need of it, we have said what we have to say, and also about the necessary sort, that it is a distinct sort, that it is a natural part of household management, being concerned with food, and that it is not unlimited like the other, but has a defining mark.[92]

I 10

Clearly, we have also found the solution to the puzzle raised at the start about whether the craft of wealth acquisition belongs to a household manager and a politician, or whether this is not so, but wealth must rather be available to him.[93] For just as politics does not make humans, but takes them from nature and uses them, so too nature must provide land or sea or something else as a source of food, so a household manager must manage what comes from these sources in the appropriate way. For it does not belong to weaving to make wool but to use it, and to know which sorts are usable and suitable or bad and unsuitable.

For someone might be puzzled as to why the craft of wealth acquisition is a part of household management, whereas the craft of medicine is not, even though the members of a household need to be healthy, just as they need to live and have every other necessity. But since there is a way in which it does belong to a household manager and a ruler to see even to health, whereas in another way it does not belong to them, but rather to a doctor, so too in the case of wealth there is a way in which it belongs to a household manager to see to it, and another in which it does not belong to him but to an assistant craft. But above all, as was said earlier, nature must ensure that this is on hand.[94] For it is a function of nature to provide food for what is born, since the leftovers of what they are born from are food for each one.[95] That is why in all cases the craft of acquiring wealth from crops and animals is in accord with nature.

But since it is of two sorts, as we said, one belonging to the craft of commerce and the other to household management, and the latter is necessary and praiseworthy, whereas the craft of exchange is justly
1258b1 blamed (for it is not in accord with nature but involves taking from others), usury is most reasonably hated, because it gets wealth from money itself, rather than just what money was provided for.[96] For money was introduced for the sake of exchange, but interest makes money itself grow bigger. That in fact is how it got its name. For offspring (*tokos*) resemble their parents, and interest (*tokos*) is money that comes from money. And so of all the sorts of crafts of wealth acquisition this one is the most unnatural.

I 11[97]

Since we have adequately discussed what relates to knowledge, we must go through what relates to use.[98] For of all such things theoretical knowledge is something free, whereas experience is something necessary.[99] The practically useful parts of the craft of wealth acquisition are: being experienced with livestock—for example, with what sorts of horses, cattle, sheep, and similarly other animals yield the most profit in different places and conditions (for one needs experience of which of these, in comparison to each other, are the most profitable breeds, and which sorts in which places, since one thrives in one place, another in another). Next, being experienced in farming, which is now divided into land planted with fruit and land planted with cereals, and in beekeeping and in the rearing of the other creatures, whether fish or fowl, from which we can derive some benefit.[100] Of the craft of wealth acquisition of the most proper and primary sort, then, these are the parts.

The most important part of the craft of exchange, on the other hand, is trading, which has three parts: ship-owning, transport, and marketing. These are distinct from each other in that some are safer, others offering greater profit. The second part is money-lending; the third is wage-earning, of which one sort involves the vulgar craftsmen, whereas the other involves those who have no craft knowledge but are useful with their bodies only.[101]

A third kind (*eidos*) of craft of wealth acquisition comes between this one and the primary one, since it contains some part of the natural one and some part of the craft of exchange. It is concerned with things that come from the earth, or are extracted from the earth, that are inedible but useful—for example, logging and every sort of mining. And this now includes many kinds (*genos*), since many kinds (*eidos*) of things are mined from the earth.

About each of these we have now spoken in universal terms. And whereas an exact accounting of each particular one might be useful for putting them into practice, it would be vulgar to spend one's time on it.[102] Now, the most craft-like of these practices are those in which there is the least luck involved; the most vulgar, those in which the body is most damaged; the most slavish, those in which the body is used the most; the most ill-bred, those least in need of virtue in addition.[103]

But since some people have written on these topics—for example, Chares of Paros and Apollodorus of Lemnos on how to farm both grain and fruit, and others on similar topics—anyone who cares to can get a theoretical grasp on them from these.[104] Still, the scattered things that are said about how people have succeeded in acquiring wealth should be collected, since all of them are beneficial for those who hold the craft of wealth acquisition in esteem. For example, the one about Thales of Miletus.[105] This involved an insight related to the craft of wealth acquisition, which, though attributed to him because of his wisdom, happens to be universally applicable. For people were reproaching him because of his poverty, claiming that it showed his philosophy was of no benefit.[106] The story goes that he apprehended from his astronomy that a good olive harvest was coming. So, while it was still winter, he raised a little money, and put a deposit on all the olive presses in Miletus and Chios, hiring them at a low rate, because no one was bidding against him.[107] When the olive season came and many people all of a sudden sought olive presses at the same time, he hired them out at whatever rate he chose. He collected a lot of money, showing that philosophers could easily become rich if they wished, but that this is not what they take seriously.

Thales, then, is said to have demonstrated his own wisdom in this way. But, as we said, this sort of insight related to the craft of wealth acquisition—namely, establishing a monopoly for oneself if one can—is universally applicable. That is why some cities also do this when they are in need of resources, since they create a monopoly on goods for sale. For there was a man in Sicily, who used some money that had been deposited with him to buy up all the iron from the foundries, and later, when the merchants came from their warehouses to buy iron, he was the only seller.[108] He did not increase his prices very much, but all the same he added a hundred talents to his original fifty. When Dionysius heard about this, he told the man to take his money, but on the condition that he remain in Syracuse no longer, as he had discovered ways of making money that were harmful to Dionysius' own affairs.[109] Yet this man's insight was the same as Thales', since each contrived to develop a monopoly for himself.

It is also useful for politicians to know about these things, since many cities need the craft of wealth acquisition and revenues of this sort just as households do, but more so. That is why indeed some people active in politics restrict their political activities to these matters alone.

I 12

Since there were three parts to household management, one being mastership (which we discussed earlier), another the science of fatherhood, and a third, marital science, [let us now discuss the other two].[110] For a wife and children are both ruled as free people, but not with the same mode of rule. Instead, a wife is ruled in a political way, children in a kingly one.[111] For a male, unless he is somehow formed contrary to nature, is by nature more capable of leading than a female, and someone older and complete than someone younger and incomplete.

Now in most cases of rule by politicians people take turns at ruling and being ruled, because they tend to be equal by nature and to differ in nothing. All the same, whenever one person is ruling and another being ruled, the one ruling tries to distinguish himself in dress, titles, and honors from the ruled—as for example in what Amasis said about his footbath.[112] Male, by contrast, is *always* related to female in this way.

The rule over the children, on the other hand, is kingly. For a begetter rules on the basis both of affection and age, and this is a kind (*eidos*) of kingly rule. That is why Homer spoke well when he addressed Zeus, who is king of them all, as "Father of gods and men."[113] For a king should be superior by nature, but belong to the same kind (*genos*), which is just the condition of older in relation to younger, and begetter to child.

I 13

It is evident, accordingly, that household management is more seriously concerned with humans than with inanimate property, with their virtue more than with the virtue (which we call wealth) of acquisition, and with the virtue of free people more than with that of slaves.

Now the first puzzle to raise about slaves is whether the slave has some other virtue, beyond those he has as an instrument or servant, that is more estimable, such as temperance, courage, justice, and other such states of character, or whether he has none beyond those having to do with the bodily assistance he provides.[114] For there is a puzzle either way. For if slaves do have these other virtues, in what respect will they differ from free? If they do not, it is strange, since slaves are human and have a share in reason. Pretty much the same question arises concerning woman and child, as to whether there are virtues proper to them—whether a woman must be temperate, courageous, and just or not, and whether there are temperate and intemperate children or not.

This question, then, about what is ruled by nature and what is ruling by nature must be investigated in universal terms, as to whether their virtue is the same or distinct. For if both of them must share in noble-goodness, why should one of them rule and the other be ruled once and for all?[115] (For it cannot be that the difference between them is one of more or less. For being ruled and ruling differ in kind (*eidos*), not in degree.[116]) On the other hand, if the one must share in it, whereas the other must not, that would be a wonder. For if the ruler is not going to be temperate and just, how will he rule well? And if the ruled is not going to be, how will he be ruled well? For if he is intemperate and cowardly, he will do none of his duties. It is evident, therefore, that both must share in virtue, though there must be differences (*diaphora*) in it, just as there are in those who are by nature ruled.[117]

Consideration of the soul leads at once to this view. For in it there is by nature a part that rules and a part that is ruled, and the virtue of each, we say, is distinct, namely, that of the part that has reason and that of the non-rational part. It is clear, furthermore, that the same holds in the other cases as well, so that most instances of ruling and being ruled are by nature such. For free rule slaves, male rules female, and a grown man rules a child in different ways, because, while the parts of the soul are present in all these people, they are present in different ways. For a slave does not have the deliberative part of the soul at all; the female has it but it lacks control; a child has it but it is incomplete.[118]

We must take it, therefore, that the same necessarily also holds concerning the virtues of character, namely, that all must share in them, but not in the same way—instead, each must have a sufficient share for his own function. That is why a ruler needs to have complete virtue of character.[119] For his function is unconditionally that of an architectonic craftsman, and his reason is an architectonic craftsman.[120] And each of the others must have as much virtue as pertains to them. So it is evident that all those mentioned have virtue of character, and that the temperance of a man is not the same as that of a woman, and neither is the courage or justice, as Socrates supposed, but rather men have ruling courage and women assistant courage, and the same holds of the other virtues.[121]

This will also be clear if we instead investigate each particular one. For people who speak in universal terms are deceiving themselves when they say that virtue is good condition of the soul, or correct action, or something of that sort. For it is far better to enumerate the virtues, as Gorgias does, than to define them in this way.[122] That is why the way the poet spoke about woman is the way we must think about every case.[123] He said, "to a woman silence is a crowning glory"—whereas to a man this does not apply. Since a child is incomplete, it is clear that his virtue too is not his in relation to himself, but in relation to his end and his leader.[124] And the same holds of a slave in relation to his master. But we said that a slave is useful in relation to the necessities, so of [ethical] virtue too he clearly needs only a little—just so much as will prevent him from being deficient in his functions because of intemperance or cowardice.

If what has now been said is true, however, someone might raise the puzzle of whether craftsmen too need to have virtue. For shortcomings often occur in their works through intemperance. Or is this case very different? For a slave shares in his master's living, whereas a craftsman is at a greater remove, and virtue pertains to him just to the extent that slavery does.[125] For a vulgar craftsman has a kind of limited slavery.[126] Moreover, a slave is among the things that exist by nature, whereas no shoemaker is, nor any other sort of craftsman. It is evident, therefore, that the cause of such virtue in a slave must be the master, not the one who possesses the science of teaching him his functions.[127] That is why those people do not speak correctly who withhold reason from slaves, but tell us to make use only of prescriptive commands.[128] For slaves should be warned more than children.[129]

Well, where these matters are concerned let them be determined in this way. As for man and woman, father and children, the virtue relevant to each of them, what is good in their relationship with each other and what is not good, and how to achieve the good and avoid the bad—it will be necessary to go through all these in connection with the constitutions.[130] For since every household is part of a city, and these are parts of a household, and the virtue of the part must look to the virtue of the whole, it is necessary to look to the constitution in educating both women and children, if indeed it makes any difference to the excellence of a city that its children be excellent, and its women too.[131] And it must make a difference. For the women are half of the free population, and from children come those who share in the constitution.[132]

So, since we have determined these matters, and must discuss the rest elsewhere, let us put aside the present accounts as complete and make a new beginning to our discussion. And let us first investigate those who have expressed views about the best constitution.

Book II

II 1

Since our deliberately chosen project is to get a theoretical grasp on which political community is superior to all others for people who are able to live as far as possible in the way they would pray to live, we must investigate other constitutions too, both some of those used in cities that are said to be in good legislative order, as well as any others that happen to have been spoken about by anyone and that seem to be in good condition. Our aim is to see what is correct and useful in them, and further, to show that we are undertaking our methodical inquiry, and seeking something else that is beyond the presently existing constitutions, not because we wish to devise subtleties but because they are not in fact in good condition.[133]

We must make a start, however, at what is just the natural starting-point of this sort of investigation. For all the citizens must share either everything, or nothing, or some things but not others.[134] Now it is evidently impossible for them to share nothing. For a constitution is a sort of community, and so they must, in the first place, share their location. For the location of one single city is a single one, and citizens
1261a1 are sharers of that one single city. But of the things that it is possible to share, is it better for all of them to be shared in a city that is to be well managed, or is it better for some of them to be shared but not others? For the citizens could share children, women, and property with each other, as in Plato's *Republic*.[135] For Socrates claims there that children, women, and property should be held communally. Is the condition we have now better, then, or one that is in accord with the law described in the *Republic*?

II 2

For the women to be common to all both involves many other difficulties, and this one especially, namely, that what causes Socrates to say that things must be legislated in this way is not evidently what follows from his arguments. Further, the end he says his city should have is impossible, as in fact described, yet nothing has been determined about how we should define it. I am talking about its being best for a city to be as far as possible entirely *one*. For this is the hypothesis Socrates adopts.[136] And yet it is evident that the more a city becomes one the less of a city it will be. For a city is in its nature a sort of multitude, and as it becomes more one, it will turn from a city into a household, and from a household into a human being. For we would say that a household is more one than a city, and an individual than a household. So even if someone could achieve this, it should not be done, since it will destroy the city.

A city consists not only of a larger number of human beings [than a household], however, but of human beings of different kinds (*eidos*). For a city does not come about from those who are alike, since a city is distinct from a military alliance. For a military alliance is useful because of the weight of numbers, even if they are all of the same kind (*eidos*), since an alliance naturally exists for the sake of providing assistance in the way that a heavier weight does when placed on a scale. A nation will also differ from a city in this sort of way, when the multitude is not separated into villages, but is like the Arcadians.[137] But things from which one thing must come about, differ in kind (*eidos*).

That is why reciprocal equality preserves cities, as we said earlier in the *Ethics*, since this is also what must exist among people who are free and equal.[138] For they cannot all rule at the same time, but each can rule for a year or in accord with some other time scheme. In this way, then, the result is that they all do rule, just as, if they changed places, all would be shoemakers and carpenters rather than the same people always being shoemakers and carpenters. But since it is better to have it this way also where a political community is concerned, it is clearly better, where possible, for the same people always to rule. But among those where it is not possible, because all are in nature equal, it is at the same time also just for all to share in ruling (regardless of whether it is good or bad (*phaulos*) to rule), and for those who are equal to take turns, and to be similar when they are out of office, imitates this.[139] For they rule and are ruled in turn, just as if they had become other people. It is the same way among those who are ruling, some hold one office, some another.

It is evident from these considerations, therefore, that a city is not in nature one in the way some people say it is, and that what is said to be the greatest good for cities destroys them.[140] Yet what is good for a given thing in fact preserves it. It is also evident in another way that to seek to produce too much oneness in a city is not a better thing. For a household is more self-sufficient than an individual, and a city than a household, and a city tends to come into being at the time when the community of its multitude is self-sufficient. If, then, what is more self-sufficient is indeed more choiceworthy, to be less one is more choiceworthy than to be more one.

II 3

But then even if this is best for a community, namely, to be as far as possible one, this does not seem to have been proved by the argument that all at the same time say "mine" and "not mine" (for Socrates takes this as an indication that his city is completely one).[141] For "all" is ambiguous. If it means "each individually," perhaps what Socrates wants will more come about, since each will call the same person his son, the same woman, of course, his wife, the same things his property, and so on, then, for each of the things that fall to him. As things stand, however, this is not how those who treat women and children as common will speak. Instead, though all [will say "mine" and "not mine"], they will not do so each individually, and similarly for property too—all, but not each individually. Therefore, it is evident that a sort of fallacy is involved in "all say."[142] For "all," "both," "odd," and "even" are ambiguous, and produce contentious deductions even in arguments.[143] That is why in one way it would be noble if all said the same, although this is not possible, whereas in another way it is not at all productive of harmony.

In addition, what is said [by Socrates] is also harmful in another way. For what is held communally by the most people gets the least care. For people give most thought to what is their own, less to what is communal, or only as much as falls to each of them to give.[144] For apart from anything else, the supposition that someone else is attending to it makes them neglect it more, just as, in the case of household services, many servants sometimes give worse service than few. Each of the citizens acquires a thousand sons, although not as an individual, but rather any random one is likewise the son of any random citizen. So all will be likewise neglected by them all.

1262ᵃ1 Further, each says "mine" of anyone among the citizens who is doing well or badly, and says "mine" in this sense, that he is whatever fraction he happens to be of a certain number.[145] What he really means is "mine or so-and-so's," referring in this way to each of the thousand or however many compose the city, and even then he is in doubt. For it is not clear who has had a child born to him, or whether any that were born survived. Yet is this way of calling the same thing "mine" as practiced by each of two or ten thousand people really better than the way they say "mine" in cities as things stand? For the same person is called "my son" by one person, "my brother" by another, "my cousin" by a third, or something else in virtue of some other sort of kinship, whether of blood or connection by marriage—his own marriage, in the first instance, or that of his relatives. Still others call him "my fellow clansman" or "my fellow tribesman."[146]

It is better, in fact, to have a cousin of one's own than a son in that [Socratic] way.

Nevertheless, it is not even possible to prevent people from having some suspicions about who their own brothers, sons, fathers, and mothers are. For the resemblances that occur between parents and children will necessarily be taken as convincing signs of this. And this is just what actually happens, according to the reports of some of those who write accounts of their world travels.[147] For they say that some of the inhabitants of upper Libya hold their women communally, and yet distinguish the children they bear by resemblances. And there are some women, as well as some females of other animals, such as mares and cows, that have a strong natural tendency to produce offspring resembling their sires, like the mare in Pharsalus called "Just."[148]

II 4

Further, there are also other such difficulties that it is not easy for those establishing this sort of community to avoid, such as voluntary or involuntary homicides, assaults, or verbal abuse. None of these is pious when committed against fathers, mothers, or not too distant relatives (just as none is so even against outsiders).[149] But they will necessarily occur even more frequently among those who do not know their relatives than among those who do—and when they do occur, the latter can perform the customary expiations, whereas the former cannot.[150]

It is also strange that while making sons communal, he forbids only sexual intercourse between lovers, but does not prohibit sexual love itself or the other practices which, between father and son or a pair of brothers, are most unseemly, since even the love alone is so. It is strange, too, that Socrates forbids such sexual intercourse not for any other causes but solely because the pleasure that comes from it is so strong, but thinks that the lovers being father and son or brother and brother makes no difference.[151]

It would seem more useful to have the farmers rather than the guardians share their women and children.[152] For there will be less friendship where women and children are held communally.[153] But, with a view to obedience and prevent rebellion, it is the *ruled* who should be like that.

In general, the results of such a law as this must of necessity be the contrary of those that a correctly laid down law should cause, and the contrary of what caused Socrates to think that matters concerning children and women should be ordered in this way. For we think friendship to be the greatest of goods for cities, since in this way people are least likely to engage in faction.[154] And Socrates most of all praises a city's being one—something that seems to be, and that he himself claims to be, the function of friendship. Similarly, in the accounts of erotic love, we know that Aristophanes says that lovers, because of their intense friendship, have an appetitive desire to grow together and become one instead of two.[155] The result in such circumstances, however, is that one or both have necessarily perished. And in a city friendship necessarily becomes watery through this sort of community, and the fact that a father hardly ever says "mine" of a son, or son of a father. For just as adding a lot of water to a drop of sweet wine makes the mixture imperceptible, so the same happens here with the kinship connections expressed in these names, it being hardly ever necessary in a constitution of this sort for a father to take care of his sons as sons, or a son his father as a father, or brothers each other as brothers. For there are two things above all that make human beings care and feel friendship, what is special [to them] and what is beloved—neither of which can exist among people under such a constitution.[156]

But then about the transference of the children, once born, from the farmers and craftsmen to the guardians, and vice versa, there is also much confusion about the way it will be done—that is, those who do the transferring and receiving must know who has been transferred to whom.[157]

Further, in these cases what we mentioned earlier—I mean assaults, love affairs, and murders—must of necessity happen even more often. For those who have been transferred to the other citizens will no longer call the guardians "brothers," "children," "fathers," or "mothers," nor will those who have been transferred to the guardians use these terms of the other citizens, so as to avoid, through kinship, committing any such offenses.

About the community of children and women, then, let this be the way our determinations are made.

II 5

The next topic to investigate is property, and the way those who are going to be governed by the best constitution should establish it, and whether property should be held communally or not. One could investigate these questions even separately from the legislation dealing with children and women. I mean whether in matters concerning property,
1263ª1 even if children and women are held separately (which is now the way it is everywhere), it still might be best for property at least, or its use, to be communal. For example, the land might be held separately, while the crops grown on it are brought into a communal store to be consumed [communally] (as happens in some nations). Or, contrariwise, the land

might be held communally and farmed communally, while the crops grown on it are divided up for private use (some barbarians are also said to share things in this way). Or both land and crops could be communal.

Now, if others worked the land, the way would be different and easier, whereas if the citizens do the work for themselves, matters concerning property will give rise to much discontent. For if the citizens happen to be unequal rather than equal both in the profits they enjoy and in the work they do, accusations will necessarily be made against those who enjoy or take a lot but do little work by those who take less but do more. In general, though, it is difficult to live together and to share in any human concern, above all in ones such as these. This is made clear by the community of travelers away from home. For pretty much the majority of them start quarreling, because they irritate each other in humdrum matters and little things. Further, the servants with whom we get most irritated are those we employ most regularly for day-to-day services.

The communal ownership of property, then, involves these and other similar difficulties. The way we have now, if adorned by [the relevant] habits and by the order characteristic of correct laws, would be superior, and not by a little, since it would have the good of both (I mean both of the property's being communal and of its being private). For while property should in a way be communal, in general it should be private, since dividing up the care of it will produce not mutual accusations, but rather will lead to greater care being given, as each will be attending to his own. But where use is concerned, it is thanks to virtue that, in accord with the proverb, "friends share everything communally."

Even now this way of arranging things exists in outline in some cities, on the supposition that it is not impossible. In well managed cities, in particular, some elements of it exist, while others could come about. For although each citizen does have his own private property, he makes available some things to be useful to his friends, and others to be useful communally. For example, in Sparta they use each other's slaves (one might almost say) as their own, and horses and dogs as well, and if they need supplies when on a journey, they may find them in the farms throughout the territory.[158] It is evident, therefore, that it is better for property to be private, but for its use to be made communal. And to see that people become disposed in such a way is the special function of the legislator.[159]

Further, it also makes an untold difference to one's pleasure to regard something as one's own. For it is not perhaps pointless that each self loves
himself, but is rather something natural. Self-love is blamed, though, and **1263ᵇ1**
justly so.[160] This is not loving oneself, however, but rather loving oneself more than one should, just as in the case of the love of money (since, one might almost say, everyone *does* love each of the things of this sort).

But then too it is very pleasant to assist one's friends, guests, or companions, and do them favors, and this happens when one has property of one's own. These things, then, do not take place for those who make the city too much one thing, and in addition it is evident that they do away with the function of two of the virtues, namely, temperance in regard to women (for to keep away from another man's woman due to temperance is noble work) and generosity with one's property (for one cannot show oneself to be generous, nor perform any generous action, since it is in the use made of property that generosity's work lies).

Such legislation indeed looks attractive and may seem to be philanthropic.[161] For anyone who hears of it accepts it gladly, thinking that all will have a wondrous friendship for all, especially when someone blames the evils now existing in constitutions on property's not being communal (I mean lawsuits against each other over contracts, perjury trials, and flattery of the rich).[162] Yet none of these bad things comes about because property is not communal but because of depravity.[163] For we see that those who own and share property communally have far more disagreements than those who own their property separately. But in theory we take those who disagree over what they own communally to be few in number, because we compare them to the many whose property is private. Further, it would be just to mention not only how many bad things people will be deprived of by sharing, but also how many good things. But their life appears altogether impossible.

The cause of Socrates going astray, we have to think, is that his hypothesis is incorrect. For a household and a city should indeed be one in a way, but not in every way. For as a city proceeds in this direction, there is a point at which it will in one way cease to be a city and at which, in another way, while it will still be a city, as it will come closer to not being a city, it will be a worse city. It is as if one were to reduce a harmony to a unison, or a rhythm to a single beat. But because a city is a multitude, as we said before, it must be unified and made into a community through education.[164] It is strange that the one who intends to introduce education, and who believes that through it the city would be excellent, should think to rectify it by measures of this sort, and not by habits, philosophy, and laws, just as in Sparta and Crete the legislator made property communal by means of communal messes.[165]

And we must not ignore this point either, namely, that we should consider the immense period of time and the many years during which it would not have gone unnoticed if these measures were any good. For pretty much everything has been discovered, although some things have not been collected, and others, though known, are not used.[166] The matter would become especially evident, however, if one could see by the facts a constitution established in this way. For it is impossible to produce a city without separating the parts and dividing [them], some into communal messes, others into clans and tribes.[167]

So nothing else will result from the legislation except that the guardians will not farm—which is just what the Spartans are trying to do even as things stand. Neither, for that matter, has Socrates said what mode of the constitution as a whole applies to those who share in it, nor is it easy to say. And yet the multitude of the other citizens is pretty much the entire multitude of his city, but nothing has been determined about whether the farmers too should have communal property or each his own private property, or, further, whether both their women and their children should be private or communal.[168]

If, in fact, all is to be held communally by all in the same way, how will the farmers differ from the guardians? And what more will they get by submitting to their rule? Or what will they learn to make them submit to it—unless the guardians adopt some clever stratagem like that of the Cretans? For they allow their slaves to have the same other things as themselves, and forbid them only the gymnasia and the possession of weapons.

On the other hand, if the farmers too are to have such things, as they do in other cities, what way will their community be ordered? For of necessity there will be two cities in one, and those opposed to each other.[169] For Socrates makes the guardians into a sort of garrison, whereas he makes citizens of the farmers, craftsmen, and the others.[170] Accusations, lawsuits, and such other bad things as he says exist in other cities will all then exist among them too. And yet Socrates claims that because of their education they will not need many regulations (for example, town or market ordinances, or others of that sort), though he gives this education only to the guardians.

Further, he gives the farmers control of their property, although he requires them to pay a tax.[171] But this is likely to make them much more difficult to deal with and full of their own ideas than the helots, serfs, and slaves that some people have today.[172]

But whether the same things are indeed similarly necessary for the farmers or not, has in fact nowhere been discussed—and neither has the related question of what constitution, education, and laws they are to have. It is not easy, either, to discover what sort of people these are, nor is the difference it makes to the preservation of the community of the guardians a small one. But if at any rate Socrates is going to make their women communal and their property private, who will manage 1264b1
the household in the way the men manage things in the fields? Who will manage it, indeed, if the farmers' women and property are communal?

It is also absurd to draw a comparison with wild beasts in order to show that women should engage in the same practices as men, since wild beasts have no share in household management.[173]

The way Socrates appoints his rulers is also unstable. For he makes the same people rule all the time, which is a cause of faction even among people who have no recognized worth, and all the more so, of course, among spirited and warlike men.[174] But it is evident that it is necessary for him to make the same people rulers. For the gold from the god has not been mixed into the souls of one lot of people at one time and another at another, but always into the same ones. For he says that the god, immediately at their birth, mixed gold into the souls of some, silver into others, and bronze and iron into those who are going to be craftsmen and farmers.[175]

Further, even though Socrates does away with the happiness of the guardians, he says that the legislator should make the whole city happy. But it is impossible for the whole to be happy unless all, or most or some, of its parts possess happiness. For happiness is not the same thing as evenness, since it is possible for the latter to be present in the whole without being present in any of the parts, whereas happiness cannot.[176] But if the guardians are not happy, who is?[177] Surely not the craftsmen or the multitude of those who are vulgar.[178]

These, then, are the puzzles raised by the constitution Socrates describes, and there are others that are not inferior to these.

II 6

Something pretty much similar holds in the case of the *Laws*, which was written later. So we had also better briefly examine the constitution there. After all, in the *Republic* Socrates has determined very few things: how things should stand concerning the community in women and children, concerning property, and the order characteristic of the constitution. For he divides the multitude of the inhabitants into two parts: the farmers and the part that goes to war for it. And from the latter comes a third, namely, the deliberative and controlling element in the city.[179] But about whether the farmers and craftsmen will share in ruling to some extent or not at all, and whether or not they too are to possess weapons and join in battle—about these matters Socrates has determined nothing.[180] He does think, though, that the women should join in battle and receive the same education as the other guardians. Otherwise, he has filled out his account with extraneous material, in particular about what sort of education the guardians should receive.

1265a1 The *Laws* consists for the most part of laws, and he has said little about the constitution.[181] And, although he wishes to make this one more generally attainable by actual cities, he gradually turns it back toward the other.[182] For, with the exception of the community in women and property, the other things he assigns to both constitutions are the same: the same education, living in abstention from the necessary functions, and the communal messes in like manner—except that in this constitution he says that there are to be messes for women too, and that those possessing hoplite weapons should be five thousand, whereas it is one thousand there.[183]

All the Socratic accounts are extraordinary, sophisticated, innovative, and exhibit a spirit of inquiry, but it is presumably difficult to do everything well. In the case of the multitude just mentioned, for example, we must not neglect to consider that it would need a territory the size of Babylon, or some other unlimitedly large territory, to nourish five thousand in idleness, and another mob of women and servants, many times as great, along with them.[184] We should assume conditions that answer to our prayers, to be sure, but not ones that are impossible.

It is stated that the legislator should look to just two things in setting up his laws: the territory and the human beings.[185] But, further, it would be good to add that he should also look to the neighboring territories, if, in the first place, the city is to live a political life and not a solitary one.[186] For it must then possess the weapons that are useful for war not only on its own territory but also against the regions outside it. If, however, one rejects this sort of life, both for the individual and for the city communally, the need to be fearsome to enemies is just as great, both when they have invaded its territory and when they have left it.

And the quantity of property should also be looked at, to see whether it would not be better to define it in another more perspicuous way.[187] For he says that there should be as much as is needed "to live temperately," which is as if one were to say, "to live well"—for this is too universal.[188] Further, it is possible to live temperately but miserably. A better definition would be "to live temperately and generously." For, when separated, the one will lead to poverty, the other to luxury. For these are the only choiceworthy states concerned with the use of property—for example, one cannot use property either in a mild-mannered way or in a courageous one, but one can do so temperately and generously. So the states concerned with its use must also be these.

Also, it is absurd that while property is equalized nothing is established concerning the number of citizens, but instead the production of children is allowed to be unlimited, on the supposition that it will remain sufficiently close to the same number, due to childlessness, no

matter how many births there are, because this seems to be what hap-
1265b1 pens in present-day cities.[189] But the exactness this requires is not the same there as in cities nowadays. For nowadays, because properties are divided among however great a number there happens to be, no one is left without resources. In this city, by contrast, properties are indivisible, so that excess children will necessarily get nothing, no matter whether they are fewer or greater in number.[190] One might well take it, though, that it is the production of children that should be restricted, rather than property, so that no more than a certain number would be born, and that this number should be fixed by looking to the chances of some of those who are born dying, and of childlessness on the part of others. To leave the number unrestricted, however, as is done in most cities, necessarily causes poverty among the citizens; and poverty produces faction and crime. In fact, Pheidon of Corinth, one of the most ancient legislators, thought that the households and the number of citizens should be kept equal, even if the allotments of land they had were of unequal size to begin with.[191] But in the *Laws*, it is just the contrary.[192] But these matters, and how we think these matters could be better handled, will have to be spoken about later.[193]

Also omitted in these *Laws* are matters concerning the rulers and how they will differ from the ruled. For he says that just as warp and woof come from distinct sorts of wool, so should ruler stand in relation to ruled.[194]

And since he permits someone's total property to increase up to five times its original value, why should this not also hold of land up to a certain point?[195]

Also, the division of homesteads needs to be investigated, in case it is disadvantageous to household management. For to each individual he assigned two homesteads, dividing them and making them separate.[196] But it is difficult to manage two households.

The whole order is intended to be neither democracy nor oligarchy but a mean between them.[197] It is called a *polity*, since it is made up of those with hoplite weapons.[198] Now if he is establishing this, in comparison with other constitutions, as the most attainable by actual cities, what he has said is perhaps correct, but if as next best after the first constitution, it is not correct.[199] For one might well give more praise to the Spartan constitution, or some other more aristocratic one.[200] Indeed, some say that the best constitution is a mixture of all constitutions, which is why they praise the Spartan one.[201] For some assert that it is made up of oligarchy, monarchy, and democracy, saying that the kingship is a monarchy, the office of senators an oligarchy, and that it is governed democratically in virtue of the office of the overseers, because the overseers come from the people as a whole, whereas others say that the overseership is a tyranny, and that the democratic governing lies in the communal messes and the rest of daily life.[202] But in these *Laws* it is said that the best constitution should be composed of democracy and tyranny—constitutions one might well take as not constitutions at all, or as the worst of all.[203] They speak better, then, who mix together a larger number, since the constitution composed of a larger number is better.[204]

Next, the constitution in the *Laws* evidently has no monarchical element at all, but only oligarchic and democratic ones, with a tendency to lean more toward oligarchy. This is clear from the appointment of officials. For while choosing by lot from a previously elected pool is common to both, to require richer people to attend the assembly and to vote for officials, or to do some other political task, without requiring these things of the others, is oligarchic.[205] The same is true of the attempt to make the majority of officials come from among the rich, with the most important ones coming from among those with the highest property assessment.[206]

He also makes the election of the council oligarchic.[207] For everyone is required to elect candidates from the first property assessment class, then again in the same way from the second, then from the third—except that not everyone is required to elect candidates from the third or the fourth, and only members of the first and second are required to elect candidates from the fourth.[208] Then from these, he says, an equal number must be designated from each assessment class. More of them, then, will come from the highest assessment classes and the better sort, because some of the people will not vote because they are not required to.

It is evident from these considerations, then, and from what will be said later, when our investigation turns to this sort of constitution, that a constitution of this sort should not be composed of democracy and monarchy.[209] But in fact where the election of officials is concerned, electing from the elected is dangerous. For if some are willing to combine, even if they are a relatively small number, the elections will always turn out according to their wish.

This, then, is the way matters stand concerning the constitution in the *Laws*.

II 7

There are also certain other constitutions, proposed either by private individuals or by philosophers and politicians, but all of them are closer to the established constitutions, by which people are governed as things stand, than either of the ones we have discussed. For no one else has ever suggested the innovations of sharing children and women, or of communal messes for women.[210] Instead, they start with the necessities. For to some of them it seems that the most important thing is to have matters concerning property ordered in a good way. For they say that it is over these matters that everyone creates factions.

That is why Phaleas of Chalcedon, the first to propose such a constitution, did so.[211] For he says that the property of the citizens should be equal. He thought this was not difficult to do when cities were just being settled, that in those already settled it would be more difficult, but that nevertheless a leveling could be very quickly achieved by the rich giving but not receiving dowries, and the poor receiving but not giving them.

Plato, when writing the *Laws*, thought that up to a certain point things should be left alone, but that no citizen should be permitted to have a property more than five times the size of the smallest, as we also said earlier.[212] But people who legislate in this way must not forget, as they now do, that, while regulating the quantity of property, they should also regulate the quantity of children. For if the number of children exceeds the size of the property, it is necessary for the law to be abrogated at least. But abrogation aside, it is a bad thing for many people to become poor after having been rich, since it is hard work for people like that not to become revolutionaries.

That is why the leveling of property does indeed have some influence on political communities. This was evidently recognized even by some in ancient times—for example, both in the legislation of Solon and in the law in force elsewhere that prohibits anyone from getting as much land as he might wish.[213] Laws likewise prevent the sale of [landed] property, as among the Locrians, where the law forbids it unless an evident misfortune can be shown to have occurred.[214] In yet other cases it is required that the original allotments be preserved. It was the abrogation of this provision at Leucas that made their constitution democratic too, since, as a result, offices were no longer filled from the designated assessment classes.[215] But equality of property may exist and yet the amount may be too great, so that it leads to luxury, or too low, so that living in a tightfisted way results.

It is clear, then, that it is not sufficient for the legislator to make property equal; he must also aim at the mean. Further, even if one were to arrange a moderate property for everyone, it would be no benefit. For one should rather level appetites than property, and that cannot happen unless people have been sufficiently educated by the laws.[216]

But perhaps Phaleas would reply that this is actually what he was saying. For he thinks that cities should have equality in these two things: property and education. But one must also say what the education is going to be, and to have it be one and the same is no benefit. For it can be the same and one, but of the sort that will produce people who are disposed to deliberately choose to get more wealth or honor or both.[217]

Further, people engage in faction not only because of inequality of property but also because of inequality of honors—although in contrary ways in each case: ordinary people do so because of inequality in property, sophisticated ones because of honors, if they are equal.[218] Hence the saying: "Noble and base are held in a single honor."[219]

Human beings, however, do not commit injustice only because of the necessities, which Phaleas thinks equality of property will remedy (in that they will not steal because of cold or hunger), they also commit them to get enjoyment and assuage their appetites. For if they have an appetite for more than the necessities, they will seek to cure it by committing injustice—and not, you may be sure, because of this alone, but rather, even without appetite, they will commit injustice in order to enjoy the pleasures that are without pain.[220] What, then, is the remedy for these three? For the first, moderate property and work. For the second, temperance. Third, if certain people wish to find enjoyment through themselves, they should not look for a remedy beyond philosophy, since all other pleasures require [other] human beings.[221] The greatest injustices, at any rate, are committed because of excess and not because of the necessities—for example, no one becomes a tyrant to escape the cold. That is why the honors are great when one kills not a thief but a tyrant. So Phaleas' mode of constitution would be a help only against minor injustices.

Further, he wishes to establish many things thanks to which the citizens will govern well in their relations with each other, whereas he should also establish things thanks to which they will do so in their relations with neighbors and outsiders as a whole. It is necessary, therefore, for the constitution to be ordered with a view to military strength, about which he has said nothing.

Matters are similar where property is concerned. There needs to be enough not only for use within the city, but also to meet external dangers. That is why the quantity of it on hand should be neither so great that stronger neighbors will have an appetite for it, and the owners unable to repel the attackers, nor so little that they cannot sustain a war even against those who are equal or similar.

Although Phaleas has not determined this, we must not neglect to consider how much property it is advantageous to have. Perhaps the best defining mark is this: that those [neighbors] who are stronger will not profit if they go to war because of the [city's] excess in property, but as they would if the property were not so great. For example, when Autophradates was about to lay siege to Atarneus, Eubulus told him to consider how long it would take to capture the place, and then to calculate what such time would cost, since he said he was willing to abandon Atarneus at once for less.[222] These words made Autophradates have second thoughts and abandon the siege.

So, while equalizing the property of citizens is among the things that are advantageous with a view to their not engaging in faction against each other, it is (one might almost say) no big thing. For sophisticated people would get vexed, on the grounds that they deserve not to be equal, which is why in fact they are often seen being on the attack and engaging in faction. Further, the wickedness of human beings is an insatiable thing, and a mere two obols is enough at first, but once that has become traditional, they always ask for more, and go on doing so without limit.[223] For it is the nature of appetite to have no limit, and satisfying it is what ordinary people live for.[224] The starting-point in such matters, then, rather than leveling property, is to establish things so that while those who are by nature decent are of such a sort that they do not wish to get more, the base ones cannot do so—which will be the case if they are weaker and not treated unjustly.[225]

But even about the equalizing of property Phaleas has not spoken correctly. For he equalizes only landed property, but wealth also exists in the form of slaves, livestock, and money, and there is a great supply of it in so-called movables. So either equality—or some moderate regulation—should be sought in all these or all should be left alone.

It is also evident from his legislation that the city he is establishing is a small one—if, at any rate, all the craftsmen are to be public slaves and are not to contribute to the full membership of the city. But if indeed those engaged in public works should be public slaves, it should be in this way, namely, just as it was in Epidamnus and as Diophantus tried to establish in Athens.[226]

Concerning the constitution of Phaleas, then, one should, on the basis of these considerations, be pretty much able to get a theoretical grasp on whether he spoke correctly on some topic or incorrectly.

II 8

Hippodamus of Miletus, the son of Euryphon, was the man who invented the division of cities and laid out the street plan for Piraeus.[227] (He was extraordinary in other aspects of his life as well, because of his love of honor, so that he seemed to some people to be overly affected, with his long hair, expensive jewelry, and furthermore with the same cheap warm clothing worn not only in winter but also in summer, and his wish, too, to be considered well versed about nature as a whole.) He was the first of those not engaged in politics who attempted to say something about the best constitution.[228]

The city he wanted to establish had a multitude of ten thousand citizens, divided into three parts. For he made one part the craftsmen, one the farmers, and a third to defend and possess weapons. And he wanted to divide the territory into three parts—one sacred, one public, and one private. That from which what is customarily rendered to the gods was produced would be sacred; that from which the ones who go to war for it would live, public; and the land belonging to the farmers, private.

He thought that there were just three kinds (*eidos*) of laws, since the things about which lawsuits arise are three in number—wanton aggression, harm, and death.[229] He also wanted to legislate a single court with [complete] control, to which all lawsuits thought not to have been well judged were to be referred, which he proposed to establish from a certain number of elected senators. Court judgments should not be rendered, he thought, by casting ballots, but rather each juror should deposit a tablet: if he simply convicts, he should write the penalty on it; if he simply acquits, he should leave it blank; if he convicts to some extent and acquits to some extent, he should make the relevant distinctions. For he thought that as things stand legislation is not well drafted, since it compels jurors to violate their oath by judging one way or the other.[230]

Further, he set up a law that those who discover something advantageous to the city should be honored, and that children of those who die in war should receive support from public funds, on the supposition that this had not been legislated elsewhere, whereas such a law actually exists both in Athens and in some other cities. The officials were all to be elected by the people, and the people to be made up of the city's three parts. Those elected were to supervise communal matters, matters relating to aliens, and matters relating to orphans.

These, then, are most of the features of Hippodamus' order, and the ones that are most worth discussing. And the first puzzle to raise would be with the division of the multitude of citizens. For the craftsmen, the farmers, and those who possess weapons all share in the constitution. But the fact that the farmers do not possess weapons, and that the craftsmen possess neither land nor weapons, makes them both nearly slaves of those who do possess weapons. So it is impossible that *every* office be shared. For the generals, civic guards, and all the officials with (one might almost say) the most control will necessarily be appointed from those who possess weapons. But if the farmers and craftsmen do not share in the constitution, how can they possibly have any friendly feelings for the constitution?[231] On the contrary, those who possess weapons have to be *stronger* than both of the other parts.[232] Yet that is not easy unless they are numerous. And, in that case, is there any need to have the others share in the constitution or control the appointment of officials?

Further, what use are the farmers to the city? Craftsmen are necessary (for every city needs them), and they can support themselves, just as in other cities, from their craft. The farmers, though, would quite reasonably have been some part of the city if they provided food for those who possess weapons, while, as things stand, they have private land and farm it privately.

Further, there is the public land, from which the ones who go to war for the city are to get their food. If they are to farm it themselves, the fighting part will not be distinct from the farming one, as the legislator wishes them to be. And if there are going to be some others to do so, distinct from those who farm privately and from the warriors, this will be a fourth part again in the city, which shares in nothing and is alienated from the constitution. But then if one were to make those who farm the private land and those who farm the public land the same, the quantity of produce from each one's farming will be inadequate for two households.[233] And why is it that they will not from the same land and the same allotments at once provide food for themselves and for the soldiers? There is much confusion in all this.

The law about judgments is not good either, requiring judging to consist in making distinctions, while the charge is written in unconditional terms—that is, making a juror into an arbitrator.[234] This is possible in arbitration, even if there are many arbitrators, since they can confer together over their judgment. But it is not possible with juries, and, indeed, most legislators do the contrary and establish things so that the jurors do *not* confer with each other.[235]

In addition, how will the judgment not be confused when a juror thinks the defendant owes something, but not as much as the plaintiff thinks? For if the plaintiff claims twenty minas, but the juror awards ten (or the former more, the latter less), another awards five, and another four, it is clear, accordingly, that they will split the award in this way, whereas some will convict for the whole sum, and others for nothing. In what way, then, will the votes be counted?

Further, nothing compels a juror who, in a just way, unconditionally acquits or convicts to perjure himself, if indeed the accusation was written in unconditional terms. For one who acquits is not judging that the defendant owes nothing, only that he does not owe the twenty minas. But a juror who convicts, without believing that he owes the twenty minas, violates his oath straightaway.

As for his suggestion that those who discover something advantageous to the city should receive some honor, such legislation is not safe, but only pretty to listen to. For it would involve "sycophancy" and might even lead to change in the constitution.[236] But this slides into another problem and another investigation. For some people raise the puzzle of whether it is advantageous or harmful to cities to change their ancestral laws, if some other is better.[237] That is why, if indeed change is not advantageous, it is not easy to give ready assent to what Hippodamus says, for it is possible that certain people might propose that the laws or the constitution be dissolved on the supposition that this is for the common good.

Since we have mentioned this topic, however, we had better expand on it a little. For, as we said, there is a puzzle here and change may seem better. In the other sciences at any rate change has certainly proved to be advantageous—for example, medicine has changed from its ancestral ways, as has athletic training, and all the crafts and capacities generally.[238] So, since politics too must be posited as one of these, it is clear that something similar must also hold of it.

An indication of this, one might claim, is provided by the facts themselves.[239] For the laws [or customs] of ancient times were exceedingly simple and barbaric. For example, the Greeks, used to both carry weapons and buy women from each other, and the pieces that remain of ancient laws in some places are quite simpleminded—such as the homicide law
in Cyme that if the prosecutor can provide a number of his own relatives **1269a1**
as witnesses, the defendant is guilty of murder.[240]

In general, everyone seeks not what is ancestral but what is good.[241] But it is probable that the first ones, whether they were "earth-born" or the survivors of some cataclysm, were like random people [today] or people who lack understanding (and this in fact is precisely what is said about the earth-born).[242] So it would be absurd to cling to *their* beliefs.

In addition, it is not better to leave written laws unchanged either. For just as it is in the other crafts, so too in [the science of] political order, it is impossible to write down everything exactly. For it is necessary to write them in universal terms, whereas actions are concerned with particulars.[243]

From these considerations, then, it is evident that some laws must sometimes be changed. But to those who investigate the matter in another way this would seem to require much caution. For if the improvement is small, and if it is a bad thing to accustom people to casual abrogation of the laws, then some of the legislators' or rulers' errors should evidently be left unchanged, since the benefit resulting from the change will not be as great as the harm of being made accustomed to disobey the rulers.

On the other hand, the paradigm involving the crafts is false. For changing a craft is not like changing a law. For the law has no strength to secure obedience except habit, and habit does not develop except over a long period of time. So to change easily from existing laws to new and different ones is to weaken the capacity of law itself.

Further, if laws are indeed to be changed, are they all to be changed, and in every constitution, or not? And by any random person, or by certain ones? For these things make a big difference. Let us therefore set aside this investigation for the present, since it belongs to other occasions.[244]

II 9

About the constitution of Sparta and of Crete, and about pretty much all the other constitutions as well, there are two investigations to be made. One is whether there is anything legislated in it that is good or not good with a view to the best order. The other is whether there is anything legislated in it that is contrary to the hypothesis or to the mode of constitution they actually have.[245]

Now it is generally agreed that a constitution that means to be governed in a good way must provide leisure from necessary functions. But the way to provide this is not easy to grasp. For the Thessalian serfs have often attacked the Thessalians, just as the helots have the Spartans (for they are forever lying in wait, as it were, for bad luck to strike their masters).[246] But nothing like this has so far happened in the case of the Cretans. Perhaps the cause of this is that the neighboring cities, though they war with each other, never ally themselves with the rebels, because it is not to their advantage to do so, since they themselves also possess subject peoples.[247] Sparta's neighbors, on the other hand—Argives, Messenians, Arcadians—were all hostile.[248] The Thessalians, too, first experienced revolts because they were still at war with their neighbors—Achaeans, Perrhaebeans, and Magnesians.[249] And it would seem, even if nothing else, that the supervision at any rate of serfs, and what way one should consort with them, is a troublesome matter. For if they are given license, they become wantonly aggressive and claim to be of equal worth to those in control; and, if they live in misery, they conspire and hate. It is clear, then, that those to whom this happens in connection with helotry have not found the best mode of it.

Further, the license where their women are concerned is also detrimental both to the deliberate choice of the constitution and to the happiness of the city as well. For just as part of a household is a man and part a woman, it is clear that a city too should be regarded as being divided into two nearly equal parts, namely, the multitude of the men and that of the women. So in all constitutions in which matters relating to women are badly handled, half the population should be regarded as not being regulated by any law. And this is just what has happened in Sparta. For the legislator, wishing the whole city to have resilience, makes this evident where the men are concerned, but has been negligent in the case of the women.[250] For they live free of discipline, giving in to every sort of intemperance, and luxuriously.[251]

The necessary result is that wealth is esteemed in a constitution of this sort, especially if they are actually controlled by the women, as most militaristic and warlike races are (excluding the Celts and some others who openly esteemed sexual relations between males).[252] For the one who first told the myth seems not to have been unreasonable in coupling together Ares and Aphrodite.[253] For all warlike men seem prone to being possesed by sexual relations either with men or women. That is why this happened to the Spartans, and in the days of their [hegemonic] rule, many things were managed by women. And yet what difference is there between women rulers and rulers ruled by women? For the result is the same. Rashness is not useful in day-to-day matters, but only—if indeed at all—in war, but Spartan women have been very harmful even in this respect.[254] This they made clear during the Theban invasion.[255] For they were no use at all, as women are in other cities, but caused more confusion than the enemy.[256]

From the start, then, it seems that this license with regard to women occurred in Sparta for explicable reasons. For Spartan men spent much time away from home during their expeditions, that is, when they were at war with the Argives, and again with the Arcadians and **1270a1**
Messenians.[257] When leisure returned, though, they placed themselves in the hands of their legislator, having been already well prepared by the military life, since it includes many of the parts of virtue.[258] As for the women, people say that when Lycurgus tried to bring them under the laws, they resisted and he retreated.[259] These, then, are the causes of what happened—and, it is clear, of the present error as well. But, of course, we are not investigating the question of whom we should excuse and whom not, but what is correct and what is not correct.

The fact that matters relating to women are not well handled seems not only to create a certain impropriety in the constitution, as we already said before, but also to contribute something to its love of money.[260] For after the things just stated one might next criticize the uneven distribution of property. For because some of the Spartans came to own far too much wealth and others altogether too little, the land passed into the hands of a few. And this is badly ordered through the laws too. For the legislator quite correctly made it not noble to buy or sell an existing land holding, but he left owners free to give or bequeath their land if they wished, even though this necessarily leads to the same results as the other.[261] Indeed, roughly two-fifths of all the land belongs to the women, both because many become heiresses and because large dowries are given. And so it would have been better if it had been ordered that there be no dowry, or a small or even a moderate one. But, as things stand, a person can give an heiress daughter in marriage to whomever he wishes, and if a man dies intestate, the person he leaves as his heir gives her to whomever he pleases. As a result, in a land capable of supporting fifteen hundred cavalry and thirty thousand hoplites, there were fewer than a thousand. And it became clear because of the facts themselves that the ordering of these things served them badly. For the city did not withstand one single blow, but was ruined because of its shortage of men.[262]

It is said that in the time of their early kings, they used to give a share in the constitution to others, so that at that time there was no shortage of men, despite the fact that they were at war for a long time. Indeed, they say that at one time the Spartiates actually had ten thousand members.[263] But regardless of whether or not this is true, a better way to keep high the number of men in a city is by leveling property. But the law dealing with the production of children is also opposed to this. For the legislator, wishing there to be as many Spartiates as possible, encourages the citizens to have as many children as possible. For there is a law exempting a father of three sons from military service, and a father of four from all taxes. But it is evident that if many children are born, and the land has been correspondingly divided, many people will necessarily become poor.

But then matters relating to the board of overseers are badly handled too.[264] For this office by itself controls their most important matters, but the overseers are drawn from among the entire people, so that often very poor men enter it, who, because of their poverty, were open to bribery. (This has been made clear on many occasions in the past as well, and in our own day among the Andrians.[265] For some, corrupted by silver, destroyed the entire city, so far as it was up to them.)

Also, because the office is too powerful—in fact, equal to a tyranny—even the kings were forced to curry favor with the overseers. And this too has harmed the constitution, since from an aristocracy a democracy was emerging.

Certainly, the board of overseers does in fact hold the constitution together. For the people remain at peace because they share in the most important office, so that, whether it came about because of the legislator or by luck, it is advantageous to Spartan affairs. For if a constitution is going to survive, every part of the city itself must wish [the constitution] to exist and endure.[266] And the kings are in this condition because of the honor given to them; the noble and good, because of the senate (since this office is a reward of virtue); and the people, because of the board of overseers (since appointments to it are made from all). Still, though the overseers should be chosen from all, it should not be in the way it is now (since it is exceedingly childish).[267]

Further, the overseers control the most important judicial decisions, though they are random people. That is why it would be better if they judged cases not on the basis of their own consideration but in accord with the letter of the laws.[268] Also, the overseers' way of life is not in keeping with what the city wishes for. For it itself is too lax, whereas among the others it is excessive in its hardness, so that they are incapable of the resilience [it requires] but secretly escape from the law and indulge in the pleasures of the body.[269]

Matters relating to the office of the senators also do not serve the Spartans well.[270] If the senators were decent people, who were sufficiently well educated in manly goodness, one might well say that this office is advantageous to the city—although, one might dispute about whether they ought to have lifelong control of important matters, since there is the old age of thought as there is that of the body.[271] But when they are educated in such a way that even the legislator himself distrusts their goodness, it is not safe. And it is evident in fact that in many matters of public concern those who have shared in this office have repeatedly taken bribes and shown favoritism. This is why it is better for the senators not to be exempt from being inspected—which at present they are.[272] It may seem that the overseers should inspect every office, but this would give too much to the board of overseers, and is not the way we say that inspections should be carried out.[273]

The election they conduct of the senators is also decided in a childish way, and for the person who is going to be considered worthy of the office to have to ask for it himself is not correct.[274] For the one worthy of the office should hold it whether he wishes to or does not wish to.[275] But as things stand the legislator is evidently doing just the same here as in the rest of the constitution. He arranges for the citizens to love honor and then uses this fact for the election of the senators. For no one would ask for office who did not love honor. Yet of most voluntary acts of injustice among human beings the majority are pretty much caused by the love of honor or by the love of money.

Where kingship is concerned, whether it is better for cities to have one or better not to have one, is a matter for another account.[276] But it is surely better at any rate to choose each new king not as now but rather in accord with his own way of life.[277] And it is clear that even the Spartan legislator himself did not think it possible to make the kings noble and good men. At any rate, he distrusts them, on the grounds that they are not sufficiently good men. That is why the Spartans used to send out a king's opponents as fellow ambassadors, and why they regarded factional conflict between the kings as tantamount to preservation for the city.

Nor were matters concerning the communal messes (or so-called *phiditia*) well legislated by the person who first put them in place.[278] For they should rather be paid for from public funds, as they are in Crete.[279] Among the Spartans, by contrast, each individual has to contribute, even though some are very poor and unable to afford the expense. So the result is the contrary of the legislator's deliberately chosen aim. For he wishes the communal messes to be democratic, but legislated as they are now they are scarcely democratic at all, since the very poor cannot easily participate in them. Yet the defining mark of this constitution, which is ancestral for them, is that those who cannot pay this contribution cannot participate in it.[280]

The law dealing with the admirals has also been criticized by others, and correctly criticized too. For it becomes a cause of faction. For over against the kings, who are permanent generals, the office of admiral has been put in place as pretty much another kinship.

One might also criticize the hypothesis of the legislator just as Plato criticized it in the *Laws*.[281] For the entire order characteristic of their laws aims at a part of virtue, namely, military virtue, since this is useful for conquest. They were able to preserve themselves, then, while they were at war, but they started to decline once they ruled supreme, because they did not have the scientific knowledge of how to be at leisure and had never undertaken any kind of training with more control than the military sort.[282] And the error involved in this is not small. For they think that the good things that people fight about are won by virtue rather than by vice, and this is correct, but they also think that these goods are better than virtue itself, and this is not correct.[283]

Matters relating to communal funds are also in a bad condition among the Spartiates. For even though they are compelled to fight major wars there is nothing in the communal fund of the city and taxes are not properly paid. For because most of the land belongs to the Spartiates, they do not examine each other's tax payments.[284] And thus the result for the legislator is the contrary of advantageous. For he has made his city poor and the private individuals into lovers of money.

Concerning the Spartan constitution, then, let this much be said, since these are the things one might particularly criticize in it.

II 10

The Cretan constitution is very close to the Spartan, and while in some small respects it is no worse, most of it is less polished. For it seems, or at any rate it is said, that the Spartan constitution is largely an imitation of the Cretan, and most older things are less fully elaborated than newer ones.[285] For they say that Lycurgus, when he had relinquished the guardianship of King Charilaus and gone abroad, spent most of his time in Crete, because of the kinship connection.[286] For the Lyctians were colonists from Sparta, and those who went to the colony adopted the order characteristic of laws existing among the inhabitants at that time.[287] That is why even now their subject peoples employ these in the same way, on the supposition that Minos first established the order characteristic of their laws.[288]

The island seems naturally well suited and situated to rule the Greek world. For it lies across the entire sea on whose shores pretty much all of the Greeks are settled. For in one direction it is not far from the Peloponnese, and in the other not far from Asia (the part around Cape Triopium) or from Rhodes.[289] That is why Minos obtained the rule over the sea as well, subjugating some islands, sending settlers to others, and finally attacking Sicily, where he met his death near Camicus.[290]

The Cretan order is analogous to the Spartan. For the helots do the farming for the latter, whereas the subject peoples do it for the former. Also, both cities have communal messes (and at any rate in 1272a1
ancient times the Spartans called these not *phiditia* but *andreia* ("men's messes") like the Cretans—a clear indication that these came from Crete).[291] Further, there is the order characteristic of the constitution. For the overseers have the same powers as the order-keepers (as they are called in Crete), except that the overseers are five in number and the order-keepers ten. The senators, whom the Cretans call the council, are the equals of the Spartan senators. As for kingship, there used to be one in earlier times, but the Cretans did away with it, and the order-keepers have the leadership in war. All share in the assembly, but it has

control of nothing except the ratification by vote of the resolutions of the senators and order-keepers.

Now, matters relating to the communal messes are better handled by the Cretans than by the Spartans. In Sparta, as we said earlier, each person must contribute a fixed per capita amount, and, if he does not, a law prevents him from sharing in the constitution, whereas in Crete they are handled in a more communal way.[292] For out of all the public crops and livestock and the tributes paid by the subject peoples, one part is set aside for the gods and for communal public services, and another for the communal messes, so that all—women and children and men—are fed at public expense.[293] The legislator regarded moderation in eating as advantageous and devoted much philosophizing to furthering it. And as regards the segregation of women, in order to prevent them from having many children, he has made a place for sexual relations between men—as to whether this was badly done or not badly done, we will investigate on another occasion.[294] It is evident, then, that matters relating to the communal messes have been better ordered by the Cretans than by the Spartans.

Matters relating to the order-keepers, on the other hand, are even worse than those relating to the overseers. For while what is bad in the board of overseers is also bad in the board of order-keepers (for it is composed of random people), what is for the advantage of the constitution there does not exist here. For there, the election being from all, the people share in the most important office, and so wish the constitution to continue.[295] Here, by contrast, the order-keepers are elected not from all but from certain families, and the senators are elected from those who have been order-keepers. And one might make the same arguments about the Cretan senators as about those who become senators in Sparta, since their exemption from inspection and their life-tenure are greater prerogatives than they are worthy of, and it is dangerous that they rule not in accord with what is written down, but on the basis of their own consideration.[296]

The fact that the people remain at peace even though they do not share in the most important office is no indication that it has been well ordered. For there is no profit in it for the order-keepers, as there is for the overseers, because they live on an island, far away indeed from any
1272b1 who might corrupt them.

As for the cure the Cretans use for this error, it is strange and characteristic not of a political constitution but of a dynasty.[297] For the order-keepers are frequently expelled by a conspiracy either of their fellow rulers themselves or of private individuals, and it is also possible for the order-keepers to resign office in the middle of their term. But surely it is better if all these things should take place in accord with law and not with the wish of human beings, since the latter is not a safe standard.[298]

Worst of all, however, is the suspension of order-keepers, which the powerful frequently put in place, when they wish to escape punishment at the hands of justice. For this makes it clear that the order has something of a constitution about it, yet it is not a constitution but more of a dynasty. Their habit is to create anarchy, form factions, and fight each other by dividing the people and their own friends into parties.[299] Yet how does this sort of thing differ from the city ceasing to be such for a period of time and the political community dissolving?

A city in this condition is in great danger, however, as those who wish to attack it are also able to do so. But, as we said, Crete is preserved by its location, since its remoteness has served to keep foreigners out.[300] That is why the institution of subject peoples survives among the Cretans, whereas the helots frequently revolt. For the Cretans do not share in external rule—although a foreign war has recently come to the island, which has made the weakness of its laws evident.[301]

About this constitution, then, let this much be said.

II 11

The Carthaginians also seem to manage their constitution well, and in many respects in an extraordinary way as compared to other people, although in some respects mostly resembling that of the Spartans.[302] For these three constitutions, the Cretan, Spartan, and, third among them, the Carthaginian, are all in a way very close to each other and very different from the others. Many of their ordinances are well handled, and it is an indication that their constitution is well ordered that the people stand by the order characteristic of the constitution, and that no faction even worth talking about has arisen among them, and no tyrant either.

Points of similarity to the Spartan constitution are these: The messes of the *hetairia* are like the *phiditia*, while the office of the one-hundred-and-four is like that of the overseers, except that it is not worse (for the overseers are drawn from random people, whereas the Carthaginians elect to this office on the basis of worth).[303] And their kings and senate are analogous to the Spartan ones. Also, it is better that the kings are neither a separate family nor a random one at that, but if any family distinguishes itself, then it is from its members that they are elected, rather than in accord with age. For, since they control the important matters, if they are worthless people, they will do great harm to the city—as they already have to the city of the Spartans.

Most of the criticisms one might make because of its deviations [from the best constitution] are in fact common to all the constitutions we have discussed. But of those that are deviations from the hypothesis of an aristocracy or a polity, some lean more in the direction of democracy, others more in the direction of oligarchy.[304] For the kings and senators control what to bring and what not to bring before the people, provided they all agree, but if they do not agree, the people control these matters too. And when the rulers make proposals, the people are allowed not only to listen to their proposals, but also have control of deciding them, and anyone who wishes may speak against the proposals being made—which is just what does not exist in the other constitutions.

On the other hand, it is oligarchic that the boards of five, which control many and important matters, elect themselves, and also elect to the office of one-hundred, which is the most important office, and, furthermore, hold office longer than the others (for they rule before taking office and after they have left it).[305] But we must take as aristocratic that they are neither paid nor chosen by lot, and anything else of that sort, and also that all lawsuits are judged by the boards of five, and not, as in Sparta, some by some and others by others.[306]

However, the order characteristic of the Carthaginians deviates away from aristocracy and toward oligarchy most of all in line with a thought held also by ordinary people. For they think that rulers should be chosen not solely on the basis of merit but also on the basis of wealth, since it is impossible for a poor person to rule well—that is, to be at leisure to do so.[307] Hence, if indeed it is oligarchic to choose rulers on the basis of wealth, and aristocratic to choose them in accord with virtue, then this will be a third sort of order, in accord with which the Carthaginians have ordered matters relating to the constitution. For they elect with a view to both [criteria], especially in the case of the most important offices, namely, the kings and the generals.

But this deviation from aristocracy must be regarded as an error on the part of the legislator. For one of the most necessary things is to see to it from the start that the best people are able to be at leisure and to avoid doing anything unseemly, not only when in office but also when in private life. But if one must look to wealth too, for the sake of leisure, it is bad that the most important offices, those of king and general, should be for sale. For this law makes wealth more estimable than virtue, and makes the entire city moneyloving, and whatever it is that the controlling element takes to be estimable, the belief of the other citizens will necessarily follow its belief. And where virtue is not esteemed most highly, the constitution cannot be stably governed as an aristocracy. It is also reasonable to expect that those who have bought office, that is, when they rule by having spent money, will become habituated to making a profit from it. For if a poor but decent person will want to profit from office, it would be strange if a worse one, who has already spent money, will not wish to do so. That is why those who are best able to rule should rule.[308] And even if the legislator neglected the wealth of the decent people, he had better take care of their leisure at any rate while they are ruling.

It would also seem to be bad for the same person to hold more than one office, which is just what is held in high repute among the Carthaginians. For one function is best completed [when it is completed] by one person.[309] The legislator should see to it that this is what happens, and not require the same person to play the flute and make shoes. So, where the city is not small, it is more political, and more democratic, if more people participate in the offices.[310] For it is more communal, as we said, and each of the same things is better carried out and more quickly. This is clear in the case of military and naval affairs, since in both of them ruling and being ruled extend through (one might almost say) everyone.

But though their constitution is oligarchic, they are very good at escaping faction, because it is forever the case that some part of the people grows rich due to their sending it out to the cities.[311] In this way they effect a cure, and make their constitution steadfast. But this is the result of luck, whereas they ought to be free of factional conflict because of their legislator. As things stand, however, if some misfortune occurs and the multitude of those who are ruled revolt, there is no remedy for restoring peace through the laws.

As regards the Spartan, Cretan, and Carthaginian constitutions, which are quite justly held in high repute, this is the way things stand.

II 12

Some of those who have had something to say about a constitution took no part whatsoever in political actions, but always lived a private life.[312] About them pretty much everything worth saying has been said. Others became legislators, some in their own cities, others in some foreign ones as well, because they engaged in politics themselves. Some of these crafted laws only, whereas others, such as Lycurgus and Solon, crafted a constitution too. For these put in place both laws and a constitution.

Now, the constitution of the Spartans has already been spoken about.[313] As for Solon, some people think that he was an excellent legislator because he abolished an oligarchy that was too unmixed, put an end to the slavery of the people, and put in place the ancestral democracy, by mixing the constitution well—for the council of the Areopagus is oligarchic, the fact that officials are elected, aristocratic, and the courts democratic.[314] It would seem, though, that Solon found the first two—the council and the election of officials—already in existence and did not abolish them, whereas by making juries open to all, he did set up the people [in power].[315]

That is why indeed some people find fault with him. For they say that when he gave juries, which were chosen by lot, control of everything, he undid the other two [elements of the constitution]. For when this element became strong, those who gratified the people as if it were a tyrant changed the constitution into the present democracy. Indeed, Ephialtes and Pericles curtailed the power of the Areopagus, and Pericles introduced payment for jurors, and in this way each popular leader developed the power of the people and led them on to the present democracy.[316]

It appears, however, that this did not come about in accord with Solon's deliberate choice, but rather by accident—for because the people were the cause of Athens' naval supremacy during the Persian Wars, they became presumptuous, and chose base people as their popular leaders when the decent ones pursued policies opposed to their own.[317] For Solon at any rate seems to have given the people only the very minimum power necessary—that of electing and inspecting officials (since if they do not even control these, the people would be slave and enemy [of the constitution]).[318] But he drew all the officials from among the notable and rich, namely, from the *pentakosiomedimnoi*, the *zeugitai*, and the third, the so-called *hippeis*, whereas the fourth, the *thetes*, had a share in no office.[319]

Others also became legislators: Zaleucus became legislator for the Epizephyrian Locrians, and Charondas of Catana for his own citizens and for the other Chalcidian cities in Italy and Sicily.[320] (Some people actually try to connect them, on the supposition that Onomacritus, a Locrian, was the first person to become an expert in legislation, having been trained in Crete when he visited there in connection with his craft of divination, that Thales was his companion, and that Lycurgus and Zaleucus were pupils of Thales, and Charondas of Zaleucus.[321] But when they say these things, they speak without regard to chronology.)

There was also Philolaus the Corinthian, who became a legislator for the Thebans: he was a member of the Bacchiad family and became the lover of Diocles, the victor in the Olympic games.[322] This Diocles left Corinth because of his bitter hatred of the erotic passion that his mother,

Alcyone, had for him, and went off to Thebes, where he and Philolaus both ended their days. Even now people point out their tombs, which are in full view of each other, although one has a view toward the land of the Corinthians, whereas the other does not. For the story goes that they arranged to be buried in this way, Diocles, because of his hatred of his mother's passion, so that the land of Corinth would not be visible from his burial mound, Philolaus so that it would be visible from his. It was due to this sort of cause, then, that the two of them dwelt among the **1274b1**
Thebans. Philolaus became legislator for them both on other matters and concerning procreation (which they call "the laws of adoption"). This is special to his legislation, its purpose being to preserve the [same] number of estates.

There is nothing special to Charondas' legislation except lawsuits for perjury. For he was the first to introduce denunciations for this. But in the exactness of his laws, he is more polished than even present-day legislators. The feature special to Phaleas is the leveling of property—whereas to Plato it is the sharing of women, children, and property, communal messes for women, and further the law about drinking, that the sober should preside at symposia, and the one requiring ambidextrous training for soldiers, on the grounds that one of the hands should not be useful and the other useless.[323]

There are also Draco's laws, but it was for an existing constitution that he set up laws.[324] There is nothing special to his laws worth talking about, except their harshness due to the magnitude of the punishments.

Pittacus too crafted laws but not a constitution.[325] A law special to him requires drunken people to be punished more severely for making a misstep than sober ones. For because more people commit acts of wanton aggression when drunk than when sober, Pittacus looked not to the fact that greater indulgence should be shown to those who are drunk but to what is advantageous.

Androdamus of Rhegium became a legislator for the Chalcidians in the region of Thrace, and to him belong those dealing with homicides and heiresses.[326] But there is nothing special to him that one might report.

Where the various constitutions are concerned, then, both those that have control and those described by certain people, let this be the way to get a theoretical grasp on them.

Book III

III 1

For someone investigating constitutions, that is, what each is and what sort of thing it is, pretty much the first investigation concerns the city, to see what on earth the city is.[327] For as things stand, there are disputes about this, some saying that it is the city that performed a certain action, whereas others say that it is not the city but rather the oligarchy or the tyrant. And we see that the entire business of the politician and the legislator concerns cities, and that the constitution is itself a certain ordering of those who inhabit the city. But since the city belongs among composite things, and things that are wholes and composed of many parts, it is clear that the first thing that must be investigated is the citizen.[328] For a city is a particular sort of multitude of citizens. So who should be called a citizen, and what the citizen is must be investigated. And in fact there is often a dispute about the citizen as well, since not everyone agrees that one and the same person is a citizen. Indeed, someone who is a citizen in a democracy is often not one in an oligarchy.

Now we should leave aside those who acquire the title of citizen in some other way—for example, the ones who are created citizens.[329] Nor is the citizen a citizen through dwelling in a place, since resident aliens and slaves share the dwelling place. Nor are those people citizens who share in matters of justice to the extent of undergoing trial or suing, since parties to treaties can also do that. (In fact in many places even resident aliens do not share completely in these things, but must find a "sponsor," so that they participate in this sort of community in an incomplete sort of way.[330]) Like children who are too young to be enrolled in the citizen lists or old people who have been discharged, these people must be said to be citizens in a way, not unconditionally so, but rather with the addition of "incomplete" or "superannuated" or something else of this sort (it makes no difference what we add, since what we mean is clear).[331] For we are inquiring about the unconditional citizen, the one who has no defect of this sort that needs to be rectified, since one can also go through and solve similar puzzles about those who have been disenfranchised or exiled.

The unconditional citizen is defined by nothing else so much as by his participation in judgment and office. But some offices are delimited in time, so that in some cases they cannot ever be held twice by the same person, or only after a definite period. Another, however, holds office indefinitely, such as the juror or the assemblyman. Now perhaps someone might say that the latter are not officials at all, and do not, because of doing what they do, share in office.[332] And yet surely it would be absurd to deny that those with the most control are officials. But let this point pass, since the argument is about a name. For what is common to a juror and an assemblyman lacks a name that could apply to both. For the sake of distinguishing it, let us call it "indefinite office." We take it, then, that those who share in office in this way are citizens.

The definition, then, that best fits all those called citizens is pretty much one of this sort. But we must not neglect to consider that in the case of things in which the underlying subjects differ in kind (*eidos*), with one coming first, another second, and so on, either the common element is not present at all, insofar as these things are what they are, or only in some slight way.[333] We see, though, that constitutions differ in kind (*eidos*) from each other, and that some are posterior and others prior. For erroneous or deviant constitutions are necessarily posterior to those that are not erroneous. (What we mean by "deviant" will be evident later.[334]) So the citizen in each constitution must also be distinct.

That is why the citizen that was mentioned is above all a citizen in a democracy, and may possibly be so in other constitutions, but not necessarily.[335] For in some constitutions there is no democratic body, nor is there a legally recognized assembly but rather specially summoned councils, and judicial cases are tried in special courts. For example, in Sparta some cases concerning contracts are tried by one overseer, others by another, whereas cases of homicide are tried by the senate, and other cases by perhaps some other official. And it is the same way in Carthage, since there particular officials judge all judicial cases.[336]

But our definition of a citizen admits of correction. For in the other constitutions, it is not the holder of indefinite office who is assemblyman and juror, but someone whose office is definite.[337] For it is either to some or to all of the latter that deliberation and judgment, whether about some or about all matters, is assigned.

Who the citizen is, then, is evident from these considerations. For whoever is authorized to share in deliberative or judicial office, we can now say, is a citizen of the relevant city, and a city, simply speaking, is a multitude of such people adequate for self-sufficiency in living.[338]

III 2

But the definition that gets used in practice is that a citizen is someone who comes from citizens on both sides, and not just on one—for example, on the father's or on the mother's. And some go even further back, looking for two or three or more generations of ancestors. But quick, political definitions of this sort lead some people to raise a puzzle about how that third- or fourth- generation ancestor will be a citizen.[339] Hence Gorgias of Leontini, half perhaps to raise a real puzzle and half ironically, said that just as mortars are things made by mortar-makers, so Larisaeans too are what are made by official craftsmen, since some craftsmen are Larissa-makers.[340] But the puzzle is a simple one. For if the ancestors shared in the constitution in the way that is in accord with the definition just given, they were citizens. For "what comes from a citizen father or mother" cannot even be applied to the first inhabitants or founders.

But more of a puzzle is perhaps raised by the case of those who come to share in a constitution after its being changed, such as the citizens created in Athens by Cleisthenes after the expulsion of the tyrants.[341] For he enrolled many foreigners and alien slaves in the tribes. But the dispute in the case of these people is not about which of them is a citizen, but whether they are justly or unjustly so. And yet a further puzzle might be raised as to whether someone who is not justly a citizen is a citizen at all, as "unjustly" and "falsely" seem to have the same force. But since we see that there are also some people holding office unjustly, whom we say *are* holding it, albeit not justly, and since a citizen is defined as someone who holds a sort of office (for someone who shares in such office is a citizen, as we said), it is clear that these people too must be said to be citizens.

III 3

The puzzle about justly and not justly is connected to the dispute we mentioned earlier.[342] For some people raise a puzzle about how to determine whether a city has or has not performed an action—for example, when from oligarchy or a tyranny a democracy comes about. At these times, some do not wish to honor treaties, as it was not the city, but its tyrant who entered into them, or many other things of the same sort, on the grounds that some constitutions exist by the exercise of power and not because of being for the common advantage.[343] Accordingly, if indeed some cities are democratically ruled in this way, it must be conceded that the actions of this constitution are the actions of this very city in the same way as those of the oligarchy or the tyranny.

This argument seems to be akin to the puzzle of when we ought to say that a city is the same, or not the same but a distinct one.[344] Now, the most obvious way to inquire into this puzzle is by looking to the location and the human inhabitants. For it is possible for a city's location and its human inhabitants to come apart, and for some to live in one place and some in another. This is why the puzzle must be taken to be a rather tame one. For the fact that something is said to be a city in many ways makes inquiry into such puzzles in a way easy.[345]

Things are similar if one asks when the humans inhabiting the same location should be considered to be one city. Not, certainly, because it is enclosed by walls, since one wall could be built around the Peloponnese. Perhaps Babylon is like this, or anywhere else that has the dimensions of a nation rather than a city.[346] At any rate, they say that after its capture a part of the city was not aware of it for three days.

But it will be useful to investigate this puzzle on another occasion. For the size of the city, both as regards numbers and as regards whether it is advantageous for it to have one or several [locations], should not be overlooked by the politician.[347]

But where the same human beings are inhabiting the same place, is the city to be called the same as long as the inhabitants remain of the same stock (*genos*), even though all the time some are passing away and others coming to be—just as we are accustomed to say that rivers and springs remain the same, even though all the time water is flowing in and flowing out? Or are we to say that while human beings can remain the same due to this sort of cause, the city is a distinct one? For if indeed a city is a sort of community, namely, a community of citizens sharing in a constitution, then, when the constitution becomes a distinct one in form (*eidos*), that is, becomes different, it would seem that the city too cannot remain the same. At any rate, just as we say that a chorus that is at one time comic and at another tragic is a distinct chorus, even though the human beings in it are often the same, so too we say that any other community or composite is distinct if the form of the composite is distinct.[348] For example, we say that a harmony composed of the same notes is a distinct harmony if it is at one time Dorian and at another Phrygian.[349] If, then, this is how things are, it is evident that we must say that a city is the same city by looking above all to its constitution. But the name to call it may be distinct or the same one whether its inhabitants are the same or completely distinct human beings.[350]

But whether it is just to honor or not to honor agreements when a city changes to a distinct constitution, requires another argument.

III 4

Connected with the topics we have just now discussed is the investigation of whether to take the virtue of a good man and that of an excellent citizen to be the same or not the same. But then if *this* is what we should investigate, surely the virtue of a citizen must first be grasped in some sort of outline.[351]

Now just as a sailor is one of the members of a community, so too, we say, is a citizen. And though sailors are dissimilar in their capacities (for one is an oarsman, another a captain, another a lookout, and others have other sorts of titles), it is clear both that the most exact account of the virtue of each sort of sailor will be special to him and that there will also be some common account that fits them all alike. For the preservation of the ship while sailing is a function of all of them, since this is what each of the sailors desires.[352] In the same way, then, the citizens too, even though they are dissimilar, have the preservation of the community as their function, and the constitution is the community. That is why the virtue of a citizen must be relative to the constitution. If, then, there are indeed several kinds (*eidos*) of constitutions, it is clear that there cannot be one virtue that is the virtue of an excellent citizen, namely, complete virtue. But the good man, we say, is such in accord with one virtue, namely, the complete one. It is evident, then, that it is possible for someone to be an excellent citizen without having acquired the virtue in accord with which someone is an excellent man.

By going through the puzzles in another way, the same argument can be made about the best constitution. For if it is impossible for a city to be composed entirely of those who are excellent, but each must at least perform his own intrinsic function well, and this is doing it out of virtue, and since it is impossible for all the citizens to be similar, then
1277a1 there cannot be one virtue of a citizen and of a good man. For that of an excellent citizen must belong to all (since this is necessary if the city is to be best), but the virtue of a good man cannot be had by all, unless it is necessary for all the citizens of an excellent city to be good men.

Further, since a city consists of dissimilar inhabitants—that is, just as an animal straightaway consists of soul and body, a soul of reason and desire, a household of man and woman, and property of master and slave, so a city too consists of all these, and of other dissimilar kinds (*eidos*) in addition—the virtue of all the citizens cannot be one virtue, just as the virtue of the leader of a chorus and that of one of its ordinary members cannot be one virtue either.[353]

Why the virtue of man and of a citizen are not unconditionally the same, then, is evident from these considerations, but will the virtue of a certain sort of excellent citizen and that of an excellent man be the same? Well, we say that an excellent ruler is good and practically-wise, and a politician is of necessity practically-wise.[354] Also, some say that the education of a ruler is distinct right from the start—as is evident in the case of the sons of kings, who are educated in horsemanship and warfare, and in Euripides, when he says, "no subtleties for me . . . but what the city needs" (the supposition being that there is a sort of education proper to a ruler).[355] But if the virtue of a good ruler and of a good man are the same, and if the one who is ruled is also a citizen, then the virtue of a citizen would not be unconditionally the same as that of a man (although that of a certain sort of citizen would be), since the virtue of a ruler and a citizen would not be the same. Perhaps this is why Jason said that he went hungry except when he was being a tyrant, on the assumption that he lacked the scientific knowledge of how to be a private citizen.[356]

But then someone is surely *praised* for being able to rule and be ruled, and being able to do both of them well seems to be the virtue of a reputable citizen. If, then, we take a good man's virtue to be ruling virtue, but a citizen's to be both ruling and ruled, then the two virtues would not be praiseworthy in the same way.

Since, then, they seem to be distinct in some cases, and that it is not the same things that should be learned by the ruler and the ruled, whereas a citizen should have scientific knowledge of both and share in both, we may see what follows from that.

For there is rule of a master—by which we mean the kind concerned with the necessities. It is not necessary for the ruler to have scientific knowledge of how to perform these [functions], but rather of how to use [those who do].[357] In fact, the former is slavish.

(By the former I mean the capacity to do in someone's service the actions of a servant.) But there are several kinds (*eidos*) of slaves, we say, since the kinds of work they do varies. Of these, one part is that done by manual laborers. These are people, as their name itself signifies, who live by their hands. The vulgar craftsman is included among them. That is why among some peoples craftsmen did not share in office in former times, until extreme democracy arose.[358] Thus the functions performed by people ruled in this way should be learned neither by the good politician nor by the good citizen, unless for himself out of some need of his own, since then it is no longer a case of one person becoming master and the other slave.[359]

But there is also a sort of rule exercised over those who are similar in kind (*genos*) and free. For this is what we say is political rule, and the ruler must learn it by being ruled, just as one learns to be a cavalry-commander by serving under a cavalry-commander, to be a general by serving under a general, and [similarly] under a major, or company-commander. That is why this too is well said, namely, that one cannot rule well unless one has been [well] ruled.[360] And while the virtues of these are distinct, the good citizen must have the scientific knowledge needed and the capacity both to be ruled and to rule, and this is the virtue of a citizen, to know the rule of free people from both sides.

In fact, the good *man* has both virtues, even if a distinct kind (*eidos*) of justice and temperance is characteristic of a ruler. For if a good man is ruled, but is a free citizen, it is clear that his virtue (justice, for example) is not one thing, but includes one kind (*eidos*) for ruling and another for being ruled, just as a man's and a woman's courage and temperance are distinct. For a man would seem a coward if he were courageous in the way a woman is courageous, and a woman would seem garrulous if she were moderate in speech in the way a good man is. Household management, indeed, is also of distinct sorts for a man and a woman. For his function is to acquire property and hers to preserve it. Practical wisdom, by contrast, is the only virtue special to a ruler. For the others, it would seem, must be common to both rulers and ruled. At any rate, the virtue of someone ruled is not practical wisdom but true belief. For those ruled are like makers of flutes, whereas rulers are like the flute players who use them.[361]

Whether, then, the virtue of a good man and that of an excellent citizen are the same or distinct, and in what way they are the same and in what way distinct, is evident from these considerations.

III 5

One of the puzzles about the citizen, though, still remains. For is it really the case that a citizen is someone to whom it is open to have a share in office, or should vulgar craftsmen also be taken as citizens? If, indeed, those who do not share in office should be taken as citizens, the sort of virtue we discussed cannot belong to every citizen, since these craftsmen will then be citizens.[362] On the other hand, if none of these sorts is a citizen, in which part of the city should they each be put? For they are neither resident alien nor foreigner.

Or shall we say that nothing absurd follows—at any rate, not because of this argument? For slaves and freed slaves are not among those just mentioned either. In fact the truth is that not everyone without whom there would not be a city is to be taken as a citizen, since not even children are citizens in the same way that men are. Instead, the latter are unconditional citizens, whereas the former are so on the basis of a hypothesis, since, though they are citizens, they are incomplete ones. Now among some peoples in ancient times the vulgar element was slave or foreign, which is why most of them are such even now. And the best city will not confer citizenship on a vulgar person. But if [in other cities] even this sort of person is a citizen, then what we have characterized as a citizen's virtue cannot be ascribed to everyone, or even to all free people, but only to those who are released from the necessary functions. Of the necessary ones, those who perform such services for an individual are slaves; those who perform them for the community are vulgar and hired laborers.[363]

It will become evident, if we carry our investigation a little further, how things stand where these people are concerned. In fact, it is clear from what we have said.[364] For since there are several constitutions, there must also be several kinds (*eidos*) of citizens, and above all of citizens who are being ruled, so that in some constitutions the vulgar element and the hired laborer must be citizens, whereas in others it is impossible—for example, in any so-called aristocracy, that is, the one in which offices are awarded in accord with virtue and in accord with worth. For it is impossible to engage in virtuous pursuits while living the life of a vulgar person or a hired laborer.[365]

In oligarchies, on the other hand, while it is not possible for hired laborers to be citizens (for participation in office is based on high property assessments), it is possible for a vulgar person, since in fact many craftsmen become rich. (In Thebes, though, there used to be a law that anyone who had not kept away from the market for ten years could not share in office.)

But in many constitutions the law goes so far as to invite even some foreigners to be citizens. For in some democracies the descendant of a citizen mother is a citizen, and in many places the same holds of bastards too. Nevertheless, since it is because of a shortage of legitimate citizens that they make such people citizens (since it is because of underpopulation that they employ laws in this way), when they are well supplied with a mob of them, they gradually disqualify, first, those with a slave as father or mother, then those with citizen mothers [alone], until finally they make citizens only of those who come from citizens on both sides.

It is evident from these considerations, then, that there are several kinds (*eidos*) of citizens, and that the one who is above all said to be a citizen is the one who shares in the honors of office, as Homer too implied when he wrote, "like some dishonored vagabond."[366] For the one who does not share is like a resident alien. And whenever this sort of thing is kept concealed, it is for the sake of deceiving their fellow inhabitants.[367]

And whether, then, to take the virtue in accord with which a man is good and a citizen is excellent as the same or as distinct is clear from **1278b1**
what has been said: in one sort of city the good man and the excellent citizen are the same, whereas in another they are distinct. And that man is not just anyone, but the politician, that is, the one who controls

or is capable of controlling, either by himself or with others, the supervision of community affairs.

III 6

Since these issues have been determined, the next thing to investigate is whether we should take it that there is one constitution or several, and, if there are several, what they are, how many they are, and what differences (*diaphora*) there are between them.

Now, a constitution is an ordering of a city's various offices, and above all of the office that controls everything. For the governing body controls the city everywhere, and the constitution is governing body.[368] I mean, for example, that in democratic cities the people are in control, whereas in oligarchic ones, on the contrary, the few are. And we say that the constitution too is different in these cases. And we shall give the same account of the others as well.

First, then, we must ascertain what a city is set up for, and how many kinds (*eidos*) of rule are concerned with human beings and their community in living.

In our first discussions, then, where determinations were made about household management and rule of a master, it was also said that a human being is by nature a political animal.[369] That is why, even when they do not need each other's assistance, people desire no less to live together. Nevertheless, it is also true that the common advantage brings them together, to the extent that some share of noble living falls to each. It is especially this, then, that is the end both of all communally and of each separately. But they also join together and maintain the political community for the sake of living itself. For there is presumably some share of the noble present even in living itself alone, as long as the hardships of life are not too excessive. In any case, it is clear that most human beings are willing to endure much misery in order to cling to living, on the supposition that there is a sort of joy in it and a natural sweetness.

But then it is also easy to distinguish at any rate the modes of rule that are spoken about, since even in the external accounts they are often discussed.[370] For rule of a master, although in truth the same thing is advantageous for what is by nature a master and what is by nature a slave, is nevertheless rule exercised with a view to the master's own advantage, though coincidentally with a view to that of the slave (since if the slave is destroyed, the mastership cannot be preserved).

On the other hand, rule over children, wife, and the household (*oikia*) generally, which we for that reason call household management (*oikonomikê*), is either for the sake of the ruled or for the sake of something common to both ruled and ruler. Intrinsically, it is for the sake of the ruled, as we also see in the various crafts—for example, medicine and athletic training. But coincidentally it may be for the **1279ᵃ1** rulers as well. For nothing prevents a coach from sometimes being one of those he is training, just as a ship's captain is always one of the sailors. A coach or a ship's captain looks to the good of those he rules, but when he too becomes one of them himself, he shares coincidentally in the benefit. For in the one case he is a sailor, and in the other, though still a coach, he becomes one of the trained.

That is why, in the case of political offices too, where they have been set up in accord with the equality of the citizens and their similarity, the citizens expect to rule in turns. In the past, as is natural, they expected to perform public service when their turn came, and then to have someone look to their good in turn, just as they had previously looked to his advantage when they were ruling.[371] Nowadays, however, because of the benefits to be had from public funds and from ruling office, people wish to rule continuously, as if they were sickly and would come to be healthy by always ruling. At any rate, the latter would presumably pursue ruling office in that sort of way.[372]

It is evident, therefore, that those constitutions that aim at the common advantage are—in accord with what is unconditionally just—correct, whereas those that aim only at the advantage of the rulers are erroneous ones, and deviations from the correct constitutions.[373] For they are like the rule of a master, whereas a city is a community of free people.

III 7

Now that these matters have been determined, the next thing is to investigate how many constitutions there are and what they are, starting with the correct constitutions. For the deviations will be evident once these have been defined.

Since "constitution" and "governing body" signify the same thing, and the governing body is what has control in cities, and the one in control must be either one person, or few, or many, then, whenever the one, the few, or the many rule for the common advantage, these constitutions must be correct, whereas if they aim at the private advantage, whether of the one, the few, or the multitude, they are deviations.[374] For either those who share should not be called citizens, or they should share in the advantages.[375]

Now of monarchies, the one that looks to the common advantage is usually called a kingship, and rule by a few, but more than one, an aristocracy (either because the best people rule, or because they rule with a view to what is best for the city and those who share in it), whereas when the multitude governs for the common advantage, the constitution is called by the name "polity (*politeia*)," which is common to all constitutions (*poleteiai*). Moreover, this happens reasonably.[376] For while it is possible for one or a few to be superior in virtue, where more people are concerned it is already difficult for them to be exact practitioners of every sort of virtue—the major exception being military virtue, since this does come about in a multitude. That is why in this constitution the element that goes to war for it is the one with the most control, and why those who possess their own weapons are the ones who share in it.

Deviations from the aforementioned are tyranny from kingship, oligarchy from aristocracy, and democracy from polity. For tyranny is monarchy for the advantage of the monarch, oligarchy for the advantage of the rich, and democracy for the advantage of the poor. But none of them is for the common profit.

III 8

We should say a little more about what each of these constitutions is. For certain puzzles are involved, and, where each methodical inquiry is concerned, it is appropriate for the person who is carrying it out in a philosophical manner, and not merely with a practical purpose in view, not to overlook or omit anything, but to make clear the truth about each.

A tyranny, as we said, is a monarchy that exercises the rule of a master over the political community, an oligarchy is when those who control the constitution are the ones who have the properties, and a democracy, on the contrary, is when those who control it do not have much property, but are poor.

The first puzzle concerns definition. For suppose that the majority were rich and controlled the city, and that it is a democracy whenever the majority control it.[377] In the same way again suppose that the poor are fewer in number than the rich, but are stronger and control the constitution, but that when a small group is in control it is said to be an oligarchy. It would seem, then, that we have not correctly defined these constitutions.

But then even if one were to combine being few with being rich, in the one case, and being a majority with being poor, in the other, and to describe the constitutions accordingly—oligarchy as that in which the rich are few in number and hold the offices, and democracy as that in which the poor are many and hold them—another puzzle arises. For what are we to call the constitutions we just described, those where the rich are a majority and the poor a minority, but each controls in its own constitution, if indeed there is no other constitution besides those we mentioned?

What this argument seems to make clear, therefore, is that it is a coincidence that the few or the many have control in oligarchies on the one hand or in democracies on the other, and that this is because the rich are everywhere few and the poor many. That is why, in fact, the causes just mentioned are not the causes of the differences (*diaphora*) between them. What does differentiate democracy and oligarchy from each other is poverty and wealth: whenever some, whether a minority or a majority, rule because of their wealth, the constitution is necessarily an oligarchy, **1280a1**
and whenever the poor rule, it is necessarily a democracy. But it turns out, as we said, that the former are in fact few and the latter many. For only a few people are rich, but in freedom all share.[378] And it is due to these causes that both groups dispute over the constitution.

III 9

The first thing one must grasp, however, is what they say the defining marks of oligarchy and democracy are, and what both oligarchic justice and democratic justice are.

For all grasp a sort of justice, but they only go to a certain point and do not discuss the whole of what is just in the strictest sense. For example, justice seems to be equality, and it is—not for everyone, however, but for equals. Justice also seems to be inequality, and in fact it is—not for everyone, however, but for unequals. They do away with this—the *for whom*—and so judge badly. The cause is that the judgment concerns themselves, and pretty much most people are bad judges about their own affairs.

So since what is just is just for certain people, and consists in dividing both things and people in the same way (as we said earlier in the *Ethics*), they agree about equality in the thing but disagree about it in the people.[379] This is mostly because of what was just mentioned, namely, that they judge badly about what concerns themselves, but also because, since they are both speaking up to a point about a sort of justice, they consider themselves to be speaking about justice in the unconditional sense. For one lot, if they are unequal in one respect (for example, wealth), think that they are wholly unequal, whereas the other lot, if they are equal in one respect (for example, freedom), think that they are wholly equal. About what has the most control, however, they do not speak. For if it were for the sake of property that people formed a community and came together, then they would share in the city to the extent that they shared in property, and the oligarchic argument would as a result seem to be a strong one. For [they would say] it is not just for someone who has contributed one mina to share equally in a hundred minas with the one who has contributed all the rest, whether of what was there at the start or of the interest.

But [1] they do not do these things only for the sake of living, but more for the sake of living well.[380] For otherwise there could also be a city of slaves and of the other animals, while as things stand there is not one, because these share neither in happiness nor in living in accord with deliberate choice.[381]

Nor [2] do they do them for the sake of an alliance, to safeguard themselves from being treated unjustly by anyone, or [3] because of exchange and their usefulness to each other. For otherwise the Etruscans, the Carthaginians, and all those who have treaties with each other would be like citizens of one city.[382] At any rate, they have import agreements, treaties about not doing injustice, and formal documents of alliance. No offices, however, that are common to all of them have been put in place to deal with these matters, but rather each city has distinct ones. Nor are those in one city concerned that those in the other should be of a certain quality, not even that those covered by the agreements should not be unjust or depraved in any way, but only that they should not act unjustly toward each other. By contrast, political virtue and vice are closely investigated by those concerned with good legislative order. Thus it is quite evident that the city must be concerned about virtue—at any rate, the city that is truly, and not just for the sake of argument, so called. For otherwise the community becomes an alliance, differing only in location from others in which the allies live far apart, and law becomes an agreement, and, as Lycophron the sophist said, "a guarantor of just behavior toward each other," but not such as to make the citizens good and just.[383]

It is evident that this is the way it is. [4] For even if their territories were brought together into one, so that the city of the Megarians and that of the Corinthians were fastened together by surrounding walls, it still would not be a single city.[384] Nor would it be so if their citizens intermarried, even though this is one of the sorts of community that is special to cities. Nor, similarly, if there were some who lived in separate places, yet not so far apart as to share nothing communally, and had laws against doing injustice to each other in their business transactions (for example, if one were a carpenter, another a farmer, another a shoemaker, another something else of that sort, and their number were ten thousand), yet their community was in nothing else besides such things as exchange and alliance—not even in this case would there be a city.

What, then, is the cause of this? Surely, it is not because their community is scattered. For even if they lived closer together while having such a community—each in fact treating his own household like a city, and the others like a defensive alliance formed merely to provide assistance against those committing injustice—even so, they would still not seem to be a city to those who get an exact theoretical grasp on such things, if indeed they continued to associate with each other in the same manner when together as they did when separated.[385]

It is evident, therefore, that a city is not [4] a community of location, nor one [3] either for the sake of preventing mutual injustice or for the sake of exchange. On the contrary, while these must be present if indeed there is to be a city, when all of them are present it is still not yet a city. Rather the city is [1] the community in living well for both households and families, namely, complete and self-sufficient living. But in fact this will not be possible unless they inhabit one and the same location and practice intermarriage. That is why marriage connections arose in cities, as well as brotherhoods, religious sacrifices, and the pastimes characteristic of living together. And things of this sort are the function of friendship, since the deliberate choice to live together is friendship. The end of the city is living well, then, but these other things are for the sake of the end. And the city is the community of families and villages in complete and self-sufficient living, which we say is living happily and nobly.

So political communities must be taken as being for the sake of noble actions, not for the sake of living together. That is why those who contribute the most to this sort of community have a larger share in the city than those who are equal or superior in freedom or family but unequal in political virtue, and those who are superior in wealth but inferior in virtue.

That all those who dispute about constitutions, then, speak about a part of justice is evident from what has been said.

III 10

There is a puzzle, though, as to which part is to be in control of the city. For surely it is either the majority, the rich, the decent people, the one who is best of all, or a tyrant. But all of these apparently involve difficulties. For what if the poor, because they are the majority, divide up the property of the rich—is this not unjust? "Well, by Zeus, it seemed just to the body in control." But what then should we say is the extreme *injustice*? Again, if the majority, having seized everything, divides up the property of the minority, it is evident that they are destroying the city. But surely virtue does not destroy what has it, nor is justice something capable of destroying a city. So it is clear that this law cannot be just. Further, all the actions done by a tyrant were necessarily just as well. For he, being stronger, uses force, just as the majority do against the rich.

Then is it just for the minority and the rich to rule? If they act in the same way, plundering and confiscating the property of the majority, and this is just, then the other case is as well. Therefore, it is evident that all these things are bad and unjust.

Then should the decent people rule and have control of everything? In that case, everyone else will necessarily be deprived of honors, since they are denied the honors of holding political office. For offices are positions of honor, we say, and when the same people always rule, the rest will necessarily be deprived of honor.

Then is it better that the one who is most excellent should rule? But this is even more oligarchic, since those deprived of honors are more numerous.

But perhaps someone might say that it is a bad thing in general for a human being rather than the law to be in control, since at any rate he has the feelings that arise in the soul. But if law is oligarchic or democratic, what difference will it make where the puzzles we raised are concerned? For the things we have described will happen all the same.

III 11

As for the other cases, we may let them be the topic of another account. But the view that the majority rather than those who are the best people, albeit few, should be in control would seem to be well stated, and to involve some puzzles, though perhaps also some truth.[386] For the many, each of whom individually is not an excellent man, nevertheless
1281b1 may, when they have come together, be better than the few best people, not individually but collectively, just as dinners to which many contribute are better than dinners provided at one person's expense.[387] For, being many, each can have some part of virtue and practical wisdom, and when they come together, the multitude is just like one human being, with many feet, hands, and senses, and so too for their characters and thought.[388] That is why the many are also better judges of works of music and of the poets. For distinct ones are better judges of distinct parts, and all of them are better judges of the whole thing.

Indeed, it is in this respect that excellent men differ from each of the many, just as noble people are said to differ from those who are not noble, and the things in paintings produced by craft knowledge from real things, namely, by bringing together what is scattered and separate into one—even though, if taken separately at any rate, this person's eye and some other feature of someone else will be more noble than the painted ones.

Now whether it is in the case of every people and every multitude that this superiority of the majority to the few excellent people can exist is not clear. Although, by Zeus, it presumably is clear that in some of them it cannot possibly do so, since the same argument would apply to wild beasts. And yet what difference is there (one might ask) between some people and wild beasts? But of some multitude there is nothing to prevent what has been said from being true.

That is why, by means of these considerations, one might also resolve the puzzle mentioned earlier as well as the one connected to it, namely, what the free and the multitude of citizens—those who are not rich and have no claim whatsoever to virtue—should be in control of, since to have them share in the most important offices is not safe. For, because of their lack of justice and lack of practical wisdom, they would of necessity act unjustly in some instances and make errors in others.[389] On the other hand, neither to give a share nor have a share is a fearful thing.[390] For when a large number of poor people are deprived of honors in this way the city is necessarily full of enemies. The remaining alternative, then, is to have them share in deliberation and judgment. That is why Solon and some other legislators arrange to have them elect and inspect officials, but do not allow them to hold office individually. For when they all come together their perception is adequate, and, when mixed with their betters, they benefit their cities, just as a mixture of impure food mixed with the pure sort makes the whole thing more useful than a little [of the latter].[391] Taken separately, however, each of them is incomplete where judging is concerned.

But this order characteristic of the constitution itself raises puzzles. In the first place, it might seem that it belongs to the very same person to judge whether someone has treated a patient correctly, and to treat patients, that is, to cure them of their present disease—namely, the doctor. And the same would also seem to hold in other areas of experience and other crafts. Hence, just as a doctor should be inspected by doctors, so others should also be inspected by their peers. A doctor, however, may be either an ordinary practitioner of the craft, an architectonic one, or thirdly, someone well educated in the craft.[392] For there are people of this third sort in (one might almost say) all crafts. And we assign the task of judging to well-educated people no less than to those who know the craft.

It might seem, therefore, that election [of officials] is the same way, since choosing correctly is also a function of those who know the craft—for example, choosing a geometer is a function of geometers, and choosing a ship's captain of ship's captains. For even if, in the case of some functions and crafts, certain private individuals also have a share in choosing, they do not have a greater share than those who know the craft. According to this argument, then, the multitude should not be put in control of the election or inspection of officials.

But presumably not all of these things are stated correctly, both because of the argument just given, provided that the multitude is not too slavish (for each individually may be a worse judge than those who know the craft, but a better or no worse one when they all come together), and also because there are some crafts in which the maker might not be either the only or the best judge—the ones where those who lack the craft nevertheless know its products.[393] For example, knowing about a house does not belong only to the maker—instead, the one who uses it is an even better judge (and the one who uses it is the household manager). A ship's captain, too, is a better judge of a rudder than a carpenter is, and a dinner guest, rather than the cook, a better judge of a feast. This puzzle, then, might seem to be adequately solved in this way.

There is another, however, connected with it. For it seems to be absurd for base people to control more important matters than decent ones do. But inspections and elections of officials are a most important thing. And in some constitutions, as we said, these are assigned to the people, since the assembly controls all such matters. And although those who share in the assembly, in deliberation, and in judging, are drawn from those with low property assessments, whatever their age, the treasurers and generals and those who hold the most important offices are drawn from those with high property assessments.

But one can, of course, also solve this puzzle in the same way, since this way of doing things does seem to have something correct about it. For the official is neither the individual juror, nor the individual councilor, nor the individual assemblyman, but rather the court, the council, and the people, whereas each of the individuals mentioned (I mean the individual councilor, assemblyman, and juror) is only a part of these. So it is just for the majority to have control of the more important matters. For the people, the council, and the court consist of many individuals. Also, their collective property assessment is greater than the assessment of those who, whether individually or in small groups, hold the important offices. These matters, then, should be determined in this way.

The first puzzle we mentioned, on the other hand, makes nothing else so evident as that the laws, when correctly laid down, should be in control, and that the ruler, whether one or many, should have control of only those matters on which the laws cannot pronounce with exactness, because it is not easy to make universal determinations concerning every case.[394] But about what laws should be like if they are to be correctly laid down, nothing is yet clear. On the contrary, the puzzle stated earlier remains to be solved.[395] For the laws must necessarily be base or excellent, just or unjust, at the same time and in the same way as the constitutions. Still, this at least is evident, namely, that it is with a view to the constitution that the laws must be laid down. But if this is so, it is clear that laws that are in accord with correct constitutions must be just, and those in accord with deviant constitutions not just.

III 12

Since in every science and craft the end is a good, and the greatest and best good is the end of the one that has the most control of all, this is the capacity of politics.[396] But the just is the political good, and this is the common advantage. Now it seems to everyone that the just is some sort of equality, and up to a point, at least, they agree with what has been determined in those philosophical accounts in which ethical matters were determined.[397] For justice is something to some people, and they say that it should be something equal to those who are equal. But what sort of equality and what sort of inequality—we should not neglect to consider that.[398] For this also involves a puzzle for political philosophy.[399]

For perhaps someone might say that offices should be unequally distributed in accord with superiority in every good, provided people do not differ in their remaining qualities but happen to be similar, since for people who are superior something other [than an equal share] is just and in accord with worth. But if this is true, then those who excel in complexion, height, or any other good whatsoever, should get more of what is distributed by political justice. And is this not obviously false? Evidently, in the case of the other sciences and capacities, it is. For where flute players are equally proficient in their craft, better flutes are not given to those who are better bred (since they will not play the flute any better); rather it is the one who is superior with respect to his function who is to be given the superior instruments. If what has been said is not yet clear, it will become still more evident if we take it further. For if someone is superior in flute playing, but is very inferior in good-breeding or beauty, then, even if each of these (I mean birth and

beauty) is a greater good than flute playing, and is proportionately more
superior to flute playing than he is superior in flute playing, he should
still be given the superior flutes. For it is to the function that the superi-
1283a1 ority should contribute, and superiority in wealth and in good-breeding
contribute nothing to it.[400]

Further, according to this argument at any rate, every good would have to be comparable in contribution to every other. For if a certain height counted more, height in general would be in competition both with wealth and with freedom. So if this person is more superior to that one in height than that one is in virtue, and in general virtue is superior to height, then all goods would be comparable. For if this much size is better than this much [virtue], it is clear that that much is equal to it. But, since this is impossible, it is clear that in the case of politics, too, it is reasonable not to dispute over political office in accord with every sort of inequality. (For if some are slow runners and others fast, they should not have any more or any less a share of office because of this—but it is in athletic competitions that this sort of superiority wins honor.) Rather, the sorts from which a city is composed are the ones in terms of which the dispute must be formulated. That is why it is reasonable for the well bred, the free, and the rich to lay claim to the honor of office. For both those who are free and those who have assessed property are needed, since a city cannot consist entirely of poor people, any more than of slaves. But then if these things are needed in a city, it is clear that justice and political virtue are as well.[401] For a city cannot be managed without these. Except that without the former a city cannot exist, and without the latter it cannot be well managed.

III 13

Now with a view to the existence of a city, all or, at any rate, some of these qualities would seem to have a correct claim in the dispute. But with a view to good living, education and virtue would seem to have the most just claim of all in the dispute, as was also said earlier.[402] But since those equal in one thing only should not have equality in everything, nor inequality either if they are unequal in only one thing, all constitutions of this sort are necessarily deviations.

Now we said before that all dispute in a way justly, but that not all do so in an unconditionally just way.[403] The rich have a claim because they own a larger share of the land, and the land is something communal, and furthermore because they are for the most part more trustworthy when it comes to treaties. The free and well bred have a claim as being closely related to each other. For those who are better bred are more properly citizens than those who are ill bred, and good-breeding is esteemed at home by everyone.[404] Further, they have a claim because the sons of better people are likely to be better, since good-breeding is virtue of family.[405] Similarly, then, we shall say that virtue has a just claim in the dispute, since justice, we say, is a virtue relating to communities, which all the other virtues necessarily accompany.[406] But then the majority also have a just claim against the minority, since they are stronger, richer, and better, when taken as the majority in relation to the minority.

If they were all to be present in a single city, therefore (I mean, for example, the good, the rich, the well bred, and furthermore a political multitude distinct from them), will there be a dispute as to who should rule, or will there not? Within each of the constitutions we have mentioned, to be sure, the judgment as to who should rule is not disputed, since these differ from each other because of the ones who are in control—for example, because in one the rich are in control, in another the excellent men, and each of the others differ the same way. Nonetheless, we were investigating how, when all these are present at the same time, the matter is to be determined. Suppose, then, that those who possessed virtue were altogether few in number, how should the matter be settled? Should the fewness be investigated with a view to the function, namely, to whether they are able to manage the city, or to whether there is a multitude of them large enough to form a city by themselves?

There is a certain puzzle, though, that faces all who dispute over political office. For it could seem that those who claim that they deserve to rule because of their wealth have no justice to their claim at all, and similarly those claiming to do so because of family. For it is clear that if someone were richer again than all the others, then, in accord with the same justice, this one person should rule all of them. Similarly, it is clear that someone who is superior when it comes to good-breeding should rule those who dispute because of freedom. And the same thing will perhaps also occur in the case of virtue where aristocracies are concerned. For if one single man were to be better than the others in the governing body, even though they are excellent men, then, in accord with the same justice, this man should be in control. Accordingly, if the majority too should be in control because they are superior to the few, then, if one person or more than one—but fewer than the many—were superior to the others, these should be in control rather than the majority.

All these considerations, then, seem to make it evident that none of the definitions in accord with which people claim that they themselves deserve to rule, whereas everyone else deserves to be ruled by them, is correct. And in fact even against those who claim that they deserve to have control of the governing body in accord with their virtue, and similarly against those who do so in accord with wealth, majorities would have an argument of some justice. For nothing prevents a majority from being sometimes better than the few and richer, not as individuals but jointly.

That is why the puzzle that some people put forward and investigate can also be dealt with in this way. For they raise a puzzle about whether a legislator who wishes to set up the most correct laws should legislate for the advantage of the better citizens or that of the majority when the case just mentioned occurs. But what is correct must be taken to mean what is equal, and what is equal is what is correct with a view to the advantage of the whole city—that is, with a view to the common advantage of the citizens. And a citizen commonly is someone who shares in ruling and in being ruled, and while in accord with each constitution he is someone distinct, in the best constitution he is the person who has the capacity, and makes the deliberate choice, to rule and to be ruled with a view to the life that is in accord with virtue.

If, however, there is one person, or more than one (though not enough to fill up a city), who is so outstanding in extreme virtue that neither the virtue nor the political capacity of all the others is comparable to his (if there is only one) or theirs (if there are a number of them), then such people can no longer be taken to be part of the city.[407] For they would be treated unjustly if they were thought worthy of equal shares despite being so unequal in virtue and political capacity. For anyone of that sort would probably be like a god among human beings.

From this it is clear that legislation too must be concerned with those who are equals both in family and in capacity, and that for the other sort there is no law, since they themselves are law.[408] For, indeed, anyone who attempted to legislate for them would be ridiculous, since they would presumably respond in the way Antisthenes tells us the lions did when the hares acted like popular leaders and demanded equality for everyone.[409]

That is why indeed democratically governed cities introduce ostracism.[410] For of all cities these are held to pursue equality most, and so they ostracized those who seem to be superior in power because of their wealth, their many friends, or any other source of political strength, banishing them from the city for fixed periods of time. The story goes, too, that the Argonauts left Heracles behind due to this sort of cause.[411] For the *Argo* refused to carry him along with the others because he greatly exceeded the other sailors.[412] That is also why those who criticize tyranny and the advice of Periander to Thrasybulus should not be considered to be simply correct in their censure.[413] For they say that Periander said nothing to the messenger who had been sent to him for advice, but rather leveled a field by taking away the ears of corn that were superior in height. When the messenger, who was ignorant of the cause of this, reported what happened, Thrasybulus understood that he was to do away with the superior men.

This practice is advantageous not only to tyrants, however, nor are tyrants the only ones who use it; instead, the same situation holds where both oligarchies and democracies are concerned. For ostracism has the same capacity in its way as cutting the superior people down to size or sending them into exile. And the same thing is done with regard to cities and nations by those in control of power—for example, Athens with regard to the people of Samos, Chios, and Lesbos (for as soon as it had a firm grip on its rule, in violation of its agreements, it humbled them); and the king of the Persians often pruned back the Medes and Babylonians, as well as any others who had grown presumptuous because they had once ruled empires of their own.[414]

The problem is a universal one that concerns all constitutions, even the correct ones. For though the deviant constitutions do what Periander advises with a view to the private good [of the rulers], those that aim at the common good proceed in the same way. But this is also clear in the case of the various crafts and sciences. For no painter would allow the animal he was painting to have a foot that was out of proportion, not even if it were one of outstanding beauty, nor would a shipbuilder allow this in the case of the stern or any of the other parts of the ship, nor indeed would a chorus master allow someone to be a member of the chorus who had a louder and more beautiful voice than the entire chorus. And so, because of this, there is nothing to prevent monarchs from being in harmony with the city they rule when they do what Periander advises, provided that their own rule benefits their cities. That is why, as regards the generally agreed upon sorts of superiority, there is a certain political justice to the argument in favor of ostracism.

It would be better, certainly, if the legislator from the start set up the constitution so that it had no need for such a remedy. But the next best path is to try to correct the constitution, should the need arise, with a corrective of this sort. This, though, is just what tended not to happen in cities. For people did not look to the advantage of their own constitutions, but used ostracisms in a factious way.

It is evident, then, that in each of the deviant constitutions ostracism is to the private advantage [of the rulers] and is just, but it is also evident presumably that it is not also unconditionally just. In the case of the best constitution, however, there is much puzzlement, not about superiority in other goods, such as power or wealth or having many friends, but about what should be done if there happens to be someone who is outstanding in virtue. For surely people would not say that someone of that sort should be expelled or banished—but then neither would they say that there should be rule over him. For that would be very close to claiming that they deserved to rule over Zeus by dividing the offices.[415] The remaining possibility, therefore, and it seems to be just the natural one, is for everyone to obey such a person gladly, so that those like him will be permanent kings in their cities.

III 14

It may perhaps be a good thing, after the arguments just discussed, to change to an investigation of kingship. For we say that it is one of the correct constitutions. What we must investigate is whether it is advantageous for a city or territory that is going to be well managed to be under a kingship or not, but rather under some other constitution instead, or whether it is advantageous for some but not for others.

First, then, it must be determined whether there is one single kind (*genos*) of kingship or whether it has several different varieties (*diaphora*). *This*, of course, is easy to see, namely, that it encompasses many kinds (*genos*), and that the mode of rule is not the same in all of them. For the one in the Spartan constitution, which seems to be most of all a kingship in accord with law, does not have control of everything, but it is only when the king leaves the territory that he does have leadership in military affairs. Further, matters relating to the gods are assigned to the kings.

[1] This kind of kingship, then, is a sort of permanent autocratic generalship. For the king does not have control of life or death, except in a certain sort of kingship, similar to that exercised in ancient times on military expeditions, by law of force.[416] Homer makes this clear. For Agamemnon put up with being abused in the assemblies, but when they went out to fight he had control even over life or death.[417] At any rate, he says:

> Anyone I find far from the battle . . .
> Shall have no hope of escaping dogs and vultures,
> For I myself shall put him to death.[418]

This, then, is one kind (*eidos*) of kingship, namely, generalship for life. And of generalships for life some are in accord with family, while others are elective.

[2] But there is another kind (*eidos*) of monarchy beyond this, such as kingships that exist among some barbarians. The powers all these have are very close to those that tyrants have, but they are in accord with law and are hereditary. Because barbarians are by nature more slavish in their characters than Greeks, those in Asia being more so than those in Europe, they submit to rule of a master with no complaint. They are tyrannical, then, because of being of this sort. But they are stable because they are hereditary and in accord with law. And their bodyguards are kingly and not tyrannical due to the same cause. For citizens guard kings with their weapons, whereas a foreign contingent guards tyrants. For kings rule in accord with law and rule voluntary subjects, whereas the latter rule involuntary ones, so that the former have bodyguards drawn from the citizens, whereas the latter have bodyguards to protect them against the citizens.

These, then, are two kinds (*eidos*) of monarchy. [3] But there is another, which is just the one that existed among the ancient Greeks, namely, the ones they call dictators.[419] This, simply speaking, is an elected tyranny, which differs from barbarian kingship not by not being in accord with law but only by not being hereditary. Some holders of this office ruled for life, others for a defined period of time or for defined actions—for example, the Mytileneans once elected Pittacus to defend them against the exiles led by Antimenides and the poet Alcaeus.[420] And Alcaeus makes it clear in one of his drinking-songs that they did elect Pittacus tyrant, since he complains that "They set up base-born Pittacus as tyrant of that gutless and ill-omened city, with great praise from the assembled throng." These dictatorships are and were tyrannical because of being like the rule of a master, but kingly because of being elective and over voluntary subjects.

[4] A fourth kind (*eidos*) of kingly monarchy, which existed in the heroic age, was over voluntary subjects, hereditary, and came about in accord with law.[421] For because the first ones were benefactors of the multitude due to their knowledge of crafts or warfare, or because of bringing them together or providing them with land, they became kings over voluntary subjects, and their descendants inherited the office from them. They were in control of leadership in war and of those religious sacrifices which were not in the hands of priests. They also judged legal cases. Some of them did so under oath, and others not—the oath consisted in lifting up the scepter. In ancient times they ruled continuously over the affairs both of the city and of its territory and over foreign affairs. But later, when the kings themselves relinquished some of these things, and others were taken away by the mob, in various cities only the sacrifices were left to the kings, and even where there was a kingship

still worthy of the name, they held leadership only in military affairs conducted beyond the frontiers.

There are, then, these kinds (*eidos*) of kingship, four in number. One belongs to the heroic age—this kind was over voluntary subjects but for certain defined purposes, the king being general, judge, and in control of matters to do with the gods. The second is the barbarian—this is rule of a master, on the basis of family, in accord with law. The third is so-called dictatorship—this is elective tyranny. And fourth among them is Spartan kingship—this, simply speaking, is permanent generalship in accord with family. These, then, differ from each other in this way.

[5] But there is a fifth kind (*eidos*) of kingship, when one person controls all matters, just as each nation and each city controls common matters. It is ordered on the model of household management. For just as household management is a sort of kingship of a household, so this kingship is household management of a city or a nation or several nations.

III 15

It is pretty much the case, then, that there are (one might almost say) just two kinds (*eidos*) of kingship that must be investigated, namely, the last one and the Spartan. For most of the others lie in between these, since they control less than absolute kingship does but more than Spartan kingship. So our investigation is pretty much about two questions: First, whether it is advantageous for cities to have a permanent general (whether chosen in accord with family or by turns), or not advantageous: second, whether it is advantageous for one person to control everything, or not advantageous. However, the investigation of this sort of generalship looks to be of a kind (*eidos*) that belongs more to an investigation of laws than of constitutions, since it can come to exist in any constitution. So the first question may be set aside. But the remaining mode of kingship *is* a kind (*eidos*) of constitution. So we must get a theoretical grasp on it and go through the puzzles it involves.

The starting-point of the investigation is this, whether it is more advantageous to be ruled by the best man or by the best laws. Those who think it advantageous to be ruled by a king hold that laws speak only of the universal, and do not prescribe with a view to particular circumstances, so that it is foolish to rule in any craft in accord with what is written down.[422] And so it is a good thing that in Egypt the doctors are allowed to change the treatment [prescribed by the manuals] until after the fourth day—although, if they do so earlier, it is at their own risk. It is evident, therefore, that the best constitution is not one that is in accord with what is written down and laws, due to the same cause.[423] But then, the rulers should possess the universal account as well.[424] And something to which the passionate element is wholly unattached is better than something in which it is innate.[425] This element does not belong to the law, whereas every human soul necessarily possesses it. But presumably it should be said, to balance this, that a human being will deliberate better about particular cases. That he must, therefore, be a legislator is clear, and that laws must be laid down, but they must not be in control insofar as they deviate from what is best, although they should certainly be in control everywhere else.

As regards cases that the law cannot judge either at all or well, though, should the one best person rule, or everyone? For even as things stand, people come together to hear cases, deliberate, and judge, and the judgments themselves all concern particulars. Taken individually, any one of these people is presumably inferior to the best person. But a city consists of many people, just like a feast to which many contribute, and is better than one that is one and simple.[426] This is why a mob can also judge many things better than any single individual.

Further, a large quantity is more incorruptible, like a larger quantity of water, and so the multitude are more incorruptible than the few. For the judgment of an individual is necessarily corrupted when he is overcome by anger or some other passion of this sort, whereas in the same situation it takes work to get all the citizens to become angry and make mistakes at the same time.

Suppose the multitude in question consists of the free, however, and that it does nothing outside the law, except where matters the law cannot cover are concerned. Granted, this is not an easy thing to arrange where numbers are large.[427] But suppose there were a number who were both good men and good citizens, which would be more incorruptible, one ruler or a larger number all of whom were good? Isn't it clear that it would be the latter? "But such a group will split into factions, whereas the single person is free of factional conflict." One should presumably oppose this objection by pointing out that they may be excellent in soul just like the one person.

If, then, the rule of a number of people, all of whom are good men, is to be considered an aristocracy, and the rule of one person as a kingship, aristocracy would be more choiceworthy for cities than kingship, both when the office involves capacity and when it is separate from capacity, provided that it is possible to find a number of people of similar quality.[428] This is presumably also why people were formerly under kingships, namely, because it was rare to find men who were very superior in virtue, especially as the cities they lived in at that time were small.

Further, they made men kings as a consequence of benefits conferred, and conferring benefits is just what it is the function of good men to do [and good men were rare].[429] When, however, there began to be many people who were similar in virtue, they no longer put up with kingship, but looked for something common and put in place a polity. But they grew worse when they began to acquire wealth from the communal funds, and it was from this, one might reasonably suppose, that oligarchies arose. For they made wealth an honored thing.[430] Then from oligarchies they changed first into tyrannies, and from tyrannies to democracy.[431] For by concentrating power into ever fewer hands because of a shameful desire for profit, they made the multitude stronger, with the result that it revolted and democracies arose. Now that cities have become even larger, it is presumably no longer easy for any other constitution to arise besides democracy.

If, though, one *does* posit kingship as the best thing for a city, how is one to handle the matter of children? Is the family as such to rule as kings? But if they turn out as some have done, it would be harmful. "But in that case, because he is in control, he will not give it to his children." But this is no longer easy to believe. For it would be a hard thing to do, and would demand greater virtue than is in accord with human nature.

There is also a puzzle about the king's power, as to whether anyone who is going to rule as king should have some force in attendance with which he can force anyone who does not wish to obey his rule? If not, how can he possibly manage his office? For even if he exercised control in accord with the law, and never acted in accord with his own wishes contrary to the law, nonetheless it would be necessary for him to have some power with which to guard the laws. Now in the case of this sort of king it is perhaps not difficult to determine the solution. For *he* should have a force, but a force so great as to be stronger than an individual, whether by himself or together with many, but weaker than the multitude. This is the way the ancients gave bodyguards when they appointed someone from the city to be what they called a dictator or tyrant, and when Dionysius asked for bodyguards, someone advised the Syracusans to give him bodyguards of this sort.[432]

III 16

The account has now arrived at the king who does everything in accord
1287a1 with his own wish, and it is he whom we must investigate. For the king,
so-called, who rules in accord with law, is not, as we said, a kind (*eidos*) of

constitution, since a permanent generalship can exist in all of them (for example, in a democracy and an aristocracy), and many put one person in control of managing affairs.[433] There is an office of this sort in Epidamnus, indeed, and to a lesser extent in Opus as well.[434]

But as regards so-called absolute kingship (which is where the king rules everything in accord with his own wish), it seems to some people that it is not even natural for one person from among all the citizens to be in control, when the city consists of similar people. For justice and worth must be by nature the same for those who are naturally similar. So if indeed it is harmful to their bodies for equal people to have unequal food or clothing, the same holds, too, where honors are concerned, and similarly, therefore, when equal people have what is unequal. This is why it is just for them to rule no more than they are ruled, and, therefore, to do so in turn.[435] But this already involves law, since the order is law.[436]

It is more choiceworthy, therefore, to have law rule than any one of the citizens. And, by this same argument, even if to have certain people rule is better, they should be appointed as guardians of the laws and assistants to them. For it is necessary for there to be some offices, although it is not just, they say, for there to be only one—at any rate, not when all are similar.

As for the things that *the law* seems unable to determine, they could not be known by a human being either. Rather, the law, having designedly educated the rulers for these eventualities, hands over the rest to be judged and managed in accord with the most just consideration of the rulers.[437] Further, it allows itself to be rectified in any way that seems, on being put to the test, to be better than the existing laws.

The one who bids the law to rule, then, would seem to be bidding the god and the understanding alone to rule, whereas the one who bids a human being to do so adds on a wild beast as well.[438] For appetite is a thing of that sort, and spirit distorts [the judgment of] rulers even when they are the best men.[439] That is why law is understanding without desire.[440]

And the comparison with the crafts, that it is bad to give medical treatment in accord with what is written down and more choiceworthy to rely on those who possess knowledge of the craft instead, would seem to invoke a false paradigm. For doctors never do anything contrary to the [medical] reason because of friendship, but earn their pay by healing the sick. Those who hold political office, on the other hand, are accustomed to doing many things out of spite or gratitude. In fact, if people suspected their doctors of being persuaded by their enemies to do away with them because of a bribe, they would seek treatment derived from what is written down instead. Moreover, doctors themselves call in other doctors to treat them when they are sick,

1287b1 and coaches call in other coaches when they are exercising, on the supposition that they are unable to judge truly because they are judging about their own cases and where feelings are involved.[441] So it is clear that in seeking what is just they are seeking the mean. For the law is the mean.[442]

Further, laws that are in accord with habits have more control and deal with things that have more control than do written laws, so that even if a human ruler is safer than written laws, he is not safer than those that are in accord with habit.[443]

Moreover, it is certainly not easy for a single ruler to oversee many things, therefore there will need to be numerous officials appointed under him. So what difference is there between having them there right from the start and having one person appoint them in this way? Further, as we said earlier, if it is indeed just for the excellent man to rule because he is better, well, *two* good ones are at any rate better than one.[444] Hence the saying "When two go together . . . ," and Agamemnon's prayer, "May ten such counselors be mine."[445]

Even as things stand, however, the judgment of officials, such as jurors, has control of some matters, namely, those that the law cannot determine. For about those matters that it *can* determine, no one disputes that the law itself would rule and judge best. But since some matters can be covered by the laws, whereas others cannot, the latter cause people to raise and investigate the puzzle as to whether it is more choiceworthy for the best law to rule or the best man (since to legislate about matters that call for deliberation is impossible). The counterargument, therefore, is *not* that it is not necessary for a human being to judge such matters, but that there should be not only one judge but rather many.

For each official judges well if he has been well educated by the law. And it would presumably seem strange if someone, when judging with one pair of eyes, one pair of ears, and doing actions with one pair of feet and hands, could see better than many people with many pairs, since, as things stand, monarchs provide themselves with many eyes, ears, hands, and feet, since they make into co-rulers those who are friendly to their rule and to themselves. Now if they are not his friends in this way, they will not do as the monarch deliberately chooses. But if they are friends of his and of his rule—well, a friend is someone equal and similar, so if he thinks they should rule, he must likewise think that those who are equal and similar to him should rule.

The arguments of those who dispute against kingship, then, are pretty much these.

III 17

But presumably these arguments hold in the case of some people, but do not hold in the case of others. For what is by nature both just and advantageous is one thing in the case of rule of master, another in the case of kingship, and another in the case of rule by a politician. In the case of tyrannical rule, however, or of the other constitutions that are deviations, nothing is just or naturally advantageous. For they come about contrary to nature. But from what has been said, it is evident at any rate that in a case where people are similar and equal, it is neither advantageous nor just for one person to be in control of all, regardless of whether there are no laws, and the king himself is law, or whether there are laws, or whether he and the laws are good, or he and the laws are not good, or even—except in a certain way—whether he is their superior in virtue. What that way is must now be stated—although we have in a sense already stated it too.[446]

First, we must determine what is suited to kingship, what to aristocracy, and what to polity. Suited to kingship, then, is a multitude of the sort that naturally yields a stock (*genos*) that is superior in the virtue appropriate to political leadership. Suited to aristocracy is a multitude that naturally yields a multitude capable of being ruled, with the rule appropriate to free people, by those who are suited to leadership by their possession of the virtue required for the rule of a politician.[447] And suited to polity is a multitude in which there naturally arises a multitude useful for war, which is capable of ruling and being ruled, under a law that distributes the offices to the rich in accord with worth.[448]

Whenever there happens to arise, then, either a whole family, or even some one individual from among the others, who is so superior that his virtue exceeds that of all the others, then it is just for this family to have the kingship and to control everything, and for this one individual to be king. For, as was said earlier, this is not only in accord with the kind of justice usually put forward by those who put in place polities, aristocracies, oligarchies, or again democracies (for they all claim to be worthy of rule in accord with superiority in something, though not superiority in the same kind of thing), but also in accord with what was said earlier.[449] For it is surely not appropriate to kill or exile or ostracize an individual of this sort, nor to claim that he deserves to be ruled in turn. For it is not natural for the part to exceed the whole, but this is what has happened to the one who is at this extreme. So the only remaining option is to obey such a person and for him to have control not by turns but simply.

Kingship, then, and its differences (*diaphoras*), and whether it is advantageous for cities or not, and if so, for which and in what way, may be determined in this way.

III 18

We say that there are three correct constitutions, and that of these the best must be the one managed by the best people. This is the sort of constitution in which there happens to be either one particular person or a whole family or a multitude that is superior in virtue to all the rest, and where the latter are capable of being ruled and the former of ruling with a view to the most choiceworthy way of living. And in our first accounts it was shown the virtue of a man must be identical to that of a citizen of the best city.[450] Hence it is evident that in the same way, and through the same things, as a man becomes excellent, one might set up a city that is ruled by an aristocracy or by a king, so that the education and habits that make a man excellent are pretty much the same as those that make him a political or kingly ruler.

Now that these matters have been determined, we must attempt to discuss the best constitution, the way it naturally arises and how it is put in place. It is necessary, then, for anyone who is going [to do this] to make the appropriate investigation.[451]

Book IV[452]

IV 1

Among all the crafts and sciences that are not partly developed but that, having become complete, deal with some one kind (*genos*), it belongs to a single one to get a theoretical grasp on what is fitting in the case of each kind (*genos*).[453] For example, in the case of training what sort is fitting for what sort of body, what sort is best (for the best is necessarily fitting for the sort of body that is by nature most noble and most nobly equipped), and what one sort of training is fitting for most bodies (for this too is a function of training). Further, if someone has an appetite neither for the [physical] state nor for the scientific knowledge appropriate for those involved in competition, it belongs no less to coaches and athletic trainers to provide this capacity too.[454] And we see something similar occurring with regard to medicine, shipbuilding, clothing manufacture, and every other craft.

So it is clear that it belongs to the same science to get a theoretical grasp on:

[1] What the best constitution is and what it would have to be like to be most of all in accord with our prayers, provided that no external impediments stand in its way.

[2] Also, which constitution is fitting for which cities. For achieving the best constitution is presumably impossible for many of them, and so neither the unconditionally best constitution nor the one that is best in the underlying circumstances should be neglected by the good legislator and true politician.

[3] Further, the constitution based on a hypothesis. For it must be able to study how any given constitution might come into existence from the start, and in what way, once in existence, it might be preserved for the longest time. I mean, for example, when some city happens to be governed neither by the best constitution (not even having the necessary resources for it) nor by the best one possible in the existing circumstances, but by a worse one.

[4] Besides all these things, the science should know which constitution is most fitting for all cities. And so most of those who have expressed views about constitutions, even if what they say is correct in other respects, certainly fail to give useful advice. For one should not get a theoretical grasp only on the best constitution, but also on the one that is possible, and similarly on the one that is easier and more attainable for all cities.

As things stand, however, some inquire only into the constitution that is highest and requires a lot of resources, while others, though they discuss a more commonly attainable constitution, do away with the actually existing constitutions and praise the Spartan or some other. But what should be done is to describe the sort of order that people will be easily persuaded to accept and be able to set in motion, given what they already have, as it is no less work to reform a constitution than to establish one from the start, just as it is no less work to correct what we have learned than to learn it from the start.[455]

[5] That is why, in addition to what has just been mentioned, a politician should also be able to help existing constitutions, as was also said earlier.[456] But this is impossible if he does not know how many kinds (*eidos*) of constitutions there are. As things stand, however, some people think that there is just one kind of democracy and one of oligarchy. But this is not true. So one must not overlook the differences (*diaphora*) in each of the constitutions, how many they are and in how many ways they can be combined.[457]

[6] And it is with this same practical wisdom that one should see both which laws are best and which are fitting for each of the constitutions.[458] For laws should be set up, and all do set them up, by looking to the constitutions and not the constitutions by looking to the laws. For a constitution is the way that cities order their offices, how they are distributed, what element is in control in the constitution, and what the end of each community is. But the separate laws, which are among the things that make clear what the constitution is, are those that the officials must rule by and guard against those who transgress them. And so it is clear that a knowledge of the differences (*diaphora*) in each constitution and of their number is also necessary for setting up laws.[459] For the same laws cannot be advantageous to all oligarchies nor to all democracies—if indeed there are several kinds of them, and not only one kind of democracy or of oligarchy.

IV 2

In our initial methodical inquiry concerning constitutions, we distinguished three correct ones (kingship, aristocracy, polity) and three deviations from them (tyranny from kingship, oligarchy from aristocracy, and democracy from polity). We have also discussed aristocracy and kingship. (Indeed, getting a theoretical grasp on the best constitution is the same as discussing these names, since each of them wishes to be set up in accord with virtue furnished with resources.[460]) Further, how aristocracy and kingship differ from each other, and when a kingship is the one we should recognize [as appropriate], was determined earlier.[461] It remains to deal with the constitution that is called by the name shared in common by all constitutions, and also with the others—oligarchy, democracy, and tyranny.[462]

It is also evident which of these deviations is worst and which second worst. For the deviation from the first and most divine constitution must of necessity be the worst.[463] But the kingship must either be in name only and not in fact or it must be due to the great superiority of the person ruling as king. So tyranny, because it is the worst, is furthest removed from being a constitution, oligarchy is second worst (since aristocracy is very far removed from oligarchy), and democracy the most moderate.

An earlier thinker has already expressed this same view, though he did not look to the same thing we do.[464] For he judged that when all these constitutions are decent (for example, when an oligarchy is good, and also the others), democracy is the worst of them, but that when they are bad, it is the best. But we say that these constitutions are wholly in error, and that it is not correct to speak of one kind of oligarchy as better than another, but as less bad.

But making a judgment about this sort of issue may be set aside for the present. Instead, we must determine: [1] First, how many differences (*diaphora*) there are in constitutions—if indeed there are several kinds (*eidos*) of democracy and oligarchy.

Next, [2] which constitution is most attainable, and which most choiceworthy after the best constitution.

And [3] if there is some other constitution that is ruled in the best way and well formed, and at the same time fitting for most cities, what it is.[465]

Next, [4] which of the other constitutions is more choiceworthy for which people (for maybe democracy is more necessary than oligarchy for some, whereas for others the reverse holds).

After these things, [5] we must determine in what way someone who wishes to do so should put in place these constitutions—I mean, each kind (*eidos*) of democracy and again of oligarchy.

Finally, when we have gone as far as we can to give a concise account of each of these topics, [6] we must try to go through the ways in which constitutions are destroyed and those in which they are preserved, both in general and in the case of each one separately, and through what causes these most naturally come about.

IV 3

The cause of there being several constitutions is that in every city the number of the parts is greater than one.[466] For, in the first place, we see

that all cities are composed of households, and next again that within this multitude there have to be some people who are rich, some who are poor, and some who are in the middle, and that of the rich and of the poor, the first lot possess hoplite weapons, whereas the second lot are without hoplite weapons.[467] We also see that the people is part farming, part trading, and part vulgar. And among the notables there are differences both in their wealth and in the extent of their property—for example, in the breeding of horses, since this is not easy for those without wealth to do. That is why, indeed, there were oligarchies among those cities in ancient times whose power lay in their cavalry, and who used horses in wars with their neighbors—for example, the Eretrians, the Chalcidians, the Magnesians on the river Maeander, and many of the others in Asia.[468] Further, in addition to differences in accord with wealth, there are differences in accord with breeding, in accord with virtue, and in accord with everything else of the sort
1290a1 that we characterized as part of a city in our discussion of aristocracy, since there we distinguished the number of parts that are necessary to any city.[469] For sometimes all of these parts share in the constitution, sometimes fewer, sometimes more.

It is evident, accordingly, that there must be several constitutions that differ in kind (*eidos*) from each other, since their parts themselves also differ in kind (*eidos*). For a constitution is an ordering of the offices, and all constitutions distribute these either in accord with the capacity of the participants, or in accord with some sort of equality common to them (I mean, for example, the capacity of the poor, or that of the rich, or some equality common to both). There must, therefore, be as many constitutions as there are orders that are in accord with the kinds of superiority and the differences (*diaphora*) of the parts.

But there seem to be two in particular. For just as in the case of the winds some are called northern and others southern, and the others deviations from these, so there seem to be two constitutions, democracy and oligarchy. For aristocracy is regarded as a sort of oligarchy, on the supposition that it is a sort of rule by the few, whereas a so-called polity is regarded as a sort of democracy, just as the west wind is regarded as northerly, and the east as southerly.[470] And something similar holds in the case of harmonies, so some people say, since there as well two kinds (*eidos*) are posited, namely, the Dorian and the Phrygian, and the other modes are called either Doric or Phrygic.[471]

People are particularly accustomed, then, to think of constitutions in this way. But it is truer and better to distinguish them as we have, and say that two constitutions (or one) are well formed, and that the others are deviations from them, some from the well-mixed "harmony," and others from the best constitution, the more tightly controlled ones and those that are more like the rule of a master being more oligarchic, and the unrestrained and soft ones, democratic.[472]

IV 4

One should not regard a democracy, in the way some people are accustomed to do now, as simply being where the majority is in control (since both in oligarchies and everywhere else, the larger part is in control), nor an oligarchy as where the few control the constitution.[473] For if the inhabitants totaled thirteen hundred, and a thousand were rich and gave no share in the honors office to the three hundred poor, although these were free people and equal to the rich in all other respects, no one would say that they were democratically governed. Similarly, if the poor were few, but stronger than the rich, who were a majority, no one would call such a constitution an oligarchy if the others, though rich, did not share in the offices. Therefore it is better to say that a democracy is when the free are in control, and an oligarchy when the rich are in control. But it happens that the former are many and the latter few, since many are free but few are rich. For otherwise there would be an oligarchy even if offices were distributed in accord with height (as is said to happen in Ethiopia) or in accord with noble stature, since people of noble stature and tall people are both few in number.

Yet it is not enough to define these constitutions by these things alone. Rather, since the parts both of democracy and of oligarchy are several, we must grasp further that it is not a democracy if a few free people rule over a majority who are not free, as, for example, in Apollonia on the Ionian Gulf and in Thera.[474] For in each of these cities the offices were held by those who were outstanding for their good-breeding and had first taken possession of the colonies, although they were few among many. And that it is not a democracy either if the rich rule because they are a majority, as was formerly the case in Colophon, where the majority possessed large properties before the war against the Lydians.[475] Rather, it is a democracy when the free and poor, who are a majority, have the control of office, and an oligarchy, when the rich and better bred, who are few, do. It has been stated, then, that there are several constitutions, and what the cause of this is. But let us now say why there are more than the ones mentioned, which they are, and due to what cause, taking as our starting-point what we stated earlier.[476] For we agreed that no city has only one part but several.

Now if we wanted to grasp the kinds (*eidos*) of animals, we would first determine what it is that every animal must have, for example, some of the sense-organs, something with which to masticate and absorb food, such as a mouth and a stomach, and in addition to these parts by which each of them moves. If, then, there were only this many parts, but there were differences (*diaphora*) in them (I mean, for example, if there were several kinds (*genos*) of mouths, stomachs, and sense-organs, and further also of parts for movement), then the number of ways of combining these will necessarily produce several kinds (*genos*) of animals. For the same animal cannot have many different sorts (*diaphora*) of mouth, nor of ears either. So, when all the possible ways of coupling them have been grasped, they will produce kinds (*eidos*) of animals, and as many kinds as there are combinations of the necessary parts. It is the same way with the constitutions we have mentioned.[477] For cities are formed not out of one but out of many parts, as we have often said.[478]

[1] Now one of these parts is the multitude concerned with food, the ones called farmers. [2] A second is the one called vulgar. This is the one concerned with the crafts a city cannot be managed without—and of these, some are necessary, whereas others contribute to luxury or noble living. [3] A third is the trading part (by which I mean the one concerned with selling and buying, retail trade and commerce). [4] A fourth is that of hired laborers. [5] A fifth is the kind (*genos*) that goes to war for the city, which is no less necessary than the others, if the inhabitants are not to become the slaves of any aggressor. For presumably it is impossible for any city that is by nature slavish to deserve to be called a city. For a city is self-sufficient, whereas a slavish thing is not self-sufficient.[479]

That is why what is said in the *Republic*, though sophisticated, is not adequate.[480] For Socrates says that a city is formed out of four most necessary parts, and these, he says, are a weaver, a farmer, a shoemaker, and a builder. Then, on the supposition that these are not self-sufficient, he adds a blacksmith, people to look after the necessary livestock, and further both someone engaged in retail trade and someone engaged in commerce. All these become the full complement of his first city—as if every city were formed for the sake of providing the necessities, not rather for the sake of what is noble, and had equal need of both shoemakers and farmers. Nor does he assign it a part that goes to war until, its territory being expanded and encroaching on that of their neighbors, they become involved in war.

[6] Yet even in these communities of four (or however many) parts, there must be the one making assignments and rendering judgment about what is just.[481] So if indeed one should regard soul as more a part of an animal than body, then, in the case of cities too, one should regard things of the following sort as parts, rather than those concerned with necessary needs: the part concerned with war, the part

that participates in administering judicial justice, and in addition to these the part that deliberates, since deliberation is a function of political comprehension.[482] (It makes no difference to the argument whether these functions belong to separate people or the same ones, since in fact it often happens that the same people both serve as hoplites and do the farming. So, if indeed both the former and the latter are to be regarded as parts of the city, it is certainly evident that the hoplite element must be a part of the city.)

[7] Seventh is the part that performs public service by means of its property, the one we call the rich.[483]

[8] Eighth is the part that renders public service in connection with the various offices, if indeed without officials a city cannot exist. There must, then, be some people who are able to rule and perform this public service for the city either continuously or in turn.

There remains the one we happened to distinguish just now, [6] the part that deliberates and renders judgment about the claims of people involved in disputes. If indeed these things must take place in cities, then, and do so in a way that is noble and just, there must also be some people who share in the virtue of politicians.[484]

As for the other capacities, many hold that they can belong to the same people—for example, that it is possible for the same people to be the ones who go to war for the city and farmers and craftsmen, and both deliberators and judges besides. And everyone claims to possess the relevant virtue too, and thinks he is capable of ruling in most of the offices.[485] But for the same people to be both rich and poor is impossible. That is why these in particular, the rich and the poor, seem to be parts of a city. Further, because the former are for the most part few in number and the latter many, it appears that of the parts of a city these two are contraries. So constitutions are formed in accord with the sorts of superiority belonging to these, and there are held to be two constitutions, democracy and oligarchy.[486]

Now it was stated earlier that there are a number of constitutions, and what the causes are of this.[487] But we may now say that there are also several kinds (*eidos*) of democracy and of oligarchy.[488] This is in fact evident from what has been said. For there are several kinds (*eidos*) both of the people and of the so-called notables. For example, of the people, one kind (*eidos*) is the farmers and another that concerned with the crafts, another is the part involved in trade, which is engaged in buying and selling, another the part concerned with the sea—of which part is navy, part is engaged in the craft of wealth acquisition, part in ferrying passengers, and part in fishing. (In many places, indeed, a particular one of these amounts to a large mob of people—for example, fishermen in Tarentum and Byzantium, navy men in Athens, traders in Aegina and Chios, and ferrymen in Tenedos.[489]) In addition to these, there is the part involved in manual labor and that has little property, so that it is not able to be at leisure. Further, the part consisting of those who are free but not of citizen parentage on both sides, and whatever other similar kind (*eidos*) of multitude there may be. Among the notables, there are kinds distinguished by wealth, good-breeding, virtue, education, and the other characteristics that are said [of things] in accord with the same sort of difference (*diaphora*) as these.

[1] The first sort of democracy, then, is the one that is said to be above all in accord with equality. For the law in such a democracy says that there is equality when the poor enjoy no more superiority than the rich, and when neither is in control but both are similar. For if indeed freedom exists above all in a democracy, as some people suppose, and equality too, then this would be particularly the case when everyone shares in the constitution in the most similar way.[490] But since the people are a majority, and the belief of the majority is in control, this constitution must be a democracy. This, then, is one kind (*eidos*) of democracy.[491]

[2] Another is where offices are filled on the basis of property assessments, but these are low, and where anyone who acquires the assessed amount may share [in the constitution], whereas anyone who loses it may not.

[3] Another kind (*eidos*) of democracy is where all the uncontested
1292b1 citizens share, but the law rules.[492]

[4] Another kind (*eidos*) of democracy is where everyone shares in office merely by being a citizen, but the law rules.[493]

[5] Another kind (*eidos*) of democracy is the same in other respects, but the multitude has control, not the law. This arises when decrees are in control instead of laws; and this happens because of popular leaders.[494] For in cities under democracies that are in accord with law, popular leaders do not arise, but rather it is the best of the citizens who take the front seats. Where the laws are not in control, however, there popular leaders arise. For the people become a monarch, one monarch composed of many people, since the many are in control not as individuals but all together.

When Homer says "to have many rulers is not good," it is not clear whether he means this sort of rule, or the sort where there are a number of individual rulers.[495] In any case, a people of this sort, because it is a monarch, seeks to exercise monarchic rule, because of not being ruled by the law, and becomes a master. As a result flatterers are held in esteem and a democracy of this sort is the analogue of tyranny among the monarchies.[496] That is why indeed their characters are the same, in that both act like masters toward the better people, the decrees of the one are like the edicts of the other, and a popular leader and a flatterer are the same or analogous. And each of these exercises great power with each, flatterers with tyrants, popular leaders with peoples of this sort. For it is popular leaders who, by bringing everything before the people, are responsible for decrees being in control rather than the laws. For they become great because of the people being in control of everything, and also because they control the belief of the people, since the majority are persuaded by them. Further, those who make accusations against officials say that the people should judge. The suggestion is gladly accepted, with the result that all the offices are destroyed.

It might, indeed, seem reasonable to object that this sort of democracy is not a constitution at all, on the grounds that where the laws do not rule there is no constitution. For the law should rule everything, while in the case of particulars the officials and the constitution should render judgment.[497] So if indeed democracy is one of the constitutions, it is evident that this state of affairs, in which everything is managed by decree, is not even a democracy in the full sense, since no decree can possibly be universal.[498]

The kinds (*eidos*) of democracy, then, should be distinguished in this way.

IV 5

Of the various kinds (*eidos*) of oligarchy, [1] one is where offices are filled on the basis of such a high property assessment that the poor do not share in the constitution, even though they are a majority, but where anyone who does acquire the assessed amount may share in it.

[2] Another is where the offices are filled on the basis of a large assessment, and the officials themselves elect someone to fill any vacancy. If they elect from among all of these, it seems more aristocratic, if from some specified group, oligarchic.[499]

[3] Another kind of oligarchy is where a son succeeds his father.

[4] A fourth is where what was just mentioned occurs, and not the law but the officials rule. This is the counterpart among the oligarchies to tyranny among the monarchies, and to the sort of democracy we spoke of last among the democracies. Such an oligarchy is called a dynasty. There are, then, these many kinds (*eidos*) of oligarchy and democracy. But one must not overlook the fact that in many places it has happened that though the constitution that is in accord with the law is not democratic, because of custom and direction they are governed democratically. Similarly, it is the reverse in other places—the constitution

that is in accord with the laws is more democratic but, because of custom and guidance, they are governed in a more oligarchic way. This happens especially after there have been constitutional changes. For the change is not immediate, but they are content at first to get more than the others in small ways.[500] So the laws that existed before remain in effect, but it is those who have changed the constitution who exercise the power.

IV 6

It is evident from what has been said, though, that there are this many kinds of democracy and oligarchy. For either all of the aforementioned parts of the people must share in the constitution, or some must and others not.

[1] When, then, the part that farms and that owns a moderate amount of property has control of the constitution, it is governed in accord with laws. For they have enough to live on as long as they keep working, but they cannot afford to be at leisure, so they put the law in charge and hold only such assemblies as are necessary. As for the other part, it is open to them to share when they have acquired the property assessment defined by the laws. That is why it is open to all those who have acquired it to share. For, generally speaking, it is oligarchic when it is not open for all to share—and of course for it to be open to them to be at leisure is impossible in the absence of revenues.[501] This, then, is one kind (*eidos*) of democracy and these are the reasons for it.

[2] Another kind (*eidos*) arises because of the following distinction. For it may be possible for everyone of uncontested family descent to share, but for only those who have the leisure to actually do so. That is why, indeed, in this sort of democracy the laws rule, namely, because there is no revenue.

[3] A third kind (*eidos*) is when all who are free may share in the constitution, but, due to the cause just mentioned, they do not share, so that the law necessarily rules in this sort too.

1293a1 [4] A fourth kind (*eidos*) of democracy was the last to arise in cities. For because of cities having become much larger than the original ones and having abundant sources of revenue, everyone shares in the constitution, because of the superiority of the multitude. And all do share and govern, because even the poor are able to be at leisure, since they get paid. A multitude of this sort is especially at leisure, indeed, since care of their own property does not impede them at all. But it does impede the rich, so that they often do not take part in the assembly or serve on juries. That is why the constitution comes to be controlled by the multitude of poor citizens, instead of by the laws.

The kinds (*eidos*) of democracy, then, are such and so many because of these necessities. And here are those of oligarchy:

[1] When a smaller number of people own property, though not an excessive amount, this is the first kind (*eidos*) of oligarchy. For anyone who acquires the amount may share, and because of the multitude of people sharing in the governing body, law is necessarily in control, not human beings. For the more removed they are from monarchy, having neither so much property that they can be at leisure without worrying nor so little that they need to be supported by the city, the more they necessarily think that the law deserves to rule them, not themselves.

[2] But if those who own property are fewer and their properties greater than those mentioned before, the second sort of oligarchy arises, since, being stronger, they claim that they deserve to get more.[502] That is why they themselves elect from among the rest of the citizens those who are to enter the governing body. But as they are not yet strong enough to rule without law, they pass a law to this effect.

[3] But if they tighten it by becoming fewer and owning larger properties, the third stage of oligarchy is reached, where they keep the offices in their own hands, but do so in accord with a law requiring deceased members to be succeeded by their sons.

[4] But when they now tighten it excessively by their property holdings and the number of their friends, a dynasty of this sort comes close to being a monarchy, and human beings are in control, not the law. This is the fourth kind (*eidos*) of oligarchy, corresponding to the final one of democracy.

IV 7

There are also two constitutions besides democracy and oligarchy, one of which is mentioned by everyone and is said to be one of the four kinds (*eidos*) of constitutions. The four they mention are: monarchy, oligarchy, democracy, and, fourth, so-called aristocracy. There is a fifth, however, which is referred to by the name shared by all constitutions, namely, the one called *politeia* (polity). But because it does not occur often, it gets overlooked by those who try to enumerate the kinds (*eidos*) of constitutions, and, like Plato, list only the four in their discussion of constitutions.[503] **1293b1**

[1] It is correct, then, to call the constitution we treated in our first accounts an aristocracy.[504] For the one consisting of those who are unconditionally best in accord with virtue, and not those who are good men relative to a hypothesis, is the only constitution that it is just to call an aristocracy. For only in it is the same person unconditionally a

good man and a good citizen, whereas those who are good in the others are so relative to their constitutions.

Nevertheless, there are some constitutions that are called aristocracies that exhibit differences (*diaphora*) both in relation to oligarchically governed constitutions and in relation to a so-called polity. For wherever officials are elected not only on the basis of wealth but also on the basis of merit, the constitution itself differs from both of these and is called aristocratic. For even in those constitutions where virtue is not a concern of the community, there are still some who are held in high repute and believed to be decent.

[2] Wherever, then, a constitution looks to wealth, virtue, and the people (as it does in Carthage) it is aristocratic, as also are [3] those, like the Spartan constitution, which look to only two, virtue and the people, and where there is a mixture of these two things, democracy and virtue.[505] There are, then, these two kinds of aristocracy besides the first, which is the best constitution; and there is also a third, namely, [4] those kinds that lean more than so-called polity toward oligarchy.

IV 8

It remains for us to speak about so-called polity and about tyranny. We have ordered things in this way, even though neither polity nor the aristocracies just mentioned are deviations, because in truth they all fall short of the most correct constitution, and so are counted among the deviations, and these deviations that we mentioned at the start of our discussions are deviations from them [that is, from polity and aristocracy].[506] On the other hand, it is reasonable to treat tyranny last, since it is least of all a constitution, and our methodical inquiry is concerned with constitutions.

The cause, then, of our ordering things in this way having been stated, we must now set forth our views on polity. For its power should be more evident now that we have determined matters concerning oligarchy and democracy. For polity, simply speaking, is a mixture of oligarchy and democracy. But it is customary to call those mixtures that lean toward democracy polities, and to call aristocracies those that lean more toward oligarchy, because education and good-breeding more commonly accompany those who are richer.

Further, the rich seem to possess already the things for the sake of which unjust people do injustice, which is why the rich are called both noble and good and notable. Since, then, aristocracies wish to give superiority to the best of the citizens, oligarchies too are said to consist primarily of noble and good men. And it seems to be impossible for a city to be in good legislative order if it is not governed aristocratically, 1294a1 but rather by wicked people, and equally impossible for one that is not in good legislative order to be governed aristocratically.[507] But good legislative order does not exist if the laws, though well laid down, are not obeyed. That is why we must take one sort of good legislative order to be when the laws that are laid down are obeyed, and another to be when the laws that are in fact obeyed are well laid down (for there is also obedience to badly laid-down laws). The latter, though, can come about in two ways, since people may either obey the best laws possible for them, or the unconditionally best ones.

Aristocracy seems above all to exist when offices are distributed in accord with virtue. For virtue is the defining mark of aristocracy, wealth of oligarchy, and freedom of democracy.[508] But [control] by the belief of the majority is found in all of them. For in oligarchy, aristocracy, and in democracies, the belief of the major part of those who share in the constitution is what is in control.

Now in most cities the kind (*eidos*) of constitution is badly named.[509] For the mixture aims only at the rich and the poor, at wealth and freedom. For among pretty much the majority of people the rich seem to occupy the place of noble and good men. But since there are *three* grounds for claiming equality in the constitution, namely, freedom, wealth, and virtue (for the fourth, which they call good-breeding, is a consequence of two of the others, since good-breeding is a combination of old money and virtue), it is evident that the mixture of the two, the rich and the poor, ought to be called polity, whereas a mixture of the three should most of all the others be called an aristocracy, after the true and first one.

It has been stated, then, that there are other kinds (*eidos*) of constitutions besides monarchy, democracy, and oligarchy, and what they are, and how aristocracies differ among themselves, and polities from aristocracy, and it is evident that they are not far apart from each other.

IV 9

Besides democracy and oligarchy, we should—in continuity with what was said—now discuss in what way a so-called polity arises, and how it should be put in place.[510] And at the same time it will be clear what things define democracy and oligarchy. For what we must do is get hold of the division of these things, and then make a composite out of these, taking as it were a token from each.

There are three defining marks of this composition and mixture: [1] One is to take the legislation of both constitutions. For example, in the case of the administration of justice, oligarchies impose a fine on the rich if they do not serve on juries, but provide no payment for the poor, whereas democracies pay the poor but do not fine the rich. Common to both constitutions, though, and a mean between them, is doing both. That is why this is characteristic of a polity, since it is a mixture formed from both. This, then, is one way to couple them.

[2] Another is to take the mean between the orders characteristic of each. For example, in democracies membership in the assembly is either not based on a property assessment at all or on a very small one, whereas in oligarchies it is based on a large property assessment. Common here is doing *neither*, but rather the assessment that is in a mean between the two of them.

[3] A third is to take things from both orders, some from oligarchic law and others from democratic law. I mean, for example, that it seems to be democratic for officials to be chosen by lot, and oligarchic by election; democratic not on the basis of a property assessment, oligarchic on such a basis. It is aristocratic, accordingly, and characteristic of a polity, to take one element from one and another from the other—from oligarchy, by making the officials elected, from democracy, by doing so not on the basis of a property assessment.

This, then, is the way to mix them. But the defining mark of a good mixture of democracy and oligarchy is when it is possible to speak of the same constitution both as a democracy and as an oligarchy. For it is clear that speakers speak of it in this way because the mixture is a good one. The mean too is like this, since each of the extremes is evident in it, which is just how things are in the case of the Spartan constitution. For many people attempt to speak of it as a democracy, because it has many democratic elements in its order.

In the first place, for example, there is the way sons are brought up. For those of the rich are brought up like those of the poor, and are educated in the way that the sons of the poor could be. Similarly, at the next age, when they have become men, it is the same way, since it is not entirely clear who is rich and who is poor. The food at the communal messes is the same for everyone, and the rich wear clothes that any poor person could also provide for himself. Further, of the two most important offices, the people elect candidates to one and share in the other, since they elect the senators and share in the overseership.

Other people, however, call the Spartan constitution an oligarchy because of its having many oligarchic elements. For example, all the officials are elected and none chosen by lot, a few have control to impose death and exile, and there are also many other such elements. In a constitution that is well mixed, by contrast, both elements should seem to be present, and also neither, and it should be preserved because of itself and not because of external factors, and because of itself not because a majority wishes it (since that could happen in a wicked constitution too), but because none of the parts of the city as a whole would even wish for another constitution.

In what way a polity should be put in place, and likewise those constitutions that are termed aristocracies, has now been stated.

IV 10

It remained for us to speak about tyranny, not because there is much argument about it, but so that it can take its place in our methodical inquiry, since we assign it too a place among the constitutions.

We dealt with kingship in our first accounts, where we made an investigation into whether what is most of all called a kinship is advantageous for cities or disadvantageous, who should be king, where he should come from, and in what way the kingship should be put in place.[511] And we distinguished two kinds (*eidos*) of tyranny while we were making our investigation of kingship, because their power in a way also overlaps with kingship, because both of these sorts of rule are in accord with law. For among some barbarian peoples they choose [1] autocratic monarchs, and in former times among the ancient Greeks there were people who became monarchs in this way, namely, [2] the ones called dictators. There are certain differences (*diaphora*) between these. But both were kingly, because they were in accord with law and involved monarchical rule over voluntary subjects, and both were tyrannical, because the monarchs ruled like masters in accord with their own judgment.

There is, though, a third kind (*eidos*) of tyranny, which is the very one that seems most of all to be a tyranny, because it is a counterpart to absolute kingship. And any monarchy is necessarily a tyranny of this sort if the monarch rules in a non-accountable way over people who are his equals or betters, with a view to his own advantage, not that of the ruled. That is precisely why it is rule over involuntary subjects, since no free person voluntarily puts up with such rule.

The kinds (*eidos*) of tyranny are these and this many, then, due to the aforementioned causes.

IV 11

What is the best constitution, and what is the best life for most cities and most human beings, comparing it neither to a virtue that is beyond the reach of private individuals, nor to an education that requires natural gifts and resources that depend on luck, nor to the constitution that is in accord with our prayers, but to a life that most people can share and a constitution in which most cities can share? For the constitutions called aristocracies, which we talked about just now, either fall outside the reach of most cities or border on so-called polities—which is why the two should be spoken about as one.

But now the judgment about all these matters depends on the same elements. For if what is said in the *Ethics* is correct, and a happy life is the unimpeded life that is in accord with virtue, and virtue is a medial state, then the middle life is best, the mean that admits of being aimed at by each sort of person.[512] These same defining marks must also define the virtue and vice of a city or constitution. For the constitution is a sort of life of a city.

In all cities, you see, there are three things that are parts of the city, the very rich, the very poor, and third those who are in the middle between these. Therefore, since it is agreed that the moderate and the middle is best, it is evident that possessing a middling amount of the goods of luck is also best of all.[513] For that makes it easiest to obey reason, whereas whatever is hyper-noble, hyper-strong, hyper-well bred, or hyper-rich, or the contraries of these, hyper-poor, hyper-weak, or exceedingly without honor has difficulty in obeying reason. For the first lot tend more toward committing wanton aggression and major vice, whereas the second lot tend too much to become malicious and pettily wicked. And injustices are caused in the one case by wanton aggression and in the other by evildoing. Further, those in the middle are least inclined either to avoid rule or to be eager to rule, both of which things are harmful to cities.

In addition, those who are superior in the goods of luck (strength, wealth, friends, and other things of that sort) neither wish to be ruled nor know how to be ruled. And this characteristic they acquire right from the start at home while they are still children. For because of their luxurious living they are not accustomed to being ruled even in school. Those, on the other hand, who are excessively deprived of such goods are too humble. So the latter do not have the scientific knowledge of how to rule, but only how to be ruled in the way slaves are ruled, whereas the former do not have it of how to be ruled in any way, but only how to rule with the rule of a master.[514]

What comes into being, then, is a city consisting of slaves and masters, but not of free people, the one group envious, the other contemptuous—which is the furthest thing from political friendship and community.[515] For community is fitted to friendship, since enemies do not wish to share even a road in common. But a city tends at any rate to consist as much as possible of people who are equal and similar, and this especially holds of those in the middle.[516] So it is necessary for this city—the one that is composed of those we say a city is by nature composed of—to be governed in the best way.

Also, of all the citizens, those in the middle are the ones that preserve themselves most in cities. For they neither desire other people's property, as the poor do, nor do other people desire theirs, as the poor desire that of the rich. And because they are neither plotted against nor plot, they pass their time free from danger. That is why Phocylides did well to pray: "Many things are best for those in the middle. In the middle is where I want to be in a city."[517]

It is clear, therefore, that the political community that is due to those in the middle is best too, and that cities can be well governed where the middle class is numerous and stronger—especially if it is stronger than both of the others, or, failing that, than one of them. For it will tip the balance when added to either and prevent opposing excesses from arising.[518] That is why it is the height of good luck if those in the governing body own a middling and adequate amount of property, because when some people own an excessive amount and the rest own nothing, either extreme democracy arises or unmixed oligarchy or—as a result of both excesses—tyranny. For tyranny arises from the most vigorous sort of democracy and from [unmixed] oligarchy, but much less often from middle constitutions or those close to them. We will state the cause of this later on when we discuss constitutional changes.[519]

It is evident that the middle constitution is best, then, since it alone is free from factional conflict. For where there are many people in the middle, conflicts and disagreements least occur among the citizens. And large cities are freer from factional conflict due to the same cause, namely, that the middle class is numerous. In small cities, on the other hand, it is easy to divide all the citizens into two, so that no middle class is left and pretty much everyone is either poor or rich. And democracies are more stable and longer lasting than oligarchies because of those in the middle (for they are more numerous in democracies than oligarchies and share in office more), since when, without these, the poor are predominant in number, failure comes about and the democracy is quickly ruined.[520] It should be regarded as an indication of this that the best legislators have come from the middle citizens. For Solon was one of these, as is clear from his poems, as were Lycurgus (for he was not a king), Charondas, and pretty much most of the others.

It is also evident from these considerations why most constitutions are either democratic or oligarchic. For because the middle class in them is often small, whichever of the others is superior—whether the property-owners or the people—distances itself from the middle class and conducts the constitution to suit themselves, so that either a democracy comes about or an oligarchy.

In addition to this, because of the factions and fights that occur between the people and the rich, whenever one side or the other happens to be stronger than its opponents, they put in place neither a communal constitution nor an equal one, but take their superiority in the constitution as a reward of their victory and make in the one case a democracy and in the other an oligarchy.

Further, those who achieved leadership in Greece have looked to their own constitutions and put in place either democracies or oligarchies in cities, targeting not the advantage of the cities but their own, so that, because of this, the middle constitution has either never come about or has done so rarely and in few places.[521] For one man alone, among those who have previously held positions of leadership, has ever allowed himself to be persuaded to introduce this kind of order, and it has now become customary for those in cities not even to wish for equality, but either to seek rule or to put up with being dominated.[522]

What the best constitution is, then, and why it is so, is evident from these considerations. As for the other constitutions (for there are, as we say, several sorts of democracies and of oligarchies), which of them is to be put first, which second, and so on in the very same way, in accord with whether it is better or worse, is not difficult to see now that the best has been determined. For one nearest to this is of necessity always better and one further from the middle constitution worse—provided one is not judging relative to a hypothesis. I say "relative to a hypothesis," because it often happens that, while one constitution is more choiceworthy, nothing prevents a distinct one from being more advantageous for some [cities].[523]

IV 12

What constitution is advantageous for what [city], and what sort for what sort, is the next thing to go through after what has been said. First, though, a general point must be grasped about all of them, namely, that the part of a city that wishes the constitution to endure must be stronger than the part that does not.[524] But every city is made up of both quality and quantity. By quality I mean freedom, wealth, education, and good-breeding; by quantity I mean superiority in numbers. But it is possible that the quality belongs to one of the parts of which a city is formed, while the quantity belongs to another. For example, the ill bred may be more numerous than the well bred or the poor more numerous than the rich, but yet the one may not be as superior in quantity as it is inferior in quality. That is why these have to be judged in relation to each other.

Where the multitude of poor people is superior in the proportion mentioned, it is natural for a democracy to exist, with each kind (*eidos*) of democracy corresponding to the superiority of each [kind of] the people. For example, if the multitude of farmers is predominant, it will be the first sort of democracy, if the vulgar ones and wage-earners are, the last sort, and similarly for the others in between these. But where the multitude of those who are rich and notable is more superior in quality than it is inferior in quantity, there an oligarchy [is natural], with each sort of oligarchy corresponding in the same way to the superiority of the multitude of oligarchs.

The legislator, however, should always add on those in the middle in his constitution.[525] For if he is setting up oligarchic laws, he should aim at those in the middle, and if democratic ones, he must draw in those in the middle by these laws. And where the multitude of those in the middle predominates either over both of the extremes together, or even only over one of them, it is possible to have a constitution that is steadfast. For there is no fear that the rich and the poor will conspire together against these, nor indeed will either want to serve as slaves to the other, whereas if they look for a constitution that is more communal, they will find none other than this one. For they would not put up with ruling in turn, because they distrust each other. Everywhere, though, an arbitrator is most trusted, and the middling person is an arbitrator.[526]

The better mixed a polity is, the more steadfast it is. But many of those who wish to produce aristocratic constitutions make the mistake not only of granting more to the rich, but also of deceiving the people. For sooner or later, false goods necessarily give rise to a true evil. For what the rich do to get more does more to destroy the constitution than what the people do.[527]

IV 13

The subtleties devised in constitutions as pretexts to deceive the people are five in number, and concern the assembly, the offices, the courts, the possession of weapons, and athletic training.[528] [1] As regards the assembly: allowing all citizens to attend assemblies, but imposing a fine on the rich for not attending, either only on them or a much heavier one on them. [2] As regards offices: not allowing those with an assessed amount of property to be excused under oath, but allowing the poor to be excused.[529] [3] As regards the courts: fining the rich for not serving on juries, but allowing the poor not to do so, or else imposing a large fine on the former and a small one on the latter—as in the laws of Charondas.[530] In some places, everyone who has enrolled may attend the assembly and serve on juries, but once they have enrolled, if they do not attend or serve, they are heavily fined. The aim is to get people to avoid enrolling because of the fine, and not to serve or attend because of not being enrolled. They legislate in the same way where possessing weapons and athletic training are concerned. [4] For the poor are permitted not to possess weapons, but the rich are fined if they do not, [5] and if they do not train, there is no fine for the former, but the latter are fined. That way the rich will share because of the fine, whereas the poor, not being in danger of it, will not share.

These subtle devices of legislation are oligarchic. In democracies, by contrast, there are subtleties devised that are contrary to these. For while the poor are paid to attend the assembly and serve on juries, the rich are not fined [for failing to]. So it is evident that if one wishes to have a just mixture, one must combine elements from both sides, and pay the poor while fining the rich. For in this way everyone would share, whereas in the other way the constitution comes to be in the hands of one side only.

A polity should, however, be composed only of those who possess weapons. But it is impossible to define the size of the relevant property assessment unconditionally, and say that it must be so-and-so much. One should instead look for what amount is the largest that would let those who share in the constitution outnumber those who do not, and fix on that.[531] For the poor are willing to keep quiet even when they do not share in office, provided that no one treats them with wanton aggression or takes away any of their property—but this is not easy to do, since those who do share in the governing body are not always refined people. And people are in the habit of shirking in time of war if they do not receive provisions and are poor—although if food is provided, they wish to fight.

In some places, the polity consists not only of those who are serving as hoplites but also of those who have so served in the past. In Malia, the constitution consisted of both, although the officials were elected from among the active soldiers.[532] Also, the first constitution that came about among the Greeks after the kingships consisted of the warriors.[533] At the start, though, it consisted of the cavalrymen, since strength and superiority in war lay in them. For without orderly formations the hoplite element is useless, and experiences in such things and orderly formations did not exist among the ancients, so that their strength lay in their cavalry. But as cities grew larger, and those with hoplite weapons became a stronger force, more people shared in the constitution. That is why what we now call polities used to be called democracies. The ancient constitutions, on the other hand, were oligarchic and kingly, and reasonably so. For because of their small population they did not have much of a middle class, and so the people, because they were small in number and poor as regards order, put up with being ruled.

[1] What the causes are, then, of there being several constitutions, and [1a] why there are others besides those spoken about (for democracy is not one in number, and likewise neither are the others), and, further, [1b] what their differences (*diaphora*) are, and [1c] due to what cause they arise, and, in addition to this, [2] which constitution, speaking for the majority of cases, is best, and [3] which among the others fits which sort of city, have now been stated.

IV 14

Let us again, in connection with what comes next, discuss constitutions in common and each one separately, taking the starting-point that is appropriate to these topics. There are, then, three parts in all constitutions by reference to which an excellent legislator must get a theoretical grasp on what is advantageous for each constitution. When these parts are in good condition, the constitution is necessarily in good condition, and constitutions differ from each other by differing in each of these parts. One of the three parts is [1] the one that deliberates about communal affairs; the second [2] concerns the offices, that is to say, which offices there should be, with control of what things, and in what way officials should be chosen; and the third [3] is the one that judges lawsuits.[534]

[1] The deliberative part has control concerning war and peace and the making and breaking of alliances, concerning laws, and concerning death, exile, and the confiscation of property, and concerning the election and inspection of officials. And it is necessary that either [1a] all these sorts of judgments be assigned to all the citizens; or [1b] all to some of them (to some single office, for example, or to several, or some to some and others to others); or [1c] some to all and some to some.

[1a] For all to deliberate about all issues is characteristic of a democracy, since this is the sort of equality the people seek. But there are several ways of having all of them do so. [1a–i] One way is by turns rather than all together, as in the constitution of Telecles of Miletus.[535] And there are other constitutions in which deliberation is carried out by boards

of officials meeting jointly, and all enter office by turn from the tribes and from the smallest parts of the city, until all have been gone through, and they all meet together only to consider legislation, and matters pertaining to the constitution, and to listen to official announcements.[536] [1a–ii] Another way is where they all meet, but only for the choosing of officials, for legislation, matters of war and peace, and for inspections, whereas other matters are deliberated on by the officials assigned to deal with the particular area in question, these being chosen from all the citizens either by election or by lot. [1a–iii] Another way is for the citizens to meet together about offices and inspections, and to deliberate about war and alliances, and for other matters to be dealt with by offices which as far as possible are filled by election, these being the ones where it is necessary to have scientifically-knowledgeable people ruling.[537] [1a–iv] A fourth way is for all to meet and deliberate about all matters, while the officials make no judgments, but only prepare issues for judgment. This is the way in which the final democracy is managed as things stand, the one we say is analogous to a dynastic oligarchy or a tyrannical monarchy.[538] All these ways, then, are democratic.

But [1b] for some people to deliberate about all matters is oligarchic. But here too there are several differences (*diaphora*). [1b–i] For when they are chosen on the basis of more moderate property assessments, and there are more of them because of the moderateness of the assessments, and where they do not attempt to make changes that the law forbids but rather follow it, and where everyone who has the assessed amount may share—such a constitution is certainly an oligarchy, but because of its moderateness, one with the character of a polity. [1b–ii] When not everyone shares in deliberation but only those elected, and when, as before, they rule in accord with law, it is oligarchic. [1b–iii] When those who have control of deliberation elect themselves, and when son succeeds father, and they have control of the laws, this order is necessarily most oligarchic. [1c] But, when some have control of some matters—for example, when all have it over war and peace and inspections, whereas officials, who are elected and not chosen by lot, have it in the other areas, it is an aristocracy or a polity.[539] But if it happens that elected officials have control in some areas, whereas officials chosen by lot, either unconditionally or from a pre-selected group, have it in others, or if elected officials and officials chosen by lot share control, some of these are features of an aristocratic constitution and others of polity itself.

This is the way, then, that the deliberative part is distinguished in the various constitutions, and each constitution administers matters in accord with the aforementioned determinations.

In the sort of democracy that now seems most of all to be a democracy (I mean the sort in which the people have control even over the laws), it is advantageous from the point of view of improving deliberation to do the very same thing as is done in oligarchies in regard to the courts. For they assign a fine for those people they want to have on juries to ensure that they serve, whereas democrats pay the poor. Absolutely the same should be done in the case of assemblies too, since they will deliberate better if all deliberate together, the people with the notables, and the latter with the multitude. It is advantageous too if those who do the deliberating are elected or chosen by lot in equal numbers from these parts. And even if the democrats among the citizens are greatly superior in numbers, it is advantageous either not to provide pay for all of them, but only for a number commensurate with the number of notables, or to exclude the excess by lot.

In oligarchies, on the other hand, it is advantageous either to choose some additional people from the multitude or to establish a board of officials (like the so-called preliminary councilors or law-guardians that exist in some constitutions), and then [have the assembly] transact only the business that these have considered first. For, in this way, the people will share in deliberation, but will not be able to abolish anything concerning the constitution. Further, it is advantageous to have the people vote on decrees that are either the same as those brought before them [by the board], or on nothing contrary to them, or else to let all give advice and have only officials deliberate. Also, one should do the opposite of what happens in polities. For the multitude should have control when vetoing decrees but not when approving them; in the latter case, they should be referred back to the officials instead. For in polities, they do the reverse, since the few have control when vetoing decrees but not when approving them, decrees of the latter sort always being referred back to the majority instead. Concerning the deliberative part, then, and the part that has control of the constitution, let matters be determined in this way.

IV 15

[2] Next after these things is the division of the offices.[540] For this part of a constitution too has many differences (*diaphora*): how many offices there are and with control of what things; and with regard to time—how long each office is to last (for some make it six months, others less, some make it a year, others a longer period), and whether the offices should be held permanently or for a long time, or neither of these, but instead the same people may hold office several times,

or the same person not even twice but only once; further, as regards the appointment of officials—from whom they should come, by whom chosen, and in what way. Concerning all these one should be able to distinguish how many modes there can be, and then fit the sorts of offices to the sorts of constitutions for which they are advantageous.

But even to determine what are to be called offices is not easy. For a political community needs many sorts of supervisors, which is why not everyone who is chosen by vote or by lot can be regarded as an official. In the first place, for example, there are the priests (for a priesthood must be regarded as something other than and beyond the political offices). Further, patrons of the theater and heralds are elected, as are ambassadors. But some sorts of supervision *are* political, either concerned with all the citizens involved in a certain action (as a general supervises those who are serving as soldiers), or some part of them (the supervisor of women or the supervisor of children). Some are related to household management (for corn-rationers are often elected), while others belong to assistants (and to these, if they have the resources, they assign slaves).[541]

Simply speaking, however, the offices most properly so called are those responsible for deliberating about certain matters, for judging, and for prescribing [what is to be done], above all the latter, since issuing prescriptions is more characteristic of ruling.[542] But this makes (one might almost say) no difference as regards use (for as yet no judgment has been handed down to anyone disputing over the name), although there is some further work for thought to do on it.[543]

What sorts of offices, and how many, are necessary for the existence of a city, and what sorts, though not necessary, are yet useful for an excellent constitution, are puzzles one might raise with regard to *any* constitution, but especially with regard to *small* cities.[544] For of course in large cities one can and should assign a single office to a single function. For because there are many citizens, there are many people to take up office, so that some offices are held again only after a long interval and others are held only once. Also, each function is better performed when its supervision is engaged in one thing rather than being engaged in many things.[545] In small cities, on the other hand, many offices have to be co-assigned to a few people, since underpopulation makes it hard to have many people in office. For who will succeed them in their turn? But sometimes small cities need the same offices and laws as large ones, except that the latter need the same ones often, whereas the former need them only at long intervals. That is why nothing prevents their assigning many sorts of supervision [to the same officials] at the same time, since they will not impede each other, and why, because of underpopulation, they must make their boards of officials like spit-lamps.[546]

If, then, we can say how many offices every city must have, and how many are not ones it must have but that it should have, it will be easier, in the light of this, to determine which offices it is fitting to combine into a single office. But it is also fitting not to overlook the question of which matters should be supervised by numerous local offices, and which a single office should everywhere have control of. For example, in the case of good order whether a market supervisor should have control of this in the marketplace, and another official in another place, or the same one everywhere; and whether offices should be distinguished by the thing or by the people [they deal with]—I mean, for example, whether there should be a single office for good order, or one for children and another for women.

And with regard to the constitutions too, whether the kinds (*genos*) of offices also differ in each kind of constitution, or not at all. For example, whether in a democracy, an oligarchy, an aristocracy, and a monarchy, the same offices have control, even though they are not filled from equal or even similar people, but from distinct sorts in distinct constitutions (from the well educated in aristocracies, from the rich in oligarchies, and from the free in democracies), or whether certain offices exist that are, for their part, in accord with these differences, with sometimes the same offices and sometimes different ones being advantageous (since it is fitting for the same offices to be large in some places and small in others).

Nevertheless, some offices are indeed special [to certain constitutions]—for example, that of the preliminary councilors, since it is undemocratic. A council, by contrast, is democratic, since there must be some body of this sort to take care of preliminary deliberation on behalf of the people, so they can do their work.[547] It is oligarchic, though, if the councilors are few in number. But the *preliminary* councilors are necessarily few in number, so that their office is oligarchic. Where both these offices exist, however, the preliminary councilors are put in place as a check on the councilors. For a councilor is a democratic [official], a preliminary councilor, oligarchic. But the power of the council is also destroyed in those sorts of democracies in which it is the people themselves who come together and transact all business. This happens when there is wealth of the sort that provides pay to those who attend the assembly, since they then have the leisure to meet often and judge everything themselves.[548] But the supervisor of women, the supervisor of children, and any other office that has control of this sort of supervision, is aristocratic, not democratic (for how can one prevent the women of the poor from going out?) or oligarchic (for the women of oligarchs live luxuriously).[549]

Concerning these topics let this much be determined for now, but concerning the appointment of officials, we must try to go through things from the start. Differences (*diaphora*) here lie in three defining marks, the combination of which necessarily yields all the modes. Of these three, the first is [2a] who appoints the officials, second, [2b] from whom, and, lastly, [2c] in what way. And of each of these three there are different varieties. Either [2a–i] all the citizens appoint or [2a–ii] some do; and they appoint either [2b–i] from all or [2b–ii] from certain determinate groups (determined by a property assessment, for example, or by breeding, or by virtue, or by some other feature of that sort—as in Megara where they appointed from those who returned from exile together and fought together against the people); and they appoint either [2c–i] by election or [2c–ii] by lot; and, again, these may be coupled—I mean that [2a–iii] all may appoint to some offices and some to others, [2b–iii] some offices may be appointed from all and others from some, and [2c–iii] some may be appointed by lot and others by election.[550]

In the case of each of these differences (*diaphora*), there will be four modes.[551] [1] Either all appoint from all by election or [2] all appoint from all by lot; or [3] all appoint from some by election; or [4] all appoint from some by lot (and, if from all, either by sections—by tribe, for example, or by deme or clan, until all the citizens have been gone through—or from all on every occasion); or [5] partly in the first way and partly in the second.[552] Again, if only some appoint, they may do so either from all by election or from all by lot; or from some by election or from some by lot; or partly in the first way and partly in the second—I mean, partly from all by election and partly by lot, and partly from some by election and partly by lot. This gives rise to twelve modes that are separate from the two couplings.[553]

Of these ways of appointing, three are democratic, namely, when all appoint from all by election, by lot, or by both (that is, for some offices by election and for some by lot). But when not all appoint at the same time, but do so from all or from some, whether by election, lot, or both, or from all for some offices and from some for others, whether by election, lot, or both (by both I mean some by lot and others by election)—it is characteristic of a polity. When some appoint from all, whether by election, lot, or both (for some offices by lot, for others by election), it is oligarchic—although it is more oligarchic to do so by both. But when some offices are appointed from all and others from some or when some are appointed by election and some by lot, this is characteristic of an aristocratically governed polity. When some appoint from some by election, it is oligarchic, also when some appoint from some by lot (even if this does not actually occur), and when some appoint from some in both ways. But when some appoint from all, and when all appoint from some by election, it is aristocratic.

These, then, are the number of modes of appointing to offices, and this is the way they are divided in accord with the constitutions. Which are advantageous for which constitutions, and how appointments are to be made, will become evident when we determine the powers of the offices, and which these are. By the power of an office I mean, for example, control of revenues or control of defense—for the kind (*eidos*) of power that is like the one belonging to a generalship is different from that belonging to control of marketplace contracts.

IV 16

Of the three parts, it remains to speak about [3] the judicial.[554] And we must grasp the modes of these [offices] in accord with the same hypothesis.[555] There is a difference (*diaphora*) between courts that lies in three defining marks: from whom; about what; and in what way. From whom: I mean whether they are appointed from all or from some. About what: how many kinds (*eidos*) of courts there are. In what way: whether by lot or election.

First, then, let us distinguish how many kinds (*eidos*) of courts there are. They are eight in number. One is [i] the court of inspection of officials. Another [ii] is concerned with anyone who in some matter concerning the community does something unjust.[556] Another [iii] with matters that bear on the constitution. A fourth [iv] is concerned with officials and private individuals in disputes about fines. A fifth [v] is concerned with private transactions of some magnitude. Besides these there is [vi] a court that is concerned with homicide and [vii] one that is concerned with aliens.

The kinds (*eidos*) of homicide court, whether having the same juries or not, are: [vi–1] that concerned with premeditated homicide, [vi–2] that concerned with involuntary homicide, [vi–3] that concerned with cases where the fact is admitted but the justice of it disputed, and a fourth [vi–4] concerned with charges brought against those who have been exiled for homicide after their return (the court of Phreatto in Athens is said to be an example), but such cases are rare at any time even in large cities.[557] The aliens' court has [vii–1] a part for aliens disputing with aliens and [vii–2] a part for aliens disputing with citizens.

Further, besides all these, there is [viii] a court that is concerned with petty transactions; those involving one drachma, five drachmas, or a little more (for judgment must be given in such cases too, but it should not fall to a multitude of jurors to give it).

But let us set aside these courts, as well as the homicide and aliens' courts, and speak about the political ones, which, when not well managed, give rise to disagreements and constitutional changes. Of necessity, either [3a] all judge all the cases just now distinguished, and are appointed either [3a-i] by lot or [3a-ii] by election; or all judge all of them and [3a–iii] some are appointed by lot and some by election; or, [3a–iv] although dealing with the same cases, some jurors may be appointed by lot and some by election. These modes, then, are four in number.

There are as many too when appointment is from only some of the citizens. For here again either [3b–i] the juries are appointed from some by election and judge all cases; or [3b–ii] they are appointed from some by lot and judge all cases; or [3b–iii] some may be appointed by lot and some by election; or [3b–iv] some courts dealing with the same cases may be composed of both allotted and elected members. These modes, as we said, are the counterparts of the ones we mentioned earlier. [3c] Further, these same ones may be conjoined—I mean, for example, some may be appointed from all, others from some, and others from both (as for example if the same court had juries appointed partly from all and partly from some); and the appointment may be either by lot or by election or by both.

We have now stated how many modes the courts admit of. Of these the first, [3a] those which are appointed from all and judge all cases, are democratic. The second [3b], those which are appointed from some and judge all cases, are oligarchic. The third [3c], those which are partly appointed from all and partly from some, are aristocratic or characteristic of a polity.

Book V

V 1

Pretty much all the other topics, then, that we deliberately decided on have been discussed. And after what has been discussed, we should next investigate: [1] the sources of change in constitutions, how many they are and of what sort; [2] what things destroy each constitution; [3] from what sort into what sort they mostly change; further, [4] what things preserve constitutions in general and each constitution in particular; and, finally, [5] the means by which each constitution is best preserved.[558]

We should first take as a starting-point that many constitutions have come into existence because, though everyone agrees about justice and proportionate equality, they are in error about it, as we also mentioned earlier.[559] For democracy arose from those who are equal in some respect thinking themselves to be unconditionally equal, since, because they are equally free, they think they are unconditionally equal. Oligarchy, on the other hand, arose from those who are unequal in some respect taking themselves to be wholly unequal, since, because they are unequal in property, they take themselves to be unconditionally unequal.[560] And so the former claim to be worthy of an equal share of everything, on the grounds that they are all equal, whereas the latter, because they are unequal, seek to get more (for a bigger share is an unequal one).[561] All these constitutions, then, have a certain sort of justice, although unconditionally they are mistaken. And it is due to this cause that, when one or other of them does not share in the constitution in accord with the supposition [about justice] they happen to have, they engage in faction. But those who would most have justice on their side in engaging in faction, though the least likely to do so, are those who are outstanding in virtue. For they alone are the ones it is most reasonable to regard as unconditionally unequal. There are also certain people, those who are superior 1301b1
in family, who suppose that they are not worthy of merely equal things, because they are unequal in this way. For people are believed to be noble when they have ancestral wealth and virtue.

These, then, are (one might almost say) the starting-points and springs of factions—the sources from which people engage in faction. This is also why the changes that are due to factions are twofold. [1] For sometimes people engage in faction against the constitution in order to change from the one that is in place to one of another sort—for example, from democracy to oligarchy, or from oligarchy to democracy, or from these to polity or aristocracy, or from the latter to the former. [2] Sometimes, though, they engage in faction not against the constitution that is in place (for example, an oligarchy or a monarchy), which they deliberately choose to keep the same, but [2a] wish to have it in their own hands. Further, [2b] it may be a question of more or less—for example, where there is an oligarchy, the aim may be to make it more oligarchically ruled or less so; where there is a democracy, to make it more democratically ruled or less so; and similarly, in the case of the remaining constitutions, the aim may be to tighten or loosen them.[562] Further, [2c] the aim may be to change a certain part of the constitution—for example, to put in place or abolish a certain office, as some say Lysander tried to abolish the kingship in Sparta, and King Pausanias the overseership.[563] In Epidamnus too the constitution was changed with regard to one part, since a council replaced the tribal rulers, though it is still the case that only those members of the governing body who hold office are obliged to attend the public assembly when election to office is taking place—the single [supreme] official was also an oligarchic feature of this constitution.[564]

Faction, indeed, is everywhere due to inequality, when unequals do not receive what is proportionate (for example, a permanent kingship is unequal if it exists among equals), since people generally engage in faction in pursuit of equality. But equality is twofold, namely, numerical equality and equality in accord with worth.[565] By numerical equality I mean being the same and equal in number or size; by equality in accord with worth, what is the same and equal in ratio. For example, in number, three exceeds two and two exceeds one equally, whereas in ratio, four exceeds two and two exceeds one equally—for two and one are equal parts of four and two, since both are halves.

But, though people agree that what is unconditionally just is what is in accord with worth, they still disagree, as we said earlier.[566] For some regard themselves as wholly equal if they are equal in a certain respect, whereas others claim to be worthy of inequality in everything if they are unequal in a certain respect. That is also why two constitutions mostly arise: democracy and oligarchy. For good-breeding and virtue are found in few people, whereas these things [freedom (democracy) and wealth (oligarchy)] are more widespread. For no city has a hundred good and well-bred men, but there are rich ones in many places.[567]

For a constitution to be ordered simply and entirely in accord with either sort of equality, however, is bad. This is evident from what actually happens, since no constitution of this kind is steadfast. The cause of this is that it is impossible, when the first thing—namely, the starting-point—is in error, for the result not to be in the end something bad.[568] That is why numerical equality should be used in some cases, and equality in accord with worth in others.

Nevertheless, democracy is more stable and freer from factional conflict than oligarchy.[569] For in oligarchies, two sorts of faction arise, one among the oligarchs themselves, and another again against the people. In democracies, on the other hand, the only faction is against the oligarchic element, since there is no faction worth mentioning among the people themselves against themselves. Further, a constitution based on those in the middle is closer to a democracy than to an oligarchy, and this one is the most stable constitution of these sorts.

V 2

Since we are investigating the sources from which both factions and changes arise where constitutions are concerned, we must first grasp in universal terms their starting-points and causes. These are, then, (one might almost say) pretty much three in number, each of which must first be defined in outline by itself. For we must grasp [1] the disposition of people who engage in faction; [2] for the sake of what they do so; and, third, [3] what the starting-points are of political disturbances and factions among people.

[1] Now we must take it that in universal terms the cause of people's being in some way disposed to change their constitution is mostly the one we have in fact already mentioned.[570] For those who pursue equality engage in faction when they believe that they get less, even though they are the equals of those who get more, whereas those who pursue inequality (that is to say, superiority) do so when they believe that, though they are unequal, they are not getting more, but rather the same or less. (It is possible, though, sometimes to desire these things justly, sometimes unjustly.) For inferiors engage in faction in order to be equal, while equals do so in order to be superior. The disposition of those who engage in faction has now been stated.

[2] The things about which people engage in faction are profit, honor, and the contraries of these. For people also engage in faction in cities to avoid dishonor and fines, either for themselves or for their friends.

[3] The causes and starting-points of the changes—the sources that dispose people to feel in the way we described about the issues we mentioned—happen in one way to be seven in number and in another more.[571] Two of them are the same as those just mentioned, but not in the same way. For people are also stirred up against each other by profit and honor not simply in order to get them for themselves, which is what we said before, but because they see others, whether justly or unjustly, getting more of these. Other causes are: wanton aggression, 1302b1

fear, superiority, contempt, and disproportionate growth. Still others, although operating in another way, are electioneering, underestimation, neglect of small things, and dissimilarity.[572]

V 3

Of these, though, the capacity that wanton aggression and profit have and how they are causes are pretty much evident. For it is when officials are wantonly aggressive and want to get more that people engage in faction both against each other and against the constitutions that gave the officials control. And their getting more is sometimes at the expense of private, sometimes at the expense of communal, funds.

It is also clear what honor has the capacity to do and how it is a cause of faction. For people engage in faction both when they are dishonored themselves and when they see others being honored. This occurs unjustly when people are honored or dishonored contrary to their worth, justly, when in accord with their worth.

Faction arises because of superiority when some individual or group of individuals is greater in power than is in accord with the city and the power of the governing body, since when there are people like that a monarchy or a dynasty usually arises. That is why some places, such as Argos and Athens, have a practice of ostracism.[573] Yet it is better to see to it from the start that no people with so great a superiority arise than to supply a remedy after the fact.[574] People engage in faction because of fear both when they have committed injustice and are afraid of punishment and when they think they are about to suffer injustice and wish to take preemptive action before they suffer injustice. The latter occurred in Rhodes when the notables united against the people because of the lawsuits being brought against them.[575]

People also engage in faction and attack each other because of contempt. For example, this occurs in oligarchies when those who do not share in the constitution are in a majority (since they consider themselves the stronger party), and in democracies, when the rich are contemptuous of the disorder and anarchy.[576] For example, the democracy in Thebes was destroyed because they were governed in a bad way after the battle of Oenophyta, as was the democracy of the Megarians when they were defeated because of disorder and anarchy, and [it was the same story] in Syracuse, before the tyranny of Gelon, and in Rhodes prior to the revolt.[577]

Constitutional changes also occur because of disproportionate growth. For a body is composed of parts, and these must grow in proportion if symmetry is to be maintained, and if it is not, the body will be destroyed—as, for example, when a foot is four cubits [six feet] long and the rest of the body two spans [fifteen inches], or, if the disproportionate growth is not only quantitative but also qualitative, its shape might change to that of another animal.[578] So, similarly, a city too is composed of parts, one of which often grows without being noticed—for example, the multitude of the poor in democracies or polities. This sometimes also happens because of luck. At Tarentum, for example, a democracy took the place of a polity when many notables were killed by the Iapygians shortly after the Persian Wars.[579] In Argos, too, after the men of the seventh were killed by the Spartan Cleomenes, the notables were compelled to admit some of their subject peoples to citizenship.[580] And in Athens, when they had bad luck fighting on land, the notables were reduced in number, because at the time of the war against Sparta service in the army was based on the citizen list.[581] This sort of change also occurs in democracies, although to a lesser extent. For when the rich become more numerous or their properties increase in size, democracies change into oligarchies or dynasties.

But constitutions also change without the occurrence of faction, both because of electioneering, as happened in Heraea (for they replaced election with selection by lot because of this, namely, because those who electioneered were getting elected), and also because of carelessness, when people who are not friendly to the constitution are allowed to occupy the offices with supreme control.[582] Thus the oligarchy in Oreus was overthrown when Heracleodorus became one of the officials and established a polity, or rather a democracy, in place of the oligarchy.[583]

Further, constitutions change because of a small difference. I mean by small that often a great change in the laws occurs unnoticed when something small is overlooked. In Ambracia, for example, the property assessment was small, but in the end people with no property came to hold office, the assumption being that the small is very close to, or no different from, none.[584]

Racial difference also tends to cause faction, until people join together. For just as a city does not arise from any random multitude, neither does it arise in a random period of time. That is why most of those who have admitted co-colonists or late-colonists have experienced factional conflict. The Achaeans co-colonized Sybaris with the Troezenians, but later, when the Achaeans became more numerous, they expelled the Troezenians (this was the cause of the curse that fell on the Sybarites).[585] In Thurii too, Sybarites came into conflict with their co-colonists, since when they claimed to be worthy of a larger share on the grounds that the territory was theirs, they were expelled.[586] In Byzantium too the late-colonists were discovered plotting against the original colonists and were expelled because of a battle.[587] The Antissaeans forcibly expelled the Chian exiles they had admitted.[588] The Zanclaeans were themselves expelled by the Samians they had admitted.[589] The Apolloniates on the Black Sea engaged in faction after admitting late-colonists.[590] The Syracusans, after the period of the tyrants, when they granted citizenship to foreigners and mercenaries, engaged in faction and broke into battle.[591] The Amphipolitans admitted late-colonists from Chalcis and were almost all expelled by them.[592]

{In oligarchies, as we said earlier, the many engage in faction on the grounds that they are treated unjustly because they do not share equally, in spite of being equal. In democracies, the notables do so because they do share equally, in spite of not being equal.}[593]

Cities sometimes also engage in faction because of their location, when the condition of their territory is not naturally well suited for there being *one* city.[594] In Clazomenae, for example, the inhabitants of Chytrus came into conflict with those on the island, as did the inhabitants of Colophon and those of Notium.[595] At Athens, too, the people are not all alike, but those in Piraeus are more democratic than those in the town.[596]

For just as in war, where crossing even small ditches breaks up the phalanx, so too every difference seems to produce disagreement. The greatest disagreement is presumably between virtue and vice; next that between wealth and poverty; and so on for the others, including the one we have just discussed, with each one greater than the next.

V 4

Factions arise, then, not *about* small things, but *out of* small things—it is about important things that people engage in faction. Even small factions become especially strong, however, when they arise among those in control—as happened for example in Syracuse in ancient times.[597] For the constitution was changed because two young men in office engaged in faction over a love affair. For, while the first was away, the second, who was his comrade, seduced his boyfriend. The first, enraged at him, retaliated by inducing the second's wife to commit adultery. The upshot was that they drew the governing body into their disagreement and split everyone into factions. That is precisely why it is that one should be circumspect when such things are starting, and dissolve the factions of leaders and powerful men. For the error arises in the starting-point, and the starting-point is said to be half the whole, so that even a small error in it is comparable to all the errors made at the later stages.[598]

Factions among the notables generally make the whole city share in the "enjoyment," as happened in Hestiaea, for example, after the Persian Wars when two brothers quarreled about the division of their inheritance.[599] For the poorer one, claiming that his brother had not declared the true value of the property, or of the treasure their father had found, enlisted the aid of the people, and the other, who had much property, enlisted the aid of the rich. In Delphi, a quarrel arising because of a marriage alliance was the starting-point of all the subsequent factions.[600] For the bridegroom came to fetch the bride, but some accident occurred that he interpreted as a bad omen, and he left without her. Her family, on the **1304a1**
grounds that they had been treated with wanton aggression, planted some sacred objects on him while he was sacrificing and killed him as a temple robber. In Mytilene, a faction concerning heiresses was the starting-point of many evils and, in particular, of the war with the Athenians, in which Paches captured their city.[601] For a rich citizen named Timophanes left behind two daughters, and when Dexander, who wanted to obtain them for his own sons, had his suit rejected, he started a faction and incited the Athenians, whose agent he was, to interfere.[602] Among the Phocians, a conflict arose over an heiress, involving Mnaseas the father of Mnason and Euthycrates the father of Onomarchus, which conflict was the starting-point of the Sacred War for the Phocians.[603] And in Epidamnus the constitution was changed because of matters having to do with a marriage.[604] For a man had betrothed his daughter, and the father of the one to whom he had betrothed her, becoming one of the officials, imposed a fine on him, whereupon the first allied himself with all those who were outside the constitution on the grounds that he had been insulted.

Constitutions also change to oligarchy, democracy, and polity as a result of some office or part of the city acquiring prestige or increasing in size. For example, the council of the Areopagus, which was held in high repute in the Persian Wars, was believed to have made the Athenian constitution tighter.[605] And, in return, the seafaring mob, through being the cause of the victory at Salamis, and, as a result of this, of the [Athenian] hegemony due to their power at sea, made the democracy stronger.[606] In Argos, the notables, having acquired prestige in connection with the battle against the Spartans at Mantinea, undertook to overthrow the democracy.[607] In Syracuse, the people, having been responsible for victory in the war against the Athenians, changed the constitution from a polity to a democracy.[608] And in Chalcis, the people, with the aid of the notables, overthrew the tyrant Phoxus, and then immediately took control of the constitution.[609] Similarly, in Ambracia, the people joined with the opponents of Periander to expel him and afterwards took the constitution into their own hands.[610] Generally speaking, then, this should not be overlooked, that the people who come to be responsible for a city's power—whether private individuals, officials, tribes, or, in general, a part or multitude of any sort whatsoever—stir up faction. For either those who envy them for being honored start a faction, or they themselves, because of their superior achievement, are unwilling to remain on equal terms.

Constitutions also undergo change when parts of a city that are believed to be opposed to each other, such as the rich and the people, become equal to each other, and there is little or no middle class. For if either of the parts becomes greatly superior, the remaining one will be unwilling to risk going up against the manifestly stronger one. That is why those who are superior in virtue do not cause (one might almost say) any faction, since they are few against many.

Universally, then, in all constitutions, the starting-points and causes of factions and changes have this mode of operation. But people change constitutions sometimes through force, sometimes through deceit. When it is through force, they use compulsion either right at the beginning or later on. In fact, deceit is also twofold. For sometimes, after having used deceit at first, they change the constitution while the consent of the others is voluntary, and then later keep hold of it by force, when the consent of the others is involuntary—for example, the Four Hundred deceived the Athenian people by telling them that the King of Persia would provide money for the war against the Spartans, and, having deceived them, tried to keep the constitution in their own hands.[611] At other times, they persuade them from the start, and later on again, due to their being persuaded, rule them with their voluntary consent.

Putting it simply, then, changes occur in all constitutions on the basis of what has been stated.

V 5

We must now take each kind (*eidos*) of constitution separately and, on the basis of what has been stated, get a theoretical grasp on what happens to it.

Well, democracies undergo change mostly because of the wanton behavior of popular leaders. For sometimes they bring malicious lawsuits against owners of substantial private property, causing them to join forces, since a common fear brings together even the bitterest enemies, and sometimes publicly setting the multitude on them. One may see this sort of thing happening in many cases. In Cos the democracy was overthrown when wicked popular leaders arose (for the notables united [against them]).[612] In Rhodes the popular leaders provided pay [to the people], preventing the naval officials from getting what they were owed, and so the latter, because of the lawsuits brought against them, were then compelled to join together and overthrow the democracy.[613] In Heraclea, right after the colony was settled, the democracy was overthrown because of its popular leaders.[614] For the notables were treated unjustly by them and went into exile, but later on the exiles grouped together, returned home, and overthrew the democracy. And the democracy in Megara was overthrown in a somewhat similar way.[615] For the popular leaders expelled many of the notables in order to have wealth to confiscate, until they made the exiles numerous. The exiles then returned, defeated the people in battle, and put in place an oligarchy. The same thing happened to the democracy in Cyme, which was overthrown by Thrasymachus.[616] And if one got a theoretical grasp on them, one would see in the case of other cities as well that changes occur in pretty much this way. For popular leaders, in order to gratify the people, sometimes treat the notables unjustly, by redistributing their properties or their profits by means of public services, and cause them to join together, and sometimes they bring slanderous accusations in order to be able to confiscate the property of the rich.[617]

In ancient times, whenever the same person was both a popular leader and a general, democracies changed to tyranny. For pretty much most ancient tyrants arose from popular leaders.[618] The cause of this happening then but not now is that then popular leaders used to come from the ranks of those who held the office of general (for no one was as yet skilled at public speaking). Now, however, with the development of rhetoric, those who are able public speakers become popular leaders. But because of their inexperience in military matters, they do not try to make an attack on anyone, although a few cases of this sort may have occurred somewhere.

Tyrannies also arose more frequently in former times than they do now because important offices were in the hands of certain individuals, as in Miletus, where a tyranny arose out of the presidency, because the president had control of many important matters.[619] Further, cities were not large then and the people lived on their farms and were unleisured because of their need to work, so whenever the leaders of the people became skilled warriors they attempted to put in place a tyranny. They all did this after gaining the people's trust, and this trust was due to their hatred of the rich. For example, in Athens Pisistratus [was thought to deserve to be tyrant] because he engaged in faction against the plains-dwellers, and in Megara, Theagenes, because he slaughtered the rich men's cattle when he caught them grazing by the river.[620] And Dionysius was thought worthy of the tyranny for prosecuting Daphnaeus and the rich—because of his hostility, he was trusted as someone who believes in democracy.[621]

Democracies also change from ancestral democracies into democracies of the most recent sort. For when officials are elected, but not on the basis of property assessments, and the people do the electing, those eager for office, by currying favor with them, bring matters to this point, namely, that the people have control even over the laws. A remedy, so that this does not occur, or occurs less often, is to have the tribes, and not the people as a whole, nominate the officials.

Pretty much all the changes in democracies, then, happen due to these causes.

V 6

Oligarchies mostly undergo change in two ways that are most evident. [1a] One is when they treat the multitude unjustly, since in this situation anyone proves to be an adequate leader, especially when he comes from the oligarchy itself, like Lygdamis of Naxos, who actually became tyrant of the Naxians later on.[622] As for faction that takes its starting-point from others, it also admits of differences (*diaphora*). [1b] For sometimes the overthrow comes from the rich themselves, although not from the ones in office, when those enjoying the honors of office are altogether few. This occurred in Massilia, Istrus, Heraclea, and other cities.[623] For those who did not share in office agitated until first elder brothers and later in turn the younger ones were admitted. (For in some cities, a father and son, and in others, an elder and younger brother, may not hold office at the same time.) And there in Massilia the oligarchy became more like a polity, whereas the one in Istrus ended in a democracy, and the one in Heraclea went from a small number to six hundred. [1c] In Cnidus, too, the oligarchy changed when the notables were engaged in faction among themselves because so few shared in office and because, as was mentioned, if a father shared, his son could not do so, nor, if there were several brothers, could any do so except the eldest.[624] For while the notables were engaged in faction, the people seized the opportunity, picked one of the notables as their leader, attacked, and were victorious, since what is engaged in faction is weak. And in Erythrae in ancient times, during the oligarchy of the Basilids, even though those with control of the constitution supervised things well, the people nevertheless resented being ruled by a few and changed the constitution.[625]

[2a] Oligarchies also undergo change from within through the rivalry of those engaged in currying favor.[626] This popular leadership is twofold. [2a–i] One exists among the oligarchs themselves, since a popular leader can arise even when they are very few. For example, among the Thirty in Athens Charicles and his followers became powerful by currying favor with the Thirty, and likewise in the time of the Four Hundred with Phrynichus and his followers.[627] [2a–ii] Or it may take place when the oligarchs curry favor with the mob. For example, in Larissa the civic guards sought popularity with the mob because it elected them.[628] And it is the same in all oligarchies where those who elect to office are not those from whom the officials are drawn, but offices are filled either from those with high property assessments or those who belong to certain political clubs, while the electors are either those who possess hoplite weapons or—as it was in Abydus—the people.[629] It also happens wherever juries are not drawn from the governing body, since, by currying their favor in order to influence judicial decisions, the oligarchs change the constitution—which is just what occurred in Heraclea on the Black Sea.[630] [2a–iii] Further, it occurs when some draw the oligarchy into fewer hands, since those who want equality are compelled to bring in the people to assist them.

[2b] Changes in oligarchy also occur when some of the oligarchs spend away their private resources on loose living. For such people seek to stir up change, and either aim at tyranny themselves or establish someone else as tyrant, as Hipparinus did for Dionysius in Syracuse.[631] In Amphipolis, a man named Cleotimus brought in late-colonists from among the Chalcidians and, after they arrived, started factional conflict between them and the rich.[632] In Aegina, the man who conducted the transaction with Chares tried to overthrow the constitution due to this sort of cause.[633] Sometimes such people try to make changes straightaway, whereas sometimes they steal public funds. In the latter case either they themselves or those who are opposed to their stealing engage in faction against the oligarchs, which is just what happened in Apollonia on the Black Sea.[634] An oligarchy that is in concord, however, is not prone to destruction from within.[635] An indication of this is the constitution in Pharsalus.[636] For though the oligarchs are few in number, they have control of many because they treat each other well.

[2c] Oligarchies are also overthrown when they produce another oligarchy within the oligarchy. This happens when, though the entire governing body consists of only a few people, not all of these few share in the most important offices, which is just what happened at one time in Elis.[637] For though the constitution was in the hands of a few, very few of them became senators, because the senators, who numbered

only ninety, held permanent office, and because their election was characteristic of a dynasty and similar to the one used to elect the senators in Sparta.[638]

[2d] Change in oligarchies occurs both in wartime and in peacetime. [2d–i] It occurs in wartime when the oligarchs are compelled, because of their distrust of the people, to employ mercenaries, since the man placed in command of them often becomes a tyrant, like Timophanes in Corinth.[639] And if several men are placed in command, they often set up a dynasty for themselves. Sometimes fear of these consequences leads the oligarchs to give a share of the constitution to the multitude, because they are compelled to make use of the people. [2d–ii] In peacetime, because of their distrust of each other, the oligarchs put the guarding of the city in the hands of mercenaries and a neutral official, who sometimes gains control of both sides. This is exactly what happened in Larissa at the time of the rule of Simus the Aleuad, and in Abydus at the time of the political clubs, one of which was that of Iphiades.[640]

[2e] Factions also arise when some members of an oligarchy are rejected by others in connection with marriages and lawsuits and are driven to engage in faction—for example, the cases mentioned earlier in which marriage was the cause.[641] And Diagoras overthrew the oligarchy of the cavalrymen in Eretria because he was treated unjustly in connection with a marriage.[642] The factions in Heraclea and Thebes arose because of a judgment in law court, when Eurytion (in Heraclea) and Archias (in Thebes) were justly but factiously punished for adultery by the courts.[643] For their enemies loved rivalry to the point that they had them bound in the pillory in the marketplace.[644]

[2f] Many have also been overthrown by those in the constitution who became disgusted because the oligarchies were too much like the rule of a master, like the one in Cnidus and the one in Chios.[645]

But changes also occur because of mischance both in so-called polities and in oligarchies, where eligibility for the council, the courts, and the other offices is based on a property assessment. For often the first assessment is set to suit existing circumstances, so that only a few will share in the oligarchy and only those in the middle class in the polity. But when peace or some other sort of good luck leads to prosperity, properties come to be assessed at many times their original value, so that all the citizens share in all the offices. Sometimes the change happens because of a small difference and is unnoticed, while sometimes it happens more quickly.

Oligarchies change and engage in faction, then, due to these sorts of causes. In general, though, both democracies and oligarchies sometimes change not into the opposing constitutions but into others of the same kind (*genos*)—for example, from democracies and oligarchies based on law into those with [complete] control, and vice versa.

V 7

[1a] In aristocracies factions arise in some cases because few people share in office, which is just what is said to change oligarchies as well, because aristocracy too is in a way oligarchy.[646] For the rulers are few in both, although not because of the same thing. At any rate, this is why an aristocracy too is thought to be an oligarchy. This necessarily happens above all [1a–i] when there is a group of people who presume themselves equal in virtue to the ruling few—for example, the so-called Sons of the Maidens at Sparta (for they were descended from the Equals), who, when discovered in a conspiracy, were sent off to colonize Tarentum.[647] Or it happens [1a–ii] when powerful men, who are inferior to no one in virtue, are dishonored by others who are held in greater honor, as Lysander was by the kings.[648] Or it happens [1a–iii] when a man of courage does not share in office, like Cinadon, who instigated the rebellion against the Spartiates in the reign of Agesilaus.[649] Or, again, factions arise [1b] when some people are very poor and others very rich, as happens especially in wartime. This also happened in Sparta at the time of the Messenian War (this is clear from the poem of Tyrtaeus called "Good Legislative Order"), since those who were hard pressed because of the war demanded a redistribution 1307a1
of the land.[650] Or, again, [1c] when there is a powerful man capable of becoming yet more powerful, who engages in faction in order to become sole ruler—just as Pausanias (who was general during the Persian Wars) seems to have done in Sparta, and Hanno in Carthage.[651]

[2] Polities and aristocracies are mostly overthrown, however, because of a deviation from what is just within the constitution itself. For the starting-point of overthrow in a polity is that democracy and oligarchy are not mixed well, and in an aristocracy, these two and virtue as well, but especially the two. I mean by the two, democracy and oligarchy, since it is these that polities and most so-called aristocracies try to mix. For aristocracies differ from what are called polities in this respect, and this is why the former of them are less and the latter more stable. For those constitutions that lean more toward oligarchy get called aristocracies, whereas those that lean more toward democracy get called polities. That is why, indeed, the latter sort are more secure than the former. For the majority are the stronger party and they are more content with an equal share; whereas if those living in riches are granted superiority by the constitution, they try to be wantonly aggressive and get more for themselves.

In general, whichever direction a constitution leans toward is the direction in which it changes when either party grows in power—for example, polity into democracy and aristocracy into oligarchy. Or they are changed into their contraries—for example, aristocracy into democracy (since the poorer people, on the supposition that they are being unjustly treated, pull it around to its contrary), and polity into oligarchy (for what is alone steadfast is equality in accord with worth and the having of what is one's own). The aforementioned change occurred at Thurii.[652] For, because the property assessment for holding office was rather high, a shift was made to a smaller one and to a larger number of offices. But because the notables illegally acquired all the land (for the constitution was still too oligarchic), they were able as a result to get more . . .[653] But the people, who had received military training during the war, became stronger than the garrison troops, until those who had more of the land than the law allowed gave it up.

Further, [3] because all aristocratic constitutions are oligarchic in character, the notables in them especially tend to get more—for example, even in Sparta properties keep passing into fewer and fewer hands. Also, the notables are absolutely free to do as they please and make marriage alliances as they please. That is why the city of the Locrians was destroyed, indeed, because a marriage alliance was formed with the tyrant Dionysius, something that would not have occurred in a democracy or a well-mixed aristocracy.[654]

[4] Most of all, however, aristocracies are apt to change unnoticed by being overturned because of a small difference, which is precisely what was said earlier about all constitutions universally, namely, that even a small difference may cause them to change.[655] For once one thing relating to the constitution is abandoned, after this people can more easily change something that is in a small degree larger, until they change the entire order. This also happened in the case of the constitution of Thurii.[656] For the law allowed the same man to be general only after a five-year interval. But when some of the young men showed military ability and were held in high repute by the multitude of garrison troops, they came to have contempt for the men who were in charge of affairs, and thought that they themselves could easily prevail. Hence they first undertook to abrogate this law, so as to make it possible for the same men to serve as generals continuously, since they saw that the people would vote for them with enthusiasm. The officials in charge of such matters, the so-called councilors, were at first inclined to oppose this. But they were won over, because they thought that once this law was changed, the rest of the constitution would be left intact. Later, however, when they wished to prevent other things from being changed,

they were no longer able to do anything more, but the entire order characteristic of the constitution was changed into a dynasty ruled by those men who had begun the process of stirring up change.

All constitutions are subject to change (sometimes from within, sometimes from outside), however, when there is a contrary constitution either nearby or far away but powerful. This is what happened in the time of the Athenian and Spartan empires. For everywhere the Athenians overthrew oligarchies, the Spartans democracies.

Where changes and factions in constitutions come from, then, has now been pretty much discussed.

V 8

Our next topic is preservation in general and of each sort of constitution separately. [1] Now it is clear, in the first place, that if we know what things destroy a constitution, we also know what things preserve it. For contraries are productive of contrary things, and destruction is contrary to preservation. In well-mixed constitutions, then, just as care should above all be taken to ensure that no one breaks the law in other ways, small [violations] should be especially guarded against. For illegality creeps in unnoticed, in just the way that property gets used up by frequent small expenditures. The expense goes unnoticed because it does not occur all at once. For thought is led to reason fallaciously by them, as in the sophistical argument, "if each is small, so too are all." In one way this is true; in another false. For the whole composed of all the parts is not small, but it is composed of small parts. One thing to guard against, then, is destruction that has a starting-point of this sort.

[2] Next, we must not put our trust in the subtle devices put together for the sake of deceiving the multitude, since they are refuted by the facts. (As to which sort of subtle devices in constitutions we mean, this 1308a1
was discussed earlier.[657])

[3] Next, we should notice that not only some aristocracies but also some oligarchies survive, not because their constitutions are secure, but because those in office treat well both those outside the constitution and those in the governing body. They treat well those who do not share in the constitution by not being unjust toward them, and by bringing their leading men into it. And they treat well those who love honor by not being unjust to them in terms of dishonor, or to the many in terms of profit. As for themselves, the ones who do share—they treat each other in a democratic manner. For what democrats seek to extend to the multitude, namely, equality, is not only just but also advantageous for those who are similar. That is why, if the governing body

is large, many democratic legislative measures prove advantageous—for example, having offices be tenable for six months, in order that all those who are similar may share in them. For those who are similar are already a sort of people, which is why popular leaders arise even among them, as we mentioned earlier.[658] Further, [with such legislative measures] oligarchies and aristocracies are less likely to fall into dynasties. For officials who rule for a short time cannot so easily do evil as those who rule for a long time, since this is what causes tyrannies to arise in oligarchies and democracies. For either the most important men in the two constitutions aim at tyranny (popular leaders in democracies, dynasts in oligarchies), or those who hold the most important offices do so, when they hold them for a long time.

[4] Constitutions are preserved not only because of being far away from the factors that destroy them, but sometimes even by being nearby.[659] For fear makes people keep a firmer grip on the constitution. So those who are concerned about their constitution should manufacture fears—so that the citizens defend the constitution, and, like sentries on night-duty, never relax their guard—and make faraway dangers seem close at hand.

[5] Further, one should try to guard against the rivalries and factions of the notables, both by means of the laws and by preventing those who are not involved in the rivalry from getting caught up in it themselves. For to recognize an evil right from the start of its emerging takes no random person but rather a man of politics.

[6] As regards change from an oligarchy or a polity because of property assessments, if it occurs while the assessments remain the same but money becomes more plentiful, it is advantageous to investigate the total communal assessment in comparison with that of the past—in those cities with an annual assessment with that of last year's, in larger cities with
1308b1 that of three or five years ago. If the total is many times greater or many times less than it was when the rates qualifying someone to share in the constitution were put in place, it is advantageous to have a law that tightens or loosens the assessment—tightening it in proportion to the increase if the total has increased, loosening it or making it less if the total has decreased.[660] For when oligarchies and polities do not do this, the result, if the total has decreased, is that an oligarchy arises from the latter and a dynasty from the former, and, if it has increased, a democracy arises from a polity and either a polity or a democracy from an oligarchy.

[7] It is something common in democracy, oligarchy, in monarchy, and every constitution, not to allow anyone to grow too great or out of all due proportion, but to try to give small honors over a long period of time rather than large ones quickly.[661] For people are corrupted by

major honors, and not every man can handle good luck. Failing that, constitutions should at least try not to take away all at once honors that have been awarded all at once, but to do so gradually. Also, they should above all try to regulate matters by means of the laws, so as to ensure that no one arises who is greatly superior in power because of his friends or wealth. Failing this, they should make their banishments be banishments to foreign parts.[662]

[8] But since people also attempt to stir up change because of their private lives, an office should be set up to keep an eye on those whose ways of living are disadvantageous to the constitution, whether to the democracy in a democracy, to the oligarchy in an oligarchy, or similarly for each of the other constitutions.

[9] Due to the same causes one must also guard against the city's flourishing only in regard to one of its parts. A remedy for this is always to place actions and offices in the hands of opposing parts—I mean that the decent are opposite to the multitude, and the poor to the rich. Another remedy is to try to mix together the multitude of the poor and that of the rich or to increase the middle class, since this dissolves factions caused by inequality.

[10] But the most important thing in every constitution is for it to have the laws and the management of other matters ordered in such a way that it is not possible for the offices to make a profit.[663] One should pay particular heed to this in oligarchies. For the many do not so much resent being excluded from office, and are even glad to be given the leisure to attend to their private affairs, but they do resent it when they think that officials are stealing public funds. At any rate, they are then pained both at not sharing in office and at not sharing in the profits. Indeed, the only way it is possible for democracy and aristocracy to coexist is if someone were to establish this [law and management], since it would then be possible for both the notables and the multitude to have what they wish for. For allowing everyone to hold office is democratic, **1309b1**
but having the notables actually be in the offices is aristocratic. And this is what will happen on the condition that it is impossible to profit from office. For the poor will not want to hold office, because there is no profit in it, but they will prefer to attend to their private affairs, whereas the rich will be able to hold it, because they need no support from public funds. The result will be that the poor will become rich through spending their time on their work, while the notables will not be ruled by random people. To prevent public funds from being stolen, then, the handing over of the money should take place in the presence of all the citizens, and copies of the accounts should be deposited with each clan, company, and tribe.[664] And to ensure that people will hold office without

seeking profit there should be a law that assigns honors to officials who are well reputed.

[11] In democracies, the rich should be treated with restraint—not only by not having their property redistributed, but by not having their profits redistributed either (as happens unnoticed in some constitutions). It is also better to prevent the rich, even if they wish to do so, from taking on expensive but useless public services, such as paying for choruses, for superintendence at torch-races, and other things of the same sort.[665]

[12] In an oligarchy, on the other hand, one should take great care of the poor, and distribute the offices to them that yield some gain. And if one of the rich treats them with wanton aggression, his punishment should be greater than if he does this to his own lot. Also, inheritances should not be passed in accord with a bequest but in accord with family, and the same person should not receive more than one inheritance. In this way, property-holdings would be more equitable, and more of the poor could join the ranks of the rich. It is advantageous, both in democracy and in oligarchy, to give either equality or precedence in all other matters to those who share least in the constitution—the rich in a democracy and the poor in an oligarchy. But the offices that have control of the constitution should be kept solely or largely in the hands of those who are from the constitution.

V 9

[13] Those who are to hold the controlling offices should possess three qualities: first, friendship toward the constitution that is in place; next, great capacity for the functions of the office; third, virtue and justice of the sort that in each constitution is with a view to the constitution. (For if what is just is not the same in all constitutions, there must be differences in the virtue of justice as well.)

But there is a puzzle, when all these qualities are not found in the same person, about how the choice is to be made. For example, if one man knows generalship but is wicked and no friend to the constitution, whereas another is just and friendly to it, how should the choice be made? It seems that one should look to two things: which of these qualities does everyone share in more and which less? That is why, in the case of the office of general, one should look to experience more than to virtue. For everyone shares in generalship less, but in decency more. In the case of guardianship or stewardship, on the other hand, the contrary holds. For these require more virtue than most possess, but the scientific knowledge they require is common to all.[666]

One might, though, raise this puzzle: if someone has the capacity for office as well as friendship toward the constitution, why does he also need virtue? For even the first two will produce what is advantageous. Or is it possible for someone who possesses these two qualities to lack self-control, so that just as people can fail to serve their own interests well, even though they have the knowledge and are friendly to themselves, so nothing prevents them from being the same way where the community is concerned?[667]

[14] Simply speaking, whatever features in laws we describe as advantageous to constitutions all preserve those constitutions, as does the most important element, so often mentioned, of keeping watch that the multitude wishing for the constitution is stronger than the one that does not wish for it.[668]

[15] In addition to all these features, one thing must not be overlooked, which is in fact overlooked by the deviant constitutions, namely, the mean. For many of the features that are believed to be democratic destroy democracies, and many that are believed to be oligarchic destroy oligarchies.[669] Those who think that this is the one and only virtue pull the constitution toward the extreme.[670] They are ignorant of the fact that just as a nose that deviates from the most noble straightness toward being hooked or snub can nevertheless still be noble and please the eye, if it is "tightened" still more toward the extreme, the part will first be thrown out of due proportion, and in the end will appear not to be a nose at all, because it has too much of one and too little of the other of these contraries.[671] And it is the same way with the other parts [of the body] as well. This, then, can also happen in the case of the constitutions. For it is also possible for an oligarchy or a democracy to be adequate even though it has diverged from the best order. But if someone tightens either of them more, he will first make the constitution worse, and in the end make it not be a constitution at all. That is why legislators and politicians should not be ignorant about which democratic features preserve a democracy and which destroy it, or which oligarchic features preserve or destroy an oligarchy. For neither of these constitutions can exist and endure without rich people and the multitude, but when a leveling of property occurs, the resulting constitution is necessarily of a different sort, so that by destroying these by laws carried to excess, they destroy their constitutions.

[16] An error, though, is made in both democracies and oligarchies. In democracies popular leaders err wherever the multitude have control of the laws. For they always divide the city in two by fighting with the rich, yet they should do the contrary, and always be regarded as spokesmen for the rich. In oligarchies, the oligarchs should be

regarded as spokesmen for the people, and should take oaths that are the contrary of the ones they take now. For in some oligarchies, they now swear, "and I will be hostile to the people and will plan whatever wrongs I can against them."[672] But they ought to hold and give the impression that they hold the contrary view, and declare in their oaths that "I will not wrong the people."

[17] But the most important of all the ways that have been mentioned to make a constitution endure, which as things stand everyone has contempt for, is for citizens to be educated in a way that looks to their constitutions. For the most beneficial laws, even when ratified by all who are engaged in politics, are of no benefit if people are not habituated and educated in the constitution—democratically if the laws are democratic and oligarchically if they are oligarchic. For if indeed lack of self-control exists at the level of a single individual, it also exists at the level of a city.[673]

But to have been educated in a way that looks to the constitution does not mean this: doing whatever pleases the oligarchs or those who wish for a democracy. Rather, it means doing the things that will enable the former to govern oligarchically and the latter to govern themselves democratically. In present-day oligarchies, however, the sons of the rulers live in luxury, whereas the sons of the poor are hardened by exercise and toil, so that the poor are more inclined to stir up change and better able to do so. In those democracies, though, that are held to be especially democratic, the very contrary of what is advantageous has been put in place. The cause of this is that they define freedom incorrectly. For there are two things by which democracy is believed to be defined, namely, by the majority being in control and by freedom. For the just is believed to consist in equality, and what the multitude believes to be equal is believed to be in control, and freedom is believed to be doing whatever one wishes. So in democracies of this sort everyone lives as he wishes, and "for what he craves," as Euripides says.[674] But this is base. For living with a view to the constitution should not be considered slavery, but preservation.[675]

The sources of change and destruction in constitutions, then, and the features because of which they are preserved and endure, are simply speaking just about this many.

V 10

It remains to go also through monarchy, both the sources of its destruction and the features because of which it is naturally preserved. What happens in the case of kingships and tyrannies, though, is pretty much

similar to what we said happens in constitutions. For kingship is in 1310b1
accord with aristocracy, and tyranny is a combination of the lastmost oligarchy and the lastmost democracy.[676] That is why, indeed, tyranny is also the most harmful to those it rules, inasmuch as it is composed of two bad constitutions and involves the deviations and errors of both.

The coming to be of each of these sorts of monarchy lies from the start in contrary sources. For kingship arose to provide help for the decent against the people, and a king is appointed from among the decent men on the basis of a superiority in virtue, or in the actions that spring from virtue, or in accord with a superiority in a family of this sort.[677] A tyrant, on the other hand, is appointed from the people (that is to say, the multitude) to oppose the notables, so that the people may suffer no injustice at their hands. This is evident from what has happened. For (one might almost say) pretty much all tyrants have come into being from popular leaders, who came to be trusted by slandering the notables. For some tyrannies were put in place in this way in cities that had already grown large, whereas other earlier ones arose from kings who deviated from ancestral customs and sought to rule more as a master does. Others were put in place by people elected to the offices that have supreme control (for in ancient times, the people appointed "doers of the people's business" and "sacred ambassadors" to serve for long periods of time).[678] Still others arose in oligarchies that gave a single elected official control of the most important offices. For in all these ways people could easily become tyrants, if only they wished, because of the power they already possessed through the kingship or through other offices of honor. Thus Pheidon of Argos and others became tyrants while there was already a kingship; the Ionian tyrants and Phalaris as a result of their high office; and Panaetius in Leontini, Cypselus in Corinth, Pisistratus in Athens, Dionysius in Syracuse , and likewise others, from popular leadership.[679]

As we said, then, kingship is an order that is in accord with aristocracy, since it is in accord with worth, whether this is individual virtue or that of family, or in accord with benefactions, or these together with capacity.[680] For all those who obtained this office either had benefited, or had the capacity to benefit, their cities or nations. Some, like Codrus, saved their people from enslavement in war; others, like Cyrus, set them free; others settled or acquired territory, like the kings of the Spartans, Macedonians, and Molossians.[681]

A king wishes to be a guardian in order that property owners suffer
no injustice and the people no wanton aggression. But tyranny, as has 1311a1
often been said, looks to no common [advantage] except for the sake of private benefit. And the aim characteristic of tyranny is the pleasant, whereas the aim characteristic of kingship is the noble. That is also why

it is characteristic of a tyrant to want to get more wealth, and of a king to get more of the things pertaining to honor.[682] Also, a king's bodyguard consists of citizens, whereas a tyrant's consists of foreigners.[683]

It is evident, then, that tyranny has the evils both of democracy and of oligarchy. From oligarchy comes its taking wealth to be its end (for, in fact, only in this way can the tyrant possibly maintain his bodyguard and his luxury), and its mistrust of the multitude. That is why, in fact, tyrants deprive them of weapons, and why mistreating the mob, driving them out of the town, and dispersing them is common to both constitutions, to oligarchy as well as to tyranny. From democracy on the other hand comes its making war on the notables, its destroying them by both covert and overt means, and its exiling of them as rivals in the craft [of ruling] and impediments to its rule. For it is from the notables that conspiracies arise, since some of them wish themselves to rule, and others not to be enslaved. Hence too the advice that Periander gave to Thrasybulus when he cut down the tallest ears of corn, namely, that it is always necessary to do away with the citizens who exhibit a superiority.[684]

As has pretty much been said, then, one should consider the starting-points of change both in constitutions and in monarchies to be the same. For it is because of injustice, because of fear, and because of contempt that many of those who are ruled attack monarchies—in the case of injustice, it is mostly because of wanton aggression, but sometimes too because of the seizure of private property. The ends sought are also the same there as in tyrannies and kingships, since monarchs possess the great wealth and honors of office, which everyone desires.

Now, some attacks are directed against the body of the rulers, others against the office. Those caused by wanton aggression are directed against the body. And though wanton aggression is of many sorts, each of them is a cause of anger; and most angry people act for the sake of revenge, not for the sake of attaining superiority. For example, the attack on the Pisistratids took place because they abused Harmodius' sister and showed contempt for Harmodius himself (for Harmodius attacked because of his sister, and Aristogeiton because of Harmodius).[685] People plotted against Periander, tyrant of Ambracia, because once while drinking with his boyfriend, Periander asked whether he was pregnant by him yet.[686] Philip was attacked by Pausanias because he allowed him to be treated with wanton aggression by Attalus and his coterie. Amyntas the Little was attacked by Derdas because he boasted of having deflowered him.[687] The same is true of the attack on Evagoras of Cyprus by a eunuch; he felt he was treated with wanton aggression because Evagoras' son had taken away his wife.[688]

Many attacks have also occurred because of the shameful treatment of the bodies of others by certain monarchs. The attack on Archelaus by Crataeas is an example.[689] For Crataeas always felt burdened by their sexual intercourse, so that even a lesser pretext would have been enough, or perhaps he did it because Archelaus did not give him one of his daughters in marriage, though he had agreed to do so. (Instead, when hard-pressed in the war against Sirras and Arrabaeus, he gave his elder daughter to the king of Elimeia and the younger one to his own son Amyntas, thinking that this would be likely to prevent Amyntas from quarreling with his son by Cleopatra.[690]) In any case, the *starting-point* of Crataeas' estrangement was that he felt burdened by his intercourse with Archelaus. And Hellanocrates of Larisa joined him in the attack for the same reason. For because Archelaus deflowered him and then persistently refused to return him to his home as promised, he thought that the king's intercourse with him was due to wanton aggression rather than to sexual appetite. Python and Heracleides of Aenus, on the other hand, killed Cotys to avenge their father, whereas Adamas revolted on the grounds of wanton aggression, because he had been castrated by Cotys when he was a boy.[691]

Many people, too, angered because their bodies have been tormented by blows, have killed or tried to kill, on the grounds of being treated with wanton aggression, even those who held office or were associated with kingly dynasties. For example, when the Penthilids of Mytilene went around beating up people with clubs, Megacles and his friends attacked and killed them.[692] Later, Smerdes killed Penthilus because he had beaten him and dragged him away from his wife.[693] Decamnichus became leader of the revolt against Archelaus, being the first to incite his adversaries—the cause of his anger was that Archelaus had handed him over to the poet Euripides for flogging (Euripides was enraged by a remark made about his bad breath).[694] Many others have been killed or plotted against due to causes such as these.

Similar attacks also occur because of fear, which is a cause of change in monarchies and constitutions, as we mentioned.[695] For example, Artapanes killed Xerxes, fearing a charge in connection with the murder of Darius, namely, that he hanged him without being ordered to do so by Xerxes, but thinking that Xerxes, not remembering on account of his dining, would pardon him.[696]

Other attacks are because of contempt, as when someone saw
Sardanapalus carding wool with the women, if what the storytellers **1312a1**
say is true (though if this is not true of him, it might well be true of someone else).[697] And Dion attacked Dionysius the Younger because of contempt, when he saw that the citizens shared his feelings, and that

Dionysius himself was always drunk.[698] Even some friends make an attack because of contempt. For because they are trusted, they feel contempt, thinking that they will not be discovered. And those who think they have the power to take over the rule attack because of contempt in a way. For because of their power, and the contempt for danger that their power gives them, they readily make their attempt. Thus generals attack monarchs. For example, Cyrus attacked Astyages because of contempt both for his way of life and for his power, which had declined while he was living in luxury.[699] And Seuthes the Thracian attacked Amadocus while he was his general.[700]

Others attack monarchs from several of these motives—for example, both because of contempt and because of profit—as Mithridates attacked Ariobarzanes.[701] {Attempts of this sort are made mostly by those of a bold nature, who are assigned to military office by monarchs, since courage possessed of power is boldness, and it is because of both of these that people attack, thinking that they will easily prevail.[702]}[703]

With those who attack because of love of honor, however, the cause operates in another way that is beyond those previously discussed. For, although some attack tyrants because they see great profit and high office in store for themselves, this is not why someone whose attack is motivated by love of honor deliberately chooses to take the risk. It is rather that, whereas the former attack due to the causes mentioned, the latter, just as they would undertake any other extraordinary action through which people become famous and notable in the eyes of others, in the same way attack monarchs because they wish to gain not a monarchy but a reputation. But then those who are impelled by this sort of cause are, to be sure, very few in number, since it presupposes giving no thought to their own preservation should the action fail. They must follow, then, the supposition of Dion, which is not easy for most people to do.[704] For accompanied by a few followers he marched against Dionysius, saying that whatever point he was able to reach, he would be satisfied to have shared that much in the action, and that if, for example, he were killed just after having just set foot on land, that death would be a noble one for him.

One way, though, that a tyranny is destroyed, just as each of the other constitutions is as well, is from the outside, if there happens to be
1312b1 a stronger constitution contrary to it. For the wish to destroy a tyranny will clearly be present, because of the contrariety between the deliberate choices of the two constitutions, and because all people do what they wish when they have the power.[705] The contrary constitutions are on the one hand democracy—as "potter to potter," as Hesiod says (for the ultimate democracy is in fact a tyranny)—and on the other hand

kingship and aristocracy, because of the contrariety between these constitutions.[706] That is why the Spartans overthrew a large number of tyrannies, as did the Syracusans during the time when they were governed in a good way.[707]

Another way a tyranny is destroyed is from within itself, when those sharing in it engage in faction, as happened in the tyranny of those around Gelon and, in our own time, in the tyranny of those around Dionysius. The tyranny of Gelon was destroyed when Thrasybulus, the brother of Hiero, curried favor with Gelon's son and impelled him toward pleasures, in order that he himself might rule.[708] The family joined together to destroy not the entire tyranny, but Thrasybulus. But those who joined with them seized the opportunity and expelled all of them. Dion, who was related by marriage to Dionysius, marched against him, won over the people, and expelled him, but was himself killed afterwards.[709]

There are two causes, though, due to which people mostly attack tyrannies, namely, hatred and contempt. But though one of these—namely, hatred—always attaches to tyrants, it is from contempt that many of their overthrows come about. An indication of this is that (one might almost say) most of those who won the office of tyrant held onto it, whereas their successors lose it straightaway. For living lives of indulgence, they readily became contemptible and gave others ample opportunity to attack them.[710] And anger should also be taken as a part of hatred, since in a way it gives rise to the same sorts of actions.[711] Often, in fact, it is more conducive to action than hatred. For angry people attack more vehemently because passion does not make use of rational calculation.[712] It happens, though, that people are particularly led by their spirited feelings because of wanton aggression—which was the cause of the overthrow of the tyranny of the Pisistratids as well as of many others.[713] But hatred employs rational calculation more than anger does. For anger involves pain, so that it is not easy to rationally calculate, whereas hatred does not involve pain.[714]

To speak summarily, the causes that we said destroy unmixed or ultimate oligarchies and ultimate democracies should also be regarded as destroying tyranny.[715] For these are in fact divided tyrannies.[716]

Kingship is destroyed least by outside factors, which is also why it is long-lasting. The sources of its destruction in most cases come from within. It is destroyed in two ways. In one, when those who share in the kingship engage in faction, and in another way when the kings try to **1313a1** manage affairs in a more tyrannical fashion, claiming that they deserve to have control of too many areas and contrary to the law. Kingships no longer arise now, but if any do happen to occur, they tend more to be tyrannical monarchies. This is because kingship is rule with the voluntary consent of the ruled and has control of more important matters. But now there are numerous men of equal quality, although none so superior as to measure up to the magnitude and worth of the office of king. So because of this people do not voluntarily put up with this sort of rule. And if someone comes to rule through force or deceit, this already seems to be tyranny.

In the case of hereditary kingships, there is something besides the factors already mentioned that should be held to be a cause of their destruction, namely, that hereditary kings easily become objects of contempt and (even though they do not possess tyrannical power but honorable kingly office) commit wanton aggression. For their overthrow was easy. For when the ones ruled do not wish it he will straightaway not be a king, but the tyrant rules even when they do not wish it.[717]

Monarchies are destroyed, then, due to these and other such causes.

V 11

It is clear that monarchies are, simply speaking, preserved by the contrary causes, and kingships in particular by drawing them toward greater moderation. For the fewer areas over which kings have control, the longer must their office endure. For they themselves become less like masters, more equal in their characters, and less envied by those they rule. This is why, in fact, the kingships of the Molossians lasted a long time, and that of the Spartans as well.[718] In the latter case it was because the office was divided into two parts from the start, and again because Theopompus, besides moderating it in other ways, in addition put in place the office of the overseers.[719] By diminishing the power of the kingship he increased it in terms of duration, so that in a way he made it greater, not lesser. Just this, in fact, is what they say he replied to his wife when she asked him whether he was not ashamed to hand over a lesser kingship to his sons than the one he had inherited from his father: "Certainly not," he said, "for I am handing over one that will be longer lasting."

Tyrannies are preserved in two entirely contrary ways. [1] One of them is traditional and is the way most tyrants exercise their rule. Many of these are said to have been established by Periander of Corinth, but many of this sort may also be seen in the Persian empire. These include both the one we mentioned some time ago as tending to preserve tyranny (to the extent that it can be), namely, [1a] cutting down the superior men and doing away with the self-confident ones.[720] Also, [1b] not allowing communal messes, political clubs, education, and other things of that sort. [1c] Guarding against everything that is wont to engender two things, namely, self-confidence and mutual trust. [1d] Not allowing places of leisure and other leisurely gatherings, and doing everything to ensure that people are as ignorant of each other as possible, since familiarity tends to produce mutual trust.[721] [1e] Also, requiring those residing in the town to be always in [public] view and to pass their time at the palace gates, since that way the actions they do will be hard to keep secret and they will be habituated to think humble thoughts by always doing slavish service.[722] [1f] Also, imposing all the other restrictions of a similar nature that are found in Persian and barbarian tyrannies (for they are all capable of producing the same effect).

[1g] Another is trying to let nothing done or said by any of his subjects escape notice, but to retain spies, like the so-called women informers of Syracuse, or the eavesdroppers that Hiero sent to every meeting or gathering.[723] For people speak less freely when they fear the presence of such spies, and if they do speak freely, they are less likely to go unnoticed. [1h] Another is to slander people to each other, setting friend against friend, the people against the notables, and the rich against the rich themselves.

[1i] It is also tyrannical to impoverish the people, so that they cannot afford a militia and are so occupied with their daily work that they lack the leisure for plotting.[724] The pyramids of Egypt, the Cypselid monuments, the construction of the temple of Olympian Zeus by the Pisistratids, and the works on Samos commissioned by Polycrates are all examples of this.[725] For all these things have the same result, namely, lack of leisure and poverty for the ruled. [1j] And there is taxation, as in Syracuse, when, during the reign of Dionysius, taxation ate up a person's entire estate in five years.[726] [1k] A tyrant also engages in warmongering in order that his subjects will lack leisure and keep being in need of a leader. And while a kingship is preserved by its friends, it is a mark of a tyrant to distrust his friends most of all, on the supposition that while all his subjects wish to overthrow him, these are above all capable of doing so.

And the things that occur in the ultimate democracy are all characteristic of a tyranny, namely, [1l] the dominance of women in matters concerning the household, in order that they may report on the men, and [1m] the license of slaves due to the same cause. For slaves and women not only do not plot against tyrants but, if they prosper under them, are necessarily well disposed toward tyrannies and toward democracies as well (for the people too wish to be a monarch). That is why a flatterer is honored in both constitutions—in democracies, the popular leader (for the popular leader is a flatterer of the people), in tyrannies, those who are obsequious in their dealings with the tyrant,

which is precisely the function of flattery. And in fact it is because of
1314a1 this that tyranny is a lover of wickedness. For tyrants delight in being flattered. But no one would do this who had free thoughts.[727] On the contrary, decent people show friendship, or [at least] do not flatter.[728] Also, the wicked are also useful for wicked things, for "nail is driven out by nail," as the proverb goes. Also, it is characteristic of a tyrant not to delight in anyone who is dignified or free. For a tyrant thinks that he alone deserves to be like that, whereas anyone who is a rival in dignity or in being free deprives tyranny of its superiority and its element of mastership, and so tyrants hate him as a threat to their rule. Also, it is characteristic of a tyrant to have foreigners rather than citizens as dinner guests and companions, on the supposition that the latter are hostile to him, whereas the former do nothing to oppose him.

These and similar things are characteristic of tyranny and preserve its rule, but there is no depravity that it leaves out. And all of these (one might almost say) fall into three kinds (*eidos*). For tyranny aims at three things. The first is for the ruled to think small, since a small-souled person would plot against no one.[729] The second is for them to distrust each other, since a tyranny will not be overthrown until some people trust each other. This is also why tyrants attack decent people, on the supposition that they are harmful to their rule, not only because they refuse as something unworthy to be ruled as by a master, but also because they are trusted both among themselves and among others, and do not inform on each other or on anyone else. The third aim is powerlessness to take any actions. For no one tries to do what is impossible, and so no one tries to overthrow a tyranny if he lacks the power. The defining marks of tyranny, then, to which the wishes of tyrants may be led back, are these three.[730] For a person might lead all the things characteristic of tyranny back to these three hypotheses: that its subjects not trust each other, that they have no power, that they think small.[731]

This, then, is one way in which the preservation of tyrannies comes about. [2] The other involves precautions that are pretty much the contrary of those just discussed. And one may grasp it by considering the destruction of kingships. For just as one way to destroy a kingship is to make its rule more tyrannical, so one way to preserve a tyranny is to make it more like a kingship, provided that one thing only is safeguarded, namely, power, so that the tyrant can rule not only subjects who wish it but also ones who do not wish it. For if he gives this up, he also gives up being a tyrant.[732] But while this must remain as a hypothesis, as regards the other things, he should do some and seem to do others, acting the part of a king in a noble manner.

[2a] First, then, he should seem to take thought for public funds. He should not squander them on gifts that enrage the multitude, as when they take from people who are laboring and toiling in penury, and spend lavishly on courtesans, foreigners, and artists.[733] He should also render an account of funds received and expended, which is just what some tyrants in the past have done. For in this way, he will give the impression of managing the city like a household manager rather than a tyrant. And he should not be afraid of running short of funds, since he has control of the city. But at any rate for those tyrants who are often away on foreign campaigns, it is more advantageous to follow this policy than to amass a great hoard of wealth and leave it behind. For those who guard the city will be less likely to attack his interests. Tyrants on a foreign campaign have more to fear from such guards indeed than from the citizens. For the citizens accompany him, while the guards stay behind. Next, it should appear that taxes and public services are for the purposes of administration, and, should he need them, for use in times of war, and, in general, a tyrant should pose as a guardian and treasurer of the public funds, not of his own private ones.

[2b] Also, he should appear not harsh but dignified, and, furthermore, of such sort that those who meet him feel not fear but rather awe. But this of course is not easily achieved if he is contemptible. That is why, even if a tyrant neglects the other virtues, he must cultivate military virtue and make himself a reputation for it.[734]

[2c] Further, not only should he himself avoid being seen behaving with wanton aggression toward any of those he rules, whether boys or girls, but neither should any of his followers. Likewise, the women of his household should also be respectful toward other women, as many tyrannies have also been destroyed because of the wanton aggression of women. Where bodily indulgences are concerned, he should do the contrary of what certain tyrants do now. For not only do they engage in this indulgence as soon as it is dawn, and continue it for many days, but they also wish to be seen doing so by others, in order that they may be admired as happy and blessed. Yet above all in such things a tyrant should be moderate, or, failing that, he should at least avoid exhibiting his indulgence to others. For it is not the sober man who is readily attacked or despised, but the drunk one, and not the one who is wide awake, but the one who is drowsy.

[2d] Indeed, a tyrant must do the contrary of pretty much all the things we mentioned before.[735] For he must establish and adorn the city as if he were a steward rather than a tyrant.

Further, [2e] a tyrant should always be seen to be outstandingly serious where matters concerning the gods are concerned. For people are less afraid of suffering something contrary to the law at the hands of such people. And if they think their ruler is a god-fearing man, and one who takes thought of the gods, they plot against him less, on the supposition that he has even the gods on his side. In appearing to be someone of this sort, however, the tyrant must avoid silliness.

[2f] A tyrant should so honor those who prove to be good in any area that they would never expect to be more honored by citizens living under their own laws. And he should bestow such honors himself, but punishments should be left to other officials and to the courts.

[2g] It is a precaution common to every sort of monarchy, however, not to make any one person great, but if indeed one, then several, since they will keep an eye on each other. And if it happens to be necessary to make one person great, at least it should not be someone of bold character.[736] For someone with such a character is most ready to attack in connection with every sort of action. And if it seems necessary to remove someone from power, his prerogatives should be taken away gradually, not all at once.

[2h] Further, a tyrant should refrain from every sort of wanton aggression, and from two in particular, namely, corporal punishment and the sort directed against the youth.[737] He should take this precaution above all where honor-lovers are concerned. For while money-lovers resent contemptuous acts affecting their property, honor-lovers and decent human beings resent those involving dishonor. That is why he should either not treat people in these ways or else should be seen to punish like a father, not out of contempt, and to engage in intercourse with young people due to erotic causes, and not as if it were a prerogative of his office. In general, he should compensate what are believed to be dishonors with yet greater honors.

[2i] Of those who make attempts to destroy his body, a tyrant should most fear, and take the greatest precautions against, those who by deliberate choice do not care about preserving their lives after destroying his. That is why he should be especially wary of people who think that he has been wantonly aggressive toward them, or those they happen to care about. For people who attack out of spirit are careless of themselves, and, as Heraclitus said, "Spirit is a hard enemy to fight, because it pays with soul."[738]

[2j] Since cities consist of two parts, poor human beings and rich ones, it is best if both suppose that they owe their preservation to the [tyrant's] rule, and that neither is unjustly treated by the other in anything. But whichever of them is the stronger these he should most attach to his rule, so that, with his power thus increased, there will be no need for the tyrant to free slaves or confiscate weapons. For either

one of the two parts added to his power will be enough to make them stronger than the attackers.

It is superfluous, though, to discuss each particular thing of this sort. For their aim is evident. A tyrant should appear to his subjects not as a tyrant but as a household manager and a kingly man, not as an 1315b1
appropriator [of other people's things] but as a steward. He should also appear to pursue the moderate things of life, not the excessive ones, maintaining close relations with the notables, while playing the popular leader with the many. For as a result, not only will his rule necessarily be nobler and more enviable by ruling over better people, who have not been humbled, and doing so without being hated and feared, but also his rule will be longer lasting, and, in addition, he himself, in his own character, will either be nobly disposed to virtue or else half good, not wicked but half wicked.[739]

V 12[740]

Yet the shortest-lasting of all constitutions are oligarchy and tyranny. For the longest-lasting tyranny was that of the sons of Orthagoras and of Orthagoras himself in Sicyon.[741] It lasted a hundred years. The cause of this was that they treated their subjects moderately and were slaves to the laws in many areas; and, because Cleisthenes was skilled in warfare, he was not readily despised; and because in many ways, by their acts of concern, they acted like popular leaders.[742] It is said at any rate that Cleisthenes gave a crown to the judge who denied him victory in a competition; some even say that the seated figure in the marketplace is a statue of the man who gave the verdict. They say too that Pisistratus once allowed himself to be summoned for trial before the Areopagus.[743]

The second longest tyranny was that of the Cypselids in Corinth, which lasted seventy-three years and six months.[744] For Cypselus was tyrant for thirty years, Periander for forty and a half, and Psammeticus, the son of Gorgus, for three.[745] The causes of its lasting are also the same. For on the one hand Cypselus himself was a popular leader and went without a bodyguard throughout his rule, and on the other Periander, though he became tyrannical, was skilled in warfare.

The third longest was that of the Pisistratids in Athens.[746] But it was not continuous. Twice, indeed, Pisistratus, while he was a tyrant, went into exile, so that in a period of thirty-three years he was tyrant for seventeen. Since his sons ruled for eighteen years, the tyranny lasted for thirty-five years altogether.

The longest lasting of the remaining tyrannies was the one associated with Gelon and Hiero at Syracuse.[747] Yet even this did not last long, but needed two more years to last for altogether twenty years. For Gelon was tyrant for seven and died in the eighth; Hiero for ten; whereas Thrasybulus was expelled after ten months. But the majority of tyrannies have all been quite short-lasting.

The various causes that destroy constitutions and monarchies, and also those that preserve them, have now pretty much all been stated.

In the *Republic* there is a discussion by Socrates dealing with [constitutional] changes, but he does not discuss them well.[748] For in the case of the first and best constitution he does not discuss the change special to it. Indeed, he claims that its cause is that nothing remains as it is, but that everything undergoes a sort of cyclical change, and that the starting-point of this lies in the elements four and three, which "married with five, give two harmonies," whenever, as he says, the number of this figure becomes cubed.[749] His supposition is that nature sometimes produces people who are base and stronger than education. Perhaps he is not wrong in saying this, since there may be some people who are uneducable and cannot become excellent men. But how could this sort of change be any more special to the constitution he says is best than common to all the others and to everything that comes to be? Yes, and is it because of time, due to which, as he says, everything changes, that even things that did not start to exist at the same time change at the same time? If something comes to be on the day before the completion of the cycle, for example, does it still change at the same time as everything else?

In addition to this, what causes the best constitution to change into a constitution of the Spartan sort? For all constitutions more often change into their contraries than into the neighboring one. And the same argument also applies to the other changes. For he says that the Spartan constitution changes to an oligarchy, then to a democracy, then to a tyranny. Yet change may also occur in the contrary direction. For example, from democracy to oligarchy, and this happens even more often than from democracy to monarchy.

Further, as regards tyranny, he does not tell us whether there will or will not be a change, what will cause it to change [if it does], or what sort of constitution it will change into. The cause of this is that he could not easily have said. For the matter is indeterminate, since, according to him, it should change into his first or best constitution. For in this way the change would be continuous and in a circle. But tyranny also changes into another tyranny, as the constitution at Sicyon changed from the tyranny of Myron to that of Cleisthenes; into oligarchy, like that of Antileon in Chalcis; and also into democracy, like that of Gelon and his family at Syracuse; and into aristocracy, like that of Charilaus in Sparta and the one in Carthage.[750]

Change also occurs from oligarchy to tyranny, as happened in Sicily with pretty much the majority of the ancient oligarchies: in Leontini, to the tyranny of Panaetius; in Gela, to that of Cleander; in Rhegium, to that of Anaxilaus; and similarly in many other cities.[751]

It is also absurd to think that a constitution changes into an oligarchy because the office holders are money-lovers and wealth-acquirers, and not because those who are far superior in property-holdings think it unjust for those who possess no property to share equally in the city with those who do possess it. In many oligarchies, in fact, office holders are not only not allowed to acquire wealth, but there are laws to prevent it. On the other hand, in Carthage, which is governed democratically, the officials do engage in acquiring wealth, and it has not yet undergone change.[752]

It is also absurd to say that an oligarchic city is really two cities, one of the rich and one of the poor. For why is this any more true of it than of the Spartan constitution, or any other constitution where the citizens do not all possess an equal property or are not all similarly good men? And even when no one becomes any poorer than he was, constitutions still undergo change from oligarchy to democracy, if the poor become a majority, or from democracy to oligarchy, if the rich happen to be stronger than the multitude, and the latter are negligent, while the former turn their thought toward [change].[753]

Although there are in fact many causes of changes, Socrates states but one, namely, that by leading a profligate life, and borrowing excessively and paying interest, they become poor—as if all or most of the citizens were rich at the start. But this is false. Rather, when men of the leading group lose their properties, they stir up change; but when some of the others do so, nothing terrible happens. And even when change does occur, it is no more likely to result in a democracy than in some other constitution.

Further, if people have no share in the honors of office or are treated unjustly or with wanton aggression, they engage in faction and change constitutions, even if they have not squandered all their property because it is open to them to do whatever they wish (the cause of which, Socrates says, is too much freedom).

Although there are many kinds of oligarchies and democracies, Socrates discusses their changes as if there were only one of each.

Book VI

VI 1

We have already discussed how many different varieties (*diaphora*) there are of the deliberative and controlling element of the constitution, the ways of ordering offices and courts, which variety has been ordered with a view to which sort of constitution, and, further, where the destruction and preservation of constitutions is concerned, from what sources and due to what causes they come about.[754]

But since it turned out that there are several kinds (*eidos*) of democracies and likewise of the other constitutions, it will be well to investigate whatever remains to be said about these, and to determine the mode that properly belongs, and is advantageous, to each of them. Further, we must also investigate the combinations of all the modes of ordering the things we mentioned. For these, when coupled, make constitutions overlap, resulting in oligarchic aristocracies and democratically-inclined polities. I mean those couplings that should be investigated, but up to now have not been—for example, where the deliberative part and the part that is concerned with the election of officials are ordered oligarchically, but the part that is concerned with the courts is aristocratic, or where the part that is concerned with the courts and the deliberative part are oligarchic, but the part that is concerned with the choice of officials is aristocratic, or where, in some other way, not all the parts properly belonging to the constitution are combined.[755]

Now we spoke earlier about which sort of democracy is fitting for which sort of city, and likewise which sort of oligarchy for which sort of multitude, and which of the remaining constitutions is advantageous for which. Nonetheless, since we should make clear not only which sort of constitution is best for a city, but also how it and the other sorts should be established, let us briefly go through this. Let us begin with democracy, since that will at the same time make evident the opposite constitution, the one that some people call oligarchy.

To carry out this methodical inquiry, we need to grasp all the features that are democratic and that are believed to go along with democracy. For it is as a result of the way these are combined that the various kinds (*eidos*) of democracy arise, and more than one different variety (*diaphora*) of each kind. For there are two causes for there being several kinds of democracy. The first is the one mentioned earlier, namely, that there are different varieties (*diaphora*) of the people.[756] For there is the farming multitude, the vulgar one, and that manual laboring one. And when the first of these is added to the second, and the third again to both of them, this not only creates a difference with respect to the democracy's being better or worse, but even with respect to its not being the same [kind of democracy]. But the second is the one we are discussing now. For the features that go along with democracy and are believed to properly belong to this constitution, when they are [differently] combined, make democracies distinct, since with one sort a few of these features will go along, with a second more, and with a third all of them. But it will be useful to gain knowledge of each of them, whether for the purpose of establishing whichever of these sorts of democracy one happens to wish for, or for that of rectifying an existing sort. For those who are putting in place a constitution seek to combine all the features that properly belong to its hypothesis, although they err in doing so, as we said earlier in our discussions of the destructions and preservations of constitutions.[757]

Now, though, let us discuss the axioms and characters [of the various kinds of democracy] and what it is they desire.[758]

VI 2

The hypothesis of the democratic constitution is freedom. For people usually say that they share in freedom only in this constitution, since all democracies, they say, aim at this. One sort of freedom is ruling and being ruled in turn. For democratic justice is equality in accord with number, not in accord with worth.[759] But if this is what is just, then the multitude must be in control, and whatever seems so to the majority, this must be the end and this must be what is just. For they say that each of the citizens should have an equal share, with the result that in democracies the poor happen to have more control than the rich. For they are the majority, and what seems [to be the case] to the majority is in control. This, then, is one sign of freedom, which all democrats take as a defining mark of their constitution. Another one is to live as one wishes. For this, they say, is the result of freedom, since indeed that of slavery is not to live as one wishes.[760] This, then, is the second defining mark of democracy. From it arises the demand not to be ruled, best of all to be ruled by no one, or, failing that, to rule and be ruled in turn. In this way the second goal contributes to freedom in accord with equality.

When these things are presupposed and the starting-point is of this sort the following features are democratic: [1] Having all choose officials from all. [2] Having all rule each and each in turn rule all. [3] Having all offices, or all that do not require experience or craft knowledge, filled by lot. [4] Having no property assessment for the offices or as low a one as possible. [5] Having no office, or few besides military ones, held twice or more than a few times by the same person. [6] Having all offices or as many as possible be short-term. [7] Having all, or bodies chosen from all, judge all cases, or most of them and the ones that are most important and involve the most control, such as those having to do with the inspection of officials, the constitution, or private transactions.[761] [8] Having the assembly control everything or all the important things, but having no office control any or as few as possible. Of the offices, the most democratic is the council, when there is ample pay for no one, since where there is ample pay, even this office is stripped of its power. For when the people are well paid, they take all judgments into their own hands (as we said in the methodical inquiry preceding this one).[762] [9] Having pay provided, preferably for all, for the assembly, courts, and public offices, or, failing that, for service in the offices, courts, council, and the controlling assemblies, or for those offices that require their holders to share a communal mess.[763] [10] Further, since oligarchy is defined by family, wealth, and education, their contraries (lack of breeding, poverty, and vulgarity) are held to be characteristically democratic.[764] [11] Further, it is democratic to have no office be permanent; and if such an office happens to survive an ancient change of constitution, at any rate to strip it of its power and make it be filled by lot instead of election.

These, then, are the features common to democracies. And from the justice that is agreed to be democratic, which consists in everyone having equality in accord with number, comes what is believed to be most of all democracy and rule by the people. For equality consists in the poor neither ruling more than the rich nor being alone in control, but in all ruling equally on the basis of equality in accord with number, since in that way they would acknowledge that equality and freedom are present in the constitution.

VI 3

The next issue is the puzzle that arises as to how they will achieve this equality. Should they divide the assessed property so that that of five hundred citizens equals that of a thousand others, and then give equal power to the thousand as to the five hundred?[765] Or is this not the way to set up equality in accord with this? Should they instead divide as before, then take an equal number of citizens from the five hundred as from the thousand and give them control of the elections and the courts? Is this, then, the constitution that is most just in accord with democratic justice? Or is it rather the one in accord with the quantity [of people]? For democrats say that this is just, namely, whatever seems so to the greater number, whereas oligarchs say that it is whatever seems so to those with the most property.[766] For they say that it is in accord with quantity of property that it should be judged. Both views, though, involve inequality and injustice. For if justice is whatever the few believe it to be, it is tyranny, since if one person has more than the others who are rich, then, in accord with oligarchic justice, he is just in ruling alone.[767] On the other hand, if justice is what the majority in accord with number believe, they will commit injustice if they confiscate the property of the rich and few (as we said earlier).[768]

What sort of equality there might be, then, that both would agree on is something we must investigate in light of the definitions of justice they both give. For they both say that the belief of the majority of the citizens should be in control. Let this stand, then, though not fully. Rather, since as it happens there are in fact two parts of which a city is composed, the rich and the poor, let whatever is the belief of both, or of a majority of both, have control. But if their beliefs are contrary, let that of the majority (that is, those whose assessed property is [collectively] greater) prevail. For example, if there are ten rich citizens and twenty poor ones, and contrary beliefs are held by six of the rich on the one hand and fifteen of the poorer ones on the other, four of the rich having been added to the poor, and five of the poor to the rich, then let whichever group's property assessment is greater when the properties of both the rich and poor on each side are added together have control. But if the amounts happen to be equal, let it be considered a common puzzle, as it is now when the assembly or the court is split. For let it be settled by lot or let something else of that sort be done.

But even if it is very difficult to discover the truth about equality and justice, still this is easier to attain than to persuade people of it when they have the power to get more.[769] For the weaker always seek the equal and the just, whereas the strong give no thought to them.

VI 4[770]

Of the four sorts of democracy, the first in order is the best, as we said in the discussions before these.[771] It is also the most ancient of them all. But I call it first in the very same way that one might distinguish peoples. For the best people is the sort that farms, and so it is also possible to create a democracy where the multitude live by cultivation or by herding. For because they do not have much property, they lack leisure and cannot attend meetings of the assembly frequently. And because they do not have the necessities, they spend their time at their work and do not have an appetite for other people's property.[772] Indeed, working is more pleasant to them than engaging in politics and holding office, where large gains are not to be had from office. For ordinary people seek profit more than honor. Evidence of this is that they used to put up with the ancient tyrannies, and continue to put up with oligarchies, so long as no one prevents them from working or takes anything away from them. For in no time some of them become rich, while the others [at least] do not live in poverty. Further, having control of the election and inspection of officials fulfills their need, if they do have any love of honor. In fact, among some peoples, even if the multitude do not share in the election of officials, but electors are chosen from all the citizens by turns, as in Mantinea, still, if they have control of deliberation, they are content.[773] This scheme too should be considered a form of democracy, as it was once at Mantinea.

That is why, then, in the aforementioned democracy, it is both advantageous and customary for all the citizens to elect and inspect officials and sit on juries, but for the holders of the most important offices to be elected from those with a certain amount of assessed property (the higher the office, the higher the assessment), or alternatively for officials not to be elected on the basis of property assessments at all, but of their capacities.[774] People who are governed in this way are necessarily governed well, since the offices will always be in the hands of the best, while the people will wish it and not envy the decent. And to the decent and notable people this ordering is satisfactory, since they will not be ruled by their inferiors, and will rule justly because the others have control of the inspection of officials. For to be dependent, and not to be able to do whatever one believes [to be good], is advantageous, since the license to do whatever one likes leaves one defenseless against the base element that exists in every human being.[775] So the necessary result, which is the very one that is most beneficial in constitutions, is that the decent people rule while being kept from error, and the multitude are in no way short-changed.

It is evident, then, that this is the best of the democracies, and also what cause this is due to, namely, because the people are of a certain sort. And with a view to establishing a farming people, some of the laws laid down in many cities in ancient times are very useful—for example, wholly prohibiting the ownership of more than a certain amount of land, or else more than a certain amount situated between a given place and the town or city. And there used to be legislation in many cities (at any rate in ancient times) forbidding even the sale of the first allotments of land, and also one, said to derive from Oxylus, with a similar sort of effect, forbidding lending against any portion of each person's land.[776] As things stand, however, one should also attempt rectification by using the law of the Amphytaeans, as it too is useful with a view to what we are talking about.[777] For they, although numerous while having little land, are nevertheless all engaged in farming, since property assessments are not of whole estates but in accord with such small sub-divisions of them that even the poor can exceed the assessment.

After the multitude of farmers, the best people consist of herdsmen, who get their living from livestock. For herding is in many respects similar to farming, and with a view to military actions, they are above all well prepared in their habits, because they have usable bodies and are able to live in the open. The other multitudes, of which the remaining kinds of democracies are composed, are pretty much all a lot more base than these. For their way of life is base, and there is no element of virtue involved in the work to which the multitude of vulgar people, tradesmen, and hired laborers put their hand.[778] Further, because they wander around the marketplace and town, (one might almost say) this entire kind (*genos*) can easily attend the assembly. Farmers, on the other hand, because they are scattered throughout the countryside, neither meet nor have the same need for this sort of meeting. And where the situation of the territory is such that the countryside is widely separated from the city, it is easy to create a democracy that is good and [like] a polity.[779] For the multitude are compelled to make their settlements out in the countryside areas, so that, even if there is a whole mob that frequents the marketplace, one should simply not hold assemblies in democracies without the multitude from the countryside.

How, then, the best or first democracy should be established has been stated. But how the others should be established is also evident. For they should deviate in order [from the best], always excluding a worse multitude.[780]

The ultimate democracy, because everyone has a share, is not one that 1319b1
every city can tolerate, nor can it easily endure if its laws and customs are not well composed.[781] (What factors cause the destruction of this and other constitutions have pretty much all been discussed earlier.[782]) With a view to putting in place this sort of democracy and making the people strong, the leaders usually admit as many as possible to citizenship, and make citizens not only of the legitimate children of citizens but also of the illegitimate ones, and those descended from citizens on only one side (I mean their mother's or their father's). For this entire element more properly belongs to this sort of people. This, then, is how popular leaders usually establish such a constitution. Yet they should accept additional citizens only up to the point where the multitude outnumber the notables and those in the middle, and not go beyond this. For when they do overshoot it, they make the constitution more disorderly and provoke the notables to such an extent that they find the democracy hard to endure—which is just what was the cause of the faction at Cyrene.[783] For

a wicked element gets overlooked when it is small, but as it grows larger it is more in one's face.

Further, also useful with a view to a democracy of this sort are the establishments that Cleisthenes used in Athens when he wanted to increase the power of the democracy, and that those setting up the democracy used at Cyrene.[784] For distinct and more numerous tribes and clans should be created, private cults should be absorbed into a few public ones, and every subtlety devised to mix everyone together as much as possible and break up their previous associations.

Further, all tyrannical establishments are held to be democratic. I mean, for example, no supervision of slaves (which may really be advantageous to a democracy up to a certain point), or of women or children, and allowing everyone to live as he wishes.[785] For numerous people will support a constitution of this sort, since it is more pleasant for ordinary people to live in a disorderly fashion than in a temperate one.

VI 5

For a legislator, however, or for those seeking to set up a constitution of this sort, setting it up is not the most important function nor indeed the only one, but rather seeing to it that it is preserved. For it is not difficult for those who govern themselves in any old way to continue for a day or even for two or three days. That is why one should take the things we got a theoretical grasp on earlier about the sorts of preservation and destruction characteristic of constitutions, and from these try to establish stability, carefully avoiding the causes of destruction, while setting up the sort of laws, both written and unwritten, that best encompass the features that preserve constitutions.[786] And one should consider a measure to be democratic or oligarchic not if it will make the city as democratically governed or as oligarchically governed as possible, but if it will make it so for the longest time.[787]

Popular leaders nowadays, however, in their efforts to gratify the people, confiscate many properties through the courts. That is why those who care about the constitution should counteract this by passing a law that nothing confiscated from a condemned person should become communal property, but is to be sacred property instead. For those doing injustice will be no less deterred, since they will be fined in the same way as before, whereas the mob will less frequently condemn defendants, since they will gain nothing. Further, public lawsuits should always be made as few as possible by deterring with large penalties those who bring frivolous ones.[788] For people usually bring them against notables, not men of the people. All citizens, though, should be well disposed toward the constitution or, failing that, they should at least not regard those in control as their enemies.[789]

Since ultimate democracies are populous and attending the assembly without wages is difficult, this situation is hostile to the notables in places where there happens to be a dearth of revenues. For the wages have to be obtained from taxes, confiscations of property, and bad courts—things that have already overturned many democracies. Where revenues are lacking, then, few assemblies should be held, and courts with many jurors should be in session for only a few days. For this helps reduce the fears of the rich about expense, provided the rich do not receive pay for jury service but only the poor. It also greatly improves the quality of judgments in lawsuits. For the rich are unwilling to be away from their private affairs for many days, but are willing to be so for brief periods.

Where there are revenues, however, one should not do what popular leaders do nowadays. For they distribute any surplus [to the poor], who no sooner get it than they need the same again, since helping the poor in this way is like pouring water into the proverbial leaking jug.[790] But the true man of the people should see to it that the multitude are not too poor (since this is a cause of the democracy being a bad one). Measures must, therefore, be crafted to ensure long-term prosperity. And, since this is also advantageous to the rich, whatever is left over from the revenues should be collected together and distributed in lump sums to the poor, especially if enough can be accumulated for the acquisition of a plot of land, or, failing that, for a start in trade or farming. And if this cannot be done for all, distribution should instead be by turns in accord with tribe or some other part. In the meantime the rich should be taxed to provide pay for necessary meetings of the assembly, while being released from pointless public services.

It is by governing in this sort of way that the Carthaginians have made a friend of the people, since they are always sending some of them out to their subject cities to become rich.[791] But it is also characteristic of notables who are refined and have understanding to divide the poor amongst themselves and give them a start in turning their hand to some line of work. It is well too to imitate the policy of the Tarentines.[792] For by giving communal use of their property to the poor they procure the goodwill of the multitude.[793] They also divided all their offices into two, some that are elected and some chosen by lot: by lot, so that the people share; elected, so that they are better governed. But this can also be done by dividing the same office between those people chosen by lot and those elected.

We have said, then, how democracies should be established.

VI 6

It is also pretty much evident from these remarks how oligarchies should be established. For each oligarchy should be put together from its contraries, by analogy with the contrary democracy, as in the case of the most well-mixed and first of the oligarchies, which is the one that is very close to so-called polity. Here the property assessments should be divided in two, some being made smaller and some larger, the smaller ones making people eligible for the necessary offices, the larger ones, for the offices with more control.[794] Anyone who acquires a qualifying property should be allowed to share in the constitution, and the assessment should be used to admit a sufficiently large number of the people that those who share in the constitution will be stronger than those who do not share in it, and those who do share should always be drawn from the better part of the people.

The next oligarchy should be established in a similar way, with a slight tightening [of the qualifications for citizenship].

As for the oligarchy that is contrary to the ultimate democracy, which is the most dynastic and tyrannical kind of oligarchy, the worse it is, the more guarding it requires. For just as bodies that are in good health and ships that are in good condition for a voyage, and as regards their sailors, can admit of more errors without being destroyed thereby, whereas diseased bodies and ships with loose timbers and bad sailors cannot survive even a small number of errors, so too the worst constitutions need the most guarding.

1321a1 Now, democracies are generally preserved by populousness, since this is opposed to justice in accord with worth.[795] But it is clear that an oligarchy must, on the contrary, attain its preservation by good order.[796]

VI 7

Since there are four principal parts of the multitude (farmer, vulgar, tradesman, and hired laborer) and four that are useful in war (cavalry, hoplite, light infantry, and naval), where the territory happens to be fit for cavalry, there conditions are naturally well suited for establishing a strong oligarchy.[797] For the security of the inhabitants depends on horse power, and horse-breeding is in the hands of those who own large estates.[798] Where the territory is fit for hoplites, on the other hand, conditions favor the next kind of oligarchy, since hoplites are more often rich than poor.[799]

Light infantry and naval forces, however, are entirely democratic.[800] Therefore, as things stand, wherever there are large numbers of these, and there is factional conflict, the oligarchs often get the worst of it. As a cure for this, one should adopt the practice of military commanders who couple a fitting contingent of light infantry to their forces of cavalry and hoplites. This is the way the people prevail over the rich during factional conflicts, since light infantry can easily take on cavalry and hoplites.[801] Oligarchs who put in place such a force drawn from these, then, are putting in place a force against themselves. But since there is a difference of age, and some are older and others younger, they should have their own sons taught lightly-armed and unarmed combat while they are young, so that when they have been taken out of the ranks of the boys they will themselves be champions in these functions.

The multitude should be given a share in the governing body, either in the way mentioned earlier, to those who own an assessed amount of property, or, as in Thebes, to those who have kept out of vulgar functions for a given period of time, or, as in Massilia, to those who are judged to be worthy of it, whether they come from inside or outside the governing body.[802]

Further, the offices with the most control, which those in the constitution should hold, should also have public services attached to them, in order that the people will voluntarily not share in them, and will sympathize with rulers on the grounds that they pay a heavy price for office. It is also fitting that, on entering office, they should offer magnificent sacrifices and establish something for the community, in order that the people, through sharing in the festivities, and seeing the city adorned here with votive statues and there with buildings, will be glad to see the constitution endure, and as result the notables too will have memorials of their expenditure. As things stand, however, those connected with oligarchies do not do these things but the contrary ones, because they seek profit no less than honor. That is why it is well to say that they are miniature democracies.[803]

This, then, is the way to determine how democracies and oligarchies 1321b1
should be put in place.

VI 8

Following what has been said there is the matter, as was said earlier, of correctly dividing what pertains to the offices, how many they are, what they are, and concerned with what.[804] For without the necessary offices a city cannot exist, and without those related to good order and arrangement it cannot be well managed.[805]

Further, in small cities the offices are necessarily fewer, while in larger ones they are more numerous, as was also said earlier.[806] The question of which offices it is fitting to combine, then, and which to keep separate should not be overlooked.

[1] The first of the necessary supervisions, then, is the one concerned with the market, over which there should be some office to supervise contracts and good order. For in pretty much all cities it is necessary that people buy and sell with a view to supplying each other's necessary needs.[807] This is also the readiest way to achieve self-sufficiency, which is believed to be what leads people to join together in one constitution.[808]

[2] Another sort of supervision, connected to this one and close to it, is the supervision of public and private property within the town, so that it may be kept in good order, also, the preservation and rectification of decaying buildings and roads, the supervision of property boundaries, so that disputes do not arise over them, and all other sorts of supervision similar to these. Most people call this sort of office town management, though its parts are more than one in number.[809] More populous cities assign distinct officials to these parts, for example, wall-repairers, well supervisors, and harbor guards.

[3] Another office is also necessary and closely akin to this one, since it is concerned with the same areas, though it concerns the countryside and matters outside the town. In some places its holders are called country managers, in others foresters.[810] These, then, are three sorts of supervision of these things. [4] But another is the office by which public revenues are received, guarded, and distributed to each branch of the administration. Its holders are called receivers or treasurers.[811]

[5] Another is the office by which both private contracts and judgments from the courts must be recorded. Judicial indictments and introductions of judicial proceedings must be recorded by these officials.[812] In some places this office too is divided into several ones, in others a single office has control of all these matters. The officials are called sacred recorders, supervisors, recorders, and other names close to these.[813]

[6] The next after this, and pretty much the most necessary and the most difficult of the offices, is the one concerned with actions against those who have been convicted in court, and those whose names are
1322a1 posted as public debtors, and with the guarding of their bodies.[814] It is a difficult office because it provokes a lot of hatred. So where it is not possible to make large profits from it, people are either unwilling to hold it, or those who do hold it are unwilling to act in accord with the laws. It is a necessary office, however, because there is no benefit in having judicial proceedings about matters of justice, if they do not achieve their end.[815] So if, when the former do not occur, people cannot live in a community with each other, they cannot do so either

when no actions are taken. That is why it is better for this not to be one office but to consist of several people drawn from different courts, and why one should try to divide up the offices connected with posting the list of debtors in a similar way.

Further, it is also better to have [other] officials take some of the actions, in particular, incoming officials should take those imposed by outgoing ones, and, in the case of sitting officials, one should pass sentence and another take the action. For example, the town managers should take the action imposed by the marketplace managers, while other officials take those imposed by the town managers. For the less hatred there is toward those who exact the penalty, the more the actions will achieve their end. To have the same people pass sentence and act on it doubles the hatred, and to have the same people do so in all cases makes them an enemy to everyone.

In many places the office that keeps prisoners in custody is different from the one that carries out the sentence, as, for example, in the case of the office of the so-called Eleven in Athens.[816] That is why it is also better to split it up, and to use the same subtle device in its case too. For though it is no less necessary than the previous one, decent people avoid this office most of all, but giving control of it to depraved ones is not safe. For they themselves are more in need of guarding than capable of guarding others. That is why there should not be a single office assigned to guard prisoners, nor the same office continuously. Instead, prisoners should be supervised by different people in turn, chosen from among the young men, in places where there is a regiment of cadets or guards, or from the other officials.[817]

These offices must be put first, then, as the most necessary. After these, though, there are others that are no less necessary, but ranked more highly, since they require much experience and trustworthiness.

[7] The offices concerned with the defense of the city are of this sort, and any that are ordered to meet its wartime needs. In both peacetime and wartime alike there should be supervisors to supervise the defense of the gates and walls, and likewise the inspection and marshaling of the citizen troops. In some places there are more offices assigned to all these areas, in others there are fewer (in small cities, for example, a single office is concerned with all of them). Such people are called generals or war-officers. Further, if there are also cavalry, light-infantry, archers, or a navy, an official is sometimes put in place for each of them. These 1322b1
are called admirals, cavalry-commanders, or regimental-commanders, whereas those in charge of the units under these are called warship-commanders, company-commanders, or tribal-leaders, and so on for their sub-units. But all of these together are included in a single kind

(*eidos*), namely, supervision of military matters. This, then, is the way things stand with regard to this office.

[8] But since some if not all of the offices handle large quantities of public property, there must be a distinct office to receive and examine their accounts, which does not itself handle any other matters. Some call these inspectors, accountants, auditors, or advocates.

[9] Besides all these offices, there is the one that has most control of everything. For the same office often has control over the implementing as well as the introduction of a measure, or else presides over the multitude where the people have control.[818] For there must be some body to convene the controlling element in the constitution. In some places, these are called preliminary councilors (*probouloi*), because they make preliminary deliberations (*probouleuein*) for the assembly.[819] But where the multitude are in control they are called a council instead.

The offices that are political, then, are pretty much this many.[820]

[10] Another kind (*eidos*) of supervision, however, is that concerned with the gods—for example, priests, supervisors of matters relating to the temples (such as the preservation of existing buildings, the restoration of decaying ones), and all other things that are ordered in relation to the gods. In some places it happens that a single office supervises all this—for example, in small cities. But in other places there are many officials who are separate from the priesthood—for example, supervisors of sacrifices, temple-guardians, and treasurers of sacred funds. Next after this is the office set aside for all the public sacrifices that the law does not assign to the priests but which have the honor [of being celebrated] from the communal hearth.[821] These officials are called archons by some, kings or presidents by others.

The necessary sorts of supervision, then, to speak in summary form, are concerned with the following: religious matters, military matters, revenues and expenditures, the market, the town, harbors, and the countryside; further, matters relating to the courts, such as registering transactions, [taking legal] actions, keeping prisoners in custody, receiving accounts, and inspecting and examining officials; and, finally, matters relating to the element that deliberates about public affairs.

Special to cities that enjoy greater leisure and prosperity, on the other hand, and that also pay attention to good order are: [11] the offices dealing with the supervision of women, [12] the guardianship of the laws, [13] the supervision of children, [14] control of the gym-
1323a1 nasia, [15] and, in addition to these, the supervision of athletic and Dionysiac contests, as well as of any other such public spectacles there may happen to be.[822] Some of these are obviously not democratic—for example, the supervision of women and that of children, since the

poor have to employ their women and children as servants, because of their lack of slaves.

There are three offices that cities use to supervise the election of the officials who are in control: [16] law guardians, [17] preliminary councilors, and [18] council. The law guardians are aristocratic, the preliminary councilors are oligarchic, and the council is democratic.

Where offices are concerned, then, pretty much all of them have been spoken about in outline.

Book VII

VII 1

Anyone who is going to make an inquiry into the best constitution in the appropriate way must first determine what the most choiceworthy life is. For if this remains unclear, what the best constitution is must also remain unclear. For it is appropriate for those people who govern themselves in the best way to do the best that their circumstances allow—provided nothing contrary to reasonable expectation occurs. That is why there should first be agreement about what the most choiceworthy life is for (one might almost say) everyone, and then determine whether it is the same or distinct for all communally as for each separately.[823]

Considering many things said about the best way of living even in the external accounts to be adequate, then, we should make use of them here as well.[824] For, to tell the truth, as regards one way of dividing them at any rate, no one would dispute that, since there are three groups—external goods, goods in the body, and goods in the soul—all of them must belong to those who are blessed.[825] For no one would say that someone is blessed who has no shred of courage, temperance, justice, or practical wisdom, but is afraid of the flies buzzing around him, stops at nothing, no matter how extreme, when he has an appetite to eat or drink, kills his dearest friends for a pittance, and has thought as foolish and deluded as a child's or a madman's.[826]

But while these claims are ones that almost everyone would agree with, people disagree about their quantity and their relative superiority. For they consider any quantity of virtue, however small, to be sufficient, whereas of wealth, property, power, reputation, and the like they seek unlimited excess. We, however, will say to them that it is easy to achieve conviction on these matters even from the facts themselves.[827] For we see that the virtues are not acquired and safeguarded by means of external goods, but rather it is the other way around, and living hap-
1323b1 pily for human beings, whether it consists in enjoyment or virtue or both, is possessed by those who have cultivated their characters and minds excessively, but have been moderate in their acquisition of external goods, rather than by those who have acquired more of the latter than they can possibly use, but are deficient in the former.[828]

But to those who investigate the matter in accord with argument, the point is also easily seen. For external goods have a limit, just like any instrument, and everything useful is useful for something, and in excess must either harm or bring no benefit to their possessors.[829] Where each of the goods of the soul is concerned, by contrast, the more excessive it is, the more useful it is—if one should assign to these goods too not only nobility but also utility.

It is generally clear too, we shall say, that the best condition of each thing relative to others is in accord with the superiority of those things whose conditions we say they are.[830] So, if indeed the soul is more estimable, both unconditionally and to us, than property and the body, its best condition must be proportionately better than theirs.[831] Further, it is for the sake of the soul that these things are naturally choiceworthy and that every practically-wise person should choose them for its sake, not the soul for theirs.

Let us take it as agreed, then, that to each person falls just as much happiness as he has virtue, practical wisdom, and action done in accord with them. We may use the [primary] god as evidence of this, who is happy and blessedly so, not because of any external goods but because of himself and by being in his nature of a certain quality.[832] This is also why good luck and happiness are necessarily distinct. For chance or luck is the cause of the goods external to the soul, but no one is just or temperate by luck or because of luck.[833]

The next point, and one depending on the same arguments, is that the happy city is the one that is best and acts nobly. But it is impossible for those who do not do noble things to act nobly, and there is no noble function, either belonging to a man or to a city, that is separate from virtue and practical wisdom.[834] But the courage, justice, practical wisdom, and temperance of a city have the same capacity and form (*morphê*) as those in which each human being who is said to be courageous, just, practically-wise, and temperate should share.[835]

But let these remarks, as far as they go, serve as a preface to our account.[836] For not to touch on these topics is impossible, but neither can we go through all the arguments pertaining to them, since that is the function of another leisured discussion.[837] But for now, let us assume this much, that the best life, both for each separately and for cities collectively, is one involving virtue that is sufficiently furnished with the resources needed to participate in actions that are in accord with virtue. With regard to those who dispute this, we must ignore them in our present methodical inquiry, but investigate their objections later, if anyone happens not to be persuaded by what has been said.

VII 2

But whether we should say that the happiness of each individual human being is the same as that of a city or not remains to be discusssed. But here too the answer is evident. For everyone would agree that they are the same. For those who suppose that living well in the case of an individual is a matter of wealth will also count blessed a whole city, if it is rich. And those who have the highest esteem for the tyrannical life would say that the city that rules the greatest number is happiest. And if someone approves of an individual because of his virtue, he will also say that the more excellent city is the one that is happier.

But now there are two questions that need to be investigated. First, which life is more choiceworthy, the one that involves being active in politics with other people and sharing in the city, or the life of an alien, detached from the political community?[838] Further, what constitution and what condition of the city should be taken to be best—regardless of whether sharing in a city is choiceworthy for everyone or for most but not for some? Since [to answer] this question, but not the one about what is choiceworthy for each, is a function of political thought and theoretical knowledge, and this is the sort of investigation we have deliberately chosen to undertake now, the first is a side issue, whereas the second is a function of our methodical inquiry.[839]

Now it is evident that the best constitution is necessarily that order in accord with which anyone might be able to do best and live blessedly. But the very people who agree that the most choiceworthy life is the life that involves virtue are the ones who dispute about whether the political and action-involving life is choiceworthy or rather the one detached from all external concerns—some sort of contemplative life, for example, which some say is the only life for a philosopher.[840] For it is evident that these two lives are pretty much the ones that the human beings most ambitious for virtue deliberately choose, both in earlier times and at present. The two I mean are the political life and the philosophic one. And it makes no small difference on which side the truth lies. For the person at any rate who thinks correctly must order his affairs by looking to the better target—and this applies to each human being and to the constitution communally.[841]

Some people think, though, that ruling as a master over one's neighbors involves one of the greatest injustices, and that political rule, while it involves no injustice, does involve an impediment to the ruler's own joy in life.[842] But others hold beliefs that are almost the contrary. For they think that the action-involving and political life is the only one for a man. For the actions resulting from each virtue are not more open to private individuals than to those who are active in
1324b1 communal affairs and participate in politics.[843] Some, then, give this reply, but others say that the mode of constitution that rules as a master or a tyrant is the only happy one. Among some peoples, indeed,

this is the defining mark of the constitution and the laws—to rule as a master over neighbors.

That is why, although most laws have been laid down in most cases (one might almost say) at random, nonetheless if there is some one thing to which the laws do to some extent look, it is the exercise of power that they all aim at.[844] For example, in Sparta and Crete it is pretty much entirely with a view to wars that education and most of the laws are ordered. Further, among all the [barbarian] nations that have the power to get more this power is esteemed—for example, among the Scythians, Persians, Thracians, and Celts.[845] For in some cases they even have laws that spur them on to this sort of virtue. In Carthage, for example, so it is said, they receive armlets as decorations for each campaign they serve in. There was once a law in Macedonia too, that any man who had not killed an enemy must wear as his belt a rope used to tether a horse to a manger. Among the Scythians, anyone who had not killed an enemy was not permitted to drink from a cup passed around at a certain feast. And among the Iberians, a warlike nation, they plant as many small obelisks around a man's tomb as the number of enemies he has killed.[846] And there are many other things of this sort among other peoples, some sanctioned by the laws, others by customs.

Yet it would presumably seem quite absurd to those wishing to investigate the matter, if the function of a politician involved being able to get a theoretical grasp on how to rule or master his neighbors, whether they wish it or do not wish it.[847] For how could this be up to a politician or a legislator, when it is not even *lawful*?[848] And it is unlawful to rule not only justly but also unjustly (although it is in fact possible to exercise power unjustly).

Moreover, this is not what we see in the other sciences either. For it is not the doctor's or the ship-captain's function to persuade or otherwise use force against his patients (in the one case) or his passengers (in the other). But many seem to think that mastership *is* politics, and the very same thing they all deny to be either just or advantageous for themselves, they are not ashamed to practice on others. For they seek just rule among themselves, but toward others they care nothing about justice. It would be strange, though, if by nature one thing were not suited to be ruled by a master and another suited not to be ruled by a master. So if indeed things are that way, one must not try to rule as a master over everyone, but only over those who are suited to be ruled by a master, just as one must not hunt human beings for a feast or a sacrifice, but rather what is suited to being hunted for this—and any wild animal that is edible is suited to being hunted.

Moreover, it is possible for a single city to be happy even by itself
1325a1 (that is, one that is governed in a good way), if indeed it is possible for a city to be settled somewhere by itself and employ excellent laws, and whose constitution will not be ordered with a view to war or to controlling its enemies—for we are assuming that it has none.

It is clear, therefore, that although all military pursuits are to be taken as noble, they are not to be taken as the highest end of all, but rather as being for the sake of that end. And [the function] of an excellent legislator is to see how a city, a race (*genos*) of human beings, or any other community can come to have a share in good living and in the happiness that it is possible for them. There will be differences, of course, in some of the laws that are prescribed, and it belongs to legislative science to see, if there are neighboring peoples, what sorts of things should be practiced in relation to what sorts of people and how the appropriate ones are to be used in relation to each.

But this topic—namely, what end the best constitution should aim at—will receive a fitting investigation later.[849]

VII 3

As regards those who agree that a life that involves virtue is most choiceworthy, but disagree about the use of it, we must say to both sides that they are both in part correct in what they say and in part incorrect.[850] For those on one side reject political offices, since they consider that the life of a free person is distinct from that of a politician and is also the most choiceworthy one of all, while those on the other side consider that the political life is best, since it is impossible for someone who does no action to do well, and that doing well in action and happiness are the same.[851]

On the one side we have that the life of a free person is better than that of a master. This is indeed true. For there is certainly nothing dignified about using a slave as a slave, since giving orders about necessities has no share in what is noble. But to consider that every rule is rule of a master is surely incorrect. For there is no less a distance between rule over free people and rule over slaves than between being by nature free and being by nature a slave. We have determined enough about these in our first accounts.[852]

On the other side, to praise inaction more than action is not correct. For happiness is action, and furthermore the actions of those who are just and temperate achieve an end of many things that are noble.[853]

Yet perhaps someone might take these determinations to imply that control of everyone is best, since in that way one would control the greatest number of the actions that are noblest.[854] And so someone who has the power to rule should not let rule pass to his neighbor, but rather take it away from him. And a father should take no account of his children, or a child of his father, or in general a friend of his friend, or give any thought to them in comparison to this. For what is best is most choiceworthy, and doing well in action is best.

Well, perhaps what they say is true, if indeed the most choiceworthy thing there is will belong to those who commit robbery and use force. But presumably it cannot belong to them, and this assumption is false. For his actions can no longer be noble if he is not as superior [to those he rules] as a man is to a woman, a father to his children, or a master to his slaves. And so the transgressor can do nothing to later correct so great a previous deviation from virtue. For among those who are similar, the noble and the just thing is to take turns [in ruling and being ruled], since this is equal and similar treatment. But unequal shares for equal people or dissimilar ones for similar people is contrary to nature, and nothing contrary to nature is noble. That is why, when someone else is more excellent in virtue and in his action-involving capacity to [implement] what is best, it is noble to follow him and just to obey him. But he must possess not virtue alone, but also the capacity in accord with which he will be a doer of action.

If the things we have said are correct, and we should take it that happiness is doing well in action, then the best life, both for the whole city collectively and for each individual, would be an action-involving life. Yet it is not necessary, as some suppose, for an action-involving life to be lived in relation to other people, nor are those thoughts alone action-involving that arise for the sake of the consequences of doing an action, rather, much more so are the acts of contemplation and thought that are their own ends and are engaged in for their own sake.[855] For doing well in action is the end, and so action of a sort is the end too. And we say that the ones who above all do actions, even external actions, in a controlling way are their architectonic craftsmen who do them by means of their thoughts.[856]

Moreover, it is not necessary for even those cities to be inactive that are situated by themselves and have deliberately chosen to live that way, since actions can take place even among their parts.[857] For the parts of the city have many communal relations with each other. Similarly, this also holds of any individual human being. For otherwise the [primary] god and the entire cosmos could scarcely be in a noble condition, since they have no external actions beyond the [internal] ones that are proper to them.[858]

It is evident, then, that the same life is necessarily best both for each human being and for cities and human beings collectively.

VII 4

Since what has just been said about these matters was by way of a preface, and since we got a theoretical grasp on the other constitutions earlier, the starting-point for the remainder of our investigation is first to discuss the sorts of hypotheses there should be concerning the city that is going to be set up so as to be in accord with our prayers. For the best constitution cannot come into existence without commensurate resources. That is why we should hypothesize many things in advance, just as when we are praying, although none of them should be impossible. I mean, for example, the size of the citizenry and of the territory. For just as other craftsmen—for example, a weaver or a shipbuilder—must also be supplied with matter suitable for the work, and the better the matter has been prepared, the nobler the product of their craft must be, so too a politician and legislator must be supplied with proper matter in a suitable condition.[859]

First among the resources belonging to politics is a multitude of human beings, how many there should be of them, and of what quality they should be by nature. And likewise for the territory, how large it should be, and of what sort. Now, most people think that it is appropriate for a happy city to be a great one, but even if what they think is true, they are ignorant of the quality that makes a city great or small. For they judge a city to be great if the number of its inhabitants is large, whereas they ought to look not to number but to capacity. For a city too has a certain function, so that the city that is best able to complete it is the one that should be considered greatest.[860] Similarly, one should say that Hippocrates is greater not as a human being but as a doctor than one who exceeds him in physical size.[861]

Yet even if one should judge the greatness of a city by looking to the multitude, this should not be any random multitude (for perhaps of necessity there are a large number of slaves, resident aliens, and foreigners present in cities), but rather to those who are part of it—that is, who form the parts proper to a city, those of which it is composed. For possessing a superior number of these is the sign of a great city. A city that can send a large number of vulgar people out to war, on the other hand, but only a few hoplites, cannot possibly be great.[862] For a great city and a populous one are not the same.

And this too is at any rate evident from the facts, namely, that it is difficult, perhaps impossible, for a city that is overly populous to be in good legislative order. Certainly, among those that seem to be governed in a good way, we see none being lax as regards [the size of] its multitude. And this is also clear from persuasive arguments. For law is a sort of order, and so good legislative order must be a [sort of] good order. But an overly large number cannot share in order. For that would be a function of a divine power, the sort that holds the universe together, since the noble at any rate is usually found in number and magnitude.[863] That is why that city is most noble where, together with magnitude, the defining mark that has been mentioned is also found.[864]

But of the magnitude of a city there is a certain measure, just as in the case of everything else—animals, plants, and instruments. For when each of them is neither overly small nor too excessively large, it will have its own capacity, but otherwise will either be wholly deprived of its nature or be in bad condition. For example, a ship that is one span [seven and a half inches] long will not be a ship at all, nor will one of two stades [twelve hundred feet], but, as it approaches a certain size, it will sail badly, in the one case because of its smallness, in the other because of its excessive size.

Likewise also in the case of a city, one that is composed of too few people is not self-sufficient (whereas a city is something self-sufficient), but one that is composed of too many, while it is self-sufficient in the necessities, the way a nation is, is still no city, since it is not easy for it to have a constitution. For who will be the general of its excessively large multitude, and who, unless he has the voice of Stentor, will serve as its crier?[865] That is why, while the first city must be the one composed of a multitude of the sort that is the first multitude large enough to be self-sufficient with a view to living well as a political community, it is also possible for a city that exceeds this one in number to be a greater city, but, as we said, this is not possible indefinitely.

What the defining mark of this excess is can easily be seen from the facts. For a city's actions are either those of the rulers or those of the ruled. And a ruler's function is prescription and judgment. But with a view to judgments in lawsuits and with a view to distributing offices in accord with worth, each citizen must know the other citizens, that is, know what sorts of people they are. For where they do not know this, the business of electing officials and judging lawsuits must go badly, since to act in an offhanded way is unjust in both these proceedings. But this is evidently precisely what occurs in an overly-populous city.

Further, it is easy for resident aliens and foreigners to get a share in the constitution, since it is not difficult for them to escape notice because of the excessive size of the population.

It is clear, therefore, that the best defining mark for a city is this: it is the greatest excess of multitude with a view to self-sufficiency in living that can be easily surveyed as a whole. Let the size of the city, then, be determined in this way.

VII 5

Similar things hold in the case of the territory. For, as regards the sort of territory it is, it is clear that everyone would praise the most self-sufficient. And such a territory must be all-producing. For self-sufficiency is having everything and needing nothing.

In quantity or extent it should be large enough to enable the inhabitants to live at leisure in a way that is generous and at the same time temperate.[866] But whether this defining mark is correctly or incorrectly stated is something that must be investigated with greater exactness later on, when we come to discuss the question of possessions generally, what it is to be well off where property is concerned, and how and in what way this is related to its use.[867] For there are many disputes about this topic of investigation because of those who draw us toward either of the two extremes of life, the one lot toward tightfistedness, the other toward luxury.[868]

The form (*eidos*) of the territory is not difficult to describe (although on some points one should listen to those experienced in generalship): it must be difficult for enemies to invade and easy for the citizens themselves to get out of.[869] Further, just as the multitude of people should, as we said, be easy to survey as a whole, the same also holds of the territory, since for a territory to be easily surveyed as a whole is for it to be easily defended.

As for the position of the city, if it is to be in accord with our prayers, it is appropriate for it to be well situated in relation both to the sea and to the surrounding territory. One defining mark was mentioned above: defensive troops must have access to all parts of the territory. The remaining defining mark is that the city should allow easy transportation with a view to the conveyance of collected crops, and furthermore materials for the wood-market, and for any other work of this sort the territory happens to possess.

VII 6

Where communication with the sea is concerned there is much dispute about whether it is beneficial or harmful to cities that are in good legislative order. For it is said that entertaining foreigners as guests who have been brought up under different laws is detrimental to good legislative order, as is populousness. For it is said that, as a result of their use of the sea for importing and exporting, a multitude of traders comes about, and this is contrary to being governed in a good way. But it is quite clear that, if these things do not come about, then it is better both with a view to safety and to ensuring a ready supply of necessities for a city and its territory to have access to the sea. For with a view to withstanding war more easily people should be readily defensible both on land and sea in order to preserve themselves. And with a view to inflicting harm on their attackers, if they are unable to do so on both, at least they will be in a better position to do so on one or the other, if they have access to both. It is also necessary for cities both to import the things that are not available at home and to export those of which they have a surplus. For a city should engage in trade for itself, not for others, whereas those that open their market to everyone do so for the sake of revenue.[870] But a city that must not be involved in this sort of getting more must not have a market of this sort either.[871]

Since, even as things stand, we see many territories and cities that have ports or harbors naturally well situated in relation to the city, so that they are neither parts of the same town nor too far away from it, but are kept under its control by walls and other similar defenses, it is evident that if any good comes from this sort of communication [with a port or harbor], it will be available to the city, whereas if there is anything harmful, it can be prevented by means of laws that specify or define the sorts of people that should or should not have dealings with each other.

As far as naval forces are concerned, it is quite clear that it is best to have up to a certain quantity of them. For a city should also be formidable on sea, exactly as it should be on land, able to aid not only itself but also some of its neighbors. But where the number and size of these forces are concerned, we must look to the life of the city. For if it is going to live a life of leadership and a political life, it must also have forces of this sort that are commensurate with its actions.[872]

There is no need, though, for cities to suffer the populousness associated with the seafaring mob, since they should not be part of the city at all.[873] For the force of marines is free and consists of infantry, and it is what has control and commands the ship. And if the city contains a multitude of subject peoples and farmers, there cannot be any shortage of sailors. We see this happening in certain cities even now, for example, in the city of Heraclea.[874] For it can man many triremes, despite being more modest in size than many other cities. Where territory, harbors, cities, the sea, and naval force are concerned, then, let matters be determined in this way.

VII 7

We spoke earlier about what the defining mark should be for the multitude of citizens.[875] Let us now discuss of what sort they should be as regards their nature.

One may, then, pretty much understand what *this* is by looking at those Greek cities that are well reputed, and at the way the entire inhabited world is divided into nations. For the nations in cold regions, particularly in Europe, are full of spirit but somewhat deficient in thought and craft knowledge, which is why they remain comparatively free, but are without a political constitution and incapable of ruling their neighbors.[876] Those in Asia, on the other hand, have souls endowed with thought and craft knowledge, but they lack spirit.[877] That is why they remain in subjection and slavery.

The Greek race (*genos*), however, occupies an intermediate position geographically, and likewise shares in both sets of characteristics. For it is both spirited and possessed of thought. That is why it remains free, governs itself in the best way, and is capable of ruling all, should it acquire one constitution.[878] The same difference (*diaphora*), though, is also found among the Greek nations in relation to each other. For some have a nature that is one-sided, whereas in others both these capacities are well blended. It is evident, accordingly, that as regards their nature people must be both spirited and possessed of thought, if they are to be easily led to virtue by the legislator.

In fact, some say that guardians should have this very quality, namely, friendly to those they know and fierce to those they do not, and spirit is what produces friendliness (*philêtikon*), since it is the capacity of the soul by which we love (*philoumen*).[879] A sign of this is that one's spirit is roused more against associates and friends than against strangers, when one regards oneself as being treated contemptuously. That is why, when Archilochus was complaining about his friends, it was appropriate for him to say to his spirit: "It is you who are choked with rage against your friends."[880] The element of ruling and the element of being free derive from this capacity in all cases, since spirit is both fit for rule and indomitable. But it is not correct to claim that guardians are to be harsh to those they do not know, since one should not treat anyone in this way. Nor are great-souled people by nature harsh, except to those behaving unjustly.[881] And furthermore they feel this more toward intimates, just as we said earlier, if they regard themselves as being treated unjustly. And it is reasonable that this should happen. For they suppose that in addition to being harmed they are deprived of the benefit that they consider they are owed. Hence the sayings: "Wars among brothers are harsh," and "Those who have loved excessively will hate excessively too."[882]

About the people who should govern themselves, then, their number and of what sort they should be as regards their nature, and about the size and sort of the city's territory, pretty much enough has been determined. For we should not seek the same exactness in accounts as in what comes through perception.[883]

VII 8

Since, as in the case of the other things that are composed in accord with nature, those things without which the whole cannot exist are not parts of the whole composite, clearly the things that are necessary for the existence of a city should not be assumed to be parts of it either, and likewise for any other community from which something one in kind (*genos*) is formed.[884] For communities should have some one thing that is common and the same for all the members, whether they share in it equally or unequally—for example, food, a quantity of territory, or something else of this sort.

But whenever one thing is for the sake of another and the other is that for whose sake it is, they have nothing in common except that one produces and the other gets produced. I mean, for example, the relationship of every instrument and craftsman to the work produced. For there is nothing that is common to the house and the builder, but rather the builder's craft knowledge is for the sake of the house.[885] That is why, though cities need property, property constitutes no part of a city—although among the parts of property are many animate things. But a city is a community of similar people, and exists for the sake of living in the best possible way.

Since the best thing is happiness, however, and it is some sort of activation or complete use of virtue, and since, as it happens, some people are able to share in happiness, whereas others are able to do so only to a small degree or not at all, it is clear that this is a cause of their being many kinds (*eidos*) and different varieties (*diaphora*) of city and of constitution.[886] For by pursuing this in different ways and by different means each group of people produces distinct ways of life and distinct constitutions.[887]

But we must also investigate the question of how many of these things there are that a city cannot exist without. For what we are calling the parts of a city would of necessity be included among them. So we must determine the number of functions there are, since this will make the answer clear. First, there should be a food supply. Second, crafts—for living needs many instruments.[888] Third, weapons—for the members of the community must also have weapons of their own, both in order to rule (since there are people who disobey) and in order to deal with outsiders who attempt to do injustice. Further, a ready supply of wealth, both for their needs among themselves and for military needs. Fifth, but of primary importance, the supervision of religious matters, which is called a priesthood. Sixth, and most necessary of all, judgment about what is advantageous and just in their relations with each other.

These, then, are the functions needed in (one might almost say) every city. For a city is not just any random multitude, but one that is self-sufficient with a view to living, as we say, and if any of these functions is lacking, a community cannot be unconditionally self-sufficient. It is necessary, therefore, for a city to be set up in accord with these sorts of work. There must, therefore, be a multitude of farmers to provide the food; and craftsmen; and a fighting element; and a rich element; and priests; and judges of what is necessary and advantageous.[889]

VII 9

Having determined these matters, it remains to investigate whether all these functions should be shared by all (for it is possible for all the same people to be farmers and craftsmen and deliberators and judges), or whether distinct people should be assigned to each of the functions we mentioned, or whether some of these are necessarily specialized, whereas others are common. It is not the same, though, in every constitution. For it is possible, as we said, for everyone to share in all, or for not everyone to share in all, but certain people in certain ones.[890] For these things also make constitutions distinct. For in democracies everyone shares in everything, whereas in oligarchies it is the contrary.

Since we are investigating the best constitution, however, the one in accord with which a city would be most happy, and happiness cannot exist separate from virtue, as was said earlier, it evidently follows that in a city governed in the best way, possessing men who are unconditionally—not relative to a hypothesis—just, the citizens should not live either a vulgar or a trading life.[891] For lives of these sorts are ignoble and entirely contrary to virtue.[892] Nor should those who are going to be citizens be farmers, since leisure is needed both for the development of virtue and for political actions.

But since the best city contains both a military part and one that deliberates about what is advantageous and renders judgment about what is just, and since it is evident that these are most of all parts of the city, should these functions also be assigned to distinct people, or are both to be assigned to the same people? [The answer to] this is evident too, because in one way the functions should be assigned to the same people and in another they should be assigned to distinct ones. For insofar as the prime time for each of the two functions is distinct, in that one requires practical wisdom and the other strength, they should be assigned to distinct people.[893] On the other hand, insofar as it is impossible for those capable of using and resisting force to tolerate being always ruled, to that extent they should be assigned to the same people. For those who control the weapons also control whether a constitution will endure or not.

The only course remaining, therefore, is for the constitution to assign both functions to the same people, but not at the same time. Instead, just as it is natural for strength to be found among younger men and practical wisdom among older ones, so it is advantageous and just to assign the functions to each group in this way, since this division is in accord with worth.[894]

Moreover, the property too should be assigned to them. For it is necessary for the citizens to be well supplied with resources, and these people are the citizens. For the vulgar element does not share in the city, nor does any other kind (*genos*) of person who is not a craftsman of virtue.[895] This is clear from our hypothesis.[896] For happiness necessarily involves virtue, and a city must not be called happy by looking at just a part of it, but by looking at all the citizens. It is also evident that the property should be theirs, if indeed the farmers must be slaves, either barbarians or subject peoples.[897]

Of the things we enumerated earlier, then, only the kind (*genos*) consisting of priests remains.[898] The order of these is also evident. For no farmer or vulgar person should be appointed as a priest, since it is appropriate for the gods to be honored by citizens. But because the political element is divided into two parts, namely, the military and the deliberative, and because it is appropriate for those who are worn out with age to render service to the gods and find rest, it is to these that priesthoods should be assigned.

We have now stated, therefore, the things without which a city cannot be formed, and how many parts of a city there are. Farmers, craftsmen, and the laboring element generally are necessary for the existence of cities, but the military as well as the deliberative elements are parts of a city. And each of these is separate from the others, some permanently, others by turns.

VII 10

It seems to be recognized among those who philosophize about constitutions—and not just nowadays or in recent times—that a city should be divided into separate kinds (*genos*), and that the military element should be distinct from the farming element. For it is still this way even 1329b1 now in Egypt, and also in Crete—Sesostris having made such a law for Egypt, so it is said, and Minos for Crete.[899]

Communal messes also seem to be an ancient order, having arisen in Crete during the reign of Minos, but those in Italy are much older.[900] For the chroniclers say that one of those who settled there, a certain Italus, became their king, and that on account of him they changed their name and were called Italians instead of Oenotrians, and the promontory of Europe that lies between the Gulfs of Scylletium and Lametius (which are a half-day's journey apart) was given the name of Italy.[901] It was Italus, they say, who made the nomadic Oenotrians into farmers, and along with enacting other laws for them, first introduced communal messes. That is why some of those descended from him still make use of communal messes even today, as well as of some of his laws. The ones who lived near Tyrrhenia were the Opicians, who were then (as now) called Ausonians. The ones living near Iapygia and the Ionian Gulf, in a region called Siritis, were the Chonians, who were related to the Oenotrians by race (*genos*). So it was in this region that communal messes were first ordered.

The separation of the multitude of citizens according to kind (*genos*), on the other hand, originated in Egypt. For the kingship of Sesostris extends much further back in time than that of Minos. We should take it, indeed, that pretty much everything else too has been discovered many times, or rather an unlimited number of times, in the long course of history.[902] For our needs themselves are likely to teach the necessities, and once they are present, the things that contribute to refinement and abundance quite reasonably develop.[903] So one should think that, where matters pertaining to constitutions are concerned, things hold in the same way.

That all such matters are ancient is indicated by the facts about Egypt. For the Egyptians seem to be the most ancient of peoples, yet they possessed laws and political order.[904] That is why one should make adequate use of what has been discovered, but also try to inquire into whatever has been overlooked. We said earlier that the territory should belong to those who possess weapons and share in the constitution, why those doing the farming should be distinct from these, and how much territory there should be and of what sort.[905] Now, though, we must first speak about the distribution of land, who the farmers should be, and what sort of people they should be, since we say that property should not be held communally, as some have claimed—but it should
1330a1 be communal in its use, as it is among friends—and that neither should any citizen be in need of food.[906]

As for communal messes, everyone agrees that it is useful for well-established cities to have them (what the cause is of our agreeing with this will be stated later).[907] All the citizens should share in these, even though it is not easy for the poor to contribute the required amount from their private resources and manage the rest of their household as well. Further, expenses relating to the gods should be shared communally by the entire city.

It is necessary, therefore, for the territory to be divided into two parts, one communal and the other belonging to private individuals. And each of these must again be divided in two. One part of the communal land should be used to support public services to the gods, the other for expenditure on the communal messes, while one part of the private land should be located near the frontiers, the other near the city, so that, with two allotments assigned to each citizen, all of them may share in both locations. For this is in accord with justice and equality and also ensures greater concord in the face of wars with neighbors.[908] For wherever things are not this way, some citizens make light of feuds with bordering cities, while others are, contrary to what is noble, give too much thought to them. That is why some cities have a law that prohibits those who dwell close to the border from sharing in deliberations about whether to go to war with neighboring peoples, on the supposition that because of their private interest they are incapable of deliberating in a noble way. It is necessary, then, for the land to be divided in this way, due to the causes we mentioned.

As for those who do the farming, it is above all necessary—if the matter is to be in accord with our prayers—that they be slaves, who neither belong to the same race nor to spirited ones, since that way they will be useful as regards work, and safe as regards not stirring up change. As a second best, they should be barbarian subject peoples, similar in nature to those just mentioned. Of these, the ones who work on private land should be private to those who possess property, whereas those who work on the communal land should be communal. The way slaves should be treated, and why it is better to hold out freedom as a reward to all slaves, will be discussed later.[909]

VII 11

We said earlier that a city should have as much access to the land and to the sea, and likewise to its entire territory, as is possible.[910] As regards its own situation, one should pray to be successful in getting a site for it, looking to four things.[911] The first is health, because it is a necessity.

For cities that slope toward the east, that is, toward the winds that blow from the direction of the rising sun, are healthier. Second healthiest are those that slope away from the north wind, since they have milder winters.

One of the remaining things to keep in view is that the city should be well sited for political and military actions. With a view to military ones, the city should be easy for the citizens themselves to get out of but difficult for their enemies to approach and blockade. It should also possess a plentiful water supply of its own, especially springs. But if it does not, a way has been discovered to construct bounteous great receptacles for rainwater to prevent the supply from running short when the citizens are kept away from the countryside by war.

Since we must give thought to the health of the inhabitants, and this depends on the location being well situated in territory of this sort and facing in this direction, and second, on using healthy water, and making this concern more than a side issue. For the things we use in the greatest quantity and most frequently for our bodies contribute most to health. And the capacity of water and air has a nature of this sort.[912] That is why in all well thought-out cities, if it happens that all the springs are not equally healthy or if the healthy ones are not abundant, one should distinguish and keep separate those for nourishment and those for other uses.

As regards fortified places, what is advantageous is not the same for all constitutions. For example, an acropolis is oligarchic or monarchical, a level-ground fortification is democratic, and neither of these, but rather a number of strongholds, is aristocratic.[913]

Where the disposition of private dwellings is concerned, the new Hippodamean way of laying them out in straight rows is considered pleasanter and more useful for other actions, but for safety in war the contrary one, which prevailed in ancient times, is more useful.[914] For it makes it difficult to enter for foreign troops and for attackers to find their way around.[915] That is why the best city should share in both of these. This is possible in fact if one establishes it in the way that farmers make the "vine clumps" (as some farmers call them), that is, if the city as a whole is not made in straight rows, but only parts and places.[916] For in this way both safety and beauty will be well served.

As for walls, those people who say that cities that lay claim to virtue should not have them are too archaic in their suppositions about things—and this though they see cities that prided themselves in this way refuted by the facts.[917] It is true that against those who are similar to ourselves and not very superior in numbers it is not noble to seek preservation through fortifying walls. But it can and does happen that the superiority of the attackers is too much for human virtue or for the virtue of a small number of people.[918] So if one is to preserve oneself and not suffer ill-treatment or wanton aggression, one should think that the safest fortification provided by walls is most appropriate for war—particularly in light of recent discoveries about projectiles and engines for improved precision in sieges.[919]

For to think it worthwhile for cities not to build surrounding walls is like seeking to make the territory easy to invade and mountainous places removed, and like not building walls around private houses on the grounds that they will make the inhabitants cowardly.

Further, we should not neglect to consider that it is open to the inhabitants of cities with surrounding walls to treat them in both ways, namely, as having walls or as not having them, whereas this is not open to the inhabitants of a city without walls. If, then, this is the way things stand, a city should not only have surrounding walls, but it should also take care to ensure that they both enhance the beauty of the city and are useful for military purposes, as well as others, and, in particular, those brought to light by recent discoveries. For just as attackers are always busily concerned with new ways to get more [of the upper hand], so too, while defenders have already discovered some things, they should seek and devise others.[920] For no one even attempts to attack those who are well prepared from the start.

VII 12

Since the multitude of citizens should be assigned to communal messes, and the walls should have guardhouses at intervals, and towers in suitable places, these things clearly suggest that some communal messes should be provided in these guardhouses. That, then, is the way one might arrange these.

As for the buildings assigned to the gods, and the communal messes for officials with the most control, it is fitting for them to be located together in an appropriate place—except in the case of temples assigned a separate location by the law or some other prophecy delivered by the Pythian god.[921] And a place like this would be one that is such as to be a conspicuous enough setting for virtue and also better fortified than the neighboring parts of the city.[922]

Below this site, it is appropriate to set up a marketplace of the sort they call by that name in Thessaly—the one they call "free."[923] This is one that should be kept clear of all merchandise, and that no vulgar person, farmer, or anyone of that sort, may come near unless summoned by the officials. The place would have added appeal if there was an order of the gymnasia for the older men there. For it is appropriate for this order to be divided into age groups, and to have some of the officials spend their time with the younger men, and have the older men spend time with the officials. For being present in the eyes of the officials is what most engenders true shame, and the kind of fear characteristic of free people.[924]

The marketplace for merchandise, by contrast, should be distinct from this free one, and should have a separate site, conveniently located for collecting together all the things sent in from both land and sea.

Since the city's pre-eminent element is divided into priests and officials, it is appropriate too for the order of the communal messes of the priests to be located in the vicinity of the sacred buildings.[925]

As for the boards of officials that are made to supervise contracts, legal accusations, summonses, and other administrative matters of that sort, as well as those that deal with marketplace management and so-called town management, one should establish their seat near the marketplace and in some public meeting place, and the area around the necessary marketplace is of this sort. For the upper marketplace is intended for being at leisure, the lower, for necessary actions.

The order that has just been mentioned should also be imitated in matters pertaining to the countryside.[926] For there too the officials that some call foresters and others country managers must have messes and guardhouses for the purposes of keeping guard on things. Further, temples must be distributed throughout the territory, some dedicated to gods and others to heroes.[927]

It would be pointless, however, to spend time now in giving an exact account and speaking about things of this sort. For they are not difficult to understand, but difficult to do, since speaking about them is a function of prayer, whereas having them come about is a function of luck.[928] That is why we should now put aside anything further concerning such matters.

VII 13

But we must now discuss the constitution itself, and of which and of what sorts of people the city that is going to be blessedly happy and govern itself in a good way should be composed.[929]

There are two things in which well-being consists in all cases: one of these is setting up the target and end of action correctly, the other is discovering the actions that carry us toward it. For it is possible for these either to clash with each other or to be in harmony. For sometimes the target is well set up, but people make an error in what they do to hit it; sometimes they achieve everything that furthers the end, but the end they set up is a base one; and sometimes they make both errors, as in connection with medicine, for example.[930] For sometimes they neither make a correct judgment about what sort of condition a healthy body should be in nor hit upon the things that are productive in furthering the defining mark they set before themselves.[931] But in the crafts and sciences both of these must be mastered, the end and the actions that are toward the end.

Now it is evident that everyone aims at living well and at happiness. But while it is possible for some to achieve these ends, it is not open to others, either because of some stroke of luck or because of nature.[932] For living in a noble way also needs certain supplies, although fewer are needed by those in a better condition, more by those in a worse one. But others straightaway seek happiness in an incorrect way, although it is possible for them to achieve it.[933]

Since what we are proposing to do is to look at the best constitution, however, and it is the one in accord with which a city will be governed in the best way, and it would be best governed in accord with a constitution that would make it most possible for the city to be happy, it is clear that we must not neglect to consider what happiness is. And we say—and have given this definition in our ethical works (if anything in those discussions is of benefit)—that it is a complete activation and use of virtue, and this not on the basis of a hypothesis but unconditionally.[934] By on the basis of a hypothesis I mean what is necessary, by unconditionally I mean those that are done nobly. For in the case of just actions, for example, just penalties and punishments spring from virtue, but are necessary, and their nobly done has the character of necessarily done. For it is a more choiceworthy situation if no man or city needs any such things. By contrast, just actions that aim at honors and prosperity are unconditionally noblest. For the former involve choosing something bad, whereas the latter are the contrary, since they establish and generate good things.[935]

An excellent man, of course, would use poverty, disease, and other sorts of bad luck in a noble way, but blessedness involves their contraries.[936] For in accord with the definition in our ethical accounts, an excellent man is the sort for whom, because of his virtue, unconditionally good things are good.[937] It is clear, then, that his use of them must also be unconditionally excellent and noble. That is why people consider the causes of happiness to be external goods—as if a lyre rather than craft knowledge were taken to be the cause of brilliant and noble lyre-playing.

It follows, therefore, from what has been said, that some things must be there to start with, whereas others must be established by the legislator. That is why we pray for the composition of the city to be successful concerning the things that luck controls (for we take it that luck does control them).[938]

The city's being excellent, however, is no longer a function of luck but of scientific knowledge and deliberate choice. But surely a *city* is excellent by its citizens—those who share in the constitution—being excellent. And in our city all the citizens share in the constitution. This, therefore, must be investigated, namely, how a man becomes excellent. For even if it is possible for all to be excellent without each citizen being so individually, the latter is still more choiceworthy.[939] For if each individually is excellent, it follows that all are.

But surely people become good or excellent because of three things. These three are nature, habit, and reason. For one must be born, first of all, a human being, and not one of the other animals. Similarly, one's body and soul must be of a certain quality. But in the case of some qualities, being born with them is of no benefit, because habits make them change. For some qualities, because of their nature, play a double game, going toward the worse or toward the better because of one's habits.[940] But, whereas the other animals mostly live by nature alone, while to a small extent some also do so by habit, the human being lives by reason as well. For the human being alone has reason. So these must harmonize with each other. For people do many actions contrary to their habits and their nature because of reason, if they are persuaded that some other way is better.

Now, we determined earlier what sort of nature people should have if they are going to be easily handled by the legislator.[941] What is left at this point is a function of education, since some things are learned by habituation and others by listening.[942]

VII 14

Since every political community is composed of rulers and ruled, this topic must be investigated, namely, whether distinct people should be rulers and ruled or whether the same ones should be both throughout life. For clearly their education must follow along with these alternatives.

Now then, if they differed from each other as much as gods and heroes are believed to differ from human beings—straightaway having a great superiority first in body and then in soul, so that superiority of the rulers in comparison to those ruled was indisputable and evident, it would clearly be altogether better if the same people always ruled and the others were always ruled. But since this is not easy to achieve, and since there are not, as Scylax says there are in India, kings who are so greatly superior to the ruled, it is evident, due to many different causes, that it is necessary for all to share alike in ruling and being ruled in turn.[943] Since, for those who are alike, equality consists in sameness, and it is difficult for a constitution to endure if it is set up contrary to justice. For along with the ruled there are all those in the surrounding territory who wish to stir up change, and one of the impossible things is that those in the governing body be numerous enough to be stronger than all these.[944]

On the other hand, that the rulers *should* be different from the ruled is indisputable. Hence the legislator should investigate the question of how this is to be achieved, and how they should share with each other. We spoke about this earlier.[945] For nature has provided the distinction by itself making part of the same kind (*genos*) younger and part older, the former suited to be ruled and the latter to rule.[946] For no one resents being ruled in accord with his age, or considers himself superior, especially when he is going to be compensated for his contribution when he reaches the proper age.

We must conclude, therefore, that rulers and ruled are in one way the same but that in another way they are distinct. So their education too must be in one way the same but in another way distinct. For if someone is going to rule well, so it is said, he must first be [well] ruled.[947]

But rule, as we said in our first accounts, is on the one hand for the sake of the ruler and on the other for the sake of the ruled. Of these, we say that the former is the rule of a master, the latter rule over free people. Now, in some cases the things prescribed differ not with respect to the works they prescribe but with respect to that for the sake of which they are to be done. That is why it is noble even for free young men to perform many of the functions that are believed to be appropriate for slaves.[948] For, as regards the noble and the not noble, the difference does not lie so much in the actions themselves as in their ends, namely, that for the sake of which [they are to be done]. Since we say that the virtue of a citizen and a ruler is the same as that of the best man, and that the same man should be ruled first and ruler later, the legislator would have to make it his business to determine how and through what practices men become good, and what the end of the best way of living is.[949]

The soul, though, is divided into two parts, one of which has reason intrinsically, whereas the other does not have it intrinsically, but is capable of listening to it.[950] It is in accord with the virtues of these, we say, that a man is called in a way good. As to whether the end lies in one of these more than the other, to those who make the distinction we mentioned it is not unclear what must be said. For the worse part is always for the sake of the better, and this is as evident in the products of the crafts as it is in those of nature.[951] But the part that has reason is better. And it, in the way that we are accustomed to divide it, is divided into two, since on the one hand there is practical reason and on the other theoretical reason.[952] So it is clear that the rational part of the soul must also be divided in the same way. Actions too, we will say, are divided proportionately, and those that belong to the part that is by nature better must be more choiceworthy to anyone who can succeed in doing all or only two of them.[953] For this is always what is most choiceworthy for each individual, to attain the topmost [good].[954]

The whole of life too, however, is divided into unleisure and leisure, war and peace, and of things doable in action some are necessary or useful, others noble.[955] And where these things are concerned it is necessary to make the same choice as in the case of the parts of the soul and their actions. War must be for the sake of peace, unleisure for the sake of leisure, necessary and useful things for the sake of noble ones.[956]

The politician must legislate, therefore, looking to all these things in a way that is in accord with the parts of the soul and their actions, but more to those that are better and those that are ends. And he should legislate in the same way as regards lives and as regards the divisions of actions.[957] For one should be able to be unleisured or to go to war, but more able to sustain peace and leisure, and one should be able to do necessary and useful actions, but noble ones more so. So these are the targets that should be kept in view when educating citizens, both when they are still children and whenever else they need education. It is evident, however, that those Greeks who are now believed to be governed in the best way, and those legislators who set up their constitutions, neither ordered the various aspects of their constitutions with a view to the best end nor their laws and education with a view to all the virtues, but instead were vulgarly inclined toward the ones believed to be useful and more conducive to getting more.[958]

Some later writers have expressed the same belief in a quite similar way to this. For they praise the Spartan constitution and admire the target of its legislator, because he legislated on all matters with a view to conquest and with a view to war. And what they say is easy to refute by argument, and has now been refuted by the facts too.[959] For just as most human beings are eager to rule as masters over many, because this provides them with a ready supply of the goods of luck, so too Thibron evidently admires the Spartan legislator, as do each of the others who have written about their constitution, because by being trained to dangers, they ruled over many.[960] And yet it is clear—now at any rate that their empire is no longer in their hands—that the Spartans are not happy, and that their legislator is not a good one.

Further, this is ridiculous, namely, if while keeping to his laws, and there being no impediment to making use of them, they lost their noble way of living. Neither are they correct in their supposition about the sort of rule a legislator should be seen to honor. For rule over free people is nobler and more involves virtue than rule of a master. Further, one should not consider a city happy or praise its legislator because he trained it to exercise power for the purposes of ruling its neighbors, since such things involve great harm. For it is clear that [on the same supposition] any individual citizen who is able should also try to acquire the power to rule his own city. Yet this is precisely what the Spartans accused their king, Pausanias, of doing, even though he held so high an office.[961]

There is, then, nothing worthy of a political [ruler] in these sorts of arguments and laws, nor anything beneficial or true. For the same things are best both individually and communally, and it is these that a legislator should produce in the souls of human beings. Military training should not be attended to for the sake of reducing those who are not worthy of it to slavery, but rather, first, in order that the trained ones themselves not be enslaved to others, second, to pursue a position of leadership in order to benefit the ruled, not to be masters of all of them, and, third, to be masters of those who are worthy of being slaves. 1334a1

Events as well as arguments testify, then, that the legislator should give more serious attention to how legislation about matters of war and other matters may be ordered for the sake of leisure and peace. For most cities of this sort are preserved while they are at war, but are destroyed once they acquire rule. For they lose their edge, just as iron does, when they remain at peace. But the one responsible is the legislator, who did not educate them to be capable of being at leisure.

VII 15

Since the end is evidently the same for human beings both communally and individually, and since it is necessary for there to be the same defining mark for the best man and for the best constitution, it is evident that the virtues for leisure must be present. For, as has often been said, the end of war is peace, and that of unleisure is leisure.[962] But the virtues useful with a view to leisure and passing the time include both those whose function lies in leisure and those whose function lies in unleisure. For many necessities must be present in order for being at leisure to be possible. That is why temperance is appropriate for our city as are courage and resilience. For as the proverb says, there is no leisure for slaves, and those who are incapable of facing danger courageously are the slaves of their attackers.

Now, courage and resilience are for unleisure, philosophy for leisure, and temperance and justice are useful during both, and particularly when people remain at peace and are at leisure. For war compels people to be just and temperate, but the enjoyment of good luck and the leisure that accompanies peace make them wantonly aggressive instead. Much justice and temperance are needed, therefore, by those who seem to do best and who enjoy all the things regarded as blessings—people like those, if there are any, as the poets say there are, who live in the Isles of the Blessed.[963] For these above all will need philosophy, temperance, and justice, to the extent that they are at leisure amidst an abundance of such goods.

It is evident, then, why a city that is going to be happy and excellent should share in these virtues. For it is shameful to be incapable of making use of good things, but it is even more shameful to be incapable of making use of them in leisure—when being unleisured or when at war appearing to be good, but slavish when at peace and leisure. That is why one must not cultivate virtue as the city of the Spartans does. For the Spartans are not different from the others in this way, namely, in not considering the same things as they do to be the greatest goods, but in considering that these are brought about particularly by means of a certain virtue. But since . . . these goods and the enjoyment of them to be greater than that of the virtues . . . and that . . . because of itself, is evident from these considerations.[964] What must be theoretically grasped, then, is how and through what means this will come about. We made a distinction earlier, accordingly, to the effect that nature, habit, and reason are needed.[965] And of these, what sort the citizens must be as regards their nature was determined earlier.[966] It remains to get a theoretical grasp on whether they are to be educated by means of reason first or by means of habits. For these must harmonize with each other, and the harmony must be the best one.[967] For it is possible for reason to be in error about the best hypothesis, and for it to be led because of habits in the same direction.[968]

This, then, is at any rate evident. First, just as in other cases, coming to be proceeds from a starting-point, and the end that proceeds from a certain starting-point is starting-point for another end. But reason and understanding are our nature's end, and so it is to further these that the coming to be and the training of our habits should be established.[969]

Second, just as soul and body are two, so we see that the soul has two parts as well: the non-rational and the one that has reason. And the states of these are also two in number, one of which is desire and the other the understanding. And just as the coming to be of the body is prior to that of the soul, so the non-rational part is prior to the rational. This too is evident. For spirit and wish, and furthermore appetite, are present in children straight from birth, whereas rational calculation and understanding naturally arise as they grow.[970] That is why supervision of the body must come first, prior to that of the soul, and then supervision of desire, but supervision of desire must be for the sake of the understanding, and that of the body for the sake of the soul.

VII 16

If indeed, then, the legislator should see to it from the start that the bodies of children being reared are to develop in the best possible way, he must first supervise the union of the sexes, and determine when, and between what sorts of people, a marital relationship should be brought about. In legislating for this marital community, he should look both to the people involved and to their time of life, so that they will reach the same stage of life at the same time and there be no dissonance between their procreative capacities, the man still being capable of procreating but the woman not, or the woman capable but the man not.[971] For these things produce conflicts and disagreements among them.

Next, he should also look to the succession of children. For children should not be too far removed in age from their fathers, since the gratitude of children is of no use to more elderly fathers, and the help of such fathers is of no use to their children, neither should they be too close in age, since this leads to many annoyances. For there is less respect in cases of this sort, just as among contemporaries, and the closeness in age is liable to cause disputes over the management of the household.

Further, to return to the point with which we started our discussion, the legislator should look to how the bodies of those who are born are to be in congruence with his wish.

Pretty much all these things come about by supervising one thing. For since it has been determined that men's fertility, to speak of the majority of cases, comes to an end at a maximum age of seventy, and women's at fifty, the starting-point of their sexual union in terms of their ages should be such that it reaches its decline at these times.

The coupling of young people, however, is a bad thing with a view to procreation. For in all animals the young are more likely to bear offspring that are imperfect, and they are more likely to give birth to offspring that are female and small in size, so that the same must occur in human beings as well. The following is a sure sign of this. In all those cities in which the coupling of young men with young women is the custom, people are imperfect and undersized as regards their bodies.

Further, young women have longer labors, and more of them die in childbirth. That is why some people say that this is the cause of the oracle that was given to the Troezenians, namely, that many were dying because of the marrying off of younger women, and was not related to the harvesting of the crops.[972]

Further, with regard to temperance, it is advantageous for women to be given in marriage when they are older, since women who have had sex when they were young are believed to be more intemperate. Also, the bodies of males seem to be harmed with respect to their growth, if they have intercourse while their body is still growing.[973] For this growth too takes a definite period of time, after which it is no longer extensive.[974] That is why it is fitting for the women to marry when they are around eighteen years of age, the men when they are thirty-seven, or a little before.[975] For, at such an age, sexual union will occur when their bodies are in their prime, and, with respect to losing their capacity to procreate, they will also decline together at the appointed times. Further, as to the succession of children, it will occur for them when they are starting their prime, if their birth takes place soon after the marriage, as can reasonably be expected, while for their fathers it will occur when these are already at the age of their decline, namely, toward the seventieth year.

We have said, then, when sexual coupling should occur. As for the season, however, one should use the time many people use, since they now correctly set aside the winter as the time to begin this sort of living together as husband and wife. In addition, couples should get a theoretical grasp for themselves on what is said about procreation by doctors and natural scientists. For doctors have adequately discussed the times that are opportune as regards the body, and natural scientists have discussed the winds, favoring northerly winds over southerly ones.[976]

As to what qualities their bodies should have if they are to be most beneficial to the offspring, we must deal with that topic at greater length in our discussion of the supervision of children.[977] It is sufficient to speak of it in outline now. For the [physical] state characteristic of athletes is not useful either with a view to the good state of a citizen or with a view to health or procreation, nor is one that is too reliant on medical treatment and poorly suited to physical exertion.[978] But the state that is in a mean between these two is useful for these purposes. One should, then, have a state that is achieved by physical exertion, but not by violent physical exertion, and that furthers not just one thing, as the state characteristic of athletes does, but rather the actions of free people.

And these things should exist for men and women alike. For even pregnant women should take care of their bodies and not stop exercising or adopt a meager diet. The legislator can easily accomplish this by requiring them to take a walk every day in order to worship the gods whose assigned prerogative is to watch over birth.[979] But with regard to their thought, as opposed to their bodies, it is fitting for them to spend their time taking things easy, since unborn children obviously draw resources from their mothers, just as plants do from the earth.[980]

Where the question of whether to rear offspring or feed them is concerned, let there be a law that no disabled one is to be reared, but that offspring not be exposed because of the number of children, if the way the customs are ordered prohibits the exposure of offspring once they are born.[981] The quantity of procreation, though, should be defined, and if some children are conceived by some of those who have intercourse contrary to this, an abortion should be induced before the onset of perception and life. For what is pious and what is not will be distinguished by perception and life.

Since we have determined the starting-point of the age at which men and women should start their sexual coupling, let us also determine for how long a time it is fitting for them to render public service by procreating. For the offspring of parents who are too old, like those of parents who are too young, are imperfect in both body and in thought, whereas those of people who have reached old age are weak. That is why the length of the time in question should be in accord with the time when thought is in its prime. In most cases, this occurs—as some of the poets who measure age in periods of seven years have said—around the time of the fiftieth year. So when they have exceeded this age by four or five years they should be released from bringing children into the light of day.[982] If they have intercourse after that, it should be evident that it is for the sake of health, or due to some other such cause.[983]

As for intercourse with another man or another woman, let it be unconditionally not noble to appear to be engaging in it in any way with anyone, when one is a husband and referred to as such.[984] If someone is found doing anything of this sort during his period of procreation, he should be punished with dishonor appropriate to his offense.[985] **1336a1**

VII 17

It should be recognized that the sort of food that children are given once they are born makes a great difference to the strength of their bodies. And it is evident to anyone who investigates the other animals or those nations concerned to cultivate a military disposition that the food that is particularly suited to [children's] bodies has a lot of milk in it but very little wine, because of the diseases [it produces].[986] Further, it is also advantageous for them to make whatever movements are possible at that age. But to prevent curvature of the limbs, due to softness, there are certain mechanical instruments, which some nations employ even today, to make their bodies straight.[987] It is advantageous, too, to habituate them to the cold right from the time they are small children. For this is very useful both with a view to health and with a view to military affairs. That is why many barbarian nations have the custom of submerging newborn children in a cold river, whereas many others—for example, the Celts—dress them in light clothing.[988] For in all cases in which it is possible to habituate, it is better to habituate right from the start, but to do so gradually. And because their bodily condition is hot, children are naturally well suited to being trained to bear the cold.[989]

In the first stage of life, then, it is advantageous to adopt this sort of supervision as well as any that is similar to it. During the following stage, which lasts until five years of age, it is not a good idea to have children engage in any kind of learning or any necessary physical exertion, lest it impede their growth.[990] But they should engage in as much exercise as will prevent laziness of the body, and this should be provided for them both through various activities and through play. But the games they play should not be either unfree or exerting or undisciplined.[991]

As for the sort of stories and fables that children of this age should listen to, let this be the concern of the officials who are called child-supervisors. For all such things should pave the way for their later pursuits. That is why many of the games they play should imitate the things they will give serious attention to later on.

Those in the *Laws* who prevent children from screaming and crying are wrong to prohibit such things, for they contribute to growth, since they are in a way an exercise for the body.[992] For holding the breath produces strength in those who are exerting themselves, and this is what happens in children when they exert themselves in screaming.[993]

The child-supervisors should investigate the way children pass the time, particularly to ensure that they are as little as possible in the company of slaves. For at this age, and until they are seven years old, it is
1336b1 necessary for them to be reared in their households. So it is quite reasonable to expect that they will pick up an element of unfreedom from what they see and hear even at that early age.

The legislator should in general banish shameful language from the city, as he would any other shameful thing, since by speaking lightly of whatever is shameful one comes closer to doing it.[994] He should above all banish it from among children, so that they neither say nor hear anything of this sort.

If, however, anyone is found saying or doing something forbidden, and is a free man who is not yet old enough to have been given a seat at the communal messes, he should be punished with loss of honors or with blows, whereas, if he is older than this, he should be punished with those dishonors usually reserved for the unfree, because he has acted in a manner characteristic of slaves.

Since we are banishing talk about anything of this sort, it is evident that we should also banish looking at pictures or stories that are unseemly.[995] Let the officials take care, then, that no statue or picture be an imitation of such actions, except in the precincts of certain gods at whose festivals custom permits even licentious raillery to occur.[996]

In addition to these, custom allows those of a suitable age to pay this sort of honor to the gods on behalf of themselves, their children, and their wives. But there must be legislation that younger people not be spectators either of iambus or of comedy until they have reached the age when it is appropriate for them to recline at the communal table and drink wine, at which time their education will make them entirely unaffected by the harm resulting from such things.[997]

To be sure, our present discussion of this issue has been cursory. Later we must stop and determine it at greater length, first going through the puzzle of whether this [namely, prohibiting the attendance of the young at such performances] should be done or not, and if so how it should be done.[998] But the present was the appropriate time, however, to have made mention of it to the extent necessary. For perhaps the remark of Theodorus, the tragic actor, was not a bad one.[999] For he said that he never allowed anyone else, not even an incompetent actor, to enter a scene before him, because audiences become accustomed to the voice they hear first. The same is true of our relationships with people and things: whatever we encounter first we like better. That is why everything base must be made alien to the young, especially if it involves depravity or ill will.

When the first five years have passed, children should spend the two years till they are seven observing the lessons they themselves will need to learn. There are then two stages in their education that should be distinguished, from seven years to puberty and from puberty to twenty-one years. For those who divide the stages of life into seven-year periods are not for the most part incorrect. And one should follow

1337a1 the natural divide, since every craft and every sort of education wishes to fill in what nature leaves out.[1000]

First, then, we must investigate whether some order should be produced that is concerned with the children; next, whether it is advantageous for the supervision of them to be made a communal matter or in some private way (as is also the case in most cities now); and third, what sort of supervision it should be.

Book VIII

VIII 1

Now, no one would dispute that legislators should be especially concerned with the education of the young. For in fact in cities where this does not occur, its absence is harmful to the constitutions. And education should, in fact, have a view to the particular constitution. For the character that properly belongs to each constitution usually both safeguards it and puts the constitution in place from the start (for example, the democratic character does so for a democracy, and the oligarchic one for an oligarchy), and a better character is a cause of a better constitution in all cases.[1001] Further, in the case of every capacity and craft there are things one must have prior education and prior habituation in, with a view to the sorts of work that each must carry out.[1002] So it is clear that this also holds with a view to the actions of virtue.

But since the end for the whole city is a single end, it is evident that education too must be one and the same for all, and that its supervision must be communal, not private as it is at present, where each individual supervises his own children privately, teaching them whatever private instruction he believes best.[1003] But for communal matters, the training too should be communal.

At the same time, one should in no way think that any citizen belongs to himself alone, but that all of them belong to the city, each being a part of the city.[1004] And it is natural for the supervision of each part to look to the supervision of the whole. One might praise the Spartans on account of this, since they pay the most serious attention to their children, and do so communally.[1005]

VIII 2

It is evident, then, that there should be legislation concerning education, and that this should be made communal. But we must not neglect to consider of what sort the education should be and how someone should be educated. For as things stand there is dispute about its functions. For not everyone supposes that the young should learn the same things, whether with a view to virtue or with a view to the best life, nor is it evident whether it is more appropriate that it be with a view to thought or with a view to the character of the soul.[1006]

Investigation on the basis of current education results in confusion, since it is not at all clear whether people should be trained in what is useful for life, in what conduces to virtue, or in something out of the ordinary. For all these proposals have acquired some advocates. Also, nothing is agreed about what furthers virtue. For, to begin with, people do not all esteem the same virtue, so that it is reasonable to expect them also to diverge about the training needed for it.

That children should be taught those useful things that are necessary, however, is not at all unclear. But it is evident that they should not be taught all of them, there being a difference between the functions of the free and those of the unfree, and that they should share only in such things as do not make those who share in them vulgar. (Any function should be considered vulgar, and so too any craft or branch of learning, if it renders the body, the soul, or the thought of free people useless for the uses and actions of virtue.[1007] That is why we call vulgar both the sorts of crafts that put the body into worse condition and the sorts of work that are done for wages. For they make thought unleisured and low.)

Even in the case of some of the free sciences, while it is not unfree to share in them up to a point, to overly apply oneself to them with a view to exactness is liable to result in the harms just mentioned.[1008] But what one does an action for the sake of, or learns for the sake of, also makes a big difference. For what one does for one's own sake, for the sake of friends, or because of virtue is not unfree, but someone who does the same thing because of others would in many cases seem to be acting like a hired laborer or a slave.

VIII 3

The sorts of learning that are now laid down as a foundation, as was said earlier, tend in two directions.[1009] And there are pretty much four that are customarily taught: reading and writing, athletics, music, and fourth, in some cases, drawing. Reading, writing, and drawing are taught because they are useful for life and have many uses, whereas athletics is taught because it contributes to courage. In the case of music, though, there is immediately a puzzle to go through. For nowadays most people share in it for the sake of pleasure. But those who at the start assigned it a place in education, did so, just as has often been said, because nature itself seeks not only the correct use of unleisure but also the capacity to be at leisure in a noble way.[1010] For this is the one starting-point of everything else, and so we should speak about it again.[1011]

If both are needed, but being at leisure is more choiceworthy than unleisure and is its end, then we should inquire into what it is people should spend their leisure doing. For surely they should not spend it amusing themselves. For then it would be necessary for amusement to be the end of life. But if that is impossible, and if amusements are more to be used in periods of unleisure (for someone who exerts himself needs relaxation, and amusement is for the sake of relaxation, whereas unleisure is accompanied by toil and strain), then we should, because of this, introduce amusement, but watch for the appropriate time to use it, as if dispensing it as a medicine [for the ills of unleisure].[1012] For this sort of movement of the soul is a loosening and, because of the pleasure it involves, a relaxation.

Being at leisure itself, though, seems to involve pleasure, happiness, **1338ª1** and living blessedly. This does not belong to those who are unleisured, however, but only to those who are at leisure. For the person who is being unleisured is being so for the sake of some end, because he does not possess it, whereas happiness is an end, and everyone thinks that it is accompanied not by pain but by pleasure. This pleasure is not taken to be the same by everyone, however, but each takes it to be what is in accord with himself and his state [of character], and the best person takes it to be the best pleasure, the one that comes from the noblest things.[1013] So it is evident both that certain things should be learned and taught with a view to the leisure spent in passing the time, and that these teachings and these sorts of learning are for their own sake, whereas those that with a view to unleisure are necessary and for the sake of things other than themselves.

That is why our predecessors assigned music too a place in education, not on the supposition that it is necessary, since it is nothing of the sort; nor on the supposition that, like reading and writing, it is useful for making money, managing a household, acquiring learning, and for many political actions, or, as drawing seems to be, useful for discerning the works of craftsmen more correctly; nor, again, on the supposition that, like athletics, it furthers health and vigor, since we see that neither of these results from music. What remains, then, is that music is for passing the time in leisure—which is manifestly just why people introduce it. For they assign it a place in what they think to be a pastime characteristic of free people. That is why Homer puts it this way: "call the bard alone to the rich banquet," and then he goes on to mention certain others "who call the bard," he says, "that he may bring delight to all."[1014] Elsewhere, Odysseus says that the best pastime is when men are enjoying good cheer and "the banqueters seated in due order throughout the hall, give ear to the bard."[1015]

It is evident, therefore, that there is a certain sort of education that sons should be given not as something useful or necessary but as something noble and free. But as to whether it is of one sort or several, which these are, and how they should be taught—these are things that must be discussed later on.[1016] But as things stand, we have come this far along the route, namely, that from the ancients we have some testimony based on the educational subjects they laid down as a foundation, since music makes this clear.

Further, it is also clear that children should be taught some of the useful things (such as reading and writing) not only because of their usefulness but also because many other sorts of learning become possible through them. Similarly, they should be taught drawing not in order not to make errors in their private purchases and avoid being cheated when buying or selling products but rather because it makes them good at contemplating the beauty of bodies. To be inquiring everywhere about usefulness is least of all fitting for those who are great-souled and free.[1017]

Since it is evident that education by means of habits must come before education by means of reason, and that education of the body must come before education of thought, it is clear from these that children must be given over to athletic training and coaching. For the first of these produces a certain quality in the state of their bodies and the other in its functions.

VIII 4

Some of the cities that nowadays seem to most supervise children produce in them a state appropriate for an athlete, damaging the form and the growth of their bodies, whereas the Spartans, though they did not make this error, nevertheless make them beast-like by the physical exertions they impose, on the supposition that this is the most advantageous thing with a view to courage. And yet, as we have said many times, the supervision of children should neither look to just one virtue nor to this one above all.[1018] But even if this were the one, the Spartans have not succeeded in procuring it either. For neither in other animals nor in [barbarian] nations do we find that courage follows along with the greatest savagery, but with a tamer, lion-like character.[1019] Many of these nations think nothing of killing and cannibalizing people—for example, of those that live around the Black Sea, there are the Achaeans and Heniochi, and there are other nations on the mainland, some similar to those, others worse, that are skilled in raiding, but in courage they have no share.[1020]

Further, we know that the Spartans themselves, as long as they persisted in their love of physical exertions, were superior to others, whereas now in both athletic and military contests they are left behind by others. For they were superior to others not because they gave athletic training to their young people in that way, but because they alone were trained people competing against untrained ones.

So what is noble, not what is beast-like, should play the leading role here. For it is not the wolf or any other wild beast that would compete against noble danger, but rather a good man.[1021] And those who throw the young too much into these [physical exertions], and leave them without direction in the necessary things, produce people who are *in truth* vulgar, since they have made them useful for one political function only, and one at which they are worse, as our argument shows, than other people.[1022] One should judge the Spartans not on the basis of their earlier works, but of their present ones. For now they have people who compete with them in education, whereas earlier they had not.

We have agreed, then, that one should make use of athletic training, and how one should make use of it. For until they reach puberty lighter athletic exercises should be given, but a strict diet and physical exertions should be forbidden, in order that nothing impede their growth. For no small indication that this can have such an effect is that in the Olympic games one can find only two or three cases in which the same people were victorious both as men and boys, because, when the young are trained, the necessary athletic exercises take away their strength.[1023] But when they have spent the three years after puberty on the other sorts of learning, it is fitting for the next period of their lives to be preoccupied both with physical exertions and strict dieting. For one should not exert thought and the body at the same time, since each of these sorts of physical exertion naturally produces a contrary effect: exerting the body impedes thought; exerting thought impedes the body.

VIII 5

As for music, although we have gone through some of the puzzles in our earlier account, it will be well to take these up again now and develop them, in order to provide a sort of keynote for the arguments one might state in an exposition of the subject.[1024] For it is not easy to determine what the capacity of music is, or what one should share in it for the sake of. [1] Is it for the sake of amusement and relaxation, like sleep and drink? (For these are not intrinsically excellent things, but rather are pleasant and, at the same time, "put an end to care," as Euripides says.[1025] In fact, that is why people class music together with these things and make similar use of all of them, namely, sleep, drink, and music—and they also include dancing among these.) [2] Or perhaps we should think instead that music contributes something to virtue, on the supposition that, just as athletic training establishes a certain quality in the body, so music has the capacity to produce a character of a certain quality, by habituating us to be capable of enjoying ourselves correctly? [3a] Or does music contribute something to passing the time and [3b] to practical wisdom? For this must be set down as third of the things mentioned.[1026]

Now, it is not unclear that the young should not be educated for the sake of amusement. For while they are learning they are not amusing themselves, since learning involves pain.[1027] But neither is it fitting to give a pastime to children of that age at any rate, since the end [as something complete] is not appropriate for anyone who is incomplete.[1028]

But perhaps it might seem that what is a serious matter for children is for the sake of the amusement they will have when they have become men and complete. If that were so, however, for the sake of what must they learn music themselves? Why should they not, like the kings of the Persians and the Medes, take part in musical learning and its pleasure through [the performances of] other people? For those who have made this very thing their function and craft will necessarily produce something better than those who devote only as much time to it as is needed for learning. On the other hand, if they have to exert themselves in such things, they would also have to prepare themselves for the business of gourmet cooking. But that is absurd.

There is the same puzzle, however, even if music is capable of making people's characters better. For why must they learn it themselves, rather than, when listening to others, enjoy it in the correct way and be able to discern [its qualities], like the Spartans? For they do not learn it themselves, but are still able, so they say, to discern which melodies are good of their kind and which are not good of their kind.

The same argument also applies if music is to be used with a view to well-being and a free passing of the time, namely, why must they learn it themselves rather than having the enjoyment of other's use of it? One may investigate the supposition we have about the gods. For Zeus himself does not sing or play the lyre to accompany the poets. On the contrary, we even say that such people [namely, the ones who play music for the entertainment of others] are vulgar, and that doing the actions is not for a [true] man, unless he is drunk or amusing himself.

But perhaps we should investigate these matters later on.[1029] Our first inquiry, though, is whether music is to be put in education or not, and in which of the three areas we puzzled about earlier its capacity lies, namely, amusement, education, or passing the time. And it seems reasonable to assign it a place—and it appears to have a share—in all of them. For amusement is for the sake of relaxation, and relaxation is necessarily pleasant, since it is a sort of cure for the pain caused by one's exertions.

Also, it is generally agreed that one's pastime should not only involve what is noble but also what is pleasant, since being happy is composed of both of these.[1030] And everyone says that music is among the very greatest pleasures, both when it is unaccompanied and when it involves singing. At any rate, Musaeus says that "singing is the most pleasant thing for mortals."[1031] That is why, indeed, it is reasonably included in social gatherings and pastimes, as having the capacity to delight. And so one might suppose from that too that young people should be educated in music. For those pleasures that are harmless are fitting not only with a view to the end, but also with a view to relaxation. But since it rarely happens that human beings attain the end, whereas they do frequently relax and make use of amusements (not only because relaxation and amusements lead to other things, but also because of pleasure), it would be useful to allow the young to find rest from time to time in the pleasures of music.[1032]

What has happened, however, is that human beings make amusements their end. For presumably the end involves a certain pleasure too, although not just a random one, and in their search for it they take amusement to be it, because it has a certain similarity to the end of actions. For the end is not choiceworthy for the sake of what *will* be, and these sorts of pleasures are not choiceworthy for what *will* be, but because of things that have happened already—for example, physical exertions and pains. One might reasonably suppose, then, that it is due to this cause that they seek to achieve happiness by means of these pleasures. But where their taking part in music is concerned, it is not because of this alone, it seems, but also because it is useful with a view to relaxation.

Yet we must surely investigate whether this effect is not coincidental and music's nature not more estimable than one that is in accord with **1340a1**
the use we just mentioned, and whether one should not merely share in the common pleasure that comes from music, of which everyone has a perception (for music has a natural pleasure, which is why the use of it is agreeable to people of all ages and characters), but see whether it contributes in some way to character and soul. This would be clear, if we come to be of a certain quality in our characters through music. But that we do come to be of a certain quality is surely evident because of many distinct things, not least indeed because of the melodies of Olympus, since it is generally agreed that they make souls become ecstatic, and ecstasy is an attribute connected to the character of the soul.[1033]

Further, everyone who listens to imitations comes to have the corresponding feelings, even in separation from the rhythms and melodies of these imitations.[1034] But since music happens to be one of the pleasures, and virtue is concerned with enjoying, loving, and hating in the correct way, it is clear that one should learn and become habituated to nothing so much as correctly discerning and enjoying decent characters and noble actions.[1035] And in rhythms and melodies there are the greatest likenesses to the true natures of anger and gentleness, and furthermore of courage and temperance, and of all the contraries of these, and of the other [components of] characters.[1036] And this is clear from the facts, since we are altered in our souls when we listen to such things. But someone who is habituated to being pained or being pleased in the case of likenesses is close to being the same way in relation to the true things. For example, if someone enjoys contemplating an image of something due to no other cause than its shape or form, he will himself necessarily enjoy contemplating the very thing whose image he is contemplating.[1037]

It happens, however, that in other perceptible objects—for example, in those of touch and taste—no likenesses of [the components of] characters are present, although the objects of sight contain faint ones. For there are a few shapes that do contain such likenesses, and everyone shares in this sort of perception.[1038] Furthermore, these are not likenesses of [the components of] character, but rather the shapes and colors that are produced are signs of the components of character, and these signs refer to the body that is in the grip of the feelings.[1039] Nevertheless, insofar as there is a difference also in the contemplation of these, the young should not contemplate the works of Pauson but rather those of Polygnotus or any other painter or sculptor able to represent character.[1040]

In melodies themselves, though, there are imitations of the [components of] characters.[1041] And this is evident. For, to begin with, the nature of the harmonies is divided, so that listeners are put into distinct states and do not have the same way of responding to each of them.[1042] Instead, they respond to some—for example, the so-called Mixo-Lydian—in a more mournful and anxious way; to others—for example, the more relaxed ones—they respond with softer thought; they are in a medial and settled state most of all to a distinct one, namely, the Dorian (which seems to be the only one of the harmonies that produces this effect); and the Phrygian makes them ecstatic.[1043] These points have been well accounted for by those who have philosophized about this sort of education, since the evidence for their accounts comes from the facts themselves.[1044] It is the same way, too, with the rhythms. For some have a character that is productive of stability, others one that is productive of movement, and of these some involve movements that are more vulgar, whereas others involve more free ones.

It is evident from all these considerations, then, that music has the capacity to produce a character of a certain quality in our souls. And if it has the capacity to produce this, it is clear that children should be introduced to it and educated in it. And instruction in music is fitting to the nature of those at that stage of life. For the young, because of their age, do not voluntarily put up with anything that is unsweetened with pleasure, and music is something naturally sweet. Also there seems to be a certain natural affinity to harmonies and rhythms, which is why many of the wise say that the soul is a harmony, others that it has a harmony.[1045]

VIII 6

We must now discuss whether they themselves should learn to sing and play an instrument or not—which is just the puzzle we raised earlier.[1046] It is not unclear, of course, that it makes a great difference to the development of certain qualities if someone shares in the works himself.[1047] For if people do not share in the works, it is difficult, if not impossible, for them to become excellent discerners of their quality. At the same time, children should have something to occupy them, and the rattle of Archytas, which they give to children to keep them from breaking things in the house, should be considered a good invention, since youth cannot keep still.[1048] This, then, is fitting for children in their infancy, and education is a rattle for older children.

It is evident from these considerations that children should be educated in music in such a way that they are capable of sharing in the works. And it is not difficult to determine what is suitable or unsuitable for the different ages, or to solve the puzzle raised by those who say that the pursuit is vulgar. For, first, since it is for the sake of discerning that one should participate in the works, because of this they should make use of the works while they are young, whereas when they are older they should give them up, but be able to discern which melodies are noble and enjoy them in the correct way, due to what they learned while they were young.

As for the criticism raised by some people, namely, that music makes people vulgar, it is not difficult to resolve by investigating the extent to which those being educated in political virtue should participate in the works, and what sorts of melodies and rhythms they should participate in, and, further, on which sorts of instruments they should do their learning, since this too is likely to make a difference. The resolution of the criticism depends on these considerations. For nothing prevents certain modes of music from producing the effect we mentioned.[1049] It is evident, then, that learning music must neither impede later actions nor make the body vulgar and useless for military and political training—for current uses on the one hand, and for later sorts of learning on the other.[1050]

This could be brought about where learning is concerned if they did not exert themselves either with a view to competitions requiring craft-like expertise and exertion or with works that excite wonder or are extraordinary (which have now made their way into competitions and from there into education), but learned such things too up to the point at which they are able to enjoy noble melodies and rhythms, and not only the common element in music, as even some of the other animals do, and, furthermore, the majority of slaves and children.[1051]

It is also evident from these considerations what sorts of instruments should be used. Flutes should not be introduced into their education, or any other instrument requiring craft-like expertise, such as the cithara or any other that may be of this sort, but rather those instruments that will make them good listeners either in their musical education or any other sort. Further, the flute has to do not with character but rather with frenzy, and so the correct occasions for its use are those where contemplation has the capacity to effect a purification rather than learning.[1052] And let us further add that a contrary factor with a view to its use in education is that playing the flute prevents speech.

That is why our predecessors correctly rejected its use by the young and by free people, even though they had used it at first. For when they came to be more at leisure because of their greater prosperity, and greater-souled as regards virtue, and, further, when on the basis of their works both before and after the Persian Wars they became presumptuous, they latched onto every sort of learning, making no distinction but pursuing them all. That is why they also included flute playing among the things they learned. Even in Sparta, indeed, a certain patron played the flute himself to accompany his own chorus.[1053] And in Athens flute playing became such a local custom that most free men pretty much participated in it, as is clear from the tablet that Thrasippus set up when he had been patron for Ecphantides.[1054]

Later, when they were better able to discern what does contribute to virtue and what does not, flute playing was rejected, because of their experience with it. And the same thing happened to many other ancient instruments, such as the pectis, the barbitos, and those that contribute to the pleasure of people who listen for expressive effects, namely, the heptagon, the trigona, the sambukai, and all those requiring a scientific virtuosity.[1055] 1341b1

The story told by the ancients about flutes is also reasonable. For they, as you know, say that Athena invented flutes but threw them away. Now, there is nothing wrong with saying that the goddess did this out of annoyance at how flute playing distorted her face, but the more likely explanation is that education in flute playing does nothing for thought, but it is to Athena that we attribute scientific knowledge and craft knowledge.[1056]

We reject craft-like education, then, both in instruments and in the works—and by craft-like I mean with a view to competitions. For the practitioner pursues this sort of education not for the sake of his own virtue, but to give his listeners pleasure, and a vulgar pleasure at that. That is why we judge its works to belong not to free men but more to hired laborers. For they do indeed become vulgar, since the target they set up as their end is a base one. For the contemplator of it, because he is vulgar, usually alters the music, so that he produces certain qualities in the craftsmen who perform for him, and in their bodies, because of the movements.[1057]

VIII 7

But further investigation must be made of harmonies and rhythms, and with a view to education, as to whether all the harmonies and all the rhythms should be used, or whether they should be divided, and next whether the same division should be set up for those who are exerting themselves with a view to education, or, third, some distinct one.[1058] Since we see that music consists of melody-making and rhythms, we must not neglect to consider what capacity each of these has as regards education, or whether we should deliberately choose music that has a good melody or the one that has a good rhythm.

Considering as correct, then, much that has been said about these things by some current experts on music as well as those from philosophy who happen to be experienced in issues pertaining to musical education, we shall deliver over those who wish to seek an exact accounting of each particular to them. At the moment, however, we shall draw distinctions in the way laws do, and speak about these things only in outline.[1059]

We accept the division made by some of those in philosophy who divide melodies into those relating to character, those relating to action, and those relating to ecstasy, claiming that the harmonies are by nature akin to these particular melodies, one being related to one melody, and another to another.[1060]

We say, though, that music should not be used for the sake of one benefit but several, since it is for the sake of both education and purification (as to what we mean by purification, we will speak of it in simple terms now, but again and more perspicuously in our discussions concerning poetics), and third, for passing the time, for rest, and for the relaxation of one's tensions.[1061]

1342a1 Hence it is evident that all the harmonies are to be used, but that they are not all to be used in the same way. Instead, with a view to education we should use the ones that most have to do with character and for listening to while others perform them, those that relate to action and those that relate to ecstasy. For any feeling that strongly affects some people's souls is present in everyone, although to a different degree, either greater or lesser—for example, pity and fear, and, furthermore, ecstasy. For there are certain people who are prone to being possessed as a result of this movement.[1062] But under the influence of sacred melodies (when they make use of the ones that induce a frenzy in their souls), we see that they calm down, as if they had received medical treatment and a purification. The same thing, then, must be undergone by those who are prone to pity or fear or to feelings generally, and by others to the extent that each of these things falls to them, and they all get a certain purification and feel their burdens lightened by pleasure.[1063] In a similar way, the action-involving melodies provide harmless enjoyment to human beings.[1064]

That is why use of these sorts of harmonies and these sorts of melodies should be permitted to competitors who perform music for the theater. But since the theater audience is twofold, one free and well educated, the other vulgar, composed of vulgar people, hired laborers, and other people of that sort, the latter too must be provided with competitions and spectacles with a view to relaxation. For just as their souls are distorted from the natural state, so too there are harmonies that are deviations and melodies that are strained and involve excessive expressive effects, and what produces pleasure for each person is what is akin to his nature.[1065] That is why authorization to use a certain sort of music of this kind (*genos*) should be given to those who compete before a theater audience of this sort.

But, as has been said, with a view to education the melodies that have to do with character should be used as well as harmonies of this sort.[1066] And the Dorian is of this sort, as we said earlier, but one should accept any other that passes the examination carried out for us by those who share in the pursuit of philosophy and musical education.[1067] The

Socrates of the *Republic* was not correct, however, to retain only the Phrygian along with the Dorian, especially since he includes the flute among the instruments he rejects.[1068] For the Phrygian has the same capacity among harmonies as the flute has among instruments, since 1342b1
both are frenzied and expressive of feeling. For all Bacchic frenzy and all movements of that sort are, among instruments, most characteristic of the flute, whereas among the harmonies, the Phrygian melodies are the ones that are suited to these.

Composition shows this clearly.[1069] For example, the dithyramb seems by general agreement to be Phrygian. And those who comprehend this matter mention many examples of this, notably the fact that when Philoxenus tried to compose a dithyramb—*The Mysians*—in Dorian, he could not do it, but as a result of its very nature fell back into Phrygian again, which is the harmony naturally appropriate to it.[1070]

As for the Dorian, everyone agrees that it is the most steady and has most of all a courageous character. Further, since we praise the mean between extremes, and say that it is what we should pursue, and the Dorian has this nature in relation to the other harmonies, it is evident that being educated in the Dorian melodies is more appropriate for younger people.[1071]

There are, though, two targets: the possible and the appropriate.[1072] And in fact each individual should more undertake things that are possible *and* appropriate. But these things are determined by one's stage of life. For example, it is not easy for people exhausted by age to sing harmonies that are strained; rather, nature suggests the relaxed harmonies at their stage of life.[1073] That is why some of those concerned with music rightly criticize Socrates for this as well, namely, that he rejected the relaxed harmonies for the purposes of education not because they have the capacity that drink has (since drink instead produces Bacchic frenzy) but because they make us weak.[1074] So, with a view also to that future stage of life, namely, old age, one should avail oneself of harmonies of this sort and melodies of this sort.

Further, if there is a certain sort of harmony that is appropriate to the age of children, because it has the capacity to provide both order and education at the same time, as appears to be particularly the case with the Lydian harmony, then it is evident that these three things must be made the defining marks in education: the mean, the possible, and the appropriate.

Notes

Book I

Note 1

Community (*koinônia*): A *koinônia* (sometimes translated as "partnership" or "association") consists of people of different sorts, who engage in a common enterprise that involves sharing something in common (*koinos*) (II 1 1260^{b}39–40), and who are bound to each other by a sort of friendship and a sort of justice: "in every community there seems to be some sort of justice and some sort of friendship as well" (*NE* VIII 9 1159^{b}26–27). Thus a household is a *koinônia*, a city is a *koinônia*, but so too are master and slave, or the partners in a business transaction, or even fellow travelers (II 5 1263^{a}17). The political *koinônia* subsumes all or most of these: "Other communities seek what is advantageous in some area—for example, sailors seek what is advantageous on a voyage related to some moneymaking occupation or something of that sort, whereas fellow soldiers seek what is advantageous in war, whether money, victory, or taking a city; and similarly with members of tribes or demes. Some communities, though, seem to come about because of pleasure—namely, religious guilds and dining clubs, since these come about for the sake of sacrifices and companionship. All of these, however, seem to be subordinate to the political community, since it seeks not the advantage that is present at hand but the one that is for all of life" (*NE* VIII 9 1160^{a}14–23).

The community that has the most control of all, and encompasses all the others, aims both at the good that has the most control of all and does so to the highest degree: "If, then, there is some end of things doable in action that we wish for because of itself, and the others because of it, and we do not choose everything because of something else (since if *that* is the case, it will go on without limit so that the desire will be empty and pointless), it is clear that this will be the good—that is, the best good. Hence regarding our life as well, won't knowing the good have great influence and—like archers with a target—won't we be better able to hit what we should? If so, we should try to grasp in outline, at least, what the good is and to which of the sciences or capacities it properly belongs. It would seem to be the one with the most control, and the most architectonic one. And politics seems to be like this, since it is the one that prescribes which of the sciences need to exist in cities and which ones each group in cities should learn and up to what point. Indeed, we see that even the capacities that are generally most honored are under it—for example, generalship, household management, and rhetoric. And since it uses the other practical sciences and, furthermore, legislates about what must be done and what avoided, its end will encompass those of the others, so that it will be the human good" (*NE* I 2 1094^{a}18–^{b}7). In our text the parallel argument is being used to define not the highest good or the most controlling or most architectonic science, but the city itself, which is controlled by that science with the aim of achieving that good.

Encompasses (*periechousa*): The primary connotation of *periechein*, which is a compound of the preposition *peri* ("around") and the verb *echein* ("have," "possess"), is that of containing by surrounding. So if that were its meaning here, the thought would be that because the city contains the other communities, the good it aims at is higher than the good they do. Just as "contain" can also mean "circumscribe" or "limit," however, so too can *periechein*. The idea would then be that by looking to its own end, city sets limits to the ends of the communities that are parts of it. Why a limiting end of this sort would have to be the best or human good would remain unclear. Other people's rights, for example, may set absolute limits to our pursuit of happiness and so be limiting ends. But it is not obvious that respecting the rights of others is the *highest* good. In addition, whatever imposes the limit would itself have to be an end that all other ends further, so that this end is a better good than the other ones. This is the idea operative at I 13 1260^{b}8–20.

Control (*kurios*): Control is fundamentally executive power or authority or the power to compel, so that a general is *kurios* over his army (*NE* III 8 1116^{a}29–^{b}2) and a politician is *kurios* over a city and its inhabitants. Since what is *kurios* in a sphere determines or partly determines what happens within it, it is one of the most estimable or important elements in the sphere, so that what is less estimable than something cannot or should not control it (VI 12 1143^{b}33–35, 13 1145^{a}6–7).

Note 2

City (*polis*): A *polis* (plural: *poleis*) is a unique political institution, something like a city and something like a modern state (hence "city," "state," and "city-state" are common translations). Unlike a typical city, however, a *polis* enjoyed the political sovereignty characteristic of a state (it could possess its own army and navy, enter into alliances, make war, and so on), whereas unlike a typical modern state, it was politically, religiously, and culturally unified and often quite small in size. Its territory included a single (typically) walled town (*astu*), with a citadel and a marketplace, which, as the political and governmental heart of things, is itself often referred to as the *polis* (*Pol.* VII provides many examples of this), and also included the surrounding agricultural land. Citizens lived there as well as inside the town proper. A *polis* is a multitude of citizens (III 1 1274^{b}41) sharing a constitution (3 1276^{b}1–2), so that *poleis* with different constitutions are distinct (1276^{b}10). But while a *polis* includes women, children, and slaves (I 13 1260^{b}8–20, II 9 1269^{b}14–19, 1277^{a}5–10), strictly speaking only the unconditional citizens, namely, those who share in judicial and deliberative office, are genuine parts of it (VII 8 1328^{a}21–^{b}2, 1329^{a}2–5, 9 1329^{a}19–24). A *polis* is the natural community for human beings to live in (I 2 1253^{a}7–18, III 6 1278^{b}19–25, *NE* VIII 12 1162^{a}17–19, *EE* VII 10 1242^{a}22–27), since they can live well and achieve the happiness that is their natural end only within it.

Note 3

Those who think that the positions of politician, king, household manager, and master [of slaves] are the same: See Plato, *Pol.* 258e–261a, Xenophon, *Mem.* III.iv.12, III.6.14.

Politician (*politikos*): *Politikê*—the art, craft, or science of politics—is the practical body of knowledge used in ruling a city (*NE* I 9 1099^{b}29–32, 13 1102^{a}18–25, II 1 1103^{b}3–6, VI 8 1141^{b}23–33, VII 11 1152^{b}1–3, X 9 1180^{b}23–1181^{b}23). Someone who knows *politikê* is a true *politikos*—a true politician or true statesman—while, in a looser sense, anyone holding the requisite office is a *politikos*. "Statesman" and "political ruler" are other common translations.

King (*basileus*): A kingship is a monarchical constitution that aims at the common advantage (III 7 1279^{a}32–34). Its deviant form is tyranny. Five kinds of kingship are discussed in III 14: (1) Spartan kingship; (2) barbarian kingship; (3) dictatorship; (4) consensual, elective, law-based kingship; (5) absolute kingship. In II 15 (1285^{b}33–37) these are reduced to two fundamental kinds: Spartan and absolute. In III 16 Spartan kingship is removed from the list of genuine kinds of kingship, on the grounds that it is not a kind of constitution (1287^{a}3–4).

Household manager (*oikonomos*): Household management (*oikonomikê, oikonomia*) when possessed by a male is (1) the craft or science of acquiring property, when possessed by a female it is (2) the craft of preserving it (III 5 1277^{b}24–25). The natural part of the craft of property acquisition is a part of (1) (I 8 1256^{b}26–27), but the craft of commerce is not. Other parts of (1) are mastership of slaves, marital science, and procreative science (see I 3, 12–13).

Master (*despotês*): A master is someone who (in the best case) exercises the rule of a master (*despotikê*) over natural slaves in accord with the craft or science of mastership (*despotikê epistêmê*). See I 7.

Note 4

They think that each of these differs with regard to large or small number: The number referred to may be either of people ruled or, as the example of king and political ruler in the next sentence shows, of people ruling.

Kind (*eidos*): *Eidos* sometimes means "form," and is contrasted with *hulê* ("matter"), and sometimes means "species," and is contrasted with *genos* ("genus"). But often, as here, *eidos*—and *genos* too—seems to have a more general meaning, and are then translated as "kind," followed by the Greek term in parenthesis. Parallel issues arise for *diaphorai*, which are sometimes the differentiae that divide a genus into species, and so define each of its species, and are sometimes simply the different features that distinguish one kind of thing from another, without necessarily suggesting that the kinds are genera or species in the strict sense or that the differences are differentiae. Again, the Greek term in parenthesis signals what is going on.

Note 5

The reasons belonging to this sort of science (*epistêmês*): *Epistêmê*, which usually means "science" or "scientific knowledge," may be being used here in a weaker sense. But since scientific knowledge may be nascent (II 5 1263^{a}39n), undeveloped

(II 8 1268^{b}34), or of something fairly insignificant (I 7 1255^{b}22–31), little may hang on the matter. Since the sciences in question are practical ones, however, the reasons belonging to them will be prescriptions that direct actions. When the relevant science does not provide such prescriptions, or when the question of how to apply them is in doubt, deliberation will be required. As a result practical reasons are sometimes the outcomes of deliberation about what to do in particular circumstances.

Reasons (*logous*): In ordinary Greek *logos* (here "reason") can refer among other things (1) to a word or organized string of words constituting a discussion, conversation, speech, explanation, definition, principle, reason, or piece of reasoning, or (2) to what such words or their utterances mean, express, or denote, such as, the ratio between quantities (*NE* V 3 1131^{a}31–32), or (3) to the capacity that enables someone to argue, give reasons, and so on (*Pol.* VII 13 1332^{b}5).

Science (*epistêmê*): (1) Aristotle usually divides sciences (*epistêmai*) into three kinds: theoretical (contemplative), practical (action-involving), and productive (crafts) (*Top.* VI 6 145^{a}15–16, *Met.* XI 7 1064^{a}16–19). But sometimes a more fine-grained classification is employed, in which theoretical sciences are divided into natural sciences (such as physics and biology) and strictly theoretical sciences (such as astronomy and theology) on the basis of the kinds of beings with which they deal (*Ph.* II 7 198^{a}21–^{b}4, *Met.* VI 1 1025^{b}18–1026^{a}32). The term *epistêmê* is sometimes reserved for the unconditional scientific knowledge provided exclusively by the strictly theoretical sciences (*NE* VI 3 1139^{b}31–34), but here, as often elsewhere, it is used in the looser sense, which encompasses the practical and productive sciences as well. To understand what a science of any of these sorts is, we must begin a few steps back.

(2) An *assertion* is the true (or false) predication of a single predicate term A of a single subject term B, either as an affirmation (*kataphasis*) (A belong to B) or a denial (*apophasis*) (A does not belong to B) (*Int.* 8). What makes a term a single subject term, however, is not that it is grammatically singular or serves as a grammatical subject but that it designates a substantial particular—a canonical example of which is a perceptible matter-form compound, such as Socrates. Similarly, what makes a term a predicate is that it designates a universal (man, pale)—something that can have many particular instances. When the role of predicate is restricted to universals, therefore, while that of subject is left open to both particulars and universals, it is more on ontological or metaphysical grounds than on what we would consider strictly logical ones. Subjects and predicates are thus ontological items, types of beings, rather than linguistic or conceptual ones, and logical principles, such as the principle of noncontradiction, are very general ontological principles, truths about all beings as such, or qua beings. Particular assertions (Socrates is a man) and general assertions (Men are mortal) have the same subject-predicate form, but when the subject is a universal, the assertion may itself be either universal (All men are mortal) or particular (Some men are mortal)—that is to say, the predicate may be asserted (denied) of the subject either universally (*katholou*) or in part (*kata meros*) or, if the quantifier is omitted (Men are mortal), indefinitely (*adihoristos*). General assertions, as a result, which are the only ones of interest to science (*Met.* VII 15 1039^{b}27–31), are of four types: A belongs to

all B (**a**AB), A belongs to no B (**e**AB), A belongs to some B (**i**AB), A does not belong to all B (**o**AB).

(3) A *science*, whether theoretical or one of the other sorts, is a state of the soul that enables its possessor to give demonstrative explanations—where a demonstration (*apodeixis*) is a special sort of deduction (*sullogismos*) from scientific starting-points and a deduction is "an argument in which, certain things having been supposed, something different from those supposed things necessarily results because of their being so" (*APr.* I 2 24ᵇ18–20). The things supposed are the argument's premises; the necessitated result is its conclusion; all three are assertions of one of the four types we looked at. In Aristotle's view, such deductions are *syllogisms* (*sullogismos*, again) consisting of a major premise, a minor premise, and a conclusion, where the premises have exactly one "middle" term in common, and the conclusion contains only the other two "extreme" terms. The conclusion's predicate term is the *major term*, contributed by the major premise; its subject is the *minor term*, contributed by the minor premise. The middle term must be either subject of both premises, predicate of both, or subject of one and predicate of the other. The resulting possible combinations of terms yield the so-called figures of the syllogism:

	First figure		Second figure		Third figure	
	Predicate	Subject	Predicate	Subject	Predicate	Subject
Premise	A	B	A	B	A	C
Premise	B	C	A	C	B	C
Conclusion	A	C	B	C	A	B

Systematic investigation of the possible combinations of premises in each of these figures results in the identification of the *moods* or modes that constitute valid deductions. In the first figure, these are as follows:

Form	Mnemonic	Proof
aAB, **a**BC | **a**AC	**Barbara**	Perfect
eAB, **a**BC | **e**AC	**Celarent**	Perfect
aAB, **i**BC | **i**AC	**Darii**	Perfect (or from Camestres)
eAB, **i**BC | **o**AC	**Ferio**	Perfect (or from Cesare)

A mood is perfect when there is a proof of its validity that is *direct*, in that it does not rely on the validity of any other mood. Only first figure syllogisms have perfect moods.

(4) Besides their logical interest as admitting of direct proof, perfect syllogisms in Barbara are also of particular importance to science. First, because "syllogisms that give the why, which hold either universally or for the most part, in most cases are carried out through this figure. That is why it is the most scientific of all; for getting a theoretical grasp on the why is most important for [scientific] knowledge" (*APo.* I 14 79ᵃ20–24). Second, "only through this figure can you hunt for

scientific knowledge of something's essence" (79^{a}24–25): essences hold universally, only perfect syllogisms in Barbara have universal conclusions, and definitions of essences, which are scientific starting-points, must hold universally.

(5) Specifically scientific starting-points are of just three types (*APo.* I 10 76^{a}37–^{b}22). Those *special* to a science are definitions of the real (as opposed to nominal) essences of the beings with which the science deals (II 3 90^{b}24, II 10 93^{b}29–94^{a}19). Because these are definitions by genus and differentia (II 13 96^{a}20–97^{b}39), a single science must deal with a single genus (*Met.* VII 12, *APo.* I 7 75^{b}10–11, I 23 84^{b}17–18, 28 87^{a}38–39). Other starting-points (so-called axioms) are common to all or many sciences (*APo.* I 2 72^{a}14–24, I 32 88^{a}36–^{b}3). A third sort of starting-point posits the existence of the genus with which the science deals, but this may often be left implicit if the existence of the genus is clear (I 10 76^{b}17–18). The source of these starting-points, in turn, is perception and experience, which lead by induction and dialectic, to a grasp by understanding of them: "From perception memory comes to be, and from many memories of the same thing, experience. For, then, memories that are many in number form one experience. And from experience, or from the whole universal that has come to rest in the soul (the one over and above the many, this being whatever is present as one and the same in all of them), comes a starting-point (*archê*) of craft knowledge and scientific knowledge—of craft knowledge if it concerns production (*genesis*), of scientific knowledge if it concerns being" (*APo.* II 19 110^{a}3–9). See Introduction, pp. xxxiii–l.

(6) To constitute a *demonstration* a deduction must be a valid syllogism in the mood Barbara, whose premises meet a number of conditions. First, they must be immediate or indemonstrable, and so must be reached through induction. Second, our confidence in them must be unsurpassed (Introduction, pp. xliii–xliv). Finally, they must be necessary (and so, of course, true) in a special sense: the predicates in them must belong to the subjects in every case, intrinsically, and universally (*APo.* I 4 73^{a}24–27): (6a) *In every case:* A predicate *A* belongs to every subject *B* if and only if there is no *B* to which it fails to belong and no time at which it fails to belong to a *B*: "for example, if animal belongs to every man, then if it is true to say that this thing is a man, it is also true to say that it is an animal, and if the former is the case now, the latter is also the case now" (73^{a}29–31). (6b) *Intrinsically:* A predicate *A* belongs intrinsically to a subject *B* just in case it is related to *B* in one of four ways: (i) *A* is in the account or definition of what *B* is, or of *B*'s substance, or essence (73^{a}34–37); (ii) *B* is a complex subject φB_1, where φ is an intrinsic coincident of B_1—for example, odd number or male or female animal (*Met.* XIII 3 1078^{a}5–11)—and *A* is in the definition of φB_1's essence; (iii) *A* just is *B*'s essence; (iv) *A* is not a part of *B*'s essence or identical to it but stems causally from it, so that being *B* is an intrinsic cause of being *A* (73^{a}34–^{b}24). (6c) *Universally:* A predicate *A* belongs to a subject *B* universally just in case "it belongs to it in every case and intrinsically, that is, insofar as it is itself" (73^{b}26–27).

(7) Because intrinsic predicates stem in various ways from essences, the subjects to which they belong must have essences. In other words, they must be *intrinsic beings*, since—stemming as they do from essences—intrinsic predicates identify or make them clear: "The things said to be intrinsically are the very ones signified

by the figures of predication" (*Met.* V 7 1017^{a}22–23). These figures of predication are the so-called *categories*: "Anything that is predicated (*katêgoroumenon*) of something must either be . . . a definition . . . if it signifies the essence . . . or, if it does not, a special property (*idion*) . . . or one of the things in the definition, or not; and if it is one of the things in the definition, it must signify the genus or the differentiae, since the definition is composed of genus and differentiae. If, however, it is not one of the things in the definition, it is clear that it must be a coincident; for a coincident was said to be that which belongs to a thing but that is neither a definition nor a genus nor a special property. Next we must distinguish the kinds (*genos*) of predication in which one will find the four mentioned above. These are ten in number: what-it-is, quantity, quality, relation, when, where, position, having, doing, and being affected. For the coincidents, the genus, the special properties, and the definition will always be in one of these kinds of predication [or *categories*]" (*Top.* I 8–9 103^{b}7–25). For each of the intrinsic beings in these ten *categories* we can state its what-it-is (*Met.* VII 4 1030^{a}17–24), even if strictly speaking only substances have definitions and essences (5 1031^{a}7–24). Specifying these is one of the tasks of *Categories*, where Aristotle explains how beings in categories other than that of substance are ontologically dependent on those in the category of substance.

Ruling and being ruled (*archôn kai archomenos*): The notion of ruling (*archôn*) and the correlative notions of being a ruler (also *archôn*), exercising rule (*archein*), or holding ruling office (*archê*) is explained in the following brief passage: "The one in accord with whose deliberate choice what is moved is moved and what is changed is changed—for example, the rulers (*archai*) in cities, dynasties, and kingships are said to be *archai*, as are crafts, especially architectonic ones" (*Met.* V 1 1013^{a}10–14). On *archê* as starting-point, see I 9 1257^{a}6n, and on architectonic, 5 1253^{b}38n, 13 1260^{a}17n.

Note 6

The method of inquiry that has guided us elsewhere: "In all methodical inquiries in which there is knowledge—that is, scientific knowledge—of things that have starting-points, causes, or elements, it comes from knowledge of these (for we think that we know each thing when we know its primary causes and primary starting-points all the way to its elements), so it is clear that in the scientific knowledge of nature our first task is to determine the starting-points. And the natural route is from things that are knowable and more perspicuous to us toward things that are more perspicuous and more knowable by nature, since the same things are not knowable to us as are knowable unconditionally. That is why we must in this way advance from things that are less perspicuous by nature but more perspicuous to us to the things that are more perspicuous by nature and more knowable. And the things that are in the first instance clear and perspicuous to us are rather compounded. It is only later, through an analysis of these, that we come to know their elements and starting-points. That is why we must proceed from the universal to the particular. For it is the whole that is more knowable by perception, and the universal is a sort of whole. For the universal embraces many things as parts. The same is true in a way of names in relation to an account. For a name like 'circle' signifies a sort of whole in an indivisible way, whereas the definition [= account] divides it into its particular [elements]" (*Ph.* I 1 184^{a}1–^{b}3). See also *HA* I 1 486^{a}5–14, *PA* II 1 646^{a}8–24.

Note 7

As in other cases, a composite must be analyzed until we reach things that are incomposite (*asunthetôn*): "Just as it is possible for A to belong to B indivisibly, so it is also possible for it not to belong indivisibly. By belonging or not belonging indivisibly I mean that there is no middle term for them, since they no longer belong or do not belong in virtue of something else" (*APo.* I 15 79^{a}33–36); "By a demonstration I mean a scientific deduction, and by scientific I mean a deduction in virtue of which we have scientific knowledge of something. . . . Demonstrative scientific knowledge must proceed from items that are true, primitive, immediate [= indivisible], and more knowable than, prior to, and causes of the conclusion" (I 2 71^{b}17–23); "It is impossible to have [scientific] knowledge until we come to indivisibles" (*Met.* II 2 994^{b}21). I take "incomposite (*asunthetos*)" and "indivisible" (*atomos*) to be more-or-less equivalent.

Whether or not it is possible to gain some craft-like expertise about each of the things we have mentioned: The "things we have mentioned" are household managers, masters, politicians, and kings, and the question is whether we can gain the sort of general or universal understanding of them that will reveal the differences between them (I 3 1253^{b}16–18).

Craft-like expertise (*technikon*): "It seems, presumably, that someone who *does* wish to become expert in a craft (*technikô[i]*) or in a theoretical science should take steps toward the universal and come to know it as well as possible, since that, we said, is what the sciences are concerned with" (*NE* X 9 1180^{b}20–23).

Craft (*technê*): A *technê* is a science concerned with production, rather than with action (dealt with by practical sciences) or truth (dealt with by theoretical sciences). See 1252^{a}15n.

Note 8

If we were to see how these things grow naturally from the start, we would in this way, as in other cases, get the best theoretical grasp on them: "All the homoeomerous bodies are composed of the elements we have mentioned [= earth, water, fire, air] as their matter, but, in accord with their substance [= essence], of their account [= form]. This is always clearer in the case of the later arrivals and, in general, in things that are instruments and for the sake of something. For example, it is clearer that a corpse is a human being homonymously [than that its flesh is so]. In the same way, accordingly, the hand of a dead person is a hand homonymously (just as flutes made of stone might still be called flutes). For these too seem to be instruments of a sort. But this is less clear in the case of flesh and bone, and still less so in the case of fire and water. For the for-the-sake-of-which is less clear where the matter predominates most. For if you take the extremes, matter is not any other thing beyond itself, and the substance is nothing other than the account [= the form], but the intermediates [= matter-form compounds] are related to each in proportion to their nearness to it" (*Mete.* IV 12 389^{b}28–390^{a}7).

Note 9

The thought, then, is that we will get a better theoretical grasp on what household managers, masters, politicians, and kings actually are when we see how the communities they rule grow naturally. For we will then understand their natural ends—the thing that they are naturally for the sake of. And this will turn out to be the city—the political community ruled not by a master, a household manager, or a king, but by a politician.

Get the best theoretical grasp on (*theôrêseien*): The verb *theasthai*, with which *theôria* is cognate, means "to look at" or "gaze at." Hence *theôria* itself is sometimes what someone is doing in looking closely at something, or observing, studying, or contemplating it. *Theôria* can thus be an exercise of understanding (*nous*), which is the element responsible for grasping scientific starting-points (*NE* VI 6 1141ᵃ7–8), such as (the definition of) right angle in the case of geometry, or (the definition of) happiness in the case of politics. Hence the cognate verb *theôrein* sometimes means "to be actively understanding" or "to be actively contemplating" something. "Get a theoretical grasp on" often seems to convey the right sense.

Note 9

They do not do so from deliberate choice (*prohaireseôs*): We wish for the end or target, we "deliberate about and deliberately choose what furthers it" (*NE* III 5 1113ᵇ3–4). Deliberate choice (*prohairesis*) is thus a matter of choosing (*haireisthai*) one thing before or in preference to (*pro*) another (III 2 1112ᵃ16–17), and so of deliberating about what things should be done earlier than or in preference to others in order to further the desired end: "someone with understanding chooses the better of two things in all cases" (*EE* VII 2 1237ᵇ37–38). The thought here is that our urge to procreate is like that of other animals. In response to the urge we can certainly deliberate, for example, whom to have children with, but that procreation is on our agenda at all is a part of our nature.

But, like other animals and plants, because the urge to leave behind something of the same sort as themselves is natural: "It is the most natural function in those living things that are complete and not disabled or spontaneously generated, to produce another like itself—an animal producing an animal, a plant a plant—in order that they may partake in the eternal and divine insofar as they can. For all desire that, and it is for the sake of it that they do whatever they do by nature. (The for-the-sake-of-which, though, is twofold—the purpose for which and the beneficiary for whom.) Since, then, they cannot share in what is eternal and divine by continuous existence, because nothing that admits of passing away can persist as the same and numerically one, they share in them insofar as each can, some more and some less. And what persists is not the thing itself but something like itself, not one in number but one in form" (*DA* II 4 415ᵃ26–ᵇ7); "Between a man and a woman, friendship seems to hold by nature, since a human being seems to be by nature more couple forming than political to the extent that household is prior to and more necessary than city, and reproduction is a characteristic more common to animals. Now with the other animals, their community only goes as far as reproduction, whereas human beings share a household not only for the sake of reproduction but also for the sake of various things necessary for life. For straight from the beginning their functions are divided, those of a man being different from those of a woman, so they assist each other by putting their special ones into the common enterprise. Because of this, both utility and pleasure seem to be found in this form of friendship. It may also exist because of virtue, however, if both parties are decent. For there is a virtue characteristic of each, and they can enjoy something like this. And children seem to be a bond of union, which is why childless unions are more quickly dissolved. For children are a good common to both, and what is common holds things together" (*NE* VIII 12 1162^{a}16–29).

Note 10

Capable of looking ahead by using its thought (*dianoia[i]*): *Dianoia* is often contrasted with the body (*Pol.* II 9 1270^{b}40, VII 16 1335^{b}16), making "mind" seem a natural translation of it. But unlike the mind, which includes perception, imagination, belief, knowledge, desire, virtues of character, and other such things, *dianoia* is contrasted with each of these. It is not perception, because all animals have that, whereas "the majority of animals do not have *dianoia*" (*DA* I 5 410^{b}24). It is not imagination, because, as we might put it, *dianoia* is propositional, or operates on things that can be true or false, asserted or denied (*Pol.* II 11 1273^{a}22), whereas imagination is a representational state that is more like perception, more "imagistic." Thus "what assertion and denial are in the case of thought, that, in the case of desire, is precisely what pursuit and avoidance are" (*NE* VI 2 1139^{a}21–22). Unlike belief and knowledge, however, "thought is in fact not yet assertion" (*NE* VI 9 1142^{b}12–13), making it natural to think of it, or some of it anyway, as a process of reasoning that can culminate in a belief or an asserted proposition (*Pol.* IV 15 1299^{a}30 and V 8 1307^{b}35 are nice examples). And this further evidenced by the fact that the virtues of thought, which are theoretical wisdom and practical wisdom (*NE* I 13 1103^{a}4–6), are (respectively) those of the scientific sub-part and the rationally calculative sub-part, of the part of the soul that has reason (VI 1 1139^{a}5–12). At the same time, the fact that scientific knowledge includes both demonstrative reasoning and a grasp on scientific starting-points by the understanding, implies that not all thinking need be in any sense inferential, since understanding is non-inferential—a grasping of something rather than something process-like (*Pol.* VII 13 1325^{b}20 is a good example). *Dianoia* is not desire, because, while desire can cause animal movement, without thought, as it does in the case of non-rational animals, "thought by itself . . . moves nothing" (*NE* VI 2 1139^{a}35–36). As a result, it is not character (*Pol.* VIII 2 1337^{a}38–39), since the latter, as involving desire, is cultivated by habituation, whereas *dianoia* is cultivated by teaching (*NE* II 1 1103^{a}14–18)—hence the common and politically important contrast between thought and character (*Pol.* III 11 1281^{b}7).

By nature a slave: A slave is an animate piece of property belonging wholly to his master (*Pol.* I 4 1254^{a}12–23)—an instrument or tool for use in matters having to do not with production but with action (1254^{a}7–8). Some people are legal slaves, or slaves simply because they have been enslaved. Others, however, because their souls lack a deliberative part (13 1260^{a}12), are natural slaves. As a result, they are not self-sufficient (IV 4 1291^{a}10) and cannot be happy (III 9 1280^{a}32–34). For such people slavery is coincidentally advantageous and just (I 4 1255^{a}1–3, III 6 1278^{b}32–37).

But it is neither just nor advantageous for merely legal slaves to be enslaved, unless perhaps if they have been living as slaves for some time (I 5 1255^{a}1–3n).

There are also various kinds of natural slaves, some of whom seem to have a larger share in virtue (or reason) than others (*Pol.* I 7 1255^{b}27–29, 13 1260^{a}14–20, VII 10 1330^{a}30–31). Similarly, there are also various kinds of free people: a vulgar craftsman is a free man, whose soul presumably has a deliberative part, yet he has "a kind of limited slavery" (I 13 1260^{a}39–^{b}1), and is not a free citizen in most constitutions (III 5). It is presumably in these doctrines, if anywhere, that we should look for an easing of the tensions that exist in Aristotle's account of natural slaves, three of which are particularly evident. First, though it is just and advantageous for natural slaves to be enslaved, all slaves, natural or legal (it seems), should be offered freedom as a reward for good service (VII 10 1330^{a}32–33). Second, though slaves lack a deliberative part, those heads of household who have the resources delegate the position of household manager (a position that seems to require both deliberative ability and foresight) to a steward, who is himself (presumably) a slave (I 7 1255^{b}35–37). Third, and related to the second, is the fact that insofar as a slave is a human being, there is even possibly a sort of friendship between master and slave (6 1255^{b}12–15).

Perhaps the thought underlying these claims is that training can, as in the case of non-human animals, make up for much of what nature fails to provide. For though these animals, too, lack a deliberative part, they are capable, because they have imagination, of making associative connections between experiences, which can guide their behavior in much the way that explicit deliberative reasons can guide mature human action: "Insofar as an animal has a desiring part, so far is it capable of moving itself. A desiring part, however, cannot exist without an imagination, and all imagination is either rationally calculative or perceptual. Hence in the latter the other animals also have a share . . . but the deliberative sort exists [only] in the rationally calculative ones (for whether to do this or that is already a work of rational calculation; and we must measure by one [standard], since we are pursuing the greater [good]; and so we must be able to make one appearance that results from many). And this is the cause of these animals seeming not to have belief, namely, that they do not have the [imagination] that results from a syllogism" (*DA* III 10 433^{b}27–11, 434^{a}11). A natural slave with an adequately stocked imagination, then, might well, even without autonomous access to deliberative reasons, make an excellent steward, a passable friend, and be ready, at a certain point, to be released from slavery.

Moreover, unlike wild animals, but like children, slaves do have reason (I 13 1260^{b}5n), in the sense that, like the desiring part of the soul (*NE* I 13 1102^{b}30–1103^{a}3), they can listen to reasons generated by others, and both understand and follow them. But it is less clear whether the same is true when we turn from practical deliberation and the deliberative sub-part (of the part of the soul that has reason) to theoretical scientific reasoning and the scientific sub-part (VI 1 1139^{a}11–14). For Aristotle allows that "while young people become geometers and mathematicians and wise in such things, they do not seem to become practically-wise" (VI 8 1142^{a}12–13). So it seems that he might allow that slaves, too, are like that—capable of autonomous theoretical scientific reasoning, but not of practical reasoning. In the absence of explicit statement on the topic it is difficult to be certain either way.

Consistency aside, Aristotle's doctrine of natural slaves, like his views on women (I 12 1259ᵇ1, 13 1260ᵃ13), are ones we do not endorse, but must nonetheless try to understand as fully as we can. It is a virtue of both doctrines that they seek a natural basis for social and political differences, and so are subject to revision when the natural basis, as in these cases, turns out to be missing.

Note 11

That is why the same thing is advantageous for both master and slave: This claim is developed at I 5–7. At III 6 1278ᵇ32–37, however, it is made clear that the rule of a master over a slave is "rule exercised with a view to the master's own advantage, though coincidentally with a view to that of the slave (since if the slave is destroyed, the mastership cannot be preserved)." This gives such rule a rather special status. From the perspective of its aim it is only coincidentally advantageous to the slave, but because of the unique nature of the relationship of slave to master, it cannot achieve its aim without also achieving what is advantageous to the slave. This distinguishes it from deviant constitutions, which aim exclusively at the advantage of the rulers and in achieving that aim need not, even coincidentally, achieve what is advantageous to the ruled. At the same time, it distinguishes rule of a master from correct constitutions. For they aim at the common advantage (III 6 1279ᵃ17n), not intrinsically at that of the ruler and coincidentally at that of the ruled. The common advantage in a correct constitution, however, is that of citizens who are separate from each other, so that each of them has an advantage that is intrinsically or non-coincidentally his. The advantage of master and slave is apparently not common in this sense, since a slave is like a part of his master (I 4 1254ᵃ8–13), and so seems to have no advantage that is intrinsically his own. Nonetheless, a slave is separate from his master (1254ᵃ17), and that may be enough to enable us to make sense of such an advantage: considered as like a part of his master, the slave's advantage is coincidentally that of his master; considered as separate, that advantage is intrinsically his. We should recall, in any case, that the separate citizens of a correct constitution or city are parts of it (1253ᵃ26–27), so that their common advantage too is that of separate *parts*.

Note 12

The Delphian knife: Apparently a multipurpose, cheaply made tool of some sort. See IV 15 1299ᵇ10n.

Nature produces nothing in a stingy way: See I 1 1253ᵃ9n.

Note 13

Every instrument will be completed best if it serves one function rather than many: "It is better, where possible, not to have the same instrument for dissimilar uses. . . . For where it is possible for two things to be used for two functions without impeding each other, nature is not accustomed to make things as does the coppersmith who, to economize, makes a spit-lamp [IV 15 1299ᵇ10n], but where this is not possible, nature makes use of the same thing for several functions" (*PA* IV 6 683ᵃ19–26).

Functions (*erga*): A function (*ergon*) is: (1) an activity that is the use or actualization of a state, capacity, or disposition; (2) a work or product that is the further result of such an activity (*NE* I 1 1094^a5–6). It is intimately related to its possessor's end or final cause: "The function is the end, and the activity is the function" (*Met.* IX 8 1050^a21–22); "each thing that has a function is for the sake of its function" (*Cael.* II 3 286^a8–9). Moreover, a thing's good or doing well "seems to lie in its function" (*NE* I 7 1097^b26–27). But this holds only when the thing itself is not already something bad (*Met.* IX 9 1051^a15–16). Finally, a thing's function is intimately related to its nature, form, and essence. For a thing's nature is "its for-the-sake-of-which" (*Ph.* II 2 194^a27–28), its form is more its nature than its matter (II 1 193^b6–7), and its essence and form are the same (*Met.* VII 7 1032^b1–2). Hence "all things are defined by their function" (*Mete.* IV 12 390^a10), with the result that if something cannot function, it has no more than a name in common with its functional self (*Pol.* I 2 1253^a20–25, *PA* I 1 640^b33–641^a6, *Met.* VII 10 1035^b14–25). Functions are thus attributed to a wide variety of things, whether living or nonliving. These include plants (*GA* I 23 731^a24–26) and animals generally (*NE* X 5 1176^a3–5), including divine celestial ones (*Cael.* II 3 286^a8–11), parts of their bodies and souls (*PA* II 7 652^b6–14, IV 10 686^a26–29), instruments or tools of various sorts (*EE* VII 10 1242^a15–19), crafts, sciences (II 1 1219^a17), philosophies (*Met.* VII 11 1037^a15) and their practitioners (*NE* VI 7 1141^b10), cities (*Pol.* VII 4 1326^a13–14), and nature itself (*Pol.* I 10 1258^a35).

Note 14

That is why the poets say: See Euripides, *Iphigenia in Aulis* 1266, 1400.

Note 15

From these two communities, then, the household was first to arise: The two are the community of man and woman and that of master and slave.
Hesiod was correct when he said: At *Works and Days* 405.
Hesiod: One of the oldest known Greek poets (c. 700 BC), author also of the *Theogony* and the *Catalogue of Women*. His works, like those of Homer, played a substantial role in Greek education.

Note 16

To poor people an ox takes the place of a servant: Indicating that there can be households that lack—at any rate, human—slaves.

Note 17

Charondas: A 6th-cent BC legislator from Catana in Chalcidice in the southern part of Macedonia.
Epimenides the Cretan: A religious teacher of the late 6th and early 5th cents BC. The works from which Aristotle quotes are lost.

Note 18

The village in accord with nature seems to be a colony (*apoikia*) **of the household** (*oikias*): *Apoikia* is etymologically related to *oikia*. See also Plato, *Lg.* 681b.
Colony: When the population of, for example, a Greek city became too large for the available resources it often sent some of its citizens out to colonize new

territory elsewhere. The resulting colony was politically autonomous but typically retained some ties with its mother city.

Note 19
Nation: See II 2 1261^{a}28n.

Note 20
The same holds in the colonies, because of the kinship [of the villagers]: Compare III 15 1286^{b}8–11.

Note 21
This is what Homer is describing: At *Iliad* X.114–115.

Note 22
Self-sufficiency: See I 2 1253^{a}26n.

Note 23
Every city exists by nature (*phusei*): Things that are "by nature are the ones whose cause is within themselves and are orderly" (*Rh.* I 10 1369^{a}35–^{b}1), which cause is an internal starting-point of "movement and rest, whether in respect of place, growth and withering, or alteration" (*Ph.* II 1 192^{b}13–15). And each such thing is a substance: "things that have a nature are those that have this sort of starting-point. And each of them is a substance. For a substance is a sort of underlying subject, and a nature is always in an underlying subject" (192^{b}32–34). Non-substantial phenomena, like the upward movement of fire, by contrast, though they occur by or in accord with nature, do not themselves have a nature: "And these things [that are by nature and have a nature] are also in accord with nature, as too is whatever belongs intrinsically to them, as spatial movement upward belongs to fire—for this neither is nor has a nature but is by nature and in accord with nature" (192^{b}35–193^{a}1).

When substantial things do have a nature, moreover, it derives not from their matter but from their distinctive manner of composition, or form: "That is why, as regards the things that are or come to be by nature, although that from which they naturally come to be or are is already present [namely, the matter], we still do not say that they have their nature if they do not have their form or shape" (*Met.* V 4 1015^{a}3–5). Thus, for example, a feline embryo has within it a starting-point that explains why it grows into a cat, why that cat moves and alters in the ways it does, and why it eventually decays and dies. A house or any other artifact, by contrast, has no such source within it; instead "the starting-point is in something else and external" (*Ph.* II 1 192^{b}30–31), namely, the understanding of the craftsman who produces it: "Nothing comes away from the carpenter to the matter of the timbers, nor is there any part of the craft of carpentry in the product, but the shape and the form are produced from the carpenter through the movement in the matter. And his soul, in which the form is and his scientific knowledge, moves his hands or some other part in a movement of a particular sort, different when the product is different, the same when it is the same, and the hands move the instruments, and the instruments move the matter" (*GA* I 22 730^{b}11–19; also *Met.* VII 7 1032^{a}32–^{b}10). Let us call such an internal starting-point a *canonical nature*.

Since a city is at least as complex as a human animal, it seems that it should be included among the things existing by nature that do have such a nature. And this seems to be borne out to some extent by the way Aristotle introduces his argument: "If we were to see how these things grow naturally from the start, we would in this way, as in other cases, get the best theoretical grasp on them (*Pol.* I 2 1252^{a}24–26). But it would certainly not be unreasonable to deny this, and to say that a city, though in some sense natural, does not have a canonical nature.

Not everything that has a canonical nature, however, realizes or perfects its nature *by* nature: craft is sometimes needed "to perfect or complete the task that nature is unable to perfect or complete" (*Ph.* II 8 199^{a}15–16). For example, human beings exist by nature and have canonical natures (1 193^{b}5–6), but to perfect these they must acquire the virtues, and these are acquired in part through habituation and in part through the craft of education (*NE* II 1 1103^{a}17–26, *Pol.* VII 13 1332^{a}39–^{b}11), since "every craft and every sort of education wishes to fill in what nature leaves out" (*Pol.* VII 17 1337^{a}1–3). To be sure, things that exist by nature are distinct from things that are the products of a craft. But things that have their canonical natures perfected by craft are not products of craft. Their forms (or formal natures) do not flow into them from the souls or minds of a craftsman, as happens in the case of genuine craft products. Instead, potentialities that are parts of their natures are further actualized by craft. Thus the mere fact of a thing's needing to have its nature completed by craft or the like is no obstacle to its nature being canonical. That is why Aristotle can comfortably combine the view that the city exists by nature with the view that "although the impulse toward this sort of community exists by nature in everyone, the person who first put one together also was the cause of very great goods" (*Pol.* I 3 1253^{a}29–31).

Once we realize, then, that even if the city has a canonical nature, craft is still needed to develop that nature, we can see that less is involved in attributing such a nature to it than we might think. For it is not as if the city will just develop in the way that a feline embryo does. But it would not be wise to overplay even this contrast. For animal natures too seem to need to be domesticated by means of the relevant crafts and sciences if their natures, as internal starting-points of growth and withering, are to be as developed as possible: "In the case of a human being and the other animals the same holds. For domestic animals are by nature better than wild ones, and it is better for all of them to be ruled by human beings, since in this way they secure their preservation" (*Pol.* I 5 1254^{b}10–13).

If the city does have a canonical nature, moreover, the question arises of what sort of being—what *category* of being—it is (I 1 1252^{a}15n(7)). Is it a substance, a quality, a quantity, a relation, or one of the others? The most plausible answer is that it is some sort of substance. For in the first place beings with natures are substances (*Met.* VIII 3 1043^{b}22–23) and in the second place the city is clearly not a quality or quantity or any of the others. Since it must be in some category, it seems that it must be a substance of some sort. And there are indeed substances of various sorts: "what is intrinsically intelligible is the one column [of opposites], and in this substance is primary, and in *this* the simple one and an activity" (XII 7 1072^{a}31–32). Matter-form compounds with natures, then, though they are agreed by everyone to be substances (VII 3 1029ᵃ33–34), are not primary—or the most primary—substances either: that is a status that belongs exclusively to substances which, like the primary god, are simple activities (*Pol.* I 4 1254ᵃ5n). It seems reasonable, therefore, to say that the city is a substance, but not a primary one, and to leave the issue there. Since Aristotle often seems to use the term *ousia* ("substance") to mean *protê ousia* ("primary substance"), this might help explain why he never explicitly categorizes the city as a substance. It is perhaps also worth mentioning that artifacts—items produced by crafts—raise similar problems: are they substances or in some other category? Again, the most reasonable answer seems to be that they are substances of a sort, but not primary substances.

Since the first communities do: Like other animals, human beings have a natural desire to reproduce. Since they are sexually dimorphic, this desire leads them to form a sexual union (a type of community or communal relation) with members of the opposite sex (*Pol.* I 2 1252ᵃ27–30). In the *Nicomachean Ethics*, this desire is further characterized as follows: "Between a man and a woman, friendship seems to hold by nature, since a human being seems to be by nature more couple forming than political to the extent that household is prior to and more necessary than city, and reproduction is a characteristic more common to animals" (VIII 13 1162ᵃ16–19). We might legitimately wonder, however, whether this is correct—whether the desire for sexual union does naturally lead to the formation of Aristotelian couples and *households*. For these have two problematic features. The first is that they involve the subordination of women to men (*Pol.* I 12 1259ᵇ1–2). The second is that the household typically contains (natural) slaves (2 1259ᵇ9–12).

Somewhat similar problems arise concerning the next stage in the emergence of the city: the village. First, the village is "the first community, consisting of several households, for the sake of satisfying needs other than everyday ones" (*Pol.* I 2 1252ᵇ15–16). So if the village is to be natural so must the needs that give rise to it. But all that Aristotle tells us is that households have to engage in exchange with each other when the need arises (I 9 1257ᵃ19–25). This does not help very much, because the things they exchange with each other seem to be just the sorts of things that the household itself is supposed to be able to supply, such as wine and corn (1257ᵃ25–28). Second, to count as a village a community of several households must be ruled in a characteristic way, namely, by a king (1252ᵇ20–22). This is natural, Aristotle explains, because villages are colonies or offshoots of households, in which the eldest is king (1252ᵇ20–22). The problem is that on Aristotle's own view households involve various kinds of rule, not just kingly rule. For example, a head of household rules his wife with political rule (I 12 1259ᵇ1n). We might wonder, therefore, why a village has to be governed with kingly rule rather than with political rule.

The final stage in the emergence of the city, and the conclusion of Aristotle's argument that the city exists by nature and that a human being is a political animal, is presented in the following terse and convoluted passage, which I reprint here for the purposes of analysis:

> [1] The community, coming from several villages, when it is complete, is the city, once it has already reached (one might almost say) the limit of total

> self-sufficiency. [2] It comes to be for the sake of living, but it exists for the sake of living well. [3] That is why every city exists by nature, since the first communities also do. For this one is their end, and nature is an end. For what each thing is when its coming to be has been completed, this we say is the nature of each—for example, of a human, of a horse, or of a household. Further, its for-the-sake-of-which—namely, its end—is best, and self-sufficiency is both end and best. [4] From these considerations, then, it is evident that a city is among the things that exist by nature, that a human is by nature a political animal, and that anyone who is without a city, not by luck but by nature, is either a wretch or else better than human. (1252^{b}27–1253^{a}4)

[1] tells us that the city, unlike the village, has pretty much reached the goal of total self-sufficiency. Yet it seems clear that enough basic human needs are satisfied outside of the city for human life to be possible there: households and villages that are not parts of cities do manage to persist for considerable periods of time (*Pol.* I 2 1252^{b}22–24, II 2 1261^{a}27–29), as do individuals (I 2 1253^{a}31–33).

[2] separates what gives rise to the city from what sustains it once it exists. Fairly basic human needs do the former, but what sustains a city in existence is that we are able to live well and achieve happiness only in it (this point is elaborated in *Pol.* III 6 1278^{b}20–30). Thus the city is self-sufficient not simply because our essential needs are satisfied there but because it is the community within which we achieve the happiness that is our natural end.

[3] tells us that household, village, and city are like embryo, child, and mature adult, in that a single nature is present at each stage but developed or completed to different degrees, until, at the end of the process, the nature is fully realized and the end achieved. Moreover, it suggests that this nature lies within the individuals who constitute the household, village, and city: they are political animals because their natural needs lead them to form, first, households, then villages, then cities. "An impulse toward this sort of community," we are told, "exists by nature in everyone" (*Pol.* I 2 1253^{a}29–30). This impulse, in fact, is part and parcel of their impulse to realize their natures fully and achieve happiness.

[4] draws the required conclusion, making it clear that if a human being is brought up outside a city, his nature will not be fully developed, and he will not achieve his natural end, or best good. It is this stunted nature that makes him a wretch (*phaulos*). Either that or, because his nature has managed to develop fully without the education and socialization that a city provides, he must be greater than human.

Let us go back now to [3], which is clearly the crucial premise. Consider a newborn baby. He is not born into a pre-social state of nature of the sort described in Thomas Hobbes' *Leviathan*, but into a family. Hence from the very beginning he is leading a sort of communal life and, as a result, acquiring virtue of a sort, which we may call *household virtue*. For "in the household we have the first starting-points and springs of friendship, of a constitution, and of justice" (*EE* VII 10 1242^{a}40–^{b}1). Thus each member of the household will have, beyond his biological (first) nature, a (second) nature of a sort that identifies him as a member of a household, and marks him off as such. This justifies us in speaking of a nature that is not simply constituted by the collective natures of the individuals living in a household, but of one that is common to them all. This common nature is the nature of the household.

The same line of argument applies in the case of the village and the city. Each community educates its inhabitants into a type of virtue that suits them to be members of it. As a result, each indexes their natures to itself. The clearest examples of this sort of indexing are provided by the various types of constitutions that cities can have: a democracy, Aristotle says, should suit its citizens to it by stamping democratic virtues into their souls by means of public education; an oligarchy should do the same with oligarchic virtues, and so on (*Pol.* V 9 1310^{a}12–36, VIII 1 1337^{a}11–18). Hence an individual who is a citizen of a democracy has a nature that marks him as such. When he realizes his nature, or performs his function, by engaging in rational activity expressing virtue, he shows himself to be, as it were, by nature democratic. But, to pick up again the point made in [3], this nature should not be thought of as wholly different from that possessed by citizens of other constitutions or by members of a village or household. Rather it is the same nature realized, developed, or perfected to a different degree.

The move from household to village to city constitutes, then, a development in human virtue. If human beings were non-rational animals, the development would itself be one that occurred through the operation of non-rational natural causes. But because human beings have a rational nature, their natural development (which is always communal, as we have seen) essentially involves a development in their rational capacities—for example, an increase in the level of practical wisdom they possess (or in the degree of their closeness to possessing practical wisdom, if you like). Imagine, then, that the household already exists. Adult males in it possess a level of virtue and practical wisdom that they bring to bear in solving practical problems. The household is not self-sufficient: it produces a surplus of some needed items, not enough of others. This presents a practical problem, which is an exercise of practical wisdom to solve. And it might be solved, for example, by noticing that other nearby households are in the same boat, and that exchanging goods with them would improve life for everyone involved. But exchange eventually leads to the need for money and with it the need for new communal roles (that of merchant, for example), new forms of communal control (laws governing commerce), new virtues of character (such as generosity and magnificence which pertain to wealth), and new opportunities for the exercise of (a further developed) practical wisdom (*Pol.* I 9 1257^{a}5–^{b}10). It is by engaging in this boot-strapping process that practical wisdom both causes new forms of communal life to emerge and causes itself to develop from the vestigial forms of it found in the household to the unconditional form of it found in Aristotle's best constitution, where alone the virtue of a good human being and a good citizen coincide (IV 7 1293^{b}1–7).

The appearance of the city at a stage in this process can now quite reasonably be thought of both as natural and as an exercise of practical wisdom or politics—as the result (say) of a legislator having crafted a constitution for a collection of suitably situated villages which, when appropriately realized by them and their members, will be a city, a self-sufficient political community (*Pol.* I 2 1253ᵃ29–31). Notice that Aristotle himself often characterizes the city as something crafted by legislators, and often likens politics to a craft (for example, II 8 1269ᵃ9–12, 12 1274ᵇ18–19, III 12 1282ᵇ14–16, IV 12 1273ᵇ32-33, VII 4 1325ᵇ40–1326ᵃ5). If things possessing canonical natures had to perfect their natures by nature, this sort of talk would be disturbing, since it would conflict with the characterization of the city as existing by nature. But many canonical natures, including our own, need to be perfected by craft. That the city's nature is among them is not only no threat to its being a canonical nature, therefore, it is just what we would expect given the close ties between our natures and its nature.

The nature of a city, understood in this way, is clearly internal to it. It thus has one of the defining marks of a canonical nature. But does it have the others? Is it a starting-point of "movement and rest, whether in respect of place, growth and withering, or alteration" (*Ph.* II 1 192ᵇ13–15). A city seems to be a matter-form compound, whose form is its constitution and whose inhabitants are its matter (*Pol.* III 3 1276ᵇ1–13). Since a thing's form "has a better claim than matter to being called nature" (*Ph.* II 1 193ᵇ6–7) than its matter, what we are really asking is whether Aristotle thinks that a city's constitution is a source of its stability and movement or change in the way that a canonical nature is. And apparently he does. A city can change its matter (population) over time, but cannot sustain change from one form of constitution to another (*Pol.* III 3 1276ᵃ34–ᵇ1), or dissolution of its constitution altogether (II 10 1272ᵇ14–15). Thus its identity over time is determined by its constitution. A population constitutes a single city if it shares a single constitution. Thus its synchronic unity, its identity at a time, is also determined by its constitution. A city can grow or shrink in size, but its constitution sets limits to how big or small it can be (VII 4–5). What causes it to decay or to survive is also determined by the sort of constitution it has (Book V discusses these constitution-specific causes in considerable detail). Thus a city's constitution does seem to be a canonical nature, and the city itself does seem to meet all of Aristotle's conditions for existing by nature. It is no surprise, therefore, to find Aristotle claiming that the various kinds of constitutions, the various kinds of natures that cities possess, are to be defined in the same way as the different natures possessed by animals belonging to different species (IV 4 1290ᵇ25–39).

Note 24

A human is by nature a political animal: Political animals are those whose function "is some one common thing" (*HA* I 1 488ᵃ7–8). It is in this sense that gregarious animals such as bees, wasps, ants, and cranes also count as political. The "common thing" in the case of human beings is the *polis* or city, making them political animals to a yet greater degree (*Pol.* III 6 1278ᵇ15–30, *NE* VIII 12 1162ᵃ17–19). But though all human beings may be political animals in the sense of having a natural impulse to form a political community (*Pol.* I 2 1253ᵃ29–30), not all have the right sort of nature, or inhabit the right sort of region, to enable that impulse to achieve its goal (VII 7 1327ᵇ20–38). Moreover, men of any region are naturally

different from women, adults from children, naturally free people from natural slaves. Some of these natural differences, such as differences in physical strength, are ethically and politically inert (III 12 1282ᵇ23–1283ᵃ14), but others are not. Women's souls have a deliberative element but it lacks control, those of free children have a deliberative element but it is immature, those of natural slaves have no deliberative element at all—as a result none of these people can have unconditional practical wisdom or ethical virtue (I 13 1260ᵃ9–ᵇ20). And because they cannot, Aristotle thinks that those of them that are political animals at all—and that excludes the natural slaves—are the sort that should be ruled not the sort that should rule (I 5 1254ᵇ13–14, III 4 1277ᵇ25–30). In the case of women, this is their permanent status; in the case of the male children of free people, it is one they enjoy only until they are mature adults. Like many claims in ethics and politics, however, these hold for the most part, not invariably and necessarily (*NE* I 3 1094ᵇ19–22). So there might well be a woman (a biologically female human being), for example, whose deliberative element did not lack control and who could, therefore, serve as a political ruler. The same goes for those who are born in a non-propitious geographical region. But even adult males who possess practical wisdom and virtue, and who could serve as political rulers, are not guaranteed to so serve. For if someone of outstanding practical wisdom and virtue emerges in their community, they are obliged to become his subjects and accept him as their king (III 13 1284ᵇ25–34). Thus a man's status as a ruler, unless he happens to have a degree of unconditional practical wisdom and virtue that is unsurpassable, is a somewhat vulnerable one; it is not absolute.
Luck (*tuchê*): See I 11 1258ᵇ36n.
Like the one Homer condemns: At *Odyssey* IX.63–64. Homer is describing a man who "loves fighting with his own people."
Clanless: See IV 15 1300ᵃ25n.

Note 25

Appetite (*epithumia*): Appetite, spirit, and wish collectively comprise desire (*orexis*) (*DA* II 3 414ᵇ2). "Appetite is concerned with what is pleasant and what is painful" (*NE* III 2 1111ᵇ16–17), and so with the apparent good, wish with what is really good (4 1113ᵃ23–ᵇ2).
Like an isolated piece (*azux*) **in a game of checkers** (*pettoi*): A *pettos* (plural: *pettoi*) is an oval-shaped stone used in playing checkers (drafts), backgammon, or the like. Since any game played with a *pettos* is a game of *pettoi*, it is not clear to which game in particular Aristotle is referring, or what precisely an *azux* is, or why someone like it has "an appetite for war."

Note 26

Nature does nothing pointlessly: A frequent claim in Aristotle—for example, *Pol.* I 5 1254ᵇ27, 6 1255ᵇ3, 9 1256ᵇ21, *PA* I 1 641ᵇ12–29. The nature referred to might be: (1) "the nature of the whole," as it is called at *Met.* XII 10 1075ᵃ11–12, considered (though perhaps not even there) as something beyond the natures of the various things that constitute the whole; (2) the nature that is constituted by those natures, but not as something beyond them; (3) some third option.

Note 27

Good (*agathos*): (1) A good X is one that possesses the virtues, or excellences, that enable it to fulfill the function (1252b4n) characteristic and definitive of X's. Thus a good human being is someone who possesses human virtue and is able to perform well the rational activities that are characteristic and definitive of human beings (*NE* I 7 1097b24–1098a20). (2) The good for human beings, the human good, is happiness, while (3) other things we aim at are good to the degree that they promote our happiness (1097a15–b22). Aristotle divides goods of the latter sort into three kinds: (3a) external goods (also called resources or goods of luck), (3b) goods of the soul, and (3c) goods of the body (*Pol.* VII 1 1323a25n). Goods of the soul are states (the virtues) and the activities that are in accord with them—for example, doing well in action (*eupraxia*) or happiness. External goods and goods of the body, on the other hand, are capacities or tools that the virtuous person uses to achieve good ends, and the vicious bad ones (1323b7–12). Although external goods, unlike goods of the soul, are the result of luck (1323b27–29), the sphere of luck can be reduced by craft and science, so that many external goods admit of at least limited human control (*NE* VI 4 1140a17–20, *Met.* I 1 981a1–5). Some external goods—such as money, honors, and bodily pleasure—are fought over or competed for, while others—such as friends, beauty, or good-breeding—are not (*NE* IX 9 1169a20–21). The former are the area of focus for many of the virtues of character.

Note 28

It is community in the perception of the good and the bad, the just and the unjust, and the rest that makes a household and a city: See III 9 1280b5–12.

Note 29

The city is prior in nature to the household and to each of us individually: "The order of coming to be and that of substance [= essence] are opposed. For what is posterior in the order of coming to be is prior in nature, and that which is first in nature is last in coming to be" (*PA* II 1 646a24–28). Households are necessary for the existence of cities and are thus prior to them in the way that matter is prior to form or essence (*NE* VIII 12 1162a18–19). Yet just as the saw does not exist for the sake of the iron that is necessary for its existence, so the city does not exist for the sake of the household, but the other way around. From that more important teleological point of view, therefore, crucial to defining what a household is, the city is prior: "It is the same way in the case of anything in which an end is present: without things that have a necessary nature it could not exist, but it does not exist because of these (except in the way that a thing exists because of its matter), but for the sake of something. For example, why is a saw such as it is? So that this may be—that is, for the sake of this end. It is impossible, however, that the end it is for the sake of should come to be unless the saw is made of iron. It is necessary, then, that it should be made of iron, if there is to be a saw and the function belonging to it" (*Ph.* II 9 200a7–13).

Note 30

If the whole body is put to death, there will no longer be a foot or a hand, except homonymously: "Things are said to be *homonymous* when they have only a name in common, but the account of the substance [= essence] that corresponds to the name is distinct—for example, both a human and a picture are animals. These have only a name in common and the account of the essence corresponding to the name is distinct. For if we are to say what it is for each of them to be an animal, we will give a special account to each" (*Cat.* 1 1ᵃ1–6).

Note 31

Capacity (*dunamis*): The term *dunamis* (plural: *dunameis*) is used by Aristotle to capture two different but related things. (1) As in ordinary Greek, it signifies a power or capacity something has, especially one to cause movement in something else (productive *dunamis*) or to be caused to move by something else (passive *dunamis*). (2) It signifies a way of being F, being capable of being F (or being F in potentiality) as distinguished from being actively F (or F in actuality) (see *NE* IX 7 1168ᵃ5–15).

Note 32

An individual is not self-sufficient when separated: The claim is not that an individual cannot live outside a city, but that he cannot live the good or happy life there: "The complete good seems to be self-sufficient. By 'self-sufficient,' however, we mean not self-sufficient for someone who is alone, living a solitary life, but also for parents, children, wife, friends, and fellow citizens generally, since a human being is by nature political" (*NE* I 7 1097ᵇ7–11). See also V 9 1310ᵃ34–36.

Note 33

Anyone who cannot live in a community with others, or who does not need to because of his self-sufficiency, is no part of a city, so that he is either a wild beast or a god: "If, as they say, human beings become gods because of an extreme of virtue, it is clear that the state opposed to the type that is beast-like will be of this sort. And just as there is in fact neither vice nor virtue of a wild beast, neither is there of a god. But his state is more estimable than virtue, while that of a wild beast is of a different kind than vice" (*NE* VII 1 1145ᵃ22–27).

Note 34

When separated from law and judicial proceeding (*dikê*): See I 2 1253ᵃ38n.

Note 35

A human grows up (*phuetai*) **possessed of weapons for practical wisdom and virtue to use:** "It is not because they have hands that human beings are most practically-wise, but because they are the most practically-wise of animals that they have hands. For the most practically-wise animal would use the greatest number of instruments well, and the hand would seem to be not one instrument but many, since it is, as it were, an instrument for [using] instruments (*organon pro organôn*). . . . For the hand becomes a talon, claw, horn, spear, sword, and any other weapon or instrument. For it can be all of these because of its capacity to grasp and hold them all. And for this the form of the hand has been adapted by nature" (*PA* IV 10 687ᵃ16–ᵇ7). See also I 4 1253ᵇ32–33.

Practical wisdom (*phronêsis*): *Phronêsis* (verb *phronein*) is used: (1) in a broad sense to refer to thought or (roughly speaking) intelligence of any sort (as at *Met.* IV 5 1009ᵇ13, 30); (2) in a narrower sense to refer to the distinctively practical wisdom discussed, for example, in *NE* VI 5; and (3) as equivalent in meaning to *sophia* or theoretical wisdom (*Met.* XIII 4 1078ᵇ15, and throughout *Protr.*). The association of *phronêsis* with virtue shows that (2) is what is being referred to here. This sort of practical wisdom is the same state of the soul as *politikê*—the craft or science of politics (*NE* VI 8 1141ᵇ23–24)—and involves the possession of all the virtues of character (13 1144ᵇ30–32). Roughly speaking, these virtues ensure that the end aimed at is correct, while practical wisdom discovers what will best further the end and effectively prescribes this, so that the agent does the best action available and so acts well (13 1145ᵃ2–6).

Virtue (*aretê*): Anything that has a function (1252ᵇ4n) has a correlative *aretê*. Thus it is possible to speak of the *aretê* of thieves, scandalmongers, and other bad things that are good at doing what they do (*Met.* V 16 1021ᵇ12–23), as well as of the *aretê* of non-living tools and instruments. For this reason *aretê* is often nowadays translated as "excellence." One advantage of the conventional translation "virtue," besides its being widely used, is that it preserves the link between Aristotle's thought and so-called virtue ethics. The sort of ethical virtue, or virtue of character, to which Aristotle is referring here, is "a deliberately choosing state, which is in a medial condition in relation to us, one defined by a reason and the one by which a practically-wise person would define it. Also, it is a medial condition between two vices, one of excess and the other of deficiency" (*NE* II 6 1106ᵃ36–1107ᵃ3).

Note 36

But justice (*dikaiosunê*) **is something political** (*politikon*): "Political virtue and vice are closely investigated by those concerned with good legislative order. Thus it is quite evident that the city must be concerned with virtue—at any rate, the city that is truly, and not just for the sake of argument, so called" (III 9 1280ᵇ5–8).

Note 37

For justice (*dikê*) **is a political community's order:** *Dikê*, in contrast to *dikaiosunê* (the virtue), seems here to be justice as embodied in laws, legal systems, and judicial proceedings: "there is no benefit in having judicial proceedings (*dikas*) about matters of justice (*dikaiôn*), if they do not achieve their end. So if, when the former do not occur, people cannot live in a community with each other, they cannot do so either when no actions are taken" (VI 8 1322ᵃ5–8).

Order (*taxis*): The notion of *taxis* ("order," "arrangement"), especially of constitutional, legal, and political order is of fundamental importance in the *Politics*—so much so, in fact, that politics itself can be described as "[the science of] political order" (II 8 1269ᵃ10).

And justice (*dikê*) **is a judgment** (*krisis*) **of what is just** (*dikaiou*): Reading ἡ δὲ δίκη with Dreizehnter for OCT ἡ δὲ δικαιοσύνη ("and justice is a judgment of what is just"). Compare: "*dikê* is a judgment (*krisis*) of what is just and what is unjust" (*NE* V 10 1134ᵃ31–32); "*dikê* is a judgment (*krisis*)" (*Rh.* II 1 1377ᵇ21).

Note 38

Free people: See III 8 1280ᵃ5n.

Note 39

What (*ti*) **each of them is and what sort of thing** (*poion*) **each must be:** The account (*Met.* I 1 981ᵃ15n) or definition of what something is consists of its genus and its differentia (VII 12 1027ᵇ29–30), of which the genus is stated first: "the genus is intended to signify the what-it-is, and is placed first of the things said in the definition" (*Top.* VI 5 142ᵇ27–29). Sometimes both elements are included in the what-something-is or the essence: "genera and differentiae are predicated in the what-it-is" (VII 3 153ᵃ17–18; also *APo.* II 5 91ᵇ28–30, 13 97ᵃ23–25). But sometimes the genus tells us what the thing is while the differentiae tell us what sort or quality of thing it is (*poion ti*): "a thing's differentia never signifies what-it-is, but rather some quality (*poion ti*)" (IV 2 122ᵇ16–17; also 6 128ᵃ26–27, *Met.* V 14 1020ᵃ33). What Aristotle is saying, then, is that in the case of master and slave, husband and wife, and the rest, we must look for their definitions by genus and differentia.

Note 40

Mastership, "marital" science (for we have no word to describe the union of woman and man), and "procreative" science: The names of these crafts or sciences are: *despotikê*, *gamikê*, and *teknopoiêtikê* ("procreative science"). The ending *-ikê*, like the corresponding "-ics" in "physics" and "politics," signifies that either *epistêmê* ("science") or *technê* ("craft") should be supplied or presupposed. Since a craft is typically a productive science (*Met.* IX 2 1046ᵇ3), it does not matter much which we choose. Marital and procreative science are shown in operation at VII 16. Rule over women, which is an exercise of the former, and rule over children, which is an exercise of the latter, are discussed in I 12–13. Mastership is discussed in I 4–7, the craft of wealth acquisition in I 2, 8–11.

Note 41

The craft of wealth acquisition (*chrêmatistikê*): The craft or science of acquiring wealth, which, because of complexity in the notion of wealth, is of at least two different kinds. The natural kind is concerned with the acquisition (but not the use) of natural wealth, and is a part of (1253ᵇ12–13) or assistant to (I 8 1256ᵃ3–7) (the craft of) household management. The unnatural kind is the craft of commerce. In I 11 a third kind, which "comes between" these two, is discussed; it deals with metals etc. extracted from the earth, and timber and other non-foodstuffs grown on it (1258ᵇ27–31).

Note 42

But let us first discuss master and slave in order to see the things that are related to necessary use: See I 11 (notice 1258ᵇ9–10).

But also to see whether we can acquire something in the way of knowledge about these things that is better than what it is supposed at present: See I 4–10.

Note 43

As we said at the start: See I 1 1252ᵃ7–16.

Note 44

Others believe that it is contrary to nature to be a master: Alcidamas of Elaea, a student of the sophist Gorgias, writes, "God set all people free; nature has made no one a slave" (*CAG* XXI:2, p. 74, 31–32 = Gagarin & Woodruff, p. 276).

Note 45

It is by law (*nomô[i]*) **that one person is a slave and another free, whereas by nature** (*phusei*) **there is no difference between them:** Laws are universal rules (II 8 1269ª11–12, *NE* V 10 1137ᵇ13–14) typically backed by sanctions that compel compliance (*NE* X 9 1180ª21). There are two kinds of law: special (*idion*) and common or universal (*koinon*). Special law is the law followed by some city, whereas common law is "in accord with nature" (*Rh.* 13 1373ᵇ6, 15 1375ª32). Thus special law and common law can conflict (13 1373ᵇ9–11, 15 1375ª27–ᵇ8), and when they do special law is revealed to be conventional only—as those who think that slavery is never anything except conventional suppose it always to be. Law that is in accord with nature is correct because, being in accord with specifically human nature among other things, it furthers human happiness. Being ruled by law, however, is generally better than being ruled by human beings, because the law is dispassionate (*Pol.* III 15 1286ª17–20, 16 1287ª28–32). Nonetheless, the law cannot cover every eventuality and cannot dictate how it is to be applied in every particular case, so "the law, having designedly educated the rulers for these eventualities, hands over the rest to be judged and managed in accord with the most just consideration of the rulers" (1287ª25–27). Judging in this way is an exercise in decency (II 7 1267ᵇ6n). Laws are contrasted with the constitution itself (II 6 1265ª1–3, III 15 1286ª2–4, IV 1 1289ª15–25) and with decrees (IV 4 1292ª6n). Finding which laws are best and which is fitting for a given constitution is one function of politics or practical wisdom (1 1289ª11–13).

That is why it is not just either, since it involves force: Also VII 2 1324ª35–37.

Note 46

The craft of property acquisition (*ktêtikê*): See I 8 1256ᵇ23–39, 9 1257ᵇ17–23.

Note 47

All assistants are like instruments for [using] instruments (*organon pro organôn*): In other words, they are like a second pair of hands. See I 2 1253ª35n.

Note 48

Daedalus: A legendary craftsman and inventor, whose statues were so lifelike that they ran away unless tied down (*DA* I 3 406ᵇ18–19, Plato, *Men.* 97d).

The tripods of Hephaestus: Hephaestus was the armorer and blacksmith to the gods. The description of his tripods is that of Homer, *Iliad* XVIII.376.

An architectonic craftsman: Aristotle distinguishes between craftsmen of different degrees of excellence or achievement: (1) The lyre player and the good lyre player have the same function, but the latter has "the superiority that is in accord with the virtue (for it is characteristic of a lyre player to play the lyre and of an excellent one to do it well)" (*NE* I 7 1098ª8–12). (2) Some craftsmen know all that is in the craft handbook, so to speak, but when it comes to problems that lie outside it, and so require deliberation, they sometimes arrive at reasons that are false (VI 5 1140^{a}28–30). These people know all the true handbook reasons but not the true deliberative ones. They may be good craftsmen for routine jobs, but, lacking the relevant sort of practical wisdom, they are not good for hard cases. (3) Some craftsmen are wise (*sophos*) in that they are the most exact practitioners of their craft (7 1140^{b}9–10). They know not just the true handbook and deliberative reasons but the ultimate explanatory ones—those that might be found in the most exact treatises on the craft's starting-points. Thus what distinguishes "those doctors who pursue their craft in a more philosophical or wisdom-loving way" is that their search for the "primary starting-points of health and disease" leads them to begin by considering nature in general (*Sens.* 1 436^{a}17–^{b}1; also *Juv.* 21 480^{b}22–30). This third class is that of the architectonic craftsmen: "It is also because of this that we consider the architectonic practitioners in each craft to be more estimable, to know in a yet more full sense, and to be wiser than the handicraftsmen, because they know the causes of the things they produce. The handicraftsmen, by contrast, we consider to be like some sort of inanimate things that produce without knowing what they produce, in the way, for example, that fire burns. But whereas inanimate things produce each result by a sort of natural tendency, the handicraftsmen do so by habit—the supposition being that architectonic craftsmen are wiser not in terms of being practically efficient, but in terms of having the account themselves and knowing the causes" (*Met.* I 1 981^{a}30–^{b}6). We can see, then, why "the ones who above all do actions, even external actions, in a controlling way are their architectonic craftsmen who do them by means of their thoughts" (*Pol.* VII 3 1325^{b}22–23). We can see, too, why—at any rate in the practical sphere—politics seems to be the most architectonic science, "since it is the one that prescribes which of the sciences need to exist in cities and which ones each class in cities should learn and up to what point. Indeed, we see that even the capacities that are generally most honored are under it—for example, generalship, household management, and rhetoric. And . . . it uses the other practical sciences and, furthermore, legislates about what must be done and what avoided" (*NE* I 2 1094^{a}26–^{b}6).

Note 49

Action-involving (*praktikon*): See VII 2 1324^{a}27n.

Note 50

Since production (*poiêsis*) **and action** (*praxis*) **differ in kind** (*eidos*): The noun *praxis* (plural: *praxeis*; verb: *prattein*) is used in a broad sense to refer to any intentional action, including one performed by a child or wild beast (*NE* III 1 1111^{a}25–26, 2 1111^{b}8–9), and in a narrower one, which is the one employed here, to refer exclusively to what results from deliberation (*bouleusis*) and deliberate choice (*prohairesis*), of which neither beasts nor children are capable (I 9 1099^{b}32–1100^{a}5, *EE* II 8 1224^{a}28–29).

What distinguishes a *praxis* from a *poiêsis* is that the latter is always performed for the sake of some further end, whereas a *praxis* can be its own end: "Thought by itself, however, moves nothing. But the one that is for the sake of something and practical does. Indeed, it even rules productive thought. For every producer produces for the sake of something, and what is unconditionally an end (as opposed to in relation to something and for something else) is not what is producible but what is doable in action. For doing well in action (*eupraxia*) [= *eudaimonia* or happiness] is the end, and the desire is for it. That is why deliberate choice is either desiderative understanding or thought-involving desire, and this sort of starting-point is a human being" (*NE* VI 2 1139^{a}35–^{b}5).

Thus the distinction between a *praxis* and a *poiêsis* is a special case of a more general distinction that Aristotle draws between an *energeia* ("activity") and a *kinêsis* ("movement"; plural: *kinêseis*): "Since, though, of the actions that have a limit none is an end, but all are in relation to an end (for example, making thin), and since the things themselves, when one is making them thin, are in movement in this way, [namely,] that what the movement is for the sake of does not yet belong to them, these [movements] are not cases of action, at least not of complete action, since none is an end. But the sort in which the end belongs *is* an action. For example, at the same time one is seeing [a thing] and has seen [it], is thinking and has thought, is understanding [something] and has understood [it], whereas it is not the case that [at the same time] one is learning [something] and has learned [it], nor that one is being made healthy and has been made healthy. Someone who is living well, however, at the same time has lived well, and is happy and has been happy [at the same time]. If this were not so, these would have to come to an end at some time, as when one is making [something] thin. But as things stand it is not so, but one is living and has lived. Of these, then, one sort should be called movements and the other activities. For every movement is incomplete, for example, making thin, learning, walking, building. These are movements and are certainly incomplete. For it is not the case that at the same time one is walking and has taken a walk, nor that one is building [something] and has built [it], or is coming to be [something] and has come to be [it], or is being moved [in some way] and has been moved [in that way], but they are different, as are one's moving and having moved [something]. By contrast one has seen and is seeing the same thing at the same time, or is understanding and has understood. The latter sort, then, I call an activity, the former a movement" (*Met.* IX 6 1048^{b}18–35). Expressed linguistically, the contrast is one of aspect rather than tense. Roughly speaking, a verb whose present tense has imperfective meaning designates a *kinêsis*, while one whose present tense has perfective meaning designates an *energeia*. The distinction itself is ontological, however, not linguistic: an *energeiai* and *kinêseis* are types of beings, not types of verbs. A *poiêsis* or *kinêsis* is something that takes time to complete and, like the time it takes, is infinitely divisible (*Ph.* III 7 207^{b}21–25, *Met.* V 13 1020^{a}26–32). It has a definite termination point or limit, before which it is incomplete and after which it cannot continue (*NE* X 4 1174^{a}21–23). A *praxis*, by contrast, does not take time to complete, and so does not really occur "in time" (*Ph.* VIII 8 262^{b}20–21) but is temporally point-like (*NE* X 4 1174^{b}12–13). Having no definite termination, while it may stop, it need never finish (*Met.* IX 6 1048^{b}25–27).

The paradigm cases of *actions*, as we understand them, are temporally extended bodily movements appropriately related to (perhaps by being caused by) beliefs, desires, and intentions. Hence "action" is clearly a somewhat misleading translation of *praxis*. Nonetheless, there is one type of action that *praxeis* seem to resemble quite closely, namely, so-called *basic actions*—actions we do directly without having to do anything else. This is especially true, if, as Aristotle himself seems to believe, these are thought to be mental acts of willing, deciding, or trying: "we say that in the most controlling sense the ones who above all do actions, even in the case of external actions, are the ones who by means of their thoughts are their architectonic craftsmen" (*Pol.* VII 3 1325ᵇ21–23). Like *praxeis*, in any case, these sorts of mental acts are not bodily movements and do not seem to take time to perform. Moreover, just as we do not perform basic actions by doing something else first, the same seems true of *praxeis*, so that a human being "is a starting-point and begetter of *praxeis* just as he is of children" (*NE* III 5 1113ᵇ18–19; also VI 2 1139ᵇ5). As in the case of productions, where the form in a craftsman's soul is transmitted to the matter via the movements of his hands and instruments (*GA* I 22 730ᵇ12–23), so the results of such *praxeis* may be transmitted via bodily movements to other things that are capable of being changed by them. These results, and the bodily movements involved in bringing them about, are what we think of as paradigm actions.

When a group of dramatic actions have a plot-structure (*mythos*) of the sort a good tragedy possesses, Aristotle says that they constitute a single action that is "one, whole, and complete" (*Po.* 23 1459ᵃ19). By being enactments of the real-life equivalent of the relevant sort of plot or plan, therefore, the same should also be true of a group of non-dramatic actions. As a group of actors can set out to perform *Oedipus Tyrannus*, so a single agent can set out to enact a unified plan of action, which involves doing many different things in some sort of sequence. The complex action that fits this plan may be what constitutes his acting well—his *eupraxia*.

To understand why the agent is doing any of the things specified by the plan, we will typically need to see it in relation to the plan as a whole. For many of these, taken individually, might not be ends or goods choiceworthy for their own sakes: some might be otherwise valueless means to ends, some might be productions of needed equipment, some might be actions whose status as intrinsically choiceworthy, because constitutive of *eupraxia*, nonetheless depends on their role in the plan. As parts of the whole complex action they help constitute, however, all *are* intrinsically choiceworthy, since the complex action is itself so. Hence the unified plan itself might be likened to the form of health in the soul of the doctor, which dictates the bodily movements that constitute, for example, producing the uniform state in a tense muscle, which is the relevant defining-mark of health (*Met.* VII 7 1032ᵇ6–10). The actualization of the plan, the setting of it in motion, is an action, as is the carrying out of the subsequent steps. In performing each of them, the agent is achieving the goal of acting well. For acting well, since it is not an external end, is not something achieved only when the plan is fully executed, as health is produced only when the muscles relax and the patient becomes healthy. At the same time, it does not seem to be an entirely internal end, either, since the plan may fail to be completely carried out.

We set the associated plan in motion, which is a basic action, but whether we will succeed in carrying it out fully is in part a matter of luck. If we fail through no fault of our own, we have in one way done what is required of us—we have tried, we have done all that we could do. In another way, though, we have failed, and may now have something more to do, such as try again, or make amends of some sort. The possibility of failure of this sort taints complex actions with unleisure, since it means there are usually obstacles or resistances to overcome in order to carry them out. Many—perhaps most—actions are surely complex. They would be unleisured, therefore, and subject to a sort of incompleteness, even if they had no additional external ends. We might think of a political constitution as a plan for a very complex action, with the citizens, who act in obedience to its laws and so on, as its executors or agents. Similarly, a household, which is part of a city with such a constitution, is also such an executor (I 13 1260^{b}8–20), and its "constitution"—its operating instructions—is itself a plan of action, which the members of the household put into effect by doing what it prescribes. Thus even when what it prescribes is a production, rather than an action proper, that production too becomes part of the complex action that is the household in activity.

Since both need instruments, their instruments must differ in the same way as they do: From an instrument of production, such as a shuttle, we get something beyond the use of it, namely, the product (cloth) it is used to produce; from an instrument of action, such as a piece of clothing or a bed, we get nothing beyond the use (1254^{a}4–5). This is because a process of production, such as weaving, since it is a *poiêsis*, essentially has a further end, whereas a *praxis* or *energeia*, such as living, does not.

Note 51

Life (*bios*): See Introduction, pp. li–lii.

Life, though, is action, not production: (1) We are alive in the sense of having a *bios* even when we are asleep or unconscious. But we are more fully alive when we are awake and conscious: "'living' is said of things in two ways, and we must take the one in accord with activity, since it seems to be called 'living' in a fuller sense" (*NE* I 7 1098^{a}5–7). (2) We are alive in the fuller sense when engaged in action or activity, rather than when producing, because living is an activity, since we both are living and have lived simultaneously.

Note 52

That is why a slave is an assistant in the things related to action: The inference seems to be this: (1) An assistant is an animate instrument. (2) A piece of property is an instrument for living. (3) A slave is an animate piece of property. (4) A slave is an assistant in living. (5) Living is action rather than production. (6) A slave is an assistant in things related to action.

Note 53

A piece of property is an instrument that is for action and separate [from its owner]: "all natural bodies—those of plants just like those of animals—are instruments of the soul, since they are for the sake of the soul" (*DA* II 4 415^{b}18–19).

What distinguishes a slave from a part of his master's body is that he is separate from it as his body parts are not (I 6 1255^{b}11–12).

Note 54

The rule is always better when the ruled are better: See V 12 1315^{b}4–7, VII 3 1325^{a}27–30, 14 1333^{b}26–29.

Note 55

Even in things that do not share in living some rule exists—for example, in a harmony: The reference is to the *mêsê* or *hêgemôn* ("leader"), which is the dominant note in a chord (*Met.* V 11 1018^{b}26–29).

Note 56

The soul (*psuchê*): Unlike souls as we conceive of them, which are found only in "higher" beings like us, Aristotelian souls are found wherever there is life and movement: souls are animators. Thus all plants and animals, however primitive or simple, have some sort of soul. Moreover, unlike Cartesian or some religious conceptions of the soul, Aristotelian souls (productive understanding aside) are tightly tied to the bodies whose souls they are. The account of them makes this apparent: "It is necessary, then, for the soul to be substance, as form, of a natural body that has life potentially. But substance is actuality. Therefore, it is the actuality of such a body. But something is said to be actual in two ways, either as scientific knowledge is or as contemplating is. And it is evident that it is as scientific knowledge is. For both sleep and waking depend on the presence of the soul; waking is analogous to contemplating, and sleep to having but not exercising [scientific-knowledge]; and in the same individual scientific knowledge is prior in coming to be. That is why the soul is the first actuality of a natural body that has life potentially" (*DA* II 2 412^{b}19–28). Thus an ensouled body is a matter-form compound whose body is matter and whose soul is form.

Although the various sorts of soul are found separated from each other in other living things, they are also found hierarchically organized within the human soul, with higher ones presupposing lower ones (*Pol.* VII 14 1333^{a}21–30, 15 1334^{b}15). On the lowest rung in the hierarchy is nutritive soul, responsible for nutrition and growth. It is the only sort of soul possessed by plants. The next rung up is perceptual soul, responsible for perception and for the feeling and appetite that cause animal movement. Together with nutritive soul it is found in all animals. In human beings, both are constituents of the non-rational part of the soul. The third sort of soul, found only in human beings, is rational soul, which comprises the part of the soul that has reason and the understanding.

Looked at from the bottom up rather than from the top down, this hierarchy is teleological: lower sorts of soul and their functions are for the sake of the higher ones. For example, the homoeomerous parts, such as flesh, and their functions exist for the sake of the non-homoeomerous or structured parts and their functions. Among the latter parts, the sense organs are particularly important with regard to survival, which is essential for all other functioning (*DA* III 12 434^{a}22–^{b}27). In animals with rational soul, the senses (especially smell, hearing, and sight) "inform us of many distinctions from which arise practical wisdom about intelligible objects as well as those of action," and so also exist "for the sake of doing well" or being happy (*Sens.* 1 436^{b}10–437^{a}3). Finally, practical wisdom itself, though it exists for its own sake, also exists for the sake of the understanding (*NE* VI 13 1145^{a}6–9). Understanding, then, is at the teleological peak of the organization, and so is the final or teleological cause of everything else in it.

The soul rules the body with the rule of a master: "What is the starting-point of movement in the soul? Just as in the whole it is the [primary] god, so it is too in us. For the divine constituent in us [= understanding or reason] in a way does all the moving. Of reason, however, the starting-point is not reason, but something superior. But what besides the [primary] god is superior to both scientific knowledge and understanding, since virtue [of character] is an instrument of understanding?" (*EE* VIII 2 1248^{a}25–29).

Whereas the understanding rules desire with political rule or kingly rule: "One part of the soul is non-rational whereas another part has reason. . . . Of the non-rational part, one part seems to be shared and vegetative—I mean, the cause of nutrition and growth. For this sort of capacity of soul is one that we suppose is present in all things that take in food, even embryos. . . . Another natural constituent of the soul, however, also seems to be non-rational, although it shares in reason in a way. For we praise the reason—that is, the part of the soul that has reason—of a person with self-control and of a person without it, since it exhorts them correctly toward what is best. But they also have by nature something else within them besides reason, apparently, which fights against reason and resists it. . . . But this part apparently also has a share of reason, as we said, at any rate, it is obedient to the reason of a self-controlled person. Furthermore, that of a temperate and courageous person, presumably, listens still better, since there it chimes with reason in everything. Apparently, then, the non-rational part is also twofold, since the vegetative part does not share in reason in any way but the appetitive part (indeed, the desiring part as a whole) does so in some way, because it is able to listen to reason and obey it. It has reason, then, in the way we are said to have the reason of our fathers and friends and not in the way we are said to have that of mathematics. The fact, though, that the non-rational part is persuaded in some way by reason is revealed by the practice of warning people and of all the different practices of admonishing and exhorting them" (*NE* I 13 1102^{a}27–1103^{a}1). The thought, apparently, is that because the desiring part of the soul shares in reason in a way, and is persuadable by it, it ought to be ruled in a way that reflects this fact. Since political and kingly rule, unlike that of a master, are over free and willing (persuaded) subjects, they are the ones appropriate to it (*Pol.* I 7 1255^{b}20, III 5 1277^{b}7–9, VII 14 1333^{a}3–6).

The understanding (*ho nous*): In the broadest sense of the term, someone with *nous* is someone with sound common sense, and the cognate verb *noein*, like *dianoeisthai*, means "to think" (*Mete.* I 3 340^{b}14, *Ph.* IV 1 208^{b}25, *NE* III 1 1110^{a}11). *Nous*, in this sense, is what enables a soul to suppose, believe, deduce, calculate, reason, and believe, so that it is possible to *noein* something false (*DA* III 3 427^{b}9). In the narrow sense, *nous* is what makes possible a type of knowledge of universal scientific starting-points that, unlike scientific knowledge proper, is not demonstrable from anything further: "About the starting-point of what is scientifically known there cannot be scientific knowledge . . . since what is scientifically known is demonstrable . . . the remaining alternative is for *nous* to be of starting-points" (*NE* VI 6 1140^{b}33–1141^{a}8); "*nous* is of the terms or definitions (*horoi*) for which there is no reason (*logos*)" (8 1142^{a}25–26).

When the starting-point in question is a practical one, such as the good or the noble, its grasp by *nous* is accompanied by wish (*boulêsis*)—a desire based on deliberation—for what in the agent's actual situation the particular good or noble thing to do is: "This is the way the object of desire and the intelligible object moves things: it moves them without being moved. Of these objects, the primary ones are the same. For the [primary] object of appetite is the apparently noble, and the primary object of wish is the really noble. But we desire something because it seems [noble] rather than its seeming so because we desire it. For the starting-point is the active understanding. And understanding is moved by intelligible objects" (*Met.* XII 7 1072^{a}26–30).

This *nous*, which is the sort referred to here, is a divine substance (*NE* I 6 1096^{a}24–25, X 7 1177^{b}19–1178^{a}8), or anyway the most divine one in human beings (X 7 1177^{a}16), and so it shares in the immortality that is characteristic of gods: "it alone [of the parts of the human soul] is immortal and eternal" (*DA* III 5 430^{a}23). Consequently, it alone of these parts is separable from the human body and can survive its death: "*Ho nous* seems to be born in us as a sort of substance, and not to pass away. . . . Understanding (*noein*) and contemplating (*theôrein*) are extinguished because something else within passes away, but it itself is unaffected" (*DA* I 4 408^{b}18–25; also *Long.* 2 465^{a}26–32). Among sublunary animals this *nous* is fully possessed only by human beings (*PA* II 10 656^{a}7–8, *NE* X 8 1178^{b}24–25). In fact, a human being is most of all his *nous* (Introduction pp. lxi–lxiii).

Although classified in these texts as a substance, *nous* is also sometimes classified as a state (*hexis*) of the soul that "grasps the truth by way of assertion and denial" (*NE* VI 3 1139^{b}15–17). For in its case the distinction between a state and its activation collapses, since it is "in substance [or essence] and activity" (*DA* III 5 430^{a}18), though it must be (in the state of being) in touch with an intelligible object in order to grasp the truth about it (*Met.* XII 7 1072^{b}18–30, notice "good state" (*eu echei*) at 1072^{b}24). On the metaphor of touching, see *Met.* IX 10 1051^{b}24.

No English term is a precise equivalent for *nous* or *noein* in this narrow sense. "Intellect," which is in many ways the best choice, lacks a cognate verb in current use. "Understanding" is better in this respect but shares with "intellect," "intelligence," "intuitive reason," "apprehension," and other common translations the defect of not being factive or truth entailing, since *nous* is one of the five states of the soul "in which the soul grasps the truth by way of affirmation and denial" (*NE* VI 3 1139^{b}15–17).

Note 57

It is better for all animals to be ruled by human beings, since in this way they secure their preservation: Compare I 8 1256^{b}15–20.

Note 58

The other animals assist not because they perceive the reason but because of feelings: Retaining αἰσθανόμενα ("they perceive") with Dreizehnter.

Note 59

Nature tends indeed to make the bodies of free people and slaves different. . . . But the contrary also often happens: See I 6 1255^{b}4n.
Nature tends: See I 2 1253^{a}10n.

Note 60

If people were to become in body alone as distinguished as the statues of the gods, everyone would say that those who fell short deserved to be their slaves: The thought—admittedly a bit obscure—seems to be this. (1) Assume that nature succeeds in making the bodies of slaves and free people different. (2) Assume that, unlike now, the bodies of all and only free people are like the bodies that the gods have in statues. (3) It would follow that those who had bodies that fell short of this would have the bodies of natural slaves. (4) Hence they would not be free people, and so would also have the souls of natural slaves and be natural slaves. (5) Everyone would agree that if there are natural slaves, they deserve to be slaves of those who are by nature free. (Those who think that all slaves are so by conventional law would accept this conditional, presumably, but would deny that there are any natural slaves.) The next sentences draw parallel conclusions about the soul. But there we return to the real world in which nature does not always succeed in correlating beauty of body with beauty of soul, so that the difference between those who are by nature free and those who are by nature slaves is harder to see.

Note 61

The contrary claim: That slavery is unjust.

Note 62

A writ of illegality: A legislative speaker in the Athenian assembly was liable to a writ of illegality or *graphê paranomôn* if he proposed legislation that contravened already existing law.

Note 63

What produces a going back-and-forth (*epallattein*) **in the arguments:** As in a tug of war with no decisive winner. The verb *epallattein* also means "overlap," and is used in this sense at IV 10 1295^{a}9.
In a way virtue, when it is equipped with resources, is most able to use force: Virtue (excellence) together with the necessary external goods or resources are what enable us to do the relevant thing well—including use force. If someone is able to conquer his enemies, this suggests that he has the virtues needed for success (VII 2 1324^{b}22–1325^{a}14).

Note 64

One side [A] believes that justice is goodwill, whereas the other [B] believes that justice is precisely this—the rule of the stronger: Reading εὔνοια with Dreizehnter and the mss. for OCT ἄνοια ("one side believes that justice is nonsense").

A and B both believe that "there is no force without virtue" (1255^a15–16). But they disagree in their accounts of justice, and hence about whether the enslavement of conquered peoples is just. B believes that such enslavement is just, because justice by his definition is always on the side of the stronger. A on the other hand believes that such enslavement is by his definition unjust, since it is not good for the slaves, and so not a case of goodwill. Both accounts are canvassed by Thrasymachus in Plato, *Rep.* I (338c, 343c). Both A and B agree, then, that those with virtue should rule, and so their arguments—once their disagreements about justice are set aside—have no force against that view.

Goodwill (*eunoia*): Goodwill consists in wishing good things for what one feels it toward, so that "friendship is said to be reciprocated goodwill" (*NE* VIII 3 1155^b33–34); "friendship and justice are concerned with the same things and involve the same people" (9 1159^b25–26); "friendship holds cities together. . . . Of just things the most just of all seem to be fitted to friendship" (1 1155^a22–28).

Note 65

Good-breeding (*eugeneia*): "Good-breeding is a virtue of stock (*genos*), and virtue is among the excellent things; and a stock is excellent in which there have by nature come to be many excellent individuals. And this happens when there is an excellent starting-point in the stock. For a starting-point has a capacity of this sort—to establish many things like itself. For that is the function of a starting-point—to produce many others like itself. Hence, when there has been one individual of this sort in the stock and he is so excellent that many generations receive his goodness, this stock is necessarily excellent. For there will be many excellent humans if the stock is human, [many excellent] horses if it is equine, and similarly also with regard to the other animals. Thus it is reasonable that neither the rich nor the good but those who are from old money or from old goodness would be of good-breeding. For the account seeks the truth, since a starting-point is higher than everything. But it is not even the case that those born from good ancestors are well bred in every case, but as many as happen to have among their ancestors starting-points that are good. When a man is good himself, but does not have the natural capacity to give birth to many men similar [to himself], the starting-point does not have in those cases this sort of capacity" (F94 R^3 = Barnes, pp. 2423–2424); "Good breeding in the case of a nation or a city, then, means that its members are indigenous or ancient, that its first leaders were distinguished men, and that from them have sprung many who were distinguished for qualities we admire. The good-breeding of an individual may result from the male side or from the female one, requires legitimacy [in birth and citizenship] on both, and—as in the case of a city—that the earliest ancestors were notable for virtue, wealth, or something else that is highly esteemed, and that many distinguished people—men, women, young and old—come from the stock" (*Rh.* I 5 1360^b31–38); "Good-breeding (*eugenes*) is in accord with the virtue of the stock (*genos*), whereas being true to one's descent (*gennaion*) is in accord with not being a degeneration from nature. This degeneration, for the most part, does not happen to the well born, although there are many who are worthless people. For in the generations of men, as in the fruits of the earth, there is a certain yield, and sometimes, when the stock is good, exceptional men are produced for a period of time, and then again later on [after a period of worthless ones]. Naturally clever (*euphua*) stock degenerates into characters disposed to madness (for example, the offspring of Alcibiades and Dionysius), whereas steady stock degenerates into stupidity and dullness (for example, the offspring of Cimon, Pericles, and Socrates)" (II 15 1390^{b}21–31). Also *Pol.* IV 8 1294^{a}21, V 1 1301^{b}2.

Note 66

Unconditionally (*haplôs*): The adjective *haplos* means "simple" or "single-fold." The adverb *haplôs* thus points in two somewhat opposed directions. To speak *haplôs* sometimes means to put things simply or in simple terms, so that qualifications and conditions will need to be added later. Sometimes, as here, to be F *haplôs* means to be F in a way that allows for no "ifs," "ands," or "buts." In this sense, what is F *haplôs* is F unconditionally speaking, or in the strictest, most absolute, and most unqualified way (*Met.* V 5 1015^{b}11–12), so that what is unconditionally F is what is intrinsically F (*NE* VII 9 1151^{b}2–3).

As the Helen of Theodectes does when she says: Fr. 3 Nauck. Theodectes was a mid-4th-cent tragic poet who studied with Aristotle. Helen is Helen of Troy, the wife of Menelaus, whose abduction by Paris precipitated the Trojan Wars.

Note 67

In just the way that human comes from human, and beast from beast, so too good people come from good ones. But, though nature tends to do this, it is nonetheless often unable to do so: "Nature tends, then, to measure the coming to be and passing away of animals by the regular movements of these bodies [the sun and moon], but nature cannot bring this about exactly because of the indefiniteness of matter, and because many starting-points exist which impede coming to be and passing away from being according to nature, and often cause things to occur contrary to nature" (*GA* IV 10 778^{a}4–9); "The [male] seed is a residue and moves with the same movement as that in accord with which the body grows through the distribution of the ultimate nourishment [namely, blood]. When it comes into the uterus it causes the female's residue [that is, the menses] to take shape and moves it in the same movement in which it itself is actually moving. For the menses is also a residue, and contains all the parts [of the body] potentially, though none actually. It even has in it potentially those parts that differentiate female from male. And just as offspring from parents with a disability are sometimes born with a disability and sometimes not, so offspring from a female are sometimes female and sometimes not female but, rather, male. For the female is like a male with a disability, and the menses is seed, only not pure. For it does not have one thing in it, namely, the starting-point of the soul" (II 3 737^{a}18–30); "It is necessary to take hold of the universal hypotheses . . . that some movements [those in the female menses] are present potentially and others [those in the male seed] actually . . . that what gets mastered changes over into the opposite; that what slackens passes into the movement that is next to it: slackening a little into a movement that is close by; more, into one that is farther away; finally, the movements so run together that it [the fetus or offspring] does not resemble any of its own or kindred, rather all that is left is what is common, and it is [simply] human" (IV 3 768^{b}5–12).

Nature tends: I 2 1253^{a}10n.

Note 68
Cases where it is advantageous and just: Retaining καὶ δίκαιον with Saunders and the mss.

Note 69
There is in fact a sort of mutual advantage and mutual friendship for such masters and slaves as deserve to be by nature so related: "Neither is there friendship toward a horse or an ox, or toward a slave insofar as he is a slave, since there is nothing in common between the parties. For a slave is an ensouled instrument, an instrument a soulless slave. Insofar as he is a slave, then, there is no friendship toward him, but insofar as he is a human being there is. For there seems to be some sort of justice on the part of any human being toward anyone capable of participating in a community of law and convention, and of friendship too, then, to the extent that he is a human being (*anthrôpos*)" (*NE* VIII 11 1161^{b}1–8). *Anthrôpos* is sometimes used to refer to the whole human animal, sometimes to the human element in human beings by contrast with the divine one (their understanding) (X 7 1177^{b}27–28), and sometimes to that divine element, since it is what makes human beings distinctively human (X 5 1176^{a}25–29). Hence a slave is more or less human depending on what his share in understanding is. That is why the more human he is, the more he is capable of friendship and the rest. Toward natural slaves neither friendship nor justice exists—or only a very minimal level of them, consequent upon the fact that even a capacity minimally to apprehend reason may qualify someone to participate to some extent in a community of law and convention. In the case of legal slaves, friendship between them and their masters is excluded by the fact that they are being treated unjustly in being enslaved—between them the contrary of friendship and mutual advantage holds (1255^{b}14–15). But there is nothing, it seems, to prevent legal slaves (to the extent that they share in understanding) from being friends with each other or with other human beings who are not their masters.

Note 70
Monarchy (*monarchia*): Rule by one person. Kingship is its correct, tyranny its deviant, form.
Free (*eleutherôn*): See III 9 1280^{a}5n.
Equal (*isôn*): See III 9 1280^{a}19n.

Note 71
Someone is said to be a master . . . in virtue of being such-and-such a sort of person: See I 6 1255^{b}6–12.

Note 72
Syracuse: A city located on the southeast corner of the island of Sicily, next to the Ionian Sea.

Note 73
More estimable (*entimiotera*): The core sense of *timios* ("estimable") is captured in the remark that ordinary people "commonly say of those they find especially

estimable and especially love that they 'come first'" (*Cat.* 12 14^b5–7). Something is thus objectively *timios* when—like starting-points and causes—it "comes first by nature" (14^b3–5). To say that something is estimable is thus to ascribe a distinct sort of goodness or value to it: "By what is estimable I mean such things as what is divine, what is superior (*beltion*) (for example, soul, understanding), what is more time-honored (*archaioteron*), what is a starting-point, and so on" (*MM* I 2 1183^b21–23). Thus happiness is "something estimable and complete . . . since it is a starting-point . . . and the starting-point and the cause of goods is something we suppose to be estimable and divine" (*NE* I 12 1102^a1–4).
As the proverb says: A line from the comic poet Philemon. Fr. 54 Kock.

Note 74
A steward takes on this office: Compare: "Practical wisdom is a sort of steward of *sophia*, procuring leisure for it and its function" (*MM* I 35 1198^b8–20).
While they themselves engage in politics or do philosophy: See VII 3.
Do philosophy (*philosophousin*): On *philosophia*, see Introduction pp. lxix–lxx.

Note 75
The science of acquiring slaves (that is, the just variety of it) is a kind of warfare or hunting: See I 8 1256^b20–26.

Note 76
Our guiding way [of inquiry]: See I 1 1252^a17–20.

Note 77
Puzzle (*aporia*): "A dialectical problem (*problêma*) is a subject of inquiry . . . about which [1] people have no belief either way, or [2] on which the many have a belief contrary to that of the wise, or [3] the wise contrary to that of the many, or [4] about which the members of either of these classes disagree among themselves. . . . Problems also occur [5] where deductions conflict, since there is a puzzle about whether the thing holds or not, because there are strong arguments on both sides. They occur, too, [6] where we have no argument because they are so vast, and we find it difficult to give an explanation—for example, is the universe eternal or not? For one may also inquire into problems of that sort" (*Top.* I 11 104^b1–17). Thus a problem is [5] a *puzzle* just in case there are strong arguments on one side of it and strong arguments on the other: "A certain sophistical argument constitutes a puzzle. For because they wish to refute in a way that is contrary to beliefs in order to be clever when they engage in ordinary discussions, the resulting deduction turns into a puzzle. For thought is tied up when it does not wish to stand still, because what has been concluded is not pleasing but cannot move forward, because of its inability to resolve the argument" (*NE* VII 2 1146^a21–27).

Note 78
Wealth (*chrêmata*): Natural wealth consists of the instruments required by household managers and politicians (1256^b36–37). Unnatural wealth is money (I 10 1258^b4–6).

And property: Reading ἥ δὲ κτῆσις with Dreizehnter and ms. Γ for OCT ἥ γε κτῆσις.
Is a part of wealth-acquisition: Reading χρηματιστικῆς with OCT and the mss. Dreizehnter reads οἰκονομικῆς ("is a part of the craft of household management").

Note 79
If then nature makes nothing incomplete (*ateles*) **and nothing pointlessly** (*matên*): See I 2 1253ᵃ9n.
It must be that nature made all of them for the sake of humans: This is entailed by following four claims, of which (1) connects being *ateles*—or without a *telos* of a certain sort—with being pointless, while (2)–(4) explain what that *telos* is and why human beings alone have it: (1) "If, then, there is some end (*telos*) of things doable in action that we wish for because of itself, and the others because of it, and we do not choose everything because of something else (since if *that* is the case, it will go on without limit so that the desire will be empty and vain), it is clear that this will be the good—that is, the best good" (*NE* I 2 1094ᵃ18–22). (2) "Happiness is the best good" (I 7 1097ᵇ22). (3) "What is unconditionally complete, then, is what is always intrinsically choiceworthy and never choiceworthy because of something else. Happiness seems to be most like this, since *it* we always choose because of itself and never because of something else" (1097ᵃ33–ᵇ1). (4) "Of the other animals, none is happy, since they in no way share in contemplation. Happiness extends indeed just as far as contemplation does, and those to whom it more belongs to contemplate, it also more belongs to be happy, not coincidentally but, rather, in accord with contemplation, since this is intrinsically estimable. And so happiness will be some sort of contemplation" (X 8 1178ᵇ27–32). (1–4) need not mean, however, that plants and animals have intrinsic natures that are adapted to human uses and purposes; the direction of adaptation may be the other way around: human beings may have the nature they do—including their capacity to develop crafts, sciences, and political communities—because it enables them to use all that nature produces. Thus camels have the sorts of tongues and stomachs they do so that they can eat the thorny bushes that grow in their desert habitats, but these bushes do not have the nature they do because there are camels around to eat them (*PA* III 14 674ᵃ28–ᵇ18). It is "differences in food have produced different ways of life among the animals" (*Pol.* I 8 1256ᵃ21–22), not the other way around (see also IV 4 1290ᵇ25–37n). Nonetheless, the fact remains that if humans did not exist, all the other natural beings would be incomplete. A point made from a different direction at I 5 1254ᵇ10–13.

Note 80
Self-sufficiency in this sort of property, with a view to living the good life, is not unlimited (*apeiros*): "In fact because a happy person needs the goods that fortune brings [= external prosperity] in addition, some people think that good luck is the same as happiness. But it is not. For even good luck is an impediment when it is excessive, and presumably it should no longer by rights be called *good* luck. For the defining mark of *good* luck is determined by relation to happiness" (*NE* VII 13 1153ᵇ21–25). This defining mark, limit, or end (*Pol.* I 9 1257ᵇ28) is happiness or

living well: "Happiness, then, is apparently something complete and self-sufficient, since it is the end of what is doable in action" (*NE* I 7 1097^{b}20–21); "[The] political philosopher . . . is the architectonic craftsman of the end to which we look in calling each thing unconditionally bad or good" (VII 11 1152^{b}1–3).
As Solon in his poetry says it is: Fr. 1.1 Diehl. Solon (c. 640–560 BC) was an Athenian statesman and poet, and architect of the Athenian constitution.

Note 81
There is no instrument of any craft that is unlimited in quantity or size: See VII 2 1323^{b}7–10.

Note 82
The other does not exist by nature, but comes more from a sort of experience and craft knowledge: See 1257^{a}41–^{b}5, I 10 1258^{a}38–^{b}8.
Experience (*empeirias*) **and craft knowledge:** A person A perceives that when X_1 is sick with a fever giving him honey-water was followed by a reduction in fever (*Met.* VI 2 1027^{a}23–24). He retains this connection in his memory. Then he perceives that giving honey-water to X_2, X_3, . . . X_n was also followed by a reduction in their fever. A also retains these connections in his memory. When as a result of retaining them A associates drinking honey-water with fever reduction, he has "one experience," since "from memory (when it occurs often in connection with the same thing) comes experience. For memories that are many in number form an experience that is one in number" (*APo.* II 19 100^{a}4–6). The "same thing" is the connection between drinking honey-water and fever reduction, which result in the capacity to treat a fever. This is what makes experience "pretty much similar" to scientific knowledge and craft knowledge (*Met.* I 1 981^{a}1–2). The difference between them is that A does not know *why* honey-water reduces fever: "experienced people know the that but do not know the why, whereas craftsmen know the why, that is, the cause" (981^{a}29–30).

Note 83
Starting-point (*archê*): In the strict sense, a scientific-starting point, or first principle, is "the cause of many things, with nothing above it being a cause of it" (*GA* V 7 788^{a}14–16). Starting-points of this sort are discussed in I 1 1252^{a}15n(5). In a more general sense, which is the one relevant here, a starting-point is a place to start an investigation that is not itself taken to need defense.

Note 84
Each piece of property has two uses, both of which are uses of it intrinsically (*kath' hauto*): Something is intrinsically F or (literally) F "all by itself" or F *in its own right* or (Latin) *per se* F if it is F unconditionally, or because of what it itself essentially is. Thus Socrates is intrinsically rational, since being rational is part of being human and Socrates is essentially human, but he is not intrinsically musical, since being musical is not part of what it is to be human.

Note 85
Exchange (*metablêtikê*): The three parts of the craft of exchange are trading (whose sub-parts are ship owning, transport, and marketing), money-lending, and

wage-earning (I 11 1258^{b}20–27). The kinds of exchange that involve bartering surplus goods for other needed goods are natural and are not a part of the craft of wealth acquisition (1257^{a}14–30). The other kinds are parts of the craft of commerce.

Note 86

The craft of commerce (*kapêlikê*): The part of wealth-acquisition, but not of household-management (1257^{a}41–1258^{a}18), that produces wealth through exchange (1257^{b}20–22). It is concerned with money as opposed to natural wealth, and involves getting wealth at the expense of others. Usury (*obolostatikê*) is a part of it (I 10 1258^{a}38–^{b}2).

Note 87

As a replenishment of a self-sufficiency that is in accord with nature: "To eat or drink random things until we are overfull is to exceed the quantity that is in accord with nature, since a natural appetite is for the replenishment of a need" (*NE* III 11 1118^{b}16–19).

Note 88

Money is the element (*stoicheion*) **and limit** (*peras*) **of exchange:** Money is the *stoicheion*—or as we would say "unit"—of exchange for obvious reasons; it is the *peras* because the price of something sets a limit on its exchange value.

Element (*stoicheion*): A *stoicheion* was originally one of a row (*stoichos*) of things and later a letter of the alphabet or an element of any complex whole (Plato, *Tht.* 201e). Aristotle uses it in these ways, and to refer to the five primary elemental bodies (earth, water, air, fire, and ether), from which all others are composed.

Note 89

It appears to be (*phainetai*) **necessary for all wealth to have a limit:** The verb *phainesthai* ("appear") with (1) a participle is endorsing of what appears to be so and is translated "it is evident," "or it is seen to be," or the like, and the cognate adjective *phaneron* as "evident." *Phainesthai* with (2) an infinitive, as here, is neither endorsing nor rejecting of what appears to be so and is translated "appears." When *phainesthai* occurs without a participle or an infinitive, it may be endorsing or rejecting. Appearances (*phainomena*) are things that appear to be so but that may or may not be so. Things that appear so to everyone or to wise people who have investigated them are *endoxa*, or reputable beliefs.

Note 90

Goes back and forth (*epallattei*) **between the two sorts of crafts of wealth acquisition:** On *epallattein*, see I 6 1255^{a}13.

Note 91

What they take seriously is living, not living well: See I 2 1252^{b}29–30, III 9 1280^{a}31–32.

Note 92

It is not unlimited like the other, but has a defining mark (*horos*): A common meaning of the noun *horos*, from which the verb *horizesthai* ("define") derives, is "term," in the logical sense, in which a syllogism has three terms. Its root meaning derives from a stone marking the boundary or limit of a territory or piece of land in a visible way. Hence the doctor's *horos* is the thing "by reference to which he discerns what is healthy for a body from what isn't" (*EE* VII 15 1249^{a}21–22).

Note 93

The puzzle raised at the start: At I 8 1256^{a}3–10.

Wealth must rather be available to him: Wealth being the various goods that the craft of wealth acquisition would make him skilled at acquiring, were they not simply available.

Note 94

As was said earlier, nature must ensure that this is on hand: At 1258^{a}20–21.

Note 95

The leftovers of what they are born from are food for each one: See I 8 1256^{b}10–12.

Note 96

But since it [the craft of property acquisition] is of two sorts, as we said: At I 8 1256^{b}26–39, 9 1257^{b}17–23.

The craft of exchange is justly blamed (for it is not in accord with nature but involves taking from others): "In regard to property our first concern is the ones in accord with nature. And of the ones in accord with nature, farming is prior to the others, second, those that deal with things that come from the earth—for example, mining and anything else of that sort. Farming is most of all so because of its justice. For it does not take from human beings, either voluntarily, as do commerce and the wage-earning crafts (*hai mistharnikai*), or involuntarily, as do the military ones. Further, farming is natural. For by nature all get their food from their mother, so that human beings get it from the earth" (*Oec.* I 2 1343^{a}25–^{b}2).

It gets wealth from money itself, rather than just what money was provided for: The wealth that usury gets from money, as the next sentence makes clear, is more money, rather than the goods that money is introduced to be exchanged for.

Note 97

I 11: Although the distinction between questions bearing on use and those bearing on knowledge has already been drawn at I 3 1253^{b}15–18, it has not exactly been trumpeted, so that the discussion of it in this chapter comes somewhat unheralded. Moreover, the account of the craft of wealth acquisition is now divided into three kinds, rather than, as previously (I 8–10) into just two. It may be, then, that this chapter is a later addition to Book I.

Note 98

Since we have adequately discussed what relates to knowledge, we must go through what relates to use: See I 3 1253^{b}14–18.

Note 99

Theoretical knowledge is something free, whereas experience is something necessary: See VIII 2 1337^{b}5–21.

Note 100

Farming, which is now divided into land planted with fruit and land planted with cereals: Ancient farming consisted of the cultivation of wheat and other cereals on flat open plains (*psilê*) and the cultivation of grapes, olives, etc. on more hilly areas (*pepehuteumenê*).

Note 101

Vulgar (*banausôn*): An exact English equivalent for *banausos* is now difficult to find. *Phortikos*, used at 1258^{b}35, and also translated as "vulgar," is a near equivalent. Here is Herodotus on the subject: "The Thracians, Scythians, Persians, Lydians, and pretty much all the barbarians think that those of their fellow citizens who learn crafts—and their descendants too—are inferior in esteem, and regard as well born those who keep themselves clear of any form of manual work, and above all those who are free to engage in warfare. All the Greeks have learned this, especially the Spartans" (II.167).

Vulgar craftsmen (*technitôn*): Vulgar craftsmen—indeed the vulgar element in general—have a rather odd position in Aristotle's scheme of things. Though they are somewhat free, and somewhat enslaved, they seem to be further removed from virtue than slaves are (I 13 1260^{a}39–^{b}1). Yet nothing in their nature fits them to do the work they do (1260^{b}1–2). Instead, it seems to be their work itself that prevents them from acquiring virtue and being happy (VIII 2 1337^{b}4–21), suggesting that if they had not become vulgar craftsmen, they might (other things being equal) have been capable of virtue and happiness. They are typically contrasted with farmers, tradesmen, hired laborers (IV 2 1289^{b}32–33, VI 1 1317^{a}24–26), as also with free people (VIII 5 1340^{b}9–10) and hoplites (VII 4 1326^{a}23), and grouped together with wage-earners (VIII 2 1337^{b}13–14).

Note 102

An exact accounting (*akribologeisthai*): Here used with the somewhat negative connotation that it has more explicitly at *NE* IV 2 1122^{b}6–8: "The magnificent person will incur such [great] expenditure for the sake of what is noble, since this is a feature common to the virtues. Further, he will do it with pleasure and lavishly, since exact accounting (*akribologia*) is niggardly."

Vulgar (*phortikon*): The opposite of noble (II 9 1270^{a}20n) and free (III 9 1280^{a}5). As with *banausos* (1258^{b}26), an exact English equivalent is hard to find.

Note 103

The most craft-like (*technikôtatai*) **of these practices are those in which there is the least luck involved:** "'Experience made craft,' as Polus says, 'and lack of experience, luck'" (*Met.* I 1 981^{a}3–5). Aristotle is quoting Polus of Acragas, a mid-5th-cent BC student of Gorgias of Leontini. Plato gives Polus' adage in a slightly different form: "experience makes our age proceed in accord with craft, inexperience in accord with luck" (*Grg.* 448b5–7).

Luck (*tuchê*): What happens by luck in the broad sense is what happens coincidentally or contingently (*APo.* I 30 87^{b}19–22, *Met.* XIII 8 1065^{a}24–28). What happens by luck in the narrower sense of *practical* luck is what has a coincidental final cause. If a tree's being by the back door is the sort of thing that might be an outcome of deliberative thought, it is a candidate final cause of action—an end we aim at (*Ph.* II 5 197ᵃ5–8, 6 197ᵇ20–22). If wish, which is the desire involved in deliberation and deliberate choice, is what causes it to be there, the tree's being by the back door is a genuine final cause. If not, its being there is a coincidental final cause. Unlike chance (*to automaton*), which applies quite generally to whatever results from coincidental efficient causes, practical luck applies only to what could come about because of action and deliberate choice. Hence it is the sphere relevant to action: "Luck and the results of luck are found in things that are capable of being lucky, and, in general, of action. That is why indeed luck is concerned with things doable in action" (II 6 197ᵇ1–2). Since the sphere of practical luck is also that of the practical and productive sciences (*PA* I 1 640ᵃ27–33, *Rh.* I 5 1362ᵃ2), it is the sort relevant here. Goods external to the soul are controlled by luck (*MM* VII 3 1206ᵇ33–34), goods internal to it, such as virtue, are not (*NE* I 10 1100ᵇ7–21, *Pol.* VII 1 1323ᵇ27–29).

Note 104

Chares of Paros: Otherwise unknown.

Apollodorus of Lemnos: A contemporary of Aristotle's who wrote on practical farming.

Note 105

Thales of Miletus: See DK 11 = TEGP pp. 17–44. He is associated with the doctrine that water is the starting-point of all beings.

Miletus: On the western coast of Anatolia, near the mouth of the Maenander River, in modern-day Turkey.

Note 106

People were reproaching him because of his poverty, claiming that it showed his philosophy was of no benefit: "Theoretical wisdom is clearly scientific knowledge combined with understanding of the things that are naturally most estimable. That is why Anaxagoras and Thales and people of that sort are said to be wise—but not practically-wise when we see them to be ignorant of what is advantageous to themselves—and why what they know is said to be extraordinary, wondrous, difficult, and worthy of worship but useless, because it is not human goods they seek" (*NE* VI 1141ᵇ2–8). The reference is to Thales' expertise in astronomy, which is termed "philosophy," because astronomy is "the mathematical science that is most akin to philosophy" (*Met.* XII 8 1073ᵇ4–5).

Note 107

He raised a little money (*chrêmatôn*): The forms of wealth (*ploutos*) are "landed property . . . slaves, livestock, and money (*nomismatos*), and . . . so-called movables" (II 7 1267ᵇ10–12). Of these only *nomisma* is money in the strict sense of minted currency. But just as we think of a wealthy person as someone with a lot of money, even if in fact most of his wealth is in other forms, so do the Greeks. Thus while the "man from Sicily" uses *nomisma* (1259ᵃ24) to make more *nomisma*

(1259ᵃ27), what he is instructed to take with him is *chrêmata* (1259ᵃ29). Hence *chrêmata* is often best translated, as it is here, not as "wealth" but as "money." **Chios:** The fifth largest of the Greek islands, just over four miles from the Anatolian coast.

Note 108

Sicily: Large island off the toe of Italy.

Note 109

Dionysius: Probably Dionysius I (430–367 BC), the ruling tyrant of Syracuse.

Note 110

Mastership (which we discussed earlier): At I 7.
Another the science of fatherhood: Called procreative science at I 3 1253ᵇ8–12.
[Let us now discuss the other two]: "Since (*epei*)" normally introduces a protasis, but no apodosis is immediately forthcoming, suggesting that there may be a lacuna in the text.

Note 111

A wife is ruled in a political way: Political rule is exercised among free and equal people who take turns ruling and being ruled (1259ᵇ4–6). This suggests that a wife should sometimes rule her husband. But this seems to be excluded (1259ᵇ9–10). It is not entirely clear, therefore, why Aristotle characterizes such rule as political rather than monarchical, as he seems to at I 2 1252ᵇ20–21, 6 1254ᵇ13–14, or as aristocratic, which is what he says it is in the following passage: "The community of man and woman is apparently aristocratic, since the man rules in accord with his worth and in those matters in which a man should rule, whereas whatever is fitting for a woman he gives over to her. If on the other hand the man controls everything, he changes it into an oligarchy, since he makes it contrary to worth and not dependent on who is better. Sometimes, though, women rule because they are heiresses. Their rule, then, is not in accord with virtue but exists because of wealth and power, as in oligarchies" (*NE* VIII 10 1160ᵇ32–1161ᵃ3). Perhaps the thought is, then, that the husband's rule is political in at least the sense that there are areas in which he delegates rule to his wife, although none in which he is ruled by her. Delegation, though, is not abrogation. Hence even in those areas where a woman rules, she does so as her husband's proxy, not autonomously. In other words, a woman's status is like that of a younger man's in the best constitution. For he too is ruled by political rule, but does not get to rule others until, having experienced rule in the city's military arm, he is old enough to acquire the practical wisdom needed to rule as a deliberator and judge (*Pol.* VII 9 1329ᵃ2–17). Thus if a woman, even in her prime, were by nature like a younger man in the relevant respects, it would be proper for her to be ruled with political rule, but improper for her ever to serve as an autonomous ruler. The fact that closeness of age between husband and wife "is liable to cause disputes over the management of the household" (VII 16 1335ᵃ3–4), and so over rule of the household generally (III 6 1278ᵇ38), might be regarded as mildly relevant evidence in this regard. See also I 13 1260ᵃ13n.

Note 112

What Amasis said about his footbath: When Amasis (596–525 BC) first became king of the Egyptians, they treated him with contempt because he was of humble origins. So he had a gold footbath made into a statue of a god. The Egyptians treated the statue with great respect. Amasis pointed out that he was like the footbath. He had once been an ordinary person, but he was now a king, worthy of honor and respect. The story is recounted in Herodotus II.172.

Note 113

Homer spoke well: For example, at *Iliad* I.544. See also *NE* VIII 10 1161ᵃ25–27.

Note 114

Temperance (*sôphrosunê*): "Where pleasures and pains are concerned (not all of them and even less so where pains are concerned), the medial condition is temperance and the excess is intemperance" (*NE* II 7 1107ᵇ3–6); "Temperance and intemperance are concerned with the sorts of pleasures that the rest of the animals share in as well (which is why they appear slavish and beast-like), namely, touch and taste" (III 10 1118ᵃ24–26).

Courage (*andreia*): "A person is courageous who endures and fears the things he should, in the way he should, when he should, and is similarly confident, since a courageous person feels and acts as things merit and in the way reason prescribes" (*NE* III 7 1115ᵇ17–20).

Justice (*dikaiosunê*): "[Justice as a whole (= general justice)] is complete virtue—not unconditionally but in relation to another person. . . . And it is complete virtue in the highest degree, because it is the complete use of complete virtue. It is the complete use because someone who possesses it is able to use his virtue in relation to another person and not solely with regard to himself. For many people are able to use their virtue in what properly belongs to themselves but unable to do so in issues relating to another person" (*NE* V 2 1129ᵇ25–1130ᵃ1); "It is evident that there is another sort of injustice beyond injustice as a whole, that is a part of it. It has the same name, because its definition places it in the same genus, since they both exercise their capacity in relation to another person. The former is concerned with honor, wealth, or preservation (or—if we had a name for it—whatever includes all these) and is concerned with them because of the pleasure of making a profit, while the latter is concerned with all the things that are the concern of an excellent person" (V 11 1130ᵃ32–ᵇ5).

Note 115

Noble-goodness (*kalokagathia*): "Noble-goodness is complete virtue" (*EE* VIII 3 1249ᵃ16–17; also *MM* II 8 1207ᵇ20–27). See also II 9 1270ᵃ20n.

Note 116

Being ruled and ruling differ in kind (*eidos*), **not in degree:** Although "things that differ in kind (*eidos*) also admit of differences in degree" (*NE* VIII 1 1155ᵇ 14–15).

In degree (*tô[i] mallon kai hêtton*): Literally "in the more and the less." See V 8 1308ᵇ6n.

Note 117

Those who are by nature ruled: Reading ἀρχομένων with Dreizehnter and Saunders for OCT ἀρχόντων.

Note 118

A slave does not have the deliberative part of the soul at all: See I 2 1252ª34n.
The female has a deliberative part but it lacks control (*akuron*): (1) People who stand by their beliefs because they are stubbornly opinionated are said to be "pained if their own beliefs lack control, insofar as these are like decrees" (VII 10 1151ᵇ15–16). (2) Like a law, a decree has prescriptive force, but rather than being universal—as a law must be—is so adapted to particular circumstances as to render any further deliberation unnecessary: "There are some cases where it is impossible to establish a law, so that decrees are needed. For . . . a decree adapts itself to the things themselves" (*NE* V 10 1137ᵇ27–32). That is why (3) "a decree is doable in action, as the last thing" (VI 1141ᵇ24–28)—that is, the last thing reached in deliberation, whether political or private. (4) When a political decree is revoked or nullified it is rendered *akuron,* so that it no longer controls action. The implication of this chain of thought is that what makes a female's deliberative part *akuron* is that the decrees it reaches in practical deliberation do not control her own actions. This would explain why those who lack self-control are likened to females: "if someone gives in to strong or excessive pleasures or pains, it is not something to wonder at. . . . But it is something to wonder at if he does this where things that ordinary people can successfully struggle against are concerned and if he gives in to and cannot struggle successfully against these—unless it is because of his congenital nature or because of disease . . . or as female differs in relation to male in this regard" (7 1150ᵇ6–16). The overall idea, then, would be that, while women are prone to lack self-control, making them unsuited to rule, nonetheless their capacity to deliberate makes them suited to be ruled in a way that recognizes that capacity. This would explain why Aristotle says both that they should be ruled in a political way, as free and equal people, while at the same time thinking that they should not rule their husbands (*Pol.* I 12 1259ᵇ1n). Similarly, a generative organ is *akuron* if it is unable to generate offspring (*GA* IV 4 772ᵇ28).

Having said that women should be ruled in a political way, however, Aristotle goes on to mention that "a male, unless he is somehow formed contrary to nature, is by nature more capable of leading (*hêgemonikôteron*) than a female" (*Pol.* I 12 1259ᵇ1–3). This suggests that a woman's deliberative decrees lack control not of herself (though that may also be true) but of *others*. For "all females are less spirited than males, except in the case of bear and leopard" (*HA* IX 1 608ª33–34) and "the element of ruling and the element of being free come from this capacity in all cases, since spirit is something fit for rule and indomitable" (*Pol.* VII 7 1328ª7).

On the other side, the fact that women have a role to play in household management suggests that they have some control at least over children and slaves: "Household management, indeed, is also of distinct sorts for a man and a woman. For his function is to acquire property and hers to preserve it" (*Pol.* III 5 1277ᵇ24–25). Since war is a sort of property acquisition (I 8 1256ᵇ23–26), we can see why this division might have recommended itself. But preservation too requires skills and crafts, which must be learned and taught by someone with the appropriate sort of control. Having made the point about household management, indeed, Aristotle first contrasts it with practical wisdom, which is "the only virtue special to a ruler" (1277^{b}25–26), and then adds that "the virtue of someone ruled is not practical wisdom but true belief," on the grounds that "those ruled are like makers of flutes, whereas rulers are like the flute players who use them" (1277^{b}28–31).

One natural way to cash this account out, then, is in terms of chain of command. The male head of household, as the user of the house, is the best judge of how it should be: "the one who uses it [a house] is an even better judge [than the one who makes it] (and the one who uses it is the household manager)" (III 11 1282^{a}20–21). Moreover, because he possesses practical wisdom, he knows what happiness is, and what best furthers it. So he also knows not just *that* it should be a certain way, but *why* it should (*NE* VI 9 1142^{b}31–33). His wife, on the other hand, has true belief about how the house should be, but not the knowledge of why it should be that way, because she is ruled directly with political rule by him. She, in turn, and by a sort of proxy, rules those below her with appropriately different sorts of rule, just as he rules them directly with the corresponding sorts of direct rule. Unlike him, then, she is not an unconditional ruler, but rather a ruler of a sort—a ruler in relation to her husband's slaves and children, but not in relation to her husband himself. In a household without a steward, most of the day-to-day management of the house would presumably be left to her. See I 7 1255^{b}35–37, VI 8 1323^{a}5–6.

As in the case of natural slaves, nothing Aristotle says here seems to preclude the possibility of a woman's having a soul with a fully functional scientific subpart. See I 2 1252^{a}34n.

Note 119

A ruler needs to have complete virtue of character: Which is a single state constituted of the various virtues of character (courage, temperance, and the rest) and practical wisdom (*NE* VI 13 1144^{b}1–21).

Note 120

A ruler's function is unconditionally that of an architectonic craftsman (*architektonos*), **and his reason is an architectonic craftsman:** "The political philosopher [≈ the political ruler who knows the craft of politics] is the architectonic craftsman (*architektôn*) of the end to which we look in calling each thing unconditionally bad or good" (*NE* VII 11 1152^{b}1–3).

His reason (*ho logos*): Literally: "the reason." But, as the texts just cited suggest, the reason that is architectonic is the one embodied in the craft of politics employed by the political ruler.

Architectonic craftsman: See I 1253^{b}38n.

Note 121

As Socrates supposed: "[*Socrates*] Will virtue differ, as regards being virtue, whether it is in a child or in an old man, in a woman or in a man? [*Meno*] Well, I somehow think, Socrates, that this is no longer like those other cases.

[*S.*] What? Weren't you saying that a man's virtue is to manage a city well, and a woman's a household? [*M.*] Yes, I was. [*S.*] Well then, is it possible to manage a city well or a household or anything else whatever, while not managing it temperately and justly? [*M.*] Certainly not. [*S.*] And if they really manage it justly and temperately, isn't it by means of justice and temperance that they will manage it? [*M.*] Necessarily. [*S.*] So both men and women will need the same things, if they are really going to be good—justice and temperance. [*M.*] Apparently. [*S.*] What about a child and an old man? If they were intemperate and unjust, could they possibly be good? [*M.*] Certainly not. [*S.*] But if they were temperate and just? [*M.*] Yes. [*S.*] So all human beings are good in the same way, since they are good if they possess the same things. [*M.*] So it seems" (Plato, *Men.* 73a6–c5).
Socrates: Here, as in II 1–5, the chief character in the majority of Plato's dialogues, but sometimes the historical figure, Socrates of Alopece 470/469–399 BC, on whom that character is based.

Note 122
It is far better to enumerate the virtues, as Gorgias does: "[*Socrates*] Meno, what do you say virtue is? Tell me, don't be begrudging. The result may be that I spoke a very lucky falsehood when I said that I had never yet met anyone who knew this, if it comes to light that you and Gorgias do know it. [*M.*] I will tell you, Socrates; it is not difficult. First, then, if you want to know a man's virtue, that is easy. This is a man's virtue: to take part in the city's affairs capably, and by doing so to benefit his friends and harm his enemies, while taking care that he himself does not suffer anything like that. If you want a woman's virtue, that is not difficult to describe. She must manage the household well, look after its contents, and be obedient to the man. There is a different virtue for a child, one for a male and one for a female, and for an older man, one for a free man, if you want to know that, and one for a slave, if you want to know that. There are very many other virtues, too, so there is no puzzle about telling you what virtue is. You see, for each of the affairs and stages of life, and in relation to each particular function, there is a virtue for each of us—and it is the same way, I think, Socrates, for vice" (Plato, *Men.* 71d5–72a5).
Gorgias: See III 2 $1275^{b}26$n.

Note 123
The way the poet spoke about woman: Sophocles, *Ajax* 293.

Note 124
A child's virtue too is not his in relation to himself, but in relation to his end and his leader: The relevant end is the one that will be the child's when he is a mature adult, namely, happiness, in which as a child he has no share: "Children who are said to be blessed are being called blessed because of their prospects, since for happiness there must be, as we said, both complete virtue and a complete life" (*NE* I 9 $1100^{a}3$–5). His father is his leader or his king (*Pol.* I 12 $1259^{b}1$).

Note 125
A slave shares in his master's living: See I 6 $1255^{b}11$–12.

A craftsman is at a greater remove, and virtue pertains to him just to the extent that slavery does: It is insofar as a craftsman serves a master that he needs some share of those states of character which, because they further happiness (in his case the happiness of a master or head of household), are in fact virtues of character. See VII 1 1323b21–23, 8 1328a37–40.

Note 126
A vulgar craftsman has a kind of limited (*aphôrismenên*) **slavery:** The idea—to us rather counterintuitive—is that a vulgar craftsman is worse off than a slave, because his share in virtue, and so in happiness, is less. Thus it is worse, not better, to be a slave in a limited way than to be fully a slave.

Note 127
The science of teaching (*didaskalikên*) **him his functions:** *Didaskalikê* is essentially a linguistic activity: "Certain animals share at once in some learning and teaching, some from each other, some from human beings, these are the ones that have hearing—not just those that hear sounds but those that further perceive the differences between signs" (*HA* IX 1 608a17–21; also *Pol.* I 2 1253a1–18, *Po.* 19 1456b5–7). In the full sense, it involves formal instruction in a craft or science that results in scientific knowledge of causes: "Teaching is what those people do who state the causes of each thing" (*Met.* I 2 982a29–30); "An indication of the one who knows, as opposed to the one who does not know, is his capacity to teach. That is why we think craft knowledge to be more like scientific knowledge than experience is, since craftsmen can teach, while experienced people cannot" (1 981b7–10); "Teaching is argument (*logos*) in accord with scientific knowledge" (*Rh.* I 1 1355a26).

Note 128
Those people do not speak correctly who withhold reason from slaves: That is, as the following sentence makes clear, who do not treat slaves as having any share of reason—not even as much as is possessed by the desiring part of the soul.
But tell us to make use only of prescriptive commands: "It is certainly necessary to punish slaves, in a just way, and not to spoil them by warning them like free people. And in speaking to a household one should pretty much always use a prescriptive command" (Plato, *Lg.* VI 777e4–778a1).

Note 129
Slaves should be warned (*nouthetêteon*) **more than children:** "The fact, though, that the non-rational part is persuaded in some way by reason is revealed by the practice of warning (*nouthetêsis*) people and by all the different practices of admonishing and exhorting them" (*NE* I 13 1102b33–1103a1). The idea, presumably, is that children should be treated in a way that respects the fact that they do have a deliberative part which, though incomplete, needs to be helped to develop, so that it will one day have the completeness it currently lacks.

Note 130
It will be necessary to go through all these in connection with the constitutions: No discussion devoted to this topic appears in the *Politics* as we have it.

Constitutions (*politeiai*): The U.S. Constitution is the highest law of the land and is embodied in a document. A *politeia* is something like that, but is not simply a set of laws, written or otherwise. Instead, it is the community of people whose laws those are. (The English word "constitution" has a parallel sense, as in "He has a strong constitution.") Aristotle gives a number of characterizations of a *politeia* which show this clearly: A *politeia* is "a sort of life (*bios*) of a city" (IV 11 1295a40–b1); "a certain ordering of those who inhabit the city" (III 1 1274b38) or of its various offices, "above all of the office that controls everything" (III 6 1278b8–10). At the same time, however, the term *politeia* sometimes refers to (1) a political system of any sort, whether constitutional or not (II 10 1271b20 with 1272b9–11), sometimes to a system of a particular sort, namely, a *polity* (II 6 1265b26–28, II 11 1273a4–5, III 7 1279a37–b4, III 15 1286b13, IV 1 1289b28), and often to any political system defined by and governed in accord with universal laws (1289a18–20). The fundamental reason why there are more constitutions than just one is that people seek happiness "in different ways and by different means" (VII 8 1328a41–b2).

Note 131

The virtue of the part must look to the virtue of the whole: See I 2 1253a18–29, VIII 1 1337a27–30.

It is necessary to look to the constitution in educating both women and children: Referred to as "the most important of all the ways that have been mentioned to make a constitution endure" at V 9 1310a12–13.

Its children be excellent: Reading τοὺς παῖδας εἶναι σπουδαίους with Dreizehnter and the mss. for OCT τὸ τοὺς παῖδας εἶναι σπουδαίους.

Excellent (*spoudaios*): Often, as here, *spoudaios* is a synonym of *agathos* ("good") but sometimes, when predicated of things, it means "serious," "weighty," or "important," as at *NE* X 6 1177a1–2.

Note 132

Those who share in the constitution (*koinônoi tês politeias*): In the best city, (1) "all the citizens share in the constitution" (VII 13 1332a34–35), suggesting a contrast with other cities in which this is not so, and thus also apparently drawing a contrast between sharing in the constitution and being a citizen. Similarly, (2) those who hold office are contrasted with "those in the governing body" and "those outside the constitution" (V 8 1308a5–7). Since "the constitution is governing body" (III 6 1278b11), and an unconditional citizen is "defined by nothing else so much as by his participation in judgment and office" (III 1 1275a22–23), the natural way to interpret (1) and (2) seems to be this: Those who share in the constitution are those participants in judgment and office (= unconditional citizens) who belong to the governing body—these being the citizens who occupy or are eligible to occupy "the offices that have control of the constitution" (V 8 1309a30). Thus in the best city all the unconditional citizens share in the constitution because all eventually become members of the governing body (VII 14 1332b35–1333a3). We must distinguish, then, between the offices that are keyed to unconditional citizenship and "the most important offices" (II 11 1273a29–30, IV 9 1294b29–31) or "the offices most properly so called" (IV 15 1299a25) that are keyed to membership in the governing body and that control the constitution.

BOOK II

Note 133

Which political community is superior to all others for people who are able to live as far as possible in the way they would pray to live: See IV 1 1288^b21–24, VII 4 1325^b35–40. That not many people are lucky enough to live in such ideal conditions is something Aristotle recognizes (VI 1 1288^b24–27).
Devise subtleties (*sophizesthai*): See IV 13.

Note 134

Citizen (*politês*): "The unconditional citizen (*politês haplôs*) is defined by nothing else so much as by his participation in judgment and office" (III 1 1275^a22–23), but different people count as such in different constitutions (13 1283^b40–1284^a3). Not all offices are equally important, however, and we need to distinguish between those keyed to citizenship and those keyed to sharing in the constitution (I 13 1260^b20n). In a kingship, for example, the king alone shares in the constitution, since he alone occupies the most important offices, but this does not prevent others from being unconditional citizens through sharing in other less important ones. That is why there can be citizens to "guard kings with their weapons" (III 14 1285^a25–26). This has consequences too, obviously, for how we are to understand the "common advantage," which all correct constitutions further. See III 6 1279^a17n.

Note 135

The citizens could share children, women, and property with each other, as in Plato's *Republic*: See 423e–424a, 449a–466d.

Note 136

The hypothesis Socrates adopts: At *Rep*. 462a. See II 9 1269^a32n.

Note 137

Nation (*ethnos*): A nation occupied a larger territory than a city, had a larger population, and a less tight political order. It need not have a single town or urban center, and may consist of many scattered villages. See VII 2 1324^b11–12 for examples.
Like the Arcadians: In Aristotle's day, these were organized into a confederacy of cities.
Arcadians: Inhabitants of Arcadia, a highland region at the center of the Peloponnese.

Note 138

That is why reciprocal equality preserves cities, as we said earlier in the *Ethics*, since this is also what must exist among people who are free and equal: "In communities based on exchange, however, what binds the parties together is what is just in this way, namely, reciprocity that is proportionate and not equal. For it is proportionate reciprocity that keeps a city together. For people either seek to return evil for evil (and if they do not, it seems like slavery) or good for good (and if they do not, no giving in exchange takes place), and it is by giving in exchange that they

keep together. . . . What produces proportionate exchange is diagonal coupling. Let A be a builder, B a shoemaker, C a house, and D a shoe. The builder, then, must get from the shoemaker the shoemaker's work and give him his own work in return. So if there is first proportionate equality and then reciprocity is achieved, the condition we mentioned will be met. But if not, there is no equality and nothing to keep the parties together, since there is nothing to prevent the work of one of them from being more excellent than that of the other. These works, then, must be equalized. For it is not from two doctors that a community comes about but from a doctor and a farmer and, in general, from people who are different and not equal. And these must be equalized. That is why everything that is exchanged must be in some way commensurable. It is for this purpose that money has been introduced and becomes a sort of mean. For since it measures everything, it also measures excess and deficiency and how many shoes are equal to a house or food. Just as builder is to shoemaker, then, so must such and such number of shoes be to a house or food. For if this does not happen, there will be no exchange and no community. And it will not happen unless the things in question are in some way equal. Hence they must all be measured by some one thing. . . . In truth, this one thing is need, which binds everything together. For if people neither needed things nor needed them to a similar extent, either there would be no exchange or not the same one. But as a sort of exchangeable representative of need, money came into existence on the basis of convention and is called 'money' (*nomisma*) because of this, because it exists not by nature but by conventional law (*nomos*), and changing it or rendering it useless is up to us" (*NE* V 5 1132^{b}31–1133^{a}31). See also III 12 1282^{b}21n.
Free: See III 8 1280^{a}5n.

Note 139
But among those where it is not possible, because all are in nature equal, it is at the same time also just for all to share in ruling (regardless of whether it is good or bad (*phaulos*) to rule), and for those who are equal to take turns, and to be similar when they are out of office, imitates this: Reading εἴτ' ἀγαθὸν εἴτε φαῦλον τὸ ἄρχειν, πάντας αὐτοῦ μετέχειν, τοῦτό δὲ μιμεῖται with the mss. for OCT reading εἴτ' ἀγαθὸν εἴτε φαῦλον τὸ ἄρχειν. πάντας αὐτοῦ μετέχειν, τοῦτό γε μιμεῖται.

Note 140
What is said to be the greatest good for cities: At *Rep*. 608e.

Note 141
All at the same time say "mine" and "not mine": At *Rep*. 462a–e.

Note 142
A sort of fallacy (*paralogismos*) is involved in "all say": In this case the fallacy is due to an ambiguity in the term "all." For a related fallacy, see V 8 1307^{b}36–39.

Note 143
Contentious deductions (*eristkous sullogismous*): "Sophistic . . . is a way of making money from apparent wisdom. . . . Contenders (*eristikoi*) and sophists use

the same arguments, but not to achieve the same goal. . . . If the goal is apparent victory, the argument is contentious; if it is apparent wisdom, it is sophistic" (*SE* 11 171^{b}27–33).

Even in arguments (*en tois logois*): *Met.* II 3 995^{a}11–12 contrasts "in arguments" with "in business transactions." The idea, presumably, is that even when the focus is on arguments themselves, as in logic or dialectic, terms such as "all," "both," "odd," and "even" can result in deductions the fallacy in which can be difficult to spot.

Note 144

Or only as much as falls to each of them to give: For example, someone might have an official responsibility for, or a special interest in, some common property.

Note 145

Each says "mine" of anyone among the citizens who is doing well or badly in this sense: See *Rep.* 463e2–5.

Note 146

"My fellow clansman" or "my fellow tribesman": See IV 15 1300^{a}25n.

Note 147

According to the reports of some of those who write accounts of their world travels: See Herodotus IV.180. *Rh.* I 4 1360^{a}33–35 comments on the usefulness of such travel writings to those drafting laws.

Note 148

The mare in Pharsalus called "Just": So-called because by producing a colt that resembled the sire she showed herself to be a just or faithful mate. Aristotle uses the same example at *HA* VII 7 586^{a}12–14.

Pharsalus: A town in Thessaly in northern Greece.

Note 149

Just as none is so even against outsiders: Reading ὥσπερ καὶ πρὸς τοὺς ἄπωθεν with the mss. The clause is ambiguous even if καὶ is omitted, as it is by OCT and Dreizehnter. But it cannot mean or imply that homicides, assaults, or verbal abuse *are* pious when committed against outsiders. Instead the implication is that they are particularly impious when committed against relatives, since they are impious even when committed against outsiders. See Plato, *Lg.* IX 868c–873c.

Note 150

The customary expiations: Reading γνωριζόντων with Saunders and the mss. for OCT γνωριζομένων.

Note 151

Socrates forbids such sexual intercourse solely because the pleasure that comes from it is so strong: "[*Socrates*] Can you think of any pleasure that is greater or keener than sexual pleasure? [*Glaucon*] No, I cannot—or of a more insane one either. [*S.*] But isn't the right sort of passion a naturally moderate and musically educated passion for order and beauty? [*G.*] Yes. [*S.*] Then nothing insane and nothing akin to dissoluteness can be involved in the right love? [*G.*] No, they cannot. [*S.*] Then sexual pleasure must not be involved, must it, and the lover and the boy who passionately love and are loved in the right way must have no share in it? [*G.*] No, by Zeus, Socrates, it must not be involved. [*S.*] It seems, then, that you will lay it down as a law in the city we are founding that a lover—if he can persuade his boyfriend to let him—may kiss him, be with him, and touch him, as a father would a son, for the sake of beautiful things. But in all other respects, his association with the one he cares about must never seem to go any further than this. Otherwise, he will be reproached as untrained in music, and as lacking in appreciation for beautiful things. [*G.*] That's right" (*Rep.* III 403a–c). See also VII 16 1335^{b}37–38.

Note 152
It would seem more useful to have the farmers rather than the guardians share their women and children: The city described in the *Republic* has three parts: producers, guardians (soldier-police), and philosopher-kings. The guardians and philosopher-kings share their women, children, and other property in common. The text is less clear about whether this is also true of the producers (see II 5 1263^{a}8–21).

Note 153
There will be less friendship where women and children are held communally: Perhaps for the reason given at II 8 1263^{a}8–21.

Note 154
We think friendship to be the greatest of goods for cities, since in this way people are least likely to engage in faction (*stasiazoien*): *Stasis* ("faction") is internal political conflict, extending all the way from political tensions to outright civil war, typically occurring between aristocrats, oligarchs, and democrats, which is sometimes severe enough to result in the overthrow or modification of the constitution.

Note 155
In the accounts of erotic love (*tois erôtikois logois*) **Aristophanes says that lovers have an appetitive desire to grow together and become one instead of two:** Aristophanes, the comic dramatist (c. 455–c. 386 BC), appears as a character in Plato's *Symposium*, and in his account of erotic love, which is one of several, expresses the views under discussion (192c–193a).

Note 156
There are two things above all that make human beings care and feel friendship, what is special [to them] and what is beloved (*to agapêton*)**—neither of which can exist among people under such a constitution:** "What is beloved . . . [is a greater good than something that is one among others]. That is why someone who puts out the eye of a one-eyed man does not do the same harm as someone who does this to a man with two eyes, since he deprives him of what is beloved" (*Rh.* I 7 1365^{b}16–19). Hence, in Aristotle's view, there is nothing beloved in the city described in the *Republic*, because everyone is just one among others.
What is special [to them] (*to idion*): As opposed to be shared with others.

Note 157

The transference of the children, once born, from the farmers and craftsmen to the guardians, and vice versa: See *Rep*. 415a–d.

Note 158

Sparta: Also called Lacedaemon. A prominent city situated on the banks of the Eurotas River in Laconia, in the southeastern Peloponnese.

The territory (*chôra*): Sometimes *chôra* refers to a city's entire territory, including its urban areas, and is translated as "territory"; sometimes it refers to the territory outside the urban areas, and is translated as "countryside."

Note 159

To see that people become disposed in such a way: See VII 13 1332a31–38.

Legislator (*nomothetês*): The legislator in the full sense of the term is someone who possesses legislative science (*nomothetikê*) in its complete, or perfected, form. Most of the actual legislators Aristotle discusses—Phaleas of Chalcedon, Hippodamus of Miletus, Lycurgus, Solon—do not come up to that high standard, as Aristotle's often decisive criticisms of them shows. Yet such truth as they do contain constitutes at least some small contribution to legislative science. They are nascent legislators, therefore, who possess nascent (or embryonic) legislative science.

Although "where the laws do not rule there is no constitution" (IV 4 1292a32) and some laws make a constitution clear (1 1289a18–20), there is nonetheless a difference between a constitution and a set of laws (1289a15–25). So there is also a difference between those who craft laws only, and those who, like Lycurgus and Solon, craft a constitution too (II 12 1273b32–34). No craft or science is singled out, however, as a specifically constitutional one. But what is said in the following text indicates the difference Aristotle has in mind: "Of the practical wisdom concerned with the city, the architectonic part is legislative science, while the part concerned with particulars has the name common to both—'politics.' This part is practical and deliberative, since a decree is doable in action, as the last thing. That is why only these people are said to take part in politics, since it is only they who do things in just the way handicraftsmen do. It also seems that the practical wisdom concerned with oneself as an individual is most of all practical wisdom, and it is this that has the name common to all the sorts. Of the other sorts, one is household management, another legislative science, another politics, and of the latter, one part is deliberative (*bouleutikê*) and the other judicial (*dikastikê*)" (*NE* VI 8 1141b24–33). It is clear, then, that while a legislator focuses exclusively on a city's laws, a designer of constitutions also includes the management of the city's households as well as its deliberative and judicial functions within his purview. It is also reasonably clear that "the practical wisdom concerned with the city" has these same things in its purview. But this practical wisdom is "the same state [of the soul]" as politics, or political science (1141b23–24), implying, surely, that the science a designer of constitutions needs is precisely politics itself—a description of which is given in *Pol.* IV 1 1288b21–1289a25. This would explain why no specifically constitutional science is introduced.

It is also worth noting in this regard that while "the law should rule everything," officials and the constitution "should judge only about particulars" (IV 4 1292ᵃ32–34). Though in this case the constitution is no doubt the governing body (III 6 1278ᵇ11, 7 1279ᵃ25–26), the point remains that law and constitution have distinct purviews.

Another distinction not to be overlooked is made in the following text: "Some of those who have had something to say about a constitution took no part whatsoever in political actions, but always lived a private life. . . . Others became legislators, some in their own cities, others in some foreign ones as well, because they engaged in politics themselves" (*Pol.* II 12 1273ᵇ27–32). Thus a nascent legislator need not have ever been active in politics (1273ᵇ27–32n), or be a citizen of the city for which he is legislating, likewise a designer of constitutions. This raises the question of whether this separation carries over from nascent legislative science and politics to the complete, or perfected, sciences themselves. Here is the start of Aristotle's answer:

> [1] Shouldn't we next investigate from what sources and in what way someone might become competent in legislative science? Or isn't it, as in other cases, from politicians? For, as we saw, legislative science seems to be a part of politics. Or is it not evident that it is the same in the case of politics as in the other sciences and the other capacities? For in the others, it is evident that it is the same people who impart their capacities to others as actively practice them themselves, just as with doctors or writers. In the case of politics, however, although [2a] it is the sophists who profess to teach it, it is practiced not by any of them but by politicians, and [2b] they seem to do so thanks to some sort of ability and experience rather than to thought. For it is evident that they neither write nor speak about such matters (and yet that would be a nobler thing, presumably, than to compose speeches for the law courts and the assembly), and furthermore it is evident that they have not made their own sons or any other friends of theirs into politicians either. But it would be quite reasonable for them to have done so, if indeed they were able to, since there is nothing better than this capacity that they could have left to their cities or could have chosen to have for themselves or, then, for their closest friends. [3] Still, experience does seem to make no small contribution, since otherwise people could not, through intimacy with politics, have become politicians. That is why those who seek to know about politics would seem to need experience in addition. (*NE* X 9 1180ᵇ28–1181ᵃ12)

Here [1] states that politics, since it is a science, should, like other crafts and sciences, be based on experience and intimacy with the pertinent field of inquiry (I 1 1252ᵃ15n(5)). A difficulty is then raised in [2]. Experience and scientific theorizing should go together, but in the case of politics they seem to come apart. For [2b] the politicians who have the experience lack the scientific knowledge, as evidenced by the fact that they neither write about political topics nor teach what they know to their sons, in the way that those with scientific knowledge would do, since scientists and craftsmen can teach while merely experienced people cannot (*Met.* I 1 981^{b}7–10), and [2a] the sophists who purport to teach politics lack experience in it. [3] responds that experience must make a difference, otherwise people could not become (even nascent) politicians on the basis of it.

The second part of Aristotle's answer about the relevance of experience to the complete science of politics, which includes legislative science, is similar in structure to the first part:

> [4] Those of the sophists who profess to teach politics, however, are evidently a long way from teaching it, since on the whole they know nothing about what sort of thing it is or what sorts of things it is concerned with. For if they did, they would not have taken it to be the same as rhetoric or even inferior to it, nor would they have thought that [5] legislating is an easy matter for anyone who has collected together laws that enjoy a good reputation, since it amounts to selecting the best ones—as if the selection did not call for comprehension and correct discernment were not, as in matters of music, the greatest thing. [6] For those with experience in a particular area discern the works in it correctly and comprehend by what means or in what way they are brought to completion, and discern what is in tune with what, whereas those who lack experience must be content not to have it escape them whether the work is well or badly made, as in the case of painting. But laws would seem to be the works of politics, so how could someone become competent in legislative science or discern which laws are best, from *them,* since it is evident that we do not become doctors from reading textbooks either? Yet these textbooks do try to say not only what the treatments are but also how each sort of patient might be cured and should be treated, distinguishing their various states. [7] But while these do seem to be of benefit to experienced people, to those who lack scientific knowledge they seem useless. [8] Presumably, then, collections of laws and constitutions might also be of good use to people who are able to get a theoretical grasp on them and discern what is correctly done or the opposite and what sorts of things fit with what. In those who go through them without being in this state, however, no correct discernment would be present, unless of course by chance, although they may become better comprehenders of them. [9] So since our predecessors have left the subject of legislation unexamined, it is presumably better if we ourselves investigate it and indeed constitutions generally, so that as far as possible our philosophy of human affairs may be brought to completion. (*NE* X 9 1181^{a}12–^{b}15)

In [4] the sophists are ruled out as having scientific knowledge of politics and as being teachers of it, because [6] they lack the political experience needed for correct discernment and comprehension of laws, and so cannot acquire political science, as [5] they think, simply by selecting good laws from collections of sets of laws and constitutions that are already in use somewhere or that have been proposed as excellent. Nonetheless, [7] to experienced people, who are able to

discern correctly, they are useful (even if to people who already have full scientific knowledge of politics they are useless—since they have already learned all there is to know from them). But [8] they are also useful to those who, like Plato and Aristotle himself, have lived private lives, and have not been active in politics, provided their theoretical grasp on them enables them to discern which ones are correct. (We learn about what sort of theoretical grasp this is in VII 1–3.) Even those who lack such a grasp, such as the nascent politicians, can gain a better comprehension of laws and constitutions by studying collections of them. Finally [9] draws the conclusion that we who have the requisite theoretical grasp, namely, Aristotle and his careful students and readers, should investigate the laws and constitutions that seem worthwhile, so as to select the best ones. We are thus led into the very sort of investigation undertaken in the *Politics*.
Function: See I 2 $1254^{b}4$n.

Note 160
Self-love (*philauton*) **is blamed, and justly so:** A more nuanced account of blameworthy, as opposed to blameless, self-love is given in *NE* IX 8 $1168^{b}15$–34: "Now those who reduce it to a term of reproach call 'self-lovers (*philautous*)' those who allocate to themselves the greater share in money, honors, and bodily pleasures. For these are the things ordinary people desire and take seriously, on the supposition that they are the best goods—which is why they are fought about. Those people, then, who are greedy where these things are concerned gratify their appetites and their feelings and the non-rational part of the soul generally. And ordinary people are like this, which is why the term has come about, deriving from the most ordinary case, which really is a base one. Those who are self-lovers in this way, then, *are* justly objects of reproach. That it is those who allocate goods of this sort to themselves that most people are used to calling 'self-lovers' is clear enough. For if someone were always taking more seriously than anything else the doing of just actions or temperate ones or whatever else might be in accord with the virtues, and in general were always keeping for himself what was noble, no one would call *this* person a 'self-lover' or blame him. A person of this sort, though, would seem to be *more* of a self-lover. At any rate, he allocates to himself the good things that are noblest and the ones that are best of all and gratifies the element in himself that has most control, obeying it in everything. But just as a city too or any other complex system seems to be most of all its most controlling part, so also does a human being. A person is most of all a self-lover, then, who likes this part and gratifies this part."

Note 161
Such legislation indeed looks attractive and may seem to be philanthropic (*philanthrôpos*): What is *philanthrôpos* is not philanthropic in our sense of the term but rather what exhibits a love of human beings. Thus woodcocks are *philanthrôpos* in that they are easily domesticated (*HA* IX 26 $617^{b}23$–27), whereas we are *philanthrôpos* if, for example, we are moved by seeing even a very bad person falling from good fortune into bad (*Po.* 13 $1453^{a}2$) or a clever villain being deceived (18 $1456^{a}21$).

Note 162

When someone blames the evils now existing in constitutions: See *Rep*. 464d–465d.

Note 163

Depravity (*mochthêria*): *Mochthêria* is much the same as vice, so that a *mochthêros* person is a vicious one. Sometimes, though, *mochthêros* is simply equivalent to *kakos* ("bad"), as at *NE* VII 14 1154ᵃ11.

Note 164

A city is a multitude, as we said before: At II 2 1261ᵃ18.

Note 165

Philosophy: See I 7 1253ᵃ3n.

Crete: The largest of the Greek islands, located in the southern part of the Aegean, separating it from the Libyan Sea.

Communal messes (*sussitiois*): *Sussitia* are groups of people who regularly eat meals together, the places where such meals are eaten, or the meals themselves. They are often organized by the city and paid for from public funds. Despite the fact that Aristotle's promised discussion of this institution is missing (VII 10 1330ᵃ4–5), it seems pretty clear from what he does say that though one of its functions was to feed the citizens, so that none went hungry (1330ᵃ1), another was to foster community among them. For having such messes tends to foster the communal use of property, which Aristotle favors (1263ᵃ21–41), while tyrants forbid them because they do not want the citizens to know and trust each other (V 11 1313ᵃ41–ᵇ6). Moreover, there was often a symposium after the meal itself, at which there was music and discussion, and it seems certain that Aristotle plans to have this practice continue in his best city (VII 17 1336ᵇ20–23, VIII 3 1338ᵃ21–30). On the political and educational significance of symposia, see Plato, *Laws* I–II.

Note 166

Pretty much everything has been discovered: See VII 10 1329ᵇ25–35n.

Note 167

Clans and tribes: See IV 15 1300ᵃ25n.

Note 168

Nothing has been determined about whether the farmers too should have communal property or each his own private property, or, further, whether both their women and their children should be private or communal: Producers (including farmers) initially seem to have a traditional family life and to own private property. But casual remarks at *Rep*. 433d and 454d–e suggest, for example, that female producers will not necessarily be housewives, but will be educated for whatever social role they have the highest natural aptitude for.

Note 169

Of necessity there will be two cities in one, and those opposed to each other: A criticism Socrates makes of other cities at *Rep*. 422e–423b.

Note 170
Socrates makes the guardians into a sort of garrison: See *Rep*. 415a–417b, 419a–421c, 543b–c.

Note 171
He gives the farmers control of their property, although he requires them to pay a tax: Reading ἀποφορὰν φέροντας with Dreizehnter and the mss. for OCT τοὺς ἀποφορὰν φέροντας. See *Rep*. 416d–e.

Note 172
Helots: The slave population of Sparta.

Note 173
It is absurd to draw a comparison with wild beasts in order to show that women should engage in the same practices as men: See *Rep*. 451d–e.

Note 174
Socrates makes the same people rule all the time, which is a cause of faction even among people who have no recognized worth, and all the more so, of course, among spirited and warlike men: The guardians, as soldier-police, are spirited and warlike. The rulers—the philosopher-kings—are chosen from among them. Aristotle thinks that those not chosen will resent this. See VII 9 1329^{a}9–12.

Note 175
He says that the god, immediately at their birth, mixed gold into the souls of some, silver into others, and bronze and iron into those who are going to be craftsmen and farmers: See *Rep*. 415a–c.

Note 176
It is possible for the evenness to be present in the whole without being present in any of the parts: Two is an even number but its parts are odd.

Note 177
If the guardians are not happy, who is?: Aristotle is presumably referring to *Rep*. 420b–421c, 519e–520d. What Socrates says there is that it is not the aim of the constitution to make the guardians, or any other group, "outstandingly happy, but to make the whole city so." But he thinks that the guardians will nonetheless be as happy as possible (465d–e).

Note 178
Surely not the craftsmen or the multitude of those who are vulgar: See I 11 1258^{b}26n.

Note 179
He divides the multitude of the inhabitants into two parts: the farmers and the part that goes to war for it. And from the latter comes a third, namely, the deliberative and controlling element in the city: See *Rep*. 412b–417b, 428c–d, 535a–536d. Also IV 4 1291^{a}10–22.
Controlling element (*kurion*): See I 1 1252^{a}5n.

Note 180
About whether the farmers and craftsmen will share in ruling to some extent or not at all, and whether or not they too are to possess weapons and join in battle—about these matters Socrates has determined nothing: Aristotle overlooks *Rep.* 434a–c, where Socrates discusses these topics.

Note 181
He has said little about the constitution: The referent of "he" is Socrates, who is not in fact a character in *Lg.*—although Aristotle includes it among the "Socratic accounts" (1265^a11).

Note 182
He wishes to make this one more generally attainable by actual cities: See *Lg.* 739a–e, 745e–746d, 805b–d, 853c.
He gradually turns it back toward the other: The one described in the *Rep.*

Note 183
The same education: See *Lg.* 961a–968b.
Living in abstention from performing the necessary functions: See *Lg.* 741e, 806d–807d, 846d, 919d–920a.
The necessary functions: Those that are unfree. See III 6 1280^a5.
And the communal messes—except that in this constitution he says that there are to be messes for women too: In *Rep.* female guardians share the same messes as the male (458c–d). In *Lg.* the female citizens have messes of their own, separate from those of the male (780d–781d, 806e–807b, 842b).
Those possessing hoplite weapons should be five thousand, whereas it is one thousand there: See *Lg.* 737e, 740c. The number one thousand probably comes from *Rep.* 423a.
Hoplite weapons: See 1265^b28n.

Note 184
Babylon: In ancient Mesopotamia, between the Tigris and Euphrates Rivers.

Note 185
It is stated that the legislator should look to just two things in setting up his laws: the territory and the human beings: This is not in fact stated in our text of *Lg.*, but Aristotle may be inferring it from 704a–708d, 747d, 842c–e.

Note 186
But, further, it would be good to add that he should also look to the neighboring territories: Something in fact mentioned at *Lg.* 737d, 738c, and 949e–953e.
If the city is to live a political life and not a solitary one: Cities typically lead a political life in part by interacting with other cities or states (VII 6 1327^b3–6). Even isolated cities, however, can lead such a life provided that their parts interact appropriately (10 1325^b23–27).

Note 187
In a more perspicuous way (*saphôs*): Perspicuity (*saphêneia*) is associated with explanation, which is ultimately from starting-points: "Beginning with things that are

truly stated but not perspicuously, we proceed to make them perspicuous as well. . . . That is why even politicians should not regard as peripheral to their work the sort of theoretical knowledge that makes evident (*phaneron*) not only the fact that but also the explanation why" (*EE* I 6 1216^{b}32–39). The same point is made at *NE* I 7 1098^{b}7–8 by noting that when we have a correct definition of the starting-point of politics much else will "at the same time become evident (*sumphanê*) through it." *Saphês* is often equivalent in meaning to *akribês* ("exact"): "it is well to replace a word with a better known equivalent, for example, instead of *akribês* in describing a supposition, *saphês*" (*Top.* II 4 111^{a}8–9). On exactness, see III 9 1280^{b}28n.

Note 188
He says that there should be as much as is needed "to live temperately": See Plato, *Lg.* 737d.
This is too universal: That is, too universal to be useful.

Note 189
The production of children is allowed to be unlimited: Aristotle overlooks *Lg.* 736a, 740b–741a, 923d.

Note 190
In this city properties are indivisible: See *Lg.* 740b, 741b, 742c, 855a–b, 856d–e.

Note 191
Pheidon of Corinth: Otherwise unknown.
Corinth: A city located on the Isthmus of Corinth, which joins the Peloponnese to the mainland of Greece, roughly midway between Athens and Sparta.

Note 192
In the *Laws*, it is just the contrary: Plato fixes the number of estates and makes them of equal size.

Note 193
These matters will have to be spoken about later: At various places in VII 5, 10, 16.

Note 194
He says that just as warp and woof come from different sorts of wool, so should ruler stand in relation to ruled: See *Lg.* 734e–735a, but also 632c, 818a, 951d–952b, 961a–c, and *Pol.* 308d–311c.

Note 195
He permits someone's total property to increase up to five times its original value: See *Lg.* 744e.

Note 196
To each individual he assigned two homesteads, dividing them and making them separate: See *Lg.* 745c–e, 775e–776b. The point of the division seems to be to provide a married son with a household of his own (776a). Aristotle adopts a similar arrangement for different reasons in his best constitution (VII 10 1330^{a}14–25).

Note 197

Democracy (*dêmokratia*): In Aristotle's view, democracy, which is the most moderate of the deviant constitutions (IV 2 1289^{b}4–5), is a deviant form of polity (1265^{b}28n). For, unlike the latter, where the many rule for the common advantage, a democracy is rule of the many "for the advantage of the poor" (III 7 1279^{b}8–9). But this definition captures its essence only coincidentally (8 1279^{b}34–39), since democracy is unconditionally the rule of the poor for the sake of the poor (1280^{a}2–3), and so of the free for the sake of the free. For "in freedom all share" (1280^{a}5; also IV 4 1290^{a}40–^{b}3), and "the hypothesis of the democratic constitution is freedom" (VI 2 1317^{a}40). Such rule, however, comes in a number of different varieties, which Aristotle distinguishes in different (and not obviously equivalent) ways: (1) At V 6 1306^{b}20–21, he distinguishes between (1a) democracy based on law and (1b) one in which the people have complete control. (2) At IV 4 1291^{b}30–1292^{a}38 he distinguishes five kinds of democracy: (2a) the rich and the poor are equal by law and neither has control; (2b) offices are filled on the basis of a low property-assessment; (2c) all uncontested citizens share in the constitution and the law rules; (2d) all citizens (contested or uncontested) share and the law rules; (2e) the same as (2d) except the citizens, not the laws are in control. (2a–d) are presumably sub-varieties of (1a), whereas (2e) is identical to (1b). (3) At IV 6 1292^{b}22–1293^{a}12, on the other hand, just four kinds of democracy are listed, which seem to correspond to (2b–e). This list, like the one given in VI 4, omits (2a), perhaps because it combines elements of democracy (rule by the many) and oligarchy (rule by the few) and so is more of a polity than a democracy—the distinctions here are somewhat fluid, as Aristotle recognizes (IV 8 1293^{b}33–38). (4) The recipe given at VI 4 1319^{a}39–^{b}1 for constructing the various kinds of democracies, which is based on the various kinds of common people distinguished at IV 4 1290^{b}39–1291^{a}10, does not seem to result in (2b–e) in any obvious way.

Oligarchy (*oligarchia*): A deviant form of aristocracy, where the rich, whether few (as is usually the case) or many, rule for their own advantage (III 8 1280^{a}1–2), so that it is the rule that "exists because of wealth and power" (*NE* VIII 10 1161^{a}2–3).

Note 198

Hoplite: A heavily armed infantryman, who carried a round shield (*hoplon*), a spear, and a sword. Since he had to provide these at his own expense, only moderately rich people could afford to be hoplites. Poorer people rowed in the navy or served as light-armored troops. Richer citizens, who could afford a horse, fought in the cavalry. Citizen hoplites were the principal fighting force in Greece until mercenaries replaced them late in the fourth century.

It is called a *polity*, since it is made up of those with hoplite weapons (*hopliteuontôn*): The hoplites are a larger class than the rich "few" who rule in an oligarchy but smaller—since hoplite weapons are expensive—than the poor "many" who rule in a democracy. That is why it is in the mean or middle between the two of them.

Polity (*politeia*): A polity is: (1) a constitution ruled by the majority for the common advantage (III 7 1279^{a}37–39); (2) a mixture of oligarchy and democracy (IV 8

1293^{b}33–34), of rich and poor (1294^{a}22–23), of wealth and freedom (1294^{a}16–17); (3) a constitution that depends on the middle class (11 1295^{b}34–1296^{a}9); (4) a constitution that depends, as here, on the hoplite or warlike class (III 17 1288^{a}12–15, IV 13 1297^{b}1–2). Although Aristotle never explicitly identifies a polity with the middle constitution described in IV 11 (except perhaps at 1297^{a}39–40), it seems for two reasons that the latter just is a (well-mixed) polity. (1) There are just six kinds of constitution: kingship, aristocracy, polity, tyranny, oligarchy, and democracy (IV 2 1289^{a}26–30). Because the middle constitution must be one of these, it is hard to see what it could be besides a polity. (2) A well-mixed polity is in the middle between an oligarchy and a democracy (9 1294^{b}14–18), so is the middle constitution (1296^{a}22–^{b}2). Since there cannot be two middles between two extremes, it seems that the middle constitution must just be a well-mixed polity.

Note 199

If he is establishing this as the most attainable by actual cities of the several constitutions, what he has said is perhaps correct, but if as next best after the first constitution, it is not correct: Plato seems to have designed his constitution to be both of these (*Lg.* 739a–e, 745e–746d, 805b–d, 853c).

Note 200

Or some other more aristocratic one: An aristocracy in the strict sense is rule by the truly best (*aristos*) people, who, in Aristotle's view, are those possessed of unconditional virtue of character and practical wisdom. The best constitution described in *Pol.* VII–VIII is an aristocracy of this sort. Other lesser sorts of aristocracies are discussed in IV 7.

Note 201

Some say that the best constitution is a mixture of all constitutions, which is why they praise the Spartan one: See IV 9 1293^{b}13–40. This constitution and the various offices mentioned in the next sentences are discussed in II 9.

Note 202

People (*dêmos*): The class that rules in a *dêmokratia* ("democracy"), which is typically the vast majority of the poorer people in the city.

Tyranny (*turannis*): A deviant kind of kingship that consists in rule of involuntary subjects (V 10 1313^{a}14–16, 11 1314^{a}34–38) by one master, who aims at his own advantage rather than that of the community as a whole (III 7 1279^{b}6–7). It is a mixture of ultimate oligarchy and ultimate democracy (V 10 1310^{b}2–7), and thus is the worst constitution of all, and the one that is furthest from being a true constitution (IV 2 1289^{b}1–2, 8 1293^{b}27–30). If a tyrant listens to good advice, however, he will rule in a more moderate way and will either be "nobly disposed to virtue or else half good, not wicked but half wicked" (V 12 1315^{b}9–10). The various kinds of tyranny, discussed in III 14 and IV 10, include foreign kingship and dictatorship.

Note 203

In these *Laws* it is said that the best constitution should be composed of democracy and tyranny: Plato describes monarchy (not tyranny) as the mother of all constitutions (*Lg.* 693d–e). He describes the constitution he is proposing, which is not the best but the second best (739a–e), as a mean between monarchy and democracy (756e). In *Rep.* IX, he agrees with Aristotle that democracy and tyranny are the worst constitutions (580a–c).

Note 204

The constitution composed of a larger number is better: The idea is perhaps this: a constitution in which principles drawn from a large number of other sorts of constitutions are mixed together will be to the advantage of more sorts of citizens (whatever their own constitutional leanings) and so will have greater equality (IV 8 1294ª15–25) and more stability (II 9 1270ᵇ17–28).

Note 205

The assembly (*ekklêsia*): The assembly of adult male citizens that had the ultimate decision-making power. Its membership and frequency of meetings varied from constitution to constitution.

To require richer people to attend the assembly to vote for officials, or to do some other political task, without requiring these things of the others, is oligarchic: See *Lg.* 756b–e, 763d–767d, 951d–e.

Note 206

The majority of officials come from among the rich, with the most important ones coming from among those with the highest property assessment: This is true of the market and city managers but it is not so clearly true of other important officials (*Lg.* 753b–d, 755b–756b, 766a–c, 946a).

Property assessment (*timêma*): A measure of wealth or property for the purposes of taxation or determining public service, often used to determine citizenship or eligibility for political office.

Note 207

He also makes the election of the council oligarchic: See *Lg.* 756b–e.

Note 208

In the same way: Reading ἴσως with Saunders for OCT ἴσους ("in equal number").
Candidates: Reading τοὺς with Saunders for OCT τοῖς.

Note 209

From what will be said later: At IV 7–9, 12 1296ᵇ34–1297ª13.

Note 210

No one else has ever suggested the innovations of sharing children and women, or of communal messes for women: Aristotle gives a longer list of Platonic innovations at II 12 1274ᵇ9–15.

Note 211

Phaleas of Chalcedon: An older contemporary of Plato.
Chalcedon: In Asia Minor, almost directly opposite Byzantium, and now a district of Istanbul.

Note 212

Plato, when writing the *Laws*, thought that no citizen should be permitted to have a property more than five times the size of the smallest, as we also said earlier: At II 6 1265^{b}21–23.

Note 213

The legislation of Solon: Discussed at II 12 1273^{b}35–1274^{a}21.

Note 214

Laws likewise prevent the sale of [landed] property (*ousian*): *Ousia* often means "substance" in the metaphysical sense of "essence," "primary being," or "primary subject of predication." But here it means "property," as in our phrase, "a man of substance."

Among the Locrians: A Greek settlement in southern Italy. Its legislator Zaleucus (mentioned at II 12 1274^{a}22–31) was famous for trying to reduce class conflict and may have been the author of the law against the sale of property.

Note 215

At Leucas: A Corinthian colony founded in the 7th cent BC.

Note 216

One should rather level appetites than property, and that cannot happen unless people have been sufficiently educated by the laws: "It is difficult for someone to get correct guidance toward virtue from childhood if he has not been nurtured under laws of the appropriate sort, since a moderate and resilient way of living is not pleasant for ordinary people, most of all when they are young. That is why laws must prescribe their nurture and practices, since these will not be painful when they have become habitual. But it is not enough, presumably, that when people are young they get the correct nurture and supervision. On the contrary, even when they have grown into adulthood they must continue to practice the same things and be habituated to them. And so there will need to be laws concerning these matters as well and, in general, then, concerning all of life. For ordinary people obey force rather than argument; and they obey penalties rather than what is noble" (*NE* X 9 1179^{b}31–1180^{a}5). Also *Pol.* VIII 1 1337^{a}10–32.

Note 217

The sort that will produce people who are disposed to deliberately choose to get more (*pleonektein*) **wealth or honor or both:** *Pleonektein* means to "get or have more," usually in the sense of more than one's fair share—although V 2 1302^{b}1 makes it clear that it is possible to get more in a just way. The corresponding disposition, or character trait, is often greed (*pleonexia*), which, even if not always a vice, has a substantial potential to lead to vicious action.

Note 218

Ordinary people (*hoi polloi*): Sometimes Aristotle uses *hoi polloi* (literally, "the many," "the multitude") to refer simply to a majority of people of whatever sort—to most people. But quite often, as here, he uses it somewhat pejoratively to refer to the vulgar masses (*NE* I 5 1095^b16) in contrast to cultivated, sophisticated, or wise people (1095^a21). "Ordinary people" often seems to convey the correct sense.

Note 219

"Noble and base are held in a single honor": Homer, *Iliad* IX.319. Achilles is complaining that if Agamemnon strips him of his war prizes, then he, though noble and deserving of such honors, is being treated as if he were base and not deserving of them.

Note 220

The pleasures that are without pain: "They also say, though, that pain is the lack of what is in accord with nature, and pleasure its replenishment. And these feelings are bodily. If, then, pleasure is replenishment of what is in accord with nature, that in which the replenishment is found will also be what is being pleased—hence, the body. But it does not seem to be. Hence the replenishment is not pleasure, although someone would be pleased when the replenishing takes place, just as he would be pained when the cutting does. This belief seems to be in accord with pains and pleasures connected with food, since when people have developed a lack, and so an antecedent feeling of pain, they are pleased by the replenishment. This does not happen in connection with all pleasures, however, since those of learning are without pain as—in the case of the pleasures of perception—are those arising through smell, and many sounds, sights, memories, and expectations are like that as well" (*NE* X 3 1173^b7–19). Compare Plato, *Rep.* 359c, 373a–d, 583b–588a.

Note 221

If certain people wish to find enjoyment through themselves, they should not look for a remedy beyond philosophy, since all other pleasures require [other] human beings: "But if happiness is activity in accord with virtue, it is quite reasonable that it should be in accord with the one that is most excellent, and this will be the virtue of the best element. Whether, then, this element is understanding or something else that seems by nature to rule, lead, and understand what is noble and divine, whether by being something divine itself or by being the most divine element in us—the activity of *it,* when in accord with the virtue that properly belongs to it, will be complete happiness. That it is contemplative activity we already said. . . . Moreover, we think that pleasure must be mixed in with happiness, and the most pleasant of the activities in accord with virtue is agreed to be the one in accord with theoretical wisdom. At any rate, philosophy seems to involve pleasures that are wondrous for their purity and stability, and it is quite reasonable that those who have attained knowledge should pass their time more pleasantly than those who are looking for it. Moreover, the self-sufficiency that is meant will belong most of all to contemplative activity. For while a theoretically-wise person as well as a just one and people with the other virtues all need the things necessary for living, when these are adequately supplied, the just one still needs people to do just actions for and with, and similarly for a temperate person, a courageous

person, and each of the others. But a theoretically-wise person, even when by himself, is able to contemplate, and the more wise he is, the more he is able to do so. He will do it better, presumably, if he has co-workers, but all the same he is most self-sufficient" (*NE* X 7 1177ᵃ12–ᵇ1).
Philosophy: See I 7 1255ᵇ37n.

Note 222
Autophradates, Atarneus, Eubulus: Eubulus was a rich money-changer who united Atarneus and Assos (two strongholds on the coast of Asia Minor) into a single kingdom, which was attacked by the Persian general Autophradates (c. 350 BC). Aristotle was resident in Assos in the late 340s BC.

Note 223
The wickedness (*ponêria*) of human beings is an insatiable thing: *Ponêria* is ethical badness or vice (*NE* VII 8 1150ᵇ36–37), here in the narrower sense of appetite-based greed.
A mere two obols is enough at first: An obol was one-sixth of a drachma, which was the average daily wage. The two-obol payment (*diôbelia*) was introduced in Athens to relieve debt after the fall of the oligarchy of 411–410 BC. See *Ath.* XXVIII 3.

Note 224
It is the nature of appetite to have no limit, and satisfying it is what ordinary people live for: See I 9 1257ᵇ40–1258ᵃ14.

Note 225
Decent (*epieikês*): *Epieikês* is sometimes used interchangeably with *agathos* ("good") (*NE* V 10 1137ᵃ34–ᵇ2). In a narrower sense (defined at 1137ᵇ34–1138ᵃ3), an *epieikês* person is characterized in particular by an attitude to legal justice that pays more attention to fairness than to the letter of the law. What makes an *epieikês* person decent is that he is fair-minded and considerate of others (VI 11 1143ᵃ19–24). When contrasted with the majority (*hoi polloi*), as here, the *epieikeis* are the ones who are better off and more respectable (IX 6 1167ᵃ35–ᵇ1).

Note 226
If indeed those engaged in public works should be public slaves, it should be in this way, namely, just as it was in Epidamnus and as Diophantus tried to establish in Athens: Epidamnus in the Adriatic was a colony of Corinth and Corcyra founded in the 7th cent BC. The identity of Diophantus is uncertain and his scheme otherwise unknown.

Note 227
Piraeus: The port of Athens.

Note 228
He was the first of those not engaged in politics who attempted to say something about the best constitution: See II 12 1273ᵇ27–32.

Note 229

Wanton aggression (*hubris*): "The person who commits wanton aggression (*hubris*) also treats with contempt; for wanton aggression consists in doing things or saying things that involve shame for the one who suffers them, not in order that something [beneficial] may come about for the agent or because something [bad] has happened to him, but for the pleasure of it; for those who are doing the same thing back are revenging themselves not committing wanton aggression. The cause of pleasure to those who commit wanton aggression is that they think that they become more superior themselves by ill-treating others (that is why young people and rich ones are prone to wanton aggression, since they think themselves superior when they commit wanton aggression)" (*Rh.* II 2 1378^{b}23–29).
Harm (*blabê*): Including both personal injury and damage to property.

Note 230

He thought that as things stand legislation is not well drafted, since it compels jurors to violate their oath by judging one way or the other: An Athenian juror took an oath whose gist was something like this: "I will cast my vote according to the laws (*kata tous nomous*) and using my most just consideration *(gnômê[i] tê[i] dikaiotatê[i])*." See *Rh.* I 15 1375^{a}29–30, ^{b}16–17, Demosthenes, *Against Aristocrates* 96. He gave his verdict by putting a ballot either in the guilty urn or not-guilty urn. The penalty for some crimes was prescribed by law. For others the jury had to choose between a penalty proposed by the prosecuting party and a counterpenalty proposed by the defendant. In neither case could a juror propose a penalty of his own devising. Thus Hippodamus is proposing to a give a juror more discretion in both sorts of cases. Since verdicts were typically determined by majority vote of the jurors, the distinction we make between judge and jury had little or no application, so that a juror was in effect a sort of judge.

Note 231

If the farmers and craftsmen do not share in the constitution (*politeias*), **how can they possibly have any friendly feelings for the constitution** (*politeian*): Farmers do share in the constitution (1268^{a}17–18), in the sense that they are included among its citizens, they do not share in the offices in which the real power resides. They are thus more like slaves of the powerful, who alone possess the weapons, than free citizens. Legally they share in the constitution, but in reality they do not.

Note 232

On the contrary, those who possess weapons have to be *stronger* than both of the other parts: Omitting with Saunders, Pellegrin, and Schütrumpf the OCT quotation marks on ἀλλὰ δεῖ καὶ κρείττους εἶναι τοὺς τὰ ὅπλα γε κεκτημένους ἀμφοτέρων τῶν μερῶν.

Note 233

The quantity of produce from each one's farming will be inadequate for two households: Because of the lost efficiency of scale a farmer can produce less from two farms than from a single one with the same acreage.

Note 234

Arbitrator (*diaitêtês*): "The arbitrator looks to decency whereas the juror looks to the law" (*Rh.* I 13 1374^{b}20–22). Also *Pol.* IV 12 1297^{a}5–6.

Note 235

Most legislators do the contrary and establish things so that the jurors do *not* confer with each other: It was not unusual, for example, for Athenian juries to have between five hundred and a thousand members.

Note 236

Sycophancy (*sukophantia*): Athenian laws provided rewards to those who successfully prosecuted cases that enriched the city (such as recovered tax revenues or property confiscated because of the offense). By the late 5th cent BC this led to the practice of sycophancy, which consisted in bringing suit against someone in hopes either of getting a bribe from him for dropping the suit or of getting a reward from the city if the suit proved successful. The idea in the present instance is that Hippodamus' law is like those Athenian ones, only broader in scope.

It might even lead to change in the constitution: See V 7 1307^{a}40–^{b}19 for an example.

Note 237

Some people raise the puzzle of whether it is advantageous or harmful to cities to change their ancestral laws, if some other is better: See, for example, Herodotus III.80, Plato, *Lg.* 772a–d, *Pol.* 298c–e, Thucydides I.71.

Note 238

Athletic training (*gumnastikê*): *Gumnastikê*, when provided by a trainer (*gumnastikos*), aims to produce a "good physical condition" in the one receiving it (*NE* V 11 1138^{a}31; also *EE* I 8 1218^{a}35–36); when provided by a coach (*paidotribês*), it includes more focused training aimed to inculcate specific physical skills (including athletic and military ones). See VIII 3 1338^{b}6–8.

Crafts and capacities: See III 12 1282^{b}16n.

Note 239

The facts themselves (*tôn ergôn*): For other meanings of *ergon*, see I 2 1252^{b}4n.

Note 240

The homicide law in Cyme: It is not clear to which of three ancient cities—Aeolian Cyme, Euboean Cyme, or Italian Cyme—Aristotle is referring. A Cyme is mentioned again at V 5 1305^{a}1.

Note 241

Everyone seeks not what is ancestral but what is good: "Every craft and every methodical inquiry and likewise every action and deliberate choice seems to seek some good. That is why they correctly declare that the good is 'that which all seek'" (*NE* I 1 1094^{a}1–3).

Note 242

Whether they were "earth-born" or the survivors of some cataclysm: The earth-born are described at Plato, *Pol.* 272c–d, *Lg.* 677b–678b, the cataclysm view at *Ti.* 22c–23d, *Lg.* 677a–d.

Note 243

It is necessary to write laws in universal terms: The revelatory contrast is between laws and decrees. A law (*nomos*) is by definition a relatively permanent enactment, universal in scope and applicable on many different occasions. A decree (*psêphisma*), by contrast, is a singular enactment, adapted to particular circumstances (*NE* V 10 1137^{b}27–32), stating what is to be done in a single particular case, and is thus the last thing reached in a piece of practical deliberation (VI 8 1141^{b}24–28).

Whereas actions are concerned with particulars: The canonical practical question bearing on action is, What particular action should I the agent or we the city do in these particular circumstances? The law may provide specific guidance in some cases, but in others deliberation, which like a decree is sensitive to the peculiarities and details of the case, is required: "Practical wisdom . . . is concerned with human affairs and what can be deliberated about. For of a practically-wise person we say that most of all this is the function—to deliberate well. And nobody deliberates about what cannot be otherwise or about the sorts of things that do not lead to some specific end, where this is something good, doable in action. . . . Nor is practical wisdom knowledge of universals only. On the contrary, it must also know particulars. For it is practical, and action is concerned with particulars. That is why, in other areas too, some people who lack knowledge—most of all, those with experience—are more effective *doers* of action than are others who have knowledge. For if someone knows that light meats are digestible and healthy but is ignorant about which sorts of meat are light, he will not produce health; but someone who knows that bird meats are healthy will produce health more. But practical wisdom is practical, so one must possess both sorts of knowledge—or this one more" (*NE* VI 1141^{b}8–22).

Note 244

It belongs to other occasions to investigate issues involved in changing laws: These occasions do not arise in the *Politics* as we have it.

Note 245

The hypothesis (*hupothesis*): At II 2 1261^{a}16 the hypothesis or basic assumption of the constitution described by Socrates in *Rep.* is identified as "its being best for a city to be as far as possible entirely *one*." Since his aim in adopting it is to make the city as a whole as happy as possible (420b), and since "by pursuing this [happiness] in different ways and by different means each group of people produces different ways of life and different constitutions" (VII 8 1328^{a}41–^{b}2), it seems reasonable to identify a constitution's hypothesis with its basic presuppositions about how happiness is to be achieved and what it consists in. Hence it can be readily identified with the deliberately chosen aim of the constitution (1269^{b}13, 1270^{b}30, 1271^{a}32).

Note 246
Thessalians: Inhabitants of Thessaly, a region bordering the Aegean on the east, Macedonia on the north, and central Greece on the south.

Note 247
Subject peoples (*perioikoi*): *Periokoi*—those who dwell (*oikoi*) around (*peri*)—were found in various Greek cities, such as Sparta and Crete. They were not citizens and so did not participate in government. They were not slaves, and could not be bought and sold, but they sometimes paid taxes, served in the army, or provided farm labor.

Note 248
Argives: Inhabitants of Argos (V 3 1302^{b}18n).
Messenians: Inhabitants of Messenia, a region in the southwestern Peloponnese.
Arcadians: See II 2 1261^{a}29n.

Note 249
Achaeans: The inhabitants of Achaea, a region in the north-central part of the Peloponnese.
Perrhaebeans: Inhabitants of Perrhaebia, the northernmost district of ancient Thessaly. Later part of Macedonia.
Magnesians: See IV 3 1289^{b}39n.

Note 250
Resilience (*karteria*): Resilience is a medial state between luxuriousness (*trupherotês*) and toughness (*kakopatheia*) (*EE* II 3 1221^{a}9). It goes along with being hard (*sklêros*) and so is the opposite of being soft (III 1 1229^{b}2, *NE* VII 7 1150^{a}14).

Note 251
Free of discipline (*akolastôs*), **giving in to every sort of intemperance** (*akolasia*): *Akolasia* ("intemperance") means "lack of discipline," from the cognate verb *kolazein* ("discipline," "punish").

Note 252
The necessary result is that wealth is esteemed in a constitution of this sort: See Plato, *Rep*. 547b–555b.
Celts: Herodotus, II.23 IV.49 mention Celts as living near the head of the Danube and in the far west of Europe. They are also mentioned as living near present-day Marseilles.

Note 253
The one who first told the myth seems not to have been unreasonable in coupling together Ares and Aphrodite: Ares, the god of war, is often portrayed as the partner of Aphrodite, the goddess of sexual love—for example, Homer, *Odyssey* VIII.266–366. Aristotle thinks that myths often contain a core of wisdom, though it may not be apparent at first glance (VIII 6 1341^{b}2–8, *Met.* XII 8 1074^{a}38–^{b}14).

Note 254

Rashness (*thrasutês*): "Someone who avoids and fears everything and endures nothing becomes cowardly, whereas someone who fears nothing at all and goes to face everything becomes rash" (*NE* II 2 1104ᵃ20–22).

Spartan women have been very harmful even in this respect: Aristotle's line of thought is apparently from the women's "freedom from discipline" (1269ᵇ22) to their lack of the "resilience" (1269ᵇ20) required for courage, and from their intemperance and luxury (1269ᵇ22–23) to their defect's being rashness rather than cowardice.

Note 255

This they made clear during the Theban invasion: Of 369 BC under Epaminondas. See Plato, *Lg.* 813e–814c, Xenophon, *Hell.* VI.5.28.

Thebes: A city in Boetia in central Greece, about thirty-one miles northwest of Athens.

Note 256

As women are in other cities: Thucydides II.4.2, III.74.2 attest to the importance of women during sieges.

Note 257

When they were at war with the Messenians: See V 7 1306ᵇ37n.

Note 258

Their legislator: Lycurgus, the (perhaps legendary) architect of the Spartan constitution.

Note 259

The women resisted and he [Lycurgus] retreated: See Plato, *Lg.* 781, 806c.

Note 260

As we already said before: At 1269ᵇ17–23.

Note 261

Noble (*kalos*): The adjective *kalos* is often a term of vague or general commendation ("fine," "beautiful," "good"), with different connotations in different contexts: "The contrary of *to kalon* when applied to an animal is *to aischron* ['ugly in appearance'], but when applied to a house it is *to mochthêron* ['wretched'], and so *kalon* is homonymous" (*Top.* I 15 106ᵃ20–22). (Similarly, the adverb *kalôs* often means something like "well," or "correct.")

Even in the general sense, however, *kalos* has a distinctive evaluative coloration suggestive of "order (*taxis*), proportion (*summetria*), and determinateness (*hôrismenon*)" (*Met.* XIII 3 1078ᵃ36–ᵇ1), making a term with aesthetic connotation, such as "beauty," seem a good equivalent: to bear the stamp of happiness one must have *kallos* as opposed to being "very ugly (*panaischês*)" (*NE* I 8 1099ᵇ3–4; also *Pol.* V 9 1309ᵇ23–25). Moreover, just as a thing need not have a purpose in order to be beautiful, a *kalon* thing can be contrasted with a purposeful one: a great-souled person is one "whose possessions are more *kalon* and purposeless (*akarpa*) than purposeful and beneficial" (*NE* IV 3 1125^{a}11–12). At the same time, it seems wrong to associate *kalon* with beauty in general, since to be *kalon* a thing has to be on a certain scale: "greatness of soul requires magnitude, just as *to kallos* ('nobility of appearance') requires a large body, whereas small people are elegant and well proportioned but not *kaloi*" (1123^{b}6–8); "any *kalon* object . . . made up of parts must not only have them properly ordered but also have a magnitude which is not random, since what is *kalon* consists in magnitude and order (*taxis*)" (*Po.* 7 1450^{b}34–37; also *Pol.* VII 4 1326^{a}33–34). It is this requirement that makes "nobility" in its more aesthetic sense a closer equivalent than "beauty."

In ethical or political contexts, the canonical application of *kalon* is to ends that are intrinsically choiceworthy and intrinsically commendable or praiseworthy (*epaineton*): "Of all goods, the ends are those choiceworthy for their own sake. Of these, in turn, the *kalon* ones are all those praiseworthy because of themselves" (*EE* VIII 3 1248^{b}18–20; also *NE* I 13 1103^{a}9–10). It is because ethically *kalon* actions are intrinsically choiceworthy ends, indeed, that a good person can do virtuous actions because of themselves (*NE* II 4 1105^{a}32) *and* for the sake of what is *kalon* (III 7 1115^{b}12–13). What makes such actions choiceworthy (VI 1 1138^{a}18–20) and praiseworthy (II 6 1106^{b}24–27), however, is that they exhibit the sort of order (X 9 1180^{a}14–18), proportionality (II 2 1104^{a}18), and determinateness (II 6 1106^{b}29–30, IX 9 1170^{a}19–24) that consists in lying in a mean (*meson*) between two extremes. This brings us full circle, connecting what is ethically *kalon* to what is aesthetically noble, lending the former too an aesthetic tinge.

Finally, what is ethically *kalon* includes an element of self-sacrifice that recommends "nobility," in its more ethical sense, as a good equivalent for it as well: "It is true of an excellent person too that he does many actions for the sake of his friends and his fatherland, even dying for them if need be. For he will give up wealth, honors, and fought-about goods generally, in keeping for himself what is *kalon*" (*NE* IX 8 1169^{a}18–22). One reason people praise a *kalon* agent, indeed, is that his actions benefit them: "The greatest virtues must be those that are most useful to others, and because of this, just people and courageous ones are honored most of all; for courage is useful to others in war, justice both in war and peace" (*Rh.* I 9 1366^{b}3–7). But since what is *kalon* is a greater good than those an excellent person gives up or confers on others, there is also a strong element of self-interest in what he does: "The greater good, then, he allocates to himself" (*NE* IX 8 1169^{a}28–29). An excellent person does *kalon* actions for their own sake, not for an ulterior motive, because it is only as done in that way that they constitute the doing well in action (*eupraxia*) that just *is* happiness.

He left owners free to give or bequeath their land if they wished: As a result some estates became very large while others became too small to support their owners.

Note 262

The city did not withstand one single blow: Aristotle is referring to the crushing defeat inflicted on the Spartans by the Thebans in the battle of Leuctra in 371 BC.

Note 263
Spartiates: Adult male citizens of Sparta.

Note 264
The board of overseers (*ephoreia*): Five ephors or overseers were elected annually by the Spartiates. These supervised the operations of the political and judicial system as a whole, and served to limit the powers of the two kings.

Note 265
In our own day among the Andrians: It is unclear to which incident Aristotle is referring.
Andros: The northmost of Cyclades, about six miles southeast of Euboea.

Note 266
If a constitution is going to survive, every part of the city must wish [the constitution] to exist and endure: Reading διαμένειν αὐτά with Dreizehnter and Pellegrin and ms. H[a] for OCT διαμένειν ταὐτά ("every part of the city must wish it to exist and remain the same"). This principle is repeated in various forms at IV 9 1294[b]34–40, VI 5 1320[a]14–17. It should probably be distinguished from the one expressed, for example, at IV 12 1296[b]14–16, 13 1297[b]4–6, V 9 1309[b]16–18, VI 6 1320[b]26–28, which requires only that the stronger party in the city wishes the constitution to remain unchanged. Generally speaking the more extreme versions of the deviant constitutions satisfy the latter principle, but not the former.

Note 267
Though the overseers should be chosen from all, it should not be in the way it is now (since it is exceedingly childish): The overseers seem to have been chosen by acclamation, like the senate, or perhaps by lot. See Plato, *Lg*. 692a.

Note 268
On the basis of their own consideration (*autognômonas*): "What is called 'consideration (*gnômê*),' due to which, people are said to be sympathetically considerate (*sungnômones*) and to have consideration, is the correct discernment of what is decent" (*NE* VI 1143[a]19–20). On decent, see II 7 1267[b]6n.

Note 269
Excessive in its hardness (*sklêron*): See 1269[b]20n.
Secretly escape from the law and indulge in the pleasures of the body: See Plato, *Rep*. 548b.

Note 270
The senators: The Spartan senate (*gerousia*) has twenty-eight members in addition to the two kings. All were over sixty years old and were probably chosen from aristocratic families. The senate prepared the agenda for the assembly of citizens and had other political and judicial functions.

Note 271
Decent people: See II 7 1267[b]6n.

Manly goodness (*andragathia*): This is the only occurrence of the word *andragathia* in Aristotle. The cognate verb *andragathizesthai* ("exhibit manly goodness") occurs in the pseudo-Aristotelian, *VV* 2 1250^{b}4: "it belongs to courage (*andreia*) to endure hardship, be resilient, and choose to exhibit manly goodness."
There is the old age of thought (*dianoias*) **as there is that of the body:** "People who are older and pretty much past their prime have characters that are mostly the contrary of those [of young people] (for because they have lived for many years, have been more often deceived, have made more errors themselves, and because most things turn out badly, not only do they affirm nothing with assurance but everything with far less assurance than they should). And they *think* things but *know* nothing. And being doubtful, they always add 'perhaps' and 'maybe,' and state everything that way, but nothing firmly. And they are cynical (for cynicism consists in taking everything in the worst way). Further, they are suspicious because they lack trust, and lack trust because of their experience. And, because of these things, they neither love nor hate intensely but, following the advice of Bias, love as if they would one day hate and hate as if they would one day love. And they are small-souled because of having been humbled by life (or they have an appetite for nothing grand or unusual but rather for things that are necessary for life). And they are ungenerous (for one of the necessities is wealth, and at the same time they know from experience that it is difficult to acquire and easy to lose). And they are cowardly and fearful about everything ahead of time. . . . And they love life, and all the more so at the end of their days, because their appetite is for what is absent, and also because what they need is what they most have an appetite for. And they love themselves more than they should (for this too is a sort of smallness of soul). And, more than they should, they live with a view to what is advantageous and not to what is noble, because of their self-love (for what is advantageous is good for the individual, whereas what is noble is unconditionally so). And they are more shameless than prone to shame (for since they do not care equally about what is noble and what is advantageous they are contemptuous of their reputation). And they expect the worst because of their experience (for most of the things that happen are bad, or at any rate turn out for the worse), and because of their cowardice too. And they live in memory more than in hope (for what is left of life is short, what is past is long, and hope is for the future, memory for what is gone by). This is precisely the cause of their garrulousness (for they keep talking about things that have gone by, since they take pleasure in reminiscences). And their outbursts of spirit, though sharp, are weak. And while some of their appetites have forsaken them, others are weak, so that they are not appetitive people, or people who act in accord with their appetites, but rather in accord with profit. That is why people of this age appear to be temperate, for their appetites have loosened and they are slaves to profit. And they live more in accord with rational calculation than in accord with their character (for rational calculation has to do with what is advantageous, character with the virtues). And the unjust actions they commit are due to malice, not wanton aggression. The old are also inclined to pity, but not because of the same thing as the young (for the latter are so because of a love of human beings, whereas the former are so because of weakness, since they think that all

sorts of sufferings are close at hand for themselves, and this . . . tends to arouse pity). As a result, they are prone to complain and are neither witty nor lovers of laughter (for proneness to complaint is the contrary of love of laughter)" (*Rh.* II 13 1389^{b}13–1390^{a}23).

Note 272

Inspect (*euthunein*): Inspection (*euthuna*) was a device designed to ensure (typically) democratic control of officials (II 12 1274^{a}15–21, III 11 1281^{b}32–34, 1282^{a}25–32, VI 8 1322^{b}6–12). In Athens a board of ten inspectors and ten assistants were elected by lot. Officials were subject to inspection by it at the end of their term in office, to see whether they had taken bribes, embezzled public funds, or been guilty of maladministration. See *Ath.* LIV 2.

Note 273

It may seem that the overseers should inspect every office, but this would give too much to the board of overseers, and is not the way we say that inspections should be carried out: The objection, presumably, is to putting inspection in the hands of the already powerful board of overseers, which judged things on the basis of their own consideration not by following the letter of the law (II 10 1272^{a}37–39), rather than in those of a separate, independently elected and law-governed body, as in Athens. It is not entirely clear who the "we" are. We in Athens? We here in the Lyceum?

Note 274

The election they conduct of the senators is also decided in a childish way: Namely, by an elaborate process of acclamation. See V 6 1306^{a}18–19, Plutarch, *Lycurgus* XXVI.

Note 275

The one worthy of the office should hold it whether he wishes or does not wish to: Similarly, in Plato, *Rep.* VIII democracy is criticized because "there is no compulsion to rule in this city, even if you are qualified to rule, or to be ruled, if you do not wish to be" (557a1–3).

Note 276

A matter for another account: See III 14–17.

Note 277

It is surely better at any rate to choose each new king not as now but rather in accord with his own way of life: Sparta had two kings, each descended from a different royal house. Both were members of the senate and ruled for life. Their functions were political and military but also religious. It would be better, Aristotle suggests, to choose the kings by looking to their way of life, rather than, as the Spartans did, by making the kinship hereditary.

Note 278

The communal messes (*sussitia*) **(or so-called *phiditia*):** The former was the usual Attic term.

Note 279

Public messes should rather be paid for from public funds, as they are in Crete: See II 10 1272ª12–27.

Note 280

The defining mark (*horos*): See I 9 1258ª18n.

Note 281

The hypothesis of the legislator: See 1269ᵇ32n.
Just as Plato criticized it in the *Laws*: At 625c–638b.

Note 282

Scientific knowledge of how to be at leisure (*epistasthai scholazein*): Aristotle's way of thinking about leisure (*scholê*) or passing the time (*diagôgê*) overlaps with ours but differs from it in important ways. We think of leisure time as time off from work in which we can do as we choose. Aristotle agrees that leisure time and work time are distinct (I 8 1256ª31–35), but thinks that activities that are entirely leisured must be choiceworthy solely because of themselves. Among these he includes such scientific activities as the exercise of theoretical wisdom or mathematical knowledge, which we might think of as work. In these, he thinks, complete happiness consists (*NE* X 7 1177ᵇ19–26). Entirely unleisured activities, he thinks, are choiceworthy solely because of some additional end, such as producing or providing the necessities of life (X 6 1176ᵇ2–3)—included among these are the canonical productive crafts (*Met.* IX 6 1048ᵇ18–35). Activities which are choiceworthy in part because of themselves, and in part because of an additional end, include activities in accord with practical wisdom and the virtues of character. These too constitute happiness, but of a less than complete or secondary sort (*NE* X 7 1177ᵇ4–18, 8 1178ª9–22). Most people would include amusing pastimes as leisured activities par excellence (X 6 1176ᵇ6–17), but Aristotle does not agree: "Happiness is not found in amusement, since it would be absurd indeed for the end to be amusement, and our life's labors and sufferings to be for the sake of amusement. For we choose almost everything, except happiness, for the sake of something else, since it is the [unconditional] end. To work hard and toil [just] for the sake of amusement, however, appears a silly and entirely childish thing to do. Rather 'play to be serious,' as Anacharsis puts it, seems to have it right. For amusement is a form of relaxation, and it is because we cannot toil continuously that we need relaxation. Relaxation, then, is not an end, since it occurs for the sake of activity [in accord with virtue]" (X 6 1176ᵇ27–1177ª1). Nonetheless, because humans do have to engage in unleisured practical and productive activities, a good political constitution "should permit amusement, but be careful to use it at the correct time, dispensing it as a medicine for the ills of unleisure" (*Pol.* VIII 3 1337ᵇ35–42; also VIII 5 1339ᵇ31–42).

Note 283

They also think that the goods people fight about are better than virtue itself, and this is not correct: This criticism of Sparta and other oligarchies is repeated in different forms at VII 2 1324ᵇ5–11, 14 1333ᵇ5–11, 1334ª2–ᵇ5.

The goods people fight about (*tagatha ta perimachêta*): "Money, honors, and bodily pleasures . . . are the things ordinary people desire and take seriously, on the supposition that they are the best goods—which is why they are fought about (*perimachêta*)" (*NE* IX 8 1168^{b}16–19).

Note 284

The Spartiates do not examine each other's tax payments: Thucydides tells us that the custom was "never to act hastily in the case of a Spartan citizen and never to come to an irrevocable decision without indisputable proof" (I.132).

Note 285

It is said that the Spartan constitution is largely an imitation of the Cretan: See Herodotus I.65, Plato, *Min.* 318c–d, 320a–b.

Note 286

King Charilaus: Charilaus was the posthumous son of Lycurgus' elder brother King Polydectes and reigned as king c. 780–750 BC. He was thought by Aristotle to have become a tyrant. See V 10 1310^{b}18–20, 1313^{a}1–3, also Herodotus VIII.131.

Note 287

Lyctians: Inhabitants of the city of Lyctus in Crete.

Note 288

Subject peoples: See II 9 1269^{b}3n.

Minos: Semi-mythical Cretan king, husband of Pasiphaë, mother of the Minotaur.

Note 289

Peloponnese: The peninsula constituting the southernmost part of mainland Greece, from which it is now separated by the Corinth Canal.

Rhodes: The largest of the Dodecanese islands, located northeast of Crete and just off the Anatolian coast of Turkey.

Note 290

Finally attacking Sicily, where he met his death near Camicus: See Thucydides I.3, 8, 15.

Camicus: A fortress town, near Acragas.

Note 291

The Spartans called these not *phiditia* but *andreia*: See II 9 1271^{a}26–27.

Note 292

In Sparta, as we said earlier, each person must contribute a fixed per capita amount: II 9 1271^{a}29–37.

Note 293

Another for the communal messes, so that all—women and children and men—are fed at public expense: Women and children did not participate in the common messes in Crete, but presumably enough was left over to feed them at

home. See II 12 1274b9–11 where common messes for women is cited as a peculiarity of Plato's constitution (Plato, *Lg.* 780e–781a).
Public services: See III 6 1279a11n.

Note 294
He has made a place for sexual relations between men: *Paiderasteia*, or boy love, between an older man (*erastês*) and an adolescent boy (*erômenos*) was an accepted practice in Classical Athens. Sex was common in such relationships, with the boy playing the passive role. Once the boy reached manhood, however, and his bloom of youth faded, that was supposed to change. On pain of losing his citizen rights, he could no longer be a passive sexual partner. Instead, he was expected to marry, have children, and became an *erastês* in his turn. Though erotic in nature, the relationship was conceived as primarily educative. By associating with someone who was already a man, a boy learned virtue or excellence and how to be a man himself. Rites of passage in some primitive warrior societies also involve sexual contact between men and boys, and it is sometimes suggested that Greek *paiderasteia* also had its roots in a warrior past.
As to whether this was badly done or not badly done, we will investigate on another occasion: Aristotle does not return to this topic in our *Politics*. But see II 4 1262a32–40, VII 16 1335b38–1336a2.

Note 295
The election being from all: See II 9 1270b17–28.

Note 296
On the basis of their own consideration (*autognômonas*): See II 9 1270b29n.

Note 297
As for the cure the Cretans use for this error: Namely, the restriction of the senators and order-keepers to certain families.
Dynasty (*dunasteia*): A *dunasteia* is a hereditary oligarchy in which not the law but the officials rule (IV 5 1292b5–10).

Note 298
It is better if all these things should take place in accord with law and not with the wish of human beings, since the latter is not a safe standard: "That is why it is not a human being we allow to rule but reason (*logon*), because a human being does so for himself and thus becomes a tyrant" (*NE* V 6 1134a35–b1). *Logon* here probably refers specifically to the reason that is embodied in law, and in fact one ms. has *nomon* ("law") in place of *logon*. See also III 15 1286a9–20.

Note 299
Create anarchy: Reading ἀναρχίαν with OCT for Dreizehnter and the mss. μοναρχίαν ("monarchy").

Note 300
Its remoteness has served to keep foreigners out (*xenêlasias*): Thereby serving as the equivalent of the Spartan practice of *xenêlasia*, or actively expelling foreigners. See Plato, *Lg.* 848a.

Note 301

The Cretans do not share in external rule—although a foreign war has recently come to the island: The thought is that external rule—ruling over people outside one's own territory—increases the chances of having to fight foreign wars, which are one cause of revolt by serfs or subject peoples (II 9 1269^b5–7).
A foreign war has recently come to the island: A reference perhaps to invasion by Phalaecus the Phocian in 345 BC.

Note 302

Carthaginians: Inhabitants of Carthage in present-day Tunisia, on the eastern shore of Lake Tunis, across from the city of Tunis.

Note 303

The messes of the *hetairia*: *Hetairos* in its non-technical sense is a term for a close personal companion or friend of any sort, but it can, as at Thucydides VIII.65.2, apply more specifically to a member of *hetairia*, which in the *Politics* and elsewhere, usually refers to a political club. Here, however, the *sussitia tôn hetairôn*, since they are like the *phiditia*, may not have been restricted to those who were companions or united politically. See V 6 1305^b32n.

Note 304

The hypothesis: See II 9 1269^a32n.
Of an aristocracy or a polity: Here, as at IV 9 1294^b10–11, aristocracy and polity (II 6 1265^b28n) are treated as equivalents.

Note 305

The office of one-hundred: Referred to as the office of the one-hundred-and-four at 1272^b34–35.
They rule before taking office and after they have left it: The meaning is not entirely clear.

Note 306

Not, as in Sparta, some by some and others by others: It is oligarchic to assign different judicial powers to different groups, because the power to, for example, execute or exile someone can then end up in the hands of a very few people (IV 9 1294^b31–34). Thus in Sparta some cases could be tried by a single overseer (III 1 1275^b9–10).

Note 307

Rulers should be chosen not solely on the basis of merit (*aristindên*) **but also on the basis of wealth** (*ploutindên*): The switch from *aristindên* (1273^a23) to *kat' aretên* ("in accord with virtue") at 1273^b26–27 indicates that we should take these two notions as equivalent. See IV 7 1293^b10n.

Note 308

That is why those who are best able to rule: Reading ἀρχεῖν with Saunders and the mss. for OCT ἀργεῖν ("That is why those who are best able to be at leisure").

Note 309

One function is best completed [when it is completed] by one person: See I 2 1252^{b}1–5n.

Note 310

It is more political (*politikôteron*) **if more people participate in the offices:** In part, no doubt, because the more people who share in office, the more politicians (*politikoi*) there are.

Note 311

It is forever the case that some part of the people grows rich due to their sending it out to the cities: The cities in question were presumably Carthaginian colonies of some sort. Just how those sent out became rich is unclear.

Note 312

Some of those who have had something to say about a constitution: Namely, Plato, Hippodamus, and probably Phaleas.

[1] Took no part whatsoever in political actions (*praxeôn politikôn*), **but [2] always lived a private life** (*idiôteuontes*): The key to understanding this deceptively simple contrast is to be found in the following text: "It certainly seems that someone who knows about and spends his time on the things that concern himself is practically-wise and that politicians are [3] busybodies (*polupragmones*). That is why Euripides says: 'How can I be practically-wise, when I could have [4] minded my own business (*apragmonôs*), and been numbered among the ranks of the army, sharing equally?'" (*NE* VI 8 1142^{a}1–6). At the same time, those who [4] mind their own business and [2] live a private life may well do all that is required of them as ordinary citizens, such as serving in the military, voting in the assembly, and being members of juries. Thus Socrates who has done all these things, and has even been a member of the advisory Council of the Five Hundred (Plato, *Ap.* 32a9–c3), describes himself as living "privately (*idiôteuein*) not publicly (*dêmosieuein*)" (32a2–3), and as being "a busybody (*polupragmonô*) in private (*idia[i]*)" (31c4–5), because he converses about ethics only with individuals, and has a daemonic sign that opposes his "doing political things (*ta politika prattein*)" (31d5) or being concerned with "the city's actions (*praxai*)" (23b8). And he describes himself this way on the grounds that he "does not dare to go before the multitude to advise the city" (31c6–7) or care about "being a general, a popular leader, or holding some other political office, or joining the cabals and factions that come to exist in a city" (36b6–9). To [1] take part in political actions, then, is to be [3] a busybody in the latter way—not just to be a responsible citizen, but to be, as we would say, "active in politics."

Note 313

The constitution of the Spartans has already been spoken about: In II 9.

Note 314

Solon: See I 8 1256^{b}32n and, on his constitution, *Ath.* V–XII.

Put an end to the slavery of the people: Many poorer people in Athens had become slaves through a process of debt bondage in which they offered their own persons as security for loans. Solon cancelled all existing debts—the so-called *seisachtheia*, or shaking off of burdens—and put an end to this practice.
The council of the Areopagus: From earliest times the council of the Areopagus (a rocky hill northwest of the Acropolis) had jurisdiction over homicide cases, but came to have "extensive supervisory powers over the important aspects of political life" (*Ath.* VIII 4 10–12). Since its members were drawn from the richer classes, it was a powerful oligarchic element in Solon's constitution.

Note 315
He did set up the people [in power] (*ton de dêmon katastêsai*): Or: "he did set up the democracy." But Solon's reforms are better seen as paving the way for democracy than actually setting it up.

Note 316
Pericles (c. 495–429 BC): The leading Athenian politician during the heyday of Athens' empire.
Ephialtes: In 462/1 BC Ephialtes joined Pericles in introducing legislation that stripped the court of the Areopagus of most of its privileges and powers. He was murdered in the same year.
Introduced payment for jurors: Allowing poorer people to serve without financial loss.
Popular leader (*dêmagôgos*): *Dêmagôgos* is sometimes, as here, a fairly neutral term used to describe an influential democratic leader, such as Pericles, but more often it has a negative connotation, referring to those who curry favor with (*dêmagôgein*) the people and undermine the rule of law (IV 4 1292^{a}4–37) in order to gain power.

Note 317
Because the people were the cause of Athens' naval supremacy during the Persian Wars, they became presumptuous: See V 4 1304^{a}22–24, Plato *Lg.* 707a–d.
Persian Wars: Between the Persian empire and the Greek cities, 499–449 BC.

Note 318
If they do not even control these, the people would be slave and enemy: See III 11 1281^{b}21–38.

Note 319
Pentakosiomedimnoi, zeugitai, hippeis: The *pentakosiomedimnoi* were those whose property produced at least five hundred measures (*medimnoi*) of corn, olive oil, or wine. The *zeugitai*, those whose property produced three hundred measures of these things, and so were able to maintain a team of oxen (*zeugos*). The *hippeis*, those whose property produced two hundred measures, and so could keep a horse and fight as cavalrymen (*hippeis*). Since these divisions were based solely on wealth or property, not on lineage, they permitted the sort of upward mobility that the earlier lineage system effectively excluded. See *Ath.* VII.

Note 320
Chalcidian cities: Cities founded by colonists from Chalcis, the chief city on the island of Euboea.

Note 321
Zaleucus, Charondas, Onomacritus, Thales: Zaleucus was a 7th-cent BC legislator for the Locrians living in southern Italy. Charondas was probably 6th cent. Onomacritus may be the poet and divine of that name who was active in Athens at the end of the 6th cent. Thales (or Thaletas), who worked in Sparta, was a 7th-cent poet from Gortyn in Crete.

Note 322
Philolaus the Corinthian: Otherwise unknown.
Thebans: Thebes was a city in Boeotia in central Greece.
The Bacchiad family: The leading oligarchic family in Corinth in the 6th cent BC.
Olympic games: Religious and athletic festival held every four years at the sanctuary of Zeus in Olympia.

Note 323
Preside at symposia (*sumposiarchein*): A symposium was, among other things, a drinking party, at which the symposiarch determined the order of toasts, the amount to be drunk, and so on. See II 5 1263^{b}41n.
A feature special to Plato is the sharing of women, children, and property: The combination is special to Plato, but the leveling or equalizing of property as such (II 7 1266^{a}34–36) is here attributed to Phaleas. He, however, seems to have leveled only landed property (II 1267^{b}9–10).
The sober should preside (*sumposiarchein*) **at drinking parties:** See Plato, *Lg.* 637a–b, 671a–672d.

Note 324
Draco's laws: Draco set up laws for Athens in 621 BC, which were notorious for their harshness. Hence our word "draconian."

Note 325
Pittacus: One of the fabled seven sages, Pittacus was appointed tyrant of Mytilene in 589 BC to restore order. He is mentioned again at III 14 1285^{a}35–^{b}1. His treatment of drunken offenses is alluded to at *NE* III 5 1113^{b}30–33 and mentioned at *Rh.* II 25 1402^{b}8–12.

Note 326
Androdamus of Rhegium: Nothing further is known about him.
Rhegium: Modern-day Reggio, located on the toe of southern Italy, separated from Sicily by the Strait of Messina.

BOOK III

Note 327
What (*tis*) **each is and what sort of thing it is** (*poia tis*): See I 3 1253^{b}8n.

Note 328

The city belongs among composite things: And so, like other composites, should be analyzed in terms of its parts. See I 1 1252^a17–21n.

Things that are wholes (*holôn*) **and composed of many parts:** A *holon* is typically a matter-form compound, which is not identical simply to the sum of its parts. Thus at *Met.* X 1 1052^a22 a whole is what has a certain shape and form by nature, and at V 6 1016^b12–13 not being "some sort of whole (*ti holon*)" is identified with "not possessing one form." At VIII 6 1045^a10 is something beyond the parts that is the cause of their being one, namely, a form ($^a23$). And at IX 8 1084^b30, whole goes together with one and form. This is why the identity of a city is determined by its constitution (= form) rather than by its inhabitants (= matter) (*Pol.* III 3 1276^b6–9).

Note 329

The ones who are created citizens: Such as honorary citizens and the like.

Note 330

Sponsor (*prostatês*): Resident aliens in Athens had to have a citizen to sponsor them, but they could represent themselves in legal proceedings. In other places, it seems that their sponsor had to do this for them.

Note 331

Citizen lists: At the age of eighteen young Athenians were enrolled in the citizen list kept by the leader of their *deme* or district. Older men were released from military service and also perhaps from jury duty and attendance at meetings of the assembly.

Note 332

Someone might say that the latter are not officials (*archontas*) **at all:** In fact, jurors and assemblymen were not called *archontes* in Athens.

Because of doing what they do: Being jurors, assemblymen, and the like.

Note 333

In the case of things in which the underlying subjects differ in kind (*eidos*), **with one coming first, another second, and so on, either the common element is not present at all, insofar as these things are what they are, or only in some slight way:** Exercise, a complexion, a certain physical condition, and also other things are all said to be healthy. Each of these is an underlying subject of which the attribute healthy is predicated and each differs in kind from the other. But exercise is healthy because it causes health, a complexion is healthy because it is a sign of health, and a bodily condition (having a temperature of 98.4° etc.) is healthy because it is health. Here the bodily condition is prior, because it figures in the accounts of why the other things, such as exercise and a complexion, are healthy. But because the explanation in each case is different there is nothing common to the three cases—there is no universal healthiness that is the same in each of them (*Met.* IV 2 1003^a21–$^b19$). In the same way non-deviant constitutions are prior to deviant ones, because the latter are defined in terms of them. A related but somewhat different argument for the same conclusion appears at *EE* I 8 1218^{a}1–8: "In things where there is priority and posteriority, there is not some common thing beyond these and separate from them. For then there would be something prior to the first, since the common separate thing would have priority because if the common one were destroyed, the first would be destroyed. For example, if multiplication by two is the first case of multiplication, the multiplication predicated of all of them in common cannot be separate from them, since it would then be prior to multiplication by two."

Note 334
What we mean by "deviant" will be evident later: See III 6–7.

Note 335
The citizen that was mentioned: Namely, the holders of indefinite office (1275^{a}26–33).

Note 336
It is the same way in Carthage: See II 11 1273^{a}18–20.
Carthage: In present-day Tunisia.

Note 337
In the other constitutions: Namely, the non-democratic ones.

Note 338
Whoever is authorized to share in deliberative or judicial office, we can now say, is a citizen: Reading ἢ with Dreizehnter and the mss. for OCT καὶ ("deliberative and judicial office"). At V 6 1305^{b}33–34 citizens are recognized who participate in judicial but not deliberative office.

Note 339
But quick, political definitions of this sort lead: Reading ταχέως with ms. Γ for OCT παχέως ("but coarse, political definitions of this sort").

Note 340
Gorgias of Leontini: c. 483–376 BC. He was a famous orator and sophist, who visited Athens in 427 (DK B82 = TEGP pp. 725–787).
Leontini: (Present-day Lentini) is a town in southwest Sicily.
Larisaeans too are what are made by official craftsmen (*dêmiourgôn*), **since some craftsmen are Larissa-makers:** In Larissa, and other places, the word *dêmiourgos*, which means "craftsman," is also the title of a certain sort of public official. A Larisaean was both a citizen of Larissa and a kind of pot made there. Hence Gorgias' joke.
Larissa: A city in Thessaly in central Greece.

Note 341
Cleisthenes: A 6th cent BC Athenian statesman whose wide-ranging reform of the Athenian constitution was as significant and abiding as that of Solon. See IV 15 1300^{a}25n.

Note 342

The dispute we mentioned earlier: At III 1 1274b34–36.

Note 343

The common advantage: See III 6 1279a17n.

Note 344

This argument seems to be akin to the puzzle of when we ought to say that a city is the same, or not the same but a distinct one: Because the problem about whether or not a city performed a given action depends on the identity conditions for cities.

Note 345

The fact that something is said to be a city in many ways makes inquiry into such puzzles in a way easy: If by a city is meant a political community, it can have a split location and population; if what is meant is a place or location, a city whose population splits into two locations will be two cities.

Note 346

Babylon: Herodotus describes Babylon as "a vast city in the form of a square with sides almost fourteen miles long" (I.178).

Note 347

Whether it is advantageous for it to have one or several [locations]: Reading ἒν with Simpson and some mss. for OCT ἔθνος ἒν ("whether it is advantageous for it to consist of more than one race or not"). Aristotle discusses the issue in VII 6.

Note 348

We say that any other community or composite is distinct if the form of the composite is different: See III 1 1274b39n.

Note 349

A harmony composed of the same notes is a distinct harmony if it is at one time Dorian and at another Phrygian: See VIII 5 1340b3–5n.

Note 350

The name to call it may be distinct or the same one whether its inhabitants are the same or completely distinct human beings: A name (*onoma*) for Aristotle signifies an account or (in some cases) a definition (*Met.* IV 7 1012a22–24, VIII 6 1045a26), which is of the form (VII 10 1035a21) or essence (4 1029b20) of the thing named. His point here, therefore, is not that Corinth can continue to be so called or have its name changed to "Argos," whether its population remains the same or not, but rather that the form or constitution of Corinth, and hence the name that signifies it, can remain the same whether or not its population remains the same.

Note 351

Outline (*tupos*): Sometimes when Aristotle gives an outline, it means that a fuller account may be forthcoming, so that the outline is merely provisional (*NE* II 7 1107b14–16). When things in a given area hold for the most part, however, it seems that the truth about them *must* be stated in outline (II 2 1104ᵃ1–5). In this case, having to outline seems to be a function of the subject matter, so that it is because we are discussing things that hold for the most part in ethics and politics (I 3 1094ᵇ19–22) that these sciences involve outlining.

Note 352

The preservation of the ship while sailing (*tês nautilias*): *Nautilia* can mean "ship," but its more usual meaning is "a sailing" or "a voyage" or "navigation." Its use here, rather than the more usual *naus*, reminds us that because "the constitution is a sort of *life* of a city" (IV 11 1295ᵃ40–ᵇ1) its analogue is the ship in action—the ship while sailing.

Note 353

Property consists of master and slave: The master is not a piece of property, as the slave is, but property, as something requiring management, involves both.
The virtue of all the citizens cannot be one virtue: The examples in this paragraph are all ruler-ruled pairs. Aristotle has already shown in I 13 that the virtues of each member of the pair must be different.

Note 354

And a politician is of necessity practically-wise: Reading πολιτικὸν with the mss. for OCT and Dreizehnter πολίτην ("and a citizen is of necessity practically-wise").

Note 355

Euripides: Athenian tragic playwright (c. 480–407/6 BC), author of some ninety plays, including the *Bacchae* and *Medea*. The quotation is from his lost play *Aeolus* (Fr. 16.2–3 Nauck). King Aeolus is apparently speaking about the education his sons are to receive.

Note 356

Jason: Tyrant of Pherae in Thessaly (c. 380–370 BC).

Note 357

It is not necessary for the ruler to have scientific knowledge of how to perform these [functions], but rather of how to use [those who do]: See I 7 1255ᵇ20–37.

Note 358

Craftsmen (*dêmiourgoi*) **did not share in office:** In the previous sentence we have "the vulgar craftsmen (*ho banausos technitês*)," suggesting that the *dêmiourgoi* (literally: "public workers") and *technitês*, which is Aristotle's usual term, are pretty much the same.
Extreme democracy (*dêmon . . . ton eschaton*): Also referred to at IV 11 1296ᵃ2. Probably not to be confused with the ultimate democracy (*dêmokratia teleutaia*) described at IV 4 1292ᵃ2–38.

Note 359

Neither by the good politician nor by the good citizen: Retaining οὐδὲ τὸν with Dreizehnter and the mss.

Unless for himself out of some need of his own: See VIII 7 1341ᵇ10–15.

Note 360
One cannot rule well unless one has been [well] ruled: A saying to this effect is attributed to Solon. See DL I [**60**], 174–175. Also VII 14 1333ᵃ2–3.

Note 361
Those ruled are like makers of flutes, whereas rulers are like the flute players who use them: See III 11 1282ᵃ17–23, Plato, *Rep*. 429b–430c, 433c–d, 473c–480a, 601d–602b.

Note 362
The sort of virtue we discussed: The one that enables a person to rule and be ruled well.

Note 363
Hired laborers (*thêtes*): Free landless laborers, who were not craftsmen, and who worked for hire. Their status in Aristotle's scheme of things, like that of vulgar craftsmen, is somewhat anomalous. See I 11 1258ᵇ26n.

Note 364
In fact, it is clear from what we have said: At III 1.

Note 365
It is impossible to engage in virtuous pursuits while living the life of a vulgar person or a hired laborer: Explained somewhat at I 13 1260ᵃ38–ᵇ1, VIII 3 1337ᵇ4–21.

Note 366
As Homer too implied: At *Iliad* IX.648, XVI.59. Achilles is complaining about how he is being treated by Agamemnon.

Note 367
Whenever this sort of thing is kept concealed, it is for the sake of deceiving their fellow inhabitants: See II 5 1264ᵃ19–22.

Note 368
The constitution is governing body: "But just as a city too or any other complex system, seems to be most of all (*malist'*) its most controlling part, so also does a human being" (*NE* IX 8 1168ᵇ31–33). See Introduction, pp. lxii–lxiii.

Note 369
In our first discussions it was also said that a human being is by nature a political animal: See I 2 1253ᵃ7–8.

Note 370
The external accounts (*tois exôterikois logois*): *Exôterikoi logoi* are also mentioned at VII 1 1323ᵃ21 and at *Ph.* IV 10 217ᵇ30, *Met.* XIII 1 1076ᵃ28, *NE* I 13 1102ᵃ26, VI 4 1140ᵃ2, *EE* I 8 1217ᵇ20, II 1 1218ᵇ32. *Cael.* I 9 279ᵃ30 mentions "the philosophical

works in circulation" and *DA* I 4 407b29 "the common accounts." The references, apparently, are to popular works written by Aristotle himself and "in circulation" (*NE* I 5 1096a3) outside the Lyceum, or to accounts or arguments, not necessarily developed by him, that are generally known. Whatever the precise reference here, it must be to accounts with which the audience of the *Politics* could be safely taken to be familiar.

Note 371

Perform public service (*leitourgein*): A *leitourgia* is any public service paid for out of private funds, such as funding a chorus for a play, equipping a trireme for the navy, or providing a feast for the city (*NE* IV 2 1122b22–23). Sometimes, though, *leitourgein* comes close in meaning to our notion of charitable giving (VIII 14 1163a29, IX 6 1167b12).

Note 372

At any rate, sick people who believe they would be cured by ruling would presumably pursue office in that sort of way: See III 4 1277a24–25.

Note 373

Those constitutions that aim at the common advantage are—in accord with what is unconditionally just—correct, whereas those that aim only at the advantage of the rulers are erroneous ones, and deviations from the correct constitutions: Aristotle does not specify the group G, whose advantage is the common advantage, nor does he tell us whether the common advantage is the advantage of the individual members of G, or that of G taken as some sort of whole. But a natural first thought is that G should consist of all the free native inhabitants of the constitution. On that account, however, even some correct constitutions, such as a polity, will count as deviant. For the common advantage in a correct constitution is a matter of having a share in noble or virtuous living (1278b20–23). Hence a polity will not aim at the advantage of its native-born vulgar craftsmen, tradesmen, or laborers, since there is "no element of virtue" in these occupations (VI 4 1319a26–28). A second natural thought, in part a reaction to the first, is that G should consist of the unconditional citizens, who share in judgment and office (III 1 1275a22–23). But if G is not then to coincide with the rulers, and the distinction between correct constitutions and deviant ones to be undercut, we need to distinguish between the offices keyed to unconditional citizenship and those keyed to sharing in the most important offices, the constitution, and rule (I 13 1260b20n). Yet even the deviant constitutions seem to aim at the advantage of a wider group than that, namely, one that includes the wives and children of those eligible for such offices (I 13 1260b8–20, III 9 1280b40–1281a1, V 9 1310a34–36).

Though these attempts to define G all fail, the last does point in a promising direction. Let us begin with the class, N, of the free native inhabitants of the constitution. There are two ways to construct the class of unconditional citizens from N. The first is on the basis of the sort of justice internal to the constitution, the second is on the basis of unconditional justice. If we proceed in the first way, and the constitution is an oligarchy, for example, the unconditional citizens will be the rich male members of N. But if we proceed in the second way, the unconditional citizens of the oligarchy will be those who have an unconditionally just claim to that status. And Aristotle thinks that the virtuous, the rich, and the poor all have such a claim, one that is proportional to their virtue (III 9 1280^b40–1281^a8, III 12 1283^a14–26, IV 8 1294^a19–20). Thus they ought to be unconditional citizens of any constitution. In fact, however, they are such only in correct constitutions, not in deviant ones.

We may now construct G as follows: all the members of N, who have an unconditionally just claim to be unconditional citizens of the constitution, are members of G; all the wives and children of members of G are members of G; no one else is a member of G. If a constitution aims at the advantage of G, it aims at the common advantage and is correct; if it aims at the advantage of the subset of G consisting of the rulers who have control of the constitution (and their families) it is deviant. This seems to be what Aristotle has in mind when he writes: "the political good is justice, and justice is the common advantage" (III 12 1282^b16–18). Nevertheless, while a correct constitution *aims* only at the advantage of G, Aristotle almost certainly thinks that it will be advantageous to all its members, whether they are members of G or not. In any case, he thinks this about household slaves (I 2 1252^a34, III 6 1278^b32–37). Presumably, then, he ought to think it about the public slaves or barbarian serfs who do all the work in his ideal constitution.

The question now is whether the common advantage is that of each member of G, or of G taken as some sort of whole. Is the common advantage to be understood individualistically or holistically? Some views espoused in the *Politics* seem to suggest that Aristotle had fairly significant holistic or organicist leanings. The argument that individual human beings are parts of the city to which they belong, for example, in the same way that hands are parts of human beings (I 2 1253^a18–29), suggests that it might be as uncontroversial (or almost as uncontroversial) to sacrifice an individual for the good of the city as it would be to sacrifice a hand for the good of the individual whose hand it is. The views expressed on the use of ostracism seem to endorse such a sacrifice. For it does not seem to be advantageous to the superior individual to be ostracized from his city, yet even correct constitutions may ostracize him, Aristotle argues, when doing so serves the common advantage (III 13 1284^b4–20). True, the ideal constitution and other well-constructed constitutions will not need such a remedy, because of the foresight of their legislators. But the point remains that correctness in a constitution seems to be no guarantee that the advantage of each individual in G will be safeguarded there. Even in such constitutions, moreover, ostracism seems not to be needed because the legislator has ensured that no superior person will emerge in the constitution (V 3 1302^b19–21), not because he has recognized that no individual, however superior, should have his advantage justly sacrificed to the common advantage.

Aristotle also uses the claim that individuals are parts of the city to justify fairly massive intrusion of the political into what we would consider to be the private sphere: "One should in no way think that any citizen belongs to himself alone, but that all of them belong to the city, each being a part of the city. And it is natural for the supervision of each part to look to the supervision of the whole"

(*Pol.* VIII 1 1337a27–30). Hence the ideal constitution should have laws that regulate or constrain the freedom of association of many of its inhabitants (VII 6 1327a 37–40), their freedom to marry, reproduce, and rear their offspring (16 1335a4–b19, 1335b22–25), their freedom to have extra-marital affairs (1336a1–2), their religious freedom (10 1330a8–9), their freedom of expression and artistic freedom (17 1336b3–23), even their freedom to dine as they choose (10 1330a3–8).

Many other texts, however, suggest that Aristotle means to be espousing some sort of individualism. The following is a small sample: "It is impossible for the whole to be happy unless all, or most or some, of its parts possess happiness. For happiness is not the same thing as evenness, since it is possible for the latter to be present in the whole without being present in any of the parts, whereas happiness cannot" (*Pol.* II 5 1264b17–22); "the common advantage brings them together, to the extent that some share of noble living falls to each" (III 6 1278b21–23); aristocrats "rule with a view to what is best for the city and those who share in it" (7 1279a35–37); "it is evident that the best constitution is necessarily that order in accord with which anyone might be able to do best and live blessedly" (VII 2 1324a23–25); "the best life, both for the whole city collectively and for each individual, would be an action-involving life" (3 1325b15–16); "a *city* is excellent by its citizens—those who share in the constitution—being excellent. And in our city all the citizens share in the constitution" (13 1332a32–35). It seems, then, that Aristotle is an individualist in at least this important sense—he believes that the best constitution, and the very intrusive laws that are part of it, promote the virtue, and so the happiness, of the individuals in G. The question is how is his apparent holism to be combined with his apparent individualism?

Aristotle's treatment of ostracism strongly suggests that he thinks that a just constitution may require members of G to do things that do not promote their individual advantage. At the same time, he thinks that such a constitution must promote the advantage of the individual members of G. These views are compatible provided that promoting the advantage of the individual members of G need be no more than generally congruent with their actually being advantaged. Thus, for example, a correct constitution that has no need of ostracism is better, Aristotle thinks, than one that does need it, presumably because the former constitution better promotes the advantage of each of the individuals in G than the latter. At the same time, if an individual in G actually threatens the stability of the correct constitution, and the justice it embodies, the constitution may have to sacrifice his advantage to that of the other members of G. What it does, in other words, is sacrifice the advantage of an individual in G in a case in which failing to do so would risk destroying a constitution that promotes the advantage of each of the other members of G. In these circumstances, that is the closest the constitution can come to preserving the congruence in question. In times of war or scarcity, this congruence is likely to be quite hard to preserve; in times of peace and plenty, much easier. But the general point remains: no constitution short of an omnipotent and omniscient one can absolutely guarantee that this congruence will always be absolute.

Aristotle does not seem, then, to be an extreme individualist, who thinks that the happiness of the city simply consists in the happiness of each of the individual members of G, so that to achieve the happiness of the former is necessarily to achieve the happiness of the latter. By the same token, he is not an extreme holist or organicist who thinks of the happiness of the whole of G as something distinct from the happiness of each of the individuals in it, so that it is possible to achieve the happiness of the former without achieving the happiness of the latter. What he is, it seems, is a moderate individualist—someone who thinks that the happiness of a city must be generally congruent with the happiness of the individual members of its G class. But whether we should call this position moderate individualism (as I have opted to do) or moderate holism is perhaps more a matter of taste than substance.

The fact—if it is a fact—that there need be no more than this sort of general congruence between a city's happiness and the happiness of the individuals in its G class also explains why Aristotle's doctrine that individuals are parts of a city is no threat to his moderate individualism. A hand can perform its task only as part of a body. So there is general congruence between the health of a body and the health of all its parts. But in some circumstances the closest we can come to preserving this congruence involves sacrificing a part. In this respect, Aristotle thinks, we are like hands. If we find this insufficiently reassuring, it can only be on the grounds, apparently, that we think that general congruence between the aim of a just city and that of an individual in G is not enough, that more is required, that congruence must be guaranteed in all circumstances. Aristotle certainly fails to provide such reassurance, but this may be a strength rather than a weakness of his view.

Note 374

Since "constitution" and "governing body" signify the same thing: See III 6 1278^b11n.

Note 375

Either those who share should not be called citizens: Reading τοὺς μετέχοντας with Dreizehnter and the mss. for OCT τοὺς μὴ μετέχοντας ("either those who do not share should not be called citizens").

Note 376

This happens reasonably: The reason Aristotle gives in the next sentence suggests that he is thinking as follows. (1) There are three correct constitutions: kingship, aristocracy, and X. (2) It would be unreasonable for X to be called a kingship or an aristocracy, since it is unreasonable to think that the multitude could all have the level of virtue required in the rulers of either of these. (3) Yet, because it is rule by the multitude for the common advantage, it has something in common with kingship and aristocracy, and so it is reasonable that it should have a name common to both of them. (4) The deviations are called *politeiai* with reference to the correct ones from which they deviate. (5) Therefore, it is reasonable for X to have a name common to all *politeiai*, correct or deviant. (6) And that name is of course *politeia*.

Note 377

The majority (*plêthos*): A *plêthos* can be just any multitude—any (typically) large group of people. But here, as elsewhere, it refers to the majority of the citizens of a city, not the majority of its total population (which may include many non-citizens, such as slaves and resident aliens). Because of this the notion inherits some of the problems inherent in the notion of a citizen. For example, when Aristotle tells us that the majority (or majority opinion) has control in all constitutions (IV 8 $1294^{a}11$–14), the majority he is referring to is the majority of the "unconditional citizens" (III 1 $1275^{a}19$–23) who participate in political office. In the case of an aristocracy or an oligarchy, this may be a relatively small number of people.

Note 378

Freedom (*eleutheria*): A free person is, in the first instance, someone who is not a slave. In this sense the farmer citizens of a democracy are free men. But a farmer must work in order to get the necessities of life—he is not a man of leisure. So there is another sense in which he is not free. A person who is free in this second sense has distinctive character traits, education, and outlook. Unlike a slavish or vulgar person, he is not obsessed with practical or useful things (VII 14 $1333^{b}9$–10, $1338^{b}2$–4), but is rather the sort of person "whose possessions are more noble and purposeless than purposeful and beneficial, since that is more characteristic of self-sufficient people" (*NE* IV 4 $1125^{a}11$–12). The fact that he is well educated gives him a broad perspective on the world, rather than a narrow-minded or overly specialized one (*Pol.* II 9 $1270^{b}37$n). Hence he is able to judge or assess the credibility and appropriateness of discussions belonging to different professions and disciplines in which he is not himself an expert, so as to be able to choose competent advisors when he needs them. Only this sort of free man can have practical wisdom and the virtues of character, so that he alone has what it takes to be an unconditional citizen in the best kind of city (VII 9 $1329^{a}2$–17). Since that city ensures that he has the resources needed for leisure ($1329^{a}17$–26), he does not need to work for a living, and so does not "live in dependence on another," which is another important mark of being free (*Rh.* I 9 $1367^{a}32$–33). The art and music he enjoys, and the use he makes of his leisure, further distinguish him from those who are vulgar or uncivilized (*Pol.* VII 15 $1334^{a}11$–40, VIII 7 $1342^{a}19$–32, *Po.* 26 $1461^{b}26$–$1462^{a}4$). But even such a citizen is often under the control of others, whom he must obey, so that there are often substantial limitations on his freedom or self-determination too.

Note 379

As we said earlier in the *Ethics*: See II 2 $1261^{a}31$n.

They agree about equality in the thing but disagree about it in the people: Suppose a piece of land is divided into two parcels, X and Y, that are then distributed to two people, A and B, respectively. The distribution is just in Aristotle's view if the ratio of the *value* of X to the *value* of Y is the same as the ratio of the *merit* of A to the *merit* of B, so that $V_x : V_y = M_a : M_b$. Aristocrats, oligarchs, and democrats agree about the conditions under which $V_x = V_y$ but disagree about those under which $M_a = M_b$. Democrats claim that all free citizens are equal in merit; aristocrats claim that merit is proportional to virtue; oligarchs claim that it is proportional to wealth (*NE* V 3 1131ᵃ14–ᵇ23). Democratic equality seems to be numerical equality, while aristocratic and oligarchic equality seem to be equality according to merit, or proportional equality (*Pol.* V 1 1301ᵇ29–30). Some of the problems involved in numerical equality are discussed in VI 3.

Note 380
But they do not do these things only for the sake of living, but more for the sake of living well: In Greek the sentence begins with *ei* ("if") and so begins a long protasis. But since there is no subsequent apodosis, I have omitted the "if."

Note 381
Slaves and animals share neither in happiness nor in living in accord with deliberate choice: Happiness, as "activity of the soul in accord with virtue and, if there are more virtues than one, in accord with the best and most complete" (*NE* I 7 1098ᵃ15–18) is either (1) contemplation in accord with theoretical wisdom or (2) practical activity in accord with practical wisdom (which includes the virtues of character) (X 7–8). Other animals do not share in (1) because they are "completely deprived of this sort of [contemplative] activity" (8 1178ᵇ25) or in (2) because they are incapable of deliberate choice (III 2 1111ᵇ9), and action in accord with practical wisdom must be deliberately chosen (II 6 1106ᵇ36–1107ᵃ2). Slaves do not share in (2) because their soul lacks a deliberative part (*Pol.* I 13 1260ᵃ12), and do not share in (1) because they cannot live the leisured life that contemplation requires (*NE* X 7 1177ᵇ22), since leisured activities require the virtues of character (*Pol.* VII 5 1334ᵃ11–40), which are in any case also required if we are to recognize as happiness what is in fact happiness: "it is virtue, whether natural or habituated, that teaches correct belief about the starting-point [= happiness]" (*NE* VII 8 1151ᵃ18–19).

Note 382
Etruscans: Ancient inhabitants of a region of Italy roughly corresponding to present-day Tuscany.

Note 383
Lycophron the sophist: The expressions attributed to him at *Rh.* III 3 1405ᵇ35–36, 1406ᵃ7–9 suggest that he was a follower or imitator of Gorgias. He is also mentioned at *Ph.* I 2 185ᵇ27–28.

Note 384
Megarians: Inhabitants of Megara, a city in the northern section of the Isthmus of Corinth, opposite the island of Salamis.

Note 385
An exact theoretical grasp (*akribôs theôrousin*): "One science is more exact than another, and prior to it, if it is both of the that and the why, and not of the that separately from the why; or if it is not said of an underlying subject and the other is said of an underlying subject (as, for example, arithmetic is more exact than harmonics); or if it proceeds from fewer things and the other from some additional

posit (as, for example, arithmetic is more exact than geometry). By from an additional posit I mean, for example, that a unit is a substance without position and a point is a substance with position—the latter proceeds from an additional posit" (*APo.* I 27 87ᵃ31–37); "We should not demand the argumentative exactness of mathematics in all cases but only in the case of things that involve no matter" (*Met.* II 3 995ᵃ14–16). As applied to craftsmen and their products, on the other hand, *akribês* means "refinement," "finish," or "sophistication." Applied to perceptual capacities, such as seeing or smelling (*DA* II 9 421ᵃ10), it means "discriminating." Applied to virtue and nature, it may have more to do with accuracy—hitting a target (*NE* II 5 1106ᵇ14–15)—as it may when applied to definitions (VIII 7 1159ᵃ3) or distinctions (II 9 1107ᵇ15–16) or units of measurement (*Met.* X 1 1053ᵃ1).

Note 386

Would seem to be well stated: Reading εὖ λέγεσθαι for OCT λέγεσθαι ("would seem to be stated").

Note 387

[1a] The many, of whom each individually is not an excellent man, nevertheless may, when they have come together, be better than the few best people, not individually but collectively, [1b] just as dinners to which many contribute are better than dinners provided at one person's expense: [1b] is the first in a series of five analogies that Aristotle gives in nuanced support of [1a]. The others are: [2] the many, when they come together, are just like one human being in character and thought (1281ᵇ5–7); [3] the case of music and poetry, where the many are better judges because "distinct ones are better judges of distinct parts, and all of them are better judges of the whole thing" (1281ᵇ9–10); [4] the case of pure and impure food, where "a mixture of impure food mixed with the pure sort makes the whole thing more useful than a little [of the latter]" (1281ᵇ36–38); [5] the case of certain crafts, where "the maker might not be either the only or the best judge—the ones where those who lack the craft nevertheless know its products" (1282ᵃ18–19). It is useful to discuss these together.

[1b] Why are dinners to which many contribute better than dinners provided at one person's expense? The answer must surely lie in what the many contribute. And this could be [1b-i] a cash contribution—the idea being that the many are collectively richer than one person (1282ᵃ39–41), and that in general a larger sum results in a better dinner. The problem with [1b-i] is that it appears to leave judgment, and with it virtue and practical wisdom, out of the equation. Yet without these the larger sum may result in a worse dinner: "A person who is excessive and vulgar exceeds by spending more than he should, as we said, since in matters of small expenditure, he spends a lot and is improperly extravagant—for example, by giving the members of his dining club a dinner appropriate for a wedding" (*NE* IV 3 1123ᵃ19–22). On the other hand, an advantage of [1b-i] is that it makes the contribution of the many co-ordinate with that of the one rich individual, in that each contributes money. But when Aristotle returns to the dinner analogy at III 15 1286ᵃ29–30, he seems to have contributions in kind rather than in cash in mind. Since money is the universal equivalent, however, this may be a relatively

small point. Another possibility, more in keeping with the other analogies, but preserving this advantage, is (1b-ii): each of the many, in contributing to the dinner, whether in cash or in kind, has a say in what goes into it, thus ensuring that the dinner as a whole will be more satisfying to the diners collectively, since each will find in it something that he likes. A third possibility is just like this, except that [1b-iii] the quality of the dinner is measured by culinary excellence rather than diner satisfaction. Here the idea is that in virtue of contributing to the expense of the dinner each individual member of the many judges the part of the dinner that he is best able to judge—if he is a cheese expert, the cheese course, if he is a wine expert, the wine, and so on. Since [1b-iii] would make the dinner analogy cognate with [2] the music and poetry analogy, it seems to be more plausible that either [1b-i] or [1b-ii].

What [2] adds to [1b] is an analogical specification of the way in which a multitude must come together if [1a] is to be supported: it must come together so as to be like an individual human being. What this entails, in the case of the virtues of character and practical wisdom, is that the various parts of these possessed by individual members of the multitude must be assembled together in such a way that the multitude collectively possesses these virtues in the way that an individual does. This means, at a minimum, that [2a] the sub-group that is analogous to the desiring part of the soul, with its constituent appetites and spirited desires, must obey [2b] the sub-group that is analogous to the part of the soul that has reason (*NE* I 13 1102^{b}13–28).

What [3], the analogy with the case of music and poetry, adds is a specification of how the collective multitude does its judging: parts of it judge parts of the whole that is being evaluated. As in [1b-iii], therefore, the natural thought is that the parts of the whole are judged by the relevantly qualified sub-group of the multitude. Nothing is said, however, about what the parts of, for example, a tragedy are, what would make a sub-group able to judge one of these parts in particular, or how these partial judgments are to result in an overall judgment. The aim of the analogy, in fact, seems quite limited, namely, to set us up for the discussion that occurs between [3] and [4] and so for [4] itself.

The first part of that discussion distinguishes the excellent man from a member of the multitude: he is an excellent judge of all the parts, whereas a member of the multitude is an excellent judge of only one, or a few, of them (1281^{b}10–15). The second part points out that [1a] is not true of every multitude, since some are like wild beasts or too slavish (1281^{b}15–20, 1282^{a}15). This raises the question, unanswered here, of what sort of multitude [1a] is true of. (But see, for example, VI 4–7.)

What [1b]–[3] are taken to show is now explained in connection with [4]. Because the individual members of the multitude lack justice and practical wisdom they are not suited as individuals to share in judgment and deliberation, which are the most important offices (1281^{b}25–28). On the other hand, to exclude them from these offices altogether is politically dangerous, since it turns them into enemies of the constitution and the city (1281^{b}28–30). The solution to the puzzle is to let them share collectively in office to the extent of electing and inspecting those who do hold them—these being members not of the multitude but of those individually possessed of virtue and practical wisdom. This allows us to see what the parts are, not now of poems or statues, but of their political analogues, namely, electing to and inspecting versus holding political offices. The multitude are collectively competent to elect and inspect, since "when they all come together their perception is adequate" for this (1281^{b}34–35), but they are not competent to hold the offices as individuals, since that would require each of them to be virtuous and practically-wise. This division, in turn, helps us to better understand [2], since we can now see that those who elect and inspect are the analogues of the non-rational parts of the soul, whereas those who judge and deliberate are the analogues of the part of the soul that has reason. That is why it is the two mixed together in the appropriate way that benefits the city, just like [4] a mixture of impure food (the multitude) with pure food (the virtuous few). For just as a mixture of these foods furthers the health of the body, so a mixture of these ways of sharing in the most important offices furthers the health and stability of the city.

Yet this solution to one puzzle itself raises a puzzle. For if we look to the various crafts it seems that those eligible to hold an office should be the ones eligible to inspect its holders, just as it is those qualified as doctors who are eligible to inspect doctors, and so on (1281^{b}38–1282^{a}3). And it might seem that election is the same way, since "choosing correctly is also a function of those who know the craft—for example, choosing a geometer is a function of geometers, and choosing a ship's captain of ship's captains" (1282^{a}8–10). It is to this puzzle that [5] is offered as a solution. For just as there are some crafts in which it is the user of the craftsman's products and not the craftsman himself who is the best judge of their quality, so in the case of a city—though this is left implicit—the multitude who collectively experience it in actual use may be better judges than the officials who control it.

Note 388
Some part of virtue and practical wisdom: In *NE* VI 13, Aristotle argues that full virtue of character, as opposed to natural or habituated virtue, involves practical wisdom and understanding, and so can be possessed only as a unified whole. Here, however, he seems to acknowledge that individual people can possess a *part* both of virtue and of practical wisdom. But since each of them does so as part of a practically-wise and virtuous whole, the apparent change in doctrine may be apparent only—a sort of synecdoche rather than a literal truth.

Note 389
Because of their lack of justice (*adikian*) **and lack of practical wisdom** (*aphrosunên*), **they would of necessity act unjustly in some instances and make errors in others:** *Adikia* is usually translated as "injustice," but here seems to have the weaker meaning of "lacking justice," since to act unjustly in some instances, it is enough to not be just. Similarly for *aphrosunê*.

Note 390
Neither to give a share (*metadidonai*) **nor have a share** (*metechein*) **is a fearful thing:** The subjects of the infinitives *metadidonai* and *metechein* should it seems

be the same. But the context seems to require them to be different, since it seems that it is the free multitude who should have a share but the others (the rich, the virtuous) who should give it to them. But perhaps it is the free who should give a share to the rich or virtuous, since the presupposition of the puzzle is that they should be in control (1281[b]23–24).

Note 391

Just as a mixture of impure nourishment (*mê kathara trophê*) **mixed with the pure sort makes the whole thing more useful than a little [of the latter]:** Pure food is already in a form in which it can be absorbed into the bloodstream, but is presumably easier to digest, or provides more of the requisite feeling of fullness, when mixed with food that needs first to be worked on by the gastric juices. See *GA* I 20 728[a]26–30.

Note 392

Someone well educated (*pepaideumenos*) **in the craft:** See Introduction, pp. lxviii–lxiv.

Note 393

Provided that the multitude is not too slavish (*andrapodôdes*): *Andrapodôdes* is opposed to *eleutherios* ("free") at *NE* IV 8 1128[a]20–21.

Note 394

The first puzzle we mentioned: See III 10 1281[a]35–39.

Note 395

The puzzle stated earlier remains to be solved: This is the puzzle of which part—the majority, the rich, the decent people, the one who is best of all, or a tyrant—should be in control (III 10 1281[a]11–13). Since before we can settle which laws, as being just or correct, as should be in control as extensively as the limits of law permit, we must first settle the question of which constitutions are just or correct. And that involves determining who the governing bodies are of the correct ones, since "the constitution is governing body" (III 6 1278[b]11).

Note 396

The science or craft that has the most control of all, and this is the capacity of politics: See I 2 1252[a]5n.

The capacity (*dunamis*) **of politics:** Often, as here, crafts or sciences are lumped together with capacities as things that can be used to achieve opposite effects, as medicine can be used to cure but also to kill (*NE* V I 1129[a]13–14). Sometimes, though, a body of knowledge is classified as a capacity (*dunamis*) rather than a science, because its subject matter lacks the requisite sort of unity: "Rhetoric is constituted from the science of the *Analytics* [= logic and scientific explanation] and from the part of politics dealing with character [= ethics], resembling dialectic on the one hand, sophistical arguments on the other. But to the extent that someone tries to set out dialectic and rhetoric not as *dunameis* but as sciences, he unwittingly obscures their nature by the change, setting them down as sciences dealing with specific subject matters, rather than with arguments alone" (*Rh.* I 4 1359[b]9–16).

Note 397
Those philosophical accounts in which ethical matters were determined: Namely, *NE* and *EE*.

Note 398
What sort of (*poiôn*) equality and what sort (*poiôn*) of inequality: Or "equality for what sort of people and inequality for what sort of people." See III 9 1280ᵃ19n.

Note 399
Political philosophy: That is, political science. Compare *NE* VII 11 1152ᵇ1–3. But see also Introduction pp. lxix–lxx.

Note 400
It is to the function that the superiority should contribute, and superiority in wealth and in good-breeding contribute nothing to it: Punctuating with Pellegrin δεῖ γὰρ εἰς τὸ ἔργον συμβάλλεσθαι τὴν ὑπεροχὴν, καὶ τοῦ πλούτου καὶ τῆς εὐγενείας συμβάλλονται δ'οὐδέν rather than with OCT δεῖ γὰρ εἰς τὸ ἔργον συμβάλλεσθαι τὴν ὑπεροχὴν καὶ τοῦ πλούτου καὶ τῆς εὐγενείας, συμβάλλονται δ'οὐδέν ("For the superiority in wealth and birth must contribute to the function, and they contribute nothing").

Note 401
Political virtue: Reading τῆς πολιτικῆς ἀρετῆς with OCT and Schütrumpf. Dreizehnter reads τῆς πολεμικῆς ἀρετῆς ("military virtue").

Note 402
As was also said earlier: At III 9 1281ᵃ1–8.

Note 403
We said before: At III 9 1280ᵃ7–25.

Note 404
Good-breeding is esteemed at home by everyone: See I 6 1255ᵃ32–37.

Note 405
Good-breeding is virtue of family: See I 6 1255ᵃ33n.

Note 406
Justice, we say, is a virtue relating to communities (*koinônikên*), which all the other virtues necessarily accompany: See I 13 1259ᵇ24n.

Note 407
Extreme (*huperbolên*) virtue: "If, as they say, human beings become gods because of an extreme of virtue, it is clear that the state opposed to the type that is beast-like will be of this sort. And just as there is in fact neither vice nor virtue of a wild beast, neither is there of a god. But his state is more estimable than virtue, while that of a wild beast is of a different kind than vice" (*NE* VII 1 1145ᵃ22–27). Compare I 2 1253ᵃ1–4. Here, however, it seems that the person outstanding in extreme virtue need not, as in the case of a god, be beyond virtue altogether. His virtue is

extreme simply in comparison to that of his fellows, among whom, therefore, he is like a god among humans.

Note 408

For the other sort [namely, those who are outstanding in extreme virtue] there is no law, since they themselves are law: "A sophisticated and free person . . . is a sort of law for himself" (*NE* IV 8 1128ᵃ31–32).

Note 409

Antisthenes: A follower of Socrates, present at his death. He wrote widely, including on topics in what we would now call the philosophy of language, and in many genres, including Socratic dialogues. It is not clear to which of his works Aristotle is referring. In Aesop, *Fables* 241, the lions' reply to the hares is, "Where are your claws and your teeth?"
Popular leaders: See II 12 1274ᵃ10n.

Note 410

Ostracism: Ostracism in the form of banishment without loss of property or citizenship for ten (later five) years was introduced in Athens by Cleisthenes. See *Ath.* XXII.

Note 411

Argonauts: A band of heroes who accompanied Jason in his quest to find the Golden Fleece. They are named after their ship, which was in turn named for its builder Argus, who built it under Athena's guidance.
Heracles: The son of Zeus and Alcmene, he was the greatest of the Greek heroes.

Note 412

The *Argo* refused to carry him along with the others: Athena had a board built into the *Argo* that enabled it to speak.

Note 413

The advice of Periander to Thrasybulus: Periander was tyrant of Corinth (625–585 BC), Thrasybulus tyrant of Miletus. The full story is told in Herodotus V.92, where the roles Aristotle attributes to Periander and Thrasybulus are reversed.

Note 414

Samos, Chios, and Lesbos: The most powerful cities in the Athenian alliance.
Samos: An island in the eastern Aegean, south of Chios, and separated from the coast of Anatolia by the one-mile-wide Mycale Strait.
Lesbos: Also called Mytilene, after its capital city, Lesbos is the third largest Greek island. It is located in the northeastern Aegean, close to the Anatolian coast.
Medes: Ancient inhabitants of Media (northwestern Iran), defeated by, and absorbed into, Persia in 550 BC.

Note 415

By dividing the offices: So that Zeus ruled and was ruled in turn.

Note 416

Except in a certain sort of kingship: Reading εἰ μὴ ἔν τινι βασιλείᾳ with the mss. for OCT εἰ μὴ ἕνεκα δειλία ("except because of cowardice").
Law of force (*en cheiros nomô[i]*): When someone is put to death by an exercise of the right that superior force or strength confers he is put to death *en cheiros nomô[i]*.

Note 417

Agamemnon: The leader of the Greek army in the Trojan Wars.

Note 418

Homer makes this clear: *Iliad* II.391–393. The last line Aristotle quotes is not in our text.

Note 419

There is another, which is just the one that existed among the ancient Greeks, namely, the ones they call dictators (*aisymnêtês*): Some barbarian cities, however, also seem to have been of this kind (IV 10 1295^{a}11–14). A dictator, as we may infer from Aristotle's discussion of this kind of kingship, was the holder of an elective tyranny that was in accord with law.

Note 420

Mytileneans: Inhabitants of Mytilene, the capital and port of the island of Lesbos.
Pittacus, Antimenides, Alcaeus: Pittacus, see II 12 1274^{b}18–23n. Alcaeus (born c. 620 BC) was a lyric poet from Mytilene in Lesbos. Antimenides was his brother. The verse Aristotle quotes is Fr. 87 Diehl.

Note 421

The heroic age: The period described in the Homeric poems.

Note 422

It is foolish to rule in any craft in accord with what is written down: See II 8 1269^{a}9–11.

Note 423

The best constitution is not one that is in accord with what is written down and laws: Aristotle returns to this argument at III 16 1287^{a}33–^{b}5.

Note 424

The rulers should possess the universal account as well: "Nonetheless, it seems, presumably, that someone who *does* wish to become expert in a craft or in a theoretical science should take steps toward the universal and come to know it as well as possible, since that, we said, is what the sciences are concerned with. Maybe, then, someone who wishes to make people—whether many or few—better because of his supervision should also try to acquire legislative science, if it is through laws that we can become good. For producing a noble disposition in anyone whoever—in anyone put before him—is not a matter for some random person, but if indeed anyone can do it, it is a person who has knowledge, just as in medicine and in all other matters that involve a sort of supervision and practical wisdom. Hence shouldn't we next investigate from what sources and in what way someone might become competent in legislative science? Or isn't it, as in other cases, from politicians? For, as we saw, legislative science seems to be a part of politics" (*NE* X 9 1181^{a}24–31).

Note 425

Something to which the passionate element is wholly unattached is better than something in which it is innate: Compare II 10 1272^{b}5–7n, III 16 1287^{a}28–32.
The passionate element (*to pathêtikon*): The non-rational element in the soul, comprising appetites, desires, and emotions.

Note 426

Just like a feast to which many contribute . . . is better than one that is one and simple: See III 11 1281^{a}42–^{b}3n.

Note 427

This is not an easy thing to arrange where numbers are large: See III 5 1278^{a}6–11, 7 1279^{a}39–^{b}4.

Note 428

Both when the office involves capacity (*meta dunameôs*) **and when it is separate from capacity** (*chôris dunameôs*): The capacity referred to is the political capacity mentioned at III 13 1284^{a}9–10, not the sort of military or coercive power that results from having an armed guard of the sort mentioned in connection with barbarian kingships (III 14 1285^{a}24–29), to which Aristotle will turn in a moment (1286^{b}27–40). Thus the argument here concerns the sort of political capacity that goes along with being good or virtuous men, not with military strength, and concludes that having more men with such capacity is better for a city than having only one.

Note 429

They made men kings as a consequence of benefits conferred: See V 10 1310^{b}10–12.
Conferring benefits is just what it is the function of good men to do: Because good men have the virtue of generosity and generosity involves conferring benefits (*NE* IV 1 1120^{a}33–34), especially when in positions of power: "No one would choose to live without friends, even if he had all the other good things. For even rich people and those who are rulers or hold positions of power seem to need friends most. For what benefit is such prosperity once the opportunity to be a benefactor—which occurs most and is most praiseworthy when it is toward friends—is removed? Or in what way could their prosperity be protected and safeguarded without friends? For the greater their prosperity is, the more precarious it is" (VIII 1 1155^{a}5–11).

Note 430

They made wealth an honored thing: See V 10 1311^{a}9–10, Plato, *Rep.* 554a.

Note 431
From oligarchies they changed first into tyrannies, and from tyrannies to democracy: For somewhat different explanations, see IV 13 1297b16–28, V 12 1316a1–b27.

Note 432
When Dionysius asked for bodyguards: See I 11 1259a28–36n.

Note 433
As we said: At III 15 1286a2–4.

Note 434
Opus: The chief city of Locris.

Note 435
This is why it is just for them to rule no more than they are ruled, and, therefore, to do so in turn: See II 2 1261a30–b6.

Note 436
The order is law (*hê gar taxis nomos*): Ruling and being ruled *in turn* involves a sort of order in ruling and being ruled, which needs to be established and enforced by law.

Note 437
Hands over the rest to be judged and managed in accord with the most just consideration of the rulers: See II 10 1272a38–39n.

Note 438
The god and (*kai*) **the understanding:** If *kai* is epexegetic or explanatory (as at *NE* I 6 1096a24–25), the meaning is "the god, that is, the understanding." See I 5 1254b5n.
The god (*ho theos*): Aristotle recognizes the existence of a number of different divine beings or gods, among whom he distinguishes a primary god, referred to as *ho theos* ("the god"), who is the one alluded to here, and who is the unmoved mover of everything else (*Met.* XII 7–8). He is an understanding that has itself as its sole object, so that he is an "active understanding of active understanding" (9 1074b34–35).

Note 439
Spirit (*thumos*): Aristotle sometime uses *thumos* and *orgê* ("anger") interchangeably (*Rh.* I 10 1369b11) and very often uses *thumos* in contexts where its aggressive side is highlighted (for example, *NE* III 8 1116b15–1117a9). In other places, however, he says that anger is only "in (*en*)" the spirited element (*Top.* II 7 113a36–b1, IV 5 126a10) alongside other feelings, such as fear and hatred (IV 5 126a8–9). In one passage, indeed, he identifies spirit as the source not just of "negative" feelings but also of love and friendship: "spirit (*thumos*) is what produces friendliness (*philêtikon*), since it is the capacity of the soul by which we love (*philoumen*)" (*Pol.* VII 7 1327b40–1328a1). This is in keeping with his claim that if hatred is in the

spirited element, then love, as its contrary, must be there too (*Top.* II 7 113ᵃ33–ᵇ3). Presumably, then, we should think of spirit as passionate—as "hot and hasty" (*NE* VII 6 1149ᵃ30)—rather than as always aggressive. At *DA* II 3 414ᵇ2 it, along with appetite and wish, is characterized as collectively comprising desire (*orexis*).
Spirit distorts (*diastrephei*) **[the judgment of] rulers:** The distortion is the sort that feelings generally produce because of their involvement with pleasure and pain: "What is pleasant or painful does not ruin or distort every sort of supposition (for example, that triangles do or do not contain two right angles) but it does do this to the one about what is doable in action" (*NE* VI 5 1140ᵇ13–16); "Depravity produces distortion and false views about practical starting-points" (12 1144ᵃ35–36). That is why to correct these distortions and establish a virtuous mean in our feelings we should investigate "what we ourselves are easily drawn toward, since different people are naturally inclined toward different things. This will become known to us from the pleasure and pain that the things bring about in us. And it is in the contrary direction that we should drag ourselves off, since it is by pulling well away from error that we shall attain the mean—as people do in rectifying distortions in pieces of wood" (II 9 1109ᵇ1–7).

Note 440
That is why law is understanding without desire: Without desire (*orexis*) because without appetite and spirit (*DA* II 3 414ᵇ2).

Note 441
Doctors themselves call in other doctors to treat them when they are sick: "We call on partners in deliberation on important questions, when we mistrust ourselves as not being adequate to determine the answer" (*NE* III 3 1112ᵇ10–11).

Note 442
The law is the mean: See *NE* V 5 1132ᵃ19–24 (quoted in IV 12 1297ᵃ5–6n).

Note 443
Laws that are in [1] accord with habits (*kata ta ethê*) **have more control and deal with things that have more control than do written laws:** *Ethê* can also mean "customs," which would give, [2] "Laws that are in accord with customs. . . ." The contrast would then be between written laws and unwritten or customary ones (on which, see IV 6 1292ᵇ11–17). Elsewhere, however, Aristotle pretty much dismisses this distinction as of little importance: "It is clear that communal types of supervision come about through laws and that decent ones do so through excellent laws. Whether the laws are written or unwritten, though, would seem to make no difference" (*NE* X 9 1180ᵃ35–ᵇ1). But since unwritten laws seems to be "character related (*êthikê*)" in nature (VIII 13 1162ᵇ21–23), and character "results from habit (*ethos*)" (II 1 1103ᵃ17), the difference between [1] and [2] may be itself of little importance. Nonetheless, when we turn to the next clause [1] seems preferable to [2]. See also II 8 1269ᵇ20–21.
Even if a human ruler is safer than written laws, he is not safer than those that are in accord with habit (*to ethos*): The idea is this. People who think that it is better to be ruled by written laws than by human beings support their case by (1) appealing to the presence in human beings but not in laws of elements, such as

spirit and appetite, that distort judgment. People who think that human rulers are better appeal to (2) the preferability of a human judge in particular cases due to the fact that the laws cannot take account of all the circumstances pertinent in them. What (2) overlooks is that human judges have characters based on habits, which are themselves the results of being brought up under laws (1287ᵃ25–26), whether written or unwritten, and so are no safer—no better—than those laws.

Note 444
As we said earlier: At 1286ᵇ3–5.

Note 445
"When two go together . . . ": Homer, *Iliad* X.224.
"May ten such counselors be mine": *Iliad* II.372.

Note 446
Although we have in a sense already stated it too: At III 13 1284ᵃ3–ᵇ35.

Note 447
That naturally yields a multitude: Reading πλῆθος with Dreizehnter and the mss. for OCT γένος ("That naturally yields a stock").

Note 448
A multitude useful for war: Reading πλῆθος πολεμικὸν with Dreizehnter and the mss. for OCT γένος πολιτικὸν ("political stock"). For the explanation of why a polity needs such a multitude, see II 6 1265ᵇ26–28, IV 13 1297ᵇ1–2.

Note 449
As was said earlier . . . what was said earlier: At III 13 1284ᵃ3–ᵇ34.

Note 450
In our first accounts: At III 4–5.

Note 451
It is necessary, then, for anyone who is going [to do this] to make the appropriate investigation: This sentence, which is incomplete without the bracketed addition supplied from the previous sentence, appears in a slightly different form as part of the opening sentence of Book VII. It is bracketed for deletion here in OCT.

BOOK IV

Note 452
Book IV: The end of III 18 prepares us for a discussion of the best constitution, but this book does not contain one. Moreover, the opening of IV 2 suggests that such a discussion has already taken place, and much has indeed been said about it in discussing other people's views about it and in discussing aristocracy and kingship. Nonetheless, Aristotle's own best constitution is not formally discussed until Books VII–VIII, leading Newman and some editors to place these immediately following Book III.

Note 453
Among all the crafts and sciences that are not partly developed but that, having become complete, deal with some one kind (*genos*), **it belongs to a single one to get a theoretical grasp on what is fitting in the case of each kind** (*genos*): See I 1 1252ᵃ15n(5).

Note 454
The scientific knowledge appropriate for those involved in competition: Boxing and wrestling are classed as sciences at *Cat.* 8 10ᵇ3–4.
It belongs no less to coaches and athletic trainers to provide this capacity too: See VIII 3 1338ᵇ6–8.

Note 455
Set in motion: Reading κινεῖν with Pellegrin and most mss. for OCT καινίζειν ("use for the first time") and Dreizehnter and some mss. κοινωνεῖν ("share in").
As it is no less work: Reading ὡς ἔστιν οὐκ ἔλαττον ἔργον with Dreizehnter and the mss. for OCT ὥστ᾽ ἔστιν οὐκ ἔλαττον ἔργον ("so that it is no less work").

Note 456
As was also said earlier: At 1288ᵇ27–33 = [3].

Note 457
One must not overlook the differences in each of the constitutions, how many they are and in how many ways they can be combined: For the explanation, see IV 4 1290ᵇ25–1293ᵃ34, VI 1 1317ᵃ18–1318ᵃ3.

Note 458
It is with this same practical wisdom: Practical wisdom is the same state of the soul as politics, or political science (*NE* VI 8 1141ᵇ23–24), explaining why Aristotle can switch from discussing one to discussing the other.

Note 459
Their number: Reading τὸν ἀριθμὸν with the mss. for OCT τὸν ὁρισμὸν ("their definition").

Note 460
Getting a theoretical grasp on the best constitution is the same as discussing these names: See III 4 1276ᵇ11–13n.

Note 461
When a kingship is the one we should recognize (*nomizein*) **[as appropriate], was determined earlier:** At III 17 1288ᵃ15–29.

Note 462
The name shared in common by all constitutions: That is, *politeia*, which is translated as "polity" when it refers to this particular sort of constitution. See II 6 1265ᵇ28n.

Note 463
The first and most divine constitution: Namely, kingship, which is the most divine, because Aristotle's primary god (III 16 1287ᵃ29n) rules the universe with

kingly rule (*Met.* XII 10 1076ᵃ3–4), which is the way in which Zeus rules the other gods (*Pol.* I 2 1252ᵇ24–27).

Note 464
An earlier thinker has already expressed this same view: Plato, *Pol.* 302e–303b.

Note 465
Some other constitution that is ruled in the best way (*aristokratikê*) **and well formed, and at the same time fitting for most cities:** Since an aristocracy in the strict sense is not fitting for most cities (II 6 1265ᵇ33n), I have followed Pellegrin in treating *aristokratikê* as having its etymological meaning here. IV 7 does suggest, however, that a polity, which is the sort of constitution being referred to, might count as a sort of aristocracy.

Note 466
The cause of there being several constitutions: This is one of several, but perhaps equivalent, explanations that Aristotle gives. See IV 6, V 1 1301ᵃ25–33, 1301ᵇ29–1302ᵃ2, VI 1–7.

Note 467
Hoplite weapons: See II 6 1265ᵇ28n.

Note 468
Eretrians: Eretria ("city of the rowers") is a town on the island of Euboea that faces the coast of Attica across the narrow South Euboean Gulf.
Chalcidians: Chalcis, situated at the narrowest point of the Euripus Strait, is the chief town in Euboea.
Magnesians on the river Maenander: Magnesia on the Maenander was in Ionia, fifteen miles from Ephesus, in present-day Turkey.

Note 469
In our discussion of aristocracy we distinguished the number of parts that are necessary to any city: Probably a reference to III 12 1283ᵃ14–26, although the topic is also discussed in VII 7–9.

Note 470
The west wind is regarded as northerly, and the east as southerly: "West winds are called northerly, since they blow from where the sun sets and are therefore colder. East winds are called southerly, since they blow from where the sun rises and are warmer. Winds are thus called northerly or southerly on the basis of this division between cold, hot, or warm" (*Mete.* II 6 364ᵃ18–27).

Note 471
Something similar holds in the case of harmonies, so some people say, since there as well two kinds (*eidos*) **are posited, namely, the Dorian and the Phrygian, and the other modes are called either Doric or Phrygic:** See VIII 5 1340ᵃ40–ᵇ5n.

Note 472
The well-mixed "harmony": Harmony is here the balanced mixture of elements in a constitution. The well-mixed constitution is identified in IV 9.

Note 473
In the way some people are accustomed to do now: See Plato, *Pol.* 291d.
Both in oligarchies and everywhere else, the larger part is in control: See IV 8 1294^{a}11–14 for an explanation.

Note 474
Thera: A city that was on the ridge of the Messa Vouno mountain on the island of Santorini.

Note 475
As was formerly the case in Colophon, where the majority possessed large properties before the war against the Lydians: The war occurred in the reign of Gyges in the first half of the 7th cent BC.
Colophon: A city in Ionia, located between Lebedos and Ephesus. Its ruins are situated south of Değirmendere Fev in the Izmir province of Turkey.
Lydians: Inhabitants of Lydia, present-day Anatolia, in western Asia Minor. Later a province of Persia.
It is not a democracy either: Reading δῆμος with Dreizehnter and the mss. for OCT ὀλιγαρχία ("it is not an oligarchy either").

Note 476
What we stated earlier: At IV 3 1289^{b}27.

Note 477
The constitutions we have mentioned: The reference could be to (1) the list of six constitutions given at IV 2 1289^{a}26–30, (2) the shorter list said to constitute the present agenda at 1289^{a}35–38, or (3) oligarchy and democracy, which are the chief focus of discussion after 1289^{b}6.

Note 478
Cities are formed not out of one but out of many parts, as we have often said: At III 1 1274^{b}38–40, 12 1283^{a}14–17, IV 3 1289^{b}27–28, 4 1290^{b}23–24.

Note 479
A city is self-sufficient: See I 2 1252^{b}27–30, II 2 1261^{b}12–13.
A slavish thing is not self-sufficient: Since a (natural) slave belongs entirely to his master (I 4 1254^{a}12–17).

Note 480
What is said in the *Republic*: At 369d–371e.

Note 481
[6]: This part is not explicitly labeled as the sixth, but the next one that is labeled is the seventh (1291^{a}33).
The one making assignments (*apodôsonta*) **and rendering judgment about what is just** (*krinounta to dikaion*): At 1291^{a}38–40, we have "the part that deliberates (*to bouleuomenon*) and renders judgment (*krinein*) about the claims of people involved in disputes," while at VII 9 1329^{a}3–4 we have "the one that

deliberates about what is advantageous (*to bouleuomenon peri tôn sumpherontôn*) and renders judgment about what is just (*krinon peri tôn dikaiôn*)." It seems, therefore, that here too we should discern two different functions performed by a single part, one that consists in making assignments on the basis of deliberation about what is advantageous, and the other in rendering judgments about what is just.

Note 482
Political comprehension (*sunesis*): "Comprehension is not concerned with what always is and is unchanging, nor is it concerned with just any of the things that come to be but with those one might puzzle and deliberate about. That is why it is concerned with the same things as practical wisdom [= politics], although comprehension is not the same as practical wisdom. For practical wisdom is prescriptive, since what *should* be done or not is its end, whereas comprehension is discerning only" (*NE* VI 10 1143^{a}4–10).

Note 483
Public service: See III 6 1279^{a}11n.

Note 484
The virtue of politicians: Reading πολιτικῶν with Dreizehnter and the mss. for OCT πολιτῶν ("the virtue of citizens"). The virtue in question is practical wisdom (III 4 1277^{b}25–26), which is the same state of the soul as politics, or political science (*NE* VI 8 1141^{b}23–24).

Note 485
The relevant virtue: Presumably, practical wisdom (1291^{b}1–2).

Note 486
Constitutions are formed in accord with the sorts of superiority belonging to these: Namely, wealth (the rich) and numbers (the poor). See III 17 1288^{a}20–24, IV 11 1296^{a}27–32.

Note 487
It was stated earlier: At III 7–13, IV 3 1289^{b}27–28.

Note 488
There are also several kinds of democracy and of oligarchy: See VI 1–7.

Note 489
Tarentum: Modern-day Taranto, a coastal city in Apulia in southern Italy.
Byzantium: Present-day Istanbul.
Aegina: An island in the Saronic Gulf, seventeen miles from Athens.
Tenedos: An island in the northeastern part of the Aegean, now belonging to Turkey.

Note 490
If indeed freedom exists above all in a democracy, as some people suppose, and equality too: See Plato, *Rep*. 557a–c, 562b–563d.

Note 491

This, then, is one kind of democracy: It does not appear on the lists given in VI 4 and 5.

Note 492

Uncontested citizens: Those whose citizen birth is clear on both sides. See III 2 1275^{b}22–26, IV 6 1292^{b}35–36.

Note 493

Everyone shares in office merely by being a citizen: So that a larger number shares in office than in [3]. See III 2 1275^{b}34–1276^{a}6.

Note 494

Decrees (*psêphismata*): A law (*nomos*) is a relatively permanent enactment, universal in scope and applicable on many different occasions. A decree (*psêphisma*), by contrast, is a singular enactment, adapted to particular circumstances (*NE* V 10 1137^{b}27–32), stating what is to be done in one particular case, and is thus the last thing reached in a piece of practical deliberation (VI 8 1141^{b}24–28).

Popular leaders: See II 12 1274^{a}10n.

Note 495

When Homer says: At *Iliad* II.204.

Note 496

Flatterers (*kolakes*): "Among those who cause pleasure to others, a person who aims at being pleasant, not because of something else, is ingratiating, while someone who does so to get some benefit for himself (in terms of wealth or what comes because of wealth) is a flatterer (*kolax*)" (*NE* IV 6 1127^{a}7–10).

Note 497

The law should rule everything: Reading πάντων with Dreizehnter and the mss. for OCT πάντων τῶν καθόλου ("the law should rule all universal matters"). See II 10 1272^{b}5–7, III 15 1286^{a}9–20.

While in the case of particulars the officials and the constitution should render judgment: τὴν πολιτείαν κρίνειν with Dreizehnter for OCT ταύτην πολιτείαν κρίνειν ("in the case of particulars the officials [should rule], and this should be judged a constitution"). The oddness of the claim that the constitution should render judgment in particular cases is reduced when we recall that "the constitution is governing body" (III 6 1278^{b}11). In the sort of democracy under discussion the people are the governing body. Alternatively, one might take the meaning to be that the officials should render judgment in particular cases *in accord with* the constitution.

Note 498

This state of affairs, in which everything is managed by decree, is not even a democracy in the full sense: See I 13 1260^{b}12n.

Note 499
If they elect from among all of these, it seems more aristocratic, if from some specified group, oligarchic: Explained at IV 15 1300a8–b7.

Note 500
They are content at first to get more (*pleonektountes*) **than the others in small ways:** See II 7 1266b37n.

Note 501
And of course for it to be open to them to be at leisure is impossible in the absence of revenues: Reading τὸ δὲ δὴ ἐξεῖναι σχολάζειν ἀδύνατον μὴ προσόδων οὐσῶν which OCT obelizes.

Note 502
Being stronger, they deserve to get more (*pleonektein*): See II 7 1266b37n.

Note 503
Like Plato: *Rep*. VIII–IX.

Note 504
The constitution we treated in our first accounts: See III 4 1276b34–1277a1, 5 1278a17–21, 1278b1–5, 15 1286b3–7, 18 1288a37–b2.

Note 505
Wherever, then, a constitution looks to wealth, virtue, and the people (as it does in Carthage) it is aristocratic: See II 11 1273a21–b1.
Those, like the Spartan constitution, which look to only two, virtue and the people: See II 9 1270b15–17, b25, 1271b2–3.

Note 506
We mentioned at the start of our discussions: At IV 2 1289a26–b5, see also III 7 1279b4–6.

Note 507
Governed aristocratically: That is, by the best (*aristos*) people.

Note 508
The defining mark: See I 9 1258a18n.

Note 509
Now in most cities the kind (*eidos*) **of constitution is badly named:** Reading τὸ τῆς πολιτείας εἶδος κακῶς καλεῖται with OCT for Dreizehnter and the mss. τὸ τῆς πολιτείας εἶδος καλεῖται ("now in most cities the kind that is called a polity exists"). The latter reading conflicts with IV 7 1293b40–41, which tells us that polities are rare. Some editors, including Lord and Pellegrin, think that the text is corrupt.

Note 510
In continuity with what was said: At IV 8 1293b22–30.

Note 511

We dealt with kingship in our first accounts: See III 14–17.

Note 512

If what is said in the *Ethics* is correct, and [1] a happy life is the unimpeded life that is in accord with virtue, and [2] virtue is a medial state: [1] is not said in so many words in the *Nicomachean Ethics*, but it is implied by the following: "What, then, prevents us from calling happy the person who is active in accord with complete virtue and is adequately supplied with external goods not for some random period of time but in a complete life?" (I 11 1101ᵃ14–16). For absence of external goods, such as wealth and power, can impede an otherwise virtuous agent from putting his virtue into action. [2], on the other hand, is explicitly stated: "Virtue, then, is a deliberately choosing state, which is in a medial condition in relation to us, one defined by a reason and the one by which a practically-wise person would define it. Also, it is a medial condition between two vices, one of excess and the other of deficiency" (II 6 1106ᵇ36–1107ᵃ3).

Then [3] the middle life is best, the medial one that admits of being aimed at by each sort of person: The qualification in the second clause ("the medial one that admits of being aimed at by each sort of person") stems from the fact that what is being looked for is the best life that is in practice achievable "for most cities and most human beings" (1295ᵃ25–31).

Note 513

The goods of luck: Aristotle recognizes three sorts of goods: those of the body, those of the soul, and external goods (*NE* I 8 1098ᵇ12–14), which are usually so-called because they are external to the soul (*EE* II 1 1218ᵇ32–33), although sometimes goods relating to the body are also classed as internal goods (*Rh.* I 5 1360ᵇ1–29). In any case, it is into this third class that goods of luck fall, since luck is in control of them: "Of goods external to the soul, chance or luck is the cause, but no one is just or temperate as a result of luck or because of luck" (*Pol.* VII 2 1323ᵇ27–29; also *MM* II 8 1206ᵇ33–34).

Note 514

The latter do not have the scientific knowledge (*epistantai*) of how to rule, but only how to be ruled in the way slaves are ruled: See I 1 1252ᵃ15n.

Note 515

The one group envious, the other contemptuous (*kataphronountôn*): *Kataphronêsis* though sometimes distinguished from (for example, V 2 1302ᵇ3–4), is often the same as (for example, VII 7 1328ᵃ13), *oligôria*, which is "the actively entertained belief that something is manifestly worthless. . . . There are three forms (*eidos*) of it: despising, spite, and wanton aggression" (*Rh.* II 2 1378ᵇ10–15).

Note 516

A city tends, at any rate, to consist as much as possible of people who are equal and similar: "Political friendship in fact tends to be in accord with equality" (*EE* VII 10 1242ᵇ30–31). Also VII 8 1328ᵃ35–36.

Note 517

Phocylides: A 6th-cent-BC poet from Miletus. The lines quoted are Fr. 10 Diehl.

Note 518

It will tip the balance when added to either and prevent opposing excesses (*huperbolas*) **from arising:** By joining the poor it prevents excessive oligarchy, by joining the rich, excessive democracy.

Note 519

When we discuss constitutional changes: At V 8 1308ᵃ20–24, 10 1310ᵇ3–7, 1312ᵇ34–38.

Note 520

Failure (*kakopragia*): Not the contrary of *eupraxia*, or "doing well in action," but of *eupragia*. See *Top*. II 2 109ᵇ37, 110ᵃ11, *EE* III 7 1233ᵇ23, 25, *Rh*. II 9 1386ᵇ10, 26.

Note 521

Those who achieved leadership in Greece: Namely, democratic Athens and oligarchic Sparta.

Note 522

One man alone, among those who have previously held positions of leadership, has ever allowed himself to be persuaded to introduce this kind of order: We do not know to whom Aristotle is referring, though Philip of Macedon is thought to be a likely candidate. Thucydides, writing about the government of the Five Thousand in Athens, which deposed that of the Four Hundred oligarchs in 411 BC, has this to say: "And now for the first time, at least in my lifetime, the Athenians clearly had their best government, since a moderate blending of the few [oligarchs] and many [democrats] came about. And this was the first thing, after so many misfortunes had occurred, that made the city raise its head again" (VIII.97.2).

Note 523

While one constitution is more choiceworthy, nothing prevents a different one from being more advantageous for some [cities]: "What is advantageous is good for the individual, whereas what is noble is unconditionally so" (*Rh*. II 13 1289ᵇ37–1390ᵃ1); "We should pray that unconditionally good things will also be good for us, while choosing the ones that are good for us" (*NE* V 1 1129ᵇ5–6). See also VII 2 1324ᵃ16n.

Note 524

The part of a city that wishes the constitution to endure must be stronger than the part that does not: Referred to as "the most important element" at V 9 1309ᵇ16–18.

Note 525

The legislator, however, should always add on (*proslambanein*) **those in the middle in his constitution:** That is, he should add them on to the class whose advantage his constitution furthers. For example, he should add them to the few rich if his constitution is oligarchic, and to the poor many if it is democratic.

Note 526

Everywhere, though, an arbitrator (*diatêtês*) **is most trusted, and the middling person is an arbitrator:** "When people are involved in dispute they take refuge in a judge. Going to a judge, however, is going to justice, since a judge is meant to be, as it were, justice ensouled. Also, they seek a judge as an intermediary—in fact, some people call judges 'mediators,' on the supposition that a person who can hit the mean is the one who will hit what is just. Hence what is just is a mean in some way, if indeed a judge is also one" (*NE* V 6 1132^{a}19–24).

Note 527

What the rich do to get more does more to destroy the constitution than what the people do: See V 7 1307^{a}12–20.

What the rich do to get more (*hai pleonexiai*): See II 7 1266^{b}37n.

Note 528

The subtleties devised in constitutions (*en tais politeiais*): *Politeiai* may refer to polities in particular rather than to constitutions generally, since at V 8 1308^{a}2–3, Aristotle refers back to the subtleties discussed here, in a warning that seems to be addressed specifically to "well-mixed constitutions" (1307^{b}30–31).

Note 529

Not allowing those with an assessed amount of property to be excused under oath: For example, a property owner might be excused from holding office by swearing under oath that it would be an undue burden (financial or otherwise) for him to do so.

Note 530

As in the laws of Charondas: See II 12 1274^{b}5–8.

Note 531

What amount is the largest: Reading ποῖον with Dreizehnter and the mss. for OCT πόσον.

Note 532

Malia: A city on the north coast of Crete, twenty-one miles east of Heraklion.

Note 533

The first constitution that came about among the Greeks after the kingships consisted of the warriors: See III 15 1286^{b}11–13.

Note 534

[1]–[3]: [1] is discussed below; [2] in IV 15, [3] in IV 16.

Note 535

Telecles of Miletus: Otherwise unknown.

Note 536

Tribes: See IV 15 1300^{a}25n.

Note 537
The ones where it is necessary to have scientifically-knowledgeable people ruling: Democratic constitutions favored election by lot, but were willing to make an exception for offices, such as generalship, which required expert knowledge (VI 2 1317ᵇ20–21).

Note 538
The final democracy: See IV 4 1292ᵃ4–37.

Note 539
It is an aristocracy or a polity: Reading ἀριστοκρατία ἢ πολιτεία with Dreizehnter and the mss. for OCT ἀριστοκρατία ἡ πολιτεία ("the constitution is an aristocracy").

Note 540
The division of the offices: Further discussed in VI 8.

Note 541
Corn-rationers are often elected: Especially in times of scarcity, but also when a gift of corn was given to a city and needed to be distributed in an equitable way.

Note 542
More characteristic of ruling (*archikôteron*): And so a good indicator of the offices (*archai*) that, as exercising rule (*archê*), are most properly so called. Obviously, not all so-called offices are like that. See I 13 1260ᵇ20n.

Note 543
This makes (one might almost say) no difference as regards use (for as yet no judgment has been handed down to anyone disputing over the name), although there is some further work for thought (*dianoêtikên pragmateian*) **to do on it:** The name or term "office" is most properly applied to those involved in deliberating, judging, and prescribing, especially the latter. But no final judgment has been reached where there is dispute about the use of the term. Where its use in practice is concerned the issue is of little importance, though theory might have more to say about it. See I 11 1258ᵇ9–11, 33–35.

Note 544
How many are necessary for the existence of a city: These are listed in VI 8.

Note 545
Each function is better performed when its supervision is engaged in one thing rather than being engaged in many things: Compare I 2 1252ᵇ1–5, II 11 1273ᵇ9–15, also Plato, *Rep*. 370a–b, 374a–c, 423c–d, 433a, 443b–c, 453b.

Note 546
A spit-lamp (*obeliskoluchnion*): A military tool that could be used either as a roasting spit or as a lamp holder.

Note 547
So they can do their work (*ascholôn*): Literally, "so they can be without leisure."

Note 548

When there is wealth of the sort that provides pay to those who attend the assembly: See VI 2 1317b30–35.

Note 549

How can one prevent the women of the poor from going out?: Well-off women in Athens were kept in a sort of purdah in the households first of their fathers and then of their husbands. Poorer ones had to work in the fields or other public places.
The women of oligarchs live luxuriously: See II 9 1269b12–39.

Note 550

[2a–c]: The nine different variations are: [2a–i] all appoint, [2a–ii] some appoint, [2a–iii] all appoint to some offices and some appoint to others; [2b–i] all are appointable, [2b–ii] some are appointable, [2b–iii] all are appointable to some office and some are appointable to others; [2c–i] appointment is by lot, [2c–ii] appointment is by election, [2c–iii] appointment is by lot to some offices and by election to others.

Note 551

There will be four modes: Reading τέσσαρες with Dreizehnter and the mss. for OCT ἕξ ("six"). The text of this paragraph (1300a22–31) is difficult, as the additions in OCT indicate.

Note 552

Tribe (*phulê*), **deme** (*dêmos*), **clan** (*phratra*): Tribes were the principal components or divisions of the citizen body. Thus in the system developed by Cleisthenes (III 2 1275b36n) for Attica in 508/7 BC, the land was divided into three zones: city, shore, and inland. Each of these was in turn divided into ten sections called *trittyes*, to each of which was assigned between one and ten of the 139 existing settlements, including villages and towns, which were all called demes. Three units, one drawn from each of the three zones, were put together to form a tribe. Each of the resulting geographically scattered ten tribes was named after a local hero, and membership of it made hereditary in the male line. These tribes were then assigned or took on various political functions, such as brigading units for the army, and constituencies for the election of magistrates. Before this reorganization, which had the effect of breaking up old political allegiances, every Athenian male belonged to a clan (or brotherhood), and clans functioned as social units concerned with family and descent. Under Draco's laws (II 12 1274b15n), for example, a clan was required to support the family of one of its members if he was a victim of unintentional homicide, or to take on the role of his family if he had none.

Note 553

This gives rise to twelve modes: All appoint from all (1) by election, (2) by lot; all appoint from some (3) by election, (4) by lot; (5) all appoint from all partly by election and partly by lot; (6) all appoint from some partly by election and partly

by lot; some appoint from all (7) by election, (8) by lot; some appoint from some (9) by election, (10) by lot; (11) some appoint from all partly by election and partly by lot; (12) some appoint from some partly by election and partly by lot.
Separate from the two couplings: Namely, [2a–iii] all may appoint to some offices and some to others, and [2b–iii] some offices may be appointed from all and others from some.

Note 554
The three parts: See IV 14 $1297^{b}36$–$1298^{a}3$.

Note 555
In accord with the same hypothesis (*hupothesin*): Namely, that used in discussing the other two parts (deliberative, offices) of a constitution and exemplified at IV 14 $1298^{a}3$–9 (= [1a–c]).

Note 556
Anyone who in some matter concerning the community (*ti tôn koinôn*) **does something unjust:** "Unjust actions and just actions are a matter of doing injustice and acting justly in two ways, either toward one definite individual or toward the community (*to koinon*). For the one who commits adultery or assault does something unjust to some definite person, whereas who avoids military service does it to the community" (*Rh.* I 13 $1373^{b}20$–24).

Note 557
The court of Phreatto in Athens: If someone exiled from Athens for involuntary homicide was charged with a second voluntary homicide, he could not enter Attica to stand trial, but he could offer his defense from a boat offshore at Phreatto on the east shore of Piraeus.

BOOK V

Note 558
[5] The means by which each constitution is best preserved: That is the steps or devices needed to implement [4] the things that preserve a given constitution. See V 11 $1313^{a}34$–$^{b}32$, VI 5 $1319^{b}37$–$1320^{b}17$.

Note 559
Though everyone agrees about justice and proportionate equality, they are in error about it, as we also mentioned earlier: See III 9 $1280^{a}7$–25, 12 $1282^{b}14$–23.

Note 560
Those who are unequal in some respect: Specifically, unequal because superior (V 2 $1302^{a}26$–27).

Note 561
Get more (*pleonektein*): See II 7 $1266^{b}37$.

Note 562

The aim may be to tighten or loosen them: See IV 6 1293ᵃ26–34, V 8 1308ᵇ3–6, 9 1309ᵇ18–1310ᵃ2.

Note 563

Lysander tried to abolish the kingship in Sparta: Lysander was a Spartan general and political leader who fought against Athens in the Peloponnesian War. He failed in his attempt to introduce elective monarchy in Sparta, and was killed in 395 BC. See V 7 1306ᵇ33n.

King Pausanias: See V 7 1307ᵃ4n.

Note 564

In Epidamnus too the constitution was changed with regard to one part: This change may be the one also referred to at 1304ᵃ13–17.

Epidamnus: See II 7 1267ᵇ18n.

Note 565

Numerical equality and equality in accord with worth: See III 9 1280ᵃ19n.

Note 566

As we said earlier: At 1301ᵃ25–28.

Note 567

There are rich ones in many places: Reading εὔποροι δὲ πολλοὶ πολλαχοῦ with Dreizehnter and the mss. for OCT εὔποροι δὲ καὶ ἄποροι πολλοὶ πολλαχοῦ ("there are rich ones and poor ones in many places").

Note 568

It is impossible, when the first thing—namely, the starting-point—is in error, for the result not to be in the end something bad: See V 4 1303ᵇ28–31n.

Note 569

Democracy is more stable and freer from faction than oligarchy: Compare IV 11 1296ᵃ13–18.

Note 570

The cause of people's being in some way disposed to change their constitution is mostly the one we have in fact already mentioned: At V 1 1301ᵃ33–35, 1301ᵇ35–39.

Note 571

[3] The causes and starting-points of the changes—the sources that dispose people to feel in the way we described about the issues we mentioned—happen [3a] in one way to be seven in number and [3b] in another more: The seven causes are profit, honor, wanton aggression, fear, superiority, contempt, and disproportionate growth in power. In [3a] profit and honor are treated as two causes; in [3b] the two ways in which these can operate are treated as distinct causes, yielding more than seven causes. Of the four causes mentioned in the final sentence of the paragraph, the first three (electioneering, underestimation, neglect of small things) cause political change, but not in the same way as the initial seven (or more than seven) do (see V 3 1303^{a}13–14). The fourth (dissimilarity) also causes faction, at least "until people join together" (1303^{a}25–26).

Note 572
Underestimation (*oligôria*). See IV 11 1295^{b}23n.

Note 573
Argos: An ancient city in the eastern Peloponnese.
A practice of ostracism: See III 13 1284^{a}17–25.

Note 574
It is better to see to it from the start that no people with so great a superiority arise: Compare V 8 1308^{b}16–19.

Note 575
The latter occurred in Rhodes: Presumably the event referred to at 1302^{b}32–33 and V 4 1304^{b}27–31.

Note 576
This occurs in oligarchies when those who do not share in the constitution are in a majority: In this case the majority are moved to start a faction by the wanton aggression exhibited by the few who exclude them from office.

Note 577
The battle of Oenophyta: With Athens in 456 BC.
The tyranny of Gelon: Which began in 485 BC. See V 10 1312^{b}10–16.
In Rhodes prior to the revolt: See 1302^{b}23–24n.

Note 578
Its shape might change to that of another animal: At *GA* IV 3 768^{b}27–37, Aristotle describes a disease called "satyriasis," which produces changes in a human face, so that it comes to resemble the face of an animal. He does not think, however, that an animal or any of its parts can change into an animal, or a part of an animal, of another species. See the discussion of so-called monsters at 769^{b}10–30, especially 769^{b}16–17.

Note 579
Iapygians: Iapygia is the heel of the Italian peninsula.
Shortly after the Persian Wars: In 473 BC. See Herodotus VII.170.

Note 580
In Argos, too, after the men of the seventh were killed by the Spartan Cleomenes: The battle referred to was fought at Sepeia c. 495 BC. It is unclear why "the men of the seventh" are so called. It may be because the battle was fought on the seventh day of the month, a day on which Apollo—who was thought to have been born on a seventh—was especially honored in Sparta. Cleomenes I was a king in Sparta c. 519–487 BC. See Herodotus VI.57.

Note 581

At the time of the war against Sparta service in the army was based on the citizen list: The war against Sparta is the Peloponnesian War (431–404 BC). Land forces were drawn from the class of citizens rich enough to afford hoplite weapons. Since these were mostly notables, defeat on land disproportionately affected their class.

Citizen list: See III 1 1275^{a}15n.

Note 582

As happened in Heraea: This event is otherwise unknown. Heraea was a city on the river Alpheus in western Arcadia in the Peloponnese.

Note 583

Oreus was overthrown when Heracleodorus became one of the officials and established a polity: Oreus, also called Hestiaea (V 4 1303^{b}33), was on the north end of the island of Euboea. The event described occurred in 377 BC, when Heraea revolted against the Spartans and joined the Athenian alliance, enabling Heracleodorus to win office and to change the constitution in a democratic (pro-Athenian) direction. See Herodotus VII.23, Thucydides I.144, Xenophon, *Hell.* V.4.56–57.

Note 584

Ambracia: Situated on the Arachthus River in northwest Greece, Ambracia was a colony of Corinth, founded by Gorgus the illegitimate son of Cypselus, the tyrant of Corinth (V 10 1310^{b}29). Gorgus, who also reigned as a tyrant, was replaced by his son Periander—on whose overthrow by a democracy, see V 4 1304^{a}31–33. The change Aristotle describes, therefore, is from a less inclusive—or more oligarchic—democracy to a more inclusive, or more extreme, one.

Note 585

The Achaeans co-colonized Sybaris with the Troezenians, but later, when the Achaeans became more numerous, they expelled the Troezenians: The Achaeans were from the north coast of the Peloponnese, the Troezenians from the Argolid peninsula. Sybaris, which was co-founded by them in c. 720 BC was in the instep of the Italian peninsula, and became renowned for its luxury—hence, "sybarite."

This was the cause of the curse that fell on the Sybarites: The precise nature of the curse is unknown, but driving out fellow colonists would have been viewed as an act of great sacrilege. In any case, in 510 BC the city was destroyed by the neighboring Croton and "due to their luxury and their wanton aggression had all their happiness taken away from them in seventy days" (Strabo VI.1.13, 9–10).

Note 586

In Thurii too, Sybarites came into conflict with their co-colonists: These Sybarites were citizens, not of the original city of Sybaris, but of its third reincarnation, which Aristotle is probably thinking of as an early stage in the foundation of the Panhellenic colony of Thurii.

Thurii: A city on the Tarentine gulf, close to Sybaris.

Note 587

In Byzantium . . .: Nothing further is known about these events.

Note 588

The Antissaeans forcibly expelled the Chian exiles they had admitted: The Antissaeans were Aeolians from the north coast of Lesbos; the Chians were Ionians from the island of Chios, south of Lesbos. The difference in race between them was presumably the cause of the conflict.

Note 589

The Zanclaeans were themselves expelled by the Samians they had admitted: The conflict at Zancle (modern-day Messina) is described in Herodotus VI.22–24.

Note 590

The Apolloniates on the Black Sea engaged in faction after admitting late-colonists: See V 6 1306^{a}7–9.

Note 591

The Syracusans, after the period of the tyrants: That is, after the fall of Thrasybulus in 467 BC.

Note 592

The Amphipolitans admitted late-colonists from Chalcis and were almost all expelled by them: Amphipolis on the river Strymon in Macedonia was founded in 436 BC as a colony of Athens. In 424 BC the city surrendered to the Spartan general Brasidas and thus became allied with Sparta. In 422 BC, Athens attempted to regain it, but was defeated in the battle of Amphipolis, in which Socrates fought (Plato, *Ap.* 28e) and Brasidas was killed. Amphipolis then became an independent city, which it remained until 357 BC. See Thucydides I.100, IV.102–108, V.6–11, 26.

Note 593

As we said earlier: At V 1 1301^{a}25–35, 1301^{b}35–40.

{In oligarchies . . . equal.} This paragraph seems out of place. Newman (IV p. 316) proposes that we read it at V 1 1301^{a}39 following the sentence that ends with "engage in faction." But it is not clear that a fully satisfactory place can be found for it.

Note 594

Their territory is not naturally well suited (*euphuôs*) **for there being *one* city:** Something is *euphuês* if it is well (*eu*) grown (*phuê*) or favored by nature in capacities, appearance, or some other respect. The situation of a bodily organ can be *euphuês* (*PA* III 4 666^{a}14), as can that of a city, as we see here; an animal can be *euphuês* as regards a function, such as reproduction (*GA* II 8 748^{b}8, 12), or the acquisition of a capacity, such as bearing the cold (*Pol.* VII 17 1336^{a}20) or becoming a poet (*Po.* 17 1455^{a}32) or a musician (*EE* VIII 2 1247^{b}22).

Note 595

Clazomenae: Located on a small island in the Gulf of Smyrna in Asia Minor, Clazomenae was the birthplace of the Presocratic philosopher Anaxagoras.

The inhabitants of Chytrus: Reading Χύτρῳ for OCT Χυτῷ.
Chytrus: Site unknown.
Colophon: Located a few miles south of Clazomenae on the coast of Asia Minor, Colophon is the birthplace of another great Presocratic philosopher, Xenophanes.
Notium: The port of Colophon.

Note 596
The town (*to astu*): See I 1 1252ᵃ6n.

Note 597
Even small factions become especially strong, however, when they arise among those in control: Compare Plato, *Rep.* 545c–d.
As happened for example in Syracuse in ancient times: The events referred to are thought to have occurred during the oligarchy of the Gomori, which was overthrown by the people shortly before Gelon's seizure of power (referred to at V 3 1302ᵇ31).

Note 598
[1] The error arises in the starting-point (*archê[i]*), **and [1a] the starting-point** (*archê*) **is said to be half the whole:** When Aristotle makes use of [1a] elsewhere, it is clear that *archê* means "starting-point": "We get a theoretical grasp on some starting-points through induction, some through perception, some through some sort of habituation, and others through other means. In each case we should follow the method of inquiry suited to their nature and make very serious efforts to define them correctly. For they are of great and decisive importance regarding what follows. It seems indeed that the starting-point is more than (*pleion*) half the whole and that many of the things we were inquiring about will at the same time become evident through it" (*NE* I 7 1098ᵇ4–8). But he is happy to connect this meaning of *archê* to the meaning it often has in political contexts: "The one in accord with whose deliberate choice what is moved is moved and what is changed is changed—for example, the rulers (*archai*) in cities, dynasties, and kingships are said to be *archai*, as are crafts, especially architectonic ones" (*Met.* V 1 1013ᵃ10–13). It is likely, then, that the sentence punningly exploits both meanings: errors in starting-points/rulers are particularly bad.

Note 599
As happened in Hestiaea: Which is referred to as Oreus at V 3 1303ᵃ18. Nothing else is known about this event, which must have occurred prior to the absorption of Hestiaea by Athens in 446 BC.

Note 600
In Delphi, a quarrel arising because of a marriage alliance (*kêdeia*) **was the starting-point of all the subsequent factions:** See Plutarch, *Precepta Gerendae Reipublicae*, Ch. 32 825b.
Delphi: A city on the southwestern spur of Mount Parnassus, in the valley of Phocis. The site of the famous oracle.

Note 601

In Mytilene, a faction concerning heiresses was the starting-point of many evils: See Thucydides III.2–50.

Paches captured their city: Paches, the Athenian general, captured Mytilene in 428 BC.

Note 602

Timophanes, Dexander: Otherwise unknown citizens of Mytilene.

Agent (*proxenos*): A *proxenos*, like a consul or ambassador, was the representative of city X to city Y, who was a citizen of Y, not of X.

Note 603

Mnaseas the father of Mnason and Euthycrates the father of Onomarchus: Onomarchus was an outstanding Phocian general, who was killed in the war with Philip of Macedon in 352 BC. Mnaseas, also a Phocian general, was killed a year later. Mnason may have been a companion of Aristotle's. See Athenaeus 264d.

Which conflict was the starting-point of the Sacred War for the Phocians: Phocis, in central Greece northwest of Boeotia, became embroiled in a lengthy war (355–347 BC) with Thebes, over an alleged sacrilege against Apollo (hence "Sacred War"), whose temple at Delphi was located on Phocian territory. It was ended by the intervention of Philip of Macedon. See Diodorus XVI.23–25, 27–33, 35–38, 56–61.

Note 604

In Epidamnus the constitution was changed because of matters having to do with a marriage: V 1 1301^{b}21–26 may describe the same change.

Note 605

The council of the Areopagus: See II 12 1273^{b}40n.

Which was held in high repute in the Persian Wars: In part because it paid eight drachmas a day to the sailors who manned the Greek ships in the battle of Salamis. See *Ath.* XXIII. 1–2.

Was believed to have made the Athenian constitution tighter: That is, less democratic. See IV 3 1290^{a}22–29.

Note 606

The seafaring mob: The navy was recruited from the poorer classes, since only strength was needed to row a trireme, and so was a powerfully democratic force in Athenian politics. See VI 7 1321^{a}13–14, Plato. *Rep.* 396a–b, *Lg.* 707b–c.

Salamis: An island in the Saronic gulf near Athens. The battle of Salamis in 480 BC was a decisive victory for the Greeks in the Persian Wars. See Herodotus VIII. 40–97.

Note 607

The battle against the Spartans at Mantinea: In this battle, in 418 BC, the pro-oligarchic Spartans defeated a pro-democratic coalition of Argive, Mantinean, and Athenian forces. The Argive notables, however, won a good reputation in the battle, and soon afterward, with Spartan help, overthrew the democracy in Argos. See Thucydides V.63–84, Diodorus XII.79, 80.1–3.

Note 608
In Syracuse, the people, having been responsible for victory in the war against the Athenians: The expeditionary Athenian force sent against Syracuse in 415 BC was totally destroyed two years later in a series of sea-battles in the harbor, responsibility for the victory is thus accorded—as in the case of the battle of Salamis—to the pro-democratic poorer citizens who manned the Syracusan ships.

Note 609
The tyrant Phoxus: Otherwise unknown.

Note 610
In Ambracia, the people joined with the opponents of Periander to expel him: In c. 580 BC. Further details are given at 1311ᵃ39–ᵇ1.

Note 611
The Four Hundred: The oligarchy that replaced the democracy in Athens in 411 BC. See Thucydides VIII.45–98.

Note 612
In Cos: Some associate these events with the defection of Cos from the Athenian Confederacy in 357 BC. Other sources mention the existence of a faction there in 366 BC. See Diodorus XV.76.2, Strabo XIV.2.19.
Cos: An island in the Dodecanese chain of islands, located in the southeastern Aegean, off the Anatolian coast of present-day Turkey.

Note 613
In Rhodes: See V 3 1302ᵇ23–24. The popular leaders needed money to pay the people to attend the assembly, since influencing the assembly was the source of their own power. They used money that should have been paid to the naval officials for this purpose, who were then unable to pay their workers and suppliers, and had lawsuits brought against them as a result. As a result, they united and overthrew the democracy that supported the popular leaders.

Note 614
In Heraclea: Many Greek cities were named "Heraclea," after the hero Heracles. V 6 1305ᵇ36 suggests that this one is the Heraclea on the Black Sea, which was founded by Megara c. 560 BC.

Note 615
In Megara: See V 3 1302ᵇ31.

Note 616
In Cyme: See II 8 1269ᵃ1n.
Thrasymachus: Perhaps the sophist, Thrasymachus of Chalcedon, who makes a memorable appearance in Book I of Plato's *Republic*, and to whom Aristotle refers

on five occasions: *SE* 34 183^{b}32, *Rh.* II 23 1400^{b}19–20, III 1 1404^{a}14, 8 1409^{a}2, 11 1313^{a}8.

Note 617
Public services: See III 6 1279^{a}11n.

Note 618
Pretty much most ancient tyrants arose from popular leaders: Compare Plato, *Rep.* 564d–566d.

Note 619
As in Miletus, where a tyranny arose out of the presidency (*prutaneia*): The tyranny may have been that of Thrasybulus. See III 13 1284^{a}27n, Herodotus I.20. The precise powers of the presidency in Miletus are not known.

Note 620
Pisistratus: The leader of the pro-democratic "hill-dwellers," against the rich landowning "plains-dwellers" (IV 15 1300^{a}25). In 561 BC he was able to persuade the Athenians to give him a bodyguard and make himself tyrant. See *Rh.* I 2 1357^{b}30–36, *Ath.* 13–14, Herodotus I.59.
Theagenes: Theagenes became tyrant of Megara in the latter half of the 7th cent BC, from which he was eventually driven out. See *Rh.* I 2 1357^{b}30–36, Thucydides I.126, Plutarch, *Aetia Roman et Graeca*, 295c–d.

Note 621
Dionysius: Dionysius I. See I 11 1259^{a}28n.
Daphnaeus: A general in Syracuse, who was supposed to relieve Acragas when it was besieged by the Carthaginians in 406 BC, but failed to do so, apparently because of his corruption. He was removed from office and killed by Dionysius in 405 BC. See Diodorus XII.96.3.

Note 622
Lygdamis of Naxos: Tyrant in Naxos c. 545–524 BC. Lygdamis, the leader of the democracy, supplied aid to Pisistratus, who later conquered Naxos and installed him as tyrant. See *Ath.* XV, *Oec.* II 2 1346^{b}7–12, Herodotus I.61, 64.
Naxos: The largest of the Cyclades group of islands, located in the central Aegean.

Note 623
Massilia: Modern-day Marseilles.
Istrus: On the Black Sea.
Heraclea: See V 5 1304^{b}31n.

Note 624
Cnidus: On the coast of southwest Asia Minor (modern-day Turkey).

Note 625
Erythrae: An Ionian city on the coast of Asia Minor.
Basilids: Probably descendants of the first kings (*basileis*), the family is also found at Ephesus and perhaps at Chios, which is opposite Erythrae.

Note 626

Those engaged in currying favor (*dêmagôgountôn*): That is, doing what a popular leader (*dêmagôgos*) does, but in this case with the aim of becoming such. See II 12 1274ᵃ10n.

Note 627

Among the Thirty in Athens Charicles and his followers became powerful: The oligarchy of the so-called Thirty Tyrants, of which Charicles was a member, was in control in Athens for a brief period in 404/3 BC. Compare Xenophon, *Hell.* II.3–4, Diodorus XIV.3–6, which portray Critias (the cousin of Plato's mother) rather than Charicles as the leader of the demagogues. See also *Ath.* XXXIV–XXXVIII, Plato, *Ap.* 32c–d.
The Four Hundred: These gained control in Athens in 411 BC. Phrynichus was one of its more extreme anti-democratic members. See *Ath.* XXXIII, Thucydides VIII.89–90.

Note 628

Larissa: The principal city of Thessaly is also mentioned at 1306ᵃ29–30 and at III 2 1275ᵇ26–30, V 10 1311ᵇ17–20.
Civic guards: See II 8 1262ᵃ22.

Note 629

Political clubs (*hetairia*)**:** Thucydides VIII.54.4 mentions "sworn associations (*xunômosiai*) which already existed in Athens for mutual support in lawsuits and in elections." To a certain extent these are the equivalent of the *hetairia* mentioned here. Thus *Ath.* XXXIV.34.3 mentions "the notables in the *hetaireiai* . . . who wanted an oligarchy," contrasting them with others "who did not belong to any *hetairia*, but were in other respects reputable citizens" and who "aimed at restoring the ancestral constitution." V 9 1310ᵃ9–10 mentions an oath that a member of certain oligarchies swears: "I will be hostile to the people and . . . plan whatever wrongs I can against them." See also II 11 1272ᵇ34n.
Abydus: On the Asiatic coast of the Hellespont. It probably became an oligarch in 411 BC when it seceded from the Athenian empire. See Thucydides VIII.62.

Note 630

Heraclea on the Black Sea: See V 5 1304ᵇ31–34.

Note 631

As Hipparinus did for Dionysius in Syracuse: Hipparinus was one of the generals from whose ranks Dionysius I (I 11 1259ᵃ28n), who later married Hipparinus' daughter Aristomache, became first supreme general then tyrant. Hipparinus' son Dion was a friend and student of Plato's, and later opposed Dionysius' son, Dionysius II. See Plutarch, *Dion* 3.

Note 632

In Amphipolis: See V 3 1303ᵇ2–3n. Nothing else is known about Cleotimus and his activities.

Note 633

Chares: A famous 4th-cent Athenian general. His activities in Aegina are otherwise unknown.

Note 634

Apollonia on the Black Sea: See V 3 1303^{a}36–38.

Note 635

An oligarchy that is in concord (*homonoousa*): "Concord (*homonoia*) seems to be something like friendship, and this is what legislators seek most, whereas faction, because it is enmity, they most seek to drive out" (*NE* VIII 1 1155^{a}24–26); "Concord too is apparently a feature fitted to friendship. That is why it is not agreement in belief, since that might occur even among people who do not know each other. Nor are people said to be in concord when they are of one mind about just anything—for example, on matters related to the heavens (for concord concerning these is not fitted to friendship). On the other hand, we do say that a city is in concord when people are of one mind about what is advantageous, deliberately choose the same things, and put into action the things they have resolved in common. Things doable in action, then, is what concord is concerned with, and of these, the ones that have a certain magnitude and where it is possible for both or all parties to attain their goals. A city is in concord, for example, when all resolve to have offices be elective, to form an alliance with Sparta, or to have Pittacus rule (when he too is willing to do so). But when each of the two parties wishes the rule for himself, like those in the *Phoenician Women*, they factionalize. For it is not concord when each of the two parties thinks the same thing, whatever it may be, but, rather, when they think it in connection with the same party (for example, when both the common people and the decent ones think that the best people should rule), since that way all the parties get what they are seeking. Concord is apparently political friendship, then, as it is in fact said to be, since it is concerned with things that are advantageous and ones that affect our life" (IX 6 1167^{a}22–^{b}4).

Note 636

Pharsalus: A city in Thessaly. At the time Aristotle is writing, Pharsalus enjoyed the favor of Philip of Macedon. Little else is known about the oligarchy there.

Note 637

Elis: In the northwestern Peloponnese.

Note 638

Their election was characteristic of a dynasty: See IV 6 1293^{a}26–30.
Similar to the one used to elect the senators in Sparta: See II 9 1270^{b}35–1271^{a}6.

Note 639

Timophanes in Corinth: During the war with Argos and Cleonae, c. 365 BC, the Corinthians hired four hundred mercenaries and put their general Timophanes in command. Timophanes then used these mercenaries to make himself tyrant, which caused his brother Timoleon to assassinate him. See Plutarch, *Timoleon* 4, Diodorus XVI.65.3–8.

Note 640

This happened in Larissa at the time of the rule of Simus the Aleuad: The Aleuads were a great Thessalian family. The Simus referred to is most probably the one who betrayed Thessaly to Philip of Macedon. See Demosthenes, *De Corona* 48. The events and people mentioned are otherwise unknown.
Abydus: See 1305b33n.

Note 641

The cases mentioned earlier in which marriage was the cause: See V 4 1303b37–1304a17.

Note 642

Diagoras overthrew the oligarchy of the cavalrymen in Eretria: Nothing further is known about these events.

Note 643

Archias: Tyrant of Thebes c. 379 BC.

Note 644

Their enemies had them bound in the pillory in the marketplace: A punishment commonly reserved for thieves. Nothing further is known about these events in Heraclea and Thebes.
Heraclea: See V 5 1304b31–34n.

Note 645

Like the one in Cnidus: See 1305b12–18.
Chios: See V 3 1303a34–35n.

Note 646

Which is just what is said to change oligarchies as well: See V 6 1306a13–22.

Note 647

The so-called Sons of the Maidens at Sparta (for they were descended from the Equals): The Equals (*homoioi*) were Spartan citizens, born of citizen parents, who possessed sufficient wealth to enable them to participate in the communal messes (see II 9 1271a26–37). Various accounts are given of the Sons of the Maidens: (1) They were the offspring of Spartans who were degraded to the rank of helots for failing to serve in the first Messenian War. (2) They were the illegitimate sons of young unmarried Spartan women who were encouraged to increase the population during that war. (3) They were sons of adulterous Spartan women conceived while their husbands were away at that war. They founded Tarentum in 708 BC.

Note 648

Lysander: The great political leader and commander of the Spartan fleet who defeated the Athenians at Aigospotami in 405 BC, thereby effectively winning the

Peloponnesian War. When the Thirty Tyrants, whom he had more or less installed in Athens, were deposed, he helped the more moderate oligarchs that succeeded them, and subsequently joined forces with them, in their struggle with a democratic group that had taken control of Piraeus. At this point King Pausanias, perhaps envious of the power that Lysander was accumulating (see Xenophon, *Hell.* II.4.29), intervened, arriving in Attica with an army of his own. He abandoned Lysander's policy of aiding the oligarchs, working out a settlement that restored democracy to Athens (*Hell.* IV.24–43, Diodorus XIV.33.5–6, Plutarch, *Lysander* 21). Later, in 398 BC, Lysander supported Agesilaus in his struggle with Leotychidas for the kingship. Once Agesilaus was elected, however, Lysander found himself once again in a subordinate position. It was this double dose of dishonor at the hands of first one then another Spartan king that seems to have led him to try to abolish the kingship (V 1 1301^{b}19–20) or replace it with an elective monarchy, open to every Spartan citizen (Diodorus XIV.13, Plutarch, *Lysander* XXIII–XXV, XXX).

Note 649

Like Cinadon, who instigated the rebellion against the Spartiates in the reign of Agesilaus: Cinadon was motivated to rebel, evidently, because he belonged to a class that was excluded from the honors of office. See Xenophon, *Hell.* III.3.4–11.

Agesilaus: Aegilsaus II was the Eurypontid king of Sparta c. 400–360 BC.

Note 650

It is also what happened in Sparta at the time of the Messenian War: The war referred to is the Second Messenian War (685–668 BC). See also II 9 1270^{a}3.

Tyrtaeus: A 7th-cent-BC elegiac poet from Sparta.

"Good Legislative Order": Fr. I.7–9 Diehl.

Note 651

Pausanias: The Spartan general who led the allied Greek forces in its victory over the Persians at Plataea in 479 BC, and in its recovery of Byzantium in the next year. This success led Pausanias to aspire to "become tyrant of Greece" (Herodotus V.32) and to enter into treasonous correspondence with Xerxes, the Persian king. He was recalled to Sparta and stripped of his leadership of the allied forces. He returned to Byzantium and renewed his intrigues. Recalled a second time to Sparta, he tried to foment rebellion among the helots by offering them freedom and citizenship. To escape arrest, he sought refuge in a temple, where he was allowed to starve to death. See Thucydides I.94–95, 128–134, Diodorus, XI.44–46.

Hanno: A leading figure in Carthage in the middle third of the 4th cent BC. He tried to poison the Carthaginian senators and, when that failed, to incite an insurrection among the slaves. He was betrayed and cruelly executed, and his entire family killed. See Justin XX.5, XXI.4.

Note 652

The aforementioned change occurred at Thurii: Little is known about these events, which seem unrelated to those mentioned at V 3 1303^{a}31–33.

Note 653

They were able as a result to get more . . . : Dreizehnter marks a lacuna in the text at this point.

Note 654

The city of the Locrians: Namely, Locri, which is on the east side of the toe of Italy. **Because a marriage alliance was formed with the tyrant Dionysius:** Dionysius I (I 11 1259^a28n) married Doris, the daughter of a prominent Locrian on the same day that he married Aristomache (V 6 1306^a12n). Dionysius II, the son of Dionysius I and Doris, on being driven out of Syracuse, sought refuge in Locri, where he promptly seized the acropolis and made himself tyrant. See Justin XXI.1–3, Strabo VI.1.8.

Note 655

What was said earlier: At V 3 1303^a20–25.

Note 656

This also happened in the case of the constitution of Thurii: Nothing beyond what Aristotle tells us is known about these events.

Note 657

This was discussed earlier: At IV 13 1297^a14–$^b1$. Aristotle himself seems to encourage the use of such a device at 1308^a28–30.

Note 658

As we mentioned earlier: V 6 1305^b24–27.

Note 659

Constitutions are preserved not only because of being far away from the factors that destroy them, but sometimes even by being nearby: See V 7 1307^b19–25.

Note 660

It is advantageous to have a law that tightens or loosens (*epiteinein ê anienai*) **the assessment:** As a musician tightens or loosens his instrument's strings until a certain target note is struck (IV 3 1290^a22–29), so it is too with vocal cords, sinews, and other string-like things (*GA* V 7 787^b10–24). Hence the notion of tightening and loosening gets employed wherever a certain tripartite structure is thought to exist, consisting of a continuous underlying subject, often referred to as "the more and the less" (*to mallon kai to hêtton*), a pair of opposed attributes that can vary in degree, and a target, typically a mean condition of some sort, that can be achieved by tightening or decreasing loosening their underlying subject so as to change the degree of the attributes. As a result, Aristotle speaks of tightening and loosening in characterizing a wide range of phenomena, from the parts of animals to political constitutions (*Pol.* V 9 1309^b18–31, *Rh.* I 4 1360^a23–30). In the case of noses and other such bodily parts, the continuous underlying subject is flesh and bone (or its shape), the pair of opposite attributes is hooked and snub, and the target—which lies somewhere in between the two, and so (as in political constitutions) in a mean of some sort—is being a straight nose, or at the very least a nose of some sort. In the case of colors, too, while many are constituted out of white and black in some definite ratio, others are constituted in "some incommensurable ratio of excess or deficiency," and so are apt for tightening and loosening (*Sens.* 3 439^{b}30).

Note 661
In monarchy: Dreizehnter with some mss. brackets καὶ ἐν μοναρχίᾳ for deletion.

Note 662
They should make their banishments be banishments to foreign parts: See 1302^{b}17–21.

Note 663
The most important thing in every constitution is for it to have the laws and the management of other matters ordered in such a way that it is not possible for the offices to make a profit: See Plato, *Rep.* 520e–521b.

Note 664
The handing over of the money should take place in the presence of all the citizens: That is, the handing over of public monies by an official leaving an office to a newly elected one.
Company (*lochos*): A *lochos* was originally a military classification, but here it is a civil administrative division of a city. On clan and tribe, see IV 15 1300^{a}25n.

Note 665
Torch-races: Relay races in which torches served in place of batons. See Plato, *Rep.* 328a1.

Note 666
Scientific knowledge (*epistêmê*): See IV 11 1295^{b}19n.

Note 667
Just as people can fail to serve their own interests well, even though they have the knowledge and are friendly to themselves, so nothing prevents them from being the same way where the community is concerned: A person who lacks self-control knows what the good is, or where his best interests lie, but does not act on his knowledge, typically because his appetite for immediate pleasure overcomes his wish for the long-term good (*NE* VII 1–3). A similar condition, Aristotle suggests, could exist, as regards the best interests of the community, in someone who has the capacity to hold a certain office and is a friend to the constitution. The result would be that he would not do what was best for it, even though he knew what was best (hence his capacity for office) and wished to do it (hence his friendship for the constitution).

Note 668
As does the most important element, so often mentioned, of keeping watch that the multitude wishing for the constitution is stronger than the one that does not wish for it: In fact it is mentioned only once, at any rate by Aristotle, at IV 12 1296^{b}14–16.

Note 669
Many of the features that are believed to be democratic destroy democracies, and many that are believed to be oligarchic destroy oligarchies: Compare Plato, *Rep.* b–c, *Lg.* 701e.

Note 670
Those who think that this is the one and only virtue pull the constitution toward the extreme: That is, virtue as conceived by democracy on the one hand and by oligarchy on the other.

Note 671
If it is "tightened" still more toward the extreme: See V 8 1308[b]4n.

Note 672
In some oligarchies, they now swear: See V 6 1305[b]32n.

Note 673
If indeed lack of self-control exists at the level of a single individual, it also exists at the level of a city: Compare VII 1 1323[b]32–36n.

Note 674
Everyone lives as he wishes: See V 1316[b]24, VI 4 1319[b]30, Plato, *Rep.* 557b.
As Euripides says: 646 Fr. 891 Nauck.

Note 675
Living with a view to the constitution should not be considered slavery, but preservation: See I 2 1253[a]26–27n.

Note 676
Kingship is in accord with aristocracy: Because both are in accord with virtue or merit (IV 2 1289[a]30–35, V 10 1310[b]32–34).
Tyranny is a combination of the lastmost (*hustatês*) **oligarchy and the lastmost democracy:** Lastmost or ultimate (*teleutaia*) oligarchy is a dynasty (IV 6 1293[a]30–34); ultimate democracy (= [4]) is where the people rule rather than the laws (1293[a]1–10). On tyranny as a mixture of these, see IV 11 1296[a]3–4, 1312[b]34–38.

Note 677
Kingship arose to provide help for the decent against the people: Reading ἐπὶ τὸν δῆμον with OCT for Dreizehnter and the mss. ἀπὸ τοῦ δήμου ("to provide help from the people for the decent"). The help a king provides is not partisan, however, but just to both parties. See 1310[b]40–1311[a]2.

Note 678
"Doers of the people's business": These so-called *dêmiourgoi* existed in many Greek cities.
"Sacred ambassadors": These so-called *theôroi* were sent to attend sacred games and to consult oracles on behalf of their city.

Note 679

Pheidon of Argos: In the mid-7th cent BC Pheidon converted the kingship of Argos into a tyranny. According to Herodotus, "this was the Pheidon who established weights and measures for the Peloponnesians and who displayed absolutely the greatest act of wanton aggression of any Greek, in that he drove out the Elean marshals of the games and set the contests at Olympia himself" (VI.127).

Phalaris: Tyrant of Acragas in Sicily in the first half of the 6th cent BC. He allegedly roasted his enemies alive inside a bronze bull (Pindar, *Pythian* I.95–96), something Aristotle cites as the action of someone with a depraved (because savagely cruel) nature (*NE* VII 5 1148^b19–24). See also *Rh.* II 20 1393^b8–23.

Panaetius in Leontini: The first Sicilian tyrant. He is mentioned again at V 12 1316^a34–37. Leontini (modern Lentini) is twenty miles northwest of Syracuse.

Cypselus in Corinth: Mentioned again at V 12 1315^b22–29. According to Herodotus, "he drove many of the Corinthians into exile, deprived many of their wealth, and many more of their lives. When he had reigned for thirty years and died in prosperity, he was succeeded by his son Periander" (V.92).

Pisistratus in Athens: See V 5 1305^a23n.

Dionysius in Syracuse: See I 11 1259^a28n.

Note 680

As we said: At 1310^b2–3.

Or on these together with capacity: See III 13 1284^a7.

Note 681

Codrus: A legendary early king of Athens, who is associated with Alcestis and Achilles by Plato, *Sym.* 208d. According to one traditional account he was already king when he gave his life to prevent Athens from being invaded by the Dorians.

Cyrus: Cyrus the Great was the first ruler of the Persian empire (559–529 BC). See Plato, *Menex.* 239d–e.

The kings of the Spartans: Probably, the first ones, Agis and Eurypon.

Of the Macedonians: The story of how Perdiccas became king of the Macedonians (mid-7th cent BC) is told in Herodotus VIII.137–139.

Macedonians: Inhabitants of Macedonia, situated on the northern periphery of Greece.

Of the Molossians: The kings of the Molossians in Epirus in northwest Greece, who were allegedly descended from Neoptolemus son of Achilles.

Note 682

That is also why it is characteristic of a tyrant to want to get more wealth, and of a king to get more of the things pertaining to honor: On the connection between wealth and the pursuit of pleasure, see I 9 1257^b40–1258^a5.

Note 683

A king's bodyguard consists of citizens, whereas a tyrant's consists of foreigners: See III 14 1285^a24–29.

Note 684

The advice that Periander gave to Thrasybulus: See III 13 1284^{a}26–33.

Note 685

Harmodius attacked because of his sister, and Aristogeiton because of Harmodius: Hipparchus, son of Pisistratus, tried to seduce Harmodius the boyfriend of Aristogeiton. When his advances were twice repulsed, he took revenge by arranging to have Harmodius' sister publicly humiliated. In revenge Harmodius and Aristogeiton plotted to kill Hipparchus and his brothers, but succeeded in killing Hipparchus only (514 BC). In the process Harmodius was killed, as later was Aristogeiton. Hippias survived as tyrant for four more years, until his expulsion by the Athenians, aided by the Spartans. Harmodius and Aristogeiton were later celebrated in Athens as tyrannicides. See *Ath.* XVIII, Herodotus V.55–65, Thucydides VI.54–59, Plato, *Sym.* 182c.

Note 686

People plotted against Periander, tyrant of Ambracia: Nephew of Periander of Corinth. See V 3 1303^{a}23n, 4 1304^{a}31–33.

Philip was attacked by Pausanias because he allowed him to be treated with wanton aggression by Attalus and his coterie: The attack took place in Aegeae (the early capital of Macedon) in 336 BC. The story involves two of Philip's boyfriends, both named Pausanias, one of whom, out of jealousy, caused the death of the other, who was a friend of Attalus, uncle of Cleopatra, one of Philip's wives. In revenge, Attalus invited the surviving Pausanias to dinner, got him drunk, and had him sexually abused by mule skinners. Pausanias complained to Philip, and, when his complaint went unheeded, stabbed him to death. See Diodorus XVI.91–94.

Note 687

Amyntas the Little was attacked by Derdas because he boasted of having deflowered him (*dia to kauchêsasthai eis tên hêlikian*): Literally "boasted in regard to his youth" or "boasted for [having taken] his [bloom of] of youth." Amyntas and Dardas are otherwise unknown.

Note 688

The attack on Evagoras of Cyprus by a eunuch: Evagoras was king of Salamis in Cyprus 411–374 BC. See Diodorus XV.47.8.

Cyprus: Large island in the eastern Mediterranean, off the coasts of present-day Syria and Turkey.

Note 689

The attack on Archelaus by Crataeas is an example: Archelaus II was king of Macedon c. 413–399 BC. For Plato (*Grg.* 470d–471d, 525d), he is the archetype of the corrupt tyrant, who gained the throne by murdering his uncle, cousin, and half-brother. Thucydides, however, praised him for strengthening his kingdom more than its previous eight kings put together (II.100.2). Socrates declined to join Archelaus' court (*Rh.* II 23 1398^{a}24–26, DL II **[25]**), but the poets Agathon, Euripides (1311^{b}30–34), and Timotheus did join it. See Plutarch, *Amatorius* 23.

Note 690
Elimeia: In central Greece, south of Macedon.
Cleopatra: See 1311^b3n.

Note 691
Aenus: A town in Thrace on the trade route between the Black Sea and the Aegean.
Adamas: Apparently a eunuch in the service of Cotys.
Cotys: King of Thrace, assassinated in 359 BC.

Note 692
The Penthilids of Mytilene: The ruling family in the early Mytilenian oligarchy in Lesbos, which claimed descent from Penthilus, illegitimate son of Orestes. The revolt by Megacles occurred sometime before 650 BC.

Note 693
Later, Smerdes killed Penthilus: Either Megacles had failed to kill Penthilus, or he was not a member of the oligarchic Penthilids.

Note 694
Decamnichus became leader of the revolt against Archelaus, being the first to incite his adversaries—the cause of his anger was that Archelaus had handed him over to the poet Euripides for flogging (Euripides was enraged by a remark made about his bad breath): Plutarch, *Sym.* II.1.9 remarks that "a jest on anyone for his stinking breath or filthy nose is irksome." But hardly sufficiently so, one would think, to merit a flogging. It may be, though, that the breath itself was less an issue than what Decamnichus implied it meant about its possessor's oral practices. This would help explain why Euripides was so angry about it. Euripides died in 406 BC; the revolt against Archelaus did not occur until seven years later in 399 BC.

Note 695
As we mentioned: At 1311^a25.

Note 696
Artapanes killed Xerxes, fearing a charge in connection with the murder of Darius: Xerxes was king of Persia (486–465 BC), Darius was his oldest son, and Artapanes (or Artabanus), the leader of his bodyguard. Presumably, Xerxes usually drank heavily at dinner, and so was prone to forget what he had said.

Note 697
As when someone saw Sardanapalus carding wool with the women: Sardanapalus was a king of the Assyrians (669–626 BC) renowned for his luxurious lifestyle. He is cited by Aristotle as a paradigm of someone devoted to the gratification of his appetites (*NE* I 5 1095^b19–22, *EE* I 5 1216^a16–19). According to the storytellers, Sardanapalus was not just carding wool, but wearing the clothes, jewelry, and makeup of a courtesan, and mimicking her voice and gestures. See Athenaeus XII.528e–530c, Diodorus II.23–27, Justin I.3.

Note 698

Dion attacked Dionysius the Younger because of contempt: Dionysius II (the Younger) was the son of Doris, one of the wives of Dionysius I (V 7 1307^{a}38–39n). Dion was the brother of Aristomache, another of his wives, and husband of Aristomache's daughter Arete. He was also, more famously, the friend and pupil of Plato (*Ep*. VII). The story is continued at 1312^{a}33–39.
Dionysius himself was always drunk: One of his drinking parties allegedly went on for ninety days (Plutarch, *Dion* VII.4).

Note 699

Cyrus attacked Astyages: Astyages was the last king of the Medes (594–559 BC). Cyrus (1310^{b}38n) was his grandson as well as his general. See Herodotus I.107–130.

Note 700

Seuthes the Thracian attacked Amadocus: Probably Seuthes II, son of Sparadocus (Xenophon, *An*. VII.2.32). The attack on Amadocus is otherwise unknown.
Amadocus: Amadocus I was Thracian king of the Odrysae (a union of Thracian tribes) from 410 BC until the beginning of the 4th cent.

Note 701

As Mithridates attacked Ariobarzanes: Probably the Ariobarzanes who was satrap of the Persian province of Pontus and led the Satrap's revolt c. 362 BC (Diodorus, XV.90). According to Xenophon (*Cyr*. VIII.8.4), he was Mithridates' father.

Note 702

Courage possessed of power is boldness (*thrasos*): In the bad sense *thrasos* is rashness, and is the extreme between which and cowardice courage is the mean (*EE* II 3 1220^{b}38–1221^{a}12). Here, however, it seems to be a sort of courage, and so not necessarily bad.

Note 703

{Others . . . prevail}: This sentence should perhaps follow the word "drunk" (*methuonta*) at 1312^{a}6 in the previous paragraph, as Newman suggests.

Note 704

Dion: See 1312^{a}4n.

Note 705

Because of the contrariety between the deliberate choices of the two constitutions: The deliberate choices in question are presumably those relating to their different conceptions of happiness and how best to pursue them (VII 8 1327^{a}37–^{b}2).
And because all people do what they wish when they have the power: On the connection between deliberate choice and wish, see IV 4 1292^{a}6.

Note 706

As Hesiod says: *Works and Days* 25.
The ultimate democracy is in fact a tyranny: See IV 4 1292^{a}2–38.

Note 707

The Spartans overthrew a large number of tyrannies: Including, among many others (Thucydides I.18.1), one in Athens. See 1311^{a}36–39n. Earlier we heard that they also overthrew a number of democracies (V 7 1307^{b}23–24).

As did the Syracusans during the time when they were governed in a good way (*kalôs*): That is, while they had an aristocracy (466–413 BC).

Note 708

The tyranny of Gelon: Gelon was tyrant of Syracuse 485–478 BC. He was succeeded by his brother Hiero (mentioned at V 11 1313^{b}13–15), who died in 467 BC. Thrasybulus became tyrant on Hiero's death, only to be overthrown ten months later, as we learn at V 12 1315^{b}34–39.

Note 709

Dion, who was related by marriage to Dionysius, marched against him: See 1312^{a}36–39.

Note 710

Lives of indulgence (*apolaustikôs*): "People seem (which is not unreasonable) to get their suppositions about the good—that is, happiness—from their lives. For ordinary people, the most vulgar ones, suppose it to be pleasure. And that is why the life they like is the life of indulgence. . . . They have an argument for their choice, though, because many of those in positions of control feel the same as Sardanapalus" (*NE* I 5 1095^{b}14–22). On Sardanapalus, see 1312^{a}1n.

Note 711

Anger (*orgê*): "Let anger be desire, involving pain, for apparent revenge, because of apparent contempt on the part of a person unfitted to treat the person himself, or one of those close to him, with contempt . . . [Where] contempt is an activation of belief concerned with what appears worthless" (*Rh.* II 2 1378^{a}30–^{b}12).

Anger should also be taken as a part of hatred, since in a way it gives rise to the same sorts of actions: Anger is not part of the definition of hatred, since we can hate people for things other than contemptuous treatment. But for present purposes we can think of attacks on tyrants that are motivated by anger as included in, or as a part of, those motivated by hatred, since they result in the same sorts of actions.

Note 712

Rational calculation (*logismos*): Rational calculation, of which deliberation (*bouleusis*) is a variety, is the function of the calculative or deliberative part (*logistikon, bouleutikon*) of the soul, of which practical wisdom is the virtue and action the primary focus (*NE* VI 1 1139^{a}11–17, 5 1140^{a}24–28). Sometimes calculation is a matter of measuring or counting, as when people use pebbles to calculate such things as the produce tax on animals (*SE* I 1 165^{a}9–10, *Oec.* II 1348^{a}23), but more often, as here, it is a matter of reasoning or constructing arguments of the sort that might bear on practical questions to which no craft or science provides an explicit answer (*Top.* VI 6 145^{b}16–20, *Rh.* I 2 1357^{a}1–4, *NE* VI 5 1140^{a}28–30). Hence it is often coupled with inquiry (*zêtêsis*), either as the means it employs or as the embodiment and justification of its outcome (*MA* 7 701ª17–20, *NE* VI 9 1142ᵇ2, 15, VII 3 1147ª25–31).

Note 713
Spirited feelings (*tois thumois*): See III 16 1287ª31n.
The tyranny of the Pisistratids: See 1311ª36–39n.

Note 714
Anger involves pain, so that it is not easy to rationally calculate: "If the appetites are large and intense, they even knock out rational calculation" (*NE* III 12 1119ᵇ10). Since "appetite is concerned with what is pleasant and what is painful" (2 1111ᵇ16–17), the pain involved in anger will be accompanied by an appetite to avoid or remove it that will disable rational calculation.

Note 715
Unmixed or ultimate oligarchies and ultimate democracies: See IV 4 1292ª4–37, 5 1292ᵇ5–10, 6 1293ª30–34, 11 1296ª1–4, 14 1298ª29–33.

Note 716
Ultimate democracies and oligarchies are in fact divided tyrannies: In the sense that the tyrant instead of being one undivided person is divided into the many individuals who make up the people in the one case and the oligarchy in the other.

Note 717
But the tyrant rules even when they do not wish it: Reading ὁ τύραννος with the mss. for OCT τύραννος.

Note 718
The kingships of the Molossians: See V 10 1310ᵇ37–40n.

Note 719
The office was divided into two parts from the start: See II 9 1271ª22n.
Theopompus: King of Sparta c. 720–675 BC.
The overseers: See II 9 1270ᵇ6–17.

Note 720
The one we mentioned some time ago as tending to preserve tyranny: At 1311ª8–22, and prior to that at III 13 1284ª26–33.

Note 721
Not allowing places of leisure (*scholai*) **and other leisurely gatherings** (*scholastikoi*): Or "schools and other scholarly gatherings." See II 9 1271ᵇ5n.

Note 722
They will be habituated to think humble thoughts (*phronein mikron*) **by always doing slavish service:** Self-confidence is *phronêmatia* (1313ª40), *phronein mikron* (literally, "think small") what militates against it.

Note 723
The so-called women informers of Syracuse: See Plutarch, *Dion* XXVIII, *De Curiositate* XVI, where these informers are men.
Hiero: See V 10 1312^{b}11n.

Note 724
They cannot afford a militia: Reading μήτε with Dreizehnter and the mss. for OCT ἤ τε.

Note 725
The pyramids of Egypt: See Herodotus II.124–125.
The Cypselid monuments: In Corinth. They included a golden statue of Zeus. See V 12 1315^{b}22–29, Plato, *Phdr.* 236b.
The construction of the temple of Olympian Zeus by the Pisistratids: Begun by Pisistratus in 6th cent BC and completed by the Roman emperor Hadrian, some of its columns are still standing. See V 5 1305^{a}23n.
Olympian Zeus: Zeus, god of sky and thunder, ruled as king of the gods on Mount Olympus. The epithet "Olympian" picks him out as having that role. As Zeus Xenios, he was the patron of hospitality to strangers (*xenia*), as Zeus Herkios, he was keeper of oaths, and so on.
The works on Samos commissioned by Polycrates are all examples of this: Including an underground aqueduct, a mole in front of the harbor, and the largest known temple. See Herodotus III.60.
Polycrates: Tyrant of Samos c. 535–522 BC.

Note 726
Dionysius: See I 11 1259^{a}28n.

Note 727
No one would do this who had free thoughts (*phronêma echôn eleutheron*): That is the sorts of thoughts that, as the opposite of humble ones, are characteristic of someone with self-confidence, as opposed to a slave. See 1313^{b}8n and, on freedom, III 9 1280^{a}5n.

Note 728
Decent people: See II 7 1267^{b}6n.
Show friendship, or [at least] do not flatter: A true friend loves someone for his qualities, for who he is. A flatterer is someone who gives the appearance of doing this, but does not. See *Rh.* I 11 1371^{a}17–24.

Note 729
A small-souled person (*mikropsuchos*): "A person who thinks himself worthy of smaller things than he is, is small-souled, whether he is worthy of great or moderate things, but also if he is worthy of small ones and thinks himself worthy of ones that are yet smaller. Also, the person who is most small-souled of all would seem to be the one who is worthy of great things. For what would he do if he were not worthy of so much?" (*NE* IV 3 1123^{b}8–13); "A small-souled person who is worthy

of good things will deprive himself of the things he is worthy of and thus does seem to have something bad in him, stemming from his not thinking of himself as worthy of good things and from being ignorant of himself. For otherwise he would have reached out for the things he was worthy of, since they are certainly good ones. Nevertheless, people like that do not seem to be silly, at least, but, rather, to be lacking in self-esteem. Their belief about themselves actually seems to make them worse, though. For each sort of person seeks what is in accord with his worth, but these people avoid even noble actions and pursuits because they think they are unworthy of them, and similarly external goods" (1125^{a}19–27).

Note 730
The defining marks: See I 9 1258^{a}18n.

Note 731
These three hypotheses: See II 9 1269^{a}32n.

Note 732
If he gives this up, he also gives up being a tyrant: Since a tyrant must rule also over subjects who do not wish it. See II 6 1265^{b}40n.

Note 733
Spend lavishly on courtesans, foreigners, and artists (*technitais*): A *technitês* in this context is not so much an ordinary craftsman (which is one meaning of the term) as a theatrical artist, whether a musician, actor, or dancer, or someone involved in the sorts of extravagant building projects mentioned at 1313^{b}21–24. The focus, in any case, is on extravagant expenditures on luxury items.

Note 734
He must cultivate military virtue: Reading πολεμικῆς with OCT and Dreizehnter for mss. πολιτικῆς ("political virtue").

Note 735
A tyrant must do the contrary of pretty much all the things we mentioned before: At 1313^{a}34–^{b}32.

Note 736
Of bold character (*êthos trasun*): See V 10 1312^{a}19n.

Note 737
Two in particular: Reading δυοῖν for OCT δυεῖν.
The sort directed against the youth: Typically sexual in nature.

Note 738
Heraclitus: DK B85 = TEGP 130 F85. Heraclitus of Ephesus (flourished c. 500 BC) was one of the greatest of the Presocratic philosophers and originator of the doctrine that everything flows or is in flux.
"It pays with soul": That is, a spirited person is willing to lay down his life for what he cares about.
Spirit: See III 16 1287^{a}31n.

Note 739

Half wicked (*hêmiponeron*): "[A person who lacks self-control] acts voluntarily (for in a way he acts knowing both what he is doing and for the sake of what), but he is not a wicked person, since his deliberate choice is decent. So he is half wicked" (*NE* VII 10 1152ᵃ15–17).

Note 740

V 12: This chapter consists of two parts: (1) a list of long-lasting tyrannies, and (2) a discussion of Plato's account of constitutional change in *Rep.* VIII. (1) omits the tyranny of Dionysius I, which lasted more or less for fifty years, and somewhat intrusively mentions oligarchy (1315ᵇ12) in a discussion devoted to monarchy. On these grounds some scholars have doubted its authenticity. In the case of the omission of Dionysius' tyranny, however, we might note that it is hardly an example of the sorts of moderate tyrannies on which Aristotle is likely focusing to illustrate his claim that these are, or tend to be, the most long lasting (11 1315ᵇ7–8). And, without the omission, the intrusion seems somewhat insignificant. (2), for its part, follows a sentence that seems to bring this chapter to a close (1315ᵇ40–1316ᵃ1), and seems oddly placed, since Aristotle usually begins discussion of a topic by listing and criticizing the views of his predecessors (as, for example, in *Pol.* II). Moreover, its characterization of Carthage (1316ᵃ34n, 1316ᵇ5n) is anomalous. So there is perhaps some reason to question its placement, as well as the authenticity of, at any rate, some of its elements.

Note 741

The longest-lasting tyranny was that of the sons of Orthagoras and of Orthagoras himself: Their tyranny was founded in Sicyon, which is just west of Corinth, in 670 BC. See Herodotus VI.126.

Note 742

Cleisthenes: The grandson of Orthagoras and the grandfather of the Athenian reformer of the same name (III 2 1275ᵇ36n).

Note 743

Pisistratus once allowed himself to be summoned for trial before the Areopagus: Pisistratus (V 5 1305ᵃ23n) was charged with murder, but his accuser was afraid to show up at the trial. See *Ath.* XVI.8, Plutarch, *Solon* XXXI.

Note 744

The second longest tyranny was that of the Cypselids in Corinth: Founded c. 657 BC.

Note 745

Periander, Gorgus: Gorgus was half-brother of Periander (III 13 1284ᵃ26n) and succeeded him as tyrant.

Note 746

The third longest was that of the Pisistratids in Athens: See V 5 1305ᵃ23–24, 10 1311ᵃ36–39, 11 1313ᵇ23.

Note 747

The longest lasting of the remaining tyrannies was the one associated with Gelon and Hiero at Syracuse: See V 3 1302^b31–33, 1303^a38–$^b2$, 10 1312^b9–17.

Note 748

In the *Republic* there is a discussion by Socrates dealing with [constitutional] changes: See Plato, *Rep.* 545c–569c.

Note 749

[Plato] claims that its cause is that nothing remains as it is, but that everything undergoes a sort of cyclical change, and that the starting-point of this lies in the elements four and three, which "married with five, give two harmonies," whenever, as he says, the number of this figure becomes cubed: "[*Socrates*] Now for the birth of a divine creature [= the universe (*Ti.* 30b–d, 32d, 34a–b)] there is a cycle comprehended by a perfect number, while for a human being, it is the first number in which are found increases involving both roots and powers, comprehending three intervals and four terms, of factors that cause likeness and unlikeness, increase and decrease, and make all things mutually agreeable and rational in their relations to each other. Of these factors, the base ones—four in relation to three, together with five—give two harmonies when thrice increased. One is a square, so many times a hundred. The other is of equal length one way but oblong. One of its sides is one hundred squares of the rational diameter of five each diminished by one, or alternatively one hundred squares of the irrational diameter each diminished by two. The other side is a hundred cubes of three. This whole geometrical number controls better and worse births" (*Rep.* 546b–c). The human geometrical number is the product of 3, 4, and 5 "thrice increased": if $(3 \times 4 \times 5) \times (3 \times 4 \times 5) = (3 \times 4 \times 5)^2$ is one increase, $(3 \times 4 \times 5) \times (3 \times 4 \times 5) \times (3 \times 4 \times 5) \times (3 \times 4 \times 5) = (3 \times 4 \times 5)^4$ is three. This formula included "increases involving both roots and powers": $(3 \times 4 \times 5)$ is a root; its indices are powers. It "comprehends" three "intervals," symbolized by $\times$, and four "terms," namely, the roots. The resulting number, 12,960,000, can be represented geometrically as: (1) a square whose sides are 3,600 or (2) an "oblong" or rectangle whose sides are 4,800 and 2,700. (1) is "so many times a hundred": 36 times. (2) is obtained as follows. The "rational diameter" of 5 is the nearest rational number to the real diameter of a square whose sides are 5. This diameter = $\sqrt{5^2 + 5^2} = \sqrt{50} = 7$. Since the square of 7 is 49, we get the longer side of the rectangle by diminishing 49 by 1 and multiplying the result by 100. This gives 4,800. The "irrational diameter" of 5 is $\sqrt{50}$. When squared (= 50), diminished by 2 (= 48), and multiplied by 100 this, too, is 4,800. The short side, "a hundred cubes of three," = 2,700. The significance of the number is more controversial. The factors "that cause likeness and unlikeness, increase and decrease, and make all things mutually agreeable and rational in their relations to each other" are probably the numbers, since odd numbers were thought to cause likeness and even ones unlikeness (*Ph.* III 4 203^a13–15). Of the numbers significant in human life, one is surely the 100 years of its maximum span (*Rep.* 615a8–b1). Another might be the number of days in a year (roughly 360), and a third might be the divisions of those days into smaller units determined by the sun's place in the sky, since it is the sun that provides for "the coming to be, growth, and nourishment" of all visible things (509b2–4). Assuming that those units are the 360 degrees of the sun's path around the earth, the number of moments in a human life that have a potential effect on its coming to be, growth, and nourishment would be 100 × 360 × 360 or 12,960,000—Plato's human geometrical number.

Note 750
The constitution at Sicyon changed from the tyranny of Myron to that of Cleisthenes: See 1315ᵇ11–22.
Into oligarchy, like that of Antileon in Chalcis: The other tyranny at Chalcis mentioned by Aristotle is that of Phoxus (V 4 1304ᵃ29–31), which was followed by a democracy, not by the tyranny of Antileon. The two tyrannies are otherwise unknown.
Into democracy, like that of Gelon: See V 3 1303ᵃ38–ᵇ2.
Into aristocracy, like that of Charilaus in Sparta: See II 10 1271ᵇ25n.
The one in Carthage: Because 1316ᵇ5–6 states that Carthage has "not yet undergone change," while II 11 1272ᵇ24–33 states that it never had a tyranny or any significant faction, some editors bracket this clause as an interpolation.

Note 751
In Leontini, to the tyranny of Panaetius: See V 10 1310ᵇ29n.
In Gela, to that of Cleander: Assassinated in 498 BC after being tyrant for seven years. See Herodotus VII.154–155.
Gela: City in southern Italy.
In Rhegium, to that of Anaxilaus: 494–476 BC. Rhegium is on the Italian side of the straits of Messina. See Herodotus VI.23, VII.165, 170.

Note 752
In Carthage, which is governed democratically: The characterization is strange, since Carthage is said to be an aristocracy (IV 7 1293ᵇ14–16), although with some democratic features (II 11 1273ᵃ6–13).

Note 753
The former turn their thought (*noun*) **toward [change]:** On *nous*, see I 5 1254ᵇ5n.

BOOK VI

Note 754
We have already discussed: At IV 14–16, V 1–12.

Note 755
Those couplings that should be investigated, but up to now have not been: These hybrid constitutions are not discussed in the *Politics* as we have it.

Note 756
The first is the one mentioned earlier, namely, that there are different varieties of the people: See IV 4 1291ᵇ14–28, 6 1292ᵇ22–1293ᵃ34, 12 1296ᵇ24–31.

Note 757

The features that properly belong to its hypothesis: See II 9 1269ᵃ32n.

As we said earlier in our discussions of the destructions and preservations of constitutions: See V 9 1309ᵇ18–35.

Note 758

Axioms (*axiômata*): "An immediate deductive starting-point I call a posit if we cannot show it but it is not necessary for anyone who is to learn anything to grasp it; and one that it is necessary for anyone who is to learn anything whatever to grasp, I call an axiom (since there are some things of this sort), for we are accustomed to use this name especially of such things" (*APo.* I 2 72ᵃ14–18). Here the meaning is close to that of *hupothesis*. See VI 2 1317ᵃ40.

Note 759

Democratic justice is equality in accord with number: Equality in accord with number involves equal participation in political office by each citizen, and so an interchange of ruling and being ruled (1317ᵇ15–16, II 2 1261ᵃ30–ᵇ6). It does not seem to have to involve equality of property, since none of the ways of establishing it in VI 3 requires a redistribution of property.

Note 760

Result (*ergon*): See I 2 1252ᵇ4n.

Note 761

Or bodies chosen from all: Reading ἢ ἐκ πάντων with some mss. for OCT καὶ ἐκ πάντων ("and bodies chosen from all").

Note 762

As we said in the methodical inquiry preceding this one: See IV 15 1299ᵇ38–1300ᵃ4.

Note 763

The controlling assemblies (*tas ekklêsias tas kurias*): The reference is to the meetings of assemblies like that of the Athenian assembly described in *Ath.* XLIII.4: "In each prytany [= one tenth of a year] there is one controlling assembly (*mian men kurian*), in which the people have to ratify the continuance of the officials in office, if they served in office (*archein*) well, and consider the funding of the corn supply and the defense of the country. On this day, too, impeachments (*eisaggelias*) are introduced by those who wish to do so, lists of confiscated properties are read out, and also applications for inheritances and wards of state, so that nobody may be ignorant of any unclaimed estates."

Note 764

[10]: This sentence is bracketed for deletion by Dreizehnter and by Keyt on the grounds that it does not fit on a list of institutions. The thought, though, may be that just as family, wealth, and education are positive factors in determining suitability for office in an oligarchy, so lack of breeding, poverty, and vulgarity are such factors in a democracy. This is not quite an institution but it does have obvious institutional impact.

Note 765

Should they divide the assessed property so that that of five hundred citizens equals that of a thousand others, and then give equal power to the thousand as to the five hundred: We are to suppose two groups, one of the rich, with five hundred members, and one of the poor, with a thousand. If we distribute political power and office so that each group has the same amount, have we treated rich and poor as equality in accord with number demands?

Note 766

Democrats say that justice is whatever seems so to the greater number: See VI 2 1317^{b}5–7.

Note 767

It is tyranny, since if one person has more than the others who are rich, then, in accord with oligarchic justice, he is just in ruling alone: See III 13 1283^{b} 13–27.

Note 768

As we said earlier: At III 10 1281^{a}14–28.

Note 769

When they have the power to get more: See II 7 1266^{b}37n.

Note 770

VI 4: On Aristotle's different accounts of the kinds of democracy, see II 6 1265^{b}27n.

Note 771

In the discussions before these: At IV 4 1291^{b}30–1292^{a}38, 6 1292^{b}25–1293^{a}10.

Note 772

And [1] because they do not have the necessities, [2] they spend their time (*diatribousi*) at their work and [3] do not have an appetite for other people's property: Reading τὸ μὴ ἔχειν in [1] with the mss. for OCT τὸ ἔχειν ("and because they have the necessities"). Generally, it is the need for necessities that drives people to work, so that if they are already supplied with these it is unclear why they would spend their time working. What makes the OCT emendation of [1] attractive is [3], since it seems difficult to see why people who lack the necessities would not have an appetite for other people's property. But an answer to this is at least suggested in [2] by the use of the verb *diatribein*: because the farmers spend their time working to supply themselves with the necessities of life, they stay isolated on their farms and have no time left over to meet their neighbors and cast covetous eyes on their property, just as they have none left over to attend assemblies or hang out in the marketplace, where the possessions of others are readily observable (1319^{a}30–32). Nonetheless, the case for emendation remains a fairly strong one.

Note 773

As in Mantinea: See also V 4 1304^{a}25–27.

Note 774
Their capacities: See III 13 1284^{a}7.

Note 775
The base element that exists in every human being: See III 16 1287^{a}28–32n.

Note 776
Oxylus: Probably the mythical ancient founder of Elis, on which see V 6 1306^{a}15–19.

Note 777
The Amphytaeans: Amphytis was a small city on the northeast coast of Pallene in Chalcidice.

Note 778
Their way of life is base, and there is no element of virtue involved in the work to which the multitude of vulgar people, tradesmen, and hired laborers put their hand: Explained at I 13 1260^{a}39–^{b}2, VIII 2 1337^{b}4–21.

Note 779
A democracy that is good and [like] a polity: Or "a good democracy or a polity" (Keyt) or "a good democracy, that is, a polity" (Pellegrin). On Aristotle's various accounts of polity, see II 6 1265^{b}28n.

Note 780
Democracies should deviate in order [from the best], always excluding a worse multitude: The best democracy includes only the best multitude, which is that of the farmers, while excluding the next best, or least worse, multitude, which is that of the herdsmen. And so on.

Note 781
The ultimate democracy, because everyone has a share, is not one that every city can tolerate: For one thing, not every city is rich enough to pay to have everyone participate. See IV 6 1293^{a}1–10.

Note 782
The factors that cause the destruction of this and other constitutions have pretty much all been discussed earlier: In V 5.

Note 783
Cyrene: A Greek colony on the Libyan coast of Africa that was founded from Thera (modern Santorini) in c. 630 BC under the leadership of Battus. Battus and his heirs ruled as kings until the Cyrenaeans called in a legislator named Demonax, who made their constitution more democratic. Later, one of Battus' heirs started a faction in response. See Herodotus IV.150–205.

Note 784
The things that Cleisthenes used in Athens when he wanted to increase the power of the democracy: See III 2 1275^{b}34–37, IV 15 1300^{a}25n, *Ath.* XIX–XXII, Herodotus V.66, 69–73.

Note 785
No supervision of slaves (which may really be advantageous to a democracy up to a certain point), or of women or children: On this sort of supervision, see IV 15 1300^{a}4–8, VI 8 1322^{b}37–1323^{a}6. The advantages to not having it in a democracy are explained at V 11 1313^{b}32–39, 1323^{a}3–6.

Note 786
The things we got a theoretical grasp on earlier about what causes the preservation and destruction of constitutions: Namely, in Book V.

Note 787
One should consider a measure to be democratic or oligarchic not if it will make the city as democratically governed or as oligarchically governed as possible: See V 9 1309^{b}20–1310^{a}2, 1310^{a}19–20.

Note 788
Public lawsuits should always be made as few as possible by deterring with large fines those who bring frivolous ones: See II 8 1268^{b}25n.

Note 789
They should at least not regard those in control as their enemies: See II 9 1270^{b}20–22.

Note 790
The poor no sooner get it than they need the same again: See II 7 1267^{b}1–5.
The proverbial leaking jug: Forty-nine of the fifty daughters of Danaus murdered their husbands on their wedding night. They were punished in Hades by having to endlessly fill leaking jars with water.

Note 791
The Carthaginians: See II 11.
Have made a friend of the people: "It also seems that friendship holds cities together and that legislators take it more seriously than justice. For concord seems to be something like friendship, and this is what they seek most, whereas faction, because it is enmity, they most seek to drive out. Also, if people are friends, there is no need for justice, whereas people who are just need friendship in addition to justice" (*NE* VIII 1 1155^{a}22–27); "In each of the constitutions there is evidently friendship to the extent that there is justice" (11 1161^{a}10–11).

Note 792
Tarentines: Tarentum (V 3 1303^{a}3) was a colony of Sparta, which had a somewhat similar provision.

Note 793
Goodwill (*eunoun*): See I 6 1255^{a}17n.

Note 794
The necessary offices: See III 13 1287^{a}17–22, VI 8 1321^{b}6–1322^{b}18.

Note 795

Democracies are generally preserved by populousness (*poluanthrôpoi*): The populousness in question is that of the *dêmos*—the poorer citizens—not of the city as a whole. When the *dêmos* is large it is typically stronger than the rich few, and so can generally remain in control and keep the democracy in place. Unless, of course, as in the ultimate democracy—which is also perforce populous in this sense (VI 5 1320ª17)—it goes too far and drives the rich to take extreme measure against it, such as bringing in supporting forces from neighboring oligarchies.

This (*touto*) **is opposed to justice in accord with worth:** *Touto* refers to the democratic justice found in democracies in which the *dêmos* is populous. See VI 2 1317ᵇ3–7.

Note 796

Good order (*eutaxia*): See VI 8 1321ᵇ7, VII 4 1326ª30.

Note 797

Naturally well suited (*euphuôs*): See V 3 1303ᵇ8n.

Note 798

Horse-breeding is the privilege of those who own large estates: See IV 3 1289ᵇ33–40.

Note 799

Hoplites are more often rich than poor: See II 6 1265ᵇ28n.

Note 800

Light infantry and naval forces, however, are entirely democratic: See V 4 1304ª22–24n.

Note 801

Light infantry can easily take on cavalry and hoplites: This is so if, as Aristotle seems to be supposing, we are talking about factional conflict occurring within the confines of a city, where cavalry and hoplites are difficult to deploy. In the open field, hoplites and cavalry are obviously superior.

Note 802

The multitude should be given a share in the governing body, in the way mentioned earlier: At VI 7 1320ᵇ25–29.

As in Thebes, to those who have kept out of vulgar functions for a given period of time: See III 5 1278ª25–26.

Or, as in Massilia, to those who are judged to be worthy of it: See V 6 1305ᵇ1–12.

Note 803

That is why it is well to say that they are miniature democracies: "Miniature," because they are ruled by the few rather than the many; "democracies," because the few in them pursue money in the way that the many do. See VI 4 1318ᵇ16–17.

Note 804

There is the matter, as was said earlier, of correctly dividing what pertains to the offices, how many they are, what they are, and concerned with what: See IV 14 1298^{a}1–3, 15 1300^{b}7–12, VI 1 1316^{b}39–1317^{a}10.

Note 805

Good order (*eutaxian*) **and arrangement** (*kosmon*): The difference in meaning between *eutaxia* and *kosmos* (which also often mean "order") is slight, so that *eutaxia* and *eukosmia* (1321^{b}14, 20, 1322^{b}39, also IV 15 1299^{b}16, 19) amount to much the same thing.

Note 806

In small cities the offices are necessarily fewer, while in larger ones they are more numerous, as was also said earlier: At IV 15 1299^{a}31–^{b}30.

Note 807

In pretty much all cities people must be able to buy and sell with a view to supplying each other's necessary needs: See I 9 1257^{a}14–30.

Note 808

This is also the readiest way to achieve self-sufficiency, which is believed to be what leads people to join together in one constitution: See I 2 1252^{b}27–1253^{a}1, III 6 1278^{b}17–30.

Note 809

Town management (*astunomia*): See VIII 12 1331^{b}6–13, *Ath.* L.2, LIV.1.

Note 810

Country managers (*agronomoi*): See VIII 12 1331^{b}14–17.

Note 811

Receivers (*apodektai*) **or treasurers:** See *Ath.* XL.5–XLVIII.2.

Note 812

[1] Judicial indictments (*graphas tôn dikôn*) **and [2] introductions of judicial proceedings** (*eisagôgas [tôn dikôn]*): A *graphê*—a writ, indictment, or legal case—could be either a private one (*dikê idia*) or a public one (*dikê demosia*). The former was a case affecting an individual, and only that individual, or, in the case of homicide, a close relative. The latter was a case regarded as affecting the city as a whole, such as embezzlement of public funds, desertion from the army, or impiety (like the *graphê asebeias*, or writ of impiety, brought against Socrates). It could be brought by any citizen, since there was no equivalent of a public prosecutor or district attorney in Athenian law. Here [2] is probably intended to refer to public cases, [1] to private ones. *Eisagôgeis* ("introducers") in the 5th cent BC were magistrates assigned to cases having to do with the amount of tribute owed to Athens by cities allied with her. In the late 4th cent magistrates with the same name were assigned to deal with financial cases of various sorts.

Note 813
Sacred recorders (*hieromnêmones*): See *Ath.* XL.2–5.

Note 814
The most difficult of the offices: These were difficult in part because the holders of them were not "professionals" but ordinary citizens elected by lot, who might find themselves having to take action against their neighbors, and in part because cities were typically small, so that a protective anonymity was difficult to achieve.
Those whose names are posted as public debtors: In Athens the names of public debtors were posted in the marketplace (Plato, *Lg.* 762c, 946d). The debtors themselves were disenfranchised until their debt was paid, and might also be subject to imprisonment or confiscation of property.

Note 815
There is no benefit in having judicial proceedings about matters of justice, if they do not achieve their end: See I 2 1253ᵃ29–39 and, on the exercise of the virtues in such offices, VIII 13 1332ᵃ7–18.

Note 816
The office that keeps prisoners in custody is different from the one that carries out the sentence: Prisoners were kept in custody pending punishment, but prison itself was not used as a punishment.
For example, the office of the so-called Eleven in Athens: The Eleven, who were chosen by lot (*Ath.* LII.1) and were in charge of the custody of prisoners, did carry out executions but not other sentences. Thus they did to some degree exemplify the separation that Aristotle is praising. But because they did not perfectly exemplify it, some editors think this clause is a marginal gloss that has made its way into the text.

Note 817
Cadets (*ephêboi*): In Athens, these were young men who at the age of eighteen began the two years of compulsory military training required of all male citizens. See *Ath.* XLII.

Note 818
Or else presides over the multitude: Reading ἢ with some mss. for OCT ἣ.

Note 819
Preliminary councilors: See IV 14 1298ᵇ26–34.

Note 820
The offices that are political, then, are pretty much this many: The supervision of religious matters is of primary importance in Aristotle's view (VII 8 1328ᵇ12), but the office exercising it is not a political office (IV 15 1299ᵃ17–23), since it does not prescribe things to the gods, with whose affairs the office is concerned: "[Practical wisdom] does not control either theoretical wisdom or the better part [of the soul (= the understanding)] any more than medicine controls health, since it does not use it but sees to its coming into being. So it prescribes for its sake, but not to it.

Besides, it would be like saying that politics rules the gods, because it prescribes with regard to everything in the city" (*NE* VI 13 1145^{a}6–11).

Note 821

The office set aside for all the public sacrifices that the law does not assign to the priests: In Athens these were assigned to various other officials, such as the so-called king (*basileus*) or the president of the council. See *Ath.* III.3, LVI.2–7, LVII.

The communal hearth (*koinê hestia*): A city's communal hearth derived from the hearth in a king's palace, which was of both practical and magical or religious significance.

Note 822

Athletic and Dionysiac contests: The athletic, musical, and dramatic competitions that were held throughout the year in many Greek cities. See VIII 6 1341^{a}9–12, *Rh.* III 15 1416^{a}28–34, *Ath.* LVI.5, LVII.1, LX.1, 3.

BOOK VII

Note 823

What the most choiceworthy life is for (one might almost say) everyone: Compare VII 2 1324^{a}18–19.

Whether it is the same or distinct for all communally as for each separately: See VII 3 1325^{b}30–32.

Note 824

The external accounts: See III 6 1278^{b}31n.

Note 825

External goods, goods in the body, and goods in the soul: External goods are usually those that are external in particular to the soul (1323^{b}7–8). But sometimes goods relating to the body are also classed as internal goods (*Rh.* I 5 1360^{b}26–27). The same triadic division is made at *NE* I 8 1098^{b}12–16: "Goods, then, have been divided into three sorts, with some said to be external, some relating to the soul, and some to the body. The goods relating to soul are most fully such, and, we say, are goods to the highest degree, and we take the actions and activities of the soul to be goods relating to soul." A similar ranking is expressed in *Protr.* B21: "A person should do other things for the sake of the goods that are in himself, and of these the ones that are in the body for the sake of those that are in the soul, and virtue [of character] for that of wisdom (*phronêsis* [= *sophia*]), since this is the highest [good]."

Goods in the soul: Namely, the various virtues of character (courage, temperance, and so on) and of thought (practical wisdom, theoretical wisdom) mentioned in the next sentence.

Note 826

Blessed (*makarios*): *Makarios* is often a synonym for *eudaimôn* ("happy"), but sometimes with the implication of being extremely happy (*NE* I 10 1101^{a}7) or in a condition like that of the gods (X 8 1178^{b}25–32).

All three sorts of goods must belong to those who are blessed: But, as we see from the following two texts, not all have an equal impact: "All the same, it [virtuous activity] apparently needs external goods to be added, as we said, since it is impossible or not easy to do noble actions without supplies. For just as we perform many actions by means of instruments, we perform many by means of friends, wealth, and political power. Then again there are some whose deprivation disfigures blessedness, such as good-breeding, good children, and noble looks. For we scarcely have the stamp of happiness if we are extremely ugly in appearance, ill-bred, living a solitary life, or childless, and have it even less, presumably, if our children or friends are totally bad or were good but have died" (*NE* I 8 1099^{a}31–^{b}6); "If, however, it is activities that control living, as we said, no blessed person will ever become wretched, since he will never do hateful or base actions. For a truly good and practically-wise person, we think, will bear what luck brings graciously and, making use of the resources at hand, will always do the noblest actions, just as a good general makes the best uses in warfare of the army he has and a good shoemaker makes the best shoes out of the hides he has been given, and the same way with all other craftsmen. If this is so, however, a happy person will never become wretched—nor *blessed*" (11 1100^{b}33–1101^{a}8).
Thought as foolish and deluded as a child's: "No one would choose to live possessing a child's level of thought throughout his life, even if he were to take the fullest possible pleasure in the things children take pleasure in or to get enjoyment from doing some utterly shameful action, even if he were never going to suffer any pain" (*NE* X 3 1174^{a}1–4).

Note 827
Even from the facts themselves: Contrasted with the findings of those "who investigate the matter on the basis of argument (*logon*)" (1323^{b}6–7). The relative weights of the two are assigned in the following text: "Accounts [or arguments] (*logoi*) of matters that lie in the sphere of actions and feelings carry less conviction than the facts, and so when they clash with what is in accord with the perceptible facts, they are despised and undermine the truth as well" (*NE* X 1 1172^{a}34–^{b}1). Aristotle is critical of people—often Platonists, in his view—who start giving accounts or producing arguments before assembling all the relevant facts: "What causes our inability to take a comprehensive view of the agreed-upon facts is lack of experience. That is why those who dwell in more intimate association with the facts of nature are better able to lay down starting-points that can bring together a good many of these, whereas those whom many arguments have made unobservant of the facts come too readily to their conclusions after looking at only a few facts" (*GC* I 2 316^{a}5–10).

Note 828
The virtues are not acquired and safeguarded by means of external goods, but rather it is the other way around: The point, as we will see in a few lines, is not that virtue invariably leads to external goods, but that without virtue external goods are harmful: "For those who are badly disposed in things related to the soul neither wealth nor strength nor beauty is good. Instead, the more superior the

possession of these [bodily and external] conditions, the more and the more often the harm the one who possesses them but does not possess wisdom (*phronêsis*). The saying 'no knife for a child' means 'do not give abundant resources to base people'" (*Protr.* B4).

Living happily for human beings is possessed by those who have cultivated their characters and minds excessively: Compare: "Those to whom it more belongs to contemplate, it also more belongs to be happy, not coincidentally but, rather, in accord with contemplation" (*NE* X 8 1178^{b}29–31).

Excessively (*eis huperbolên*): *Huperbolê*—from the verb *huperballein*, which means "to throw beyond, or further than, others"—often carries the negative connotation of going beyond what is good or proper, as it does at 1323^{a}38 and 1323^{b}8. But it can, as it presumably does here, carry no such connotation, since—as the thought seems to be—one simply cannot go too far in cultivating one's character and one's thought.

Note 829

External goods have a limit: See 1256^{b}35–36, 1257^{b}28. The limit in question is determined by happiness, since what quantity of other goods it is good to have is the one that best furthers happiness: "[The] political philosopher . . . is the architectonic craftsman of the end to which we look in calling each thing unconditionally bad or good" (*NE* VII 11 1152^{b}1–3); "even good luck is an impediment when it is excessive, and presumably it should no longer by rights be called *good* luck. For the defining mark of *good* luck is determined by relation to happiness" (13 1153^{b}23–25).

Note 830

The best condition of each thing relative to others is in accord with the superiority of those things whose conditions we say they are: This is a consequence of the following more general view: "What belongs to the better and more estimable thing is more choiceworthy than what belongs to the worse—for example, to a god rather than to a human, and to the soul rather than to the body" (*Top.* III 1 116^{b}12–13).

Note 831

The soul is more estimable, both unconditionally and to us, than property and the body: See I 5 1254^{a}34–^{b}10 with: "That which is more fitted to rule (*archikôteron*) and more of a leader, as a human being is in relation to the other animals. Therefore soul is better than body (since it is more fitted to rule), and of soul that which has reason and thought. For it is the sort of thing that commands and forbids, and says what we should and should not do" (*Protr.* B61).

More estimable: See I 7 1255^{b}28n.

Note 832

We may use the [primary] god as evidence of this: Aristotle recognizes the existence of a number of different divine beings or gods, among which he distinguishes a primary god, referred to as *ho theos* ("the god"), which is the one under discussion here. See *Met.* XII 7–10.

Since he is happy and blessedly so, not because of any external goods but because of himself and by being in his nature of a certain quality: "If, then, that good state [of activity], which we are sometimes in, the [primary] god is always in, that is a wonderful thing, and if to a higher degree, that is yet more wonderful. But that is his state. And life too certainly belongs to him. For the activity of understanding is life, and he is that activity; and his intrinsic activity is life that is best and eternal. We say, then, that the god is a living being that is eternal and best, so that living and a continuous and everlasting eternity belong to the god, since this is the god" (*Met.* XII 7 1072^b24–30); "But that complete happiness is some contemplative activity will also be evident from the following considerations. The gods, in fact, we suppose to be the most blessed and happy of all. But what sorts of actions should we assign to them? Just ones? Won't they appear ridiculous if they engage in transactions, return deposits, and so on? Courageous ones, then, enduring what is frightening and facing danger because it is a noble thing to do? Or generous ones? To whom will they give? It will be a strange thing, if they actually have money or anything like that. And their temperate actions, what would they be? Or isn't the praise vulgar, since they do not have base appetites? If we were to go through them all, it would be evident that everything to do with actions is petty and unworthy of gods. Nonetheless, everyone supposes them to be living, at least, and hence in activity, since surely they are not sleeping like Endymion. If, then, living has doing actions taken away from it and still more so producing, what is left except contemplating? So the activity of a god, superior as it is in blessedness, will be contemplative. And so the activity of humans, then, that is most akin to this will most bear the stamp of happiness" (*NE* X 8 1178^b7–23).

Note 833

Chance or luck is the cause of the goods external to the soul: See I 11 1258^b36n.

Note 834

It is impossible for those who do not do noble things to act nobly: It is possible to do noble actions (produce a grammatical sentence) without acting nobly (doing so in a grammatical way): "It is possible to produce something grammatical either by luck or on someone else's instruction. Someone would be a grammarian, then, if he produced something grammatical and produced it in the way a grammarian would. And this is to do it in accord with the craft knowledge of grammar that is internal to himself" (*NE* II 4 1105^a22–26). Aristotle's point here is that the converse does not hold.

Noble function (*kalon ergon*): See I 2 1252^b4n.

Note 835

The courage, justice, practical wisdom, and temperance of a city have the same capacity and form (*morphê*) **as those in which each human being who is said to be courageous, just, practically-wise, and temperate should share:** This could mean (1) the city is an agent in just the way that an individual human being is, and has virtues that are the very same as those in a human being—that is, they are states of the soul concerned with feelings and actions (*NE* II 6 1106^b16–17).

Or it could mean (2) the citizens of a city—or at any rate the governing body, with which its constitution is identified (III 6 1278^b11)—have human virtues that are states of their souls and, as a result, the city they constitute or govern has these virtues, albeit in a derivative way. If (1) were correct, then a city would have to have a soul, and so, since a soul is a starting-point of life, it would have to be non-derivatively alive, it would have to be an animal of some sort. But on Aristotle's view a city is a multitude of citizens (III 1 1274^b41) sharing a constitution (3 1276^b1–2), whose identity determines its identity (1276^b2–3), not an animal of which they are animate parts. No Aristotelian animal, indeed, has other animals as its parts. (3) A third possibility, which is in between these two, is scouted in III 11—on which see 1281^a42–$^b3$n. It allows that when a multitude whose individual members are not fully virtuous or practically-wise have come together in a certain way (1281^b1), they may collectively exhibit virtue and practical wisdom, since they are then just like one human being in their "characters and thought" (1281^b7). However exactly (3) might be best elaborated, it at least provides a basis for attributing virtue and practical wisdom to a city whose individual citizens lack them, without, as in (1), attributing souls to cities. The fact remains that "a city is excellent at any rate by its citizens—those who share in the constitution—being excellent" (VII 13 1332^a32–34), and that in Aristotle's best city and constitution all the citizens must be virtuous and practically-wise. See also V 9 1310^a18–19.

Note 836

Let these remarks, as far as they go, serve as a preface to our account: In fact, VII 1–3 is all prefatory, as 1325^b33 makes clear.

Note 837

That is the function of another leisured discussion (*scholês*): The sort of discussion we find in the *Nicomachean Ethics*. *Scholê* can refer to leisure itself, or to that in which leisure is employed, especially learned discussion. Hence our words "scholar" and "scholastic." The implication is that the discussion in the *Politics* is a leisured one. See II 9 1271^b5n and V 11 1313^b3–4n.

Note 838

Alien (*xenikos*): *Xenikos* is often best translated as "foreign," as, for example, at I 9 1257^a31, II 10 1272^b20, and sometimes "foreign (*xenos*)" is contrasted with "resident alien (*metoikos*)," as at III 5 1277^b38 and VII 4 1326^a20. Here, however, *xenikos* seems to refer specifically to someone who is a resident alien in a city, not to someone who, as "no part of a city" at all, is either "a wild beast or a god" (I 2 1253^a28–29). This was the sort of status that Aristotle himself had in Athens. See Introduction, p. lxxxix.

Detached from (*apolelumenos*) **the political community:** The verb *apoluein* is used at I 9 1257^a40 to mean "save themselves from the trouble," and probably preserves some of that connotation here.

Which life is more choiceworthy, the one that involves taking part in politics with other people and sharing in the city, or the life of an alien, detached from the political community: As not self-sufficient a human being needs to live in a community with others (I 2 1253ᵃ26–29). But he could do that in two ways: (1) by being a citizen of a city, actively participating in its political life—for example, by attending the assembly, holding office if elected, and so on; (2) by being a resident alien, excluded from such participation. Politics is concerned with the question of which constitution it is unconditionally best for all or most human beings to live in, and so has something to say about (1). But it is not concerned with (2). For what life is best for a given individual depends on the particularities of his nature, character, and circumstances. For him therefore the question is not which life is unconditionally best for human beings universally, but which of the lives actually available to him is best for him. This might well be the life of a resident alien in, say, a democratic city. The difference between the two questions is nicely highlighted in the following two texts: "We should pray that unconditionally good things will also be good for us, while choosing the ones that are good for us" (*NE* V 1 1129ᵇ5–6); "In the sphere of action the work is to begin from things that are good for each particular person and make things that are wholly [= unconditionally] good good for each particular person" (*Met.* VII 3 1029ᵇ5–7).

Note 839

A function of political thought and theoretical knowledge (*theôria*): Politics, though it is a practical science (I 1 1252ᵃ15), does have a theoretical component, interested not so much in practice as in knowledge and truth. For the contrast, see I 3 1253ᵇ15–18, 11 1258ᵇ33–35. Notice too *ta êthikês theôrias*—"theoretical knowledge of ethics" at *APo.* I 33 89ᵇ9.
Theoretical knowledge (*theôria*): See I 1 1252ᵃ26n.
Of our methodical inquiry: I 1 1252ᵃ18n.

Note 840

The political and action-involving (*praktikos*) **life:** What makes something *praktikos* for Aristotle is that it appropriately involves *praxis* or action, considered as an end choiceworthy because of itself, and not—as with "practical"—that it is opposed to what is theoretical, speculative, or ideal. That is why, paradoxical as it may sound, *theôrêtikos* activities are more *praktikos* than those that are widely considered to be most so (VII 3 1325ᵇ16–21).

Note 841

The person who thinks correctly, at any rate, must order his affairs by looking to the better target: "Everyone able to live in accord with his own deliberate choice should posit some target for living nobly, whether it is honor, reputation, wealth, or education, which he will look to in doing all his actions, since not to order one's life in relation to some end is a sign of great foolishness" (*EE* I 2 1214ᵇ6–11); "someone with understanding chooses the better of two things in all cases" (VII 2 1237ᵇ37–38).

Note 842

Joy in life (*euêmeria*): *Euêmeria* is sometimes best translated as "prosperity," as at VI 8 1322ᵇ38, VII 2 1324ᵃ38. It is in this sense that *NE* X 8 1178ᵇ33 speaks of "external prosperity (*ektos euêmerias*)." Here, however, the sense seems closer to that in which it is used at III 6 1278ᵇ29: "most human beings are willing to endure much misery in order to cling to living, on the supposition that there is a sort of joy (*euêmerias*) in it and a natural sweetness."

Note 843

The actions resulting from each virtue are not more open to private individuals than to those who are active in communal affairs and participate in politics: Any action resulting from virtue open to a private individual is also open to someone active in politics, but—the implicit suggestion is—*not vice versa*. Aristotle seems not to agree with this: "private individuals seem to do decent actions no less, or even more, than people in positions of power" (*NE* X 8 1179ᵃ6–8).

Note 844

It is the exercise of power that they all aim at: Which is as much an error in a city or constitution as it is in an individual person, and for the same reasons: "We should not think that a person who is going to be happy needs many things and grand ones, even if it is not possible for him to be blessed without external goods. For self-sufficiency does not lie in an extreme amount of these and neither does action. But it is possible to do many noble actions even without ruling land and sea, since even from moderate resources a person can do actions in accord with virtue" (*NE* X 8 1179ᵃ1–6).

The exercise of power (*tou kratein*): Namely, "for the purposes of ruling its neighbors" (VII 14 1333ᵇ30–31).

Note 845

Scythians: Nomads inhabiting the northern Black Sea and fore-Caucusus region.
Thracians: Inhabitants of Thrace, a geographical area on the Black Sea, centered on the present-day borders of Bulgaria, Greece, and Turkey.

Note 846

Iberians: A people inhabiting the east and southeast Transcaucasus, ancestors of present-day Georgians.

Note 847

It would presumably seem quite absurd if the function of a politician involved being able to get a theoretical grasp on how to rule or master his neighbors, whether they wish it or do not wish it: Those who rule over subjects who do not wish it are tyrants or masters (V 10 1313ᵃ14–16, 11 1314ᵃ34–38), and it is an error to think that these are politicians, in the full sense of the term (I 1 1252ᵃ7–9n).

Note 848

How could this be up to a politician or a legislator, when it is not even *lawful* (*nomimon*): "It is clear that all lawful things (*nomima*) are somehow just, since the things defined by legislative science are lawful and each of these, we say, is just. The laws, for their part, pronounce about all matters, aiming either at the common advantage of all or at that of the best people or of those who—in accord with their virtue or in accord with some other such thing—are in control. So, in one way, the things we call 'just' are the ones that produce and safeguard happiness and its parts for the political community" (*NE* V 1 1129^{b}12–19). The injustice involved in ruling over subjects who do not wish it is not that of violating the laws of the land, but is rather the natural injustice involved in enslaving those who are not by nature slaves. See I 3 1253^{b}14–23, 5 1254^{a}17–^{b}26.

Note 849

But this topic—namely, what end the best constitution should aim at—will receive a proper investigation later: See VII 13–15.

Note 850

As regards those who agree that a life that involves virtue is most choiceworthy, but disagree about the use (*chrêseôs*) **of it:** "[One sort of justice] is complete virtue in the highest degree, because it is the complete use (*chrêsis*) of complete virtue. It is the complete use because someone who possesses it is able to use his virtue in relation to another person and not solely with regard to himself" (*NE* V 1 1129^{b}30–33). The disagreement, then, is about whether happiness for a city or an individual lies in the use of virtue in relation to another or in the use of it with regard to himself.

Note 851

Those on one side reject political offices, since they consider that the life of a free person is distinct from that of a politician and is also the most choiceworthy one of all: Being a free person and having a life of leisure go together (III 9 1280^{a}5n). Hence, in the following passage, Aristotle sides to some degree with those who oppose the life of a free person to that of a politician: "Happiness seems to reside in leisure, since we do unleisured things in order to be at leisure, and wage war in order to live in peace. Now the activity of the practical virtues occurs in politics or in warfare, and the actions concerned with these seem to be unleisured and those in warfare completely so (for no one chooses to wage war for the sake of waging war, or to foment war either, since someone would seem completely bloodthirsty, if he made enemies of his friends in order to bring about battles and killings). But the activity of a politician too is unleisured and beyond political activity itself he tries to get positions of power and honors or, at any rate, happiness for himself and his fellow citizens—this being different from the exercise of politics and something we clearly seek on the supposition of its being different" (*NE* X 7 1177^{b}4–15).

Note 852

In our first accounts: See I 4–7.

Note 853

The actions of those who are just and temperate achieve an end of many things that are noble: Because a virtuous person desires and loves the noble and acts for its sake (*NE* III 7 1115^{b}13, X 9 1179^{b}9).

Note 854

Yet perhaps someone might take these determinations to imply that control of everyone is best, since in that way one would control the greatest number of the

actions that are noblest: The actions an agent controls are his, even if it is not his body that moves in accord with that control. See 1325^{b}21–23.

Note 855

It is not necessary, as some suppose, for an action-involving life to be lived in relation to other people: This is because it can be a contemplative life, about which the point is developed more fully in the following text: "The self-sufficiency that is meant [as a defining mark of happiness] will belong most of all to contemplative activity. For while a theoretically-wise person as well as a just one and people with the other virtues all need the things necessary for living, when these are adequately supplied, the just one still needs people to do just actions for and with, and similarly for a temperate person, a courageous person, and each of the others. But a theoretically-wise person, even when by himself, is able to contemplate, and the more wise he is, the more he is able to do so. He will do it better, presumably, if he has co-workers, but all the same he is most self-sufficient" (*NE* X 7 1177^{a}27–^{b}1). **Nor are those thoughts alone practical** (*praktikas*) **that arise for the sake of the consequences of doing an action:** If some things are *praktikos*, because, like practical ones, they are useful, effective, or feasible means to some end, others are yet more *praktikos* because they further an end by constituting it or being identical to it: "We term both health and wealth as *prakton*, as well as the actions we do for their sake, the ones that further health or the making of money, so it is clear that happiness should be set down as the best for human beings of things *prakton*" (*EE* I 7 1217^{a}37–40). Though the term used here is *prakton* rather than *praktikos*, as in our text, the point remains the same: means to ends are practical, as—preeminently—are the ends themselves.

Note 856

We say that the ones who above all do actions, even external actions, in a controlling way are their architectonic craftsmen who do them by means of their thoughts: "It is also because of this that we consider the architectonic practitioners in each craft to be more estimable, to know in a yet more full sense, and to be wiser than the handicraftsmen, because they know the causes of the things they produce. The handicraftsmen, by contrast, we consider to be like some sort of inanimate things that produce without knowing what they produce, in the way, for example, that fire burns" (*Met.* I 1 981^{a}30–^{b}3). See also I 4 1253^{b}38n.
External actions (*exôterikôn praxeôn*): Actions that are external to the agent or his soul. Compare "external goods (*exôterikôn agathôn*) . . . goods external to the soul (*ektos agathôn tês psuchês*)" at VIII 1 1323^{b}25–28. See also 1325^{b}28n.

Note 857

It is not necessary for even those cities to be inactive that are situated by themselves and have deliberately chosen to live that way: Although normally a city lives a political life in relationship to other cities. See VII 6 1327^{b}4–6.

Note 858

For otherwise the [primary] god and the entire cosmos could scarcely be in a noble condition, since they have no external actions beyond the [internal] ones

that are proper to them: "We must also investigate which way the nature of the whole possesses the good and the best [= the primary investigate in god]—whether as something separated and intrinsic, or as its order. Or is it rather in both ways, like an army? For the good of an army is in its order, and is also the general—and more so the latter. For he is not due to the order, but it is due to him. All things are jointly ordered in a way, although not in the same way—even swimming creatures, flying creatures, and plants. And the order is not such that one thing has no relation to another but rather there is a relation. For all things are jointly ordered in relation to one thing—but it is as in a household, where the free men least of all do things at random, but all or most of the things they do are ordered, while the slaves and beasts can do a little for the common thing, but mostly do things at random. For this is the sort of starting-point that the nature is of each of them" (*Met.* XII 10 1075^{a}11–23).

Note 859

Other craftsmen—for example, a weaver or a shipbuilder—must also be supplied with matter suitable for the work: All crafts presuppose the existence of suitable materials: "Just as the producer does not make the underlying subject (the bronze), so he does not make the sphere either, except coincidentally, because the brazen sphere is a sphere and he does make the former. For to make the this something is to make a this something from what is wholly the underlying subject. I mean that to make the bronze round is not to make the round or the bronze but a distinct thing, namely, this form in something else. For if the producer makes something, he must make it from something else (for we assumed this). For example, he makes a brazen sphere, but in such a way that from this, which is bronze, he makes this, which is a sphere. If, then, he also made this [matter] itself, it is clear that he will make it in the same way, and the productions will go on without limit. It is evident, therefore, that neither does the form—or whatever we ought to call the shape that is in the perceptible thing—come to be, nor is there any process of coming to be of it, and the essence does not come to be either (for it is this that comes to be in something else, whether as a result of craft or as a result of nature or of some capacity). But the producer does make a brazen sphere to exist. For he produces it from bronze and sphere. For in this specific thing he produces this specific form, and the result is a brazen sphere" (*Met.* VII 8 1033^{a}28–^{b}10). Some crafts, moreover, produce suitable materials for other crafts to work on, so that a hierarchy of crafts emerges: "But since there are many sorts of actions and of crafts and sciences, their ends are many as well. For health is the end of medicine, a ship of shipbuilding, victory of generalship, and wealth of household management. Some of these fall under some one capacity, however, as bridle making falls under horsemanship, along with all the others that produce equipment for horsemanship, and as it and every action in warfare fall under generalship, and, in the same way, others fall under different ones. But in all such cases, the ends of the architectonic ones are more choiceworthy than the ends under them, since these are pursued for the sake also of the former" (*NE* I 1 1094^{a}6–16). It is at the pinnacle of this hierarchy that politics is found, directing and arranging all of them, so that they further human happiness to the greatest extent possible in the circumstances (*Pol.* I 1 1252^{a}3–7n).

Note 860

A city too has a certain function: Namely, to ensure the most choiceworthy, because happiest, life for its citizens (VII 1 1323^{a}14–21).

Function: See I 2 1252^{b}4n.

The city that is best able to complete its function is the one that should be considered greatest: "The function of a sort of thing, we say, is the same in kind (*genos*) as the function of an excellent thing of that sort (as in the case of a lyre player and an excellent lyre player), and . . . each [function] is completed well when it is in accord with the virtue that properly belongs to it" (*NE* I 7 1098^{a}8–15).

Note 861

Hippocrates: A famous 5th-cent doctor from the island of Cos. Little is known about him, however, and none of the many writings in the so-called Hippocratic corpus can with confidence be attributed to him.

Note 862

A city that can send a large number of vulgar people out to war, on the other hand, but only a few hoplites, cannot possibly be great: Not because a force of vulgar people could not triumph in battle, even over hoplites (VI 7 1321^{a}20n), but because a city composed largely of such people, with only a few rich enough to be hoplites (II 6 1265^{b}28), could not have the virtues needed to function well as a city. See VII 9 1328^{b}33–1329^{a}2.

Note 863

Divine power: See VII 3 1325^{b}28–30n.

The universe (*to pan*): *To pan* refers not to the totality of things, but to those in the spatio-temporal realm—the universe. That is why Aristotle can claim that everything (= everything that is a part of the universe) has matter and a moving cause (*Met.* XII 5 1071^{a}33–34)—something that is false of all substances. For substances, such as the primary god, "must be without matter" (6 1071^{b}20–21).

The noble at any rate is usually found in number and magnitude: See II 9 1270^{a}20n.

Note 864

The defining mark that has been mentioned: No defining mark has been mentioned as such, but the reference is clearly to the limit imposed on the population of the best city that enables it to complete its function best (1326^{a}10–14). See 1326^{b}23–25.

Note 865

Who, unless he has the voice of Stentor: A Homeric hero gifted with a very powerful voice.

Will serve as its crier (*kêrux*): The *kêrux* announced proclamations and kept order in the assembly.

Note 866

To live at leisure in a way that is generous and at the same time temperate: See II 9 1271ᵇ5n (leisure); III 9 1280ᵃ5n (generous, free); I 13 1259ᵇ24n (temperate).

Note 867

Whether this defining mark is correctly or incorrectly stated is something that must be investigated with greater exactness later on: The more exact discussion of property advertised here does not appear in our *Politics*. The defining mark mentioned, however, is endorsed at II 6 1265ᵃ28–38, 7 1266ᵇ24–38 and the relationship between the ownership of property and its use is discussed at II 4 1262ᵇ37–1263ᵃ40.

Note 868

Those who draw us toward either of the two extremes of life, the one lot toward tightfistedness (*glischrotêta*): When generosity (*eleutheria*) is the virtuous mean, the extremes are usually wastefulness (*asôtia*) and acquisitiveness (*aneleutheria*) (*NE* IV 1 1119ᵇ27), but other alternatives, including tightfistedness, are also mentioned (1121ᵇ22).
The other toward luxury (*truphên*): *Truphê* in *NE* goes along with softness and is a sort of effeminacy (*NE* VII 1 1145ᵃ35, 7 1150ᵇ2).

Note 869

Easy . . . to get out of (*euexodon*): Aristotle, however, seems to mean "easy to get out to." See 1327ᵃ6–7.

Note 870

A city must engage in trade for itself, not for others: See III 4 1277ᵇ3–7, VIII 2 1337ᵇ19–21.
Whereas those that open their market to everyone do so for the sake of revenue: See I 9 1257ᵃ34–1258ᵃ14.

Note 871

A city that must not be involved in this sort of getting more (*pleonexias*): As the best city under discussion must not. On getting more, see II 7 1266ᵇ37n.
Must not have a market of this sort: See I 9 1257ᵃ14–34.

Note 872

A life of leadership: See VII 14 1333ᵇ38–1334ᵃ1.
A political life: See II 6 1265ᵃ22n.

Note 873

The seafaring mob: See V 4 1304ᵃ17–24.

Note 874

The city of Heraclea: See V 5 1304ᵇ31n, 6 1305ᵇ11–12.

Note 875

We spoke earlier about what the defining mark should be for the multitude of citizens: At VII 4 1326ᵃ5–ᵇ25.

Note 876

The nations in cold regions, particularly in Europe, are full of spirit but somewhat deficient in thought and craft knowledge: (1) "Cold hardens and solidifies [the bodies of animals] by drying them, since as the heat is pressed out the moisture evaporates, and both hair and skin become earthy and hard" (*GA* V 3 783ª15–18); (2) "Animals that have overly many thick fibers in their blood are of an earthier nature and are spirited in character and are excitable because of their spirit" (*PA* II 4 651ª33–35).

Spirit (*thumos*): See III 16 1287ª31n.

Which is why they remain comparatively free: Their spiritedness makes them difficult to conquer: "Because of spirit, the Celts, for example, take up arms and march against the waves" (*EE* III 1 1229ᵇ28–30).

But are without a political constitution (*apoliteuta*): The virtues of thought—those states of the soul that make thought excellent—are practical wisdom and theoretical wisdom (*NE* I 13 1103ª5–6). Practical wisdom is the same state of the soul as politics (I 2 1253ª34n). Hence those deficient in thought will also be without a political constitution, since producing such a constitution is a function of politics.

And incapable of ruling their neighbors: Incapable, that is, of ruling them in a political as opposed to a tyrannical fashion. For this too requires the sort of knowledge of politics that these people are being supposed to lack.

Note 877

Those in Asia, on the other hand, have souls endowed with thought and craft knowledge, but they lack spirit: "Some of the animals, at least whose blood is watery, are capable of very subtle thought. This is due not to the coldness of their blood but rather to its thinness and purity, neither of which qualities belong to what is earthy. For the thinner and purer its fluid [= blood], the more easily moved its perceptual capacity" (*PA* II 4 650ᵇ18–24). See also III 14 1285ª19–22.

Note 878

That is why it [the Greek race] remains free, [1] governs itself in the best way (*beltista politeuomenon*) **and [2] is capable of ruling all** (*pantôn*), **should it acquire one constitution:** The meaning of "governs itself in the best way" is somewhat obscure, since different Greek cities had different sorts of constitutions, and none was the sort of aristocracy that Aristotle thinks best of all, or even the sort of well-mixed polity that he thinks to be the best of those achievable by most cities. [2] is yet more obscure, since it is difficult to see what the one constitution referred to could possibly be. For even Greece itself was too large, and Greeks too numerous, to form a single well-governed city. Perhaps the idea is that if all Greek cities had constitutions of the same good sort, so that they were less prone to the sort of inter-Greek political conflict exemplified in the Peloponnesian War, then an alliance of them, like the alliance that defeated the Persian empire, could rule all the other nations.

Note 879

Some say that guardians should have this very quality, namely, friendly to those they know and fierce to those they do not: See Plato, *Rep.* 375b–376c.

Spirit is what produces friendliness: See III 16 1287[a]31n.

Note 880
"It is you who are choked with rage against your friends": Fr. 78 Diehl. Archilochus was a 7th-cent poet from Paros, an island in the central Aegean, west of Naxos.

Note 881
Great-souled people (*megalopsuchoi*): "A great-souled person seems, then, to be someone who thinks himself worthy of great things and is worthy of them. . . . For greatness of soul requires magnitude, just as nobility of appearance requires a large body, whereas small people are elegant and well proportioned but not noble in appearance. . . . Great-souled people also appear to be concerned with honor, since it is most of all of honor that they think themselves worthy—but in accord with their worth. . . . A truly great-souled person must be good. Indeed, it would seem characteristic of a great-souled person to be great in each virtue. . . . Greatness of soul, then, seems to be like a sort of adornment of the virtues, since it makes the virtues greater and does not come about without them. That is why it is difficult to be truly great-souled, since it is not possible without noble-goodness" (*NE* IV 3 1123[b]2–1124[a]4).
Nor are great-souled people by nature harsh, except to those behaving unjustly: The assumption, apparently, is that guardians in the best city, whether Plato's or Aristotle's own, having all the virtues, must be great-souled people.

Note 882
"Wars among brothers are harsh": Euripides 672 Fr. 975 Nauck.
"Those who have loved excessively will hate excessively too": 854 Fr. 67b Nauck (author unknown).

Note 883
We should not seek the same exactness in accounts as in what comes through perception: Since accounts are always of universals (*Met.* VII 10 1035[b]34, XI 1 1059[b]26), whereas perception is always of particulars (I 1 981[b]10–11, *NE* VII 3 1147[a]25–26), the contrast is cognate with the one being made in the following text: "It is not a person who deviates [from the mean] a little—whether toward excess or toward deficiency—who is blamed, however, but one who does so a lot, since someone like that does not escape notice. But up to what point and to what extent a person's deviation is blameworthy is not easy to define in an account—nor indeed is anything else among perceptibles, for such things lie in the particulars, and their discernment lies in perception" (*NE* II 9 1109[b]18–23). Hence perception here has to do not with the defining mark for determining what the size and nature of the body of citizens should be, since that is a universal matter, but with the particular circumstances, and with determining what the body of citizens should be like given these.

Note 884
Things that are composed in accord with nature (*kata phusin*): See I 2 1252[b]30n.

The whole composite: "Something is said to be a whole if: [1] None of the parts of which it is said to be by nature a whole is absent from it. [2] It is what encompasses the things it encompasses in such a way that they are one, and this in two ways—either [2a] as each being one or [2b] as together composing one. For [2a] what is universal, or in general what is taken as such when we say "as a whole," is universal as encompassing many things by being predicated of each of them, and by all of them—each one of them—being one thing, as human, horse, and god are, because all are living things. But [2b] what is continuous and limited is a whole when it is one thing composed of many things, especially if they are present in it potentially, but, failing this, if they are actively present in it. Of these themselves, those which are by nature of such a sort are wholes to a higher degree than those are so by craft, as we also said in the case of what is one, wholeness being in fact a sort of oneness" (*Met.* V 26 1023^{b}26–36).

Note 885

There is nothing that is common to the house and the builder, but rather the builder's craft knowledge is for the sake of the house: When X and Y have something common between them of the relevant sort, they share a common end or function, in the way that political animals do (I 2 1253^{a}3n). That is why "in cases where there is nothing in common between ruler and ruled, there is no friendship, since there is no justice either—for example, of craftsman toward instrument, soul toward body, or master toward slave. *Benefited* by their users all these things certainly are, but there is no friendship toward soulless things nor justice either. Neither is there friendship toward a horse or an ox, or toward a slave insofar as he is a slave, since there is nothing in common between the parties" (*NE* VIII 12 1161^{a}32–^{b}3; also *EE* VII 9 1241^{b}17–24). Hence, where there is friendship and justice, as there is in a political community, there is something common to those who share in it.

Note 886

The best thing is happiness, however, and it is some sort of activation or complete use of virtue: "[Happiness is] activity of the soul in accord with virtue and, if there are more virtues than one, in accord with the best and most complete, furthermore, in a complete life, for one swallow does not make a spring, nor does one day. Nor, similarly, does one day or a short time make someone blessed and happy" (*NE* I 7 1098^{a}15–20); "[Justice as a whole (= general justice)] is complete virtue—not unconditionally but in relation to another person. . . . And it is complete virtue in the highest degree, because it is the complete use of complete virtue" (V 2 1129^{b}25–31).

Some people are able to share in happiness, whereas others are able to do so only to a small degree or not at all: Depending on what share of virtue they are by nature capable of. See I 13 1260^{a}14–17, also III 9 1280^{a}32–34n.

Note 887

By pursuing happiness in different ways and by different means each group of people produces different ways of life and different constitutions: (1) Happiness is "some sort of activation or complete use of virtue" (1328^{a}37–38); (2) Virtue is different in different kinds of constitution (I 13 1260^{b}8–20). Compare Plato, *Tht.* 177e4–6: "Whatever name a city applies to the good, that surely is what it aims at when it legislates."

Note 888
Living needs many instruments: Recall that wealth (I 8 1256^{b}36), property, and slaves (4 1253^{b}31–33) are all instruments.

Note 889
A multitude of farmers to provide the food: But see I 8 1256^{a}40–^{b}2.
Judges of what is necessary and advantageous: The mss. have κριτὰς τῶν ἀναγκαίων καὶ συμφερόντων, which Ross and Dreizehnter both follow. Susemihl and Kraut read κριτὰς τῶν δικαίων καὶ συμφερόντων ("judges of what is just and advantageous"). VII 9 1329^{a}3–4 supports this reading, but VII 13 1332^{a}11–18 suggests that the mss. reading is correct.

Note 890
As we said: 1328^{b}24–28.

Note 891
Happiness cannot exist separate from virtue, as was said earlier: See VII 1 1323^{b}29–36, 8 1328^{a}37–^{b}2.
Unconditionally—not relative to a hypothesis—just: See IV 7 1293^{b}1–7, also II 9 1269^{a}32n.
The citizens should not live either a vulgar (*banauson*) **or a trading life:** See I 11 1258^{b}26n (vulgar); 9 1257^{a}34–1258^{a}34 (trading).

Note 892
Ignoble (*agennês*): The opposite of *eugenês* ("well bred") on which see I 6 1255^{a}33n.

Note 893
Strength (*dunameôs*): *Dunamis* is usually translated as "capacity" or "power," and occasionally as "force," but here, as at 1329^{a}15, VII 17 1336^{a}4, and VII 4 1339^{a}4, "strength" better captures the intended meaning.

Note 894
It is natural for strength to be found among younger men and practical wisdom among older ones: "Young people become geometers and mathematicians and wise in such things, they do not seem to become practically-wise. The explanation is that practical wisdom is concerned also with particulars, knowledge of which comes from experience. But there is no young person who is experienced, since it is quantity of time that produces experience" (*NE* VI 8 1142^{a}12–16); "We attribute consideration, comprehension, practical wisdom, and understanding to the same people and say they actually have consideration and understanding when they are practically-wise and able to comprehend. . . . [But] while nobody seems wise by nature, people do seem to have consideration, comprehension, and understanding by nature. An indication of this is that we also think that these states correspond

to the stages of life and that a particular stage brings understanding and consideration, as if nature were the cause" (11 1143ᵃ26–ᵇ9).

Note 895

Craftsman of virtue: An allusion perhaps to Plato, *Rep.* 500d7–9.

Note 896

This is clear from our hypothesis: See VII 4 1325ᵇ35, also II 9 1269ᵃ32n.

Note 897

Either barbarian or subject peoples: Reading ἢ βαρβάρους ἢ περιοίκους with the mss. for OCT and Susemihl ἢ βαρβάρους περιοίκους.

Note 898

The things we enumerated earlier: At VII 8 1328ᵇ2–23.

Note 899

Sesostris having made such a law for Egypt, so it is said, and Minos for Crete: See Herodotus II.164–167, Plato, *Ti.* 24b. Sesostris, or Senusret III, was pharaoh of Egypt c. 2099–2061 BC.

Note 900

Minos: See II 10 1271ᵇ31.

Note 901

The promontory of Europe that lies between the Gulfs of Scylletium and Lametius: This is the toe of modern Italy between the Gulfs of Squillace and Eufemia.

Note 902

Pretty much everything else too has been discovered many times, or rather an unlimited number of times, in the long course of history: "Each craft and each philosophy has often been developed as far as possible only to pass away again" (*Met.* XII 8 1074ᵇ11–12). For (1) the world and human beings have always existed (*Mete.* I 14 352ᵇ16–17, *DA* II 4 415ᵃ25–ᵇ7, *GA* II 1 731ᵇ24–732ᵃ3); (2) human beings are naturally adapted to form largely reliable beliefs about the world and what conduces to their welfare in it (*Met.* II 1 993ᵃ30–ᵇ11, *Rh.* I 1 1355ᵃ15–17).

Note 903

Our needs are likely to teach the necessities, and once they are present, the things that contribute to refinement and abundance quite reasonably develop: "As more crafts were discovered, some of which were related to necessities, others to passing the time, it is quite likely that the discoverers of the latter were always thought to be wiser, because their sciences did not aim at utility. Hence when all such crafts were already developed, the sciences that aim neither at pleasure nor at necessities were discovered, first in the places where people had leisure. That is why the mathematical crafts first arose in Egypt, since there the priestly class were allowed to be at leisure" (*Met.* I 1 981ᵇ17–25).

Note 904

Yet they possessed laws and political order: Rejecting with Dreizehnter and the mss. the OCT addition of ἀεὶ ("yet they always possessed laws and political order").

Note 905

We said earlier that the territory should belong to those who possess weapons and share in the constitution: At VII 9 1329ᵃ17–26.
Why those doing the farming should be distinct from these: At VII 9 1329ᵃ34–39, 10 1329ᵇ1–2.
And how much territory there should be and of what sort: At VII 5–6.

Note 906

We say that property should not be held communally: See II 5.
As some have claimed: See II 1 1261ᵃ4–8.
But it should be communal in its use, as it is among friends, and that neither should any citizen be in need of food: This is compromise between the Platonic position (all—at any rate guardian—property is communal) and the position that all property should be privately owned, is supposed to resolve the problems of each (II 5 1263ᵃ21–30). To own or hold property, however, is to have the power to alienate or dispose of it through either gift or sale (*Rh.* I 5 1361ᵃ21–22). But, though each unconditional citizen in the best constitution (each male head of household) is given an equal allotment of land, one part of which is near the town, the other near the frontier (*Pol.* VII 10 1330ᵃ14–18), these allotments seem to be inalienable (II 7 1266ᵇ14–31, II 9 1270ᵃ15–34). But if they are, so that one cannot sell them or give them away, what does owning them actually consist in? The natural thought is that it must lie in the use of them. And even though in the best constitution that use is communal, it is so because the owner grants it to his fellow citizens out of virtue and friendship and not because the law requires him to do it (II 5 1263ᵃ29–30). The expectation, however, is that the one to whom he grants it will also treat the property and its further use in the way that virtue requires. In the best constitution, where all the citizens have complete virtue, this is a reasonable expectation. But it is not one that carries over to less virtuous constitutions.

Note 907

What the cause is of our agreeing with this will be stated later: A promise unfulfilled in our *Politics*.

Note 908

Greater concord (*homonoêtikôteron*) **in the face of wars with neighbors:** See V 6 1306ᵃ9n.

Note 909

The way slaves should be treated, and why it is better to hold out freedom as a reward to all slaves, will be discussed later: This discussion does not appear in our *Politics*, but the following text from the *Economics*, which may not be by

Aristotle, provides us with a few more thoughts on the topic: "The first and most necessary sort of property is also the best and most suited to household management (*oikonomikôtaton*)—this is the human sort. That is why one should first provide oneself with excellent slaves. But slaves are of two kinds (*eidos*), steward (*epitropos*) and worker (*ergatês*). And since we see that methods of education produce a certain character in the young, it is necessary, when one has provided oneself with slaves, to nurture the ones who are to be assigned the functions of free people. Intercourse with slaves, though, should be such as to allow them neither to be wantonly aggressive nor relaxed. And a share of honor should be given to the ones who are more free, and plenty of food to the workers. And since the drinking of wine makes even free people wantonly aggressive, so that in many nations they keep away from it (as, for example, the Carthaginians do when they are on military campaigns), it is evident that wine should never, or very seldom, be given to slaves. Three things [make up the life of a slave], work, punishment, and food. For them to have food but neither punishment nor work makes them wantonly aggressive, whereas for them to have work and punishment but no food is [to be a victim of] force and produces a lack of strength. It remains, then, to give them work and sufficient food. For it is impossible to rule without giving wages, and food is a slave's wage. And just as other people become worse when better conduct is not followed by better treatment, and there are no rewards for virtue and vice, so it is too with servants. That is why we should make inquiry and bestow and withhold each thing in accord with worth, whether it is food or clothing, leisure or punishment. And both in word and in deed we should imitate the capacity of doctors in prescribing medicine, while keeping in mind at the same time that food is not medicine, because it must be given continually. The slave best suited to his work is the kind (*genos*) that is neither too cowardly or too courageous. For both traits cause injustice [to the owner]. For those who are cowardly lack endurance, while the spirited ones are not easy to rule. And every slave should have a definite end. For it is just and advantageous to offer slaves their freedom as a prize. For they wish to work when there is a prize and a time defined [for its attainment]. One should bind slaves to one's service by the pledges of wives and children, and by not acquiring many slaves of the same nationality, in just the way that cities also do. And one should provide religious sacrifices and give treats more for the slaves' sake than for the sake of those who are free. For the former have larger shares of the very things for the sake of which these have been instituted" (5 1344ᵃ23–ᵇ11).

Note 910

We said earlier that a city should have as much access to the land and the sea, and likewise to its entire territory, as is possible: See VII 5 1327ᵃ3–10, 6 1327ᵃ11–40.

Note 911

As regards its own situation, one should pray to be successful in getting a site for it: Reading αὐτῆς δὲ πρὸς αὐτὴν τὴν θέσιν εὔχεσθαι δεῖ κατατυγχάνειν with Kraut and Schütrumpf for OCT αὐτῆς δὲ προσάντη εἶναι τὴν θέσιν εὔχεσθαι δεῖ

κατ᾽ εὐχήν ("as regards its own situation, one should pray to get a site for it that is sloping"). Dreizehnter reads κατὰ τύχην for κατατυγχάνειν.
Looking to four things: The four could be: (1a) fresh air, (1b) fresh water, (1c) political requirements, and (1d) military requirements, or (2a) health (which requires fresh air and water), (2b) political requirements, (2c) military requirements, and (2d) beauty (1330ᵇ31, 1331ᵃ12).

Note 912
The capacity of water and air has a nature of this sort: That is, they are of a nature to be capable of being used frequently and in great quantities by us.

Note 913
An acropolis is oligarchic or monarchical, whereas a level-ground fortification is democratic: An acropolis (or hill fort) does not provide equal protection for all of a city's inhabitants when the city is under attack, since those in the hill fort (typically a privileged few) are better protected than those on level ground. A fort on level ground, by contrast, provides equal (or more nearly equal) protection for all, and so is more democratic. It is aristocratic, in turn, to have a number of strongholds, one for each aristocratic family or clan, and of a quality that is in accord with the worth of each.

Note 914
The new Hippodamean way of laying them out: The way designed by Hippodamus of Miletus, on whom see II 8 1267ᵇ22–1268ᵇ31.

Note 915
Difficult to enter: Reading δυσείσοδος with OCT. Dreizehnter reads δυσέξοδος "difficult to get out of" with the mss. Compare 1330ᵇ2–3.

Note 916
Vine clumps: A vine clump or cluster was laid out like the five spots on a die.

Note 917
Those people who say that cities that lay claim to virtue should not have walls: See Plato, *Lg.* 778d–779b.
Cities that prided themselves in this way: Probably an allusion to Sparta, which had no walls, and suffered humiliating defeat when it was invaded by the Thebans under Epaminondas. See II 9 1269ᵇ37n.

Note 918
Too much for human virtue (*anthrôpinês aretês*): "People are sometimes even praised . . . when they endure something shameful or painful for great and noble things, whereas if it is the reverse, they are blamed, since to endure the most shameful things for something not at all noble or only moderately so is characteristic of a base person. And to some people it is not praise we give but, rather, sympathetic consideration, when someone does some action he shouldn't do because of things that overstrain human nature and that no one could endure" (*NE* III 10 1110ᵃ19–26); "Where the contrary of beastliness is concerned, it would most fit the

case to speak of a virtue that is beyond us, one of a heroic even a divine sort—as when Homer has Priam say that Hector was exceptionally good: 'nor did he seem the son of a mortal man but, rather, one of a god.' So if, as they say, human beings become gods because of an extreme of virtue, it is clear that the state opposed to the type that is beast-like will be of this sort" (VII 1 1145^{a}18–25).

Note 919

In light of recent discoveries about projectiles and engines for improved precision in sieges: Catapults, siege towers, and battering rams had all fairly recently been introduced.

Note 920

They should seek and devise (*philosophein*) **others:** If *philosophein* meant, as it usually does, "do philosophy" or "philosophically consider," then it would refer, presumably, to the way in which Aristotle considers whether a city should or should not have walls. Its meaning here, however, seems to be the somewhat looser one, in which it means "discuss," "investigate," "study," "work at something," or the one I have chosen, "devise."

Note 921

Some other prophecy delivered by the Pythian god: The oracle of Apollo (the Pythian god referred to) at Delphi was one of the most famous in antiquity; both cities and individuals consulted it in matters of importance, whether religious or secular. The inscriptions on the walls well convey the spirit the oracle stood for: know thyself; nothing in excess; observe the limit; hate wanton aggression; bow before the divine; glory not in strength.

Note 922

A place like this would be one that is such as to be a conspicuous enough setting for virtue and also better fortified than the neighboring parts of the city: The thought, as at VII 11 1330^{b}17–21, is that the qualities of places in the best city, which, as an aristocracy based on virtue, should match the virtue or merit of the citizens assigned to them, so that the best and best fortified places go to the most important officials.

Setting for virtue: Reading τὴν ἀρετῆς θέσιν with Dereizehnter, Kraut, and the mss. for OCT τὴν τῆς θέσεως ἀρετὴν.

Note 923

The sort they call by that name in Thessaly: Reading ὀνομάζουσιν with Dreizehnter and the mss. for OCT νομίζουσιν.

Note 924

Shame (*aidôs*): "Shame is not properly spoken about as a sort of virtue, since it is more like a feeling than a state. Shame is defined as a sort of fear of disrepute at any rate, and its effects are somewhat similar to those of the fear of frightening things. For people who are ashamed of themselves blush, and those who fear death turn pale. Both shame and fear appear, then, to be somehow bodily, which seems to be precisely what is characteristic of a feeling rather than a state. The feeling is fitting not to every age, however, but to the young. For we think that young people should have a sense of shame because they live by their feelings and so make many errors but are restrained by shame. Also, we praise those young people who have a sense of shame. No one would praise an older person for being prone to shame, however, since we think that he shouldn't do any action that gives rise to shame" (*NE* IV 9 1128^{b}10–21).

Note 925

Pre-eminent group: Reading τὸ προεστὸς with OCT and Newman. Dreizehnter and the mss. read τὸ πλῆθος ("multitude").

Note 926

The order that has just been mentioned should also be imitated in matters pertaining to the countryside: Reading μεμιμῆσθαι with Dreizehnter and the mss. for OCT νενεμῆσθαι ("the order that has just been mentioned should also be established in matters pertaining to the countryside").

Note 927

Heroes: Heroes were conceived of as beings with a special status, a bit like that of Christian saints, intermediate between gods and ordinary human beings.

Note 928

Speaking about them is a function (*ergon*) **of prayer, whereas having them come about is a function of luck:** The best city is the one that is in accord with, or that answers to, our prayers, so that when we see which one we would pray to have, we see what to say about it. Bringing it about is another matter, since it depends on the availability of suitable resources, which with luck will be on hand, but may not be. See VII 13 1332^{a}28–32 for a more careful statement.

Note 929

Of which and of what sorts of people: See I 3 1253^{b}8n.

Note 930

Sometimes the target is well set up, but people make an error in what they do to hit it; sometimes they achieve everything that furthers the end, but the end they set up is a base one; and sometimes they make both errors: "It is possible for one's target to correct but for there to be errors in what promotes [hitting] the target; and it is possible for the target to be in error but for one to be correct about what will further [hitting] it. It is also possible for neither to be correct. What, though, does virtue make correct, the target or what furthers [hitting] the target? We take it that it makes the target correct, since the target is not arrived at by deduction (*sullogismos*) or by reason (*logos*). Let us, then, posit the target as a starting-point. For the doctor does not investigate whether to make someone healthy or not, but whether he should take walks or not, nor does the trainer investigate whether to produce a good physical condition in someone or not, but whether he should practice wrestling. Similarly, no other science is concerned with the end. For just as in the theoretical sciences the hypotheses are the starting-points, so in the productive sciences the end is starting-point and hypothesis. Given, then, that so-and-so needs to be healthy, if that is to come about such-and-such must be the case, just as, in the other sphere, if a triangle [has interior angles equal to] two right angles, then such-and-such must be the case. The starting-point of understanding, then, is the end, whereas that of action is where understanding ends. So if the cause of all correctness is either reason or virtue, and if reason is not the cause, then the correctness of the end, although not of what furthers the end, would be due to virtue. Now, the end is the for-the-sake-of-which. For every deliberate choice is *of* something and *for the sake of* something. Well, the for-the-sake-of-which is the mean, and virtue is the cause of this, in that it deliberately chooses what we act for the sake of. However, deliberate choice is not of the mean, but of what furthers it" (*EE* II 11 1227^{b}19–36); "There is, then, a capacity called cleverness, and this is the sort of thing that, when it comes to the things that further hitting a proposed target, is able to do these and to hit upon them. If, then, the target is a noble one, this capacity is praiseworthy, but, if it is a base one, it is unscrupulous. That is why both practically-wise people and unscrupulous ones are said to be clever. Practical wisdom, however, is not the capacity of cleverness but does not exist without this capacity" (*NE* VI 12 1144^{a}23–29).

Note 931

The defining mark (*horos*) **they set before themselves:** The ethical or medical *horos* seems to be something that brings the target itself within reach of perception. "Health is the account [of the form or essence] in the soul and the scientific knowledge. So what is healthy comes to be when one has understood as follows: Since this is what health is, necessarily if the thing is to be healthy, this must be present—for example, a uniform state—and if the latter is to be present, there must be heat, and the doctor goes on, always understanding in this way, until he is led to a final this that he himself is able to produce. Then the movement from this point onward is called a production—the one that leads to being healthy" (*Met.* VII 7 1032^{b}5–10). The doctor's *horos* is the thing "*by reference to which he discerns* what is healthy for a body from what isn't" (*EE* VIII 3 1249^{a}21–22)—the thing that must be "looked to in saying what the correct reason is" (II 5 1222^{b}7–8). Thus the doctor can tell by touch, we may suppose, whether the muscle is in a uniform state, which is a mean between being too tense and too limp, so it becomes his *horos*. He then has to find something he can do directly, and can tell by perception that he is doing "when actually doing" it (10 1226^{a}37), that will produce the requisite uniform state, such as making the muscle hot by rubbing it. Health itself, by contrast, which is his target, need not be defined in a way that makes it accessible to perception. In the same way, the politician must have "certain *horoi*, derived from nature and from the truth itself, by reference to which he will discern what is just, what is noble, and what is advantageous" (*Protr.* B47). See also I 9 1258^{a}18n.

Note 932

While it is possible for some to achieve these ends, it is not open to others, either because of some stroke of luck or because of nature: "Even if happiness is not a godsend but comes about through virtue and some sort of learning or training, it is evidently one of the most divine things, since virtue's prize and end is evidently something divine and blessed. At the same time, it would also be something widely shared, since it is possible for it to be acquired through some sort of learning or supervision by all those not disabled in relation to virtue" (*NE* I 9 1099ᵇ14–20). However, someone may be disabled as the result of an injury, disease, or accident, or because of an unlucky natural defect, such as being born blind. No one who lacks virtue because he is disabled in these ways is reproached or blamed for this, although someone who lacks it because he had disabled himself would be (III 5 1114ᵃ25–28). The same is true of those who are by nature disabled where full virtue is concerned. A female, for example, is by nature a sort of disabled male (*GA* II 3 737ᵃ27–28), since in the process of embryogenesis she is formed because of a disabling or deforming, by the menstrual fluid of her female progenitor, of the form transmitted in her male progenitor's semen (IV 3). Human females, as a result, cannot develop full virtue, since the deliberative part of their souls "lacks control (*akuron*)" (*Pol.* I 13 1260ᵃ13). They thus have a share in virtue and happiness that is less than that of males. The same is true to an even greater extent of natural slaves, whose souls lack a deliberative part altogether (1260ᵃ12), and may also be true of people native to northern or southern regions (VII 7 1327ᵇ20–38).

Note 933
Others straightaway seek happiness in an incorrect way, although it is possible for them to achieve it: "For by pursuing this in different ways and by different means each group of people produces distinct ways of life and distinct constitutions" (VII 8 1328ᵃ41–ᵇ2); "Those constitutions that aim at the common advantage are—in accord with what is unconditionally just—correct, whereas those that aim only at the advantage of the rulers are erroneous ones, and deviations from the correct constitutions" (III 7 1279ᵃ17–20).

Note 934
We say, and have given this definition in our ethical works, that happiness is a complete activation and use of virtue: The ethical writings we possess do not give exactly this definition of happiness, but they do more or less imply it. See VII 8 1328ᵃ37–38n.
And this not on the basis of a hypothesis but unconditionally: This important rider is not found in the other ethical writings.

Note 935
The former involve choosing something bad: Reading αἵρεσίς with Pellegrin and the mss. for OCT ἀναίρεσίς ("the former involve removing something bad").

Note 936
An excellent man, of course, would use poverty, disease, and other sorts of bad luck in a noble way, but blessed happiness involves their contraries: "If, however, it is activities that control living, as we said, no blessed person will ever become wretched, since he will never do hateful or base actions. For a truly good and practically-wise person, we think, will bear what luck brings graciously and, making use of the resources at hand, will always do the noblest actions, just as a good general makes the best uses in warfare of the army he has and a good shoemaker

makes the best shoes out of the hides he has been given, and the same way with all other craftsmen. If this is so, however, a happy person will never become wretched—nor *blessed* certainly—if he runs up against luck like Priam's. He will not, then, be variable or easily subject to reversals of fortune, since he will not be easily shaken from his happiness by just any misfortunes that chance to come along but only by great and repeated ones. And from these he will not return to being happy again in a short time but—if indeed he does do so—in a long and complete one in which he achieves great and noble things" (*NE* I 10 1100^{b}33–1101^{a}13).

Note 937

An excellent man is the sort for whom, because of his virtue, unconditionally good things are good: "Should we [not] say that unconditionally and in truth the proper object of wish is the good, but to each person it is the apparent good? To an excellent person, it is what is truly the proper object; to a base one, it is whatever random thing it happens to be. It is just the same in the case of bodies. The things that are healthy for those in good condition are the things that are truly healthy, whereas for those that are diseased, it is different ones, and similarly with bitter, sweet, hot, heavy, and each of the others. For an excellent person discerns each of them correctly and, in each case, what is true is apparent to him" (*NE* III 4 1113^{a}23–31).

Note 938

That is why we pray for the composition of the city to be successful: Reading διὸ κατατυχεῖν with Coraes and εὐχόμεθα τὴν τῆς πόλεως σύστασιν with the mss. for OCT διὸ κατ' εὐχὴν εὐχόμεθα τῇ τῆς πόλεως συστάσει ("that is why, with regard to the things that luck controls [for we take it that luck does control them], we pray for the composition of the city to be in accord with our prayers"). Compare εὔχεσθαι δεῖ κατατυγχάνειν at VII 11 1330^{a}37.

The things that luck controls: Namely, external goods (VII 1 1323^{a}25n): "a happy person needs to have . . . external goods—the ones luck brings" (*NE* VII 13 1153^{b}17–18).

Note 939

Even if it is possible for all to be excellent without each citizen being so individually: See II 5 1264^{b}15–24.

The latter is still more choiceworthy: Compare: "Even if the good is the same for an individual and for a city, that of a city is evidently a greater and, at any rate, a more complete good to acquire and preserve. For while it should content us to acquire and preserve this for an individual alone, it is nobler and more divine to do so for a nation and city" (*NE* I 2 1094^{b}7–10).

Note 940

Some qualities, because of their nature, play a double game (*epamphoterizonta*): The verb *epamphoterizein* is used to characterize ambiguous statements (Plato, *Rep.* V 479c3) and to describe things that lie halfway between others: "Seals and bats lie half-way between, the former between land and water animals, and the latter between land animals and fliers" (*PA* IV 14 697^{b}1–4). Here, however, the suggestion seems to be that these qualities can run with the hares and hunt with the hounds—that they can play a double game.

Note 941
We determined earlier what sort of nature people should have if they are going to be easily handled by the legislator: See VII 7 1327^{b}18–38.

Note 942
Some things are learned by habituation (*ethizomenoi*): Habituation is a process, typically involving pleasure (reward) and pain (punishment), by which we acquire a habit that is at once cognitive (as in the case of induction) and conative, because what we experience as pleasurable we tend to desire and pursue and what we experience as painful we tend to be averse to and avoid (*DA* III 7 431^{a}8–^{b}10, *NE* III 5 1114^{a}31–^{b}3, III 12 1119^{a}25–27, *Pol.* VIII 5 1340^{a}23–28).
And others by listening: See I 13 1260^{b}4n.

Note 943
Scylax: Scylax of Caryanda in Caria was a late-6th-cent geographer. See Herodotus IV.44.

Note 944
One of the impossible things: See VII 4 1325^{b}38–39.

Note 945
We spoke about this earlier: At VII 9 1329^{a}2–17.

Note 946
The distinction: Reading διαίρεσιν with Dreizehnter for the mss. and OCT αἵρεσιν ("the choice").

Note 947
If someone is going to rule well, so it is said, he must first be [well] ruled: See III 4 1277^{b}11–13.

Note 948
It is noble even for free young men to perform many of the functions that are believed to be appropriate for slaves: See III 4 1277^{b}5–6, VIII 2 1337^{b}17–21.

Note 949
We say that the virtue of [1] a citizen and [2] a ruler is the same as that of the best man: [1] is true only in the best political system, which is the one currently under consideration. See IV 7 1293^{b}1–7. However, III 4 1277^{a}20–21 claims, albeit in the antecedent of a conditional, that "[3] the virtue of a good ruler and of a good man are the same," suggesting that [2] may be true more broadly, perhaps in all constitutions. If we mean by "good ruler" someone who is "unconditionally a good ruler," then this would obviously be the case. For "practical wisdom is the only virtue special to a [political] ruler" (*Pol.* III 4 1277^{b}25–26), and "[4] it is neither possible to be fully good without practical wisdom nor practically-wise without [full or unconditional] virtue of character" (*NE* VI 13 1144^{b}30–32). But if we run

[4] in the opposite direction, we can say that those rulers—anyway in non-deviant or correct constitutions—who have the virtues that are *relative to their constitutions*, also have a sort of constitution-relative practical wisdom. If we take that step, as it seems we should, then [2] will, like [1], be true only in the best constitution.

Note 950

The soul, though, is divided into two parts, one of which has reason intrinsically, whereas the other does not have it intrinsically, but is capable of listening to it: "Another natural constituent of the soul [beyond the vegetative part mentioned below], however, also seems to be non-rational, although it shares in reason in a way. For we praise the reason—that is, the part of the soul that has reason—of a person with self-control and of a person without it, since it exhorts them correctly toward what is best. But they also have by nature something else within them besides reason, apparently, which fights against reason and resists it. For exactly as with paralyzed limbs (when their owners deliberately choose to move them to the right, they do the contrary and move off to the left), so it is in the case of the soul as well, since the impulses of people who lack self-control are in contrary directions. In the case of the body, to be sure, we see the part that is moving in the wrong direction, whereas in the case of the soul we do not see it. But presumably we should nonetheless acknowledge that in the soul as well there is something besides reason, countering it and going against it. How it is different, though, is not important. But this part apparently also has a share of reason, as we said, at any rate, it is obedient to the reason of a self-controlled person. Furthermore, that of a temperate and courageous person, presumably, listens still better, since there it chimes with reason in everything. Apparently, then, the non-rational part is also twofold, since the vegetative part does not share in reason in any way but the appetitive part (indeed, the desiring part as a whole) does so in some way, because it is able to listen to reason and obey it. It has reason, then, in the way we are said to have the reason of our fathers and friends and not in the way we are said to have that of mathematics. The fact, though, that the non-rational part is persuaded in some way by reason is revealed by the practice of warning people and of all the different practices of admonishing and exhorting them. If we should say that it too has reason, however, then the part that has reason will be double as well—one part having it fully and within itself, the other as something able to listen to it as to a father. Virtues are also defined in accord with this difference, since we say that some are of thought, others of character. Theoretical wisdom, comprehension, and practical wisdom are virtues of thought; generosity and temperance virtues of character. For when we talk about someone's character we do not say that he is theoretically-wise or has comprehension but that he is mild-mannered or temperate. But we do also praise a theoretically-wise person with reference to his state, and—among the states—it is the praiseworthy ones that we call virtues" (*NE* I 13 1102^{b}13–1103^{a}10).

Note 951

The worse part is always for the sake of the better, and this is as evident in the products of the crafts: See *NE* I 1 1094^{a}6–16, quoted in VII 4 1325^{b}40–1326^{a}5n.

As it is in those of nature: "Just as every instrument is for the sake of something, the parts of the body are also for the sake of something, that is, for the sake of some action, so that the whole body must evidently be for the sake of some complex action. Just as the saw is there for the sake of sawing, not sawing for the sake of the saw, since sawing is a certain use [of a saw], so the body, too, is somehow for the sake of the soul, and the parts of the body for the sake of those functions for which each is naturally adapted" (*PA* I 5 645b14–20); "The perceptual capacities that operate through external media, such as smell, hearing, and sight, are characteristic of animals capable of movement. In all that have them they exist for the sake of preservation, in order that they may perceive their food before they pursue it, and avoid what is bad or destructive, while in those that also happen to have practical wisdom (*phronêseôs*), they exist for the sake of doing well, since they make us aware of many differences, from which arises practical wisdom concerning both intelligible things and things done in action" (*Sens.* 1 436b18–437a3).

Note 952

In the way that we are accustomed to divide it, the part of the soul that has reason intrinsically is divided into two, since on the one hand there is practical reason and on the other theoretical reason: "Previously, then, we said that there are two parts of the soul, one that has reason and one that lacks reason. Let us now divide in the same way the part that has reason. Let us take it that there are two parts that have reason—one through which we get a theoretical grasp on those beings whose starting-points do not admit of being otherwise and one through which we do so on those that do admit of being otherwise, since where beings differ in kind, parts of the soul that differ in kind are naturally suited to each of them, since it is on the basis of a certain similarity and kinship that they have knowledge. Let us call one of these 'the scientific part' and the other 'the rationally calculative part.' For deliberating is the same as rationally calculating, and no one deliberates about what does not admit of being otherwise. So the rationally calculative part is one distinct part of the part that has reason" (*NE* VI 1 1139a3–15). The virtue of the scientific part is theoretical wisdom, that of the rationally calculative part, practical wisdom.

Note 953

Actions too, we will say, are divided proportionately: See VII 3 1325b16–23.

Note 954

This is always what is most choiceworthy for each individual, to attain the topmost [good] (*akrotatou*): "Since every sort of knowledge and every deliberate choice reaches after some good, let us say what it is politics seeks—that is, what the topmost (*akrotaton*) of all the good things doable in action is" (*NE* I 4 1095a14–17).

Note 955

Leisure: See II 9 1271b5n.

Note 956

War must be for the sake of peace, unleisure for the sake of leisure, necessary and useful things for the sake of noble ones: "Happiness seems to reside in leisure, since we do unleisured things in order to be at leisure, and wage war in order to live in peace. Now the activity of the practical virtues occurs in politics or in warfare, and the actions concerned with these seem to be unleisured and those in warfare completely so (for no one chooses to wage war for the sake of waging war, or to foment war either, since someone would seem completely bloodthirsty, if he made enemies of his friends in order to bring about battles and killings). But the activity of a politician too is unleisured and beyond political activity itself he tries to get positions of power and honors or, at any rate, happiness for himself and his fellow citizens—this being different from the exercise of politics and something we clearly seek on the supposition of its being different. If, then, among actions in accord with the virtues, those in politics and war stand out in nobility and magnitude but these are unleisured and seek some end rather than being choiceworthy because of themselves, whereas the activity of understanding seems to be superior in excellence because it is contemplative, to seek no end beyond itself, and to have its own proper pleasure, which increases the activity by its own increase, and if in addition the self-sufficiency, leisured quality, and unweariness (so far as this is possible for a human being), as well as all the other attributes assigned to the blessed, are evidently attributes of it, then this activity will be the complete happiness of a human being, if it receives a complete span of life (since nothing is incomplete that is characteristic of happiness)" (*NE* X 7 1177^{b}4–26).

Note 957
The divisions of actions: Reading διαιρέσεις with Newman and Kraut for OCT and Dreizehnter αἱρέσεις ("the choice of actions").

Note 958
More conducive to getting more (*pleonektikôteras*): See II 7 1266^{b}37n.

Note 959
And has now been refuted by the facts too: See II 9 1270^{a}33–34n.

Note 960
Thibron: Otherwise unknown.
The goods of luck (*eutuchêmatôn*): See IV 11 1295^{b}5n.
Each of the others who have written about their constitution: These include Xenophon, *Lac.*

Note 961
This is precisely what the Spartans accused their king, Pausanias, of doing: See V 7 1307^{a}4n.

Note 962
For, as has often been said, the end of war is peace, and that of unleisure is leisure: Most recently at VII 14 1333^{a}35–36. On leisure, see II 9 1271^{b}5n.

Note 963
Much justice and temperance are needed: Rejecting with Dreizehnter and the mss. the OCT addition of μετέχειν.

The Isles of the Blessed: A paradise where good people, usually after their death, were thought to live in eternal happiness. See Hesiod, *Works and Days* 168–173.

Note 964

But since . . . these goods and the enjoyment of them to be greater than that of the virtues . . . and that . . . because of itself, is evident from these considerations: The dots indicate what seem to be gaps in the mss. The meaning is probably something like this: But since they consider these goods and the enjoyment of them to be greater goods than the enjoyment (or use) of the virtues, they train only in the sort of virtue that is useful in war, whereas that they should also train in the sort that is useful in peace and that they should do so because of itself is evident from the foregoing considerations.

Note 965

We made a distinction earlier, accordingly, to the effect that nature, habit, and reason are needed: At VII 13 1332ᵃ35–ᵇ8.

Note 966

What sort the citizens must be as regards their nature was determined earlier: At VII 7 1327ᵇ18–38.

Note 967

The harmony must be the best one: That is, the harmony must not be the one between the non-rational part (which habituation targets) of the soul and the part that has reason (which formal teaching targets) that exists in a self-controlled person, but the superior one that exists in the virtuous person, whose feelings and actions are both in a mean: "[The non-rational part] is obedient to the reason of a self-controlled person [but] that of a temperate and courageous person, presumably, listens still better, since there it chimes with reason in everything" (*NE* I 13 1102ᵇ26–28).

Note 968

The best hypothesis: Namely, the hypothesis about what end is best, or what happiness consists in. See II 9 1269ᵃ32n.

Note 969

Reason and understanding are our nature's end: See VII 14 1333ᵃ21–30n.

Note 970

Spirit (*thumos*) **and wish** (*boulêsis*)**, and furthermore appetite:** Aristotle's official view is that "wish is always found in the rationally calculative part" (*Top.* IV 5 126ᵃ13), whereas spirit and appetite are in the non-rational part: "in the rationally calculative part there will be wish, and in the non-rational part appetite and spirit. And so if the soul is tripartite there will be desire (*orexis*) in each part" (*DA* III 9 432ᵇ5–7; also *Rh.* I 10 1369ᵃ2–4). This is perhaps the only place where he deviates from that view. But the explanation for the deviation is not far to seek. For when he discusses wish in the process of trying to explain deliberate choice (*prohairesis*), he writes: "[Deliberate choice] is not *wish* either, although it appears

to be a close relative of it. For there is no deliberate choice of impossible things, and if someone were to say he was deliberately choosing them, he would seem silly. But there is wish for impossible things—for example, immortality. There is also wish concerning the sorts of things that could never come about through ourselves—for example, that a certain actor or athlete should win a victory prize. No one deliberately chooses things like that, but things he thinks can come about through him. Further, wish is more for the end, whereas deliberate choice is of the things that further the end" (*NE* III 2 1111^{b}19–27). Understood in this non-technical way, there is nothing especially rational about wish, and we can easily see why children are said to have it. The wish, however, that is a "desire involving rational calculation" (*Rh.* I 10 1369^{a}2; compare *NE* III 1112^{a}10–12) is clearly an Aristotelian regimentation of the non-technical notion, which is the one employed here. Its attribution to children, who lack rational calculation, makes this especially clear.
Are present in children straight from birth, whereas rational calculation and understanding naturally arise as they grow: Compare Plato, *Rep.* 441a–b.

Note 971
In legislating for this marital community: Namely, the community of man and woman. See I 2 1252^{b}10.

Note 972
The oracle that was given to the Troezenians: The oracle alleged said, "Do not plow the young furrow." An Athenian father gave his daughter in marriage with the words: "I give you this woman for the plowing of legitimate children."
The Troezenians: See V 3 1303^{a}29n.

Note 973
While their body is still growing: Reading σώματος with Pellegrin, Schütrumpf, Kraut and the mss. for OCT and Dreizehnter σπέρματος ("while their seed is still growing"). In Aristotle's view male seed, or semen, is a very concentrated or "concocted" blood product: "In blooded animals, blood is the final form of the nourishment . . . and since seed too is a residue from nourishment, that is, from its final form, surely it follows that seed will be either blood or something analogous to it or something constituted out of these. Every one of the parts of the animal is constituted out of blood as it becomes concocted and somehow divided into portions. . . . Therefore, seed is evidently a residue from that nourishment which is a type of blood—that which is finally distributed to the parts. This is why seed has great potentiality . . . and why it is reasonable that offspring should resemble their parents. For that which goes to all the parts [namely, blood] resembles what is left over [seed]. Hence the seed of the hand or of the face or of the whole animal is in an undifferentiated way a hand, or a face, or a whole animal—that is, what each of the latter is in actuality, such the seed is in potentiality" (*GA* I 9 726^{b}1–18). As a result it takes a lot of nourishment to replace. If a young man has frequent sexual intercourse, therefore, his growth is likely to suffer, because the nourishment required for it will be expended in making his seed.

Note 974

After which it is no longer extensive: Rejecting with Dreizehnter and the mss. the OCT addition here of ἢ μικρόν ("after which it is not longer extensive, or is small").

Note 975

Or a little before: Reading ἢ μικρόν πρότερον with Pellegrin and Kraut. OCT brackets ἢ μικρόν for deletion here, transposing it to follow πληθύον ἔτι at 1335ᵃ27, and does not read πρότερον. Dreizehnter reads ἡλικίαν ("[years of] age").

Note 976

Favoring northerly winds over southerly ones: Especially so, in Aristotle's view, if male offspring are desired: "The northern wind produces more males than the southern one, since bodies are moister during southern winds, so that they also have more residues. And more residue is more difficult to concoct. That is why in the men the seed and in the women the menstrual discharge is more moist" (*GA* IV 2 766ᵇ34–767ᵃ1). See also Plato, *Lg.* 747d–e.

Note 977

We must deal with that topic at greater length in our discussion of the supervision of children: A promise unfulfilled in our *Politics*.

Note 978

The [physical] state characteristic of athletes is not useful either with a view to the good state of a citizen: See VII 4 1338ᵇ9–1339ᵃ10.

Note 979

The gods whose assigned prerogative is to watch over birth: For example, Artemis and Eileithuia. See Plato, *Lg.* 789e.

Note 980

With regard to their thought, as opposed to their bodies, it is fitting for them to spend their time taking things easy, since unborn children obviously draw resources from their mothers, just as plants do from the earth: The thought is that mental exertions, when coupled with physical ones, would draw too many resources away from the developing fetus. See VII 4 1339ᵃ7–10.

Note 981

Whether to rear offspring or expose them: Exposure or abandonment of newborns was a fairly common form of family planning in ancient Greece. Aristotle does not approve of this practice, and goes on to forbid even the abortion of fetuses once perception and life are both present. Like Plato, *Rep.* 459d–461c, however, he requires that disabled newborns be exposed, and that fetuses resulting from illegal intercourse be aborted.

Let there be a law that no disabled one (*pepêrômenon*) is to be reared: Just how serious a disability (*pêrôsis*) has to be for this law to come into effect is unclear. For example, a normal female, in Aristotle's view, is a sort of disabled, or deformed, male (*GA* II 3 737ᵃ27–28), since in the process of embryogenesis she is formed because of a partial disabling of the form transmitted in her male progenitor's semen

(1335ᵃ26n) by the menstrual fluid of her female progenitor. But Aristotle is clearly not advocating that no female child should be reared.
If the way the customs are ordered: Reading ἐάν ἡ τάξις τῶν ἐθῶν with Dreizehnter and some mss. for OCT ἡ τάξις τῶν ἐθῶν.

Note 982
When they have exceeded this age by four or five years they should be released from bringing children into the light of day: "[*Socrates*] But when women and men have passed breeding age, I imagine we will leave them free to have sex with whomever they wish—except that a man may not have sex with his daughter, mother, daughters' daughters, or mother's female ancestors, or a woman with her son and his descendants or her father and his ancestors. And we will permit all that only after telling them to be very careful not to let even a single fetus see the light of day, if one should happen to be conceived; but if one does force its way out, they must dispose of it on the understanding that no nurture is available for such a child" (Plato, *Rep*. V 461b–c).

Note 983
If they have intercourse after that, it should be evident that it is for the sake of health, or due to some other such cause: Hippocrates, *The Seed* 4 (= Lonie, pp. 319–320), describes the pleasures and health benefits of intercourse as follows: "In the case of women, it is my contention that when the vagina is rubbed during intercourse and the womb is disturbed, an irritation is set up in the womb that produces pleasure and heat in the rest of the body. . . . [T]he woman's heat flares up in response to the man's seed, and then dies away. The pleasure experienced by the woman during intercourse is considerably less than the man's, although it lasts for a longer time. What causes the man to feel more pleasure is that the secretion from the bodily fluid in his case occurs suddenly, and as the result of a more violent disturbance than in the woman's case. Another point about women: if they have intercourse with men their health is better than if they do not. For in the first place, the womb is moistened by intercourse, whereas when the womb is drier than it should be it becomes extremely contracted, and this extreme contraction causes pain to the body. In the second place, intercourse by heating the blood and rendering it more fluid gives an easier passage to the menses, whereas, if the menses do not flow, women's bodies become prone to sickness." We might think, therefore, that Aristotle would hold somewhat similar views and that the other causes he mentions would include pleasure. In fact, though, his views are quite different: "In most men, and speaking for the most part, the result of intercourse is tiredness and weakness rather than relief, due to the cause we mentioned [see 1335ᵃ24–26n]. Further, seed does not exist in them either in childhood or in old age or in sickness—in the last case because of weakness, in old age because their constitution does not concoct enough, and in childhood because they are growing, and so all the nutriment is used up too soon" (*GA* I 18 725ᵇ16–23). This suggests that sexual intercourse, at any rate for older men (post fifty-five or so?), has few health benefits, although 726ᵃ21–24 suggests that, like urination and defecation, ejaculation of seed may help cleanse the body of waste products—which are roughly speaking

the undigested parts of food that are included in the male seed, because it is a concentrated blood product (*Pr.* IV 29). The emission of seed in intercourse is indeed pleasant for males (*GA* I 20 728^{a}9–10), as is genital friction for both sexes, although not in the penis in one case and in the womb (as Hippocrates thought) in the other: "the pleasure of intercourse is caused by touch in the same place (*kata ton auton topon*) in the female as in the male" (728^{a}31–33). But it is not clear to what extent that could provide the male citizens of Aristotle's best city, who must be temperate and practically-wise, with a reason to have it: "The arguments that a temperate person avoids pleasure, that a practically-wise person pursues a painless life, and that children and wild beasts pursue pleasure, are all resolved in the same way. For we have said in what way pleasures are good and in what way not all of them are unconditionally good, and it is the latter sort that both wild beasts and children pursue, and it is painlessness in their case that a practically-wise person pursues. These are the ones involving appetite and pain, that is, the bodily ones (since they are of that sort) and their excesses, regarding which the intemperate person is intemperate. That is why a temperate person avoids *these* pleasures, since there are pleasures that are characteristic of a temperate person too" (*NE* VII 12 1153^{a}27–35).

Note 984

As for intercourse with another man: See II 10 1272^{a}24–25n.
When one is a husband: Rejecting with Dreizehnter, Kraut, and the mss. the OCT addition of ἀνὴρ ("when a man is a husband").

Note 985

If someone is found doing anything of this sort during his period of procreation: Aristotle thinks that all adultery is wrong (*NE* II 8 1107^{a}9–17), not just female adultery. On the topic of male adultery, indeed, which is the only sort under discussion here, his views are quite radical. For while male adultery was unregulated in ancient Athens, Aristotle criminalizes it—at any rate during the period of procreating as a part of public service.
He should be punished with dishonor (*atimia[i]*) **appropriate to his offense:** *Atimia* is used here in the legal sense to refer to the loss of the various rights and privileges pertaining to citizenship. Presumably, the intent of the legislative proposal is to protect the legitimacy of children, or to restrict the number of illegitimate ones. If so, a man who commits homosexual adultery during this period would seem to deserve a smaller penalty than one who commits heterosexual adultery.

Note 986

But very little wine, because of the diseases [it produces]: "It is customary for most babies to be subject to convulsions, and more so those that are more thriving and get milk that is more plentiful and thicker and whose wet-nurses are well fleshed. What is harmful, as leading to the condition, is wine—and more so red wine than white, and wine taken without water—and most of the wind-producing vegetables, and constipation" (*HA* VII 12 588^{a}3–8). Also *Somn.* 3 457^{a}4–21.

Note 987
There are certain mechanical instruments, which some nations already employ, to make their bodies straight: The precise nature of these instruments is unknown.

Note 988
Many others dress them in light clothing: Including the Spartans. See Xenophon, *Lac.* II.4.

Note 989
Because their bodily condition is hot, children are naturally suited to being trained to bear the cold: "Like those drinking wine the young are of a hot temperament due to their nature" (*Rh.* II 12 1389ᵃ19–20). Also *Pr.* III 7 872ᵃ3–6, Plato, *Lg.* 664e, 666a.

Note 990
It is not a good idea to have children engage in any kind of learning or any necessary physical exertion, lest it impede their growth: See VIII 4 1338ᵇ38–1339ᵃ10.

Note 991
Unfree: See III 9 1280ᵃ5n.

Note 992
Those in the *Laws* who prevent children from screaming and crying are wrong to prohibit such things: See Plato, *Lg.* 791d–792e.

Note 993
Holding the breath produces strength in those who are exerting themselves: See *GA* III 4 737ᵇ36–738ᵃ1.

Note 994
Shameful language (*aischrologia*): Obscene but also abusive language. See *NE* IV 9 1128ᵃ9–ᵇ1, *Rh.* III 2 1405ᵇ8–16.

Note 995
Looking at (*theôrein*): See I 2 1252ᵃ26n.

Note 996
An imitation of such actions: Namely, the unseemly ones imitated or represented in the forbidden stories or pictures.
Except in the precincts of certain gods at whose festivals custom permits even jeering to occur: Ritualized obscenity and scurrilous mockery played a role in certain religious festivals honoring Dionysus, Demeter, and other gods.
Licentious raillery (*tôthasmon*): The verbal form *tôthazein* is used at *Rh.* II 4 1381ᵃ33, where it means to "mock" or "jeer" at someone, or "engage in a slanging match" with them. Here, though, the jeering seems to be of an obscene or licentious nature.

Note 997
There must be legislation that younger people not be spectators either of iambus or of comedy: Reading νομοθητέον with Dreizehnter and some mss. for OCT θετέον ("But it should not be granted to younger people to witness iambus or comedy").

Iambus: A figure named "Iambe" is mentioned in the *Homeric Hymn to Demeter*, who uses language so abusive that the goddess is overcome by laughter and forgets her sorrows. Iambus is associated especially with scurrilous personal humor of the sort exemplified by the work of Archilochus.
Comedy: "The types of comedy are: old-style, which is greedy for what causes laughter; new-style, which abandons this, and tends more toward the dignified; and middle-style, which is a mixture of both" (*Po.* II = Janko, p. 42); "The amusement of the free person differs from that of the slavish one, and that of the well-educated person from that of the uneducated one. We can also see this from old-style and new-style comedies, since in the former what caused laughter was shameful language, whereas in the latter it is more innuendo, and there is no small difference between these as regards graciousness" (*NE* IV 9 1128ᵃ20–25). The greatest representative of old-style comedy is Aristophanes (c. 446–386 BC), that of new-style is Menander (344–392 BC).

Note 998
Later we must stop and determine it at greater length: A promise unfulfilled in our *Politics*.

Note 999
Theodorus: A famous 4th-cent actor. The quality of his voice is praised at *Rh.* III 2 1404ᵇ22–24.

BOOK VIII

Note 1000
Every craft and every sort of education wishes to fill in what nature leaves out: "Craft in some cases completes what nature is unable to complete" (*Ph.* II 8 199ᵃ15–16).

Note 1001
The character (*êthos*) **that properly belongs to each constitution:** "Rhetoricians should know the characters of each of the constitutions. . . . And we shall grasp these through what we mentioned [namely, the ends of each constitution]. For the characters are made evident by the deliberate choice, and the deliberate choice is referred back to the end it has in view" (*Rh.* I 8 1366ᵃ12–16). See V 10 1312ᵇ3n. The deliberate choices of a constitution, however, seem to depend on those of the governing body of the citizens. See VII 13 1332ᵃ31–38. Compare Plato, *Rep.* 544d–e: [*Socrates*] Are you aware, then, that there must be as many forms of human character as there are of constitutions? Or do you think constitutions arise from oak or rock and not from the characters of the people in the cities, which tip the scales, so to speak, and drag the rest along with them? [*Glaucon*] No, they could not possibly arise from anything other than that. [*Soc.*] So if there are five cities, there must also be five ways of arranging private individual souls." It goes without saying, however, that constitutions shape souls just as they are shaped by them.

Note 1002
Capacity and craft: See III 12 1282^{a}16n.

Note 1003
The end for the whole city is a single end: See VII 1 1323^{b}40–1324^{a}2.

Note 1004
One should in no way think that any citizen belongs to himself alone, but that all of them belong to the city, each being a part of the city: The idea is the one expressed more fully at I 2 1253^{a}18–29. See also III 6 1297^{a}17n.

Note 1005
One might praise the Spartans on account of this: But see VII 14 1333^{b}5–1334^{a}10.

Note 1006
Nor is it evident whether it is more appropriate that education be with a view to thought or with a view to the character of the soul: See VII 13 1332^{a}41–^{b}11.

Note 1007
The body, the soul, or the thought of free people: Retaining ἢ τὴν ψυχὴν with Dreizehnter, Pellegrin, Schütrumpf. A compelling reason to retain ἢ τὴν ψυχὴν, beyond that provided by the mss., is that because there is more to the soul than the part responsible for thought, more than just thought and the body can be affected by vulgar functions. See I 2 1252^{a}32n.
The uses and actions of virtue: See VII 8 1328^{a}37–38n.

Note 1008
Some of the free sciences: "We do not inquire into it [namely, the wisdom of which philosophy is the love] because of its having another use, but just as a human being is free, we say, when he is for his own sake and not for someone else, in the same way we pursue this as the only free science, since it alone is for its own sake" (*Met.* I 2 982^{b}24–28). Compare: "Fine and free arguments that vigorously seek the truth in every way, so as to acquire knowledge" (Plato, *Rep.* VI 499a); "the science that free people have" (Plato, *Sph.* 253c–d).
To overly apply oneself to them with a view to exactness: That is, to become an exact practitioner of them rather than well educated about them. See III 11 1282^{a}4n, also IV 1 1288^{b}16–19.
Exactness (*akribeia*): See III 9 1280^{b}28n.

Note 1009
The sorts of learning that are now laid down as a foundation, as was said earlier, tend in two directions: In OCT this is the last sentence of VIII 2.
As was said earlier: At VIII 2 1337^{a}39–42.
Tend in two directions: Since nothing out of the ordinary (VIII 2 1337^{a}42) was part of established education, the two directions are being useful and promoting virtue.

Note 1010
Just as has often been said, nature itself seeks not only the correct use of work but also the capacity to be at leisure in a noble way: See II 9 1271^{a}41–^{b}10, VII 14 1333^{a}30–^{b}5, 1334^{a}2–^{b}28, *NE* X 7 1177^{b}2–18.
Nature itself seeks: See I 1 1253^{a}9n.

Note 1011
This (*hautê*) is the one starting-point of everything else: The reference of the feminine demonstrative pronoun *hautê* is *scholê* ("leisure") from *scholazein* ("to be at leisure") in the previous sentence, rather than to *phusis*. It is a starting-point because leisure is the end or goal of politics. See VII 14 1334^{a}4–5.
We should speak about it again: A reference to VII 13–15.

Note 1012
Dispensing it as a medicine [for the ills of unleisure]: "Happiness does not lie in amusement, since it would indeed be strange if the end were amusement and we did all the work we do and suffered evils all our lives for the sake of amusing ourselves. For, in a word, we choose everything—except happiness, since end *it* is—for the sake of something else. But to engage in serious matters and to labor for the sake of amusement would evidently be silly and utterly childish. On the contrary, 'amusing ourselves so as to engage in serious matters,' as Anacharsis puts it, seems to be correct. For amusement is like relaxation, and it is because people cannot labor continuously that they need relaxation. End, then, relaxation is not, since it occurs for the sake of activity" (*NE* X 6 1176^{b}27–1177^{a}1).

Note 1013
This pleasure is not taken to be the same by everyone, however, but each takes it to be what is in accord with himself and his state [of character], and the best person takes it to be the best pleasure, the one that comes from the noblest things: "For each state [of character] has its own special set of things that are pleasant or noble, and an excellent person is perhaps distinguished most by his seeing what is true in each case, since he is like a standard and measure of them. In the case of ordinary people, however, deception seems to come about because of pleasure, which appears to be a good thing when it is not. So they choose what is pleasant as good and avoid what is painful as bad" (*NE* III 4 1113^{a}31–^{b}2).

Note 1014
Homer puts it this way: *Odyssey* XVIII.382–385. The first line Aristotle quotes is not in the poem as we have it.

Note 1015
Elsewhere, Odysseus says: *Odyssey* IX.7–8.
Odysseus: A prominent Greek hero in the Trojan Wars.

Note 1016
These are things that must be discussed later on: A promise unfulfilled in our *Politics*.

Note 1017
Free: Reading ἐλευθέροις with Dreizehnter and the mss. for OCT ἐλευθερίοις.

Note 1018
As we have said many times, the supervision of children should neither look to just one virtue nor to this one above all: See II 9 1271ᵃ41–ᵇ10, VII 14 1333ᵇ5–10, 1334ᵃ2–ᵇ28.

Note 1019
A tamer, lion-like character: Lions, in Aristotle's view, are "free, courageous, and well bred" (*HA* I 1 488ᵇ16–17), "dangerous while feeding, gentle when no longer hungry" (IX 44 628ᵇ8–9).

Note 1020
Around the Black Sea: "Some of the savages who live around the Black Sea . . . eat raw meats, some human flesh, while others are said to reciprocally lend their children to each other to be eaten at festivities" (*NE* VII 5 1148ᵇ21–24).
The Heniochi: These were believed to be an offshoot of the Spartans. See Strabo XI.2, 12.
In courage they have no share: Because courage requires its possessor to endure dangers "for the sake of what is noble, since this is the end characteristic of virtue" (*NE* III 7 1115ᵇ12–13). See 1338ᵇ29–31.

Note 1021
It is not the wolf or any other wild beast that would compete against noble danger, but rather a good man: "The person who is called 'courageous' in the full sense, then, is the one who is unanxious where noble death is concerned and the things that are an imminent threat of death" (*NE* III 6 1115ᵃ32–34).

Note 1022
The necessary things: See VIII 2 1337ᵇ4–21, 3 1337ᵇ25–27.

Note 1023
The training of the young and the necessary athletic exercises involved take away their strength: "Both athletic training regimens that are excessive and those that are deficient will ruin our strength" (*NE* II 2 1104ᵃ15–16).

Note 1024
Keynote (*endosimon*): An *endosimon* is both a prelude or an introduction and what establishes the pitch for musicians at the beginning of a performance. See *Rh.* III 14 1414ᵇ24, 1415ᵃ7.

Note 1025
As Euripides says: Aristotle paraphrases *Bacchae* 381.

Note 1026
This must be set down as third of the things mentioned: [1] Amusement is mentioned at VIII 3 1337ᵇ36–1338ᵃ1. [3a] Passing the time at VII 15 1334ᵃ11–ᵇ5. [3b] Practical wisdom at VII 14 1333ᵃ16–30, VIII 3 1337ᵇ22–33. [2] Virtue of character

has not been explicitly mentioned in so many words. But since practical wisdom necessarily involves the virtues of character (*NE* VI 13 1144^{b}30–32), [3b] already speaks somewhat to [2]. Insofar as [2] and [3b] are distinct points, however, the difference between them must hinge, it seems, on the fact that—as the mention of habituation (1339^{a}24) strongly suggests—virtues of character are inculcated through experience and habituation, virtues of thought, like practical wisdom, through teaching (*NE* II 1 1103^{a}14–23, X 9 1179^{b}20–31). The issue between [2] and [3b], then, is whether music is part of habituation or part of the education of thought through teaching. On Aristotle's own view, [1]–[3] are all important reasons to provide education in music. See 1339^{b}11–15, VIII 7 1341^{b}36–38.

Note 1027

Learning involves pain: Contrast 1340^{b}15–17.

Note 1028

The end (*telos*) **[as something complete] is not appropriate for anyone who is incomplete** (*ateles*): See I 13 1260^{a}12–14.

Note 1029

But perhaps we should investigate these matters later on: See VIII 6.

Note 1030

Being happy is composed of (*ex*) **both what is noble and what is pleasant:** "The things pleasant to lovers of what is noble are naturally pleasant. And actions in accord with virtue are like this, so that they are pleasant both to such people and intrinsically. Their life, then, has no need of a pleasure that is superadded to it, like some sort of appendage, but has its pleasure within itself. For besides what we have already said, the person who does not enjoy doing noble actions is not good. For no one would call a person just who did not enjoy doing just actions, or generous if he did not enjoy doing generous ones, and similarly as regards the others. If that is so, however, actions in accord with virtue will be intrinsically pleasant. But they are also good, of course, and noble as well. Further, they are each of these things to the highest degree, if indeed an excellent person discerns them correctly—and he does discern them that way. Hence happiness is what is best, noblest, and most pleasant. And these qualities are not distinguished in the way the Delian inscription says: 'The noblest thing is the most just; the best, to be healthy. The most pleasant, however, is to get the thing we desire.' For the best activities possess them all. And it is these—or the one among them that is best—that we say is happiness" (*NE* I 8 1099^{a}13–25).

Note 1031

Musaeus: A semi-legendary bard to whom a number of sayings and verses were attributed.

Note 1032

It rarely happens that human beings attain the end: See VII 13 1331^{b}39–1332^{a}3. **Relaxation and amusements lead to other things:** See VIII 3 1337^{b}35–42n.

Note 1033

Olympus: A 7th-cent poet from Phrygia. "Alexander in his *Collection of Information about Phrygia* said that Olympus first brought instrumental music (*kroumata*) to the Greeks" (Pseudo-Plutarch, *De Musica* 5 = Barker 209); "Some people think that Olympus also invented the Bacchic [dance] rhythm" (29 = Barker 235).

It is generally agreed that they make souls become ecstatic (*enthousiastikas*): *Prob.* XIX 48 922[b]22 describes the Phrygian mode as "ecstatic (*enthousiastikê*) and Bacchic (*bakchikê*)," while in a fragment *enthousiasmos* (1340[a]11) is combined with "powers of divination (*tas manteias*) [in sleep]" (F10 R^3 = Barnes, p. 2391). It seems likely, then, that *enthousiasmos*, which derives etymologically from *theos* ("god"), is in particular a state similar to the feeling of ecstatic possession by a god experienced by a participant at the orgiastic feasts of Dionysus (Bacchus), and other such gods, at which intoxicating music, like that of Olympus, figured. See also 1340[b]4–5, VIII 6 1341[a]21–22, 7 1342[a]2–16.

Ecstasy is an attribute (*pathos*) **connected to the character of the soul:** What X *paschei* ("suffers" or "undergoes") is what happens to him, so that he is passive with respect to it, as opposed to what he *poiei* ("does as an agent," or "produces"). When Y does something to X, X is affected by it, so his *pathê* as a result are, in one sense, his affections or attributes and, in another, his passions or feelings. Since Aristotle is trying to show that "we come to be of a certain quality in our characters because of music" (1340[a]7–8), "attribute" (= "quality") seems to convey the right meaning, though in the next sentence *sumpatheis* must be translated as "corresponding feelings."

Note 1034

Everyone who listens to imitations comes to have the corresponding feelings, even in separation from the rhythms and melodies of these imitations: Words alone, when, for example, they describe a sympathetic character suffering injustice, can arouse our anger on his behalf, although they may do so to a greater extent when they are appropriately melodious and rhythmic. Melodies and rhythms can have similar effects, even in separation from words. See 1348[a]38–[b]10.

Note 1035

Virtue is concerned with enjoying, loving, and hating in the correct way: "It seems too that with regard to virtue of character the biggest thing is enjoying what we should and hating what we should. For these extend throughout the whole of a person's life and have a powerful influence with regard to both virtue and the happy life, since people deliberately choose pleasant things and avoid painful ones" (*NE* X 1 1172[a]21–26).

Note 1036

In rhythms and melodies there are the greatest likenesses to the true natures of anger and gentleness, and furthermore of courage and temperance, and of all the contraries of these, and of the other [components of] characters: (1) "The affections of the soul are enmattered accounts. So their definitions will be of this sort, for example: 'Being angry is a sort of movement of such-and-such a sort of body, or of a part or a capacity, as a result of something for the sake of something.' And this is why it already belongs to the natural scientist to get a theoretical grasp on the soul, either all soul or this sort of soul" (*DA* I 1 403ᵃ25–27). (2) "Why does what is heard alone among perceptibles have ethical character (*êthos*)? For even if there is a melody without words, it has ethical character all the same, whereas neither color nor smell nor flavor have it. . . . And this movement has a likeness [to ethical character] both in the rhythms and in the order of high and low notes, whereas a concord [since it consists of notes played simultaneously and so is not a movement] has no moral character. . . . The movements themselves, though, pertain to action (*praktikai*), and actions are indications (*sêmasia*) of ethical character" (*Pr.* XIX 27 919ᵃ27–37). (3) "Virtue [of character] is also this sort of condition, namely, the one that comes about as a result of the best movements of the soul, and from which comes the putting into action of the soul's best functions and feelings" (*EE* II 1 1220ᵃ29–31). Thus (1) tells us that our feelings are movements in a certain sort of body, namely, one with a soul of the right perceptual sort; (2) that the movements in certain sorts of music are likenesses, or structural analogues, of these; and (3) that the virtues of character are produced by such movements. The likenesses in the musical movements, then, are to the movement in an ensouled body that underlie, or realize, the feelings that we experience, and not (or only coincidentally) the feelings as we experience them.

The other components of character (*tôn allôn êthôn*): Literally, "the other characters." But the use of the plurals *êthôn* (genitive) here and at 1340ᵃ33, *êthesin* (dative) at 1340ᵃ29, suggests that the reference is to the states, including those of feeling, that constitute a character rather than to the character they constitute.

Note 1037

If someone enjoys contemplating an image of something due to no other cause than its shape or form, he will himself necessarily enjoy contemplating the very thing whose image he is contemplating: "And in fact it would be unreasonable, even absurd, for us to enjoy contemplating likenesses of animals, because we are co-contemplating the craft that made them, such as painting or sculpture, while not liking even more the contemplation of the things formed by nature, at any rate when we can see their causes" (*PA* I 5 645ᵃ10–15).

Note 1038

And everyone shares in this sort of perception: Rejecting with Dreizehnter, Pellegrin, Kraut, and the mss. the OCT addition of οὐ ("not everyone shares in this sort of perception").

Note 1039

And these signs refer to the body that is in the grip of the feelings: Reading (1) καὶ ταῦτ' ἐστὶν ἐπὶ τοῦ σώματος ἐν τοῖς πάθεσιν with Dreizehnter and the mss. for OCT (2) καὶ ταῦτ' ἐστὶν ἐπίσημα ἐν τοῖς πάθεσιν ("and these signs serve as marks to distinguish the feelings"). I take the preposition ἐπὶ, which has many meanings with the genitive, to have here the meaning that it does in λέγειν ἐπὶ τινος—"speaking on (with reference to) some subject." (3) One manuscript, Π[1], reads ἀπὸ in place of ἐπὶ, which gives the meaning: "these signs derive from the body that is in the grip of the feelings." Both (1) and (3) make the credible claim that colors and shapes are (in combination) likenesses of feelings only by representing bodies (people) that are (or are pretending to be) in the grip of those feelings.

Note 1040

Pauson: Aristotle mentions Pauson—about whom little is otherwise known—as having produced a trompe-l'oeil painting of Hermes, which made it difficult to determine whether the figure of Hermes was inside (or behind) the plane of the canvas or outside (in front of) it, between the viewer and the canvas (*Met.* IX 8 1050ᵃ20). At the same time, he tells us that "the figures of Polygnotus are better than we are, those of Pauson are worse" (*Po.* 2 1448ᵃ5–6). It is presumably the combination of the two features—realistic or illusionistic representation of bad characters—that makes the paintings of Pauson particularly inappropriate for young people to look at.

Polygnotus: Born c. 500 BC in Thasos, died c. 440 BC in Athens. Pausanias, *Graeciae Descriptio* X.25.1–30.9, gives a very detailed description of his monumental wall painting in the hall of the Cnidians at Delphi, which depicted the sack of Troy. He is described as "a good drawer of character (*êthographos*)" at *Po.* 6 1450ᵃ28, and this is evidenced by Pausanias, who describes many of the figures in the painting in terms of the feelings and emotions they express.

Note 1041

In melodies themselves, though, there are imitations of the [components of] characters: "Even if there is a melody without words, it has ethical character (*êthos*) all the same" (*Pr.* XIX 27 919ᵇ26–27).

Note 1042

The nature of the harmonies (*tôn harmoniôn*): *Harmonia* is used to refer to music generally, as consisting of orderly melodic relationships, and as a name for the octave, the analysis of which reveals all the other relations on which melody is based. The *harmoniai* are the melodic counterparts to the rhythms: "The name for order in movement is 'rhythm,' and, again, the order belonging to the voice, when high and low are mixed together, is given the name 'harmony'" (Plato, *Lg.* 665a).

Note 1043

Mixo-Lydian . . . Dorian . . . Phrygian: d = ditone (the interval of a major third); q = quartertone; s = semitone; t = tone:

Mixo-Lydian:	q, q, d, q, q, d, t
Dorian:	q, q, d, t, q, q, d
Phrygian:	d, q, q, d, t, q, q.

These can be represented as two tetrachords, each of the form q, q, d, together with a tone that disjoins them. See Barker, pp. 163–68.

The Phrygian makes them ecstatic: See 1340ᵃ11n.

Note 1044

Those who have philosophized about this sort of education: Including Plato, *Ion*, 533b–535a, *Rep.* 397a–401b, 401d–402a, 410a–412b, 423d–425a, *Lg.* 653c–660c, 664b–671a, 700a–701b, 798d–799b, 799e–802e, 812b–e, and—though his writings are lost to us—Damon (later 5th cent), to whom Plato refers at *Rep.* 400b–c, and on whom see Barker, pp. 168–69.

Note 1045

Many of the wise say that the soul is a harmony: Including Pythagoras of Samos. See *DA* I 4 407^{b}30–408^{a}28, Plato, *Phd.* 85e–86d, 92a–95a.
Others that it has a harmony: Including Plato, *Phd.* 93c–94b.

Note 1046

The puzzle we raised earlier: At VIII 5 1339^{a}33–^{b}11.

Note 1047

The works (*tôn ergôn*): These are the things that a professional practitioner of an art or craft does, which include reciting, singing, dancing, and playing a musical instrument, so that "performance" often seems to capture the intended meaning of the phrase. But *ta erga* also include the works of such non-performing arts as writing and painting, and works done as part of private practice as well as those done for an audience, or with an audience in mind.

Note 1048

The rattle of Archytas: The rattle in question may have been invented by the Pythagorean philosopher Archytas of Tarentum (IV 4 1291^{b}23n), who was born sometime between 435 and 410 BC and died sometime between 360 and 350 BC. But it is also possible that it was invented by a different Archytas, who was a carpenter: "A rattle of Archytas: Given to those who are not capable of keeping still. For Archytas, being a carpenter, contrived a clapper, which they gave to children so that they would not upset any of the furnishings of the house" (= Hoffman **Text A**, p. 302).

Note 1049

Nothing prevents certain modes (*tropous*) **of music from producing the effect we mentioned:** That of making those who play them vulgar.

Note 1050

For current uses on the one hand, and for later sorts of learning on the other: Reading πρὸς μὲν τὰς χρήσεις ἤδη πρὸς δὲ τὰς μαθήσεις ὕστερον with Dreizehnter, Pellegrin, Schütrumpf, Kraut, and the mss. for OCT πρὸς μὲν τὰς μαθήσεις ἤδη πρὸς δὲ τὰς χρήσεις ὕστερον ("for current sorts of learning on the one hand, and for later uses on the other").

Note 1051

But learned such things too: Rejecting with Dreizehnter, Schütrumpf, Kraut, and the mss. the OCT addition of μὴ ("but learned things that are not of this sort").
The common element in music: See VIII 5 1340^{a}2–3.

Note 1052

The flute (*aulos*): Though "flute" is the standard translation, an *aulos* was actually a reed instrument, rather like a modern oboe. This is why Plato can describe it as "the most multi-stringed" instrument (*Rep.* 399d), and so ban it from his best city, where the only harmonies permitted do not require the accompaniment of instruments capable of excessive expressive effects. See VIII 7 1342ᵃ32–ᵇ6.

Has to do with frenzy (*orgiastikon*): See VIII 5 1340ᵃ11n.

The correct occasions for its use are those where contemplation (*theôria*): In this case the contemplation takes the form of listening.

Has the capacity to effect a purification (*katharsin*): See VIII 7 1341ᵇ38–1342ᵃ28.

Rather than learning: This is because its effects are on our character, which is shaped by habituation, rather than on those elements in us, such as our thoughts and intellect, that are shaped by formal teaching. See I 13 1260ᵇ4n, VIII 5 1340ᵃ18–22n.

Note 1053

Patron (*chorêgos*): The *chorêgos* was usually a rich man who paid for a chorus as part of his public service. The chorus' flute accompanist, by contrast, was usually a professional flute player—a vulgar craftsman, in Aristotle's view, not a free or liberal person.

Note 1054

The tablet that Thrasippus set up for Ecphantides: Ecphantides was an early playwright of old-style comedy (VII 17 1336ᵇ20n). After 458 BC he won four times in competition at the Athenian festival of Dionysus. Only a few small fragments of his plays are extant. Presumably Thrasippus, who is otherwise unknown, set up a tablet, as patrons sometimes did, to celebrate the victory of a play of Ecphantides that he had financed.

Note 1055

Pectis, the barbitos, the heptagon, the trigona, the sambukai: Stringed instruments of various sorts, akin to the harp.

Those that contribute to the pleasure of people who listen for expressive effects: Reading (1) χρωμάτων with Immisch and Kraut for OCT and Dreizehnter (2) χρωμένων ("those that contribute to the pleasure of people who listen to the ones who use them"). In relation to (1) see VIII 7 1342ᵃ18–28; in relation to (2), 1341ᵃ14–15, 1341ᵇ11–12, VIII 5 1340ᵃ2–5.

Scientific virtuosity (*cheirourgikês epistêmês*): Or, "scientific dexterity." The sort of scientific knowledge—on a par with that possessed by masters of the science of boxing or wrestling (*Cat.* 8 10ᵇ3–4)—that enables a performer to play technically demanding pieces or instruments that are difficult to master.

Note 1056

It is to Athena that we attribute scientific knowledge and craft knowledge: Athena was the goddess of these, among other things.

Note 1057

He produces certain qualities in the craftsmen who perform for him, and in their bodies, because of the movements: See VIII 5 1340ᵃ18–22n.

Note 1058

Investigation must be made of harmonies and rhythms, and with a view to education, as to [1] whether all the harmonies and all the rhythms should be used, or whether they should be divided, and next [2] whether the same division should be set up for those who are exerting themselves with a view to education, or, third, some distinct one: The division mentioned in [1] is between [1a] the harmonies and rhythms to be used in the best city for some purpose, such as for inducing ecstasy or for relaxation, and [1b] those not to be used there for any purpose. The question in [2] is whether all the harmonies and all the rhythms in [1a] are to be used in education or whether a third group is needed, consisting of the subclass of those in [1a] that are useful in education.

Or, third, some distinct one: Reading τρίτον with Dreizehnter and the mss. OCT brackets it for deletion.

Note 1059

We shall draw distinctions in the way laws do: "All law is universal, but about some sorts of things it is not possible to pronounce correctly in universal terms. So in the sorts of cases where it is necessary to pronounce in universal terms but not possible to do so correctly, the law picks what holds for the most part, not unaware of the error involved" (*NE* V 10 1137ᵇ13–16).

Note 1060

[1] Those relating to character (*êthika*), **[2] those relating to action** (*praktika*): To preserve the distinction between [1] and [2], we should probably understand *praktika* not as referring specifically to actions (*praxeis*) that stem from a state of character, whether virtue or vice, but rather as referring to actions involved in dancing or in marching in military formation. See I 4 1254ᵃ5n.

Note 1061

As to what we mean by purification, we will speak of it in simple terms now, but again and more perspicuously in our discussions concerning poetics: This extended discussion does not appear in the *Poetics* as we have it. See 1342ᵃ11–15n. On simplicity, see I 6 1255ᵃ36n, and on perspicuity, II 6 1265ᵃ29n.

Note 1062

This movement: The movement in question could be (1) the movement that constitutes the melody or (2) the movement in the soul that constitutes the feeling produced by the melody. See VIII 5 1340ᵃ18–22n.

Note 1063

The same thing, then, must be experienced, when listening to frenzy-inducing sacred melodies, by those who are prone to pity or fear or to feelings generally, and by others to the extent that each of these things falls to them, and

they all get a certain purification (*tina katharsin*) **and feel their burdens lightened by pleasure:** "Tragedy, then, is an imitation of an action that is serious, complete, and of a certain magnitude . . . in the mode of dramatic enactment and not narrative, effecting (*perainousa*) through [the arousal of] pity and fear the purification (*katharsis*) of such feelings" (*Po.* 6 1449^{b}24–28). Presumably, the effect attributed to sacred melodies in our text is of the same sort as the one attributed here to tragedy. But, in the absence of the advertised more perspicuous discussion of it (1341^{b}38–40), its precise nature is difficult to determine. Nonetheless, the outlines of an intelligible account can be reconstructed with at least moderate confidence. The movements in purifying music produce correlative movements in the appropriate sort of ensouled body, which can, when the movements are excellent, produce through repetition and habituation a corresponding virtuous—and so mean—state in the soul (VIII 5 1340^{a}18–22n). If we think of the souls of listeners as initially "distorted (*parestrammenai*) from the natural state" (1342^{a}22–23), as those of people who are prone (overly susceptible) to pity and fear are bound to be, we can think of the—perhaps temporary—purification they experience as stemming from the purging, or correction, of those distortions, "since it is by pulling well away from error that we shall attain the mean—as people do in rectifying distortions (*diestrammena*) in pieces of wood" (*NE* II 9 1109^{b}6–7). Now tragedy, since it involves rhythm and harmony, dance and song (*Po.* 6 1449^{b}29–31), can surely have these very same sorts of effects. But though the whole complex imitation that is the tragedy itself, comprising all its various elements, is "an imitation of an action that is serious, complete, and of a certain magnitude" (*Po.* 6 1449^{b}24–25), it is the plot (*muthos*) that primarily imitates that action and that primarily arouses pity and fear (1450^{b}18–19, 14 1453^{b}1–6). Hence it seems that it must also be primarily the plot that effects the purification of these feelings. The account of music's purifying power, therefore, does not directly carry over to tragedy. However, just as certain movements in an appropriately ensouled body are correlated with, or realize, certain feelings, so words that evoke those feelings in us are correlated with those same movements, just as pictures are (*Pol.* VIII 5 1240^{a}25–28). By operating in the right way, then, namely, by imitating or representing a good person moving from good luck to bad luck, not because of his character but because of an isolated mistake (*Pol.* 13 1452^{b}33–1453^{a}10), it can (even if only temporarily) purge the distortions, restoring the movements associated with pity and fear to their natural or mean condition (or one closer to it), thereby purifying the associated feelings. This sort of purification, this expulsion of distortions, is not itself a sort of teaching, since it does not involve the learning of causes (*Pol.* VIII 6 1341^{a}23–24n), but it does have significant cognitive effects. For feelings that are in a mean (or closer to a mean), unlike those that are not, are better discerners of the things—such as danger—that evoke the feelings. That is why, when we have the virtues of character, we measure the danger of something correctly, seeing it for what it is, and feeling the correspondingly correct amount of fear toward it, "since a courageous person feels and acts as things merit and in the way reason prescribes" (*NE* III 7 1115^{b}19–20).

Note 1064

The action-involving melodies: Reading πρακτικὰ with OCT for καθαρτικὰ ("the purifying melodies") read by Dreizehnter, Schütrumpf, and the mss.

Note 1065

Excessive expressive effects (*parakekchrôsmena*): The use of the metaphor of color (*chrôma*) to describe music seems to refer to expressive effects involving either tone color or nuances of tuning. See Barker, p. 143n61.
What produces pleasure for each person is what is akin to his nature: See VIII 3 1338^{a}7–9n.

Note 1066

As we said: At 1342^{a}2–3.

Note 1067

The Dorian is of this sort, as we said earlier: See VIII 3 1340^{b}3–4.
One should accept any other that passes the examination carried out for us (*dokimazôsin*) **by those who share in the pursuit of philosophy and musical education:** *Dokimasia* in Athens was the process of determining whether, for example, someone should be admitted to citizenship, or was eligible for military service, or to hold the office to which he had been elected.

Note 1068

The Socrates of the *Republic* was not correct, however, to retain only the Phrygian along with the Dorian, especially since he includes the flute among the instruments he rejects: "[*Glaucon*] It looks as though you have got the Dorian and Phrygian left. [*Socrates*] I do not know the harmonies, so just leave me that harmony that would appropriately imitate the vocal sounds and speech-melodies of a courageous person engaged in battle or in other work that he is forced to do, and who—even when he fails and faces wounds or death or some other misfortune—always grapples with what chances to occur in a disciplined and resolute way. And also leave me another harmony for when he is engaged in peaceful enterprises, or in those he is not forced to do but does willingly, or when he is trying to persuade someone of something, or entreating a god through prayer, or a human being through instruction and advice; or for when he is doing the opposite—patiently listening to someone else, who is entreating or instructing him, or trying to change his mind through persuasion. Leave me the harmony that will imitate him, when he does not behave arrogantly when these things turn out as he intends, but, on the contrary, is temperate and moderate in all these enterprises, and satisfied with their outcomes. Leave me these two harmonies, then—the forced and the willing—that will best imitate the voices of temperate and courageous men in good fortune and in bad. [*G.*] You are asking to be left with the very ones I just mentioned. [*S.*] Well then, we will have no need for multi-stringed or polyharmonic instruments to accompany our odes and songs. [*G.*] No, it seems to me we won't. [*S.*] Then we won't maintain craftsmen who make triangular lutes, harps, and all other such multi-stringed and polyharmonic instruments. [*G.*] Apparently not. [*S.*] What about flute makers and flute players? Will you allow them into the city? Or isn't the flute the most multi-stringed of all? And aren't polyharmonic instruments all imitations of it? [*G.*] Clearly, they are. [*S.*] You have the lyre and the cithara left, then, as useful in our city; and in the countryside, by contrast, there would be a sort of pipe for the herdsman to play. [*G.*] That is what our argument suggests, anyway. [*S.*] Well we are certainly not doing anything new, my friend, in preferring Apollo and his instruments to Marsyas and his" (*Rep.* 399a–e).

Note 1069

Composition shows this clearly: Reading δηλοῖ δ' ἡ ποίησις here with OCT rather than following "feeling" at 1342^{b}3–4 with Dreizehnter and the mss.

Note 1070

Philoxenus: A dithyrambic poet from the island of Cythera, c. 435–380 BC. See Barker 94–95.

A dithyramb: A hymn to the god Dionysus (Bacchus).

Note 1071

We praise the mean between extremes, and say that it is what we should pursue: "In everything continuous and divisible, then, it is possible to take more, less, and equal, and these either *in relation to the thing itself* or *in relation to us*—where equal is some sort of mean between excess and deficiency. By 'the mean in relation to the thing,' I mean what is equidistant from each of its two extremes, which is precisely one in number and the same for all. The mean in relation to us, by contrast, is what takes neither too much nor too little. It is not one thing and is not the same for all. For example, if ten are many and two are few, we take six as the mean in relation to the thing, since it exceeds and is exceeded by an equal amount. That is the mean in accord with arithmetical proportion. But the mean in relation to us must not be ascertained in that way. For if ten minae is a lot to eat and two minae a little, the trainer will not prescribe six minae. For that is presumably also a lot or a little for the person who is to eat it—a little for Milo but a lot for someone starting his athletic training regimen. Similarly in the cases of running and wrestling. In this way, then, everyone with scientific knowledge avoids excess and deficiency and looks for the mean and chooses it—the mean not in the thing but in relation to us. . . . [Thus] the mean is subject to praise and is on the correct path" (*NE* II 6 1106^{a}26–^{b}27).

Note 1072

There are, though, two targets . . . the mean, the possible, and the appropriate: This paragraph and the next (1342^{b}17–34) is thought by Newman (vol. III, pp. 571–572) and some others to be an interpolation because: (1) Here the Lydian harmony is recommended for use in educating "children (*paidôn*)" (1342^{b}32), whereas earlier the Dorian was rcommended for educating "younger people (*tois neôterois*)" (1342^{b}16–20). (2) Earlier, people were characterized as responding to relaxed harmonies with "softer thought (*malakôterôs tên dianoian*)" (VIII 5 1340^{b}2), which seems somehow negative, whereas here Socrates is criticized for rejecting the use of such harmonies in education (1342^{b}23–29). (3) Earlier, adult citizens were required to give up "works" or performance, whereas here relaxed harmonies are recommended for the old to sing (1342^{b}20–23). The supposed conflict in (1), however, seems easily removed, since what is appropriate for children (think of the rattle of Archytas) need not be appropriate for younger people. Similarly, as regards (2), education in the softer harmonies, restricted perhaps to childhood, is recommended also with a view to their use in old age, when softer or more tender thought might be entirely appropriate, even if it might not be so to people in their prime, with a city to govern or defend. Finally, (3) needs to be seen in the light of the comment that ends VIII 2: "what one does for one's own sake, for the sake of friends, or because of virtue is not unfree, but someone who does the same thing because of others would in many cases seem to be acting like a hired laborer or a slave" (1337^{b}19–21). Old men singing for their own pleasure or for that of their friends are not like people performing for the pleasure of a perhaps vulgar audience. In any case, the very fact that they are old might make it permissible for them to do things forbidden to those in their prime.

Note 1073
It is not easy for people exhausted by age to sing harmonies that are strained: That is, to reach the high pitches that strain their vocal cords. See V 8 1308^{b}4n.

Note 1074
Socrates rejected the relaxed harmonies for the purposes of education not because they have the capacity that drink has but because they make us weak: "[*Socrates*] Now, surely drunkenness is also entirely inappropriate for our guardians, and softness and idleness as well. [*Glaucon*] Of course. [*S.*] What, then, are the soft harmonies, and the ones suitable for drinking-parties? [*G.*] There are some Ionian ones that are called 'relaxed,' and also some Lydian ones. [*S.*] Could you use any of them, my friend, on men who are warriors? [*G.*] No, never. So it looks as though you have got the Dorian and Phrygian left" (Plato, *Rep.* 398e).

Further Reading

Detailed and regularly updated bibliographies of works on Aristotle's *political theory* (compiled by Fred Miller), on his ethics (compiled by Richard Kraut), and on his philosophy generally (compiled by Christopher Shields) are available online at: http://plato.stanford.edu/entries/aristotle-politics/
http://plato.stanford.edu/entries/aristotle-ethics/
http://plato.stanford.edu/entries/aristotle/

Thesaurus Linguae Graeca (http://www.tlg.uci.edu) has excellent searchable Greek texts and English translations of Aristotle's writings, with linked dictionaries and grammars.

Editions of the *Politics*, translations of it, and commentaries on it are listed under Abbreviations at the beginning of the present volume.

The following are the works that I have found especially worthwhile:

Background

Austin, N., P. Vidal-Naquet. *Economic and Social History of Greece* (Berkeley, 1977).

Burkert, W. *Greek Religion* (Cambridge, Mass., 1985).

De Ste. Croix, G. *The Class Struggle in the Ancient Greek World* (Ithaca, 1981).

Dover, K. *Greek Homosexuality* (Cambridge, Mass., 1978).

Ferrar, C. *The Origins of Democratic Thinking: The Invention of Politics in Classical Athens* (Cambridge, 1988).

Forrest, W. *A History of Sparta 950–192 BC* (New York, 1968).

Garlan, Y. *Slavery in Ancient Greece* (Ithaca, 1988).

Golden, M. *Children and Childhood in Classical Athens* (Baltimore, 1990).

MacDowell, D. *The Law in Classical Athens* (Ithaca, 1978).

———. *Spartan Law* (Edinburgh, 1986).

Ober, J. *Mass and Elite in Democratic Athens: Rhetoric, Ideology, and the Power of the People* (Princeton, 1991).

———. *Democracy and Knowledge: Innovation and Learning in Classical Athens* (Princeton, 2008).

Okin, S. *Women in Western Political Thought* (Princeton, 1979).

Rowe, C., and M. Schofield. *The Cambridge History of Greek and Roman Political Thought* (Cambridge, 2000).

Stockton, D. *The Classical Athenian Democracy* (Oxford, 1991).

Wiedemann, T. *Greek and Roman Slavery* (Baltimore, 1981).

Aristotle Life and Works

Lear, J. *Aristotle: The Desire to Understand* (Cambridge, 1988).

Natali, C. *Aristotle: His Life and School* (Princeton, 2013).

Shields, C. *Aristotle* (New York, 2007).

Books on Aristotle's Political Thought

Kraut, R. *Aristotle: Political Philosophy* (Oxford, 2002).

Leunissen, M. *From Natural Character to Moral Virtue in Aristotle* (Oxford, 2017).

Meikle, S. *Aristotle's Economic Thought* (Oxford, 1995).

Miller Jr., F. *Nature, Justice, and Rights in Aristotle's Politics* (Oxford, 1995).

Riesbeck, D. *Aristotle on Political Community* (Cambridge, 2016).

Yack, B. *The Problems of a Political Animal: Community, Justice and Conflict in Aristotelian Political Thought* (Berkeley, 1993).

Collections of Essays

Barnes, J., M. Schofield, R. Sorabji (eds.), *Articles on Aristotle. Vol. 2. Ethics and Politics* (London, 1977).

Deslauriers, M., P. Destrée (eds.), *The Cambridge Companion to Aristotle's Politics* (Cambridge, 2013).

Keyt, D., F. Miller Jr. (eds.), *A Companion to Aristotle's Politics* (Oxford, 1991).

Lockwood, T., T. Samaras (eds.), *Aristotle's Politics: A Critical Guide* (Cambridge, 2015).

Patzig, G. (ed.), *XI Symposium Aristotelicum: Aristoteles Politik* (Göttingen, 1990).

Relevant Works of Mine

"Philosophy, Politics, and Rhetoric in Aristotle." In A. O. Rorty (ed.), *Essays on Aristotle's Rhetoric* (Berkeley, 1996): 191–205.

"Aristotelian Education." In A. O. Rorty (ed.), *Philosophers on Education* (London, 1998): 51–65.

Practices of Reason: Aristotle's Nicomachean Ethics (Oxford, 1992).

Action, Contemplation, and Happiness: An Essay on Aristotle (Cambridge, Mass., 2012).

Aristotle on Practical Wisdom (Cambridge, Mass., 2013).

Aristotle: Nicomachean Ethics (Indianapolis, 2014).

Aristotle: Metaphysics (Indianapolis, 2016).

Index of Names

Note: Page numbers beginning with 12 and ending with 52^{a}–99^{b} omit the 12—for example, 1279^{a} = 79^{a}. Those beginning with 13 and ending with 00^{a}–42^{b} omit the 13. Line numbers are to the Greek text, but are closely approximate in the translation. References are typically to key doctrines or discussions in the text and, when in bold, in the associated notes.

Index of Terms

Note: Page numbers beginning with 12 and ending with 52a–99b omit the 12—for example, 1279a = 79a. Those beginning with 13 and ending with 00a–42b omit the 13. Line numbers are to the Greek text, but are closely approximate in the translation. References are typically to key doctrines or discussions in the text and, when in bold, in the associated notes.